INVESTMENT
PRINCIPLES

INVESTMENT PRINCIPLES

Second Edition

TIMOTHY E. JOHNSON

Professor of Finance
University of Cincinnati

Prentice-Hall, Inc., Englewood Cliffs, N.J. 07632

Library of Congress Cataloging in Publication Data

JOHNSON, TIMOTHY E. (date)
   Investment principles.
   Includes bibliographies and index.
     1. Investments. 2. Investment analysis.
I. Title.
HG4521.J654 1982   332.6'78   82-13129
ISBN 0-13-504522-3

Editorial/production supervision and
   interior design by Richard C. Laveglia
Cover design by Judith A. Matz
Manufacturing buyer: Ed O'Dougherty
Cover Photo by Ed Gallucci, FPG

© 1983, 1978 by Prentice-Hall, Inc., Englewood Cliffs, N.J. 07632

Printed in the United States of America

10 9 8 7 6 5 4 3 2 1

ISBN 0-13-504522-3

Prentice-Hall International, Inc., *London*
Prentice-Hall of Australia Pty. Limited, *Sydney*
Editora Prentice-Hall do Brasil, Ltda., *Rio de Janeiro*
Prentice-Hall Canada Inc., *Toronto*
Prentice-Hall of India Private Limited, *New Delhi*
Prentice-Hall of Japan, Inc., *Tokyo*
Prentice-Hall of Southeast Asia Pte. Ltd., *Singapore*
Whitehall Books Limited, *Wellington, New Zealand*

To my wife, Janet
and our children, Paul, Sarah, Susan, and Linnea

Contents

12 ' ECONOMIC AND INDUSTRY ANALYSIS 290

13 MARKET ANALYSIS AND TIMING 337

14 TRADITIONAL SECURITY PORTFOLIO MANAGEMENT 368

Preface

The study of investments is of growing importance to every individual, for almost all Americans are investing in the securities market either directly or indirectly. This text is for the person who wants to understand what investing is all about. The material begins at a basic level and works toward a comprehensive description of how the securities markets work and how an investor can approach the markets systematically and prudently in order to achieve his or her investment goals.

In recent years, the field of investments has seen a variety of new approaches and philosophies. While these new approaches have aroused considerable debate among the members of the investment community, and have added a much needed quantitative aspect to investment management, some are nevertheless too hypothetical and unrealistic to be of much aid to a sound investment management program. Those of us who are actively involved in both the academic and the investment management professions know perfectly well that investing still remains primarily an art and not a science and cannot be reduced totally to a buy, hold, sell, statistical equation, or technical chart pattern. The strong fixation for quantitative approaches to security analysis and portfolio management has left a gap in the coverage of more traditional investment principles. The purpose of this book is to fill the gap created by the swing toward highly quantitative texts for the introductory investments course. This book will ground students in basic investment principles through a proper integration of practical descriptive material and relevant theoretical applications. Thus prepared, the student will be able to move to more advanced courses in security analysis and portfolio management.

This second edition has revised a large amount of the text by updating the material to relate the principles of investing to all the changes that have taken place in the field over the past five years. A large part of the book has been reorganized to improve the flow of the material covered. The redundancy among several chapters has been consolidated and a more workable relationship between security descriptions and security analysis has resulted.

Investment Principles, second edition, retains the widely accepted level of presentation of the first edition with emphasis on the descriptive approach to the sound understanding of investment principles. A new chapter on Traditional Portfolio Management has been included so as to give a more realistic balance to the chapter on Modern Portfolio Management. The entire text is updated to include the significant changes included in the Economic Recovery Act of 1981. Also, the impact of inflation is dealt with where appropriate.

The second edition has been reorganized into a more workable sequence. It begins with an introduction to the investment environment with steps involved in the analytical process. A description of the securities industry follows, leading up to a discussion of both traditional and modern portfolio theory.

Chapter One introduces the student to the topics that he or she will be confronting in the study of investments. Chapter Two covers investing from the perspective of the individual and includes the calculations necessary for a proper understanding of various investments. Although many students may have been exposed to these mathematical concepts in previous studies, a review is usually helpful.

Chapters Three and Five describe fixed and variable return securities with Chapters Four and Six outlining the process by which these securities are analyzed. Some students may have encountered part of the security description before, but it is unlikely that the exposure has been as comprehensive and accompanied by the analysis of securities.

Chapter Seven is an introduction to more speculative investment opportunities in options, warrants, rights, and the commodity market. The investor will have to decide whether to participate in these vehicles in his or her investment planning, so he or she should be aware of the nature of these investment media and their advantages and disadvantages. Although most of these items can be considered speculative, the more conservative side of options and an analytical section on convertibles is also included.

Chapters Eight and Nine describe the securities markets and how they function as well as the mechanics of the brokerage business and the execution of a security order.

Chapter Ten is devoted to a discussion of investment companies. Many investors, after dealing with securities markets, recognize that they do not have the time or talent or proper emotions to manage their own investment portfolios. This chapter should help them to choose investment companies in accordance with their long-term goals, desired diversification, and professional management needs.

Chapter Eleven discusses the regulatory bodies which oversee the securities industry. These topics, which are a necessary foundation for the analysis of investments, are generally of great interest to students.

Chapter Twelve provides an overview of the analysis of the economy and industries. Sources of information for this analysis is provided along with the general approach to an understanding of these areas. Chapter Thirteen moves to the technical approach, by which technicians use analysis of security prices and other market data as primary indicators for investment decisions.

Chapters Fourteen and Fifteen provide an overview for the investor in both the traditional and modern approaches to portfolio management. The investor who understands the securities markets and has a reasonable grasp on the analysis of the economy, industries, and securities, may nevertheless find difficulty in creating an appropriate portfolio to meet his or her overall goals. These chapters complete the investment process by showing investors how to properly construct and manage the overall portfolio.

Although the majority of the text is devoted to security investing, Chapter Sixteen, dealing with real estate investment, has been included since this is one of the most common forms of investment that may confront the individual.

Chapter Seventeen covers the important aspects of taxation and estate planning, which are of growing concern to individual investors as they reach higher tax brackets and as they attempt to plan their estates so as to properly provide the necessary assets for their families. The importance of determining the best possible means of passing the estate after death with the least tax impact is covered. Many investors have spent a considerable amount of time investing and building their assets without the proper consideration of the tax and estate implications. The text emphasizes the need for the individual to integrate his total financial planning with the investment decision process.

I am indeed grateful to a large number of people who have helped make this text possible, both from the academic community and the professional investment community. An enormous amount of assistance was provided by the wide range of reviewers who made significant contributions in their critique of the manuscript: Professor Gary G. Schlarbaum (Purdue

University), Professor Richard W. McEnally (University of North Carolina), Professor H. Russell Fogler (University of Florida), Professor Glenn A. Wilt, Jr. (Arizona State University), Professor J. Ronald Hoffmeister (University of Missouri), Professor Edward A. Dyl (University of Wyoming), Professor Michael F. Dunn (California State University), Professor Donald A. Nast (Florida State University), Professor Edwin Grossnickle (Western Michigan University), Professor David E. Risch (Florissant Valley Community College), Professor Peter Goulet (University of Northern Iowa), Professor Joe Grissom (Tarrant County Junior College), Professor Ronald Charvonia (Glendale Community College), Professor Thomas J. McKenna (Fresno City College), and Professor Gary Cain (St. Mary's College). It would be impossible to give thanks here to the many individuals within the investment community and others who were of great help; however, special thanks goes to James Roetenberger, Robert Knecht, Greg Ambro, Geoffrey Strauss, Dixie Mills, Mona Gardner, Lew Melnyk, and Al Simone.

A special word of appreciation goes to the many people at Prentice-Hall who patiently and painstakingly cultivated this project. In particular I wish to thank David Hildebrand and Rick Laveglia for their integral part in the formation of this edition.

Timothy E. Johnson
Cincinnati, Ohio

1

The Investment Environment

Investments can be a fascinating and stimulating field of study for those who are interested in gaining knowledge and expertise in investment decision making. The same basic investment principles and procedures apply to both the individual and institutional investor. The study of investments prepares individuals to operate in the securities markets either on their own behalf or on behalf of an institution employing their services. Institutions invest funds on behalf of other investors through pension funds, mutual funds, trust departments of banks, insurance companies, or other indirect investing by the individual. The majority of the emphasis and examples in this text will be from the viewpoint of the individual investor operating in the securities market, although for most investment principles no distinction is necessary.

The study of investments presupposes specific objectives. If we assume that the individual is rational and has an aversion to risk, we can assume that this person starts putting together an investment portfolio only after he or she has established the essential elements of a personal financial plan, for example, cash reserves and a life insurance program. The desire to participate in any investment program presupposes that a person wants to accumulate assets and expand net worth. However, the financial goals of an investment program differ widely among individual investors, depending upon the investors' financial needs and, to a significant extent, on social, family, and moral views on the use of money. For example, some investors participate in investment programs to accumulate money for the sake of accumulation and have no special need or goal. They derive satisfaction from the experience of successful investing. Some view investment as a means of providing a fund for their children's college education, supplementing retirement income, or fulfilling other financially related needs. Others view investment as a means of increasing their net worth in order to be able to provide increasing sources of funds for future family members, for religious organizations that need expanding funds to better serve their objectives, and for community-related organizations and programs that need private funding. Whatever the goal of the investor, the purpose of the study of investments is to equip the individual for making intelligent investment decisions.

Successful investing can be a difficult task even for professionals. Although this text presents the objective evidence of the data and the principles necessary for the correct approach to successful investing, there can be no assurance of an easy road to successful investing. Nevertheless, a prudent and informed approach to investment should allow realistic and objective investors to achieve their goals.

The study of investments is of growing importance to every individual. Almost all American workers are investing in the securities market either directly or indirectly. If an individual participates in a company pension program, purchases a life insurance policy, or deposits money in a bank or savings and loan institution, he or she is participating in the securities market. All these financial institutions are continually dealing in the securities market. When they invest the funds made available to them, they try to receive a reasonable rate of return in relation to the expected risk level assumed.

This text is for the individual who wants to understand what investing is all about. The material works toward a general understanding of how the securities markets work and how an investor might approach them systematically and prudently to achieve personal goals. The basic question facing every investor is which securities to buy. The answer depends upon many factors. Successful security investing requires careful study of the economic forces bearing upon each investment decision, the industry being investigated, and the company and security involved in the analysis. Any successful investment strategy must begin with the individual. One must be able to evaluate personal financial circumstances objectively and determine how they relate to a total financial plan lasting throughout a lifetime.

This text outlines the investment principles that are the bases of any investment program followed by a conservative and prudent investor. Unfortunately, many individuals who participate in the securities markets have very little understanding or knowledge of what they are doing, and the risks they assume result more from a gambling instinct than a prudent approach to long term investing. Many small investors have not accepted the responsibility of accumulating good basic securities. Instead, they have engaged in the most hazardous, unorthodox ventures imaginable in an attempt to gain wealth quickly. They fail to realize that investing and building a solid, well-diversified portfolio is a gradual process. Only after the basic foundation has been prepared should investors begin to accept higher levels of risk.

A major point of this text is to expose the reader to the large number of available investments in which one can participate. Some of these tend to be very speculative (see Chapter 7 in which options and the futures markets are discussed). The investor must have a working knowledge of many of the alternatives so as to be able to recognize and analyze them whenever one confronts them.

INVESTMENT, SPECULATION, AND GAMBLING

It is important to distinguish among investment, speculation, and gambling because they have a tendency to overlap. Many investors think that they are investing, when actually they are either speculating or gambling. An **investment** involves some positive rate of return that can be reasonably expected after sufficient analysis has been made. **Speculation** involves a higher level of risk and a more uncertain expectation of returns. In many cases, it is difficult to distinguish between an investment and a speculation. The distinction revolves around the investor's ability to determine the future probability of a return and the ability to make a thorough analysis of the situation. In addition, the length of time the investor plans to hold a security often determines whether it is an investment or a speculation. The same stock can be purchased as an investment or as a speculation, depending upon the purchaser's motivation. For example, an investor may attempt to make a short-term gain on a high-quality stock that other investors have been holding for many years for a combination of appreciation and dividend yield. Traditionally, investment involves a known degree of risk, which dictates that the principal and future income values be relatively certain. Speculation involves taking higher risks with a lesser degree of certainty and safety.

A difficulty with the distinction is that the degree of uncertainty must be measured differently for different types of investments. On one hand, for many corporate bonds and real estate mortgages, the probability of receiving the future stream of income payments and the principal at maturity may be appraised accurately and an appropriate yield may be received that will adequately reward the investor for the risk assumed. On the other hand, variable securities can recover only principal in the marketplace; any income is a distribution of potential profit at the discretion of management. It is, therefore, difficult to measure the safety of a stock or bond, because the investor is submitting to the risks of the marketplace. The reward for risk taking (in the form of an acceptable rate of return being measured in terms of both a dividend or interest payment and the appreciation or depreciation of the security's price) may actually be significantly less than for risk-free federal government securities that have produced higher yields than many widely held stocks.

Speculators who are interested in short-term price appreciation are less concerned with dividends. They add a significant amount of liquidity to the marketplace because they buy and sell securities in their portfolios frequently. Speculators help provide a market for securities and give it greater depth and a wider distribution of ownership, which enhances the capital markets of our economy.

An investor should be able to analyze a particular security situation. The appraisal of the qualitative and quantitative factors should permit the investor to make a rational choice, and even a reasonable valuation of the security. A speculator is more interested in the market action than its valuation. The investor is generally more concerned with fundamental financial analysis; the speculator tends to be more technically oriented and examines the market price action over the short run. The investor is concerned with the worth of the security; the speculator is more concerned with how the price of the security will move in the short run. It is important to note, however, that the speculator also investigates a situation thoroughly, although the amount of data needed to make a decision may be less and the risk may be greater than for an investment.

To make no analysis before purchasing a security would be to gamble. Gambling is generally unacceptable in the securities industry because it is a game of chance whose odds are no greater than that of rolling dice.

To distinguish between an investment and a speculation, the investor must identify financial objectives, decide how much risk he or she is willing to assume, and plan a course of action for both the near and the longer term. Certain investors should accept very little risk and must therefore be content with a modest return. Other investors can assume considerable risk and can base their plans on the possibility of high returns, always recognizing that they may suffer high losses. Certain investors must concentrate on high-grade bonds and other relatively safe commitments to ensure the income that their plans require and to assure that the principal value of the investment is safe.

THE INVESTMENT PROCESS

To be successful, the investor must understand each procedure in the investment process. When an individual approaches the securities market to make an investment, an entire series of decisions and activities begins. Long before the investor decides to select a particular security, the decision was made to allocate part of his or her net worth to a savings program, which now gives sufficient cash to launch an investment program.

Many investors are afforded the opportunity to invest when relatives leave them their estates. The average estate ranges from a few hundred dollars to many thousands of dollars. Many inheritances consist of only the value of a home, a savings account, and proceeds from a life insurance policy. Individuals who have little or no investment experience can have great difficulty in feeling content about the proper placement of such funds. Those whose cash resources have been built up over time usually have more opportunity to think through a more organized investment plan.

Once the necessary funds have been obtained, the individual must understand the nature of the various risks associated with any investment. One of the new risks that investors will discover is their own attitude toward the investments they make. Many individuals see certain aspects of their personalities for the first time when they begin to invest. Some become very uneasy and worry constantly about their investments; they tend to base their decisions on emotions rather than on sound security and portfolio analysis and objective evaluation. The major classifications of risk are discussed later in this chapter.

Investors must become familiar with the variety of investments that are available, ranging from stocks and bonds in the security markets to real estate, coins, stamps, art, and commodities. Investors must determine for themselves the investment media with which they are most comfortable. Because a significant number of investments are available (see Chapters 3 and 5), some professional investment analysts spend their entire lives in a small segment of the securities markets, perhaps studying and analyzing only bonds or a subset of municipal bonds or the computer industry. Therefore, for average investors to believe that they can be experts in a number of investment alternatives can be the beginning of their ultimate downfall. The investor is encouraged to focus attention on a limited number of investment opportunities. A degree of specialization is necessary for continuous positive results over a long-term program.

Since most of this text is devoted to investment in marketable securities, let us assume that investors have narrowed their interests to the securities markets. They must now determine a method of analysis. First, no investment program can be successful without an understanding of the economy within which the securities markets operate. Only after the investor has determined that the economic conditions are appropriate for investing should the analysis of alternatives begin.

Next, the investor should analyze industries to determine which industries are most appropriate for the present- and intermediate-term economic conditions and are the strongest in light of forecasted economic conditions. Since most industries differ considerably in their characteristics, some industries will expand and respond positively in certain economic conditions while others will perform poorly. Therefore, an examination of industries should include sufficient opportunities within which the investor can diversify to take advantage of the economic climate.

Only after economic and industry analyses have been completed should the investor consider specific firms. The investor should concentrate on the best-situated firms within the industries. Companies within an industry are both strong and weak in terms of financial strength, marketing efforts, product mix, and adequate production facilities. Once the investor has determined the strongest companies among those within an industry, selecting the appropriate security within each company can begin. For example, an investor may determine that for his or her objectives a convertible preferred stock may be superior to the underlying common stock. A more speculative investor may select a company's warrant. Another may choose a firm's bond.

The focal point of the analysis of a particular equity security is a forecast of the company's future earnings potential and the degree of risk associated with the estimate. In this case, risk is measured by the degree of uncertainty that the expected earnings are likely to occur. No single factor is more important in security analysis than the earning power of the corporation. Without a strong and continuing base of corporate earning power, any security within that firm is subject to price decline. If the earning power of the company is sporadic and weak, the investor will have difficulty in achieving the objective.

Every decision an investor makes in the investment process should be based on an analysis of expected future events. An individual's success in an investment program is predicated on the ability to forecast adequately and accurately a pattern of future events based on an analysis of the past and present and on predictions based on solid analysis about the future.

An investor's ability to analyze the economy, industry, or security adequately depends upon the sources of information. It is imperative that investors have an information system that keeps them up to date on the developments within the industries and companies for the securities in their portfolios. Many investors simply read the quotations of their securities in the financial pages of the newspaper, somehow believing that they are keeping up to date with the company. The quotation of a company's security price is secondary to fundamental security analysis.

Investors may use the *Wall Street Journal,* the company's annual reports, which include historical financial data, financial services (they may either subscribe to them or read them in a library), and information obtained from research departments of brokerage houses.

An investor should also understand the mechanics of the securities market and the relationships involved in the industry, including the relationship between broker and investor. Selecting a broker and executing an order correctly are important elements in the investment process because various amounts of money can either be gained or lost. In addition, the investor should understand the behavior of the stock market itself. Technical analysts exclusively look at the market prices to determine whether a security should be purchased or sold. The thrust of our study is fundamental analysis, although Chapter 13 addresses itself to the movements of the market and the opportunities for gauging the timing of transactions. The psychology of the market and the participants' expectations have an important bearing on the timing of any investment program. Because short-term movements in securities prices are common, the investor should be aware of many of the forces that cause fluctuations.

Once the investor has come this far in understanding the investment process, he or she must then understand the importance of portfolio management. Portfolio management dictates that the investor select from among all available alternatives those securities that will give the best combination of risk and reward to meet the stated objective. The investor brings the entire knowledge together to formulate a portfolio. It is through portfolio management that the investor has the opportunity to achieve the stated goals.

The remainder of this chapter will investigate some of the fundamental tenets of the investment process. The following chapters are organized and developed around a logical investment process for the individual. This process begins with a basic understanding of the investment environment and securities, moves through the analysis stage, and culminates with the portfolio management and investment planning decision-making process.

INVESTMENT ALTERNATIVES

There is a wide array of alternatives from which the investor may choose. They range from low-risk alternatives such as savings and loan associations, to high-risk alternatives, such as the commodity markets. In addition to an investor's concern for the rate of return and the risk of an investment, there is concern for **liquidity.** Liquidity is the ability to convert an investment to cash quickly and with little loss in value. The liquidity of a savings and loan investment will vary, depending upon whether the investor puts money in a passbook account or purchases savings certificates. Investments in real estate can have varying degrees of liquidity, depending upon the nature of the investment. Other investments, such as stamp collections, art, or rare coin collections, can have varying degrees of liquidity, depending upon their marketability.

Between the extremes of both high and low risk and high and low liquidity are literally thousands of investments. Each investor must determine the types of investments that are best able to meet his or her objectives.

Life Insurance

The prudent, conservative investor who attempts to have a long-range personal family financial plan will consider purchasing life insurance and acquiring adequate living quarters before venturing into more risky investments. For most individuals, life insurance is a key element to building a sound financial program. The lack of an adequate life insurance program can be devastating for remaining family members should a key member of the household die at a young age. Every individual must carefully examine the positive and negative aspects of life insurance in relation to an overall investment and financial plan, keeping estate planning in mind.

Although it is beyond the scope of this text to examine insurance in any detail, the investor will want to determine the desirability of ordinary (whole life) life insurance versus term insurance. For example, whole life insurance may be desirable for those in high tax brackets, because the cash value return on a life insurance policy usually accumulates at a tax-free rate. In addition, whole life insurance may provide the least expensive form of estate liquidity if an individual's assets are fixed and create problems for raising sufficient cash to pay estate taxes. On the other hand, the individual will want to determine whether or not the purchase of term insurance at a significantly lower annual premium may be desirable. This can depend upon the individual's ability to invest the premium difference between whole life and comparable term insurance at a significantly higher rate than the guaranteed and projected tax-free rate offered by ordinary life insurance.

Home Ownership

Another common investment for most individuals is the purchase of a home. For many individuals, this will be the largest investment they will ever make. Naturally, the more expensive the home purchased, the more items necessary to furnish and operate the home, and so the less cash there will be for any further investment program. The individual investor must be sure to analyze and estimate accurately the full financial impact of a home purchase decision. Chapter 16 addresses in greater detail the factors to be considered.

Savings Program

A savings program affords the individual the liquidity and opportunity for changes in occupation, emergencies, and general transactions. The individual must determine which savings vehicle will give the appropriate balance between liquidity and an acceptable rate of return. A decision must be made whether to put savings in a commercial bank, savings and loan association, mutual savings bank, credit union, money market fund, or series EE or HH savings bonds. Each person must decide just how much will be needed for these purposes before venturing into any additional investment media. The more liquid a security portfolio is, the less necessary it will be for the individual to accumulate substantial funds in a savings media. However, if the individual ventures into a number of fixed investments, such as undeveloped land, apartment buildings, or other illiquid investments, the necessity for cash reserves may be more desirable.

Once the investor has taken care of these basic investments, consideration can be given to a securities portfolio or other investment media. In addition, various forms of real estate, even mortgage lending (the individual lends money to others to purchase real estate), can be investigated.

Small Business Ventures

Increasing numbers of individuals are interested in small-business opportunities. One of the basic reasons for the industrial growth of the United States has been the entrepreneurial drive of its citizens. Those individuals who want either to create their own business or to purchase an ongoing business will need to commit personal funds before they are able to find others who are willing to lend money to purchase or start a business. Many individuals passively participate in business investments by lending money to others and receiving either notes, bonds, or stock in very local privately held businesses.

Individuals with interests in the business field who actively seek investments in other businesses on a passive basis will have little difficulty finding proposals to compete for their funds. A careful financial analysis must precede any investment, but particularly that of a closely held business investment.

This discussion of investment alternatives is by no means exhaustive, but it does present the alternatives usually available to the individual investor. As the individual becomes more acquainted with the business world and continues to seek a better understanding of it, many variations of the basic investment alternatives will appear. Much of the criteria for analysis and risk determination discussed here can be applied to almost any investment.

Securities

A major portion of this book will be devoted to the analysis and valuation of securities investment. Securities include evidence of debt, such as bonds; ownership of a business, such as common stocks; and a legal right to sell or buy an ownership of a business, such as options, warrants, and rights. Securities can be divided also into two large categories: (1) variable-return securities, or equity securities, which include stocks, warrants, and rights

(Chapters 5 and 6), and (2) fixed-return securities, which include bonds and preferred stocks (Chapters 3 and 4).

CAPITAL MARKETS

Private investment in the free enterprise system is central to any capitalist economy. The expansion of the U.S. economy depends on the ability of firms to attract funds from the private sector. A delicate balance exists between the suppliers and users of funds in the economy. Suppliers of capital funds will only be attracted if the total rate of return in terms of an interest or dividend yield and a perceived capital appreciation are sufficient to reward the suppliers for the degree of risk they assume.

Capital markets are a complex of institutions and mechanisms through which funds for purposes longer than one year are pooled and made available to business, government, and individuals and through which instruments already outstanding are transferred. Capital markets are well organized and are local, regional, national, and worldwide in scope. Figure 1-1 illustrates the flow of funds among the participants in the capital markets.

Because capital markets deal with long-term investment instruments, they play a key role in the economy's capital-formation process. Funds raised through debt instruments by businesses and individuals are primarily invested in fixed assets and inventories. Furthermore, the capital market for long-term and permanent funds, such as equity items, includes securities, mortgages, and other long-term loans. The greatest part of the long-term business debt in the capital market is acquired by financial institutions, particularly life insurance companies and the trust departments of commercial banks, which act as trustees for pension funds and private trust funds. Residential mortgages are usually held by savings and loan associations, life insurance companies, commercial banks, and mutual savings

Figure 1-1 Flow of Funds from Suppliers to Users in a Capitalistic Economy

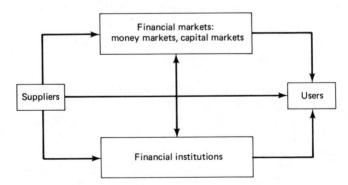

banks. Because these institutions derive their funds from the investing public, they are treated as financial intermediaries.

Equity items such as common stock, unlike corporate bonds, are mainly held by individuals, although institutions are gaining a greater percentage of the holdings of common stocks. A large share of the funds placed by individuals in common stocks is being channeled through investment companies (discussed in Chapter 10).

If the economic environment is favorable and if corporate management expectations are optimistic, companies will seek to expand their operations. Expansion can take many forms, from enlarged physical facilities with expanded production capabilities to an increased sales force. If conditions are favorable, this expansion will eventually lead to higher earnings and higher prices for the firm's securities that trade in the secondary marketplace. The financing of such expansion requires smooth operation of the capital markets, which allows the firm to sell stock or bonds to raise the necessary capital. Investors who have earned reasonable rates of return on previous investments in securities of expanding companies and industries or who have observed others doing this will be inclined to finance the expansions.

After securities have been issued to finance a firm's growth, it is important that there be an organized secondary market where previously issued securities can be traded. This secondary market facilitates investor participation, adds liquidity to the market, and allows the free exchange of security instruments either by investors or speculators.

The investor should be aware of the importance that the capital markets have to the smooth functioning of a free-enterprise economy in which all investments and reinvestments are dictated by the individuals and institutions that hold the nation's wealth. A complete explanation of the primary and secondary capital markets is given in Chapter 8.

SOURCES OF SAVINGS

A key factor that gives rise to the existence of capital markets is the ability of the economy to save. There are three sources of savings in the economy: the individual (the largest source), business corporations, and government bodies.

Prudent financial management dictates that, to readily accept the risks associated with investment in securities, an investor should be in a strong financial position before establishing an investment program. If an individual is fortunate enough to have a rising income and adequate financial protection, a program of retaining as much of the income as possible should be instituted. Whether savings accumulate rapidly or slowly, the usual source of money for investment is savings from current income or funds accumulated in the past. For the capital-formation process to run smoothly, the aggregate savings habits of individuals and corporations must provide sufficient funds for expansion and replacement investment.

Tables 1-1 and 1-2 contain data that give the allocation of disposable personal income and the percentage of disposable income that individuals save. These data help in understanding the role of the individual in the economy and in the flow of funds among segments of the economy and financial institutions.

Individuals save for a number of reasons. Many want to have emergency funds to help through difficult periods. Others accumulate funds for expenditures requiring large outlays, such as the purchase of a home or an automobile or for vacation travel, education, or retirement. A growing number of people want an income over and above their current salary or retirement benefits. With lengthening life expectancy in the United States and a lessening tendency to care for older individuals within the traditional family, the desire to build a retirement fund beyond the normal Social Security benefits and/or company retirement plan has become an increasingly important factor affecting the supply of available funds. These are the major reasons why savings accounts and life insurance policies have expanded continuously over the last three decades.

Table 1-1
Distribution of Total Personal Income (Dollar Amounts in Billions)

Year	Personal Income	Personal Taxes	Disposable Personal Income	Personal Outlays	Personal Savings	
					Amount	As a % of Disposable Income
1960	$ 402.3	$ 50.4	$ 352.0	$ 332.3	$ 19.7	5.6%
1965	540.7	64.9	475.8	442.1	33.7	7.1
1970	811.1	115.8	695.3	639.5	55.8	8.0
1971	868.4	116.7	751.8	691.1	60.7	8.1
1972	951.4	141.0	810.3	757.7	52.6	6.5
1973	1,065.2	150.7	914.5	835.5	79.0	8.6
1974	1,168.6	170.2	998.3	913.2	85.1	8.5
1975	1,265.0	168.9	1,096.1	1,001.8	94.3	8.6
1976	1,391.2	196.8	1,194.4	1,111.9	82.5	6.9
1977	1,538.0	226.5	1,311.5	1,237.5	74.1	5.6
1978	1,721.8	258.8	1,462.9	1,386.6	76.4	5.2
1979	1,943.8	302.0	1,641.7	1,555.5	86.2	5.3
1980*	2,161.0	338.7	1,822.2	1,718.7	103.6	5.7

Source: Department of Commerce data as reprinted in *Savings and Loan Fact Book,* 1981, p. 17, © United States League of Savings Associations 1981.
*Preliminary.

Table 1-2
Allocation of Household Funds (Dollar Amounts in Billions)

Item	1977	1978	1979	1980*
Disposable Personal Income	$1,311.5	$1,462.9	$1,641.7	$1,822.2
Plus: Increase in Credit	173.7	200.6	210.9	139.7
Equals: Total Funds Available	$1,485.2	$1,663.5	$1,852.6	$1,961.9
Less: Spending on Nondurable Goods and Services	1,026.7	1,149.4	1,298.5	1,459.6
Less: Increase in Currency and Demand Deposits	22.7	18.3	14.2	2.0
Leaves: Amount Available for Investment in Tangible and Financial Assets	$ 435.8	$ 495.8	$ 539.9	$ 500.3
Invested in:				
Tangible Assets	$ 230.7	$ 254.0	$ 279.0	$ 240.9
Financial Assets	205.1	241.8	260.9	259.4
Financial Assets Placed in:				
Savings Accounts	$ 109.2	$ 105.2	$ 81.1	$ 126.7
Insurance and Pension Funds	65.3	77.8	74.7	85.7
Credit and Equity Instruments	30.4	51.9	70.7	17.8

Source: Department of Commerce and Federal Reserve Board data as reprinted in *Savings and Loan Fact Book,* 1981, p. 17 © United States League of Savings Associations 1981.
*Preliminary.

Accumulating capital has always been a difficult and time-consuming process for the individual. Those who have achieved financial success know that it is difficult to maintain and expand capital because of the progressive federal income tax rates. The investment process is intimately associated with the individual's ability to save and the condition of the personal financial position that dictates just where such savings may be placed.

Pension funds and life insurance reserves are important vehicles by which people save a portion of their income each year. Accumulated funds are invested in securities on behalf of the individuals even if they do not elect to invest directly themselves. Over a long period of time these funds are expected to accumulate to large amounts that eventually will be available for either current consumption or for purchasing securities directly. Many elderly individuals who no longer need the protection of life insurance cash in their life insurance policies. They receive the cash value that has built up over the years and reinvest the proceeds for supplemental income during retirement. This can also be the case with pension funds, because many employees have the choice of either taking a cash lump-sum settlement or receiving periodic payments over the remaining years of their lives.

Figure 1-2 illustrates the relationship of the savings element to the protection element for ordinary life insurance. As the policyholder continues to make the premium payments, a cash value is created and continues to

Figure 1-2 Ordinary Life Insurance Policy

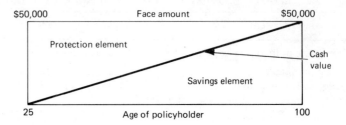

Source: Charles L. Barngrover and Timothy E. Johnson, *Personal Finance,* Grid, Inc., 1974, p. 279.

grow to the face amount at age 100. Counter to the cash value is the protection element that decreases in proportion to the rise in the policy cash value. Since the policyholder may cancel the insurance contract at any time and receive the cash value, the savings element of ordinary life insurance can be of significant value. It is obvious that an individual who has developed a savings program throughout the working career has many additional options available at retirement.

The distribution of personal savings among the various financial institutions is shown in Table 1-3. Shifts in these distributions have been considerable over the past 25 years as both individual financial objectives have changed and as the individual's perceived financial reward from the financial institutions has changed.

Business and government also save and invest. When a part of the profit of a business is reinvested, the result is a savings by stockholders, just as if the profit were paid out in the form of dividends and then reinvested. Government savings are represented by both the federal and the state and local governments and the retirement funds they administer. The gross savings of governments in the United States are very small in relation to those of personal savings and undistributed business profits.

INVESTMENT RISK

Concept of Risk

Understanding and measuring risk are fundamental to the investment process. Frequently, the risk associated with security investments is ignored and only the rewards are emphasized. An investor who does not fully appreciate the risks in security investments will find it difficult to obtain continuing positive results. An individual who is considering investing money is immediately faced with the conflict between the desire for safety of principal and the desire of a future return. All investment decisions

Table 1-3
Annual Change in Financial Assets of Households
(Dollar Amounts in Billions)

Year	Savings Associations	Mutual Savings Banks	Commercial Banks	Credit Unions	Life Insurance Reserves	Pension Fund Reserves	Credit and Equity Instruments	Total†
1960	$ 7.6	$ 1.4	$ 2.7	$0.5	$3.2	$ 8.3	$ 6.2	$ 29.9
1965	8.5	3.6	14.9	1.0	4.8	12.1	2.8	47.7
1970	11.0	4.4	27.0	1.2	5.5	18.4	− 1.2	66.3
1971	28.0	9.9	28.1	1.7	6.3	21.1	− 8.9	86.2
1972	32.7	10.2	29.0	2.5	6.9	22.6	6.0	109.9
1973	20.2	4.7	35.3	3.6	7.6	25.4	32.0	128.8
1974	16.1	3.1	34.1	2.6	6.7	29.6	36.6	131.2
1975	42.8	11.2	24.6	5.4	8.7	34.9	27.0	155.9
1976	50.6	13.0	40.2	5.5	8.4	44.2	19.5	181.4
1977	51.0	11.1	40.2	6.9	11.6	53.7	30.4	205.1
1978	44.9	8.6	44.1	7.6	12.0	65.8	51.9	241.8
1979	39.3	3.4	36.0	2.4	12.7	62.0	70.7	260.9
1980*	41.4	7.5	70.5	7.3	12.0	73.7	17.8	259.4

Source: Federal Home Loan Bank Board and Federal Reserve Board data as reprinted in *Savings and Loan Fact Book*, 1981, p. 18. © United States League of Savings Associations 1981.

†Note: Components may not add to totals due to rounding.
*Preliminary

revolve around the trade-off between risk and return. All rational investors want a substantial return from their investment, but they are not always willing to accept the risks associated with the high returns desired. The risk in holding securities is that the actual realized returns might be less than the expected returns.

Investors attempt to secure the largest possible rate of return at the highest level of risk that they are willing and able to assume. **Risk** is the uncertainty about the size of future returns on a principal amount of money invested. The **rate of return** is the relationship between the total annual return and the equity amount invested. It is expressed as an annual percentage rate.

Risk-Return Trade-Off

There is a positive relationship between the amount of risk assumed and the amount of expected return. That is, the greater the risk, the larger is the expected return and the larger the chances of a substantial loss. One of the more difficult problems for an investor is to estimate the highest level of risk that he or she is able to assume. Any such estimate is essentially subjective, although an attempt at quantifying investor risk can be made.

Figure 1-3 Positive Relationship Between Risk and Return

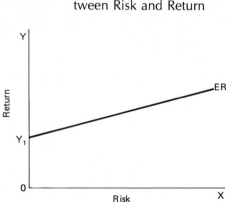

The relationship between the amount of expected return is depicted in Figure 1-3.

Risk is measured along the horizontal axis X and increases from left to right. Expected rate of return is measured on the vertical axis Y and rises from bottom to top. The line from the point 0 to Y_1 is generally called the expected rate of return on riskless investments and is commonly associated with the yield on U.S. treasury securities. The diagonal line from Y_1 to ER illustrates the concept of expected rates of return increasing as levels of risk increase. The purpose of Figure 1-3 is to illustrate the positive relationship between risk and return, although the expression is usually nonlinear. Also, as will be discussed later, there is really no security that is totally "riskless," because one or more types of risk always have the potential of affecting a security's price or income performance.

Another problem is to select individual security issues with known risk characteristics so that, when the issues are placed in a securities portfolio, the risk level of the portfolio will be averaged to the highest that the investor can afford to assume. Because this is generally a difficult task, many investors ignore this approach. The investor must select from among all security issues at a given level of risk that she or he believes will provide the highest returns. In addition, issues should be selected that are least likely to be adversely affected by the same hazards in the economy or industry or by other factors that might influence expected returns. The modern approach to portfolio management and construction is detailed in Chapter 15.

Measurement of Risk

As previously defined, risk is the uncertainty about the size of future returns (i.e., the expected rate of return) from an investment. Therefore, risk can be analyzed in terms of a probability distribution that indicates the **possible** returns and assigns probabilities to each of them. The probabilities of a specific return range from 0 (no chance of this return) to 1 (complete certainty). The assignment of probabilities can be either subjective, that is, estimated by investors, or it can be based on past frequencies (e.g., about 40 percent of the time the return on this particular investment was 15 percent). Hence, the expected rate of return is simply the weighted average of all possible returns assigned to this investment, using the associated probabilities as the weights. Mathematically,

$$\text{expected return} = (\text{probability of return})\ (\text{possible return})$$

Furthermore, the **dispersion** of those returns can be measured in terms of the variance of the estimated distribution of possible returns:

$$\text{variance (return)} = (\text{probability of return})\ (\text{possible return} - \text{expected return})^2$$

Traditionally, this measure is used to represent the **risk** of the investment.

Recently, many theorists and analysts use another approach to measure the risk of an investment in terms of **beta**. This approach will be explained fully when modern portfolio theory is discussed (Chapter 15). The basic reason for using beta is that it is more important to consider the particular investment's contribution to the risk of the portfolio to which this security belongs than the risk of the investment considered alone. If diversification is effective, that is, some securities in this portfolio are not perfectly positively correlated, then part of the risk of a security in this portfolio can be diversified. The portion of the risk that is diversifiable, in a portfolio context, is the unsystematic risk of that investment; and the portion that is undiversifiable is the systematic risk of that investment. **Systematic risk** is that portion of a security's total variability in return caused by factors affecting the price of all securities of like kind. Economic, political, business, interest rates, and inflation changes are sources of systematic risk. Their effect is to cause prices of all like securities to move together in the same manner. **Unsystematic risk** is the portion of total risk that is unique to a firm or industry, such as management's capability, labor difficulties, and changes in consumers' preferences.

Firms with high systematic risk tend to be those whose sales, profits, and stock prices follow the level of economic activity and the level of securities markets. These companies include most firms that deal in basic industrial goods and raw materials. Higher proportions of unsystematic risk are found in firms that produce nondurable consumer goods, for example, the utility industry, communications industry, and food industry.

The investor must also be aware of the concept of diversification.

Almost all types of unsystematic risk can be diversified away in a properly balanced portfolio. However, many types of systematic risk cannot be diminished, regardless of the amount of diversification among certain categories of securities.

SYSTEMATIC RISKS

Purchasing-Power Risk

Whether an individual buys securities or holds surplus funds in a bank or under the mattress, all individuals suffer from **purchasing-power risk.** This loss of income and principal because of the decreasing purchasing power of the dollar has been a basic problem for many years and is likely to continue. Therefore, the individual should construct a portfolio to help combat this risk.

For certain investors, purchasing-power risk is extremely important. Individuals and institutions that use income from their investments to buy goods and services are greatly concerned over any changes in the purchasing power of their income. Other investors, such as commercial banks and life insurance companies whose chief concern is the ability to meet fixed-dollar liabilities, will wish to achieve stable dollar values rather than be primarily concerned with protection from purchasing-power risk. Traditionally, investors who fear the effects of inflation usually invest part of their funds in a variable-return investment with the hope that these investments will rise in value over time. Generally, over the long run, well-selected investments of these equity types may increase in market price and either totally or partially offset a price level rise.

Investors who attempt to solve the problem of inflation within their investment holdings realize that fixed-income securities are of little help because they do not increase in value to compensate for the rising cost of living. Traditionally, common stock has been a good hedge against inflation, but during the period from 1965 through 1981 very little hedge against inflation was afforded holders of common stock. Therefore, one must be careful not to assume that the correlation between increasing stock prices and the consumer price index is constant, because stock prices tend to be more cyclical than do consumer prices. Nevertheless, over several decades the trend of stock prices, more than any other security investment, has tended to compensate for the trend of increasing consumer prices. In addition to real estate, precious metals, art objects, or other valuable commodities, certain stocks and convertible bonds have compensated for purchasing-power risk. The extent to which inflation governs the individual investor's policy will determine where funds should be invested.

Market risk is the loss of capital resulting from changes in price. It is not uncommon to find stock prices falling from time to time while a company's earnings are rising, and vice versa. The price of a stock may fluctuate widely within a short time even though earnings remain unchanged or relatively stable. The causes of this phenomenon are varied, but usually result from changes in the investor's attitudes and expectations.

Most market risk is caused by investor reactions to tangible as well as intangible events. For example, expectations of lower corporate profits throughout the economy may cause common stocks in general to fall in price. Investors are expressing their judgment that too much is being paid for earnings in light of anticipated events, and, therefore, this may cause a greater supply than demand for securities. Events related to market psychology are generally intangible. The emotional instability of investors acting collectively can lead to overreaction when the market rises to extreme heights or swings to extreme lows relative to the true worth of the securities.

All investors in common stock are subject to market risk, regardless of the financial condition of the particular firms or earning growth rates. However, most professional investors agree that over the long run owning common stock of financially sound and growing firms will eventually result in higher prices, even though the intermediate swings can be very sharp and deep. Instead of falling victim to panic and unloading their common stock, many experienced investors wait for a sharp setback in the market to accumulate additional stock.

An investor can do a number of things to compensate for market risk. One must carefully examine the history of each security's price behavior. Stocks that have demonstrated high volatility or a cyclical pattern in the past will likely follow that same pattern in the future. Stocks that have demonstrated a growth pattern in the past should continue to do so in the future unless there is a basic change in the company's expectation for its products or the market it serves.

The investor might choose stocks that have the lowest amount of market risk. Common stocks that are growth oriented or that offer a combination of growth and income might not have the same degree of market risk as cyclical stocks. This enables the investor to analyze market behavior and select stocks that offer both growth and income but not the traditional risks associated with cyclical stocks. Nevertheless, high-growth stocks will generally experience a sharp market price decline when a firm's growth rate slows and the market places a lower demand for that company's or industry's securities. For example, during the 1970s, the automobile industry experienced a slackening in demand for their product. Many analysts suggested that the automobile industry had matured and should no longer be considered a growth industry. The stock prices of all automobile companies dropped continually and sharply from their mid-1960 peak prices while the investment community reexamined the industry's desirability.

Investors can also reduce market risk by being careful in the timing of their purchase or sale of stock. Timing, however, is one of the most difficult tasks confronting the investor. Individual investors are traditionally poor market performers, mostly because their timing is generally incorrect. Most small individual investors buy more at market highs than they sell, and they sell considerably more shares at market bottoms than they buy. Chapter 13 examines the various timing approaches to the market, including the technician's approach.

In distinguishing between investors and speculators, it was noted that investors must be prepared to invest for a relatively long period of time if they are to benefit from a rising trend of stock prices and avoid the market's intermittent cyclical activity. The longer-term approach will usually minimize market risk if the investor is holding the stock of a quality firm that is experiencing rising earnings and a good rate of return on assets and equity.

Interest-Rate Risk

Interest-rate risk is the risk of loss of principal brought about by changes in the prevailing interest rate paid on new securities that are currently being issued. Although all investments are subject to interest-rate risk, long-term fixed-income securities are the most vulnerable. Although the rate of interest rises or falls in the marketplace as a result of the supply and demand for money, purchasers of fixed-income securities (such as bonds) receive only the fixed rate of interest specified in the contract (indenture). Therefore, the current rate of interest in the marketplace represents an **opportunity cost** to investors, because it is the rate of return that they could have earned by investing now had they not put the money into previous bonds. For example, an investor in 1976 could have purchased a AA rated industrial bond of 8 percent due in 30 years; but 5 years later, in 1981, the market interest rates went very high, and a similar bond due in 25 years (therefore, with the same maturity date) would have a coupon of 16 percent. Hence, to provide 1981 purchasers of the 8 percent bond with the same rate of return, the price of this bond will drop until the yield to maturity equals 16 percent. This drop creates a loss of principal to the original bondholders (those who bought the bond in 1976) if they decide to sell the bond in 1981. Nevertheless, the bonds whose price has decreased will eventually rise to $1,000 (the principal) at maturity date because the issuer of the bond is obligated to pay the holder at maturity $1,000.

In general, investors of fixed-income securities will find the price of their holdings rising at times when interest rates are decreasing and the price of their securities decreasing when interest rates in the marketplace are rising. This inverse relationship between interest rates and bond prices will be discussed further in Chapter 4.

The shorter the period of time is until a bond matures, the less susceptible the owners will be to interest-rate risk. The period of exposure to interest-rate fluctuation is shorter, and the closer the bond is to the maturity date, the more certain the bond's price will be. (It should be closer to $1,000) Short-term fixed-income securities will minimize the effect of interest-rate risk on the value of the investment since investors will be able to reinvest the funds at prevailing market rates. However, investors are then subject to income risk (or reinvestment risk) in that, when the short-term investment matures, the market rate may have fallen so that less income can be purchased with the same amount of money. This is also pertinent to the coupon reinvestment for all bonds. Purchasers of bonds receive interest payment periodically. If they invest those interest payments ("interest on interest") in the market, they are also susceptible to the fluctuation of market rates. To eliminate this type of reinvestment risk, zero-coupon bonds were first issued in 1981. These bonds do not pay holders any interest. Instead, they are sold at a discount when issued and pay $1,000 at maturity. An example would be the General Motors Acceptance Corporation's $1,000 zero-coupon bond issued in 1981 maturing in 1991. It was sold for $252 a bond when issued; therefore, its yield to maturity is equivalent to 14.75 percent annual compounded rate. Since there is no coupon interest payment, the purchasers are not subject to coupon reinvestment risk.

UNSYSTEMATIC RISKS

Business Risk

Changes in a company's earning power may result in a loss in income or capital to the investor. The inability of a company to maintain its competitive position and the growth or stability of its earnings is called **business risk.** Business risk is a function of the operating conditions of a firm, and the lack of stability of these operating conditions will determine operating income and dividends.

Business risk can be divided into two categories: external and internal. **External** business risk is the result of operating conditions imposed upon the firm by economic circumstances. Each firm faces its own set of external risks, depending upon the specific operating environment in which it functions. The external factors are various, but the most powerful single factor is the general business cycle of the economy.

Internal business risk is largely associated with the efficiency with which a firm conducts its operations within the broader operating environment imposed upon it. Each firm has its own set of internal risks, and the degree to which the firm is successful in dealing with them is reflected in its operating efficiency.

The operating efficiency of International Business Machines or Procter & Gamble is widely and highly regarded, and the internal business risk for these firms has been minimal. But their external business risk is considered higher than for a firm like American Telephone & Telegraph, because the predictability of economic influences is higher for American Telephone & Telegraph than for IBM or Procter & Gamble.

Internal business risk can be difficult to determine over the short run because it depends upon management ability. The management efficiency of a firm can be analyzed by comparing how the firm utilizes its assets with how other firms in the same industry utilize their assets.

External business risk, however, is more easily determined because investors can examine the economic conditions within which a firm or industry operates. There is no doubt that general economic conditions influence the level of revenues for a firm.

Before investors select an investment, they should decide what degree of business risk they wish to assume. They have a choice between stable industries (utilities) or cyclical industries (construction, paper, chemical, and steel). Investors may choose between a strong leader in an industry or a smaller firm with a poor earnings record that shows significant signs of improvement. They may also choose among securities of a particular firm: bonds, preferred stock, common stock, warrants, and options. If they choose to be defensive in their approach to business risk, they may limit their risk and reduce both the chance for loss and generally the opportunity for substantial gain. If investors choose to be more aggressive, they may undertake greater risk and may receive a greater return.

Financial Risk

Financial risk is associated with the way in which a company finances its operations. A firm's financial risk is usually determined by an examination of its capital structure (the right-hand side of the balance sheet). Debt in the capital structure creates fixed payments in the form of interest, principal, and leases that must be met by the firm, regardless of fluctuations in revenue. These fixed charges cause the amount of earnings remaining for common-stockholders to be more variable than if no interest payments were required. Financial risk can be avoided entirely if management decides not to borrow any funds and, therefore, to have no debt in the firm's capital structure. The accounting and finance student will recognize that financial risk is associated with a firm's leveraged capital structure. Debt financing affects the returns to common-stockholders because it increases the variability of common stock returns and affects common-stockholders' expectations of their return.

The firm's ability to meet its financial obligations is the central concern for the individual examining financial risk. The degree of financial risk also varies between different securities issued by one corporation. If a corporation becomes insolvent, the owners of one type of security may have a superior claim to the assets of the corporation. For example, it is possible for stockholders of an insolvent corporation to receive virtually nothing for their stock while bondholders might receive full reimbursement for the face amount of the bonds. As a result, bondholders assume a smaller financial risk than stockholders do.

The degree of a company's financial risk can be measured by its ability to meet its fixed payments. The company's total fixed charges should be compared with its earnings before interest and taxes are deducted. The higher the amount of earnings before interest and taxes relative to fixed payments, the less financial risk there is. This relationship is generally called the **fixed-charge coverage ratio.** The investor should also examine the relationship between a firm's debt and its stockholder equity. The greater management's dependence upon outside financing relative to the owner's contribution, the higher is the financial risk and the higher the interest charges. This relationship is generally called the **debt-equity ratio.** Conservative investors will generally avoid companies with a combination of high business and financial risk, because the variability of earnings will generally be large as the firm encounters different phases of the business cycle.

KEY TERMS

business risk	liquidity
capital markets	market risk
debt-equity ratio	purchasing-power risk
financial risk	rate of return
fixed-charge coverage ratio	speculation
interest-rate risk	systematic risk
investment	unsystematic risk

QUESTIONS

1. Explain the differences among investment, speculation, and gambling.
2. In what way does an investor differ from a speculator?
3. What are the first three steps that an investor should take in analyzing a security?
4. What is the single most important aspect of the analysis of an equity security? Why?
5. What should an investor consider before he invests in securities?
6. Why would an investor buy a whole life insurance policy?

7. What is the importance of secondary markets?
8. What are some of the reasons why people save?
9. Explain the importance of savings in a capitalistic system.
10. Define the following:
    a. Risk and the rate of return
    b. Systematic and unsystematic risk
    c. Purchasing-power risk
    d. Market risk
    e. Interest-rate risk
    f. Business risk
    g. Financial risk

SELECTED READINGS

American Institute for Economic Research. *Life Insurance from the Buyer's Point of View and Annuities from the Buyer's Point of View*. Great Barrington, Mass.: The Institute (revised occasionally).

BEJA, AVAHAM. "On Systematic and Unsystematic Components of Financial Risk." *Journal of Finance*, March 1972, 37.

BLUME, MARSHALL E. "On the Assessment of Risk." *Journal of Finance*, March 1971, 1.

CRAWFORD, PETER H. "Money and Household Liquidity." *Financial Analysts Journal* January–February 1967, 117.

GRAHAM, BENJAMIN, D.L. DODD, and SIDNEY COTTLE. *Security Analysis*, 4th ed. Chapters 4 and 8. New York: McGraw-Hill, 1962.

HAYES, DOUGLAS A. "The Multi-dimensional Aspects of Risk." *Journal of Portfolio Management*, Summer 1976, 23–28.

HEINLEIN, CARSTON. "Beta to Omega: Here's a Simple Way to Figure a Stock's Volatility." *Barron's*, May 30, 1977, 9, 18.

MODIGLIANI, FRANCO, and GERALD A. POGUE. "An Introduction to Risk and Return." *Financial Analysts Journal*, March–April 1974, 68–80, Part I, and May–June 1974, 69–86, Part II.

MOFFITT, DONALD. "Volatility, Beta for the Individual Investor." *Wall Street Journal*, June 20, 1977.

MUELLER, EVA, and JANE LEAN. "The Savings Account as a Source of Financing for Larger Expenditures." *Journal of Finance*, September 1967, 467–470.

"Taking Big Risks for Big Profits." *Money*, December 1976, 48–50.

"Term Insurance vs. Whole Life." *Forbes*, March 15, 1975, 45–50.

2

The Individual's Investment Perspective

The characteristics and limitations of individual investors are the primary concern of this chapter. Decisions regarding the rate of interest and its true determination affect every investor both in analyzing a security for possible investment and in analyzing the investor's personal financial affairs. Therefore, every investor should be able to perform various basic mathematical calculations in order to understand the total position of an investment and the opportunities it presents. This chapter will discuss a few basic calculations of interest rates. Calculations related to valuation of specific types of securities will be discussed later in the book when each security is analyzed.

TIME VALUE OF MONEY

The essence of investment and savings resides in the trade-off between current consumption and a larger future consumption. A person who is willing to sacrifice a portion of the current consumption demands a higher level of future consumption to compensate for the deferment. If both the current and future consumption levels are certain, the exchange rate between the two represents the pure time value of money, or the pure interest rate. For example, if the compensation for sacrificing $100 today is 105 "certain" dollars one year later, provided the price level does not fluctuate at all, then the pure time value of money is 5 percent (105/100 − 1).

However, in the real world, the price level rises as time passes. Investors suffer from purchasing-power risk when giving up current consumption for the future. To continue the example, assume that the investor perceives that the price level will rise by 10 percent annually for the future years, thereby imposing an extra 10 percent on the original 5 percent rate of interest in order to compensate for the purchasing-power risk. Hence, the rate of interest is 15 percent [(100)(1.15)/100 − 1] for this investor, provided that there is no chance for the future payment to be in default. Finally, if the investor has doubts concerning the future payment, he or she may want to add a "risk premium," say 4 percent, and make the total interest rate 19 percent per annum.

INTEREST CALCULATIONS

A great number of investment decisions depend upon interest considerations. Much of a security's market price behavior is attributable to its sensitivity to interest. The payment or receipt of interest can be looked at from several points of view. For example, the recipient of an interest payment is concerned with interest as the return that will be realized from ownership. A security's return comes from two sources: (1) periodic payments of dividends or interest, and (2) market value changes in the dollars invested. Individual securities differ in the total amount of return that can be realized and in the relative amounts provided from these two sources.

Simple Interest Calculation

Interest received on any investment is affected by the length of time the investment is held. Unless otherwise specified, interest is always calculated on an annual basis. The basic calculation is the determination of **simple interest** over a period of time. For any specified time period, the ratio of interest earned in that time period in relation to the principal invested is called the **interest rate.** It is determined by the following formula:

$$\text{interest rate} = \frac{\text{interest earned on principal per period}}{\text{principal}}$$

For example, if the interest earned on the principal over a 1-year period is $40 and the principal invested is $500, the resulting interest rate would be 8 percent.

An initial investment of any kind can grow over time and is expressed by the end value V, determined by the following calculation:

where: $V = P(1 + g)^n$
V = ending or terminal value
n = number of compounding periods
g = rate of compounding (percent)
P = initial value

Thus, $1.00 placed in the bank at 6 percent interest will grow to $1.06 at the end of 1 year because $V = \$1.00(1 + .06)^1 = \$1.06$.

Effective Interest Calculation

If individuals are to be successful with an investment program during their lifetime, they must understand the concept of **effective interest rate** as it applies to the various loans that will confront them. Whether individuals are obtaining a loan for the purchase of an automobile, appliances, or securities, it is important for them to be aware of the effective rate of interest that they will have to pay. Interest is expressed in a variety of ways. The formula for effective interest rate reduces the figures to the annual rate of interest actually paid after considering the important element of the time value of money. The formula for the effective annual rate of interest is commonly expressed as

$$r = \frac{2mni}{mn + 1}$$

where: r = effective rate of interest
m = number of payment periods in 1 year
i = annual interest rate stated
n = number of years over life of loan

To demonstrate how the effective rate of interest is computed, consider the common example of a loan for the purchase of a car. If the purchaser is financing $3,000 of the price of the automobile, the lending company or bank may state that the charge is $7\frac{1}{4}$ percent interest. However, the Truth-in-Lending Law requires that the individual be given a written statement of the effective interest rate. Thus, in addition to the rate, the lender would state that the loan is for 3 years and that a total of $3,652.50 [3,000($7\frac{1}{4}$ %)(3)

+ 3,000] will be paid over the life of the loan. Using the formula for the effective rate of interest, we find that the rate is 14.11 percent.

$$r = \frac{2(12)(3)(7\frac{1}{4}\%)}{(12)(3) + 1}$$
$$= \frac{522\%}{37}$$
$$= 14.11\%$$

Compound Interest Calculation

Compound interest is interest paid on interest already earned. Compound interest is one of the most important and dramatic factors in building a lifetime investment portfolio. For example, if one of the investor's objectives is to provide retirement funds, it is important for the investor to start putting money aside early, because funds will then receive compound interest over a long period of time. In such a situation, compounding will have the greatest impact on the investment program in the years just before retirement.

The equation for determining the terminal value (V) can be used to determine the ending value of a sum of money earning compound interest over various time periods. For example, if $1.00 is compounded over a period of 10 years at 6 percent, the terminal value would be $1.79, because $V = \$1.00(1 + .06)^{10} = \$1.79$.

Appendix A-1 shows how $1.00 can be compounded over various time periods using various interest rates. For example, the table shows that $1.00 compounded at 6 percent over 10 years is $1.791. It also simplifies the task of calculating the terminal value of amounts other than $1.00. For example, using this table, it can be determined that if $8.55 is placed in a bank at 6 percent interest, the terminal value at the end of 6 years will be $12.13. First, select the appropriate factor for a 6 percent compounding rate in the sixth year: 1.419. Then multiply that factor by the amount invested, $8.55; the resulting terminal value is $12.13. The formula from the previous section on simple interest rate shows the calculation as

$$V = p(1 + g)^n$$
$$= \$8.55(1 + .06)^6$$
$$= \$8.55(1.49)$$
$$= \$12.13$$

For convenience and simplicity, the assumption is that in each of these calculations the frequency of compounding is once per period at the end of each period. Therefore, annual compounding is used rather than shorter periods such as semiannual or quarterly. If, for example, semiannual compounding is used, select an interest rate of 3 percent, but use 12 periods (rather than a rate of 6 percent for 6 periods).

Present values can be thought of as the reverse of compounding or as discounted future values. For example, how much should be deposited in a bank today at 6 percent interest in order to accumulate $5.00 in 1 year? The appropriate values can be substituted in the present-value formula:

$$PV = \frac{V}{(1 + i)^n}$$

where:
PV = present value
V = terminal value
i = interest or discount rate
n = number of periods

Thus:
$$PV = \frac{\$5.00}{(1 + .06)^1}$$
$$= \$4.72$$

Appendix A-2 provides the sum of an annuity factor for various interest rates over various periods of time (eliminating the necessity of compounding each dollar deposited). For example, the fifth-year factor at 8 percent is 5.867; this factor can be multiplied by the annuity investment of $1,000 per period at the end of each period to obtain the sum of $5,867. Appendix A-3 can illustrate the impact of compounding on an individual investment program. If the individual has 30 years of earning power remaining, if this person can save $1,000 per year in each of those 30 years, the table indicates that the individual will accumulate $113,283 before taxes at an 8 percent rate.

If an individual approaches the investment program prudently and allows the necessary time to achieve his goals, a difference of 1 or 2 percentage points in the rate of return on investment over a 30-year period can have a dramatic effect on the total dollars accumulated. For example, if an individual invests at a rate of 5 percent, he or she will have only $66,439 at the end of 30 years, rather than the $113,283 had the selected investments yielded 8 percent compounded over the same period. The difference of 3 percentage points in the compound rate of return means a difference of more than $46,000 accumulated on the investment.

An investment application of the concept of the compound sum of an annuity is the appropriation of sufficient dollar amounts to meet a bond sinking-fund obligation. For example, if a company issues a 20-year bond for $50 million and the bond indenture (the legal contract) requires that the firm set aside sufficient funds to retire the bond by the twentieth year, the company must decide how much money to appropriate from their cash flow each year. If the entire $50 million must be available in the twentieth year of the bond issue and the sinking-fund payments begin in the fifth year, the firm has 15 years to set money aside to provide for the $50 million repayment. If the company believes that the sinking fund can grow at a compounded rate of 8 percent over the 15-year period, it will have to set aside $1,841,484 per year. That figure can be derived by dividing $50 million by the factor 27.152, which is the sum of an annuity compounded at 8 percent for the 15 years, as shown in Appendix A-3. Appendix A-3, which has been constructed on the basis of the present-value formula, indicates a factor of .943 for $1.00 discounted at 6 percent over a 1-year period. To determine the present value of $5.00 discounted at 6 percent, the factor .943 is multiplied by $5.00, which gives a present value of $4.72.

To determine whether that $4.72 will grow to $5.00 in 1 year at 6 percent, refer back to Appendix A-1 (the compound sum of $1).

$$V = \$4.72(1 + .06)^1$$
$$= \$5.00$$

The compounding and present-value formulas describe the future and present values of single sums. In other words, the future value of an invested single lump sum that is compounded for a number of periods can be determined. Also, the present value of a single sum to be received at some point in the future can be determined.

In the investment field, annuity investments or payments are quite common. For example, an individual may decide to save an equal dollar amount from each paycheck so that the amount will be compounded over a number of years until it is sufficient to meet one or more financial objectives. If the individual is able to save $1,000 per year, at a compounded interest rate of 8 percent to meet a particular need at the end of 5 years, the funds accumulated would amount to $5,867. This can be determined by calculating each $1,000 compounded at the end of the 5-year period:

$1,000 invested at end of 1st year = $1,361 at end of 5th year
1,000 invested at end of 2nd year = 1,260 at end of 5th year
1,000 invested at end of 3rd year = 1,166 at end of 5th year
1,000 invested at end of 4th year = 1,080 at end of 5th year
1,000 invested at end of 5th year = 1,000 at end of 5th year
Compounded sum = $5,867

Annuities

Furthermore, there are investment situations in which equal periodic sums are invested or received. The method of compounding an annuity to determine the sum of a constant-dollar investment will be discussed later. Also, there are times when the investor will want to know the present value of an annuity. This involves dealing with the present value of a stream of future payments. For example, the present value of a series of payments of $1.00 received at the end of each of the next 3 years at a rate of 6 percent is $2.673. This contrasts with the present value of a single payment of $1.00 at the end of the third year at 6 percent, which is $.84. The present value of an annuity of $1.00 is shown in Appendix A-4, which is simply the sum of the present values of $1.00 given in Appendix A-2.

Suppose that an individual wants to know how much to deposit today in order to provide $1.00 of benefits in each of the next 5 years at an interest rate of 6 percent. Using Appendix A-4, it can be determined that $4.21 must be deposited at 6 percent in order to withdraw $1.00 at the end of each of the next 5 years.

The present value of an annuity is commonly used by insurance companies to determine the size of death-benefit payments on a life insurance policy. For example, if a beneficiary is entitled to $50,000, he or she may elect to receive the payout, including interest, over a 10-year period. If the insurance company assumes a 6 percent rate of interest, the beneficiary will receive $6,793.48 per year. This can be determined by finding the appropriate factor in Appendix A-4, which is 7.360, and dividing it into $50,000.

INDIVIDUAL INVESTORS

If investors are to accomplish prudent investment planning, they must set forth and define their overall investment goals and objectives. This text attempts to set forth the basic investment principles by which investors can achieve their basic objectives. Throughout the text the emphasis is on an integrated approach to the investment process.

INVESTOR CHARACTERISTICS

Individuals differ greatly in their circumstances. Therefore, a financial program well suited to one individual may be inappropriate for another. An analysis of an individual's investment situation requires a study of his or her personal characteristics, such as age, health conditions, personal habits, marital status, business or professional situation, and tax status, all of which affect a willingness to assume risk.

Age and Health

Major factors affecting an individual's investment objective are age and state of health. A person in poor health or advanced in age may prefer to keep the investments in a fairly liquid form, emphasizing income and safety of principal instead of growth. This investor may not be particularly concerned about purchasing-power risk. A young person, however, may put great emphasis on growth and purchasing-power protection and place less emphasis on liquidity. Immediate cash income is subject to income taxes, but any appreciation in a securities portfolio at least postpones and usually reduces the tax if the securities are held longer than 1 year.

The younger individual can also afford to be patient for the realization of capital gains. Younger investors usually tend to be less cautious than older ones, perhaps because they are willing to accept risk, but also perhaps because they lack experience. Often, younger investors experiment in the marketplace in an attempt to become reasonably sophisticated, but in the process they often lose substantial amounts. As investors approach retirement, most of them tend to become more conservative because they feel that their poor past experiences are indicators of their future potential.

Principal may be jeopardized by an investor's poor health. If demands for current income are large, the growth potential of the investment will diminish.

Family Responsibilities

The investor's marital status can have a large impact on the investment needs and goals. Because an employed spouse usually has to provide for the physical and emotional needs of the family, this person tends to be a more conservative investor and is less likely to speculate. The number and age of dependents and their potential educational requirements can have a significant impact on investment planning. The cost of buying a home and providing life insurance often makes the development of an investment program difficult for a family during the early years. The investment needs of a single person are less complex, usually because the financial needs are less complex.

Investor's Experience

The investment objective and the success of the portfolio depend upon the investor's knowledge and experience in business and financial matters. If an investor has an aptitude for business affairs, he or she may wish to be more aggressive in investments. If talents are in other fields, and if portfolios are of moderate size, he or she may prefer to be more conservative. If the portfolio is large, an individual may wish to have the investments handled by an investment counselor. However, just because an individual has business and financial expertise does not guarantee success in the securities markets. It does, however, indicate a more mature ability to understand and evaluate the risks involved.

Also to be considered are the time the investor has to devote to investments and the temperament of the investor. The time available directly affects the investment choices, unless, of course, the investor decides to delegate the management of his or her portfolio. An investor's temperament could have a significant effect upon the performance of selected securities because inevitable fluctuations of the stock market, even if of a minor nature, do cause some people to worry considerably. For such people, less volatile security commitments, such as bonds or income-producing equities, may be preferable to common stocks, even though fixed-income securities may contain financial disadvantages for the investor.

Willingness to Assume Risk

A person's emotional makeup and financial position indicate the ability to assume the risks of an investment. As discussed in Chapter 1, there are a variety of risks to which some or all securities are subject. Since risks are always present, the investor should understand their nature, be willing to accept them, and make the necessary provisions against them. Some investors eagerly accept risk and are not alarmed if they lose large sums of money. These people are prepared financially and emotionally to invest in the more volatile securities. Others are so security conscious that they could not risk the loss of any amount; therefore, they should avoid the stock market entirely.

Many small investors do not take the responsibility of first accumulating good basic securities. They forget that investing and building a solid and well-diversified portfolio of securities takes time. Only after the basic foundation has been prepared should most investors begin to accept higher degrees of risk. The problem is that most investors find it very difficult to establish these permissible levels of risk, because changing patterns and levels do not allow risk to be examined in a static state.

INDIVIDUAL INVESTOR CONSTRAINTS AND ATTITUDES

The investor's objective is to obtain the highest possible total rate of return at the highest acceptable level of risk. The problem of determining one's ability to assume risk is difficult. All the principal conditions that affect the ability of people and institutions to absorb the impact of low rates of return and loss of principal must be examined.

The problem of an investor's ability to assume risk is complicated because adverse investment outcomes take several forms. Most frequently, adverse risks take the form of a decline in the market price of securities. This means a loss of the investor's principal. In addition, there may be a decrease in the amount of income payments that may be derived from an investment.

Adverse investment outcomes have not only financial consequences but also emotional impacts. An investor might reason that he or she should achieve greater returns by assuming more risk. The individual may not have the financial stability, psychological makeup, or knowledge and experience to withstand increased risk. In such a case, increased risk may lead to financial disaster. When investors evaluate the risks inherent in a security, they must know how these risks will affect them and how they will respond to such risks. The investor's ability to accept risk is called **investor constraint.**

Financial Constraints

For investors to evaluate the impact of various risks on their financial circumstances, they must understand the budget restrictions on their long-range overall financial plans. The investor's budget should contain an estimate of the amount of funds, if any, that can be appropriated from savings for investment. If investment funds are accumulated each year for important future family obligations, such as children's college education, the degree of risk that can be assumed may be less than if the funds had no significant future requirement.

It is, of course, difficult for young persons to predict their salary, number of children, house payments, retirement benefits, and so forth, 30 or 40 years hence. Nevertheless, it is important that they make a long-term projection and continually revise it if they are to have a viable investment program designed to meet future needs.

If high liquidity is a requirement in the short term, this financial constraint may require that investments be limited to securities that can be easily converted into cash without loss of principal. The total financial plan will dictate the appropriate amount of types of investments. The investment program must be flexible if the individual's financial circumstances change over the years. Nevertheless, high-risk investments should not be included in an investment portfolio until a good foundation of quality securities has been established. Futhermore, high-risk investments should only comprise a small percentage of any individual's investment portfolio, regardless of the individual's financial position.

Psychological Constraints

An individual's temperament affects the ability to withstand risk. The higher the risk is, the more volatile the market performance of a security will be and the greater the opportunity for high gain or loss. Although all investors try to maximize their returns with the least amount of risk and, therefore, tend to be risk averters, some are never able to make rational decisions about risky investments. Even with low-risk securities, many individuals cannot divorce emotions from the investment decision. Small investors do not usually time their purchases and sales well. As indicated earlier, small

Figure 2-1 Small-Investor Syndrome

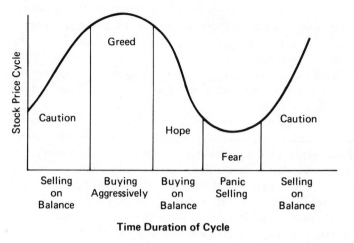

Source: Charles L. Barngrover and Timothy E. Johnson, *Personal Finance*, Grid, Inc., 1974, p. 405.

Adapted from Wilbur E. Widicus, Jr., and Thomas E. Stitzel, *Personal Investing*, revised edition (Homewood, Ill.: Richard D. Irwin, Inc., 1976), p. 426.

investors usually buy more securities than they sell when the market is at its top and sell significantly more shares than they buy when the market is at a bottom. Figure 2-1 illustrates the small-investor syndrome. It shows how emotions enter the investment picture and cause the investor to make a wrong decision.

Management Constraints

There is little doubt that the more experience and expertise an investor has the more likely success will be over the long run. The knowledgeable investor will be less likely to construct an investment portfolio of securities that is highly risk oriented or is based on speculation. This does not mean that there are any guarantees for those investors who have a great deal of experience and knowledge in investments. However, over the long run, most investors cannot afford to speculate with their resources; therefore, investment decisions must be based on sound fundamental principles that take into consideration the total financial picture.

Many investors know that they lack expertise in the investment process. The analysis section of this text instructs the investor to begin with an analysis of the economy, to select the strongest industries within the economic environment, and then to select those companies that are the major participants within those industries.

The investor may conclude that any long-term success can only come with the help of outside experts. Careful consideration must be given to select a broker whose experience in investment management is grounded in a good understanding of the securities market and security analysis. Although there are a number of excellent brokers available, the investor must keep in mind that brokers are salespersons foremost, not analysts or portfolio managers. Sometimes the research department of the broker's firm will provide the necessary investment advice that will help the individual investor to be successful.

In seeking professional advice, investors may use the services of an investment company (discussed in Chapter 10) or they may go to one of the many professional investment advisory services. The advisory services usually manage individual investment accounts of $50,000 and up. Very few of them provide individual attention for small accounts. A number of the professional investment advisory services do, however, publish investment information and recommend individual securities and portfolios to aid the small investor who is trying to manage his or her own portfolio.

PERSONAL OBJECTIVES OF INVESTMENT MANAGEMENT

A logical approach to understanding an individual investor's needs is to examine the usual steps in a financial program and the factors involved in formulating investment objectives. Almost all rational investors strive to fulfill certain needs through an investment program. Some of these needs are financial, some are emotional, and some psychological. The central issue in investment is a positive return to meet various objectives. The needs may be for education, to improve one's standard of living, for retirement, or for contributions to religious and/or social causes. Often the motive is the desire for economic power and control over assets. Some investors seek status. They want their friends to think that they are knowledgeable and important.

The amount of funds available for investment either restricts or expands the ability to meet the investor's needs. Individuals who discipline themselves to operate their daily activities within a realistic financial budget generally have more funds available for investment than do those who allow their standards of living to consume the available funds. As their savings increase and accumulate, investors' objectives can be widened and more risk assumed. Certainly, as individuals become older, their needs and their rankings of objectives may change, either because their perspectives change or because the circumstances surrounding them change.

Insurance Protection

An early step in most people's financial programs is to purchase life insurance. Life insurance provides a family with financial protection if the breadwinner dies prematurely. The need for this protection is greatest for relatively young people who have young children. For a person whose children are grown and who is approaching retirement age, insurance may be of little importance. Life insurance may also be purchased as a means of investment. However, the relatively low rate of return of the reserve account and the cost associated with purchasing protection leads most analysts to conclude that insurance is not a good investment, because other vehicles better achieve investment goals. Insurance is also purchased to provide liquidity for an estate settlement. The tax-free accumulation of cash reserves is usually of secondary importance to those who want an investment program.

Providing a Home

The purchase of a home is probably the largest single investment made by the majority of families. The financial aspects of home ownership are discussed in Chapter 16. An individual who decides to purchase a home as part of the investment portfolio should be aware of the large continuing cash requirements that are necessary to meet the needs of home ownership. These include mortgage payments, increased expenditures for furniture, lawn care, upkeep, utilities, taxes, and so on. Nevertheless, if a home is purchased in an area where property values are expected to rise during the anticipated period of home ownership, a person may potentially do as well in the long run with owning a home as living in a rental unit and investing the additional cash savings.

The modern method of amortizing the purchase of a home through a long-term mortgage solves many of the problems of investing in a home and relieves the home buyer of the responsibilities of managing the funds. The required payments of interest plus principal are a budget item that for most people ranks in importance second only to food.

Once a substantial equity in a home has been acquired, the investor has a considerable sum of money tied up in fixed property. This portion of the savings is subject to the risks of changing land values, obsolescence, neighborhood decline, and swings in the real estate market. One negative aspect is that the investor has put a substantial portion of his or her assets into one item and has thus sacrificed diversification. The owner of a well-selected, well-maintained property, however, may offset these risks by enjoying a hedge against the decline in the purchasing power of the dollar and by reaping tax benefits because the interest on the mortgage and the property taxes can be deducted from ordinary income.

Liquid Reserves

During the early stages of lifetime financial planning, the individual should be concerned with providing a reserve fund to meet unexpected needs. The size of the fund may range from three to twelve months' average living expenses and depends partly upon the amount and stability of the individual's income and the liquidity of other assets. As the amount of liquid assets increases, the need for providing an emergency fund decreases, because most individuals can liquidate sufficient funds to meet an emergency without substantially reducing their assets. This assumes, of course, that the investor has adequate medical and life insurance coverage to provide substantial funds for large emergencies. In other words, if the investor has adequate insurance protection and increasing liquid assets, the need for an emergency fund diminishes accordingly.

The major requirement of an emergency fund is to recover dollars when needed. Therefore, the rate of return on an emergency fund is usually low. The emergency fund is held in the form of bank savings deposits, accounts in savings and loan institutions, and U.S. savings bonds. The cash surrender value of life insurance policies should never be relied on as a regular segment of the emergency fund because any use of these funds lowers the death benefit and therefore the level of protection desired.

Large Needs before Retirement

One specialized objective for many family investment plans is the education of children. Funds saved for education should generally be directed to investments that can accumulate a definite sum by a definite time in the future. Many investors provide for education by purchasing fixed-income securities, such as high-quality corporate bonds or U.S. savings bonds. The earlier a family plans for educational needs, the less money it will need to deposit in such a fund in order to accumulate the desired amount. The investors, however, must remember that by providing for educational needs many years into the future, they may lose the purchasing power of the accumulated dollars. The purchase of well-selected common stocks may combat this risk if investors have a long enough period of time in which to allow the variable portfolio to appreciate.

Providing for Retirement

A main objective for a great number of investors is to provide sufficient funds to supplement any pension benefits that may be received from an employer and/or Social Security. The importance of this objective varies from one individual to another. Young families give it little attention because other needs are more pressing, but with the passage of time they begin to consider the need for establishing retirement income. Some individuals rely substantially on Social Security benefits or other public retirement plans and on private pension plans. Therefore, their flexibility during retirement is limited. Investors who feel the need to supplement retirement income accumulate funds in their investment program.

For individuals who want a minimum of risk and complete freedom from asset management, U.S. government bonds, savings accounts, fixed-dollar annuity programs, and certain mutual funds are likely to produce reasonable long-run results. But the returns are limited and purchasing-power risk is one of the major risks. The investor who cannot assume anything but the absolute minimum in risk, or who is not in a position to assume the responsibilities of managing an investment fund, must generally rely heavily on fixed-annuity or fixed-return securities.

Other investors prepare for retirement through long-range programs of direct security purchases, which include a combination of bonds, stocks, and real estate, or the selection of investment company shares. The hope is that over the long run the value of the portfolio will rise at a greater rate than inflation and that the accumulation will be large enough to provide the desired level of income during retirement.

Individuals who are managing their own retirement funds are faced with the problem of determining just how large the funds should be to produce a desired level of income during retirement. How can they know the rate of inflation before and during retirement? How can they know how long they will live? Because estimating life expectancy is virtually impossible, life insurance companies provide a desirable alternative. Life insurance companies are not concerned with the life expectancy of individual annuity holders. They are more concerned with the mortality rates of the group as a whole. Therefore, at retirement, an investor might find purchasing an annuity contract from a life insurance company desirable. Just as with funds for college education for children, the earlier that funds can be set aside, the larger the retirement fund will be.

FINANCIAL OBJECTIVES OF INVESTMENT MANAGEMENT

The previous section dealt mainly with the investor's personal needs. It is important for investors to consider their personal needs because of the impact they have on the parameters of their investment programs. This section will deal with the investor's financial needs.

Safety of Principal

The protection of the dollar value of the investment is of prime importance to most investors. The principal of any investment may be recovered through resale only if the security instrument is readily marketable and enjoys price stability. Securities that have a fixed maturity date provide the eventual recovery of principal at maturity, except in the case of default or reorganization. If the investor is attempting to meet personal objectives over the short term, safety of principal is assured only through purchasing fixed-income securities that have very short maturities.

Emergency funds require complete liquidity, but liquidity is achieved only with some sacrifice of income. The same is true of institutional investments, such as banks that must meet payments on demand or on relatively short notice. Immediate recovery of funds held as protection against the death of the income producer for a family is likely to be necessary for only part of the total family needs. Investments made for educating children generally require considerable safety of principal and availability at a specific time in the future. In most cases, the investor should be unwilling to risk dollars saved if the need is relatively short term.

Although funds may not be required immediately, ultimate recovery of principal is usually a major requirement. The importance of avoiding loss of principal varies greatly from one individual situation to another.

Safety of principal means more than just maintaining the original value of the investment. It also means protecting the purchasing power of the funds. Therefore, the investor should invest in securities that are anticipated to increase in value if the purchasing power of the dollar declines over the long run. Although common stocks are not a perfect hedge against inflation, especially over the short term, they usually provide a better hedge than do fixed-income securities.

Assurance of Income

In establishing the investment fund, an investor should attempt to achieve stability of income. Stability of income allows the investor an opportunity to enjoy the benefits of the investment portfolio now. These benefits are in the form of income or a contingency fund available for reinvestment. Income received now in the form of dividends and interest is generally more valuable than a promise of future dividends and interest. Stability of income allows the investor to plan his total investment program more accurately and logically.

Investors who require an assured income should select safe securities to provide the level of income they desire. In this case, emphasis is usually placed on fixed-return securities, but some common stocks that pay a high dividend yield but lack strong growth prospects may be appropriate. For example, the common stocks of utility companies may be appropriate for these investors.

Capital Appreciation

Generally, the investor's objective is to have the principal amount of his or her investment portfolio grow in value. This does not necessarily mean that every investor should have growth stocks in the portfolio, because this would be inconsistent with many investors' needs. A fund can be built through reinvested income and through the purchase of growth shares, although tax considerations can make the income reinvestment less desirable if the investor is in a high tax bracket. Generally, the investor's short- and long-run needs dictate whether or not capital appreciation is the right goal.

Capital growth is needed to improve the investor's long-range position in achieving personal objectives, as well as to maintain the purchasing power of the investment fund. In the search for capital appreciation, the investor must be careful not to become involved in unnecessary risk in the pursuit of long-term goals. The equity portion of a portfolio tends to have greater degrees of adverse risk than does the fixed-income portion of a portfolio in terms of the probability of having a larger fund of absolute dollars at the end of an investment program.

Inflation Protection

Protection against the effects of inflation is a constant concern for investors. The loss of purchasing power is of major concern to those who depend upon an income-producing fund as a main source of income. In formulating the components of their portfolios, investors must take into consideration the fact that the purchasing power of the dollar is constantly being eroded. Thus investors must obtain a balance among the different types of securities they select. They should be sure to include issues that have the possibility of providing a reasonable hedge against inflation.

The difficulty for investors is in selecting a balance among the various securities. For example, if investors want a high level of income, it will be difficult for them at the same time to achieve growth in the value of the portfolio to combat the potential loss of purchasing power in the future. If investors plan for a growth portfolio to combat inflation pressures, they must generally forgo a high level of income. Therefore, investors must determine just how much they need to protect themselves against inflation and still accomplish their overall long-term goals.

Liquidity of Portfolios

A most difficult goal for the individual investor, and also for any profit-oriented corporation, is to balance the desire for liquidity with the desire for profitability. The desire for liquidity dictates that funds be placed in securities that can be easily converted into cash without losing principal. Liquidity is desirable in an investment portfolio because it generally offers the investor an opportunity to take advantage of attractive investment opportunities as they arise or to provide for either unexpected or planned personal needs.

The greater the investment portfolio's liquidity, the less need there may be for an emergency fund because the securities can be easily converted to cash. In addition, the investor would not have to keep a significant amount of funds in a savings institution.

Marketability of the Portfolio

Closely related to the portfolio's liquidity is the marketability of the securities in the portfolio. Marketability refers to whether or not a security can be sold with little price change. The degree to which a security is marketable depends upon several factors. For example, the securities of a large, well-known company are generally more marketable than the securities of a small firm. Also, the size of the investor's security position may have a direct effect on marketability. If the investor owns many thousands of shares of a small company, marketability of those shares at a reasonable price may be nearly impossible. Thousands of shares of a company like American Telephone & Telegraph, however, are relatively easy to trade because there is a great deal of market activity in that company's securities.

Portfolio Diversification

Whether investors choose to emphasize income or to emphasize growth, or to emphasize a combination of growth and income, they must understand the risks involved in the volatility of a portfolio if they do not have sufficient diversification among security issues. If at all possible, investors should strive to attain diversification among at least 10 securities (preferably 15 to 20). Empirical evidence has suggested that the market risk of portfolios of fewer than 10 issues is extremely high, because an adverse price movement of one security may have a large impact on the return of the total portfolio.

The investor's portfolio may also show poor performance if the portfolio is overdiversified. The more securities there are in a portfolio, the more the portfolio may perform no better or no worse than a broad market index. However, many investors who have large numbers of securities in their portfolios may have a difficult time keeping up to date on each company and the numerous data and information each company provides. It has also been stated that overdiversification can be a refuge for inadequate or incompetent portfolio management by an individual or institution. Nevertheless, for most individual investors the problem is one of insufficient diversification instead of overdiversification.

Many individuals who work for publicly owned companies accumulate shares of stock in their companies either through a sense of identification or because their employers have stock purchase plans in which the employers contribute part of the purchase price. The negative aspect of this plan is that because the investors accumulate a larger and larger portion of their securities in this one company their financial future may depend upon the performance of only one firm.

Investor's Tax Status

For investors in low tax brackets, tax considerations have little influence on their investment decisions. However, the higher the investor's income, the more tax considerations determine the character of the investments made. For investors in extremely high taxable brackets, tax considerations may be the dominating factor. The importance of the impact of taxation, as discussed in Chapter 17, suggests the investor cannot afford to ignore the prospects for high personal income taxes and substantial estate taxes. Tax-exempt municipal bonds, special capital-gain provisions, and tax-sheltered investments are of special interest to investors in higher tax brackets.

Investors must be able to retain as much of the income and capital gains as possible from their portfolios, because the progressive tax rates on income make it difficult to retain a substantial portion of a dollar earned.

KEY TERMS

annuity	investor constraints
compound interest	present value
effective rate of interest	rate of return
interest rate	simple interest
	time value of money

QUESTIONS

1. What are the two sources of return on securities?
2. a. What is the formula for simple interest?
   b. What is the formula for determining how much an initial investment will be worth when interest is compounded?
   c. What would be the terminal value of $1,000 invested at 8 percent for 2 periods (years)?
   d. What would be the terminal value for the investment of part c if it was compounded semiannually instead of annually?
3. a. What is an annuity?
   b. If an investor puts $1,000 in a savings account at 7 percent interest annually for 10 years, how much money will he have at the end of the tenth year?
   c. If an investor needs to accumulate $10,000 within 5 years, how large an annual annuity payment will he have to make to a savings account receiving 6 percent interest in order to reach his goal?
4. a. What is effective rate of interest?

     b. What is the formula for determining the effective rate of interest?

     c. If a person buys a $1,000 appliance on credit and pays 8 percent on level monthly installment payments for 2 years, what is the effective rate of interest?

5. a. What is present value?

     b. What is the importance of present value?

     c. What is the formula for finding present value?

     d. What is the present value of $1,000 to be received in 5 years if the discount rate is 8 percent?

     e. If an investor wants to receive an annuity of $1,000 a year for 10 years, how much money will he have to put into a savings account at 6 percent interest?

6. What is the coupon rate of a bond?

7. Why does the price of a bond change?

8. Why would an older investor probably be interested in more liquid investment than a younger investor?

9. What factors should an investor have in mind when he is considering the types of investments he should make?

10. List the advantages and disadvantages of owning a home strictly as a long-term investment.

11. What is the purpose of liquid reserves and how are they invested?

12. Why would an investor purchase bonds to pay for future education costs? Why might he choose another type of security?

13. What security issues must an investor deal with when he is providing for retirement?

14. An investor is usually very concerned with the safety of the principal of his investment. What does safety of principal depend upon?

15. Why might income stability be important to an investor?

16. Capital growth can be a desirable objective for an investor. Why would an investor be interested in capital growth? What sacrifice must the investor make? What other way is there to achieve capital growth in addition to purchasing growth stocks?

17. Explain why it is difficult to obtain portfolio balance in order to protect against purchasing-power risk.

18. Why is the liquidity of his portfolio important to an investor?

19. If the investor's portfolio contains no diversification, what does the investor risk? Is there such a thing as overdiversification?

20. What procedures should an investor follow when he chooses stocks?

21. Why should an investor review his portfolio periodically?

SELECTED READINGS

BERNSTEIN, PETER L. "What Rate of Return Can You Reasonably Expect?" *Journal of Finance*, May 1973, 273–282.

CISSELL, ROBERT, HELEN CISSELL, and DAVID C. FLASPOHLER. *Mathematics of Finance*, 5th ed. Boston: Houghton Mifflin, 1978.

CLAYTON, GARY E., and CHRISTOPHER B. SPIVEY. *The Time Value of Money*. Philadelphia: Saunders, 1978.

GRAHAM, BENJAMIN. *The Intelligent Investor*, 4th rev. ed. New York: Harper & Row, 1973.

LEASE, RONALD C., WILBUR G. LEWELLEN, and GARY C. SCHLARBAUM. "The Individual Investor: Attributes and Attitudes." *Journal of Finance*, May 1974, 413–433.

LEWELLEN, W., R. LEASE, and G. SCHLARBAUM. "Patterns of Investment Strategy and Behavior among Individual Investors." *Journal of Business*, July 1977, pp. 296–333.

"Term or Cash Value Insurance—Picking the Better Buy." *Changing Times*, 1978, 33–37.

"Where to Get Help in Financial Planning." *Business Week*, March 17, 1980, 186–190.

"Why You May Be Paying Too Much for Your Life Insurance." *Changing Times*, November 1979, 39–41.

3

Fixed-Return Investments

Various investment instruments available to individual and institutional investors provide a limited return on the investment. Generally, an investor selects a fixed-return investment because he or she prefers the certainty of a predetermined rate of return to the substantial risks that can accompany investment in variable-return securities. Participation in any investment program depends upon the individual's willingness to set aside a reasonable proportion of earnings for investment. Thus, in the initial stages of an investment program, the investor usually prefers to concentrate on fixed-return securities. In this way, the individual can build a good foundation from which to move on to the riskier variable-return securities. This chapter examines the various alternatives available to an investor who is interested in fixed-return investment.

SAVINGS ALTERNATIVES

A number of savings alternatives will allow an investor to accumulate cash at a predetermined compound rate of interest. The most common institutions are the savings and loan associations, mutual savings banks, employee credit unions, and commercial banks. They all offer the saver the right to collect interest on deposits. But the interest rate varies according to the legal limits imposed on the particular institution by certain state and federal regulatory agencies and according to the length of time the deposits are held. Individuals have found savings institutions an aid in achieving many personal financial goals because they provide a convenient and reliable method for accumulating funds. Over the past 25 years, savings and loan associations have experienced the most rapid growth among all savings institutions.

Most savings institutions provide the saver a high degree of flexibility and liquidity in depositing excess funds and making withdrawals for emergency needs. The ease of deposit and withdrawal from these institutions and the federal insurance of $100,000 per account have contributed substantially to their growth.

Interest earned at savings institutions has been calculated by various methods. The most popular method used today is from the date of deposit to the date of withdrawal, giving the depositor the maximum earnings available on a daily basis. However, federal law requires that in the case of deposits subject to time constraints (such as time certificates of deposit) a penalty must be imposed if funds are withdrawn before the specified date of maturity. In most instances, that penalty is the loss of interest over the last 180 days.

Since August 1981, interest offered on time certificates of deposit for periods ranging from 30 months to 10 years changes every two weeks, depending on the rates on comparable Treasury securities. The 6-month money market certificates of deposit pay a slightly higher rate than the 6-month Treasury bill and are fixed on a weekly basis for new purchases.

Employee credit unions are available at certain companies for the benefit of employees who require loans for the purchase of appliances, cars, home improvements, and so forth. Generally, only credit union members can make short- and intermediate-term loans. To become a member (shareholder) of the credit union, an employee must become a depositor; this gives the employee the right to obtain a loan. The interest paid on deposits and charges for loans depend on the earnings of the loan portfolio. The credit union is a self-supporting institution; therefore, the interest on loans must be sufficient to pay administrative expenses and the interest on the deposits of the credit union's shareholders.

FEDERAL SAVINGS INSTRUMENTS

The major federal program to help individuals save is the issue of U.S. savings bonds. During World War II, U.S. savings bonds grew in popularity.

For many people, they were the best means of saving and were purchased through a payroll deduction program.

Originally, there was a number of series of U.S. savings bonds, but only Series E and H bonds were still available up to 1980. Beginning in January 1980, the U.S. government started issuing Series EE and HH bonds to replace the old Series E and H bonds. These bonds are not marketable (i.e., they cannot be sold in the secondary market after the original purchase), but they are redeemable 6 months after purchase if necessary. They represent a debt of the U.S. government, which makes them very secure. If these bonds are lost or stolen, they can be replaced without any loss to the investor. They are available at any bank or post office and at the Treasury itself. They are free of commission.

Series EE bonds have a maturity of 11 years, and the yield to maturity (i.e., the return of the bond if held for the entire life of the bond) is about 7 percent. If the bond is redeemed after the first 6 months, the yield is about 4 percent, with a gradually increasing rate to maturity (up to 7 percent). The denominations of Series EE bonds range from $50 to $10,000. They are purchased at 50 percent of the denomination and are redeemed at par when matured. This difference is the interest that has accrued during the holding period.

Series HH bonds have a maturity of 10 years and have an 8 percent rate of interest. The denominations are $500, $1,000, $5,000, and $10,000. They are purchased and redeemed at par. Interest is paid semiannually to the bondholder and is taxable as current income.

Both Series EE and HH bonds are exempt from state and local taxes. However, for certain reasons they are most attractive to those individuals who have retirement plans in mind. First, taxes on the accrued interest of Series EE bonds can be deferred until redeemed. Second, the exchange provision of Series EE bonds allows Series EE to be exchanged for Series HH in multiples of $500. Therefore, a person with a high tax bracket may invest in Series EE bonds and postpone federal income taxes on the interest, exchange Series EE for Series HH bonds, thereby deferring the income tax again, and then pay income tax only on the interest payments received from Series HH bonds each year. Third, the holder would pay income tax on the appreciation in principal of the original Series EE bonds when the exchanged Series HH bonds mature. If by this time this person is retired, he or she should be in a much lower tax bracket. Table 3-1 demonstrates a retirement plan for periodic income by purchasing Series EE bonds and then exchanging them for Series HH bonds.

Finally, an additional tax feature available to the holder of Series EE is to claim the accrued interest each year on the tax return. This spreads the tax liability over all the years the bonds are held, which may be desirable for individuals in low tax brackets.

Table 3-1
Series EE Government Bond Accumulation and Exchange

Monthly Purchase Series EE Bonds for 15 Years	Principal	Interest	Total Accumulation	Exchange for HH Bonds[a]	Monthly HH Bond Interest for 10 Years
$ 25.00	$ 4,500.00	$ 3,885.28	$ 8,385.28	$ 8,500.00	$ 53.12
37.50	6,750.00	5,827.92	12,577.92	13,000.00	81.25
50.00	9,000.00	7,770.56	16,770.56	17,000.00	106.25
75.00	13,500.00	11,655.84	25,155.84	25,500.00	159.37
100.00	18,000.00	15,541.12	33,541.12	34,000.00	212.50

Source: "Take Stock in America: Buy U.S. Savings Bonds." SBD 1439.
[a]Add cash to purchase the next multiple of $500.

FIXED-RETURN GOVERNMENT SECURITIES

The federal government is an active participant in the securities market through various vehicles. The government's need for ready cash for government activities necessitates its participation on a weekly basis. This is accomplished by selling different types of securities offering various characteristics and maturity dates. The cost of money to the federal government is dictated by the forces of supply and demand in the economic marketplace, because these forces determine the interest rate that must be paid. There are five classifications of fixed-return government securities:

1. Treasury bills
2. Treasury notes
3. Treasury bonds
4. Federal agency securities
5. State and municipal bonds.

Treasury Bills

Treasury bills, more commonly referred to as T-bills, are issued to winning bidders in auctions conducted every Monday. They are non-interest-bearing debt instruments of the federal government sold at a discount from face value in order to provide the investor with an acceptable yield over the life of the bills. The investor's return is the difference between the discount purchase price and the higher maturity value. Normally, T-bills are sold for maturities of 3, 6, and 12 months at minimums of $10,000 with $5,000 increments, and the Treasury accepts the best bids on the various maturities.

Treasury bills are one of the more popular investments for financial institutions and investors who require a high-quality, temporary investment for excess cash. Many investors purchase them during periods when the market is declining. That is, as they sell other securities, investors purchase treasury bills to obtain a reasonable rate of interest while normal investment instruments remain undesirable. Dealers and major banks are some of the largest purchasers. They purchase directly from the Treasury and provide a continuous market for T-bills. Treasury bills are negotiable and can be traded over the counter. They are exempt from state and local income and property taxes but are subject to all federal income taxes.

Since T-bills are sold at a discount, they are quoted on a discount basis. It is important for investors to realize that their equivalent coupon rates (the bond equivalent yield) are actually higher than the quoted discount rates. For example, a 3-month (90 days) T-bill at a 16.5% discount is equivalent to a bond yield of 17.45%. The derivation procedure is as follows: first, the bank discount rate is determined or the discount received per dollar of par:

$$16.5\% \times \frac{90 \text{ days to maturity}}{360\text{-day T-bill year}} = 4.125\% \quad \text{or} \quad \$.04125 \text{ per } \$1$$

Therefore, the price per dollar of par is

$$1 - .04125 = .95875$$

Then the discount earned per bond year is calculated (365 days):

$$4.125\% \times \frac{365\text{-day bond year}}{90 \text{ days to bill maturity}} = 16.729\%$$

Finally, the equivalent yield is obtained:

$$\frac{\text{discount earned per bond year}}{\text{price per dollar of par}} = \frac{16.729\%}{.95875} = 17.45\%$$

To summarize, the preceding equations can be reduced to

$$\text{equivalent coupon yield} = \frac{(365)(d)}{360 - (d)(n)}$$

where d is the quoted discount rate and n is the number of days to bill maturity.

Treasury Notes and Bonds

Both treasury notes and treasury bonds are interest bearing and pay interest semiannually. A major difference between these two is their longevity. Treasury notes have an original maturity of approximately 1 to 7 years; treasury bonds have an original maturity usually in excess of 5 years. Both are subject to federal taxes. There is a ready market for treasury notes and bonds. An investor can buy issues either on their original issue date or later in the marketplace. Furthermore, an investor may sell treasury notes and bonds in the marketplace before their maturity date.

Whereas U.S. Treasury bills are quoted in 1/100ths of a point (1 percent), U.S. Treasury notes and bonds are usually quoted in 1/32nds, and sometimes 1/64ths, of a point. This method of quotation also applies to federal agency securities, which will be introduced in the next section. For example, if a particular U.S. Treasury bond is quoted at 96.04, it means that the price for this bond is at 96 and 04/32 percent (= 96.125 percent) of its par value.

Federal Agency Securities

A number of government agencies offer short-, intermediate-, and long-term bonds to various investors in order to finance agency operations. These organizations were established to help certain segments of American society and to fulfill the country's responsibilities both nationally and internationally. They include the Federal Land Banks, the Federal Intermediate Credit Banks, the Federal National Mortgage Association, Federal Home Loan Banks, Banks for Cooperatives, World Bank (the International Bank for Reconstruction and Development), Inter-American Development Bank, Government National Mortgage Association, and the U.S. Postal Service. These agency securities offer an additional limited-return opportunity for investors to choose from.

There has been wide acceptance of U.S. government agency securities, which has resulted in a very large amount of securities outstanding. Yields of U.S. government agency securities are slightly higher than those on U.S. Treasury obligations because the principal and interest on agency securities are generally not guaranteed by the federal government. Nevertheless, the Treasury maintains a very close link with these agencies in the event that they need additional funding.

Two government agencies play an important part in the country's mortgage credit structure, and they offer a wide variety of securities that are of growing interest to the investment community. The Federal National Mortgage Association (FNMA or Fannie Mae) is perhaps the best known. It was created in 1938 under the National Housing Act. In 1968, the FNMA was split into two separate corporations, one privately owned but government sponsored, the other wholly owned by the federal government. The private corporation retained the original name. The new federally owned corporation became known as the Government National Mortgage Association (GNMA or Ginnie Mae).

Fannie Mae is exempt from regulation by the Securities and Exchange Commission (SEC), but it is subject to regulation by the Department of Housing and Urban Development. The majority of Fannie Mae's stockholders are banks and other financial institutions that deal in mortgages and use the agency as a mortgage market facility. They are required by law to own the stock as a precondition for dealing with FNMA. However, FNMA stock is listed on the New York Stock Exchange and can be purchased by the individual investor.

Fannie Mae is designed to bolster the home mortgage market by buying mortgages insured by the Federal Housing Administration and the Farmer's Home Administration and mortgages guaranteed by the Veterans Administration. Although private investors are the principal source of capital used to purchase these mortgages, Fannie Mae can also borrow from the Treasury. Most of the funds are raised through sale of unsecured bonds and short-term discount notes. In addition, Fannie Mae issues mortgage-backed bonds that can be purchased by individual investors, but these bonds are subordinated to the regular debentures and discount notes with regard to interest and principal payments. That is, payment of interest and principal on unsecured bonds and notes take precedence over payment on mortgage-backed bonds.

Ginnie Mae was created to assume some of the functions originally performed by Fannie Mae. Ginnie Mae assumes responsibility for mortgage assistance that cannot be carried out economically in the private sector. In addition, Ginnie Mae is the guarantee agent for its own mortgage-based securities and for those issued by Fannie Mae. To finance these activities, Ginnie Mae sells mortgage-backed bonds and serial notes and borrows from the U.S. Treasury.

Exhibit 3-1 is a report of quotations of government, agency, and miscellaneous securities as carried in the *Wall Street Journal*.

State and Municipal Securities

Municipal bonds are bonds issued by state and local governments to finance the construction of capital improvement projects that the municipality or state wishes to undertake. The most attractive feature of municipal bonds is that the interest is exempt from federal income taxes and from state and local taxes in the issuing state and municipality. Although the exemption from federal income taxes is not specified on the face of the bond, and hence is not guaranteed, the present income tax laws do not require taxpayers to report the interest income from municipals. In this sense, the municipals are considered tax-exempt bonds. For persons in high tax brackets, this tax-exemption feature makes municipals very attractive. The interest rates specified in the municipals are usually lower than those for other types of fixed-income securities before taxes are computed. For example, if a person in the 40 percent tax bracket purchases a municipal bond with a yield of 9 percent, he or she will receive the entire interest; no federal taxes will be due. However, if the same investor places funds in a corporate bond that

Exhibit 3-1 Government, Agency and Miscellaneous Securities

Government, Agency and Miscellaneous Securities

Friday, June 25, 1982
Mid-afternoon Over-the-Counter quotations; sources on request.
Decimals in bid-and-asked and bid changes represent 32nds; 101.1 means 101 1/32. a-Plus 1/64. b-Yield to call date. d-Minus 1/64. n-Treasury notes.

FNMA Issues

Rate	Mat	Bid	Asked	Yld
9.45	7-82	99.17	99.25	14.48
15.50	8-82	100.4	100.12	11.56
6.80	9-82	98.6	98.14	14.54
8.40	9-82	98.21	98.25	14.31
8.60	10-82	98.10	98.14	14.02
9.00	10-82	98.14	98.18	13.96
13.75	11-82	99.12	99.16	14.91
7.35	12-82	97.1	97.9	13.71
17.50	2-83	101.16	101.24	14.34
7.75	3-83	95.6	95.14	14.80
9.50	3-83	96.5	96.15	14.93
8.75	4-83	95.10	95.18	14.89
9.25	4-83	95.23	95.31	14.81
9.50	5-83	95.20	95.28	14.70
18.00	5-83	102.14	102.22	14.51
6.75	6-83	92.22	93.6	14.68
7.30	6-83	93.6	93.22	14.64
8.10	6-83	93.28	94.12	14.64
10.85	7-83	95.28	96.12	14.74
9.70	8-83	94.14	94.30	14.75
6.75	9-83	91.2	91.18	14.61
8.50	9-83	92.28	93.12	14.66
9.25	10-83	93.12	93.28	14.62
8.00	12-83	91.1	91.17	14.66
8.40	12-83	91.15	91.31	14.72
14.05	1-84	99.2	99.10	14.55
14.10	2-84	98.30	99.6	14.65
9.50	3-84	91.18	92.2	14.91
7.35	4-84	87.28	88.12	15.00
8.20	4-84	89.6	89.22	14.98
14.25	5-84	98.24	99.4	14.77
6.25	6-84	85.6	85.22	14.97
9.25	6-84	90.4	90.20	14.95
8.20	7-84	87.30	88.14	15.00
9.05	7-84	89.16	90	14.93
11.10	8-84	92.30	93.16	14.77
7.95	9-84	86.26	87.10	14.91
9.75	9-84	90.6	90.18	14.92
11.70	10-84	93.14	93.20	14.90
14.90	10-84	99.20	100.4	14.80
17.20	11-84	104.10	104.26	14.69
6.90	12-84	83.2	84.2	14.90
7.55	12-84	84.2	85.2	15.06
15.05	12-84	100.8	100.16	14.79
9.90	1-85	89	89.16	15.03
17.00	2-85	103.14	104.14	14.87
7.65	3-85	83.18	84.2	15.03
14.25	3-85	98.4	98.20	14.86
13.75	4-85	97	97.16	14.85
15.25	5-85	100.14	100.30	14.81
8.60	6-85	84.24	85.8	14.96
9.95	6-85	88	88.16	14.90
7.25	7-85	81.8	81.24	14.95
15.65	7-85	100.12	100.28	15.27
14.10	8-85	96.24	97.8	15.17
7.45	9-85	80.20	81.4	15.09
15.00	9-85	99	99.16	15.14
7.90	10-85	81.8	81.24	15.14
8.80	10-85	83.20	84.4	15.09
13.00	11-85	93.20	94.4	15.28
14.90	12-85	98.16	99	15.27
13.00	1-86	93.20	94.4	15.20
8.20	3-86	80.16	81	15.07
9.50	3-86	83.28	84.12	15.16
9.20	4-86	82.24	83.8	15.16
14.63	6-86	97.14	97.18	15.46
7.95	7-86	78.24	79.8	14.99
13.90	8-86	95.16	96	14.20
7.90	9-86	77.12	78.12	15.02
7.30	12-86	74.16	75.16	15.05
7.75	3-87	74.16	76.8	14.95
14.30	4-87	96.10	96.18	15.48
11.15	5-87	86	86.16	15.16
7.65	6-87	74.4	75.4	14.93
9.10	7-87	77.16	79.16	15.05
7.50	10-87	71.12	73.12	14.95
14.40	2-88	96	97	15.20
10.50	6-88	82.12	83.12	14.79
16.38	8-88	103.4	104.4	15.30
8.55	9-88	74	75	14.84
9.30	6-89	75.24	76.24	14.76
7.80	10-91	65.20	66.20	14.43
7.00	3-92	60	62	14.38
7.05	6-92	60	62	14.33

Fed. Home Loan Bank

Rate	Mat	Bid	Asked	Yld
9.60	7-82	99.18	99.26	11.56
15.90	7-82	100.4	100.12	10.35
11.25	8-82	99.16	99.18	13.55
13.10	8-82	99.28	100	12.54
16.50	9-82	100.14	100.18	13.58
11.85	10-82	99.7	99.11	13.68
8.25	11-82	99.17	99.21	14.18
16.50	12-82	100.30	101.6	13.94
5.50	1-83	99.28	100.4	14.21
9.00	2-83	96.18	96.26	14.19
15.55	2-83	100.16	100.24	14.22
14.80	3-83	100.2	100.10	14.25
14.20	4-83	99.19	99.23	14.36
7.30	5-83	93.20	94.4	14.41
11.60	5-83	97.8	97.16	14.60
14.20	6-83	99.11	99.15	14.61
13.35	7-83	98.24	99	14.36
9.30	8-83	94.2	94.14	14.66
12.25	8-83	97.2	97.18	14.57
13.95	9-83	98.28	99	14.82
14.05	10-83	98.30	99.14	14.48
14.40	10-83	99.10	99.14	14.88
7.38	11-83	90.22	91.6	14.50
9.50	11-83	93.8	93.20	14.65
15.40	12-83	100.22	100.30	14.68
15.80	1-84	100.28	101.12	14.76
11.75	2-84	95.4	95.16	14.87
9.05	2-84	91.2	91.18	14.94
9.85	3-84	92.4	92.14	14.90
12.90	4-84	96.26	97.2	14.76
7.75	5-84	88.1	88.2	14.75
8.75	5-84	89.18	90.6	14.83
11.00	5-84	93.6	93.22	14.90
14.00	6-84	98.6	98.22	14.78
15.55	7-84	100.26	101.10	14.77
7.85	8-84	86.30	87.22	14.68
16.00	8-84	101.16	102	14.85
13.85	9-84	97.12	97.28	14.96
16.40	9-84	102.12	102.28	14.81
14.45	10-84	99.2	99.6	14.85
7.38	11-84	84.22	85.14	14.76
13.55	1-85	97.2	97.18	14.68
7.38	2-85	83.18	84.18	14.57
10.80	3-85	90.20	91.4	14.83
14.55	4-85	98.28	99.12	14.80
8.13	5-85	84.12	84.28	14.68
15.00	6-85	99.30	100.14	14.81
12.80	7-85	94.12	94.28	14.93
9.35	8-85	86	86.16	14.84
14.15	9-85	97.12	97.20	15.08
8.10	11-85	82.4	82.20	14.74
14.70	12-85	98.16	98.20	15.22
13.85	1-86	96	96.16	15.14
9.55	2-86	84.20	85.4	14.96
13.10	2-86	99.16	100	15.28
15.75	3-86	100.24	101.8	15.27
15.50	5-86	100.8	100.24	15.22
15.35	7-86	99.24	100.8	15.25
14.60	8-86	97.24	98.8	15.15
16.40	9-86	102.16	103	15.39
11.30	11-86	87.28	88.12	14.99
10.45	2-87	84.20	85.4	14.99
11.10	3-87	86.20	87.4	14.97
7.65	5-87	75	76	14.67
7.60	8-87	74.4	75.4	14.63
14.20	11-88	95.10	95.18	15.30
15.10	2-89	99	100	15.09
14.25	4-89	95.28	96.12	15.11
14.55	9-89	97.4	97.20	15.08
7.38	11-93	59.8	61.8	14.38
7.88	2-97	58.28	60.28	14.32

World Bank Bonds

Rate	Mat	Bid	Asked	Yld
7.13	8-82	98.24	99.8	15.00
10.17	9-82	98.16	99	15.00
14.00	3-83	98.16	99	15.50
15.75	9-83	99.16	100	15.75
14.51	3-84	98	98.16	15.50
8.15	1-85	85.4	85.20	15.25
5.00	2-85	81.4	82.4	15.25
8.60	7-85	83.24	84.8	15.25
8.85	12-85	82.24	83.8	15.25

Rate	Mat	Bid	Asked	Yld
7.80	12-86	76.8	76.24	15.20
14.63	12-86	96	96.16	14.74
7.65	5-87	74.8	74.24	15.20
7.75	8-87	73.24	74.8	15.20
15.00	12-88	96.16	97	15.75
4.50	2-90	54.12	55.12	14.35
5.38	7-91	54	55	14.50
16.63	11-91	102.28	103.12	15.90
15.13	12-91	97.16	98	15.53
14.75	6-92	95	95.16	15.65
5.38	4-92	52.4	53.4	14.50
5.88	9-93	51.20	52.20	14.60
6.50	3-94	53.24	54.24	14.70
6.38	10-94	52.8	53.8	14.70
8.63	8-95	63.12	63.28	15.00
8.13	8-96	59.20	60.4	15.00
9.35	12-00	64	64.16	15.10
8.85	7-01	60.4	60.28	15.20
8.38	12-01	57.28	58.28	15.15
8.25	5-02	56.20	57.4	15.10
8.35	8-02	57	57.16	15.15

Bank for Co-ops

Rate	Mat	Bid	Asked	Yld
7.75	1-86	82.8	83.24	13.74

Federal Farm Credit

Rate	Mat	Bid	Asked	Yld
13.55	7-82	99.25	100.1	9.19
16.70	7-82	99.26	100.4	0.00
14.30	8-82	100	100.4	12.25
15.45	8-82	99.31	100.3	13.12
7.20	9-82	98.21	98.25	14.01
9.65	9-82	99.3	99.7	13.79
11.65	9-82	99.15	99.19	13.14
13.90	9-82	99.26	99.30	13.65
10.95	10-82	98.26	99.2	13.81
13.80	10-82	99.23	99.27	13.52
14.50	10-82	100	100.4	13.53
13.65	11-82	99.24	99.28	13.75
14.50	11-82	99.28	100	13.69
11.60	12-82	98.26	98.30	14.13
12.90	12-82	99.6	99.10	14.48
14.00	12-82	99.20	99.24	13.99
14.50	1-83	99.24	99.28	14.26
13.80	2-83	99.16	99.20	14.19
8.05	3-83	95.24	96	14.43
13.25	3-83	98.30	99.2	14.63
10.90	4-83	97.4	97.12	14.38
13.40	4-83	99.8	99.4	14.34
13.75	9-83	98.24	99.4	14.53
9.30	12-83	92.28	93.8	14.71
14.10	12-83	98.30	99.10	14.63
9.00	1-84	91.24	92.4	14.79
9.50	1-84	92.12	92.24	14.83
13.85	3-84	98.6	98.18	14.81
17.00	3-84	102.24	103.4	14.78
9.45	4-84	91.10	91.22	14.80
15.50	4-84	100.20	101	14.81
9.70	6-84	91.4	91.16	14.91
14.80	7-84	99.22	99.30	14.82
15.25	7-84	100.16	100.24	14.80
11.75	9-84	93.30	94.12	14.83
14.35	10-82	98.14	98.18	15.08
9.55	12-84	89.2	89.18	14.81
10.65	12-84	91.6	91.22	14.84
10.90	1-85	91.14	91.30	14.78
13.20	3-85	96.4	96.20	14.74
13.25	4-85	96.6	96.22	14.70
14.80	4-85	99.20	100.4	14.74
9.20	6-85	86.22	87.6	14.73
11.60	7-85	91.8	91.24	15.05
12.75	9-85	94.4	94.20	14.91
14.90	9-85	98.28	99.12	15.13
14.30	12-85	97.12	97.28	15.10
17.00	12-85	104	104.16	15.25
15.80	1-86	101	101.16	15.23
13.95	3-86	96.12	96.28	15.07
14.00	4-86	97	97.8	14.98
15.10	4-86	99.8	99.24	15.18
13.35	9-86	94.4	94.20	15.11
14.50	9-86	97.24	98.8	15.06
10.75	10-86	86.4	87.4	14.89
10.00	12-86	83.20	84.20	14.86
14.63	1-87	97.24	98.8	15.16
14.38	4-87	96.30	97.6	15.20
12.65	4-88	90.16	91.16	14.87
11.70	7-88	84.8	87.8	14.97
13.05	1-89	91.4	92.4	14.97
7.75	9-89	68.24	70.8	14.55
10.60	10-89	81	82	14.68
15.65	10-89	101.4	102.4	15.14
10.95	1-90	81.24	82.24	14.81
14.10	6-90	95.6	95.10	15.24
10.40	7-90	79.4	80.4	14.68
14.10	4-91	94.20	95.20	14.95
9.10	7-91	71.28	72.28	14.58
14.70	7-91	97.12	98.12	15.03
13.65	12-91	92.12	93.12	14.98
15.20	1-92	99.20	100.20	15.07
14.25	4-94	95.4	96.4	14.95

FIC Bank Debs.

Rate	Mat	Bid	Asked	Yld
7.95	4-86	82.16	83.16	13.70
6.95	1-87	77.8	78.8	13.54

Federal Land Bank

Rate	Mat	Bid	Asked	Yld
8.70	7-82	99.12	99.20	13.34
7.30	10-82	97.22	97.26	14.45
8.00	10-82	97.30	98.2	14.29
7.20	1-83	96.1	96.9	14.31
8.20	1-83	96.20	96.28	14.16
8.65	7-83	94.6	94.14	14.47
7.30	10-83	91.18	91.26	14.35
7.35	10-83	91.20	91.28	14.34
8.10	7-85	83.10	84.10	14.62
7.95	10-85	81.26	82.26	14.67
8.80	10-85	83.28	84.28	14.72
7.60	4-87	75.4	76.4	14.68
7.25	7-87	73.4	74.12	14.58
7.85	1-88	73.20	75.4	14.52
8.20	1-90	70.16	72.16	14.25
7.95	4-91	67	69	14.22
7.95	10-96	60	62	14.23
7.35	1-97	56.4	58.8	14.24

Inter-Amer. Devel. Bk.

Rate	Mat	Bid	Asked	Yld
4.25	12-82	94.12	95.12	15.00
4.50	4-84	86	87	13.00
4.50	11-84	82.12	83.12	13.06
8.25	1-85	85.4	85.20	15.20
8.00	3-85	84	84.16	15.30
8.38	2-86	81	81.16	15.25
14.00	12-86	94	94.16	15.76
10.75	8-87	83.24	84.8	15.30
15.00	4-89	96.24	97.8	15.66
5.20	1-92	64	66	11.06
6.50	11-92	56.12	57.12	14.60
6.63	11-93	55.12	56.12	14.60
8.63	10-95	63.8	63.24	15.00
9.00	2-01	61.12	61.28	15.20
8.75	7-01	59.28	60.12	15.15
8.38	6-02	57.4	57.20	15.15
9.63	1-04	64.4	64.4	15.25

Asian Development Bank

Rate	Mat	Bid	Asked	Yld
8.63	8-86	79.28	80.12	15.25
7.75	4-96	57.24	58.8	15.00

GNMA Issues

Rate	Mat	Bid	Asked	Yld
8.00		62.2	62.18	14.95
9.00		66.4	66.20	15.21
9.50		68.4	68.20	15.34
10.00		70.15	70.31	15.39
11.00		75.20	75.28	15.45
11.50		78	78.8	15.50
12.50		82.30	83.6	15.56
13.00		85.4	85.12	15.65
13.50		87.14	87.22	15.72
14.00		89.7	89.15	15.89
15.00		93.17	93.25	16.07
16.00		98.4	98.12	16.19

yields 14 percent interest, 40 percent of the amount received will go for taxes; the investor will be left with a return equal to 8.4 percent [= 14% × (1 − 40%)] on the investment. Therefore, it is more advantageous for such an investor to own the 9 percent municipal bond than the 14 percent corporate bond. In other words, the 9 percent municipal bond is as attractive as a 15 percent [= 9%/(1 − 40%)] corporate bond to the eyes of the investor in a 40% tax bracket, provided other features such as riskiness and maturity of these bonds are very similar.

The higher the investor's tax bracket, the more desirable municipal securities become. In fact, the higher the tax bracket, the less desirable any income-producing security, other than municipals, becomes. Generally, this investor will therefore strive for capital appreciation, of which 40 percent will be taxed at his or her marginal taxable rate. Capital appreciation is the increase in market value of an asset held for investment.

General Obligation Bonds

There are different types of municipal bonds. General obligation bonds (GO bonds) are backed by the full faith and credit of the issuer. The issuing political unit unconditionally guarantees the interest and the principal. Funds to pay the bond debt are raised through the taxing power and authority of the issuer. Taxes may take the form of an income tax or sales tax enacted solely to retire a debt over a period of time, but these bonds are usually supported by the issuer's ability to tax the real estate underlying the geographic boundaries of the particular project.

Although default seldom occurs on a full faith or credit bond, the investor who purchases municipal bonds must be careful to analyze fully the issuer's ability to repay. Because the repayment of debt is dependent upon the issuer's taxing power, the investor should be concerned with the quality of the tax base and the amount of burden it can bear. A few of the more important aspects of the tax base that the investor should investigate are the following:

1. Assessed value of the property available to tax
2. Amount of taxes currently being supported by the property
3. Amount of debt already contracted for by the issuer
4. Relative wealth of the inhabitants of the municipality or state
5. Issuer's prospects for future economic growth

All these factors interact to determine how good a credit risk the issuer is. Exhibit 3-2, Moody's key to municipal bond ratings, gives an indication as to their ranking system. All rating services carefully look into the listed areas for any state or municipality to determine the risk that the investor may have relative to the securities issued.

Revenue Bonds

Unlike general obligation bonds, revenue bonds are not backed by the full faith and credit of the issuer. The funds needed to pay the interest and repay the principal are generated solely by the project (such as toll road, transit system, waterworks, or stadium) that they were issued to finance. There is some business and financial risk associated with revenue bonds because the revenue generated by the project may not be sufficient to meet the fixed obligations. However, default is rather uncommon.

Revenue bonds can be divided into different classes according to the source of the revenues generated to support them. Utility revenue bonds are used to finance public utility facilities such as sewage systems or waterworks. Revenues from these bonds are generated by charging a user's fee for the service or the product provided by the facility. Turnpike bonds are utility bonds issued to finance construction. Revenues are derived from tolls charged for using the roadway. Quasi-utility bonds derive their revenues from projects benefiting, but not necessarily used by, the general public. For example, the Port of New York Authority, which runs and finances the docks, bridges, and airports of the city, is an example of a quasi-utility. Nonutility revenue bonds are those in which a general tax, such as an excise tax, on a certain product is used to generate needed funds.

Exhibit 3-3 shows an example of different municipal securities traded in the market.

Assessment Bonds

Assessment bonds are issued to finance improvements to public properties. The interest and principal on these bonds are paid through taxes and are levied on the property owners. Assessment bonds are a common issue when a new sewage system is installed in a community; the property owners are assessed a proportional amount for the frontage on their property. The construction of certain public buildings such as schools has also been financed by assessment bonds.

FEATURES OF CORPORATE BONDS

There are basically two types of corporate limited-return securities: **corporate bonds** and **preferred stock.** A bond is a certificate that reflects an agreement between two parties in which one party agrees, in return for the use of the other party's money for a predetermined period of time, to make fixed interest payments each year, and then repay the borrowed funds at the end of the bond's life. When issued, most corporate bonds have a lifetime

Exhibit 3-2 Key to Moody's Bond Ratings

MOODY'S BOND RATINGS

Purpose: The system of rating securities was originated by John Moody in 1909.

The purpose of Moody's Ratings is to provide the investors with a simple system of gradation by which the relative investment qualities of bonds may be noted.

Rating Symbols: Gradations of investment quality are indicated by rating symbols, each symbol representing a group in which the quality characteristics are broadly the same. There are nine symbols as shown below, from that used to designate least investment risk (i.e., highest investment quality) to that denoting greatest investment risk (i.e., lowest investment quality):

| Aaa Aa A | Baa Ba B | Caa Ca C |

For explanation of municipal rating symbols, in particular the **A 1** and **Baa 1** groups see page 137

Absence of Rating: Where no rating has been assigned or where a rating has been suspended or withdrawn, it may be for reasons unrelated to the quality of the issue. Should no rating be assigned, the reason may be one of the following:
1. An application for rating was not received or accepted.
2. The issue or issuer belongs to a group of securities or companies that are not rated as a matter of policy.
3. There is a lack of essential data pertaining to the issue or issuer.
4. The issue was privately placed, in which case the rating is not published in Moody's publications.

Suspension or withdrawal may occur if new and material circumstances arise, the effects of which preclude satisfactory analysis; if there is no longer available reasonable up-to-date data to permit a judgment to be formed; if a bond is called for redemption; or for other reasons.

Changes in Rating: The quality of most bonds is not fixed and steady over a period of time, but tends to undergo change. For this reason changes in ratings occur so as to reflect these variations in the intrinsic position of individual bonds.

A change in rating may thus occur at any time in the case of an individual issue. Such rating change should serve notice that Moody's observes some alteration in the investment risks of the bond or that the previous rating did not fully reflect the quality of the bond as now seen. While because of their very nature, changes are to be expected more frequently among bonds of lower ratings than among bonds of higher ratings, nevertheless the user of bond ratings should keep close and constant check on all ratings-both high and low ratings-thereby to be able to note promptly any signs of change in investment status which may occur.

Limitations to Uses of Ratings: Bonds carrying the same rating are not claimed to be of absolutely equal quality. In a broad sense they are alike in position, but since there are only nine rating classes used in grading thousands of bonds, the symbols cannot reflect the fine shadings of risks which actually exist. Therefore, it should be evident to the user of ratings that two bonds identically rated are unlikely to be precisely the same in investment quality.

As ratings are designed exclusively for the purpose of grading bonds according to their investment qualities, they should not be used alone as a basis for investment operations. For example, they have no value in forecasting the direction of future trends of market price. Market price movements in bonds are influenced not only by the quality of individual issues but also by changes in money rates and general economic trends, as well as by the length of maturity, etc. During its life even the best quality bond may have wide price movements, while its high investment status remains unchanged.

The matter of market price has no bearing whatsoever on the determination of ratings which are not to be construed as recommendations with respect to "attractiveness." The attractiveness of a given bond may depend on its yield, its maturity date or other factors for which the investor may search, as well as on its investment quality, the only characteristic to which the rating refers.

Since ratings involve judgments about the future, on the one hand, and since they are used by investors as a means of protection, on the other, the effort is made when assigning ratings to look at "worst" potentialities in the "visible" future, rather than solely at the past record and the status of the present. Therefore, investors using the rating should not, expect to find in them a reflection of statistical factors alone, since they are an appraisal of long term risks, including the recognition of many non-statistical factors.

Though ratings may be used by the banking authorities to classify bonds in their bank examination procedure, Moody's Ratings are not made with these bank regulations in view. Moody's Investors Service's own judgment as to desirability or non-desirability of a bond for bank investment purposes is not indicated by Moody's Ratings.

Moody's Ratings represent the mature opinion of Moody's Investors Service, Inc. as to the relative investment classification of bonds. As such, they should be used in conjunction with the description and statistics appearing in Moody's Manuals. Reference should be made to these statements for information regarding the issuer. Moody's Ratings are not commercial credit ratings. In no case is default or receivership to be imputed unless expressly so stated in the Manual.

KEY TO MOODY'S CORPORATE RATINGS

Aaa

Bonds which are rated **Aaa** are judged to be of the best quality. They carry the smallest degree of investment risk and are generally referred to as "gilt edge." Interest payments are protected by a large or by an exceptionally stable margin and principal is secure. While the various protective elements are likely to change, such changes as can be visualized are most unlikely to impair the fundamentally strong position of such issues.

Aa

Bonds which are rated **Aa** are judged to be of high quality by all standards. Together with the **Aaa** group they comprise what are generally known as high grade bonds. They are rated lower than the best bonds because margins of protection may not be as large as in **Aaa** securities or fluctuation of protective elements may be of greater amplitude or there may be other elements present which make the long term risks appear somewhat larger than in **Aaa** securities.

A

Bonds which are rated **A** possess many favorable investment attributes and are to be considered as upper medium grade obligations. Factors giving security to principal and interest are considered adequate but elements may be present which suggest a susceptibility to impairment sometime in the future.

Baa

Bonds which are rated **Baa** are considered as medium grade obligations, i.e., they are neither highly protected nor poorly secured. Interest payments and principal security appear adequate for the present but certain protective elements may be lacking or may be characterisically unreliable over any great length of time. Such bonds lack outstanding investment characteristics and in fact have speculative characteristics as well.

Ba

Bonds which are rated **Ba** are judged to have speculative elements; their future cannot be considered as well assured. Often the protection of interest and principal payments may be very moderate and thereby not well safeguarded during both good and bad times over the future. Uncertainty of position characterizes bonds in this class.

B

Bonds which are rated **B** generally lack characteristics of the desirable investment. Assurance of interest and principal payments or of maintenance of other terms of the contract over any long period of time may be small.

Caa

Bonds which are rated **Caa** are of poor standing. Such issues may be in default or there may be present elements of danger with respect to principal or interest.

Ca

Bonds which are rated **Ca** represent obligations which are speculative in a high degree. Such issues are often in default or have other marked shortcomings.

C

Bonds which are rated **C** are the lowest rated class of bonds and issues so rated can be regarded as having extremely poor prospects of ever attaining any real investment standing.

Note: Moody's applies numerical modifiers, **1**, **2** and **3** in each generic rating classification from **Aa** through **B** in its corporate bond rating system. The modifier **1** indicates that the security ranks in the higher end of its generic rating category; the modifier **2** indicates a mid-range ranking; and the modifier **3** indicates that the issue ranks in the lower end of its generic rating category

Source: Moody's Investors Service, Inc., *Moody's Bond Record*, 1982.

Exhibit 3-3

Tax-Exempt Bonds

Here are current prices of several active tax-exempt revenue bonds issued by toll roads and other public authorities.

Agency	Coupon	Mat	Bid	Asked	Chg.
Bat Park City Auth NY	6⅜s	'14	51½	54½	.....
Chelan Cnty PU Dist	5s	'13	50½	52½	.....
Chesapeake B Br&Tun-f	5¾s	'00	59	64	.....
Columbia S.P.E.	3⅞s	'03	60	64	.....
Dela. River Port Auth	6½s	'11	58½	62½	.....
Douglas Cnty PU Dist	4s	'18	36½	38½	.....
Florida Turnpike Auth	4¾s	'01	73	76	.....
Illinois Toll	4¾s	'98	48	51	.....
Indiana Toll	3½s	'94	92	94	.....
Intermountain Pwr	14s	'21	102½	104½	.....
Kansas Turnpike	3⅜s	'94	73	76	.....
Kentucky Turnpike Auth	4¾s	'06	67	70	.....
La. Offsh Terminals	6½s	'08	56	59	.....
Munic. Assist. Cp. NY	7½s	'92	72	76	.....
Munic. Assist. Cp. NY	7½s	'95	66½	70½	.....
Munic. Assist. Cp. NY	8s	'86	90	94	.....
Munic. Assist. Cp. NY	8s	'91	78	82	.....
Munic. Assist. Cp. NY	8⅜s	'08	64½	68½	.....
Munic. Assist. Cp. NY	9¼s	'90	101	105	.....
Munic. Assist. Cp. NY	9¾s	'92	86	90	.....
Munic. Assist. Cp. NY	10¼s	'93	91	95	.....
Munic. Assist. Cp. NY	10⅝s	'08	82	86	.....
Mass Port Auth	6s	'11	58½	62½	.....
Mass Turnpike Auth	3.3s	'94	96	99	.....
Massachusetts G.O.	6½s	'00	57	60	.....
NJ Turnpike Auth	4¾s	'06	47½	49½	.....
NJ Turnpike Auth	5.2s	'08	50	52	.....
NJ Turnpike Auth	5.7s	'13	57½	59½	.....
NJ Turnpike Auth	6s	'14	55½	57½	.....
NY State Power Auth	5½s	'10	53	55	.....
NY State Power Auth	6⅝s	'10	56½	58½	.....
NY State Power Auth	8s	'09	68	71	.....
NY State Power Auth	9½s	'01	86	88	.....
NY State Power Auth	9⅞s	'20	77	79	.....
NY State Thruway	3.1s	'94	55	58	.....
NY State Urban Devlp	6s	'13	48	51	.....
NY State Urban Devlp	7s	'14	54½	58½	.....
Okla Turnpike Auth	4.7s	'06	51	53	.....
Port of NY & NJ	4¾s	'03	46	48	.....
Port of NY & NJ	5½s	'03	48½	51½	.....
Port of NY & NJ	6s	'08	53	56	.....
Port of NY & NJ	6½s	'12	56	59	.....
Port of NY & NJ	7s	'11	62	65	.....
Port of NY & NJ	8.2s	'11	74	78	.....
Salt River Project	9¼s	'20	74½	78½	.....
So. Carolina PS Auth	10¼s	'20	76½	79½	.....
Valdez (Exxon)	5½s	'07	53	55	.....
Valdez (Sohio)	6s	'07	52½	54½	.....
Wshngtn PPSS #4-5	6s	'15	36	40	.....
Wshngtn PPSS #4-5	6¾s	'10	40	44	.....
Wshngtn PPSS #4-5	9⅞s	'12	57	61	.....
Wshngtn PPSS #4-5	12½s	'10	72	76	.....
Wshngtn PPSS #2	6s	'12	44½	48½	.....
Wshngtn PPSS #2	6¾s	'12	49½	53½	.....
Wshngtn PPSS #1	7¾s	'17	55	59	.....
Wshngtn PPSS #1	15s	'17	99	102	.....
Wshngtn PSSS R2	9¼s	'11	65½	69½	.....
Wshngtn PPSS R3	11⅛s	'10	78	82	.....

Source: Reprinted with permission of The Wall Street Journal, ©Dow Jones & Company, Inc. (1982). All rights reserved.

of more than 7 years. At maturity, all the borrowed funds are returned to the bondholder, who surrenders the certificate to the issuing company.

Corporate bonds are issued when a company needs additional funds to operate the business over the long run and prefers to raise the money through bonds rather than through common stock. Corporate bonds are usually sold with the help of an investment-banking syndicate, which is a group of firms joining together in an effort to sell the one corporate issue.

Although bonds can be purchased by anyone, the vast majority are purchased by banks for their trust accounts, by insurance companies making purchases from the premiums on insurance policies, and by a variety of other institutions that have funds to be invested in fixed-income securities.

Most bonds issued in the United States are issued in multiples of $1,000. Bonds can be purchased by the investor in the market because they are traded among bondholders. Bonds, like stocks, are traded on national exchanges and over the counter. The market price of bonds will fluctuate in response to changes in the level of interest rates. If interest rates begin to rise, the market price of lower-yielding coupon bonds will fall until their yield-to-maturity reaches the market rate of interest.

Coupon rates on bonds are the stated rate of interest to be paid by the issuing company to holders over the life of the issue. For example, if a 20-year bond was issued in 1965 with a coupon rate of 6 percent, the issuing firm will continue to pay $60 per year per $1,000 bond for the entire life of the bond, regardless of any fluctuation in the market price of the bond. If, during the 20-year period, interest rates rise to a higher level than 6 percent for the same type and quality of bond, bondholders will become disenchanted with the 6 percent yield and will begin selling their bonds, reinvesting the proceeds in bonds that offer a higher yield. If many bond-holders do this — and they will — the price of the bond falls and will decline as low as necessary to attract investors once again on the basis of its yield. If the bond falls to 80 (the price, $800, is quoted as a percent of par value), the purchaser will receive $60 interest every year for the $800 investment, which is a current yield of 7.5 percent ($60 divided by $800). However, the investor must recognize that a bond will be priced on the basis of yield to maturity, not merely on current yield. Therefore, the price of the bond will rise and fall as interest rate levels change. On the date of maturity in 1985, all bondholders will receive the face value of the bond, $1,000. Therefore, the purchaser of the bond at the discount price of $800 will make a profit of $200 in addition to receiving $60 interest annually.

All market prices for limited-income marketable securities are determined by prevailing market interest rates. Therefore, holders of long-term maturity, fixed-income securities run a substantial risk that rising interest rates will result in market prices that will diminish the value of their bond holdings (interest-rate risk).

Indenture

A formal agreement called an **indenture** specifies the terms of the contract and the steps that can be taken by the bondholder if the issuing company fails to meet any of these terms. Certain types of government securities do not have formal indenture contracts because the payment of interest and principal is guaranteed by the government's taxing powers. The riskier the issuing company, the more important are the terms of the indenture. The contractual nature of bonds and the right of the bondholders to receive payment before any common-stock holders upon liquidation of the company or before dividend payments, makes them a much more secure investment than common stock. However, the lower the potential risk of a particular security, the lower the expected return to the investor.

Trustee

The trustee serves a major function in the issuance of bonds. The **trustee** is an independent party, usually a bank, that serves as a representative of the bondholder and participates in the designing of the indenture contract and evaluating the quality of the assets that serve as collateral for the bond. If the issuing company fails at any time to comply with the terms of the bond indenture, the trustee represents the bondholder to see that appropriate steps are taken against the issuer to protect the bondholder's investment.

The trustee may foreclose on any assets mortgaged or secured under the indenture. **Foreclosure** means that if the issuing company fails to make interest payments as provided or to meet other requirements, the trustee may institute legal proceedings to seize the asset, sell it, and return the proceeds to the bondholder. It is hoped that the proceeds will be sufficient to reimburse the bondholder for his or her total investment. If the issuing company files for bankruptcy, the trustee will represent the bondholder's interest in the liquidation or reorganization settlement.

Investors will rarely need to be concerned about the possibility of such a procedure if they invest in companies that are in sound financial condition. But the more precarious the financial health of the issuing company, the more important the provisions of the indenture become. Not all bonds have designated security behind them in the form of specific assets. When a bond is purchased, it is important to know whether it is secured or unsecured. This does not mean that the best bonds are secured bonds. Many unsecured bonds are of high quality and can be strongly recommended for purchase.

Registered and Bearer Bonds

Most bonds are registered and bear the name of the holder. The **registered bond** ensures the right of the holder to receive interest and the principal upon maturity. The bondholder receives a check semiannually for the interest payment. If the bond is lost or stolen, no one else has the right to claim ownership. However, there are coupon bonds that do not carry the bondholder's name and may be easily transferred. These are called **bearer bonds.** The holder of bearer bonds must exercise great care to be sure that the bonds are not lost or stolen. Interest is collected by clipping the coupons attached to the bond and presenting them for payment at a designated bank. Upon maturity of the coupon bond, the certificate may be presented to the bank for redemption and cancellation.

Bond Quotations

Exhibit 3-4 is a portion of a *Wall Street Journal* list of quotations for bonds listed on the New York Stock Exchange. The AT&T bond outlined is a $3\frac{7}{8}$ percent interest-bearing bond that matures in 1990 and that currently sells at 53, or $530 per bond.

In 1990, this bond will mature, and the person holding the bond at the time will receive $1,000. However, in the meantime, the holder will receive interest of $38.75 per year, or a current yield of 7.3 percent on the invested funds if the bond was purchased on October 22, 1981. The approximate yield to maturity is 13.09 percent. An individual or institution that purchased the bond when originally issued in 1956 ran an enormous interest rate risk. Although $3\frac{7}{8}$ percent was a good rate at that time, it is a very low rate today. The investor has lost the ability to receive a good interest return and might have sold the issue at a reduced price, which, of course, would have resulted in a loss for the investment. However, AT&T has enjoyed the payment of the low interest rate for the entire life of the bond. It will certainly be unhappy to make the principal repayment in 1990, but must do so. More recent bonds have sold at substantially higher interest rates; other AT&T bonds have a coupon rate as high as 13.25 percent.

Call Feature

Other important factors for corporations include a **call feature** for all bonds. This gives the issuing company the right to call a bond before it reaches maturity. For example, a corporation originally issued bonds for $1,000 each at a high rate of interest, but since the date of issue, market interest rates have fallen, and the market value of the bond has risen. It may be to the benefit of the company to recall the bonds, retire them, and then issue new bonds at a lower interest rate. In that case, the investor would be unable to continue to receive an interest rate that is higher than the prevailing market rate.

The call feature usually does not take effect until five or six years after the bond has been issued. Once it takes effect, the call feature generally lasts through the day of maturity. During the noncallable period, the investor has the opportunity to adjust his or her investment portfolio to take into account potential call issues during the early years of the bond's life. However, history has usually seen interest rates rise, and the call provision has not been exercised for most bonds. As Exhibit 3-4 demonstrates, most older bonds are selling for prices much lower than the face value (par) unless

Exhibit 3-4

New York Exchange Bonds

Thursday, October 22, 1981

Total Volume $24,400,000

SALES SINCE JANUARY 1		
1981	1980	1979
$4,297,939,000	$3,899,510,000	$2,763,826,000

Issues traded	Domestic			All Issues	
	Thurs	Wed	Thurs	Wed
Issues traded	946	954	1004	1012
Advances	237	308	241	310
Declines	506	508	599	514
Unchanged	203	187	204	188
New highs	6	6	9	
New lows	47	41	49	43

Dow Jones Bond Averages

	—1981—		—1980—		—1979—				THURSDAY			
	High	Low	High	Low	High	Low		—1981—	—1980—		—1979—	
										Net Chg.		
20 Bonds	65.78	54.99	60.60	54.99	86.10	73.35	55.54	— .48	77.32	+ .12		
10 Utilities	61.78	53.61			88.60	72.40	54.31	— .86	76.60	+ .17		
10 Industrial	66.15	56.37			84.28	74.25	56.77	— .10	78.05	+ .05		

maturity will occur within the next few years. The inverse relationship of interest and market prices will always hold true except for convertible bonds. As interest rates go up, the price of existing bonds will go down, and vice versa.

The call price for most bonds is a few points above par value, at about 105 or 106, depending on the number of years remaining to maturity. As the bond gets closer to maturity, the amount of the call premium becomes less and less. The call feature is most commonly exercised with convertible bonds, which will be discussed later in this chapter.

Sinking Fund

Another widely used indenture clause is the **sinking-fund requirement.** The sinking fund is a special appropriation of cash made by the issuing corporation for use in retiring outstanding bonds either at maturity by purchase at a discount in the market or by calling them to meet the sinking-fund requirement. If a company sells $50 million of 30-year bonds at 8 percent, it is required to pay $4 million interest each year, for a total of $120 million, over the entire life of the bond. In addition, the company must repay the $50 million at the end of 30 years. Because it is difficult for firms to generate that much cash at one time, many bond indentures require the company to set aside a certain portion of the principal repayment annually from about the eighth or ninth year to the maturity date. That cash may be permitted to be placed in a fund to earn interest; then, at the end of the life of the bond, there will be a sufficient amount in the sinking fund to cover most of the repayment. This feature is desirable from the standpoint of the bond-holder because risk is reduced as the years progress. If there is a default in the terms of the bonds, the trustee generally has the right to distribute the money in the sinking fund to the bondholders.

At times, a company may find it desirable to use the cash deposits to purchase a limited number of the bonds in the open market and cancel them. In this way, the company can achieve the gradual retirement of its total dollar indebtedness. In fact, most bond indentures that contain a sinking-fund requirement demand that annually a certain portion of the outstanding bonds be retired. This means the bonds must be acquired and retired, not just cash set aside for maturity.

American Telephone & Telegraph is one of the few companies that does not have sinking-fund provisions included in its indentures. The company is so well respected and financially sound that the investment community readily purchases AT&T bond issues without the sinking-fund clause. When AT&T's bonds mature, they simply issue new bonds and use the proceeds to repay the maturing bond. This type of AT&T debt then becomes rather permanent, and the only item that really changes from one bond issue to the next is the rate of interest (the coupon rate).

TYPES OF CORPORATE BONDS

Secured Bonds

Secured bonds are backed by some type of assets as collateral. They are classified according to the type. For example, mortgage bonds are those in which the issuer pledges real property to guarantee the loan; a collateral trust bond is secured by collateral other than real estate; equipment trust obligations are secured by specific pieces of equipment.

When two companies merge or when one company acquires another, very often the surviving firm will assume the debt obligations of the acquired firm. This provides the bondholder of the acquired company with an additional company to look to for payment of interest and principal. An investor must be careful that the resulting combined firm continues to have at least the same minimum financial strength.

Mortgage Bonds

A **mortgage bond** is secured by one or more specific assets of the issuing company. The term mortgage refers to real property, such as plant and equipment, pledged as collateral for the loan. A deed of trust on the property is designated and given to the trustee. If there is a default on the bond issue, the trustee can foreclose and sell the mortgage property. He then distributes the proceeds among the bondholders in proportion to their holdings. If there is a loss on the sale of the mortgage property, or if the amount received is insufficient to cover the claims of all the bondholders, the bondholders become general creditors of the company for the remaining portion of the debt. For example, if each bondholder received only $700 per bond upon liquidation of the secured asset, the bondholder would then become a general creditor of the corporation for the remaining $300. In liquidation proceedings, stockholders receive funds only after all bondholders' and general creditors' claims have been fully met. Common-stockholders are residual holders in that they receive what (if anything) is left over after preferred-stockholders are paid. Therefore, from a credit standpoint, bondholders have a more secure investment than stockholders.

There are different types of mortgage bonds. **First-mortgage bonds** (also called **senior bonds**) have the first claim on specific collateral. **Second-** or **third-mortgage bonds** have a second-priority or junior claim to the pledged collateral. In case of default, the senior bondholders (creditors) are paid in full before the junior claimants are entitled to any remaining portion of the dissolved assets.

A bondholder who holds a junior mortgage claim always runs the risk that the asset cannot be sold for enough to pay both the senior and junior claims. Because of this risk, the company will have to pay a higher interest rate on second- or third-mortgage obligations than on corresponding first-mortgage obligations on the same real property. Not all second mortgages are inferior to first mortgages of other firms, however, and an investor may well prefer to hold a second mortgage on a public utilities generating plant than to hold a first mortgage on a troubled real estate investment.

Collateral Trust Bonds

A **collateral trust bond** is secured by collateral other than real estate. The collateral may consist of stock in another corporation, promissory notes or accounts receivable of the issuing corporation, or any asset or property that is not considered real estate.

Equipment Trust Obligations

The **equipment trust obligation** is secured by a specific piece of equipment. It had its beginnings with the railroad industry, and the equipment was called **rolling stock.** Railroad cars were used as the security for the bonds. Title to the railroad cars was transferred to the trustee, who returned the title to the company when all the terms of the indenture had been met and the principal amount of the bonds had been repaid.

Equipment trust certificates are generally issued so that maturities occur at different times. This feature is called **serial retirement.** Each bond has a serial number, and each number has a maturity date. This allows the railroad or other issuing company to stagger the principal repayment amounts. In more recent years, the airline industry has issued equipment trust certificates for the purchase of the 747 jumbo jets. In essence, the bondholders own the jets. At maturity, the jets can be purchased by the airline or can be sold to another airline.

Unsecured Bonds

Unsecured or **debenture bonds** are not secured by any specific type of collateral. Rather, they are secured by the general credit of the corporation. It might seem that there is less financial risk involved in the purchase of a secured bond than in the purchase of an unsecured bond, because a secured bond has a senior claim against a specific asset. However, this is not necessarily the case. The value of most secured assets is dependent upon the viability of the corporation, because the asset is worth the most when actively used. For example, the marketability of real property or some other secured asset may be much different from the purchase price. A machine that originally cost $3 million may net only $1 or $2 million in a forced sale because the machine is so specialized that there is no market for it except at a sharply reduced price.

Financially healthy firms generally have no need to issue secured bonds, whereas corporations that cannot attract investors with unsecured bonds will often issue secured bonds. Therefore, unsecured bonds can be the less risky of the two types of securities.

Many of the largest and most financially sound companies in the United States issue debenture bonds almost exclusively. These may be of the highest quality and are issued as unsecured because (1) the issuers do not want to bother assigning an interest in specific assets and, therefore, do not need to keep detailed records of those interests, and (2) the issuers enjoy the flexibility of being able to sell assets without first having to have the title released and perhaps subject to question. However, the investor should always evaluate the general credit standing and expected profitability of a company before buying any bond, secured or unsecured.

Subordinated Debentures

Debentures can be senior or junior to the company's other debts. **Subordinated debentures** are junior to secured bonds and to senior debentures. They are liens against the issuer's unsecured assets, but the claims are settled only after secured creditors and debenture holders' obligations have been met in full. Even though the holders of subordinated debentures have a junior claim to the assets of the corporation, the securities are not necessarily of poor quality. They do, however, carry higher risk. One example is convertible bonds, which are usually subordinated debentures, because the likelihood of the company's needing to make a principal repayment at maturity is reduced; the firm hopes that the issue will eventually be converted into common stock, which is viewed riskier than straight bonds of the same company. In general, all liabilities of a company must be ranked in order of priority as a precautionary measure in the event that bankruptcy proceedings become necessary in the future. The indenture details the conditions and relationship to the firm's other existing and future debts. Large institutional investors examine these provisions closely; the small investor should follow their example. The main concern is that the bondholder may hold the security for many years and that a great deal can adversely affect a company over a 30- or 40-year period. Although the firm may be financially sound today, the investor may want the added safety of knowing that his or her investment represents a senior debt; thus, if a firm becomes involved in serious difficulties in the future, the bondholder will have better assurance of recouping his or her initial investment.

The railroad industry is a good example of business and financial risk. In the early 1900s, few industries were as solid as the railroads; they were considered by many to be the backbone of the American economy. However, by the 1930s, about one-third of the total railroad trackage was in bankruptcy. During the 1960s, the railroads ran into further difficulty, and their securities became increasingly risky. The famous Penn Central bankruptcy is a prime example of this risk.

Income Bonds

Although there are not many income bonds in existence, the investor should be aware of the distinction that is uniquely theirs. The indenture for income bonds does not guarantee the payment of interest; interest is paid only when earned. Therefore, failure to make an interest payment does not mean default on the bond. Most income bonds are cumulative. If interest is not paid when due, the amounts accumulate; and if the firm becomes profitable again, all back interest on bonds must be paid before any dividends are paid to stockholders. Income bonds are, by their very nature, high-risk bonds and considered speculative.

Convertible Bonds

Convertible bonds can be one of the finest holdings for the investor looking for both appreciation of investment and income. A **convertible bond** is a cross between a bond and stock. The holder can, at his or her option, convert the bond into a predetermined number of shares of common stock at a predetermined price. Almost all convertible bonds are debenture bonds, and the indenture contract specifies the terms of conversion and the period during which the conversion privilege can be exercised, which is usually for the life of the bond.

For example, an investor purchases a $1,000 convertible bond that pays 7 percent interest annually on the face value, or $70 per year. The bond has a 20-year maturity from the original date of purchase. The terms of conversion state that the bond may be converted into 50 shares of common stock any time up to the date of maturity. Thus, if an investor were to purchase the bond at $1,000 and convert the bond into 50 shares of common stock, this person would in essence be paying $20 per share for the common stock ($1,000/$50 = $20).

Two things will make the bond price rise or fall: (1) a change in the market price of interest, and (2) a change in the price of the underlying common stock. For example, if the common stock rises to a price of $30 per share, investors would want to buy a bond at $1,000, convert it, and sell the 50 shares of common stock at $30 each for an instant profit of $10 per share, or $500 (less commissions). But this would not happen because there would be such a rush to buy the bond, that the bond's price would rise to a level that, upon conversion, would equal the price of the common stock. In this case, the bond's price would rise to $1,500 ($30 × 50 = $1,500).

In addition to the 50 percent rise in the price of the bond, the investor would still continue to collect the interest payment each year. In fact, there is no reason to convert the bond as long as the yield received on it exceeds the yield that the investor would receive on the dividends paid on the common stock.

If, however, the price of the common stock remained below $20 per share for the entire life of the bond and conversion was undesirable, the worst possibility (short of bankruptcy) would be that the investor would collect interest annually and $1,000 upon maturity. If the price of the common stock declined substantially below $20 per share, the convertible bond would rise and fall just as any other bond does, relative to changes in the market rate of interest. If the price of the common stock is significantly under $20 per share (conversion value) and the market rate of interest for convertible bonds rises above 7 percent, the price of the bond will fall below $1,000. In this case, the investor is incurring interest-rate risk. But the investor will always receive the $1,000 at maturity if the firm is financially sound.

The call feature is most often exercised for convertible bonds. For example, if the price of common stock actually does rise to $30 per share, the bond will rise to $1,500. A call price of 105 ($1,050 per bond) is substantially below the market price of $1,500. All bondholders are notified that the bond will be called, and they must accept $1,050 per bond. The bondholders would be foolish to surrender their bonds at the call price, so they either sell the bond in the open market for $1,500 or convert the bond into common stock and receive 50 shares worth $30 per share. In this way, a company can force conversion, eliminate the debt obligation, and thus increase its permanent ownership funds. In other words, any convertible issue is intended as a delayed sale of common stock.

If, however, the company's financial performance is poor and the price of the common stock does not rise, the unexpected extra debt represented by the convertible bonds could be a serious burden to the company.

Exhibit 3-4 outlines an American Medical International 8 percent convertible debenture maturing in 2000 and selling at a price of $1,500 per bond. The "cv" indicates that this is a convertible bond. The volume for the day was 15 bonds, all traded at $1,500 per bond. To determine whether the price of the convertible bond is reasonable relative to its conversion value, the value of the underlying common stock would have to be examined. (For a more detailed analysis of convertible bonds, see Chapter 7.)

PREFERRED STOCK

Preferred stock is an ownership (equity) security with most of the characteristics of bonds. Preferred stock, as its name implies, receives preferential treatment over common stock. In general, common-stock holders may not receive dividends until dividends on preferred stock have been fully paid.

In addition, preferred-stock holders are usually entitled to a superior lien against the assets of the corporation in cases of bankruptcy at liquidation. In most circumstances, holders of preferred stock do not have voting rights unless their dividends have been omitted over a certain period of time.

There are a number of classifications of preferred stock that help to clarify the ways in which it differs from common stocks and bonds. Holders of straight preferred stock are entitled to dividends before holders of common stock, and the corporation's board of directors has the right to declare preferred dividends. Usually, preferred stock is expressed as having a certain percent of cash dividend attached to it, such as 5 or 8 percent.

Most preferred-stock issues have a cumulative feature, so if preferred dividends are skipped in any year, they become cumulative and must be fully paid before any dividends on common stock are declared. Investment in preferred stock entails more risk than investment in bonds primarily because of the lack of contractual agreement that dividends must be paid or that default will occur as with a bond. Furthermore, preferred stocks do not enjoy the status of bonds in liquidation proceedings, and their holders must wait until all bondholder obligations are satisfied in full before receiving any funds. Almost all preferred stock has the cumulative feature. But if the company experiences financial difficulty and the firm is reorganized, a proposed settlement must receive the majority of preferred-stock holder votes. Therefore, if dividends are in arrears (have not been paid) for a number of years, the preferred-stock holder might receive no dividends at all or only partial dividends.

Thus, the risk element is an important consideration in judging the wisdom of investing in preferred stock. Because preferred stocks are riskier than bonds, their dividend yield should be higher than the interest yield on bonds issued by the same company, but that has not always been the case. A reason for the lower yield on preferred stock relative to a corresponding bond is the fact that, if a corporation owns preferred stock in another company, 85 percent of the dividend received is tax exempt. Therefore, a company owning the preferred stock of another firm may realize a higher net yield after taxes on the preferred stock than could be realized on a corresponding bond. Nevertheless, because preferred stocks do not carry a maturity date, the risk of fluctuation over an extended period is greater than the risk with bonds over a comparable period.

Another feature of preferred stock is the **participating clause.** It allows the preferred-stock holder to receive the regular dividend; then, after the common-stock holders receive the same proportional amount, any excess dividend declared by the company's board of directors is split between the two groups of stockholders, thus allowing the preferred stockholder to share in large profits during certain successful years. However, there are not many participating preferred issues outstanding at the present time.

Like bonds, preferred stocks may have a call feature. This allows the corporation to recall the issue at a stated call price above the par value of the preferred stock. For this reason, the price of preferred stock seldom exceeds the call price; no one wants to buy a preferred stock at a higher price and then have it called at a lower price.

Preferred stock may be convertible into common stock. In this case, the situation is very similar to that of a convertible bond, although it may also have some of the features unique to preferred stock. Once the underlying common stock nears the conversion point (parity), the market price of the preferred stock will follow the movement of the common stock.

Unless preferred stock is convertible or has a significantly higher yield than a corresponding bond, there is little reason for the individual investor to own preferred stock. Very few investment advisory firms recommend the purchase of straight preferred stock for individuals.

For the issuing company, preferred stock is a flexible device. For the investor, the evaluation of preferred stock is very difficult because it may possess some of the characteristics of both bonds and stocks. Many financial analysts use the same criteria for preferred stocks that they use for bonds unless the issue is convertible. Although legally they represent ownership, most of the characteristics of preferred stock are similar to bonds and should be evaluated as such. The critical examination should center on the firm's ability to meet its fixed obligations, such as interest, principal, and preferred dividend payments, and to have sufficient earnings remaining to pay common-stock dividends or to retain for use in future corporate expansion. If earnings have been sufficient and stable over the past decade and the firm continues to have steady growth and commands a reasonable position within its industry, financial and business risk is minimized.

COMMERCIAL PAPER

Commercial paper consists of unsecured promissory notes sold by large corporations and finance companies to meet short-term cash needs. Denominations generally begin at $100,000, and maturities range from 5 to 270 days. Many times, individual investors can participate in the commercial-paper market in denominations of $1,000. Some local finance companies offer this service to attract investors, especially when money is difficult for financial institutions to obtain. Many financial institutions and individual investors prefer commercial paper to Treasury bills as a temporary investment for cash when they are in between investments because of a higher rate of interest. The risk is higher than it is with Treasury bills, because commercial paper is a direct obligation of the issuing corporation. However, if the investor is careful to select issuing companies that are in sound financial condition, the risk is minimized considerably.

Any security sold in the United States on an interstate basis with a maturity of more than 270 days must go through a formal security registration with the SEC, which involves the publishing of a preliminary prospectus for potential investors. The major reason why companies rarely issue commercial paper with maturity exceeding 270 days is to avoid the troubles of going through the normal registration process with the SEC.

Although default on commercial-paper obligations is rare, the dramatic default in 1970 by Penn Central on more than $50 million of its paper is a reminder of the risk involved in all aspects of fixed-security investing.

KEY TERMS

bearer bond	mortgage bond
call feature	municipal bond
collateral trust bond	preferred stock
commercial paper	registered bond
convertible bond	revenue bond
corporate bond	secured bond
coupon rate	Series EE bond
equipment trust obligation	Series HH bond
Fannie Mae (FNMA)	sinking-fund requirement
foreclosure	subordinated debenture
general obligation bond	Treasury bill
Ginnie Mae (GNMA)	Treasury notes and bonds
income bond	trustee
indenture	unsecured or debenture bond

QUESTIONS

1. Why would an investor choose a limited-return investment?
2. What are the four most common savings institutions?
3. What are Series EE and Series HH U.S. Savings Bonds?
4. What are treasury bills?
5. What is the difference between treasury notes and treasury bonds?
6. What are Fannie Mae and Ginnie Mae?
7. What are the different types of municipal bonds?
8. Why do bond prices fluctuate?
9. What is an indenture?
10. What is a sinking fund?
11. What kinds of corporate bonds are there, and what are their main features?
12. What will cause the price of convertible bonds to rise or fall?
13. What is the difference between preferred stock and common stock?
14. Why might the yield on preferred stock be lower than the yield on a comparable bond?
15. What are the distinguishing characteristics of commercial paper?

SELECTED READINGS

CRETIEN, PAUL D., JR. "Convertible Premiums vs. Stock Prices." *Financial Analysts Journal*, November–December 1969, 90.

CONNELLY, JULIE. "The Irrepressible Growth of Commercial Paper." *Institutional Investor*, March 1978, 25–27ff.

DARST, DAVID M. *The Complete Bond Book*. New York: McGraw-Hill, 1975.

First Boston Corporation. *Handbook of Securities of the United States Government and Federal Agencies*. New York: The Corporation, biennial.

FISHER, LAWRENCE. "Determinants of Risk Premiums on Corporate Bonds." *Journal of Political Economy*, June 1959, 217–237.

HORTON, JOSEPH J., JR. "Rating Index for Municipal Bonds." *Financial Analysts Journal*, March–April 1962, 72.

JEN, FRANK C., and JAMES E. WERT. "Sinking Funds and Bond Yields." *Financial Analysts Journal*, March–April 1967, 125.

KASRIEL, PAUL L. "New Six-Month Money Market Certificates—Explanations and Implications." *Economic Perspectives, Federal Reserve Bank of Chicago*, July–August 1978, 3–7.

MARSHALL, WILLIAM J. "Risk and Return in the Government Bond Market." *Journal of Portfolio Management*, Summer 1977, 48–52.

Moody's Bond Survey. New York: Moody's Investors Services, Inc., 1982

Moody's Municipal and Government Manual. New York: Moody's Investors Services, Inc., monthly.

POGUE, THOMAS F., and ROBERT M. SOLDOFSKY. "What's in a Bond Rating?" *Journal of Financial and Quantitative Analysis*, June 1969, 201–208.

4

Fixed-Return Security Analysis

This chapter describes the different types of limited-return securities available to an investor, their relative advantages and disadvantages, and the factors an investor must consider when analyzing them. As introduced in Chapter 3, fixed-return securities are issued by two groups of borrowers. One group consists of government entities, such as the federal government and its agencies and the various states and their political subdivisions. The other group consists of corporations that borrow to finance business activity and growth. A brief summary is given here.

U.S. Government and Agency Obligations.

Treasury bills, notes, and bonds are negotiable obligations of the federal government. Because they are direct obligations, they are backed by the full faith and taxing power of the U.S. government and are, therefore, risk free. Federal agencies have been empowered to borrow funds directly from the investment community and, therefore, issue debt obligations. Although they are not guaranteed by the federal government, they have the implied backing of the government.

Municipal Bonds.

Obligations of states and their political subdivisions are grouped under the heading of municipal bonds. Traditionally, the securities have lower interest rates than those of any other issuer owing to their tax-free characteristics. These securities are backed by the taxing power of the issuer, by its guarantor, or by the revenue-generating project and can vary substantially in quality.

Corporate Bonds and Preferred Stock.

Corporate bonds are the obligations of corporations and can take many forms. The holders of these bonds have primary claim in the distribution of assets in the event of business failure. Like municipal bonds, the quality can vary widely, depending upon the financial condition of the issuer. Preferred stock of a corporation has preference only to common stock in payment of dividends and in liquidation of distributions of a failed firm. Preferred stock does not have any preference to a company's outstanding bond issues and derives its only investment favor in that its claim has priority over common stock.

BASIC PRINCIPLES OF BOND PRICE BEHAVIOR

As mentioned previously, there is an inverse relationship between market interest rate and the price of a bond. That is, when interest rates rise, the price of bonds will decline, and vice versa. This inverse relationship is the core of bond price principles. However, other features that a bond possesses also influence its price behavior. The important features are the number of years to maturity of the bond, and the stated coupon rate.

When the market interest rate changes (rises or declines), the price fluctuation of a bond (decrease or increase) is greater if the time remaining to maturity of the bond is longer. Given a market interest rate change (increase or decrease by a certain percent), the bond price changes (declines or rises) at a decreasing rate as maturity shortens. For example, when the market rate of interest rises, the price of a bond decreases. The longer the maturity remaining, the larger the degree of price decline will be; however, the marginal decline of the price diminishes as the remaining years to maturity shorten. This relationship is shown in Figure 4-1. Given interest rate increases from c to $c + k$, the price decline from maturity m to $m + 1$ is less than the price decline from maturity $m - 1$ to m (as shown in the graph, $d_1 \geq d_2$).

For any given maturity and magnitude of interest rate change (i.e.,

Figure 4-1 Price Behavior of a Bond

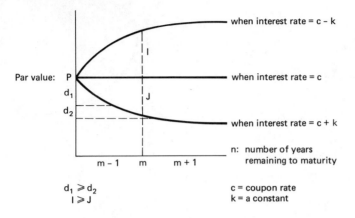

increase by a certain percent or decrease by the same percent), the resulting price increase is larger in volume than the resulting price decrease. As shown in Figure 4-1, for a given maturity m, when the interest rate decreases by k percent, the price increases by I; when the rate increases by k percent, the price decreases by J. It is always the case that I is greater than or equal to J.

The price fluctuation of a bond is greater when the market interest rate is changing from a relatively high level than from a relatively low level. For example, if the prevailing interest rate is 20 percent, a 1 percent decrease in the rate would result in a price appreciation that is greater than that of an appreciation resulting from a 1 percent market rate decrease if the rate was at 10 percent.

For a given market interest rate change, the lower the coupon rate on a bond, the greater is the resulting price fluctuation. This principle is implied by the interest-rate risk, as discussed in Chapter 2.

TERM STRUCTURE OF INTEREST RATES

When an investor contemplates placing funds in a fixed-return security, a major consideration is the rate of return that can be earned. The market rate of interest that an investor can expect to receive is constantly changing. The structure of the interest rates that faces a borrower varies considerably over time and among various fixed-return securities.

There are four basic types of interest-rate structure, or shape of the yield curve. Figure 4-2 shows these four types: (a) normal yield curve, (b) negative yield curve, (c) humped-back yield curve, and (d) horizontal yield curve.

Figure 4-2 Term Structure of Interest Rates

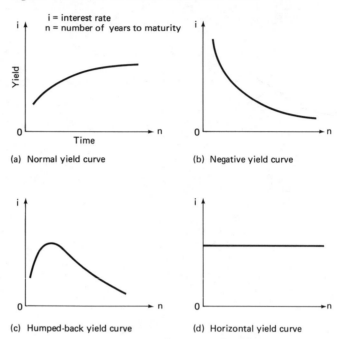

(a) Normal yield curve   (b) Negative yield curve

(c) Humped-back yield curve   (d) Horizontal yield curve

There are three generally accepted schools of thought that attempt to explain the changing yield patterns on fixed-income securities and their shift in position.

Unbiased-Expectation Theory

The **unbiased-expectation theory,** simply stated, claims that the yield on any maturity today is the geometric mean of all the 1-year yields expected to exist between today and the security's maturity date. According to the theory, investors have expectations regarding future short-term rates, and the investor is indifferent between investing in one long-term maturity security and a series of securities with 1-year maturities.

If investors are expecting a higher yield in the future, they will demand a long-term maturity to carry a higher interest rate than the current short-term rate. If investors are expecting the yield to drop in the future, the long-term rate will be lower than the current short-term rate. In summary, according to this expectation theory, investors are indifferent to the maturity of the securities. The only factor that determines whether the long-term rate is higher or lower than the short-term rate is the investors' expectation of the future interest rate.

An example of the expectation theory is that if 1-year interest rates are now 6 percent and are expected to be 8 percent in 2 years, then today's rate on 2-year bonds will be a 2-year average of 6.93 percent:

$$\sqrt[2]{(6\%)(8\%)} = 6.93\%$$

Liquidity-Preference Theory

The **liquidity-preference theory** claims that, although expectations are important, the principal factor for interest rates is the investor's aversion to liquidity risk. It holds that an investor will accept a smaller yield for short-term maturities than for long-term maturities, because securities with long-term maturities expose the investor to more interest-rate risk as a result of the larger dollar-value changes following interest-rate fluctuations in the market. For example, in Table 4-1 we can examine the change in the market value of a security having a 5 percent coupon with a maturity of 1, 5, 10, and 20 years when interest rates change in the market from 5 percent to 6 percent.

Table 4-1

Maturity	1 Year	5 Years	10 Years	20 Years
Market value before change	$1,000.00	$1,000.00	$1,000.00	$1,000.00
Market value after change[a]	$ 990.57	$ 957.88	$ 926.39	$ 888.15
Percent of change in market value	0.943%	4.212%	7.361%	11.485%

[a]Derived from the application of yield to maturity.

The security with a 20-year maturity is more price volatile than that with a shorter maturity, because longer maturities magnify the price change caused by interest-rate changes. This phenomenon is in conformity with the first bond principle that was previously introduced. The liquidity-preference theory claims that an investor will not expose himself to such price volatility without demanding a premium. Therefore, the 20-year bond would rarely sell for $1,000 if a 1-year bond with the same coupon rate sold for $1,000. The 20-year bond would sell for less, thus providing a larger yield than 5 percent. The liquidity-preference theory has come under attack, since long-term interest rates during the mid-1970s and early 1980s yielded less than short-term securities. That condition is directly opposed to the theory and has forced its supporters to reevaluate their position. Nevertheless, historically, long-term interest rates have yielded a higher rate than short-term securities.

Segmented-Markets Theory

The third widely supported theory is the **segmented-markets theory.** It is built around the concept that different groups of investors might have aversion to investing in either short- or long-maturity securities, or they might have different maturity preferences. These supporters argue that although some investors are averse to principal risk, others are averse to income uncertainty. The investor who purchases only short-term maturity issues will be constantly reinvesting at different rates of return. Segmented-market theorists point out that some large institutional investors, such as pension funds and insurance companies, do not need vast liquid assets, but rather unvarying long-term holdings with a greater concern for the safety of principal. This would indicate that two markets exist: (1) a market for short-term maturity issues dominated by individuals and institutions requiring great liquidity, and (2) a market for longer-term maturity issues comprised of institutions with little liquidity needs and long-term commitment with the major concern the safety of principal.

YIELD CALCULATIONS

One of an investor's primary concerns is the yield from a particular investment. The choice from among alternative investments often hinges on the available yield in relation to the security's risk category. A first measure of the return earned on an investment is the stated rate of return or nominal yield on the face or par value of the issue. This is the interest rate that the borrower promises to pay on the principal of a bond or the dividend rate on the par value of the preferred stock. In the case of bonds, the stated or nominal rate is also called the **coupon rate** or **coupon yield.** The terms **dividend rate** or **dividend yield** are applied to preferred stocks because they have par value.

Current Yield

A frequently used calculation is the **current yield** of an investment, which indicates the percentage relation of the cash income received to the security's market price. The current yield is computed by dividing the annual dollar income by the current market price. The current yield varies with daily changes in market price and also with the less frequent changes in the annual payment. Current yield may also vary according to the method used to determine the annual payment. Some analysts use the dividends paid in the last 12 months; others annualize the most recent dividend declaration.

Holding-Period Yield

The benefits any investor receives from holding a security consist of income received and any change in the security's price during the holding period. For example, assume that one share of XYZ Company's stock is purchased at the beginning of the year for $20 and that the stock is held for the entire year and then sold for $21.50. During the year, $1 in dividends was collected. Therefore, the rate of return achieved is the sum of the dividend yield and the change in the security's price. In this case, the total yield is $12\frac{1}{2}$ percent. The equation for the calculation is

$$\text{HPY} = \frac{(P_1 - P_0) + I}{P_0} = \frac{(21.50 - 20) + 1}{20} = 12.5\%$$

where

$\text{HPY} = $ holding-period yield
$I = $ income received during period
$P_0 = $ beginning price
$P_1 = $ ending price

When this formula is used on fixed-income securities (securities whose annual income is fixed in dollar terms), any shifts in an investor's required HPY must come from changes in the price of the fixed-income security. However, this is not true of common stocks because their dividends can fluctuate.

The HPY formula is simplified because it does not take into consideration the timing of the income payments or length of the holding period. The formula should be adjusted according to the length of the holding period and the frequency with which income is received. If the 12.5 percent return from the earlier example occurred over a 2-year period, the annual average rate of return would be approximately half as much.

Yield to Maturity

The previous discussions on approaches to understanding the movements in yield relative to interest rates are extremely important for fixed-income security investors whose primary question is, "What is the return on the investment?" Return on bonds is referred to as **yield to maturity,** which is the rate of return that an investor will realize on an annual basis if this person buys a security and holds it to maturity. In other words, the yield to maturity of a bond on a certain day is the rate of return used to discount all the future income streams (in the form of periodic coupon interest receipts and the principal repayment) and equate the former with the prevailing market price of the bond on the same day. Mathematically,

$$M = \sum_{t=1}^{n} \frac{C}{(1 + r)^t} + \frac{P}{(1 + r)^n}$$

where M = current market price of the bond
                                 n = number of years remaining to maturity
                                 C = annual coupon receipts
                                 P = principal (par value) of the bond
                                 r = rate of return, yield to maturity

Readers may recall that the calculation of yield to maturity is actually a present-value concept in application. Therefore, given the current market price of a certain bond and knowing the coupon rate and the number of years to maturity of that bond, with the preceding equation we can solve for r, the yield to maturity of the bond. However, the procedure of solving for r is very tedious and cumbersome; therefore, a shortcut is introduced here to approximate the true yield to maturity. The approximate yield to maturity can be determined by the following formula:

$$\text{approximate YTM} = \frac{C + [(P - M)/n]}{(P + M)/2}$$

This formula recognizes that yield to maturity is made up of two component parts: (1) the coupon or annual interest payment, and (2) the average appreciation or depreciation in the market price to the maturity value of par. When investing in bonds, it is important to remember that the individual components are subject to different types of taxation. The interest payments received are ordinary unearned income and are thus taxed at the investor's highest marginal rate. When a bond is purchased at a discount, any appreciation in value from purchase price to par value is subject to the lower capital gains tax treatment. When the bond is purchased at a price above par, the interest is ordinary income, and the premium may be amortized over the remaining years to maturity to reduce the interest subject to taxation.

Yield to Call

Often when bonds are issued, the indenture contains a provision that permits the issuer the option to call the bonds at sometime in the future before the maturity date. When this provision exists, the bond investor will also want to calculate the yield to call. This can be approximated by using the formula for yield to maturity in which P equals the call price and n equals the number of years to the call date. This yield can then be compared with the yield to maturity. The lesser yield is the minimum yield to be expected on the security.

Yield to Average Life

Many bonds have a sinking-fund provision that requires the issuer to retire the issue gradually at a certain schedule. For example, an issue of 10 years maturity may have a retirement schedule of calling the bond for the sinking-fund purposes from the sixth year on, and 20 percent of the entire issue will be retired annually. The issuer may either purchase the bonds in the secondary market, if the bond is sold below par, or it may call on a random basis in a lot-drawing fashion. If the latter situation occurs, an investor is not sure as to when his or her bonds would be called, since the redemption process is random. Therefore, a yield to average life is appropriate for estimating the expected value of the yield to call. The calculation of the average life of the bond is to take the summation of each year's percentage being called times the number of the year.

$$\text{average life} = \sum_{i=1}^{n} (i \times P_i)$$

where P_i is the percentage of bond retired in year i, and n is the number of years to maturity.

Using our preceding example, the retirement schedule looks like this:

(1) percentage of retirement	(2) years	(1) × (2)
0	1	0
0	2	0
0	3	0
0	4	0
0	5	0
.2	6	1.2
.2	7	1.4
.2	8	1.6
.2	9	1.8
.2	10	2.0
	Total	8.0

Therefore, the average life is 8 years. The yield to average life is then obtained by substituting 8 for the parameter n in the approximate yield to maturity equation, where P represents the call price.

ACCRUED INTEREST ON BONDS

The prices of most bonds are quoted on an **and-interest** basis. In addition to the agreed price, the buyer pays the seller the amount of interest accrued since the preceding interest date, because interest for the full six months (interest on bonds is paid semiannually) will be paid to the buyer of a bond on the next interest date.

Accrued interest on bonds is calculated on the basis of a 360-day year (in the case of certain U.S. government bonds, accrued interest is calculated on the basis of a 365-day year.) Under the 360-day basis, each month is considered to have 30 days, regardless of its calendar days. The seller is entitled to interest up to, but not including, the day of delivery. Thus, if a 5 percent bond with interest-payment dates of January 1 and July 1 is sold on Monday, October 12, and the regular five-business-day delivery is adhered to on Monday, October 19, the seller is entitled to interest for 3 months (July, August, and September) and 18 days (up to, but not including, October 19) at 5 percent, or $14.99.

If the buyer does not receive interest on the subsequent payment date, he or she cannot recover the amount advanced to the seller but must, instead, endeavor to recover the amount from the issuing company. This situation arises when bonds are sold flat; that is, the quoted price excludes any accrued interest. Such bonds are most likely either in default or income bonds whose income is uncertain.

GOVERNMENT SECURITIES

Government securities have one clear advantage over all other investment vehicles: they are free of financial risk to the purchaser. Investors who purchase these securities know that they will receive their money when the maturity date is reached because the government can always rely on its unlimited borrowing authority to retire the bond if no other way is available. An additional advantage of investing in federal government securities is their marketability. Because of their lack of risk and the large dollar amount of such securities outstanding, a ready market exists for trading in any government issue. The federal government's obligations are the most liquid securities an investor can own because they are easily and quickly convertible to cash, either by selling or by using them as security for loans.

For the speculator, government bonds have favorable margin requirements. An individual is required to put up only 10 percent of the purchase price for government securities; the other 90 percent is borrowed through a broker or bank. This procedure can be most useful when an investor is speculating on interest-rate changes, but it offers no advantage for long-term holders because few people can borrow at as favorable rates as the government. In other words, investors will generally pay more on their margin loan than will be received on the government securities and, therefore, any profit must be derived in the short run.

To obtain the investment advantages that government securities contain, the investor has to accept disadvantages. The largest disadvantage of investing in government debt instruments is their lower rate of return. The government can borrow at a lower rates than any other entity, which means that the investor will receive a lower yield than would be available from other issuers, such as corporations.

Another disadvantage of investing in government securities is inherent in all fixed-income securities. That is, the investor is vulnerable to both purchasing-power risk and interest-rate risk. Every investor must determine the advantages that liquidity offers in the ownership of government securities and their relatively risk free nature. If these advantages are important to an investor, he or she must forgo the opportunities to hedge against purchasing-power and interest-rate risks.

The securities of U.S. government agencies are subject to the same advantages and disadvantages as the government's direct obligations. However, they will usually yield a slightly higher return than the government's direct debt. This is perceived as offsetting the risk associated with the possible but highly unlikely event that the government would choose not to honor an agency's securities if for some reason they were unable to pay interest and/or principal.

Analyzing Municipal Securities

When investors analyze revenue bonds, they must be very careful and thorough. If investors do not analyze correctly or if they miscalculate the possibility that a project cannot cover its cost, there is no recourse to the municipality nor any possibility that a community's or state's tax base will make up any difference. Analysis of revenue bonds should take on two aspects. The first aspect to be considered is whether or not the project will generate sufficient revenues to repay the principal invested. The investors may be able to risk the income flow, but rarely should they risk principal. Only after the investors are sure that the principal is safe should they look to the rate of interest being paid. The probability that a project is a safe investment is determined by calculating the interest coverage, that is, how many times the interest payment is earned in a single year before the payment of interest. If the earnings available for the payment of interest equals the interest expense, the project is very risky; if the interest expense is covered by more than four times, the investment is favorable.

The second aspect to be considered in analyzing revenue bonds is the degree of asset or principal protection. For municipal bonds, this analysis can be subjective if the appropriate government entity does not provide a detailed report of its financial condition. Nevertheless, an investor should attempt to determine the degree of protection of the principal. Municipal bond industry experts and the rating services can be of great help to the investor.

Yields on Municipal Bonds

As a general rule, a given quality of municipal bonds will have a lower yield to maturity than other fixed-income securities of the same quality available to the investor because of the favorable tax treatment the investor receives on municipal interest. Under federal tax law, interest received on municipal bonds is tax exempt to the recipient. Therefore, if investors wish to compare a municipal security with another type of interest-bearing security, they must use a formula that converts both securities to a before-tax yield:

$$\text{before-tax equivalent yield} = \frac{\text{tax-exempt yield}}{1 - \text{marginal tax rate}}$$

An investor can convert a tax-exempt yield to its corresponding yield for any other type of taxable security. Table 4-2 indicates the before-tax equivalent of tax-exempt securities for various taxable income brackets. For example, if a married taxpayer in 1984 has taxable income between $20,200 and $24,600 a year, he or she is in a marginal tax bracket of 22 percent. If this person has the opportunity to buy a tax-exempt security yielding 9 percent, he or she would have to receive a before-tax return of 11.54 percent on a taxable security to give the equivalent yield. As the tax bracket of an investor increases, the desirability of tax-exempt securities increases. If the marginal income tax bracket is 50 percent, the investor would have to receive 18 percent on a taxable security to net a 9 percent after-tax yield equivalent to a 9 percent municipal bond.

Although tax exemption is a very favorable aspect of municipal bonds, the investor should not forget that there are disadvantages. The first disadvantage is the low yield to maturity that municipals generally offer. Before an investor can really take advantage of the tax-exempt nature of the municipals, he or she should be in a reasonably high tax bracket. Generally, unless an investor is in at least a 32 percent marginal tax bracket (as shown in Table 4-2), tax-exempt securities may be undesirable. This, however, will

Table 4-2

Value of Tax-Exempt Income Relative to Taxable Income, 1984

Taxable Income Married (Joint Return)	Marginal Income Tax Bracket	Tax-Exempt Yield														
		7.50%	8.50%	9.50%	10.00%	10.50%	11.00%	11.50%	12.00%	12.50%	13.00%	13.50%	14.00%	14.50%	15.00%	15.50%
$11,900– 16,000	16%	8.93	10.12	11.31	11.90	12.50	13.10	13.69	14.29	14.88	15.48	16.07	16.67	17.26	17.86	18.45
16,000– 20,200	18%	9.15	10.57	11.59	12.20	12.80	13.41	14.02	14.63	15.24	15.85	16.46	17.07	17.68	18.29	18.90
20,200– 24,600	22%	9.62	10.90	12.18	12.82	13.46	14.10	14.74	15.38	16.03	16.67	17.31	17.95	18.59	19.23	19.87
24,600– 29,900	25%	10.00	11.33	12.67	13.33	14.00	14.67	15.33	16.00	16.67	17.33	18.00	18.67	19.33	20.00	20.67
29,900– 35,200	28%	10.42	11.81	13.19	13.89	14.58	15.28	15.97	16.67	17.36	18.06	18.75	19.44	20.14	20.83	21.53
35,200– 45,800	33%	11.19	12.69	14.18	14.93	15.67	16.42	17.16	17.91	18.66	19.40	20.15	20.90	21.64	22.39	23.13
45,800– 60,000	38%	12.10	13.71	15.32	16.13	16.94	17.74	18.55	19.35	20.16	20.97	21.77	22.58	23.39	24.19	25.00
60,000– 85,600	42%	12.97	14.66	16.38	17.24	18.10	18.97	19.83	20.69	21.55	22.41	23.28	24.14	25.00	25.86	26.72
85,600–109,400	45%	13.64	15.45	17.27	18.18	19.09	20.00	20.91	21.82	22.73	23.64	24.55	25.45	26.36	27.27	28.18
109,400–162,400	49%	14.71	16.67	18.83	19.61	20.59	21.57	22.55	23.53	24.51	25.49	26.47	27.47	28.43	29.41	30.39
162,400 and over	50%	15.00	17.00	19.00	20.00	21.00	22.00	23.00	24.00	25.00	26.00	27.00	28.00	29.00	30.00	31.00

Source: Internal Revenue Serivce; author's computations.

vary, depending on the prevailing rates for taxable securities of comparable quality and risk.

As explained before, municipal bonds are attractive to those investors in a higher tax bracket. Due to the tax-exempt feature, municipals usually have a much lower before-tax yield. However, since late 1981, the tax-cut program carried out by the Reagan administration has lowered the maximum tax to 50 percent from the previous 70 percent. This reduction on individual's taxes has made the tax-exempt securities less attractive. Therefore, state and the local governments now have to issue bonds with higher coupon rates in order to attract the same amount of capital needed.

The second disadvantage concerns the issuers themselves. Often, a municipal issue is very small, a few million dollars or less; and once the investors have purchased part of a small issue, they will have difficulty liquidating their positions should they so desire. Only a very few, large, selected municipal issues are quoted on a regular basis. Substantial amounts of municipal issues are traded on a local basis, but their liquidity is sometimes in jeopardy. There are, however, large amounts of certain city and state obligations, such as New York City's, but the city's poor fiscal condition has substantially increased the risk of default.

CORPORATE BOND ANALYSIS

Payment of Debt and Interest Obligations

When determining the desirability of investing in a specific bond, the investor is concerned with two basic questions: Will the issuer be able to repay the debt? Will the issuer be able to pay the interest annually?

The investors' prime concern in analyzing a bond is determining the degree of security in recovering their investments in the event that the issuer fails. Loss of principal is the ultimate concern for bond investors, because they will have lost not only the interest due them but also any opportunity to generate future income on the principal lost. If there is any reasonable basis for assuming that the issuer could possibly be unable to repay the principal, the investors should avoid such a bond issue. To evaluate the issuer's ability to repay necessitates an examination of the market value of the assets relative to the total dollar value of outstanding debt. It is important that investors attempt to utilize market value and not merely the book value for these purposes, because they may differ considerably. Investors will want to look to market value as a basis for covering the debt obligations. Because assets are usually recorded at historical cost, market value of the assets can be substantially higher than book value.

Ratio analysis is very useful in determining the company's ability to repay, and investors should calculate the **debt-to-net-worth ratio** of the company compared to the industry norm and to acceptable standards as dictated by the rating services. If the issuer has more debt relative to net worth than the comparable industry group, the potential investor should view this as a warning. An additional test is to compare the debt to the company's net fixed assets. Fixed assets are traditionally financed from long-term debt and equity. There should be comfortable margin between debt and net fixed assets so that the debt holders are well protected if the company is forced to liquidate its fixed assets or if the firm is reorganized. The investor must be careful in comparing a company with its industry because the industry in general may be in difficulty; in such a case, ratios that reflect the norm of the industry may be unsuitable as a basis for an investment decision.

Since investors make their investments with the intention of generating income, they are understandably concerned about the issuer's ability to make timely interest payments. To evaluate that ability, investors must examine the corporation's earning power. If the issuer is not earning a sufficient income to pay the interest payments and also retire the principal, either through a sinking fund or serial retirement, investors have good reason to be concerned about future interest payments.

For these purposes the investor can utilize two types of ratio analysis. The first is an examination of the **times-interest-earned ratio,** which informs the investor about the size of the protective safety margin that exists between the earnings available for fixed charges. For these purposes, earnings before interest and taxes (EBIT) are divided by the annual fixed charges. For most companies the largest segment of fixed charges is interest on debt, and, therefore, the ratio is often referred to as the interest-coverage ratio. If the ratio is small, the issuer is barely earning an amount sufficient to cover the fixed interest payments and has difficulty generating funds to retire the principal amount of the debt. Also, a small interest-coverage ratio indicates that little cushion exists, and that if the issuer should have a difficult year in terms of revenues or increasing expenses, it may not be able to cover interest payments.

When investors use the fixed charges ratio, they must also consider the degree of seniority of their claims. If other bondholders have a superior claim on earnings, those charges should be deducted from the EBIT before utilizing the earnings figure in computing the coverage for the specific bond in question. This is most important because an investor should not look at all bonds for a particular firm as having the same interest coverage. Table 4-3 shows the calculation that the investor should initially use to determine the specific interest coverage of the bond in question.

In addition to the debt-to-net-worth ratio and the fixed-charge-coverage ratio, the investor should be concerned with the corporation's earning power. Investors will want to determine the rate of return on assets and the rate of return on equity as a gauge of management's ability to run the firm

Table 4-3
Times Interest Earned

BALANCE SHEET

Assets (in thousands)		Liabilities (in thousands)	
Current Assets	$ 500,000	Current Liabilities	$ 300,000
		Long-Term debt:	
		Primary 7%	200,000
		Subordinated 10%	300,000
Fixed Assets	1,000,000	Preferred Stock	100,000
		Common Stock	100,000
		Retained Earnings	500,000
Total Assets	$1,500,000	Total Liability Equity	$1,500,000

INCOME STATEMENT (in thousands)

Sales	$2,000,000
Cost of Goods Sold	1,900,000
Earnings Before Interest and Taxes	100,000
Interest Expense	44,000
Earnings Before Taxes	56,000
Income Taxes	28,000
Net Income	$ 28,000

$$\text{Interest coverage} = \frac{100,000}{44,000} = 2.272 \text{ times}$$

$$\text{Interest coverage, primary} = \frac{100,000}{14,000} = 7.143 \text{ times}$$

$$\text{Interest coverage, subordinated} = \frac{86,000}{30,000} = 2.867 \text{ times}$$

efficiently. In addition, they will want to determine the degree of variability in the firm's income from year to year as an indicator of the riskiness of the income stream. Many ratios can be examined, and investors should make a sufficient analysis to determine for themselves the risk class of the bonds under consideration.

The investor will also be concerned with the firm's ability and plan to repay the principal amount of the bond issue. The indenture of a bond issue often contains a sinking-fund provision that requires the firm to set aside a portion of the total dollar obligation into a separate fund. This fund will increase in value so that there will be a substantial portion of the total dollar obligation available upon maturity date for the repayment to bondholders. Not all firms use sinking funds, but they are almost always found in indentures of industrial companies. A sinking fund gives greater security to bondholders, because the firm will not have to produce the total amount of the debt principal at maturity from operations, and the firm will not be forced to float an additional bond issue to raise the necessary funds for the principal repayment. Firms such as American Telephone and Telegraph, however, do not have sinking-fund provisions. They float additional bond issues prior to the maturity of an older outstanding issue and use funds from the new issue to repay the holders of the older bond issue.

Corporate Bond Ratings

In addition to their own analysis of the quality of the firm and its ability to pay interest and principal, investors may choose to consult other sources. For example, Moody's and Standard and Poor's are two well-known professional investment services that rate bond issues. These services rate the securities of a corporation with regard to the issuer's ability to pay interest and principal.

Table 4-4 shows these two services' rating symbols for bonds with different grades. Speculative-grade bonds have small or no assurance of continued payment of interest; therefore, investors have to exercise extreme care in selecting among them.

Exhibit 4-1 describes the Standard & Poor's bond-rating definitions. A rating of a bond is based upon historical data and trends. Therefore, the investor must strive to be aware of any developments concerning a particular issuer that may change the risk characteristics of its debt securities. These rating firms issue monthly bulletins of their ratings and weekly announcements of rating changes. The services rate the outstanding issues. Bonds rated AAA are considered to be of the highest quality and those rated C to be of highly dubious quality. Investors should be aware that the market for

Table 4-4
Bond Ratings

Investment-grade Bonds		Speculative-grade Bonds	
Moody's	S&P	Moody's	S&P
Aaa	AAA	Ba	BB+
Aa	AA+		BB
	AA		BB−
	AA−	B	B+
A	A+		B
	A		B−
	A−	Caa	CCC
Baa	BBB+	Ca	CC
	BBB	C	C
	BBB−		

Exhibit 4-1

STANDARD & POOR'S Corporate and Municipal Bond Rating Definitions

A Standard & Poor's corporate or municipal bond rating is a current assessment of the creditworthiness of an obligor with respect to a specific debt obligation. This assessment may take into consideration obligors such as guarantors, insurers, or lessees.

The bond rating is not a recommendation to purchase, sell or hold a security, inasmuch as it does not comment as to market price or suitability for a particular investor.

The ratings are based on current information furnished by the issuer or obtained by Standard & Poor's from other sources it considers reliable. Standard & Poor's does not perform any audit in connection with any rating and may, on occasion, rely on unaudited financial information. The ratings may be changed, suspended or withdrawn as a result of changes in, or unavailability of, such information, or for other circumstances.

The ratings are based, in varying degrees, on the following considerations:

I. Likelihood of default-capacity and willingness of the obligor as to the timely payment of interest and repayment of principal in accordance with the terms of the obligation;

II. Nature of and provisions of the obligation;

III. Protection afforded by, and relative position of, the obligation in the event of bankruptcy, reorganization or other arrangement under the laws of bankruptcy and other laws affecting creditors' rights.

AAA Bonds rated AAA have the highest rating assigned by Standard & Poor's to a debt obligation. Capacity to pay interest and repay principal is extremely strong.

AA Bonds rated AA have a very strong capacity to pay interest and repay principal and differ from the highest rated issues only in small degree.

A Bonds rated A have a strong capacity to pay interest and repay principal although they are somewhat more susceptible to the adverse effects of changes in circumstances and economic conditions than bonds in higher rated categories.

BBB Bonds rated BBB are regarded as having an adequate capacity to pay interest and repay principal. Whereas they normally exhibit adequate protection parameters, adverse economic conditions or changing circumstances are more likely to lead to a weakened capacity to pay interest and repay principal for bonds in this category than for bonds in higher rated categories.

BB, B, CCC, CC Bonds rated BB, B, CCC and CC are regarded, on balance, as predominantly speculative with respect to capacity to pay interest and repay principal in accordance with the terms of the obligation. BB indicates the lowest degree of speculation and CC the highest degree of speculation. While such bonds will likely have some quality and protective characteristics, these are outweighed by large uncertainties or major risk exposures to adverse conditions.

C The rating C is reserved for income bonds on which no interest is being paid.

D Bonds rated D are in default, and payment of interest and/or repayment of principal is in arrears.

Plus (+) or Minus (–): The ratings from "AA" to "B" may be modified by the addition of a plus or minus sign to show relative standing within the major rating categories.

Provisional Ratings: The letter "p" indicates that the rating is provisional. A provisional rating assumes the successful completion of the project being financed by the bonds being rated and indicates that payment of debt service requirements is largely or entirely dependent upon the successful and timely completion of the project. This rating, however, while addressing credit quality subsequent to completion of the project, makes no comment on the likelihood of, or the risk of default upon failure of, such completion. The investor should exercise his own judgment with respect to such likelihood and risk.

NR Indicates that no rating has been requested, that there is insufficient information on which to base a rating, or that S&P does not rate a particular type of obligation as a matter of policy.

Debt Obligations of issuers outside the United States and its territories are rated on the same basis as domestic corporate and municipal issues. The ratings measure the creditworthiness of the obligor but do not take into account currency exchange and related uncertainties.

Bond Investment Quality Standards: Under present commercial bank regulations issued by the Comptroller of the Currency, bonds rated in the top four categories (AAA, AA, A, BBB, commonly known as "Investment Grade" ratings) are generally regarded as eligible for bank investment. In addition, the Legal Investment Laws of various states impose certain rating or other standards for obligations eligible for investment by savings banks, trust companies, insurance companies and fiduciaries generally.

Standard & Poor's publication "CreditWeek" contains a section entitled "Credit Watch" indicating whether certain events have positive or negative implications with respect to the ratings of the debt of certain companies.

Standard & Poor's does not act as a financial advisor to any issuer in connection with any corporate or municipal debt financing. Standard & Poor's receives compensation for rating debt obligations. Such compensation is based on the time and effort to determine the rating and is normally paid either by the issuers of such securities or by the underwriters participating in the distribution thereof. The fees generally vary from $1,000 to $10,000 for municipal securities, and from $1,500 to $20,000 for corporate securities. While Standard & Poor's reserves the right to disseminate the rating, it receives no payment for doing so, except for subscriptions to its publications.

Source: Standard & Poor's Stock Guide, Standard & Poor's Corporation, New York, New York, 1982.

bonds rated BB and lower may be rather small because certain institutional investors are not permitted to hold bonds rated lower than BBB.

Call Protection

The bond indenture contains information pertaining to any call provisions to which the bond is subject. Investors should strive to be aware of the bond's current standing regarding call provisions, because those provisions may affect the bond's investment value. If a bond is issued without call provisions, investors know that they will be permitted to hold the bond until maturity. It is very uncommon, however, to find a bond issue that does not contain a call provision. As previously indicated, investors should always calculate both yield to maturity and yield to call for an investment. This enables them to know exactly what the minimum yield on the investment will be. If investors anticipate that a bond will eventually be called prior to maturity, they must decide whether that minimum yield is satisfactory.

Investors must recognize that if the bonds are called they will be forced to relinquish them and that the alternatives for reinvestment of the funds will probably be at a lower yield for a bond of equal quality and maturity. A call provision establishes an upper limit to which the bond price will rise if the callable feature is in effect. If the call feature is not exercisable by the company for several years, the bond may trade slightly in excess of its future call price.

Marketability of Corporate Bonds

When investors consider corporate bonds as investment, they also consider the length of time they tentatively plan to hold the security. A large number of bond issues floated by small companies are very small in terms of dollars outstanding, and they may not have a ready secondary market. Investing in securities listed on organized exchanges (such as the New York Bond Exchange) will generally enable investors to sell their holdings readily, even if the size of the order is not large and many listed issues are not traded frequently. As a general rule, the larger the size of the bond issue, the more trading volume and the less will be its price volatility for a given day.

Advantages and Disadvantages of Corporate Bonds

In analyzing corporate bonds, the investor must be aware of their advantages and disadvantages compared with other investment possibilities. Corporate bonds offer a higher return on investment than do federal and municipal bonds. The yield differentials are shown in Figure 4-3. A wide variety of corporate bonds exists, which provides investors with the opportunity to acquire different grades of securities to meet their needs. Since large cor-

Figure 4-3 Long-Term Interest Rates

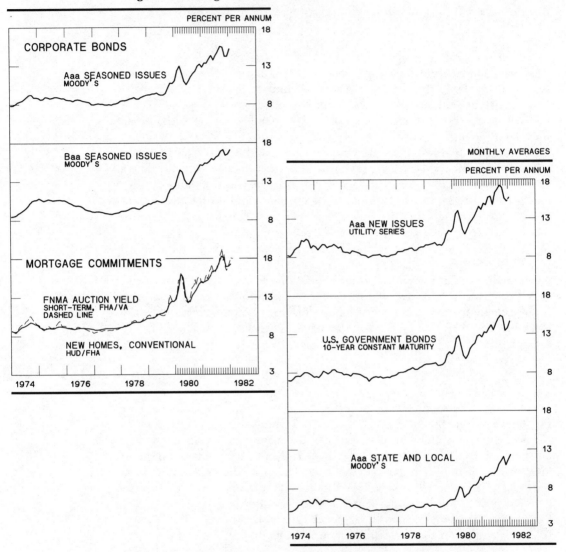

Source: Federal Reserve System, *Federal Reserve Chart Book*, 1982.

porate issues can be more marketable, they have greater liquidity than many issues of states or municipalities.

Chapter 3 emphasized many of the advantages and disadvantages of corporate bonds and pointed out that their fixed rate of return causes them to be sensitive to changes in the market rate of interest. Therefore, interest-rate risk is one of the largest concerns for the bond investor. Even as interest rates decline, bonds will be prohibited from advancing in a proportional amount because of the call-provision ceiling. In addition, the call feature increases the risk that the investor may be forced to liquidate prior to maturity and thus suffer a lower interest rate on a subsequent investment. The investor is, however, somewhat compensated for this risk by the call premium, which most bond issues possess.

Bond Portfolio Performance

Table 4-5 shows the results from a study of the annual returns from a high-quality bond portfolio for various periods from 1925 through 1974. Although certain short-term periods experienced historically high rates of return, the overall average for the entire period under study was 3.3 percent.

PREFERRED STOCK ANALYSIS

Preferred stock is a hybrid security that is not heavily utilized by corporations as a means of raising capital. It is a hybrid because it combines some of the characteristics of debt and some of equity. This section will examine the attributes of preferred stock as an investment instrument and how it fits the investor's needs.

Characteristics of Preferred Stock

Preferred stock is an ownership security that conveys to the stockholder preferential treatment as to the earnings of the issuer and to priority of claim over common stockholders in any liquidation proceeding.

Because preferred stock has a priority claim to receive cash dividends, no dividends can be paid on common stock unless and until the preferred dividend is paid in full. If the preferred-stock issue has a cumulative feature, any dividends that the board of directors have not declared on preferred stock in the past must be paid in full before any common dividends are paid. Preferred-stockholders also hold a priority claim on assets of the company in the event of liquidation. Thus, preferred-stockholders have a safety cushion equal in size to the common-stockholders' tangible equity.

Preferred stock typically has no stated maturity date, but it may be callable or possess a sinking fund. When the stock is callable, the call price is usually expressed as a percent of par. Since the call price is above par, the owners of preferred stock are afforded some protection if the issue is called from them.

Table 4-5

Long-Term Corporate Bonds

Rates of Return for All Yearly Holding Periods from 1926 to 1974

(Percent Per Annum Compounded Annually)

To The End of	From The Beginning of																
	1926	1927	1928	1929	1930	1931	1932	1933	1934	1935	1936	1937	1938	1939	1940	1941	1942
1926	7.4																
1927	7.4	7.4															
1928	5.9	5.1	2.8														
1929	5.2	4.5	3.1	3.3													
1930	5.8	5.4	4.7	5.6	8.0												
1931	4.4	3.9	3.0	3.1	2.9	−1.8											
1932	5.3	5.0	4.5	4.9	5.5	4.3	10.8										
1933	6.0	5.8	5.5	6.0	6.7	6.3	10.6	10.4									
1934	6.8	6.7	6.6	7.3	8.1	8.1	11.7	12.1	13.8								
1935	7.1	7.0	7.0	7.6	8.3	8.4	11.2	11.3	11.7	9.6							
1936	7.0	7.0	7.0	7.5	8.1	8.1	10.3	10.1	10.0	8.2	6.7						
1937	6.7	6.6	6.5	7.0	7.4	7.4	9.0	8.6	8.2	6.3	4.7	2.7					
1938	6.6	6.6	6.5	6.9	7.3	7.2	8.6	8.2	7.8	6.3	5.2	4.4	6.1				
1939	6.4	6.4	5.3	6.6	6.9	6.8	8.0	7.6	7.1	5.8	4.9	4.3	5.0	4.0			
1940	6.2	6.2	6.1	6.3	6.6	6.5	7.5	7.0	6.6	5.4	4.6	4.1	4.5	3.7	3.4		
1941	6.0	5.9	5.8	6.1	6.3	6.1	7.0	6.6	6.1	5.0	4.3	3.8	4.0	3.4	3.1	2.7	
1942	5.8	5.7	5.6	5.8	6.0	5.8	6.6	6.2	5.7	4.7	4.0	3.6	3.8	3.2	2.9	2.7	2.6
1943	5.6	5.5	5.4	5.6	5.8	5.6	6.2	5.8	5.4	4.5	3.9	3.5	3.6	3.1	2.9	2.7	2.7
1944	5.6	5.5	5.4	5.5	5.7	5.5	6.1	5.8	5.3	4.5	4.0	3.6	3.8	3.4	3.3	3.2	3.4
1945	5.5	5.4	5.3	5.5	5.6	5.4	6.0	5.6	5.2	4.5	4.0	3.7	3.8	3.5	3.4	3.4	3.6
1946	5.3	5.2	5.1	5.2	5.4	5.2	5.7	5.3	5.0	4.3	3.8	3.5	3.5	3.3	3.1	3.1	3.2
1947	5.0	4.9	4.7	4.8	4.9	4.7	5.2	4.8	4.4	3.7	3.3	2.9	3.0	2.6	2.4	2.3	2.2
1948	4.9	4.8	4.7	4.8	4.9	4.7	5.1	4.8	4.4	3.8	3.3	3.0	3.1	2.8	2.6	2.5	2.5
1949	4.9	4.8	4.6	4.7	4.8	4.6	5.0	4.7	4.3	3.7	3.3	3.1	3.1	2.8	2.7	2.6	2.6
1950	4.8	4.6	4.5	4.6	4.7	4.5	4.9	4.5	4.2	3.6	3.2	3.0	3.0	2.8	2.6	2.6	2.6
1951	4.5	4.3	4.2	4.3	4.3	4.2	4.5	4.1	3.8	3.2	2.9	2.6	2.6	2.3	2.2	2.1	2.0
1952	4.4	4.3	4.2	4.2	4.3	4.1	4.4	4.1	3.8	3.3	2.9	2.7	2.7	2.4	2.3	2.2	2.2
1953	4.4	4.3	4.2	4.2	4.3	4.1	4.4	4.1	3.8	3.3	2.9	2.7	2.7	2.5	2.4	2.3	2.3
1954	4.4	4.3	4.2	4.3	4.3	4.1	4.4	4.1	3.8	3.4	3.1	2.9	2.9	2.7	2.6	2.5	2.5

Year																	
1955	4.3	4.2	4.1	4.1	4.1	4.0	4.2	4.0	3.7	3.2	2.9	2.7	2.7	2.5	2.4	2.4	2.3
1956	3.9	3.8	3.7	3.7	3.7	3.6	3.8	3.5	3.2	2.8	2.4	2.2	2.2	2.0	1.9	1.8	1.7
1957	4.1	3.9	3.8	3.9	3.9	3.7	4.0	3.7	3.4	3.0	2.7	2.5	2.5	2.3	2.2	2.2	2.1
1958	3.9	3.8	3.6	3.7	3.7	3.5	3.7	3.5	3.2	2.8	2.5	2.3	2.3	2.1	2.0	1.9	1.9
1959	3.7	3.6	3.5	3.5	3.5	3.4	3.6	3.3	3.0	2.6	2.3	2.2	2.1	1.9	1.8	1.8	1.7
1960	3.9	3.8	3.7	3.7	3.7	3.6	3.7	3.5	3.3	2.9	2.6	2.4	2.4	2.3	2.2	2.1	2.1
1961	3.9	3.8	3.7	3.7	3.7	3.6	3.8	3.5	3.3	2.9	2.7	2.5	2.5	2.4	2.3	2.2	2.2
1962	4.0	3.9	3.8	3.8	3.9	3.7	3.9	3.7	3.5	3.1	2.9	2.7	2.7	2.6	2.5	2.5	2.5
1963	3.9	3.9	3.8	3.8	3.8	3.7	3.9	3.6	3.4	3.1	2.9	2.7	2.7	2.6	2.5	2.5	2.5
1964	4.0	3.9	3.8	3.8	3.8	3.7	3.9	3.7	3.5	3.1	2.9	2.8	2.8	2.7	2.6	2.6	2.6
1965	3.9	3.8	3.7	3.7	3.7	3.6	3.8	3.5	3.3	3.0	2.8	2.7	2.7	2.5	2.5	2.5	2.4
1966	3.8	3.7	3.6	3.6	3.6	3.5	3.6	3.4	3.2	2.9	2.7	2.6	2.6	2.5	2.4	2.4	2.3
1967	3.5	3.5	3.4	3.4	3.4	3.3	3.4	3.2	3.0	2.7	2.6	2.3	2.3	2.2	2.1	2.1	2.1
1968	3.5	3.4	3.3	3.4	3.4	3.2	3.4	3.2	3.0	2.7	2.5	2.3	2.3	2.2	2.1	2.1	2.1
1969	3.2	3.2	3.1	3.1	3.1	2.9	3.1	2.9	2.7	2.4	2.1	2.0	2.0	1.9	1.7	1.7	1.7
1970	3.6	3.5	3.4	3.4	3.4	3.3	3.4	3.2	3.1	2.8	2.6	2.5	2.4	2.3	2.2	2.2	2.2
1971	3.7	3.6	3.6	3.6	3.6	3.5	3.6	3.4	3.3	3.0	2.8	2.7	2.7	2.6	2.5	2.6	2.5
1972	3.8	3.7	3.6	3.7	3.7	3.6	3.7	3.5	3.4	3.1	2.9	2.8	2.8	2.7	2.7	2.7	2.7
1973	3.7	3.7	3.6	3.6	3.6	3.5	3.6	3.5	3.3	3.0	2.9	2.8	2.8	2.7	2.6	2.6	2.6
1974	3.6	3.5	3.4	3.4	3.4	3.3	3.5	3.3	3.1	2.9	2.7	2.6	2.6	2.5	2.5	2.4	2.4

Table 4-5
Long-Term Corporate Bonds
Rates of Return for All Yearly Holding Periods from 1926 to 1974
(Percent Per Annum Compounded Annually)

To The End of	From The Beginning of															
	1943	1944	1945	1946	1947	1948	1949	1950	1951	1952	1953	1954	1955	1956	1957	1958
1943	2.8															
1944	3.8	4.7														
1945	3.9	4.4	4.1													
1946	3.3	3.5	2.9	1.7												
1947	2.2	2.0	1.1	-0.3	-2.3											
1948	2.5	2.4	1.9	1.1	0.8	4.1										
1949	2.6	2.6	2.1	1.7	1.7	3.7	3.3									
1950	2.5	2.5	2.1	1.8	1.8	3.2	2.7	2.1								
1951	2.0	1.8	1.4	1.0	0.9	1.7	0.9	-0.3	-2.7							
1952	2.1	2.0	1.7	1.4	1.3	2.0	1.5	0.9	0.4	3.5						
1953	2.2	2.2	1.9	1.6	1.6	2.3	1.9	1.6	1.4	3.6	3.4					
1954	2.5	2.5	2.2	2.0	2.1	2.7	2.5	2.3	2.4	4.1	4.4	5.4				
1955	2.3	2.3	2.1	1.9	1.9	2.4	2.2	2.0	2.0	3.2	3.1	2.9	0.6			
1956	1.6	1.6	1.3	1.0	1.0	1.4	1.0	0.7	0.5	1.1	0.5	-0.4	-3.2	-6.8		
1957	2.1	2.0	1.8	1.7	1.7	2.1	1.8	1.7	1.6	2.3	2.1	1.7	0.6	0.6	8.6	
1958	1.8	1.8	1.5	1.4	1.3	1.7	1.4	1.2	1.1	1.7	1.3	0.9	-0.1	-0.3	3.1	-2.2
1959	1.7	1.6	1.4	1.2	1.1	1.4	1.2	1.0	0.9	1.3	1.0	0.6	-0.3	-0.5	1.7	-1.6
1960	2.1	2.0	1.8	1.7	1.7	2.0	1.8	1.7	1.7	2.2	2.0	1.8	1.2	1.3	3.5	1.8
1961	2.2	2.2	2.0	1.9	1.9	2.2	2.1	2.0	1.9	2.4	2.3	2.2	1.7	1.9	3.8	2.6
1962	2.5	2.5	2.3	2.2	2.3	2.6	2.5	2.4	2.4	2.9	2.8	2.8	2.5	2.8	4.4	3.6
1963	2.5	2.4	2.3	2.2	2.3	2.6	2.5	2.4	2.4	2.8	2.8	2.7	2.4	2.7	4.1	3.4
1964	2.6	2.6	2.4	2.4	2.4	2.7	2.6	2.5	2.6	3.0	3.0	2.9	2.7	2.9	4.2	3.6
1965	2.4	2.4	2.3	2.2	2.2	2.5	2.4	2.4	2.4	2.7	2.7	2.6	2.4	2.6	3.7	3.1
1966	2.3	2.3	2.2	2.1	2.1	2.4	2.3	2.2	2.2	2.6	2.5	2.4	2.2	2.4	3.3	2.7
1967	2.0	2.0	1.9	1.8	1.8	2.0	1.9	1.8	1.8	2.1	2.0	1.9	1.5	1.7	2.5	1.9
1968	2.1	2.0	1.9	1.8	1.8	2.0	1.9	1.9	1.8	2.1	2.0	1.9	1.7	1.8	2.5	2.0
1969	1.7	1.6	1.5	1.4	1.4	1.5	1.4	1.3	1.3	1.5	1.4	1.3	1.0	1.0	1.7	1.1

To The End of	1959	1960	1961	1962	1963	1964	1965	1966	1967	1968	1969	1970	1971	1972	1973	1974
1970	2.2	2.2	2.1	2.0	2.0	2.2	2.1	2.1	2.1	2.3	2.3	2.2	2.0	2.1	2.8	2.4
1971	2.5	2.5	2.4	2.4	2.4	2.6	2.5	2.5	2.5	2.6	2.7	2.7	2.5	2.7	3.3	2.9
1972	2.7	2.7	2.6	2.5	2.6	2.8	2.7	2.7	2.7	3.0	2.9	2.9	2.8	2.9	3.6	3.2
1973	2.6	2.6	2.5	2.5	2.5	2.7	2.6	2.6	2.6	2.9	2.9	2.8	2.7	2.8	3.4	3.1
1974	2.4	2.4	2.3	2.3	2.3	2.5	2.4	2.4	2.4	2.6	2.6	2.5	2.4	2.5	3.0	2.7

(Percent Per Annum Compounded Annually)

To The End of	From The Beginning of															
	1959	1960	1961	1962	1963	1964	1965	1966	1967	1968	1969	1970	1971	1972	1973	1974
1959	-1.0															
1960	3.9	9.1														
1961	4.2	6.9	4.8													
1962	5.1	7.3	6.4	7.9												
1963	4.5	6.0	5.0	5.0	2.2											
1964	4.6	5.7	4.9	4.9	3.5	4.8										
1965	3.8	4.7	3.8	3.6	2.1	2.1	-0.5									
1966	3.4	4.0	3.2	2.9	1.7	1.5	-0.1	0.2								
1967	2.4	2.9	2.0	1.5	0.3	-0.2	-1.8	-2.4	-4.9							
1968	2.4	2.8	2.1	1.7	0.7	0.4	-0.7	-0.8	-1.3	2.6						
1969	1.4	1.7	0.9	0.4	-0.6	-1.1	-2.2	-2.7	-3.6	-2.9	-8.1					
1970	2.7	3.1	2.5	2.3	1.6	1.5	0.9	1.2	1.5	3.7	4.3	18.4				
1971	3.4	3.7	3.3	3.1	2.6	2.6	2.3	2.8	3.3	5.5	6.5	14.6	11.0			
1972	3.6	4.0	3.6	3.5	3.0	3.1	2.9	3.4	4.0	5.8	6.7	12.1	9.1	7.3		
1973	3.5	3.8	3.4	3.3	2.9	2.9	2.7	3.1	3.6	5.0	5.6	9.3	6.4	4.2	1.1	
1974	3.0	3.3	2.9	2.8	2.4	2.4	2.1	2.4	2.7	3.9	4.1	6.7	3.9	1.7	-1.0	-3.1

Source: Roger G. Ibbotson and Rex A. Sinquefield "Stocks, Bonds, Bills and Inflation: Year-by-Year Historical Returns (1926–1974)," Journal of Business, January 1976, 26–28.

Evaluating Preferred Stock

Preferred stock should be evaluated in much the same manner as a corporate bond, but with a few exceptions. The yield on a preferred stock is calculated by the following formula:

$$\text{yield} = \frac{\text{preferred dividend}}{\text{price of preferred}}$$

This formula holds under the assumption that the preferred stock is not callable and, therefore, has a maturity to infinity. However, if this is not the case, and the preferred stock is callable, the appropriate yield should be calculated in the same manner as for a callable bond. The formula of yield to call introduced previously is appropriate here. Since there is generally no maturity date on preferred stock, holders can only depend upon a constant annual income return with capital gains limited to fluctuation in the market price caused by changes in the market rate of interest.

Ratings of Preferred Stock

In October 1973, Moody's Corporation began issuing ratings for preferred stock based upon dividend coverage and asset protection. This analysis is calculated just as for corporate bonds, with the exception that the dividend coverage is after the payment of tax. Therefore, preferred dividends are divided into net income to determine the dividend coverage. Exhibit 4-2 briefly explains Moody's preferred-stock ratings. The ratings are based on the ability of the firm to pay the preferred dividend and indicate the degree of asset protection. Standard and Poor's (S&P) also provides ratings for preferred stocks. The criteria used are similar to those of Moody's. Exhibit 4-3 shows the rating definitions of S&P.

Disadvantages of Preferred Stock

The individual investor should be aware that there are certain disadvantages to preferred-stock ownership. In the event of default on a bond interest payment, preferred-stockholders, by their lower priority than bondholders, stand to lose considerably if the firm is highly leveraged. The higher the firm's financial leverage, the lower the protection for preferred-stockholders in liquidation or reorganization.

A concern for any potential investor in preferred stocks should be the fact that there is usually no maturity date, and, therefore, preferred-stock prices will rise and fall with the long-term market rate of interest for the risk level of the security. Because of the additional risk, the preferred-stockholder should receive a higher yield than for a bond of the same com-

Exhibit 4-2

Moody's Preferred Stock Ratings

Moody's Rating Policy Review Board Extended its rating services to include quality designations on preferred stock, which Moody's had done prior to 1935, was prompted by evidence of investor interest. Moody's believes that its rating of preferred stock is especially appropriate in view of the ever-increasing amount of these securities outstanding, and the fact that continuing inflation and its ramifications have resulted generally in the dilution of some of the protection afforded them as well as other fixed-income securities.

Because of the fundamental differences between preferred stock and bonds, a variation of our familiar bond rating symbols is being used in the quality ranking of preferred stock. The symbols, presented below, are designed to avoid comparison with bond quality in absolute terms. It should always be borne in mind that preferred stock occupies a junior position to bonds within a particular capital structure and that these securities are rated within the universe of preferred stocks.

Note: Moody's applies numerical modifiers 1, 2 and 3 in each rating classification from "aa" through "b" in its preferred stock rating system. The modifier 1 indicates that the security ranks in the higher end of its generic rating category; the modifier 2 indicates a mid-range ranking; and the modifier 3 indicates that the issue ranks in the lower end of its generic rating category.

Preferred stock rating symbols and their definitions are as follows:

"aaa"

An issue which is rated "aaa" is considered to be a top-quality preferred stock. This rating indicates good asset protection and the least risk of dividend impairment within the universe of preferred stocks.

"aa"

An issue which is rated "aa" is considered a high-grade preferred stock. This rating indicates that there is reasonable assurance that earnings and asset protection will remain relatively well maintained in the foreseeable future.

"a"

An issue which is rated "a" is considered to be an upper-medium grade preferred stock. While risks are judged to be somewhat greater than in the "aaa" and "aa" classifications, earnings and asset protection are, nevertheless, expected to be maintained at adequate levels.

"baa"

An issue which is rated "baa" is considered to be medium-grade, neither highly protected nor poorly secured. Earnings and asset protection appear adequate at present but may be questionable over any great length of time.

"ba"

An issue which is rated "ba" is considered to have speculative elements and its future cannot be considered well assured. Earnings and asset protection may be very moderate and not well safeguarded during adverse periods. Uncertainty of position characterizes preferred stocks in this class.

"b"

An issue which is rated "b" generally lacks the characteristics of a desirable investment. Assurance of dividend payments and maintenance of other terms of the issue over any long period of time may be small.

"caa"

An issue which is rated "caa" is likely to be in arrears on dividend payments. This rating designation does not purport to indicate the future status of payments.

"ca"

An issue which is rated "ca" is speculative in a high degree and is likely to be in arrears on dividends with little likelihood of eventual payment.

"c"

This is the lowest rated class of preferred or preference stock. Issues so rated can be regarded as having extremely poor prospects of ever attaining any real investment standing.

Source: Moody's Investors Service, Inc., *Moody's Bond Record*, June, 1982, p. 83.

Exhibit 4-3

100

STANDARD & POOR'S PREFERRED STOCK RATING DEFINITIONS

A Standard & Poor's preferred stock rating is an assessment of the capacity and willingness of an issuer to pay preferred stock dividends and any applicable sinking fund obligations. A preferred stock rating differs from a bond rating inasmuch as it is assigned to an equity issue, which issue is intrinsically different from, and subordinated to, a debt issue. Therefore, to reflect this difference, the preferred stock rating symbol will normally not be higher than the bond rating symbol assigned to, or that would be assigned to, the senior debt of the same issuer.

The preferred stock ratings are based on the following considerations:

I.   Likelihood of payment—capacity and willingness of the issuer to meet the timely payment of preferred stock dividends and any applicable sinking fund requirements in accordance with the terms of the obligation.

II. Nature of, and provisions of, the issue.

III. Relative position of the issue in the event of bankruptcy, reorganization, or other arrangements affecting creditors' rights.

"AAA"   This is the highest rating that may be assigned by Standard & Poor's to a preferred stock issue and indicates an extremely strong capacity to pay the preferred stock obligations.

"AA"   A preferred stock issue rated "AA" also qualifies as a high-quality fixed income security. The capacity to pay preferred stock obligations is very strong, although not as overwhelming as for issues rated "AAA."

"A"   An issue rated "A" is backed by a sound capacity to pay the preferred stock obligations, although it is somewhat more susceptible to the adverse effects of changes in circumstances and economic conditions.

"BBB"   An issue rated "BBB" is regarded as backed by an adequate capacity to pay the preferred stock obligations. Whereas it normally exhibits adequate protection parameters, adverse economic conditions or changing circumstances are

more likely to lead to a weakened capacity to make payments for a preferred stock in this category than for issues in the "A" category.

"BB," "B," "CCC"   Preferred stock rated "BB," "B," and "CCC" are regarded, on balance, as predominately speculative with respect to the issuer's capacity to pay preferred stock obligations. "BB" indicates the lowest degree of speculation and "CCC" the highest degree of speculation. While such issues will likely have some quality and protective characteristics, these are outweighed by large uncertainties or major risk exposures to adverse conditions.

"CC"   The rating "CC" is reserved for a preferred stock issue in arrears on dividends or sinking fund payments but that is currently paying.

"C"   A preferred stock rated "C" is a non-paying issue.

"D"   A preferred stock rated "D" is a non-paying issue with the issuer in default on debt instruments.

NR   indicates that no rating has been requested, that there is insufficient information on which to base a rating, or that S&P does not rate a particular type of obligation as a matter of policy.

Plus (+) or Minus (−)   To provide more detailed indications of preferred stock quality, the ratings from "AA" to "B" may be modified by the addition of a plus or minus sign to show relative standing within the major rating categories.

The preferred stock rating is not a recommendation to purchase or sell a security, inasmuch as market price is not considered in arriving at the rating. Preferred stock *ratings* are wholly unrelated to Standard & Poor's earnings and dividend *rankings* for common stocks.

The ratings are based on current information furnished to Standard & Poor's by the issuer, and obtained by Standard & Poor's from other sources it considers reliable. The ratings may be changed, suspended, or withdrawn as a result of changes in, or unavailability of, such information.

Standard & Poor's Corporation receives compensation for rating securities. Such compensation is based on the work done and is paid either by issuers of such securities or by the underwriters participating in the distribution thereof. The fees generally vary from $1,500 to $20,000 for corporate securities.

Source: *Standard & Poor's Stock Guide.* Standard & Poor's Corporation, New York, New York, 1982.

pany or same risk class. There are, however, times when the yield on preferred stock is less or equal to the yield on bonds of the same corporation.

This phenomenon is brought about by the fact that dividends on preferred (or common) stock owned by corporations are 85 percent tax exempt. For example, if a corporation owns the preferred stock of another firm, 85 percent of the preferred dividend received is tax exempt. Therefore, for corporations in a 50 percent tax bracket, the purchase of another firm's preferred stock will generally have a significantly higher net yield after tax than a company's corresponding bond. Therefore, individual investors, who do not receive the same desirable tax treatment on preferred dividends, may find that the preferred dividend yield is undesirable. In that case, an individual investor would be wise to select the company's bond issue, because the yield would be more desirable and the investor would have a greater degree of security upon potential liquidation. In addition, the bond issue would have a maturity date that would decrease any downside risk potential in the long run.

The question that confronts anyone considering a fixed-income investment is the protection that the issue affords. The investor should be mostly concerned with the preservation of principal and then should attempt to obtain the highest possible yield within a risk category. Certainly, the fixed-payment nature of these income-producing securities is directed to investors who have income needs or to funds, such as pension plans or profit-sharing plans, that can accumulate tax-exempt interest and/or dividends. Those individual investors who are overly attracted to high-yielding fixed-income securities may find themselves in a higher risk category than desirable because of their acute dependence upon the income derived from various fixed-income securities and the additional risk associated with high-yielding fixed-return securities.

Commercial Paper Ratings

Commercial paper should be evaluated in a similar manner to a commercial bond. The most important consideration is on the issuer's ability to meet the debt obligations. Moody also offers ratings for commercial paper with maturities not exceeding 270 days based on the safety of the paper. According to Moody's system, issuers rated Prime-1 (P-1) have the best capacity for repayment of short-term promissory obligations, which is evidenced by such characteristics as being a lender in a well-established industry, having a high rate of return on funds employed, low debt-to-equity ratio, broad margins in earnings coverage of fixed financial charges and high internal cash generation, and well-established access to a range of financial markets and assured sources of alternate liquidity. Companies (or issuers) rated Prime-2 (P-2) are considered to have strong capacity for repayment, whereas issuers with acceptable capacity for repayment are rated P-3. The ratings are published monthly in *Moody's Bond Record* by Moody's Investors Service.

KEY TERMS

accrued interest
coupon rate (or yield)
current yield
debt obligation
debt-to-net-worth ratio
direct obligation
dividend rate (or yield)
EBIT
interest-coverage ratio
interest-rate structure
liquidity-preference theory

municipal general obligation bond
municipal revenue bond
preferred stock
price fluctuation
segmented-markets theory
times-interest-earned ratio
unbiased-expectation theory
yield to average life
yield to call
yield to maturity

QUESTIONS

1. Identify the two groups of borrowers that issue fixed-return securities?
2. Explain direct obligation securities. What direct obligation securities are issued by the U.S. government?
3. Why are debt obligations considered riskier than direct obligations? How does this affect the interest rate of debt obligations?
4. Explain the unbiased-expectation theory.
5. How does the liquidity-preference theory differ from the unbiased-expectation theory?
6. What is the segmented-markets theory?
7. What is yield to maturity, and how is it measured?
8. How is yield to call measured? Why should an investor always measure the yield to call of a bond?
9. Explain the major advantages and disadvantages in purchasing government securities.
10. How are municipal revenue bonds different from municipal general obligation bonds?
11. What two aspects of a revenue bond should the potential investor consider?
12. Why do quality municipal bonds usually have a lower yield to maturity than any other fixed-income security?
13. If an investor earns $14,000 and has the opportunity of buying a tax-exempt security yielding 6 percent, how great a return would he have to return (before tax) on a taxable security? What if his income was $25,000 and the tax-exempt yield was 9 percent?
14. What are secured bonds and unsecured bonds? Explain how the different types of secured and unsecured bonds are classified.
15. How can ratio analysis be useful to an investor in bonds?
16. What is a sinking fund? Why is a sinking-fund requirement important to a potential bondholder?

17. How are bonds rated?
18. What are the advantages and disadvantages of corporate bonds as an investment?
19. How is preferred stock evaluated?
20. Why would the yield on preferred stock be lower than the yield on a bond issued by same company?

SELECTED READINGS

BILDERSEE, JOHN S. "Some Aspects of the Performance of Non-Convertible Preferred Stocks," *Journal of Finance*, December 1973, 1187–1201.

DE PAMPHILIS, DONALD, M. "Long-Term Interest Rates and the Anticipated Rate of Inflation," *Business Economics*, May 1975, 11–18.

EDERINGTON, LOUIS H. "The Yield Spread on New Issues of Corporate Bonds," *Journal of Finance*, December 1974, 1531–1543.

Expanded Bond Values Tables. Boston: Financial Publishing Co., 1970.

FERRI, MICHAEL G. "How Do Call Provisions Influence Bond Yields?" *Journal of Portfolio Management*, Winter 1979, 55–57.

FOGLER, H. RUSSELL, and MICHAEL JOEHNK. "Deep Discount Bonds: How Well Do They Perform?" *Journal of Portfolio Management*, Spring 1979, 59–62.

KAPLAN, ROBERT S., and GABRIEL URWITZ. "Statistical Models of Bond Ratings: A Methodological Inquiry," *Journal of Business*, April 1979, 231–261.

NAGDEMAN, JULIAN J. "Cut-Rate Preferreds," *Barron's*, November 1, 1978, 11ff.

PINCHES, GEORGE E., and KENT A. MINGO. "A Multivariate Analysis of Industrial Bond Ratings," *Journal of Finance*, March 1973, 1–18.

REILLY, FRANK K., and MICHAEL D. JOEHNK. "The Association between Market-Determined Risk Measures for Bonds and Bond Ratings," *Journal of Finance*, December 1976, 1387–1403.

STEVENSON, RICHARD A. "Retirement of Non-Callable Preferred Stock,"*Journal of Finance*, December 1970, 1143–1152.

ZWICK, BURTON. "The Market for Corporate Bonds," *Quarterly Review*, Federal Reserve Bank of New York, Autumn 1977, 27–36.

5

Variable-Return Investments

When a prospective investor shifts attention from fixed-return investments to variable-return investments, a different set of criteria and objectives is used. This chapter describes the major forms of variable-return investments available to investors.

When considering variable-return investments, the investor's central concern is usually with the investment characteristics of common-stock ownership. Bondholders are lenders (creditors to the corporation), whereas stockholders are owners of the corporation. Bondholders have a legal claim against a corporation for interest and principal payments, and when the obligations are not met, the trustee can take legal action against the company. However, stockholders, whether they own common or preferred stock, are entitled to dividends only when dividends are declared by the company's board of directors. Common-stock holders have only a residual claim against the company, which limits their ownership to the net assets of the corporation after all creditors' and preferred-stock holders' claims are met.

The residual nature of common stock is what gives it the riskiness that is generally not inherent in the ownership of fixed-return investments. Inasmuch as the corporation's liability to bondholders and other creditors is fixed, the more profitable the company, the more value there is in the common-stock holders' investment because all earnings over and above the fixed claims of the creditors belong to the common-stock holders.

CORPORATE FORM OF OWNERSHIP

There are three basic forms of ownership for a company. The business may be a sole proprietorship; that is, one individual owns and runs the company. The nature of a sole proprietorship dictates that the company will be rather small. The second form of ownership is the partnership. It is a voluntary association of two or more persons to operate a business for profit. The general partnership form of ownership is rather typical and can be established with ease, but its very nature restricts the flexibility of transfer of ownership.

The third form of ownership is the **corporation.** The creation of a corporation forms an artificial being, a legal entity in and of itself. The corporation can hold property, buy and sell property, engage in legal contracts, conduct business operations, and generally replace the legal obligations assumed by sole proprietors and partners.

A corporation is chartered under state laws and has a life independent from the lives of its owners. Ownership in a corporation is evidenced by stock certificates, the number of which indicates the individual's proportion of ownership relative to the total number of shares issued by the corporation. Stock certificates give the owner the right to receive dividends if and when the board of directors properly declares them. In addition, corporate ownership gives the stockholders the right to vote for members of the **board of directors,** which is the governing body of the corporation and represents the stockholders. The board of directors, in turn, elects the officers of the firm to manage the daily operations of the corporation. The board of directors establishes the general policies and procedures by which the officers operate the firm.

A major advantage of the corporate form of organization is the limited liability of the stockholders for the debts of the company. In the case of large corporations, stockholders are seldom involved in corporate financial liability beyond the market value of the stock certificates they hold. However, in the case of a small, new company, the financial capacity can be limited, and the ability for the firm to borrow funds frequently depends on the financial strength and depth of a few corporate stockholders.

Taxes are many times cited as a reason for incorporation. At certain levels of income, tax rates are lower for a corporation than for an individual acting either as a proprietor or as a partner.

The corporation also offers the ease of ownership transferability, which is difficult in the case of a proprietorship or a partnership. The simple exchange of shares of stocks (certificates) is all that is required for the transfer

EXHIBIT 5-1 American Telephone and Telegraph Company Stock Certificate

Exhibit 5-1 American Telephone and Telegraph Company Stock Certificate (cont.)

The Company will furnish to any shareholder, upon request to its principal office or to any of its transfer offices and without charge, a full statement of the designation, relative rights, preferences and limitations of its common and preferred shares, and of each series of its preferred shares so far as the same have been fixed and the authority of the board of directors to designate and fix the relative rights, preferences and limitations of other series of its preferred shares. As specified in such statement, the affirmative vote or consent of two-thirds of the holders of preferred shares or a series of preferred shares is required in order to take certain actions affecting preferred shares.

The following abbreviations shall be construed as though the words set forth below opposite each abbreviation were written out in full where such abbreviation appears:

TEN COM — as tenants in common
TEN ENT — as tenants by the entireties
JT TEN — as joint tenants with right of survivor-
ship and not as tenants in common

(Name) CUST (Name) UNIF - (Name) as Custodian for (Name) under the
GIFT MIN ACT (State) (State) Uniform Gifts to Minors Act

Additional abbreviations may also be used though not in the above list.

For Value received, ___ *hereby sell, assign and transfer* ___ *Shares represented by the within Certificate unto*

PLEASE PRINT OR TYPE TAXPAYER-IDENTIFYING NUMBER AND NAME AND ADDRESS OF ASSIGNEE	FOR AT&T USE ONLY:	
	RIN:	
	CTF. NOTE:	YR. ☐
SHARES	CLASS ACCT:	E ☐
PLEASE PRINT OR TYPE TAXPAYER-IDENTIFYING NUMBER AND NAME AND ADDRESS OF ASSIGNEE	RIN:	
	CTF. NOTE:	YR. H ☐
SHARES	CLASS ACCT:	E ☐
PLEASE PRINT OR TYPE TAXPAYER-IDENTIFYING NUMBER AND NAME AND ADDRESS OF ASSIGNEE	RIN:	
	CTF. NOTE:	YR. H ☐
SHARES	CLASS ACCT:	E ☐

and do hereby irrevocably constitute and appoint ___

___ *Attorney to transfer the said shares on the records of the within named Company, with full power of substitution in the premises.*

Dated ___

IMPORTANT { BEFORE SIGNING, READ AND COMPLY CAREFULLY WITH REQUIREMENTS PRINTED BELOW.

THE SIGNATURE(S) TO THIS ASSIGNMENT MUST CORRESPOND WITH THE NAME(S) AS WRITTEN UPON THE FACE OF THE CERTIFICATE IN EVERY PARTICULAR WITHOUT ALTERATION OR ENLARGEMENT OR ANY CHANGE WHATEVER. THE SIGNATURE(S) SHOULD BE GUARANTEED BY A COMMERCIAL BANK OR TRUST COMPANY, OR BY A NEW YORK, BOSTON, MIDWEST, PBW OR PACIFIC STOCK EXCHANGE MEMBER FIRM, WHOSE SIGNATURE IS KNOWN TO THE TRANSFER OFFICE.

Courtesy of American Telephone & Telegraph Company.

of ownership. In large corporations, the transfer of ownership goes on continually from day to day. The constant transfer of stock certificates has created the need for the nation's stock exchanges and organized over-the-counter markets. The transfer of stock in a large corporation rarely affects the smooth operation of the company. Daily stock-ownership transfers do not affect the financial condition of the firm; however, the financial condition of the firm can directly affect the price movement of a stock as the balance of supply and demand for the company's stock certificates changes.

When a stockholder sells common stock registered in the holder's name, he or she endorses the back of the stock certificate or attaches a signed stock power of attorney to the certificate. The stock certificate and the owner's endorsement are then forwarded to the broker, who, in turn, sends the items to the corporation's transfer agent. The transfer agent cancels the old certificate, revises the records to show the new owner, and issues the new owner a new stock certificate. Exhibit 5-1 is a specimen of both sides of a stock certificate for the American Telephone and Telegraph Company.

OWNERSHIP RISK OF COMMON STOCK

Because common stock is an ownership security, the investor in the security has accepted a position of substantial risk. It is the common-stockholder's equity that gives bondholders the cushion that reduces their creditorship risk. For example, the higher the proportion of common-stock equity in a company's capital structure, the more protection bondholders have in laying claim to the marketable value of a firm's assets. If liquidation occurs, common-stock holders will receive funds only after bondholders have been rewarded 100 cents on the dollar. It is this residual characteristic of ownership that gives the common-stockholders their high level of risk. It is the common-stockholder who stands to lose the most if a firm becomes unprofitable because there is nothing available for a return on the investment. Also, upon the firm's liquidation, the likelihood that common-stockholders will receive much after all fixed claims are settled is rather remote.

For example, in the early 1980s, the financial viability of Chrysler Corporation was much in question. The concern centered on both the stockholders and bondholders positions, since substantial operating losses mounted and the senior claims of bondholders were in jeopardy.

Chapter 1 discussed the concepts of systematic and unsystematic risk. Systematic risk encompasses the factors that are beyond the control of the company or investor to change and are common to all common stocks. These factors include market risk, interest-rate risk, purchasing-power risk, and, to some extent, financial risk.

Market risk is perhaps the most troublesome for the holder of common stock, because the market price of stock in the short run can easily drop even though earnings remain constant or rise. This is exemplified by the market-emotion events that occur at random. For example, even with utility stocks, there can be significant price fluctuations, as was seen in 1974 when Consolidated Edison omitted its quarterly dividend, which had been paid continuously since before 1900. This action by the board of directors of Consolidated Edison had a dramatic negative effect on the prices of many electric utility stocks. For such a stable industry as electric utilities, a price drop of any magnitude is an extremely important development for investors who seek constant and rising income.

COMMON STOCK

Common stock generally represents a more risky investment than limited-return investments. The market value and dividends paid on common stock are highly dependent upon the earning power of the corporation, which is a reflection of the financial health of the firm and the industry that it serves. If a company is financially successful, the profit that remains after paying interest to bondholders and dividends to preferred-stockholders will usually give added value to the common-stockholders in terms of dividends and/or stock appreciation. If an investor owns stock in a company that has an excellent growth record, such as Digital Equipment Corporation, the rewards to holders of common stock can be quite large over a long period of time. Growth attracts additional buyers, and that drives the stock price higher. Some of the risk of ownership of common stock in well-established firms is minimized if their records of earnings and sales have grown at a stable rate over a sufficiently long period of time and if forecasts indicate a continued pattern of growth.

Almost all experienced investors agree that the underlying value of any common stock is the earning power of the company. If earnings are erratic or not present, the price-appreciation potential of the common stock over the long run is minimal. Many investors, perhaps more appropriately named speculators, chase stocks that are currently hot to new high market values. Many times the small investor is hurt by such speculation, especially when the earnings growth slows down or perhaps disappears completely.

Cash and Stock Dividends

Interest or dividend income is of primary importance to a bondholder or preferred-stockholder, but the same may not be true for the investor in common stock. Many common-stockholders pay high prices for stocks that pay no dividends because they believe the company can earn a greater return by reinvesting its earnings than the stockholder could earn through alternative investments. As long as the rate of return on retained earnings is in excess of the return that a common-stockholder can obtain, the earnings ought to be retained, and there likely will be an increase in the price of the shares.

However, many common-stockholders prefer to receive cash dividends. Cash represents a tangible return, whereas reinvested earnings represent a future uncertainty. Some common stocks yield very high cash dividends and are considered by the investment community to be almost fixed-income securities with the possibility of some small growth. Utility company common stocks are a prime example of those with high yields.

Cash Dividends

Several technical aspects of dividends are important to the investor. Dividends usually take the form of either cash or stock. Cash dividends are paid out of the company's earnings, usually on a regular quarterly basis. The dividend must first be declared by the company's board of directors; it then becomes a legal liability of the corporation. Most companies prefer to pay a fixed-amount cash dividend on a regular basis until the firm's earnings increase sufficiently to justify a higher payout. They are careful to avoid a position in which dividends must be reduced because of insufficient earnings. A reduction in a corporation's dividends is usually a clear indication of increased business risk and perhaps financial risk. Many firms are proud of the fact that over many decades they have never missed a dividend payment and have never lowered their payout. These companies certainly have earnings stability and generally are of investment-grade quality, although historical dividend stability is a poor measure in and of itself. The investor must examine the future earning power potential along with the dividend history.

The percent of earnings paid out in dividends for all firms over the years has averaged between 50 and 60 percent. In their more profitable years, some firms, such as General Motors, often pay an extra dividend at the end of the year over and above their regular quarterly dividends. This eliminates the problem of raising the regular quarterly dividend in exceptionally good years and then lowering the amount to a prior level in less successful years, although the auto industry problems of the early 1980s resulted in a sharp dividend reduction for all auto companies, including General Motors.

Special Dates

There are four dates associated with a dividend that are important to stockholders. The date that the board of directors decides to authorize the payment of a dividend is the **date of declaration.** On that date, the board of directors announces the dividend will be paid to stockholders of record. The **record date** is the cutoff date for the names of the persons owning the stock. In addition, the board announces the **payable date,** which is the date that dividend checks will be mailed to the stockholders by the company's bank trustee.

The fourth date is the **ex dividend date,** which occurs five business days before the record date. Because it takes five business days to clear a stock transaction on any of the nation's major exchanges and with the transfer agents, ownership of a stock on the date of record will include only those individuals who have purchased the stock before the ex dividend date. If the stock is purchased on or after the ex dividend date, the stockholder will not receive the dividend that has been declared. For example, companies ABC and XYZ are listed on the NYSE and both have recently declared dividends. If the ex dividend date is September 14, the following two lines can be found in the "Stocks Ex dividend September 14" section of the financial sections of leading newspapers before the ex dividend date:

(Company)		(Amount)
ABC	$1.88pf	.47
XYZ		.05

Then, on September 15, a section of the listing of daily activity on the New York Stock Exchange for September 14, might state:

52 Weeks				Yield	P/E	Sales			Net	
High	Low	Stock	Div.	%	Ratio	100s	High	Low	Close	Chg.
$23\frac{1}{8}$	$18\frac{1}{2}$	ABC pf	1.88	9.3	6	×24	$20\frac{3}{4}$	$20\frac{1}{8}$	$20\frac{1}{8}$	$-\frac{5}{8}$
$5\frac{1}{4}$	$4\frac{1}{4}$	XYZ	.20	4.1	10	×20	$4\frac{7}{8}$	$4\frac{7}{8}$	$4\frac{7}{8}$	....

The small letter x to the left of the daily volume totals of 2,400 shares traded for ABC preferred and 2,000 shares traded for XYZ indicates that the stocks have gone ex dividend. Anyone who owned the stock before September 14 will receive the quarterly dividend. Note also that the dividends paid on the **annual** basis are shown as $1.88 and $.20 per share per year, respectively. Because the ex dividend date usually represents quarterly payments, $.47 and $.05, respectively, will be paid per share on the date of payment, which will probably occur a few weeks after the ex dividend date.

Stock Dividends

The second type of dividend is the stock dividend. The mechanics of declaring and paying a stock dividend are the same as those for a cash dividend. The major difference is in the form of payment and its value.

Cash dividends represent a return to the owners of part of their holdings in the corporation. If no cash dividends were paid, the funds would remain with the firm and would be owned by the stockholders. A stock dividend is simply a distribution of additional shares of stock that does not change the total value of the stockholder's position. For example, if a company declared a 10 percent stock dividend and an investor owned 100 shares, he or she would receive, on the payment date, 10 additional shares. The investor would now own 110 shares, and the total value of the company remains the same. However, the value per share is less because 110 percent of the original shares is being divided into the value of the company. Therefore, the investor is no better off with a stock dividend than he or she would have been had there not been a stock distribution. This is contrary to the popular belief that a higher number of shares is worth more to an investor.

The figure derived from this division is commonly called **book value per share.** In addition, the stock exchange makes an appropriate adjustment to the closing market price per share. If the stock was traded at $10 per share the day before ex dividend date, then at the opening of the market on ex dividend date the stock would sell at $9 or $9\frac{1}{8}$ per share. Because shares sell in $\frac{1}{8}$ fractions of a dollar, a 10 percent adjustment in this case is not possible to an exact amount.

Of course, if the market price increases to $10 per share from $9, there would have been a rise from $10 to $11 + if the stock dividend had not been paid. Nevertheless, once a stock distribution has been made, all calculations of earnings per share automatically show a smaller number. Many people mistakenly believe that the value of a stock dividend is based on the same criteria as the value of a cash dividend.

Sometimes, stock dividends can be expressed as 100 percent stock dividends, which indicates the investors would receive an amount of new shares equal to the number of old shares that they hold. In such a case, it should be clear that the investors will not increase their wealth by 100 percent overnight, because the market price on the exchange will be cut in half that day.

Stock Splits

Another way to accomplish the 100 percent stock dividend is a two-for-one stock split. A stock split has exactly the same effect upon the investor as a stock dividend; the only difference is the manner in which it is recorded on the corporation's books for accounting purposes. For tax purposes, a stock split is considered a distribution of new shares, and the stockholder's cost basis per share is reduced. For example, if a stockholder has purchased 100 shares at $40 per share and a two-for-one stock split occurs, he or she must reduce the cost basis for each of the 200 shares to $20. If the split is four for one, the investor would then reduce the cost basis on 400 shares to $10 each.

If the cash dividend per share on the old stock is maintained on the new stock, or if the cash dividend rate per share is not reduced proportionately, the stockholder receives an increased cash return in subsequent cash dividend payments. But the stockholder's position is otherwise unchanged from what it was before the stock dividend or split, except that the investor's proportionate equity is evidenced by a greater number of shares. A stock dividend itself theoretically does not give increased value to the investor's holdings.

Sometimes the market price of a stock appears to rise in anticipation of a stock dividend or split. Such increased prices could reflect the expectation of increased dividends or of earnings growth. However, a mere increase in the number of shares outstanding does not change the fundamental investment value of the common stock equity. The only certain effect of a substantial stock dividend or stock split is to lower the price per share of stock in the marketplace. This creates a wider market for selling the stock at a lower price, and there are usually more buyers for shares at the lower price than there are for the same shares at a higher price before a stock dividend or stock split. The general purpose of lowering the market price of a stock is to increase interest in the company's shares, widen the distribution of the shares, and possibly raise the market value of the total shares outstanding. A number of empirical studies have been conducted to determine whether stock splits and stock dividends affect the market price of stock. The consensus is that any effect would be temporary and minor, and that over the long run stock dividends and splits have little effect on the market price.

Special Dividends

There are a number of special dividends that a firm might distribute. One of the most common is a **property dividend.** Instead of distributing cash or stock in its own firm, the company may distribute shares of stock in another firm in which they have majority or minority ownership interest. Sometimes the property dividend takes the form of an actual product that the company manufactures or distributes, but this is not very common.

When a company finds itself in severe financial difficulty, it may be forced out of business for a number of reasons. During the final legal proceedings, there may be a number of **liquidating dividends** or distributions. These are merely periodic payments to the shareholders. Once the assets of the company have been sold and liabilities paid for, there may be an amount left for the stockholders. Generally, liquidating dividends are not subject to ordinary income taxes because liquidating dividends are a return of the investor's capital. Therefore, the investor could claim either a capital gain or capital loss, depending on the original cost basis of his investment.

SUBSCRIPTION RIGHTS

Periodically, a firm may wish to sell additional securities, either bonds or common stock, to raise funds for expansion. If the additional securities offered are common stock, the company may offer the stock first to existing stockholders by means of subscription rights. These rights allow present stockholders to maintain their proportional share ownership in the company by purchasing a percent of the new issue that equals the proportion they already hold. Because a subsequent issue of stock could dilute their percentage of ownership, subscription rights can be a desirable feature for stockholders who own a large proportional share of a company's stock.

Generally, if a shareholder owns 100 shares of old stock, he or she would receive 100 rights, entitling the shareholder to buy a percent of the new shares offered. If the terms of the rights offering permits the purchase of 1 new share of stock for each 20 shares held, the stockholder owning 100 original shares could buy 5 new shares.

Before a company can issue additional shares of common stock, it must have a sufficient number authorized in the state charter. The number of authorized shares must be sufficient for a rights offering, as well as for stock dividends or stock splits. If not, the company must request the stockholders to approve a change in the authorized number of shares. Many companies have substantially more authorized shares than they have issued. This allows a company to have some flexibility in future distribution of stock, whether in the form of a rights offering, a stock dividend, a stock split, or acquisition of another company through the exchange of stock. The number of outstanding shares being held by the public can be less than the total number of shares issued, because the corporation may have purchased some of their own shares, called **treasury stock,** in the open market.

Because the terms of a rights offering are fixed, speculators may trade the rights in the open market. And because rights are exercised directly with the issuing corporation, they allow the purchase of additional shares of common stock without the need to pay a brokerage commission. Therefore, speculators hope for substantial gains as the market price of the underlying common stock fluctuates before expiration of the rights.

Three choices are available to the stockholders regarding the disposition of subscription rights. They can exercise the rights by submitting the rights and necessary cash to the corporation, which will mail them new shares; they can sell the rights in the open market to other investors who will exercise them; or they can let the subscription rights expire, which is the least desirable choice. Every year, many rights are allowed to expire because their owners do not understand their value. (For a discussion of the determination of the theoretical value of a right, see Chapter 7.) Subscription rights generally have a life of only a few weeks.

A firm might issue an investor 100 rights for every 100 shares owned. The terms of the rights offering may state that it takes 10 rights and $25 to purchase 1 additional share of stock. If today's date is October 1 and the date of the rights' expiration is November 30, the investors have two months in which to decide what to do. What they do may depend on the price of the common stock. If the market price of the common stock is less than $25, the rights are worthless. There is no reason to take 10 rights and $25 to buy a share of stock that the investor could buy through a broker for less cash and no rights. However, if the market price goes above $25 per share, the rights begin to have some value. For example, if the market price of the common stock rises to $35 per share, each right would then be worth $1, because it takes 10 rights and $25 to buy a share of new stock.

STOCK-PURCHASE WARRANTS

Warrants are very similar to rights except that they usually originate from the sale of bonds or preferred stock and have a life expectancy of many years. Some stock-purchase warrants are perpetual; that is, they have no expiration date. Like a rights offering, a warrant gives the owner the privilege of buying additional shares of common stock in the company at a predetermined price. Usually, the public owners of warrants have purchased them in the open market rather than owning them from the original distribution by the corporation. The reason rights and warrants are listed as speculative securities is that they can yield exceptional leverage potential.

Using the earlier example, if the price of common stock rises from $25 to $30, the rights value increases from zero to $.50. If the common stock price continues to rise from $30 to $35, each right is then worth $1, or a gain of 100 percent, even though the common stock price rose only a little more than 15 percent (from $30 to $35). Because the percentage gains can be exceptionally high, some people participate regularly in speculating with rights and warrants. Often, the value of a warrant will increase 500 percent while the stock itself is increasing 30 or 40 percent. Warrants are more popular than rights because there are more of them and a longer period exists for an opportunity of significant price rise.

But it is important to remember that the warrant value can decline just as fast (if not faster) when the common stock price declines or as the expiration date gets closer. Generally, stock-purchase warrants trade significantly above their true value when the expiration date is many years in the future. The anticipation by speculators is that the common stock will rise during that period, thus giving the warrants a significantly larger dollar value.

Table 5-1
Common Stocks
Rates of Return for All Yearly Holding Periods from 1926 to 1974
(Percent Per Annum Compounded Annually)

To the End of	From the Beginning of																
	1926	1927	1928	1929	1930	1931	1932	1933	1934	1935	1936	1937	1938	1939	1940	1941	1942
1926	11.6																
1927	23.9	37.5															
1928	30.1	40.5	43.6														
1929	19.2	21.8	14.7	−8.4													
1930	8.7	7.9	−0.4	−17.1	−24.9												
1931	−2.5	−5.1	−13.5	−27.0	−34.8	−43.3											
1932	−3.3	−5.6	−12.5	−22.7	−26.9	−27.9	−8.2										
1933	2.4	1.2	−3.8	−11.2	−11.9	−7.1	18.9	54.0									
1934	2.0	0.9	−3.5	−9.7	−9.9	−5.7	11.7	23.2	−1.4								
1935	5.9	5.2	1.8	−3.1	−2.2	3.1	19.8	30.9	20.6	47.7							
1936	8.1	7.8	4.9	0.9	2.3	7.7	22.5	31.6	24.9	40.6	33.9						
1937	3.6	3.0	0.0	−3.9	−3.3	0.2	10.2	14.3	5.1	8.7	−6.7	−35.0					
1938	5.5	5.0	2.5	−0.9	−0.0	3.6	13.0	16.9	10.7	13.9	4.5	−7.7	31.1				
1939	5.1	4.6	2.3	−0.8	−0.1	3.2	11.2	14.3	8.7	10.9	3.2	−5.3	14.3	−0.4			
1940	4.0	3.5	1.3	−1.6	−1.0	1.8	8.6	11.0	5.9	7.2	0.5	−6.5	5.6	−5.2	−9.8		
1941	3.0	2.4	0.3	−2.4	−1.9	0.5	6.4	8.2	3.5	4.3	−1.6	−7.5	1.0	−7.4	−10.7	−11.6	
1942	3.9	3.5	1.5	−1.0	−0.4	2.0	7.6	9.4	5.3	6.1	1.2	−3.4	4.5	−1.1	−1.4	3.1	20.3
1943	5.0	4.7	2.9	0.6	1.3	3.7	9.0	10.8	7.2	8.2	4.0	0.4	7.9	3.8	4.9	10.2	23.1
1944	5.8	5.5	3.8	1.7	2.5	4.8	9.8	11.5	8.3	9.3	5.7	2.6	9.5	6.3	7.7	12.5	22.0
1945	7.1	6.9	5.4	3.5	4.3	6.6	11.5	13.2	10.4	11.5	8.4	5.9	12.5	10.1	12.0	17.0	25.4
1946	6.3	6.1	4.7	2.8	3.5	5.6	10.1	11.6	8.8	9.7	6.8	4.4	10.1	7.7	8.9	12.4	17.9
1947	6.3	6.1	4.7	3.0	3.7	5.6	9.8	11.2	8.6	9.4	6.7	4.5	9.5	7.5	8.5	11.4	15.8
1948	6.3	6.1	4.7	3.1	3.8	5.6	9.6	10.8	8.4	9.1	6.6	4.6	9.2	7.3	8.2	10.6	14.2

Year																	
1949	14.8	11.5	9.2	8.3	10.0	5.6	7.4	9.7	9.0	11.3	10.1	6.3	4.5	3.8	5.3	6.6	6.8
1950	16.6	13.4	11.1	10.1	11.5	7.3	8.9	11.0	10.2	12.3	11.1	7.4	5.6	4.9	5.4	7.5	7.7
1951	17.3	14.3	12.1	11.1	12.4	8.4	9.8	11.7	11.0	12.9	11.7	8.2	6.4	5.7	7.1	8.1	8.3
1952	17.4	14.6	12.6	11.6	12.8	9.0	10.3	12.1	11.3	13.2	12.0	8.6	6.9	6.2	7.5	8.5	8.6
1953	15.7	13.4	11.5	10.7	11.9	8.3	9.6	11.4	10.7	12.4	11.4	8.2	6.5	5.9	7.2	8.1	8.3
1954	18.2	15.8	13.9	12.9	13.9	10.4	11.6	13.1	12.4	14.0	12.9	9.7	8.1	7.4	8.6	9.5	9.5
1955	19.1	16.8	14.9	13.9	14.8	11.5	12.5	13.9	13.2	14.7	13.7	10.5	8.9	8.2	9.3	10.2	10.2
1956	18.2	16.1	14.4	13.5	14.4	11.2	12.2	13.6	12.9	14.4	13.4	10.4	8.8	8.2	9.2	10.1	10.1
1957	16.2	14.3	12.8	12.1	13.0	10.0	11.0	12.4	11.8	13.2	12.3	9.5	8.1	7.4	8.5	9.3	9.4
1958	17.6	15.8	14.3	13.5	14.3	11.4	12.3	13.5	12.9	14.3	13.3	10.6	9.1	8.5	9.5	10.2	10.3
1959	17.3	15.6	14.1	13.4	14.2	11.4	12.3	13.5	12.9	14.2	13.3	10.6	9.2	8.6	9.5	10.3	10.3
1960	16.4	14.8	13.5	12.8	13.5	10.9	11.8	13.0	12.4	13.7	12.8	10.3	8.9	8.3	9.3	10.0	10.0
1961	16.9	15.3	14.0	13.4	14.1	11.5	12.3	13.4	12.9	14.1	13.3	10.8	9.4	8.8	9.7	10.4	10.5
1962	15.5	14.1	12.9	12.3	13.0	10.7	11.4	12.6	12.1	13.3	12.5	10.1	8.8	8.3	9.2	9.9	9.9
1963	15.8	14.5	13.3	12.7	13.4	11.1	11.8	12.9	12.4	13.5	12.8	10.5	9.2	8.7	9.5	10.2	10.2
1964	15.8	14.5	13.5	12.9	13.5	11.3	12.0	13.0	12.5	13.6	12.9	10.6	9.4	8.9	9.7	10.4	10.4
1965	15.7	14.5	13.4	12.9	13.5	11.3	12.0	13.0	12.5	13.6	12.9	10.7	9.5	9.0	9.8	10.4	10.4
1966	14.5	13.4	12.4	12.0	12.6	10.5	11.2	12.2	11.8	12.8	12.2	10.1	8.9	8.4	9.2	9.8	9.9
1967	14.9	13.8	12.8	12.4	12.9	10.9	11.6	12.5	12.1	13.1	12.5	10.4	9.3	8.8	9.6	10.2	10.2
1968	14.7	13.7	12.8	12.3	12.9	10.9	11.6	12.5	12.1	13.1	12.4	10.4	9.3	8.9	9.6	10.2	10.2
1969	13.8	12.8	12.0	11.6	12.1	10.3	10.9	11.8	11.5	12.4	11.8	9.9	8.9	8.4	9.1	9.7	9.8
1970	13.5	12.5	11.7	11.3	11.9	10.1	10.7	11.6	11.2	12.2	11.6	9.7	8.7	8.3	9.0	9.6	9.6
1971	13.5	12.6	11.8	11.4	12.0	10.2	10.8	11.7	11.3	12.3	11.7	9.9	8.9	8.4	9.1	9.7	9.7
1972	13.7	12.8	12.0	11.6	12.1	10.5	11.0	11.9	11.5	12.4	11.9	10.1	9.1	8.7	9.3	9.9	9.9
1973	12.7	11.8	11.1	10.8	11.3	9.7	10.3	11.1	10.8	11.7	11.1	9.4	8.5	8.1	8.7	9.3	9.3
1974	11.2	10.5	9.8	9.5	10.1	8.5	9.1	10.0	9.7	10.6	10.1	8.4	7.5	7.2	7.8	8.4	8.5

Table 5-1B
Common Stocks
Rates of Return for All Yearly Holding Periods from 1926 to 1974
(Percent Per Annum Compounded Annually)

From the Beginning of

To the End of	1943	1944	1945	1946	1947	1948	1949	1950	1951	1952	1953	1954	1955	1956	1957	1958
1943	25.9															
1944	22.8	19.7														
1945	27.2	27.8	36.4													
1946	17.3	14.5	12.0	-8.1												
1947	14.9	12.3	9.9	-1.4	5.8											
1948	13.2	10.9	8.8	0.9	5.6	5.5										
1949	14.0	12.2	10.7	5.1	9.9	12.0	18.8									
1950	16.1	14.8	14.0	9.9	16.0	18.2	25.1	31.7								
1951	17.0	15.9	15.3	12.2	16.7	19.6	24.7	27.8	24.0							
1952	17.1	16.2	15.7	13.0	17.0	19.4	23.1	24.6	21.1	18.3						
1953	15.3	14.3	13.7	11.2	14.2	15.7	17.9	17.6	13.3	8.3	-1.0					
1954	18.0	17.4	17.1	15.2	18.4	20.4	23.0	23.9	22.0	21.4	22.9	52.6				
1955	19.0	18.5	18.4	16.7	19.8	21.7	24.2	25.2	23.9	23.8	25.7	41.7	31.5			
1956	18.1	17.5	17.3	15.7	18.4	19.9	21.9	22.3	20.8	20.2	20.6	28.8	18.4	6.6		
1957	15.9	15.2	14.9	13.3	15.4	16.4	17.7	17.6	15.7	14.4	13.5	17.5	7.7	-2.5	-10.8	
1958	17.5	16.9	16.7	15.3	17.5	18.7	20.1	20.2	18.8	18.1	18.1	22.3	15.7	10.9	13.1	43.4
1959	17.1	16.6	16.4	15.1	17.1	18.1	19.3	19.4	18.0	17.3	17.2	20.5	15.0	11.1	12.7	26.7
1960	16.1	15.6	15.3	14.0	15.8	16.6	17.6	17.5	16.2	15.3	14.9	17.4	12.4	8.9	9.5	17.3
1961	16.7	16.2	16.0	14.8	16.5	17.3	18.3	18.3	17.1	16.4	16.2	18.6	14.4	11.7	12.8	19.6
1962	15.3	14.7	14.4	13.3	14.8	15.4	16.1	15.9	14.7	13.9	13.4	15.2	11.2	8.5	8.9	13.3
1963	15.6	15.1	14.9	13.8	15.2	15.8	16.6	16.4	15.3	14.6	14.3	15.9	12.4	10.2	10.8	14.8
1964	15.6	15.2	15.0	13.9	15.3	15.9	16.6	16.4	15.4	14.7	14.4	16.0	12.8	10.9	11.5	15.1
1965	15.5	15.0	14.8	13.8	15.1	15.7	16.3	16.2	15.2	14.6	14.3	15.7	12.8	11.1	11.5	14.7
1966	14.3	13.8	13.6	12.6	13.7	14.2	14.7	14.4	13.4	12.7	12.4	13.4	10.7	9.0	9.2	11.7
1967	14.7	14.2	14.0	13.1	14.2	14.6	15.1	14.9	14.0	13.4	13.1	14.2	11.6	10.1	10.5	12.9
1968	14.5	14.1	13.9	13.0	14.0	14.5	14.9	14.7	13.8	13.3	13.0	14.0	11.6	10.2	10.5	12.7
1969	13.6	13.1	12.9	12.0	13.0	13.3	13.7	13.4	12.5	11.9	11.6	12.4	10.1	8.8	8.9	10.8
1970	13.2	12.8	12.5	11.7	12.6	12.9	13.2	13.0	12.1	11.5	11.1	11.9	9.7	8.4	8.6	10.2

To the End of	1959	1960	1961	1962	1963	1964	1965	1966	1967	1968	1969	1970	1971	1972	1973	1974
1971	13.3	12.8	12.6	11.8	12.6	12.9	13.3	13.0	12.2	11.6	11.3	12.0	10.0	8.8	8.9	10.5
1972	13.5	13.0	12.8	12.0	12.9	13.2	13.5	13.3	12.5	12.0	11.7	12.4	10.5	9.4	9.5	11.1
1973	12.4	12.0	11.7	10.9	11.7	12.0	12.2	12.0	11.2	10.6	10.3	10.8	9.0	7.9	7.9	9.2
1974	10.9	10.5	10.2	9.4	10.1	10.2	10.4	10.1	9.3	8.7	8.2	8.7	6.9	5.7	5.7	6.7

From the Beginning of

To the End of	1959	1960	1961	1962	1963	1964	1965	1966	1967	1968	1969	1970	1971	1972	1973	1974
1959	12.0															
1960	6.1	0.5														
1961	12.6	12.9	26.9													
1962	6.8	5.2	7.6	-8.7												
1963	9.8	9.3	12.4	5.9	22.8											
1964	10.9	10.7	13.4	9.3	19.6	16.5										
1965	11.1	11.0	13.2	10.1	17.2	14.5	12.4									
1966	8.2	7.7	9.0	5.7	9.7	5.6	0.6	-10.0								
1967	9.9	9.6	11.0	8.6	12.4	9.9	7.8	5.6	24.0							
1968	10.0	9.8	11.0	8.9	12.2	10.2	8.6	7.4	17.4	11.1						
1969	8.2	7.8	8.7	6.6	9.0	6.8	5.0	3.2	8.0	0.9	-8.4					
1970	7.8	7.5	8.2	6.3	8.3	6.4	4.8	3.4	7.0	1.9	-2.4	3.9				
1971	8.3	8.0	8.7	7.1	9.0	7.4	6.1	5.1	8.4	4.9	2.9	9.0	14.3			
1972	9.0	8.8	9.5	8.1	9.9	8.6	7.7	7.0	10.1	7.5	6.7	12.2	16.6	19.0		
1973	7.3	6.9	7.5	6.0	7.4	6.0	4.9	4.0	6.2	3.5	2.0	4.8	5.1	0.8	-14.7	
1974	4.8	4.3	4.6	3.0	4.1	2.5	1.2	0.1	1.4	-1.5	-3.4	-2.4	-3.9	-9.3	-20.8	-26.4

Source: Roger G. Ibbotson and Rex A. Sinquefield. "Stocks, Bonds, Bills, and Inflation: Year-by-Year Historical Returns (1926–1974)," *Journal of Business,* January 1976, 20–22.

HISTORICAL RATE OF RETURN

The investor should be concerned with estimating the total rate of return available from a common stock portfolio. Total return is derived from a combination of the dividends available (if any) and the appreciation or decline in the price of the common stock.

It is this author's belief that an individual investor can receive an acceptable rate of return on a common stock portfolio if he or she has the time and expertise to manage a long-term investment program. If not, it will be extremely difficult to have an overall rate of return over the long run greater than that available in fixed-income securities.

The stock market has a great deal of glamour. Therefore, it is important at this point to remind the investor of the risks associated with the variable-securities market. One of the most eye-opening studies, summarized in Table 5-1, was completed in the mid 1970's. This study calculated the annual compounded rate of return that an investor would have received had an equal amount of funds been invested in every security listed on the New York Stock Exchange with all dividends being reinvested. The study included the period from 1926 through 1974 and concluded that a 8.5 percent annual compounded rate of return for all securities listed could have been realized over that period. Their research indicated that one of the best periods within the study was the 1940s and 1950s. There were several years that showed spectacular rises, for example 1933. That was the year that signaled the end of the Great Depression, and since stocks had declined approximately 80 percent between 1929 and 1932, the experience for 1933 was dramatic.

For almost any period chosen from Table 5-1, the rate of return is very good. Common stocks have been promoted as a good hedge against inflation pressures if there are more than a handful of securities in a portfolio and if they are held long enough. There have been periods however, when the opposite has been true; for example, from 1960 through 1982 increases in common stock portfolios were difficult to achieve, although many individual securities had substantial gains.

There have been very few times since 1926 when the yield an investor could receive on bonds or preferred stock has been as high as 8.5 percent, and the annual return on bonds since 1926 has not even approached that level.

An update of the previous study concerning the historical rates of return on common stocks was conducted and the results indicate the rate of return for the period of 55 years (1926 through 1980) on common stocks is 9.4 percent per annum and is 10.9 percent per annum for the 30-year period from 1951 through 1980. The compounded annual growth rate of common stock was 14 percent for the last 5 years (1976–1980) and 8.5 percent for the 10-year period ending 1980. The update also points out that the annualized rates of return on long-term bonds and the rate of inflation

Table 5-2
Annualized Rates of Return (%)

	Common Stocks	Long-term Bonds	CPI[a]
5 years (1976–1980)	14.0	2.4	8.1
10 years (1971–1980)	8.5	4.2	7.5
30 years (1951–1980)	10.9	2.8	4.0
55 years (1926–1980)	9.4	3.7	2.8

[a]Consumer Price Index

measured by the consumer price index (CPI) are lower than the rates of return on common stocks for the 55-, 30-, 10-, and 5-year periods that were specified before. Table 5-2 summarizes the result of this update.

Obviously, the potential exists for investors to realize a higher rate of return on common stock investments, particularly if they are adept in the selection and timing of their investments. Nevertheless, there is no guarantee that the individual investor can match such a historical rate or do better than fixed-income securities. One cause suggested for the stagnant common stock market is the competition that bond rates have offered from the latter half of the 1960s into the 1980s. For example, during the period from 1975 to 1982, many top-quality corporate bonds were yielding between 14 and 16 percent. Many investors who had done poorly over the past in the stock market felt that it was in their best interest to switch to bonds yielding a very attractive rate of return with substantially reduced risk.

Many investors talk about trying to beat the market, and while this may be possible to achieve over the short run in certain instances, it is extremely difficult to achieve over the long run. There are only a few institutional investors, such as pension funds, insurance funds, mutual funds, and others of similar nature, that have been able to attain a compound long-term growth rate higher than 10 percent. Most members of the investment community who can achieve an overall compound growth rate of 8 to 9 percent have done well over the past 20 years. It makes little sense to continue investing in the common stock market if the overall rate of growth for an individual has been 5 to 7 percent, because these rates of return are no better than those available on fixed-income investments, which have a considerably smaller degree of risk. However, for the investor who is in a high tax bracket, many fixed-income investments would be undesirable.

TYPES OF COMMON STOCK INVESTMENTS

Since there are numerous types of common stocks available, investors can tailor-make a portfolio to best fit their investment needs. **Growth stocks** are usually chosen by those seeking long-term capital gains through price appreciation. These stocks are usually characterized by high price/earnings ratios (P/E), low dividend payout ratios, and, consequently, a low dividend yield. High-growth stocks are often associated with smaller companies clustered in young, technical, or research-oriented fields with products in high demand and a potential for repeat business. Nevertheless, some very large companies, such as those in the office equipment industry and the drug industry, continue to have growth potential.

Income stocks are suitable for investors who seek current income. Utility stocks are a very popular form of investment for those who seek income-producing securities. The characteristics of the stocks in this group are a low P/E ratio and a high dividend payout ratio. The combination of these two characteristics results in a high dividend yield and very little growth in terms of potential price appreciation. Income stocks are usually concentrated in the public utility field or other areas subject to regulation that not only restricts the firm's income potential but also tends to establish a maximum rate of return that the firm is permitted to earn. Companies in mature industries usually have a reasonable dividend yield.

Blue-chip stocks give the investor the opportunity to derive some of the advantages of both growth and income to a limited extent. The large industrial corporations exemplified by the 30 stocks that make up the Dow-Jones Industrial Average are typically considered to be in this group. The stocks are usually those of long-established companies holding positions of dominance and maturity within their particular industry. These companies provide the investor with a reasonable dividend yield, low market price volatility, and some appreciation potential, which together might give an acceptable total rate of return. However, due to the mature nature of many industries in this Average, performance has been disappointing.

Defensive stocks refer to those that remain stable or even rise during economic downturns. In other words, during difficult periods of the business cycle, the prices of these stocks remain rather stable compared to the average in the market. They either rise or decline but at a lower rate than the market in general. Beverages, food, and drug industries are considered to be on the defensive side.

There are, of course, stocks that are issued by companies with highly unstable earnings records and very uncertain future earnings. These stocks are considered to be **speculative** in nature. The companies are usually in a small and relatively new industry, and pay little or no dividends to their investors. This type of stock is the most risky among all types of common stock investments.

REAL ESTATE INVESTMENT

Real estate is a major area of variable-return investment because it represents an extremely large segment of investment dollars. It is difficult for an active investor to ignore real estate alternatives. The decision to enter into the ownership of rental property confronts many investors each year. With inflation and an expanding population, the value of real estate can make it one of the finest available. However, such an investment can be both rewarding and frustrating in terms of problems and finances. Real estate qualifies as a variable-return investment because the value of various real estate investments rises and falls during different economic periods and in different physical settings. For example, the value of real estate over time has been on an upswing with short pauses and downturns at times, such as the depression of 1929–1932. However, in the early 1980s, real estate declined sharply in some parts of the central portions of large U.S. and foreign cities. During the first half of the 1970s, real estate in Great Britain showed a sharp decline in market value. (Although the majority of this text is devoted to security investments, Chapter 16 examines real estate because of its considerable importance to investors.)

There are a number of methods by which the individual can participate in real estate investments either directly or indirectly. Direct real estate investment commits the investor to seek out, develop, and manage a particular investment on a time basis, whether the property is an apartment building, a warehouse facility, a farm, or vacant land. Indirect investing became widespread during the 1960s through real estate investment trusts (REITs), which were established to give the individual investor an opportunity to participate in large real estate ventures. A REIT is a form of investment company that pools investors' funds and, in turn, invests in various real estate properties. REITs give owners limited liability and the opportunity to participate in ownership of income-producing property and in the appreciation of the property over a long period of time.

However, in 1974, most REITs found themselves with huge deficits. Many of the properties owned by the trusts were not producing sufficient income and could not be rented or sold. Thus, obligations of the trusts to various banks were in default. In 1974, many REIT stocks listed on the New York Stock Exchange declined sharply. As a group, most lost over 90 percent of their market value in a very short period of time.

FOREIGN INVESTMENTS

Foreign investments are of growing importance to many investors as the U.S. economy and the economies of other nations become more interdependent. There are two forms of foreign investment: direct and indirect. Investors have participated in indirect foreign investment for many years because most large U.S. corporations have foreign operations whose sales and earnings are dependent upon the economies of other nations. These foreign operations are much more than sales organizations; they include many manufacturing facilities that contribute to the economies of those countries.

An American investor can also acquire securities of foreign corporations directly, and there are currently about 30 foreign companies listed on the New York Stock Exchange. Many of these foreign corporations do not issue stock certificates to American owners; rather, they issue **American depository receipts** (ADRs), which give evidence of stock certificates held on deposit in a major bank either in New York or in the foreign country.

Investing in foreign corporations can involve risks not associated with investing in companies located in the United States. For example, the fluctuations in currency valuations can add or deduct a significant amount of earnings to a company's income statement. In addition, political uncertainties in many foreign countries add significant risk to the investment.

As Table 5-3 indicates, there has been an increasing dollar volume of transactions in U.S. stocks by foreigners and in foreign stocks by Americans.

Table 5-3
International Transactions (millions)

	Transactions in U.S. Stocks•			Transactions in Foreign Stocks■		
Year and Quarter	Foreigners' Purchases from Americans	Foreigners Sales to Americans	Net Capital Flow◆	Foreigners' Purchases from Americans	Foreigners' Sales to Americans	Net Capital Flow◆
I 1980	$10,394	$ 8,229	$2,165	$2,128	$ 2,781	− $ 653
II	6,501	6,094	407	1,353	1,809	− 456
III	10,184	9,430	754	1,953	2,789	− 835
IV	13,241	11,291	1,950	2,436	2,729	− 294
1980	$40,320	$35,044	$5,276	$7,870	$10,108	− $2,239
1979	$22,781	$21,123	$1,658	$4,615	$ 5,401	− $ 786
1978	20,145	17,723	2,423	3,666	3,139	527
1977	14,154	11,479	2,675	2,255	2,665	− 410
1976	18,227	15,475	2,753	1,937	2,259	− 323
1975	15,355	10,678	4,678	1,542	1,730	− 188
1974	7,636	7,096	540	1,907	1,723	184
1973	12,767	9,978	2,790	1,729	1,554	176
1972	14,361	12,173	2,188	2,532	2,123	409
1971	11,626	10,894	731	1,385	1,434	− 49
1970	8,927	8,301	626	1,033	998	35

•Excludes transactions between foreigners, but includes transactions between Americans on foreign markets.
■Excludes transactions between Americans, but includes transactions with other foreigners on American markets.
◆Negative figures indicate an outflow of capital from the United States.
Source: The New York Stock Exchange Fact Book (New York, 1981), p. 21; originally appeared in Treasury Bulletin.

American depository receipt (ADR)	income stock
blue-chip stock	liquidating dividend
board of directors	payable date
book value per share	property dividend
cash dividend	record date
common stock	REITs
corporation	speculative stock
date of declaration	stock dividend
defensive stock	stock-purchase warrant
dividends	stock split
ex dividend date	subscription rights
growth stock	treasury stock
	variable return

QUESTIONS

1. What are the major differences between bondholders of a corporation and stockholders?
2. What are the three basic forms of business ownership, and what are their distinguishing characteristics?
3. What are the major (potential) advantages of the corporation form of ownership?
4. What do most investors consider the most important factor in determining the price of a stock?
5. Why might a stock with small dividends sell for a high price?
6. Why do many firms pay a fixed-amount cash dividend on a regular basis rather than pay dividends that reflect profits?
7. What are the four special dates associated with a dividend?
8. What is the difference between a 100 percent stock dividend and a two-for-one stock split?
9. What are subscription rights?
10. What alternatives are available to a stockholder concerning his subscription rights?
11. What is the difference between stock purchase warrants and stock subscription rights?
12. What is the difference between direct real estate investment and indirect real estate investment?
13. What is an REIT?
14. What is an ADR?

SELECTED READINGS

"The Death of Equities: How Inflation Is Destroying the Stockmarket," *Business Week*, August 13, 1979, 54–59.

EHRBAR, A. F. "The Trouble with Stocks," *Fortune*, August 1977, 89–93.

FISHER, L. "Rates of Return on Investments in Common Stocks: The Year by Year Record, 1926–65," *Journal of Business* 41, no. 3, 1968, 291–316.

GRAHAM, BENJAMIN. "The Future of Common Stocks," *Financial Analysts Journal*, September–October 1974, 20–30.

KELLER, PHILIP R. "Utility Stocks vs. Bonds," *Financial Analysts Journal*, May–June 1968, 127.

MALKIEL, BURTON. "Common Stocks—The Best Inflation Hedge for the 1980's," *Forbes*, February 18, 1980, 118–128.

REILLY F.K., G.L. JOHNSON, and R. E. SMITH. "Inflation Hedges and Common Stocks," *Financial Analysts Journal*, January–February 1970, 104.

SCHULZ, JOHN W. "Who Needs the Blue Chips?" *Barron's*, April 2, 1979, 11–14.

6

Variable-Return Security Analysis

The central focus for many individuals approaching the securities market is common stocks. Common stocks are at the heart of variable-return security analysis, and therefore this chapter focuses on those elements that affect the desirability of owning common stock. Remember from Chapter 4 that bondholders are only concerned about the yield to maturity of the bond and the safety of their principal (the ability of the issuer to meet its fixed obligations). However, since the risk level of variable-return securities is usually higher than that of fixed-income securities, common stock investors need to consider various aspects of the issuing company. Investors should perform company analysis, a careful examination of the company's working capital management, liquidity, operating efficiencies, leverage, management-labor relationships, profitability, dividend policy, and the growth potential of the issuer, before investment decisions are made. This is why it is very important for investors who are interested in investing in common stocks to know *where* to look for company data and *how* to analyze them.

Specific Company and Security Data

A basic source of data concerning a specific firm is the company itself. Publicly held companies are required by law to make certain financial information available to their stockholders and bondholders. Annual reports and periodic reports issued throughout the year are the most common sources of this information. Annual reports are audited to assure that they adhere to standardized accounting principles. The Federal Securities Act of 1933 requires that companies selling new issues of securities must register with the SEC. Moreover, the seller must make available to the public a **prospectus,** which is a condensation of the registration statement. This prospectus must contain all information that the SEC feels is essential to enable the average investor to make a reasonable decision on the purchase of the proposed security. Thus, balance sheets and income statements for several years are included in a prospectus. Certifications by independent auditors are given, as are important notes to the financial statements describing the accounting processes used in composing the statements. Normally, a prospectus also includes a complete description of the company's property, its management, special management compensation plans, depreciation policies, and capital expenditure plans.

In accordance with the Securities Exchange Act of 1934, each company files form 10-K with the SEC annually. The 10-K report is a detailed description of a company's operations and finances that is available to prospective investors who wish to pursue their investigations in more detail.

In addition to executing orders, it is common for brokerage firms and securities dealers to provide data about specific companies and securities. These data are for their clients' use, but they are also distributed to others who might be prospective clients. Most firms publish an advisory letter that contains general market appraisals and specific security suggestions.

Two large standard financial services, Moody's and Standard & Poor's, publish daily, weekly, monthly, and yearly summaries about industries and individual companies. Moody's Investors Service is best known for its annual manuals, which contain a summary of past financial statements and other important information about leading companies and their securities. Separate manuals are issued annually for companies in the following classifications: industrials, public utilities, transportation, over-the-counter, and bank and finance. The manuals are kept up to date by the issuance of biweekly supplements. Moody's also publishes separate weekly bond and stock surveys.

Standard & Poor's Corporation publishes similar data, but in looseleaf form in what is called the Standard Corporation Records. Supplements are issued regularly. Reports on individual companies, usually reviewed quarterly, are condensed to two pages and contain important information that traces the 10-year history of the company's sales, earnings, assets, liabilities, and various ratios useful in investment analysis. The *Outlook*, a weekly publication, gives information on the economy, industries, companies, and investment opportunities. Exhibits 6-1 and 6-2 are examples of a

Exhibit 6–1

Dover Corp. 769

35,714

NYSE Symbol DOV

Price	Range	P-E Ratio	Dividend	Yield	S&P Ranking
Feb. 12'82 28	1982 33-26¼	10	0.66	2.4%	A+

Summary

Dover is the third largest in the U.S. elevator industry, and a leading factor in that business in Canada. The company also sells oil field products, nozzles and valves for petroleum marketers, bearings, seals, air conditioning parts, and automated electronic circuitry assembly equipment. Earnings increased for the 21st consecutive year in 1981. The shares were split 2-for-1 in September, 1981.

Business Summary

Dover Corp. is the third largest U.S. elevator manufacturer and a leading producer of oil well equipment, hydraulic service station lifts, and various hardware for industrial markets. Contributions by business segment in 1980 were:

	Sales	Profits
Building industry	34%	23%
Petroleum products:		
Production equipment	16%	28%
Marketing equipment	10%	11%
Machinery and equipment	22%	24%
Liquids handling equipment	8%	9%
Other fabricated metal products	10%	5%

Foreign business accounted for some 15% of total sales and 12% of profits.

The building division makes geared and gearless traction elevators, hydraulic elevators, and home and industrial lifts. Replacement parts and service contracts provide an important part of profits.

The petroleum production division produces Norris sucker rods, valves and fittings, and subsurface oil pumps. The petroleum marketing division manufactures OPW gasoline nozzles, valves, fittings and vapor recovery equipment; Rotary hydraulic automobile lifts; C. Lee Cook piston rings and packings for natural gas compressors; and Blackmer rotary pumps.

The machinery and equipment segment includes automatic screw machines, welding guns, toggle clamps, reed valves, specialized bearings and seals, and, through the 1979 acquisition of Universal Instruments Corp., automated electronic circuitry assembly equipment.

Liquids handling products include flow meters,

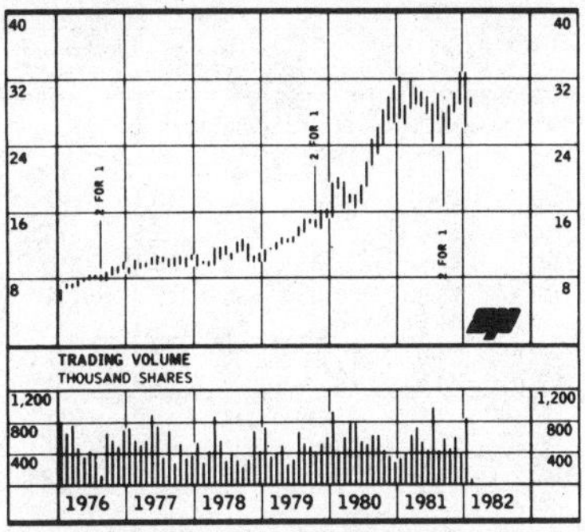

filtration equipment, and liquid handling products.

Fabricated metal products include automotive wreckers, railroad cranes, cooking and processing vessels, kettles and heat transfer and cooling equipment.

Important Developments

Sep. '81—DOV distributed a 2-for-1 stock split, and raised the dividend 27%, to $0.16½ quarterly from $0.13 (both adjusted).

Sep. '81—Dover purchased for an undisclosed amount of cash the Tipper Tie division of Rheem Manufacturing (a City Investing Co. subsidiary). Tipper Tie is the leading manufacturer of metal fasteners and clip-closing systems for packaging food and other products.

Next earnings report due in mid-April.

Per Share Data ($)

Yr. End Dec. 31	1981	1980	[1]1979	[1]1978	1977	1976	1975	1974	[1]1973	[1]1972
Book Value	NA	7.37	5.77	5.10	4.18	3.54	2.84	2.55	2.04	1.90
Earnings	2.69	2.05	1.60	1.26	1.05	0.88	0.69	0.63	0.50	0.40
Dividends	0.59	0.47½	0.39	0.32½	0.26⅜	0.20	0.16⅜	0.14	0.11⅞	0.10
Payout Ratio	22%	23%	24%	26%	25%	23%	24%	22%	24%	25%
Prices—High	33	31½	16½	12⅞	11	10⅛	6⅛	5¼	6⅞	7⅜
Low	24¼	15½	10	9½	8¾	5½	3¼	3⅛	3⅝	6½
P/E Ratio—	12-9	15-8	10-6	10-8	10-8	12-6	9-5	8-5	14-7	18-16

Data as orig. reptd. Adj. for stk. div(s). of 100% Sep. 1981, 100% Oct. 1979, 100% Sep. 1976. 1. Reflects merger or acquisition. NA-Not Available.

Standard NYSE Stock Reports
Vol. 49/No. 35/Sec. 13

February 22, 1982

Standard & Poor's Corp.
25 Broadway, NY, NY 10004

Exhibit 6–1 *(cont.)*

769   Dover Corporation

Income Data (Million $)

Year Ended Dec. 31	Revs.	Oper. Inc.	% Oper. Inc. of Revs.	Cap. Exp.	Depr.	Int. Exp.	Net Bef. Taxes	Eff. Tax Rate	Net Inc.	% Net Inc. of Revs.
1980	835	160	19.2%	32.5	16.0	6.77	139	47.5%	73.2	8.8%
¹1979	667	123	18.5%	28.6	13.1	4.38	109	47.5%	57.1	8.6%
¹1978	526	101	19.2%	30.9	10.9	2.63	89	49.6%	44.8	8.5%
1977	411	83	20.1%	22.3	6.7	2.32	75	50.2%	37.6	9.1%
1976	362	71	19.6%	9.5	5.9	2.14	64	51.3%	31.2	8.6%
1975	326	58	17.7%	8.1	5.1	2.60	49	50.3%	24.5	7.5%
1974	334	54	16.2%	6.0	5.2	3.50	46	51.6%	22.4	6.7%
¹1973	285	43	15.2%	10.4	5.1	2.88	36	50.4%	17.8	6.2%
¹1972	198	32	16.4%	10.3	3.1	0.98	28	49.5%	14.3	7.2%
1971	173	29	17.0%	2.1	3.0	1.11	26	50.3%	12.9	7.5%

Balance Sheet Data (Million $)

Dec. 31	Cash	Current Assets	Current Liab.	Ratio	Total Assets	Ret. on Assets	Long Term Debt	Common Equity	Total Cap.	% LT Debt of Cap.	Ret. on Equity
1980	18.3	317	112	2.8	475	16.5%	35.4	318	360	9.8%	25.3%
1979	17.4	275	116	2.4	414	15.8%	30.1	261	296	10.2%	23.8%
1978	25.2	202	53	3.8	306	15.9%	31.2	217	252	12.4%	22.3%
1977	34.5	170	42	4.1	260	15.6%	29.5	186	218	13.6%	21.8%
1976	37.8	154	36	4.3	223	15.1%	26.1	158	185	14.0%	21.4%
1975	9.5	125	26	4.9	190	13.1%	28.4	134	164	17.3%	19.7%
1974	2.5	130	37	3.5	183	12.8%	29.4	115	145	20.2%	21.1%
1973	7.2	113	39	2.9	167	12.3%	30.6	98	128	23.8%	19.4%
1972	2.2	84	26	3.2	125	12.6%	11.7	87	99	11.8%	17.6%
1971	4.5	71	16	4.5	103	12.7%	11.7	75	87	13.4%	18.3%

Data as orig. reptd. 1. Reflects merger or acquisition.

Net Sales (Million $)

Quarter:	1981	1980	1979	1978
Mar.	236	202	151	121
Jun.	263	207	160	135
Sep.	256	205	166	131
Dec.	271	221	189	139
	1,026	835	667	526

Sales for 1981 (preliminary) advanced 23%, year to year. Despite first half softness in petroleum marketing, strength in other market segments led to a rise in pretax income of 31%. After taxes at 47.2%, versus 47.5%, net income was also up 31%. Share earnings were $2.69, against $2.05 (as adjusted for the September, 1981 2-for-1 stock split).

Common Share Earnings ($)

Quarter:	1981	1980	1979	1978
Mar.	0.60	0.51	0.39	0.27
Jun.	0.72	0.51	0.41	0.33
Sep.	0.67	0.49	0.36	0.28
Dec.	0.71	0.54	0.45	0.39
	2.69	2.05	1.60	1.26

Dividend Data

Dividends have been paid since 1955.

Amt. of Divd. $	Date Decl.	Ex-divd. Date	Stock of Record	Payment Date
0.26	May 5	May 21	May 28	Jun. 15'81
0.33	Aug. 3	Aug. 21	Aug. 27	Sep. 15'81
2-for-1	Aug. 3	Sep. 28	Aug. 27	Sep. 25'81
0.16½	Nov. 5	Dec. 7	Dec. 11	Dec. 31'81
0.16½	Feb. 9	Feb. 22	Feb. 26	Mar. 15'82

Next dividend meeting: early May '82.

Finances

A purported class action suit was filed in March, 1981 against DOV in California seeking punitive damages of $50 million and alleging that the use of OPW vapor recovery nozzles resulted in overcharges by service stations. DOV believed that there was no merit to the claim and was vigorously defending the suit.

Capitalization

Long Term Debt: $33,623,000.

Common Stock: 35,786,737 shs. ($1 par). Institutions hold about 44%; some 15% owned by officers and directors. Shareholders: 4,300.

Office—277 Park Ave., N.Y. 10172. Tel—(212) 826-7160. Pres & CEO—G. L. Roubos. Secy—C. Laporte, Jr. VP-Treas—R. S. Bethe. Dirs—T. C. Sutton (Chrmn), M. O. Bryant, G. W. Davidson, M. C. Devas, K. N. LaVine, G. L. Ohrstrom, R. R. Ohrstrom, A. J. Ormsby, G. L. Roubos, D. Thomas. Transfer Agents—Chemical Bank, NYC; First Tennessee Bank, Memphis. Registrars—Chemical Bank, NYC; Union Planters National Bank, Memphis. Incorporated in Delaware in 1947.

Information has been obtained from sources believed to be reliable, but its accuracy and completeness are not guaranteed.   N.J.DoV.

Source: Standard & Poor's Corporation, *Standard N.Y.S.E. Stock Reports.*

Exhibit 6–2

SUPERVISED MASTER LIST OF RECOMMENDED ISSUES

GROUP 1: FOUNDATION STOCKS FOR LONG-TERM GAIN

These issues are basic building blocks for the portfolio. They offer the prospect of long-term appreciation, along with moderate but growing income. The investor seeking to build an estate should start with stocks from this list, augmenting them with issues from other groups according to one's objectives and temperament.

Earnings Per Share ($) 1980	1981	E1982	Indicated Div. $	1980-82 Price Range	Recent Price	P/E Ratio	Yield %		Annual Growth Rates for Latest 5 Years: Sales	Earn.	Div.	▼Price Action vs. Mkt. 3-6-78 to 11-28-80	Since Nov. 28, '80	Listed Options Traded	Last Page Ref.
[1]4.08	[1]4.40	[1]5.80	1.72	30⅜- 17	25	4.3	6.9	• Citicorp	8%	7%	10%	0.65	1.49	C	696
4.14	4.57	5.30	2.10	38¾- 27⅜	35	6.6	6.0	• CPC Int'l	11	13	11	0.87	1.40	..	893
4.42	3.00	↓2.50	1.80	39¼- 20	21	8.4	8.6	• Dow Chemical	17	3	13	0.92	0.79	C	830
7.15	7.66	8.25	3.50	85⅜- 42⅞	71	8.6	4.9	Eastman Kodak	15	16	12	0.99	1.33	C	770
3.62	E4.10	4.65	1.44	33¾- 17½	32	6.9	4.5	• Heinz (H.J.) (Apr.*)	11	16	19	0.71	1.89	..	830
6.10	5.63	6.75	3.44	72¾- 48¾	60	8.9	5.7	Int'l Business Machines	12	8	12	0.67	1.14	C	794
5.97	[4]5.74	3.50	2.40	51½- 30½	35	10.0	6.9	International Paper	8	3	5	0.75	1.01	C	753
[4]6.62	5.72	4.50	2.00	44⅞- 20⅛	24	5.3	8.3	Mobil Corp.	20	21	18	1.75	0.71	C	718
7.78	8.08	9.40	4.20	89¾- 62¾	84	8.9	5.0	• Procter & Gamble (June)	13	11	13	0.55	1.55	A	777
3.43	4.24	5.00	1.10	37¼- 20⅛	25	5.0	4.4	Sonat Inc.[3]	30	17	19	1.35	0.94	..	753

GROUP 2: STOCKS WITH PROMISING GROWTH PROSPECTS

These stocks promise to enjoy well above average growth rates in earnings per share for the foreseeable future. Stocks in the second category carry a higher degree of risk, but by the same token offer greater reward potential. Income is not a consideration here.

Established Growth

Earnings Per Share ($) 1980	1981	E1982	Indicated Div. $	1980-82 Price Range	Recent Price	P/E Ratio	Yield %		Latest 5-Year Growth Rates Sales	Earn.	No. of Earn. Gains '77-'81	Interim ▪Earn. Trend	▼Price Action vs. Mkt. 3-6-78 to 11-28-80	Since Nov. 28, '80	Listed Options Traded	Last Page Ref.
1.73	2.01	2.40	↑0.84	32¼- 17⅛	29	12.1	2.9	Abbott Laboratories	17%	20%	5	+16%	1.20	1.41	Ph	791
2.05	2.57	2.95	↑0.72	38 - 18¾	19	6.4	3.8	• Big Three Industries	24	22	5	+15	1.37	0.74	..	791
4.08	5.58	5.25	↑2.10	59⅜- 30½	54	10.3	3.9	Bristol-Myers	12	14	5	+14	0.95	1.54	C	870
3.20	3.61	4.15	1.62	39⅜- 20	37	8.9	4.4	• PepsiCo, Inc.	20	14	5	+14	0.61	1.90	C	714
4.63	5.41	6.35	2.40	55⅛- 29⅛	49	7.7	4.9	• Philip Morris	27	19	5	+12	0.80	1.55	A	830
[5]3.23	4.37	5.25	0.96	87⅛- 27½	41	7.8	2.3	• Schlumberger Ltd.	29	34	5	+20	1.80	0.62	C	742
5.75	6.04	6.00	2.28	69 - 41½	42	7.0	5.4	Upjohn Co.	14	19	5	− 4	1.16	0.84	C	888

More Speculative Growth

Earnings Per Share ($) 1980	1981	E1982	Mill. Shs. Outst.	1980-82 Price Range	Recent Price	P/E Ratio	Yield %		Latest 5-Year Growth Rates Sales	Earn.	No. of Earn. Gains '77-'81	Interim ▪Earn. Trend	▼Price Action vs. Mkt. 3-6-78 to 11-28-80	Since Nov. 28, '80	Listed Options Traded	Last Page Ref.
5.45	6.70	7.60	54.7	113¾- 56¾	72	9.5	..	Digital Equipment (June)	33	27	5	+12	1.38	1.02	A, C	846
2.63	[3]2.97	2.40	31.3	60¼- 24⅝	25	10.4	3.5	Harris Corp. (June)	25	21	5	−20	1.41	0.62	C	853
1.24	E1.60	2.10	46.9	28¾- 4¼	14	6.7	2.9	• Nat'l Med. Enter. (May*)	53	32	5	+38	3.20	0.98	A	697

• Best situated currently for the objectives described in the paragraph introducing each group of stocks.

EARNINGS are for calendar years or for fiscal years ending as indicated after names. Unless otherwise noted, they are based on common and common share equivalents, excluding nonrecurring items and including restatements. A—Actual. E—Estimated. ↑Estimate revised upward since last publication of the Master List; ↓estimate revised downward. *Of the following year.

Listed options traded: C—Chicago Board Options Exchange; A—American Stock Exchange; Ph—Philadelphia Stock Exchange; Pac—Pacific Stock Exchange.

INDICATED DIVIDENDS include actual or possible extras. ↑Dividend increased; ↓dividend decreased. PRICE/EARNINGS RATIOS are based on latest shown estimated or actual earnings. GROWTH RATES for sales and earnings are through latest completed years reported; for dividends, through 1981.

All stocks currently in the Supervised Master List are listed on the New York Stock Exchange.

▼A figure above 1.0 indicates that the stock outperformed the S & P industrial stock price index in this period. It is computed by taking the ratio of the stock's price at the end of the period vs. the beginning of the period and dividing it by the corresponding ratio of the index. The time periods covered are updated periodically to conform to the latest major market cycle.

▪This column compares share earnings of the latest six months with those of the corresponding year-earlier period.

Exhibit 6–2 *(cont.)*

GROUP 3: CYCLICAL/SPECULATIVE STOCKS

This group comprises stocks selected for high reward potentials stemming from a variety of considerations — including emerging opportunities, turnaround situations, stocks to benefit from cyclical upswings, and the like. Readers can expect to see more frequent changes in this list than in the others. The risk factor in some of the issues in this group may be high and the stocks recommended may not be suitable for those concerned with income or with investment grade securities.

Earnings Per Share ($)			Indi-cated Div. $	1980-82 Price Range	Recent Price	P/E Ratio	Yield %	Listed Options Traded	Last Page Ref.		Remarks
1980	1981	E1982									
6.54	3.97	2.00	1.80	38¼-21⅞	23	11.5	7.8	C	767	● Aluminum Co. of Amer.	Cyclical upturn in aluminum demand to develop before long.
5.68	4.07	2.00	2.20	43¾-21¾	22	11.0	10.0	..	742	American Standard	Modestly valued on long-term profit prospects.
5.18	5.13	↑5.75	1.60	39 -25⅝	36	6.3	4.4	Pac.	718	● Amer. Broadcasting	TV network benefiting from strong ad background.
4.73	4.97	↓1.50	1.80	41¾-16½	18	12.0	10.0	..	734	Armco Inc.	Diversification and strong management benefit outlook.
¹8.66	¹7.06	¹7.85	2.05	37⅞-18	28	3.6	7.3	..	730	● Bankers Trust	Poised for strong earnings gain; stock undervalued.
1.88	2.47	3.05	1.00	37⅜-12¼	30	9.8	3.3	A	818	● Browning-Ferris (Sept.)	Regulation of waste disposal methods aids growth prospects.
7.55	7.02	↓7.35	↑1.67	77 -25¾	44	6.0	3.8	C	742	● Burlington Northern	Superior rail and natural resource potentials.
2.43	2.65	↓2.70	0.56	30¾-17¾	22	8.1	2.5	..	905	● Engelhard Corp.	Favorable prospects for most catalytic products.
2.85	3.36	3.75	1.40	24⅛-10¾	23	6.1	6.1	A	810	Goodyear Tire & Rub.	Best-situated in industry with improved outlook.
3.40	3.86	4.10	1.40	55⅝-28¼	34	8.3	4.1	C	730	Raytheon	Strong growth likely in missile & defense electronic systems.
2.47	1.67	1.50	1.30	40¾-23⅞	24	16.0	5.4	C	846	Weyerhaeuser Co.	Timber self-sufficiency enhances long-term prospects.
4.31	4.78	5.10	1.80	65⅞-27½	29	5.7	6.2	..	777	Wheelabrator-Frye	Engineering/construction projects expanding.

GROUP 4: INCOME WITH INFLATION PROTECTION

If high yield alone were the goal, it would be easy to compile a list of high-grade bonds returning 14% or more. But bonds afford no protection against inflation. While it was hard to beat inflation in recent years, the list below comprises quality stocks that in our opinion offer the prospect of dividend growth sufficient to compensate for the degree of inflation we envisage for the period ahead.

Earnings Per Share ($)			Indi-cated Div. $	1980-82 Price Range	Recent Price	P/E Ratio	Yield %		5-Year Growth Rate	No. of Ann. Incr. 1977-81	5-Year Avg. Payout	Latest Increase	Infla-tion Hedge Ratio††	Listed Options Traded	Last Page Ref.
1980	1981	E1982													
1.19	8.55	↓9.30	5.40	61½-45	51	5.5	10.6	American Tel. & Tel.	7%	4	61%	4- 1-81	0.81	C	722
3.08	3.19	↓3.40	2.20	23½-15⅞	22	6.5	10.0	● Duke Power	6	5	65	12-14-81	0.84	Ph	767
6.49	6.44	5.00	3.00	44½-26	28	5.6	10.7	Exxon Corp.	17	5	46	12-10-80	0.97	C	758
7.21	6.37	6.50	2.80	54½-27¾	33	5.1	8.5	Gulf Oil	9	5	38	7-14-81	0.99	A	770
⁵5.82	⁵6.41	¹7.05	2.24	40 -22	29	4.1	7.7	Mellon National	11	5	34	12- 7-81	0.97	..	870
6.23	7.08	7.95	2.80	53 -27	44	5.5	6.4	● Reynolds (R.J.) Indus.	10	5	37	12- 5-81	1.05	C	818
5.95	6.01	6.25	2.60	58⅜-24⅞	25	4.0	10.4	Tenneco	7	5	43	12- 9-80	0.75	A	856
°3.53	°4.39	°5.40	2.91	32¾-19	31	5.7	9.4	● Wisconsin Elec. Pwr.	6	5	64	6- 1-81	0.77	..	718

††This figure shows the degree to which the stock's dividend and price change offset the sharp increase in the consumer price index in the 5 years through 1981. A figure of 1.0 would indicate that the impact of inflation was completely offset.

¹Net operating earnings. ²Formerly Southern Natural Resources. ³Excludes $0.40 gain from sale of an investment. ⁴Excluding capital gains. ⁵Excludes $0.24 gain from sale of Rowan Cos. shares. °Before proposed 3-for-2 stock split.

Source: Standard & Poor's Corporation, *Outlook,* June 16, 1982, pp. 704-705.

Standard and Poor's company report and recommended securities selections.

The *Value Line Investment Survey* offers a service that analyzes the stock performance of 1,700 leading companies; the analysis is presented in chart form and indicates the performance of those companies' stocks in relation to the stocks of other companies in the same industry and to securities in general. *Value Line* predicts stock performance in the coming year and in the next 3- to 5-year period. The stocks are rated according to quality, probable performance for the next 12 months, desirability of holding for 3 to 5 years, and yield. Exhibit 6-3 is a sample of a typical company report.

United Business & Investment Report, a product of United Business Service Company, produces a mix of business indicators and information such as factory orders, unemployment figures, company surveys, commodity price forecasts, Washington political views, and even a summary of competing services' recommendations. The service is directed to specific company and security recommendations.

Although Dow-Jones & Company is not normally classed as a standard financial service, its importance in providing financial information to the investor merits special mention. Famous for its daily, *the Wall Street Journal,* and *Barron's,* a financial weekly, this company also owns the Dow-Jones new tickers, which are located throughout the country and the world and which provide minute-to-minute information. Dow-Jones also publishes a weekly securities market letter designed for the individual subscriber.

Investors who have large amounts of funds available and who have insufficient time, knowledge, or temperament to analyze securities themselves may engage the services of a professional investment counselor to supervise the development and management of their portfolios. The fee charged is usually scaled to the aggregate amount of money involved and is small compared with the amount of capital usually saved by minimizing injudicious transactions.

Although bank trust officers are characteristically more familiar with conservative investment possibilities, some can also furnish helpful advice concerning common stocks. They can be especially helpful in appraising the finances and management of local corporations with whom they have business contact. In addition, many large banks issue security, industry, and economic reports that can be helpful.

Most large brokerage houses have research departments that attempt to enlarge upon the data furnished by the standard financial services. Visits to plant locations and in-depth interviews with company officers add dimension to the raw data. Such thorough research attempts to take into account government regulations, consequences of changes in the laws, competitive prospects, and, in general, any event that may or may not influence individual stocks or groups of issues. Usually, an in-house economist's report and opinion sets the stage for a variety of industry analysts who continually monitor their areas and publish reports and comments. Exhibit 6-4 is an example of the cover page of a brokerage house research report.

Exhibit 6–3

GENERAL ELECTRIC NYSE-GE | RECENT PRICE **66** | P/E RATIO **8.7** (Trailing: 9.9 Median: 12.0) | EARN'S YLD **11.5%** | DIV'D YIELD **5.2%** | 1014

BUSINESS: General Electric Co. manufactures consumer products (appliances, televisions, lighting products), industrial machines, electric motors, generating and transmission equip., aircraft engines, military equip., locomotives, medical equip. Produces man-made materials. Has interests in natural resources, esp. coking coal (Utah Internat'l). Provides financing (G.E. Credit) and information services. Foreign business (incl. exports): 37% of sales, 35% of net pft. R&D: 3.0% of sales. '81 deprec. rate: 6.9%. Est'd plant age: 7 yrs. Has 404,000 employees, 502,000 shrhldrs. Directors own 1% of stk. Chrmn.: J.F. Welch, Jr. Inc.: N.Y. Address: Fairfield, CT 06431.

GE hasn't had a down quarter since 1975. Despite the current recession, we don't expect a reversal this year. In the first quarter, the company recorded a 6% gain in share earnings despite a 1% drop in sales and a 5% decline in operating income. The main positive factors were an 89% rise in net profit at the nonconsolidated finance subsidiary (GE Credit) and lower interest charges. **The second-quarter comparisons will be tough, though,** since both operating and nonoperating income were strong in the 1981 period. But we look for another modest bottom-line gain, thanks in part to the same positive factors. GE should also continue to benefit from margin improvement in power systems (the nuclear power business is now profitable) and from easier comparisons for electronics businesses that have heavy acquisition and new program charges. **Consumer demand is the key to the second half.** GE's important major appliance business, which depends heavily on new housing construction, is severely depressed. We look for second-half improvement here, combined with continued growth in recession-resistant businesses such as medical equipment and data processing.

Higher sales to the military will also help. **The stock is a solid choice for troubled times:** It rates Highest for Safety and Above Average for Timeliness. Diversification and superb financial management have led to continued earnings growth despite high interest rates and a weak economy, and the pace will pick up as demand for consumer and capital goods rises. **GE is building for the future** with heavy investments in R&D and productivity improvements, combined with entry into new markets such as industrial automation and export services. In the 1970s, GE was a leader in recognizing the impact of inflation on corporate profits. Now, management is trying to put the company in shape for the disinflation—and the stiff competition—it foresees for the 1980s. *T.R.J./T.W.P.*

CAPITAL STRUCTURE as of 12/31/81
Total Debt $2230.0 mill. Due in 5 Yrs $1529.0mill.
LT Debt $1059.0 mill. LT Interest $92.0 mill.
Incl. $50 mill. 4¼% debs. ('87) callable
104, conv. into 12.38 shs. at $80.75.
Excl. obligations of G.E. Credit Corp.
(Total interest coverage: 7.3x) (10% of Cap'l)

Pension Liability None in '81 vs. None in '80

Pfd Stock None

Common Stock 227,761,000 shs. (90% of Cap'l)

ANNUAL RATES of change (per sh)	Past 10 Yrs.	Past 5 Yrs.	Est'd '79-'81 to '84-'86
Sales	8.5%	9.0%	10.0%
"Cash Flow"	10.5%	12.0%	12.0%
Earnings	13.0%	13.5%	12.5%
Dividends	8.5%	12.5%	11.0%
Book Value	9.5%	10.5%	12.0%

CURRENT POSITION	1979	1980	12/31/81
Cash Assets	2576.6	2201.0	2471.0
Receivables	3646.6	4339.0	4872.0
Inventory (LIFO)	3161.3	3343.0	3461.0
Current Assets	9384.5	9883.0	10804.0
Accts Payable	1476.7	1671.0	2012.0
Debt Due	995.9	1093.0	1171.0
Other	4399.2	4828.0	5551.0
Current Liab.	6871.8	7592.0	8734.0

Calendar	QUARTERLY SALES ($ mill.) Mar. 31	June 30	Sept. 30	Dec. 31	Full Year
1978	4443	4963	4842	5403	19653
1979	5081	5642	5608	6127	22460
1980	5881	6197	5963	6918	24959
1981	6088	6955	6636	7561	27240
1982	6023	6950	7150	8477	28000

Calendar	EARNINGS PER SHARE Mar. 31	June 30	Sept. 30	Dec. 31	Full Year
1978	1.09	1.40	1.31	1.59	5.39
1979	1.33	1.69	1.50	1.68	6.20
1980	1.50	1.77	1.58	1.80	6.65
1981	1.57	1.92	1.78	1.99	7.26
1982	1.66	2.05	1.99	2.20	7.90

Calendar	QUARTERLY DIVIDENDS PAID Mar. 31	June 30	Sept. 30	Dec. 31	Full Year
1978	.55	.55	.65	.65	2.40
1979	.65	.65	.70	.70	2.70
1980	.70	.70	.75	.75	2.90
1981	.75	.75	.80	.80	3.10
1982	.80	.80			

(A) Based on average shares outstand'g. Next egs. rep't due early July. Est'd constant-dollar egs./sh.: '81 $4.95. (B) Next div'd meet'g about May 21. Goes ex about June 1. Div'd payment dates: Jan. 25, Apr. 25, July 25, Oct. 25. ■ Div'd reinvestment plan available. (C) Incl. deferred charges and intangibles. In '81: $536 mill., $2.35/sh. (D) In millions, adjusted for stock splits & div'ds. (E) Before eliminations and corp. items; incl. other income.

	1979	1980	1981	1982
Consumer Products	5990.0(12.4%)	6342.0(12.0%)	6643.0(10.7%)	8000(10.0%)
Power Systems	5124.0(9.5%)	5815.0(8.9%)	5982.0(10.5%)	6000(11.0%)
Indust'l Products	4375.0(9.5%)	4690.0(11.1%)	4871.0(12.1%)	4000(11.5%)
Technical Systems	2761.0(10.1%)	3252.0(9.4%)	3979.0(8.9%)	4000(9.0%)
Aircraft Engines	2190.0(10.1%)	2660.0(12.2%)	2950.0(13.8%)	3000(11.0%)
Services/Mater'ls	1901.0(24.5%)	2115.0(23.5%)	2464.0(24.5%)	2700(23.0%)
Natural Resources	1260.0(40.8%)	1374.0(36.2%)	1372.0(35.1%)	1000(35.0%)
Ge Credit Corp	90.0(100.0%)	115.0(100.0%)	129.0(100.0%)	200(100%)
Company Total	23691.0(13.6%)	26363.0(13.4%)	28740.0(14.0%)	30000(14.0%)

Company's Financial Strength	A++
Stock's Price Stability	95
Price Growth Persistence	15
Earnings Predictability	95

Factual material is obtained from sources believed to be reliable but cannot be guaranteed.

Source: Value Line Investment Survey, Arnold Bernhard & Company, Inc., Edition 7 May 14, 1982, p. 1014.

Exhibit 6–4

Merrill Lynch   June 14, 1982

Ponderosa System, Inc.

Review

Intermediate Opinion: OK to Buy (2)
Long Term Opinion: OK to Buy (2)

Recent Price: 15 3/4 (PON-NYSE)   52 Week Range: 17 1/4 – 12

FY Feb	Earnings Per Share		P/E Ratio		Indicated Annual	
1982	1983E	1984E	1983E	1984E	Dividend	Yield
$2.01	$2.20	$3.00	7.2	5.3	$0.40	2.5%

Shares Outstanding: 4.21 mil.   LT Debt % of Capital: 56%
Market Value: $66.3 mil   Est. Return on Avg FY83 Equity: 13%
Book Value/Sh.: $17.24   Est. 5 Yr. EPS Growth: 12%

Suitability: High Risk   Invest. Character: Cyclical Growth
Industry Class: Restaurant   Options: None

SUMMARY

We continue to view the common stock of Ponderosa as offering limited downside
risk (basically that of the market) and above average upside potential. We
believe that the company has successfully weathered to date ten quarters of
dismal economic conditions in its heartland markets--the industrial North.
Past twelve months' earnings of $1.95 are well below existing earnings power,
yet reflect substantial improvement from 60 cents earned in fiscal 1981.
While our intermediate term outlook for further substantial profit gains has
been stretched out by the delayed economic recovery, we believe that the
downside earnings risk is limited to the $1.90 p.s. area. On the upside,
incremental real growth in volume per store will have a substantial leverage
effect on profits. The economic conditions necessary for this to occur are
not expected until fiscal 1984. In past economic recoveries, the stock has
been highly responsive to improved volume trends and rapid recovery in
earnings. Accordingly, we believe that initial purchases can be made at
current prices to achieve above average market appreciation over the
intermediate and long term (OK to Buy /2/).

Russell C. Mosteller, Jr., C.F.A.
Industry Analyst
(212) 637-8121

Merrill Lynch, Pierce, Fenner & Smith Inc
Securities Research Division
L11/ 613/ 610/ 002/ 001

Source: Merrill Lynch Research Department, June 14, 1982.

INTERPRETATION OF FINANCIAL DATA

Because a corporation's periodic financial statements are the primary sources of practically all the statistical material regarding a given stock, the wise investor becomes familiar with the essential components of a financial statement.

Balance Sheet

The **balance sheet** is an itemized statement of a company's financial condition at a given date, usually the last day of the year or quarter. As its name implies, it presents a balance between the company's assets and liabilities and the owners' net worth. Studying a firm's balance sheet over a period of time allows the investor to determine whether the company's financial condition is improving or deteriorating.

Assets

Assets include the various items that the corporation owns, such as properties, machinery inventories, securities, accounts receivable, and cash. Generally, assets are classified as either current or fixed. Current assets are liquid assets, such as cash, marketable securities, accounts receivable, and inventories. Fixed, or noncurrent, assets are those that are used in the normal operation of the business over a period of years; such items include land, buildings, fixtures, and machinery. Typically, fixed assets are shown on the balance sheet at cost with a reduction over the period of time that the asset depreciates. Depreciation is a charge against current income based on the original cost of operating equipment or plant that wears out over time or becomes obsolete through technological improvements.

Liabilities

Liabilities consist of the debt currently owed, the money borrowed from bondholders and other creditors, and, in general, all claims against the company such as wages and salaries, accounts payable, and accrued taxes payable. Liabilities are further subdivided into current and long term. Current liabilities are payable within 1 year and include accounts payable to suppliers, notes payable to banks and other lenders, and taxes and wages owed as of the date of the balance sheet. Long-term liabilities are those that will not fall due within a year's time; they include mortgages, long-term notes payable, and bonds payable.

Stockholder's Net Worth

Any difference between the assets and liabilities is referred to as **net worth**, because it is that portion of value in the company to which owners have claim. Common-stockholders have a claim to all the net worth of the company when there is no preferred stock. When debts exceed assets, a negative net worth exists; that condition cannot be tolerated for very long. Exhibit 6-5 shows the 1981 balance sheet of International Business Machines Corporation.

Income Statement

Whereas the balance sheet presents the financial picture of the corporation at a specific time, the **income statement** furnishes a synopsis of the revenues and expenses during a given period of operations and includes a final calculation of the net profit or loss for the period. It is also called a profit-and-loss statement, because it measures the ability of the company to sustain an acceptable level of earnings. This information helps the investor to determine whether the company is a desirable investment prospect.

The net income for the period being measured increases the net worth of the company as reflected on the balance sheet. This increase may be only temporary, however, because there may be distributions in the form of dividends paid to the stockholders. Exhibit 6–6 presents the 1981 income statement of International Business Machines Corporation.

Financial Statement Relationships

Equipped with a basic understanding of financial statements, the investor can analyze the financial condition of a firm to determine its suitability as an investment. An important step in this analysis is the comparison of the relationships existing between various items of the financial statements.

Many of these relationships can be analyzed by the use of ratios. Although the ratio between two pertinent items on the financial statements is more significant than either item considered alone, the real importance of the ratio can be determined only by comparison with the corresponding ratio norm of the company's industry group. Comparisons within a company from year to year reveal the prevalent trend in the company's financial affairs. By the same token, a comparison with similar ratios for other companies in the same field indicates whether the corporation's progress is superior or inferior to that of its competitors. However, it is important not to limit the comparison to the particular industry, because all firms represented may be in financial difficulty.

Exhibit 6–5

International Business Machines Corporation and Subsidiary Companies		Consolidated Statement of Financial Position at December 31:	
		1981	**1980**
		(Dollars in millions)	
Assets			
Current Assets:	Cash	$ 454	$ 281
	Marketable securities, at lower of cost or market	1,575	1,831
	Notes and accounts receivable–trade, less allowance:		
	1981, $187; 1980, $195	4,382	4,562
	Other accounts receivable	410	315
	Inventories	2,805	2,293
	Prepaid expenses	677	643
		$ 10,303	$ 9,925
Rental Machines and Parts		17,241	15,352
	Less: Accumulated depreciation	7,651	6,969
		9,590	8,383
Plant and Other Property		12,895	11,018
	Less: Accumulated depreciation	5,207	4,384
		7,688	6,634
Deferred Charges and Other Assets		2,005	1,761
		$ 29,586	$ 26,703
Liabilities and Stockholders' Equity			
Current Liabilities:	Taxes	$ 2,412	$ 2,369
	Loans payable	773	591
	Accounts payable	872	721
	Compensation and benefits	1,556	1,404
	Deferred income	389	305
	Other accrued expenses and liabilities	1,318	1,136
		$ 7,320	$ 6,526
Deferred Investment Tax Credits		252	182
Reserves for Employees' Indemnities and Retirement Plans		1,184	1,443
Long-Term Debt		2,669	2,099
Stockholders' Equity:	Capital stock, par value $1.25 per share	4,389	3,992
	Shares authorized, 650,000,000		
	Issued: 1981–592,293,624; 1980–584,262,074		
	Retained earnings	13,772	12,491
		18,161	16,483
	Less: Treasury stock, at cost	—	30
	1980–455,242 shares		
		18,161	16,453
		$ 29,586	$ 26,703

Source: International Business Machines Corporation, *1981 Annual Report*, p. 24.

Exhibit 6–6

International Business Machines Corporation and Subsidiary Companies		Consolidated Statement of Earnings for the year ended December 31:		
		1981	1980	1979
		(Dollars in millions except per share amounts)		
Gross Income:	Sales............................	$ 12,901	$ 10,919	$ 9,473
	Rentals	10,839	10,869	10,069
	Services.........................	5,330	4,425	3,321
		$ 29,070	$ 26,213	$ 22,863
	Cost of sales.....................	5,321	4,197	3,267
	Cost of rentals...................	4,152	3,771	3,491
	Cost of services	2,543	2,181	1,655
	Selling, development and engineering, and general and administrative expenses.......	11,027	10,324	9,205
	Interest expense.................	407	273	141
		23,450	20,746	17,759
		5,620	5,467	5,104
	Other income, principally interest	368	430	449
	Earnings before income taxes	5,988	5,897	5,553
	Provision for U.S. Federal and non-U.S. income taxes..................	2,680	2,335	2,542
Net Earnings......................		$ 3,308	$ 3,562	$ 3,011
	Per share	$ 5.63	$ 6.10	$ 5.16

Average number of shares outstanding:
1981–587,803,373
1980–583,516,764
1979–583,373,269

Source: International Business Machines Corporation, *1981 Annual Report*, p. 22.

Table 6-1 lists selected financial ratios central to an understanding of a firm's financial condition. The ratios can be divided into five categories of analysis: (1) liquidity ratios, (2) profitability ratios, (3) return-on-investment ratios, (4) leverage and capital structure ratios, and (5) common-stock security ratios.

Liquidity Ratios

A **liquidity ratio** attempts to measure the ability of the firm to meet its short-term obligations by the conversion of current assets into cash in the relatively near future. Short-term creditors are especially interested in the firm's liquidity. Bondholders are also concerned about the firm's liquidity, because interest and principal payments depend upon the firm's ability to generate sufficient cash. The **turnover ratio** indicates management's ability to utilize short-term assets in generating revenues. The faster the turnover of inventory and receivables, the less capital the firm will have tied up in these assets and, therefore, the less likelihood there will be of a problem of bad inventory or receivables.

Profitability Ratios

The maintenance of adequate profit margins is necessary if a firm is to be able to service its debt obligations, pay dividends to stockholders, and reinvest sufficient earnings to sustain an acceptable rate of growth. **Profitability ratios** help to determine a firm's ability to control costs and keep the profit margins at acceptable levels. Profitability is the central issue for both bondholders and stockholders because the underlying quality of a firm's securities is dependent upon its earning power.

Return-on-Investment Ratios

Calculations of rate of return are important to investors because they are concerned with the company's ability to generate an acceptable level of earnings with the investment available. Management's ability to utilize the firm's assets in an efficient manner will be reflected in the **return-on-investment ratios.** Companies that can maintain good margins by controlling costs or that can maintain revenues while selling in large quantities can experience good rates of return on investment.

Leverage and Capital Structure Ratios

A firm's use of debt to improve earnings for common-stock holders is demonstrated by the **leverage and capital structure ratios.** These ratios indicate the company's dependence upon debt sources of financing and, therefore, the financial riskiness of the firm for both bondholders and stockholders. The firm's ability to cover its interest and sinking-fund obligations is a central concern to any bondholder, because it measures the extent to which fixed obligations are protected by the firm's earning power.

Common-Stock Security Ratios

Most of the **common-stock security ratios** listed in Table 6-1 help to determine the security of the common stock. Asset, income, and dividend security are measured by these ratios. The potential market risk of a common stock can be partially determined by the price-earnings ratio.

VALUATION OF COMMON STOCK

The investment value of a stock, also known as the stock's **intrinsic value,** is what the individual investor tries to determine as the real, or true, worth of a particular stock. This value is usually different from the current market price of the stock. Also, different investors, owing to different expectations and different required rates of return, will have different views as to what the intrinsic value of the stock really is. Nevertheless, the calculation of the intrinsic value of a particular stock plays an important role in the fundamental approach to common stock investment, because it serves as the **cutoff price** for investment decisions. If the calculated intrinsic value of a given stock exceeds its current market price, the investor should consider buying. Similarly, if the value is below the market price, the investor should not buy the stock at the current price, because he or she will not be able to realize the required rate of return.

Calculation of the Intrinsic Value of a Common Stock

The calculation of the intrinsic value of a common stock is similar to that of the price of a bond. It is based upon the essential concept of the present value (introduced in Chapter 2). In other words, the present value of a security is determined by the future cash flows the investor can expect to receive, discounted by the investors required rate of return. For a bond,

Table 6–1
Selected Financial Ratios

Ratio	Method of Computation	Interpretation
LIQUIDITY RATIOS		
Current ratio	$\dfrac{\text{Current assets}}{\text{Current liabilities}}$	Ability to meet current debts with current assets
Cash ratio	$\dfrac{\text{Cash + short-term securities}}{\text{Current liabilities}}$	Ability to meet current debts with cash on hand
Quick ratio (acid-test ratio)	$\dfrac{\text{Cash + short-term securities + receivables}}{\text{Current liabilities}}$	Ability to meet current debts with more liquid current assets
Total asset turnover	$\dfrac{\text{Net sales}}{\text{Total assets}}$	Ability of invested capital to produce gross revenue
Average collection period	$\dfrac{\text{Average receivables} \times 365 \text{ (or 360)}}{\text{Net credit sales}}$	Period required to collect average receivables
Inventory turnover	$\dfrac{\text{Cost of goods sold}}{\text{Average inventory}}$	Liquidity of inventory and tendency to overstock
Average day's inventory	$\dfrac{\text{Average inventory} \times 365 \text{ (or 360)}}{\text{Cost of goods sold}}$	Holding period of average inventory
PROFITABILITY RATIOS		
Gross profit margin	$\dfrac{\text{Net sales} - \text{cost of goods sold}}{\text{Net sales}}$	Gross profit per dollar of sales
Operating-income ratio	$\dfrac{\text{Net sales} - \text{cost of goods sold} - \text{selling and administrative expenses}}{\text{Net sales}}$	Operating profit before interest and taxes per dollar of sales
Operating ratio	$\dfrac{\text{Operating expenses (cost of goods sold} + \text{selling and administrative)}}{\text{Net sales}}$	Operating expenses per dollar of sales
Net profit margin	$\dfrac{\text{Net income}}{\text{Net sales}}$	Net income per dollar of sales
RETURN-ON-INVESTMENT RATIOS		
Rate of return on assets	$\dfrac{\text{Net income}}{\text{Total assets}}$	Net earning power of invested capital

Ratio	Formula	Significance
Earning power of total investment	$$\dfrac{\text{EBIT (earnings before interest and taxes)}}{\text{Total assets}}$$	Ability of invested capital to produce income for all investors (bondholders and stockholders), eliminates leverage effect from net-profit-to-total-assets ratio
Rate of return on equity	$$\dfrac{\text{Net income}}{\text{Total common equity}}$$	Net earning power of common capital
LEVERAGE AND CAPITAL STRUCTURE RATIOS		
Total-debt-to-equity ratio	$$\dfrac{\text{Current liabilities} + \text{long-term debt}}{\text{Total common equity}}$$	Total amount of debt leverage per dollar of common equity
Times-interest-earned ratio	$$\dfrac{\text{EBIT}}{\text{Long-term debt interest}}$$	Income security of long-term debt
Coverage of interest and sinking-fund payments	$$\dfrac{\text{EBIT} + \text{depreciation}}{\text{Interest} + \text{sinking fund}}$$	Coverage of interest and sinking-fund payments when depreciation exceeds sinking-fund payments
COMMON-STOCK SECURITY RATIOS		
Book value per share of common stock	$$\dfrac{\text{Total common equity}}{\text{Number of shares outstanding}}$$	Asset security of the common stock
Net tangible assets per share	$$\dfrac{\text{Total common equity} - \text{intangible assets}}{\text{Number of shares outstanding}}$$	Tangible asset security of the common stock
EPS ratio	$$\dfrac{\text{Net income available for common}}{\text{Number of shares outstanding}}$$	Earnings per share of common stock
DPS ratio	$$\dfrac{\text{Dividends paid on common stock}}{\text{Number of shares outstanding}}$$	Dividends per share of common stock
Payout ratio	$$\dfrac{\text{Dividends paid on common stock}}{\text{Net income available for common stock}}$$	Dividend security of the common stock and the dividend policy of the corporate management
Price-earnings ratio	$$\dfrac{\text{Market price of common stock}}{\text{Dollars earned per share of common stock}}$$	Price of common stock relative to earnings

the future cash flows are the periodic coupon interest receipts and the payment of the principal (or the selling price of the bond) at the end of the holding period. For the common stock, future cash flows include expected annual dividend payments and the expected future selling price at the end of the holding period. Therefore,

$$\text{intrinsic value} = \frac{D_1}{(1+i)^1} + \frac{D_2}{(1+i)^2} + \cdots + \frac{D_n}{(1+i)^n} + \frac{SP}{(1+i)^n}$$

$$= \sum_{t=1}^{n} \frac{D_t}{(1+i)^t} + \frac{SP}{(1+i)^n} \tag{1}$$

where: D = expected dividend paid in year t

i = investor's required rate of return

n = number of years in the holding period

SP = expected future selling price at the end of year n

In this equation, it is assumed that the investor's required rate of return remains constant throughout the entire holding period. Furthermore, for simplicity, it is assumed that the company's dividend payment grows at a constant rate, say g; then the preceding equation may be rewritten as follows:

$$\text{intrinsic value} = \frac{D_0(1+g)^1}{(1+i)^1} + \frac{D_0(1+g)^2}{(1+i)^2} + \cdots + \frac{D_0(1+g)^n}{(1+i)^n} + \frac{SP}{(1+i)^n}$$

$$= \sum_{t=1}^{n} D_0 \frac{(1+g)^t}{(1+i)^t} + \frac{SP}{(1+i)^n} \tag{2}$$

where D is the company's present annual dividend per share.

A special case of common-stock investment occurs when the investor does not plan to sell the stock at all. The stock, once purchased, would be held forever. In this case, there is no future selling price (SP), but the expected dividend payment would go to infinity.

$$\text{intrinsic value} = \sum_{t=1}^{\infty} D_0 \frac{(1+g)^t}{(1+i)^t}$$

$$= \frac{D_0(1+g)}{i-g} \tag{3}$$

This equation holds if g is constant and i is greater than g (i.e., the investor's required rate of return is greater than the expected growth rate of the dividend). If either of these two assumptions is not true, the third equation is no longer appropriate.

Having reviewed the basic concept and assumptions underlying the intrinsic value formulas, the value of each of the five variables needs to be determined (commonly, equation 2 is used as the representative formula). D, the dividend at the present time, can be known with certainty; n, the length of the holding period, can be determined by the investor's time requirements for funds. The required rate of return, i, or the discount rate, the growth rate, and the future selling price are difficult to estimate accurately. However, the investor must have some criteria to determine whether the current market price of the stock is justified. Therefore, a further analysis of these three factors follows.

Determining the Growth Rate

The growth rate of a company can be measured by using earnings, sales, or dividends. It is generally assumed by traditional security analysis that the growth of dividends is the true underlying determinant of the growth rate of any firm over time. Although there has been considerable criticism of the dividend growth rate being used as an important determinant of investment value, it is traditionally argued that the only measurable and significant return that an investor can receive over the long run is dividends. The position holds that, if a firm is truly growing, the dividend over time will also grow and the common-stock price will react accordingly. However, many firms do not pay dividends, and it is alleged that when a company is in its infancy stage it generally defies analysis because there are so many unknown factors.

Traditional security analysis holds that the investor will have a difficult time analyzing any security during its initial years of operations; it is only after the company has stabilized and entered a more sustained growth period that analysis can truly take place. Therefore, we shall use the dividend growth rate as a measure for determining the overall long-term growth of a firm. The dividend growth rate for a company's common stock is determined by the firm's rate of return on its total investment, coupled with its dividend payout policy. If we assume a constant rate of return on investment, the lower the payout ratio is (also assumed to be constant), the higher the dividend growth rate. The following formula can be used for determining a firm's dividend growth rate:

$$g = \text{ROI}(1 - \text{PO ratio})$$

where
g = dividend growth rate
ROI = rate of return on investment
PO ratio = dividends per share/earnings per share

For example, if company A realizes a rate of return on investment of 12 percent and it follows the policy of paying out 60 percent of its earnings as cash dividends, the growth rate is $g = 0.12(1 - 0.06) = 4.8$ percent. If company A's payout ratio was reduced to 30 percent, the initial dividend would be only one-half as much, but the growth rate would increase to 8.4 percent, assuming the company could utilize the additional 30 percent retained in the business and earn 12 percent on those funds [12% × (1 − 30%) = 8.4%].

Determining the Discount Rate

The discount rate used in calculating the present value of the stream of future dividends will vary with individual investors, because each has his or her own opinion of what is required in the way of a return on an investment. Although this factor is largely up to the individual investor's personal choice, there are some identifiable lower limits. Most large listed companies have at least one outstanding publicly held debt issue. Investors can calculate the present yield to maturity from the market quotation of that debt issue. There is no reason investors should expose themselves to the additional risk of common-stock ownership of that firm if they cannot achieve a higher after-tax rate of return than that of bondholders. A lower limit can also be established for many investors by the after-tax rate of return on money-market funds or insured savings accounts, which usually is higher than the riskless after-tax yield on Treasury bills. Generally, the riskier the investment and the longer the time horizon, the higher the selected discount rate should be. However, choosing a discount rate is a personal preference for each investor, and it is based on the risk level the investor is willing to assume. Many growth-oriented common-stock investors find themselves selecting a discount rate within the range of 12 to 16 percent.

Estimating the Future Selling Price

Estimating the future selling price of a common stock is by far the most difficult part in deriving the investment-value formula. It is difficult to forecast the future market price of a common stock with any degree of accuracy or confidence. Fortunately, even though estimating the future selling price becomes more difficult the longer the investment horizon, the price also becomes less meaningful, because its value is reduced by the larger discounting factor for many years into the future. In other words, proceeds from the sale of the common stock next year will have considerably higher present value than the sale of the same security for the same price 15 or 20 years into the future.

Assume that earnings will continue to grow at a constant historical rate for the next 10 to 15 years. Using that growth rate to project earnings at a given future date and assuming that a historical P/E ratio remains constant, a future projected price can be determined. This provides the investor with a rough estimate of the future price, which can then be discounted back to the present value and added to the discounted dividend cash flow. Because it will have been heavily discounted, any inaccuracy in the future selling price will have little effect.

The difficulty in this procedure is the accuracy of assuming that a firm's growth rate will indeed continue to increase at the historic rate and that the firm will command the same P/E ratio in the future. If the investor believes that the growth rate will either increase or decrease, an appropriate adjustment should be made in the price estimate. In spite of these difficulties, the investor has few other practical tools available to make an estimate of the future price.

Decision Criteria on Investment Value

After all the variables have been assigned values, the analyst should solve the investment-value formula. The investor should then check the market price to see its relationship with the calculated intrinsic value.

If the market price of the common stock falls within the range of the intrinsic value, the individual can conclude that the security is currently selling for exactly what its true worth is to the investor and that it might be a reasonable investment. If the present market price were greater than the computed investment value, the investor would determine that the stock is overpriced and, therefore, should not be purchased. In this case, if the investor already owned that stock, he or she would either sell it and reinvest the funds in a more desirable investment or place a stop order below the current market price, which would protect the investor from any reversal in the market-price trend.

On the other hand, if the market price is less than the investment value calculated, the investor would consider the stock a good candidate for purchasing. If the investor already owned the stock, then perhaps purchase of additional shares ought to be considered.

EVALUATING THE COMPANY

Many quantitative models and techniques have been of invaluable assistance to the analyst in the study of the broad aspects of the security industry. The difficulty with such analysis is that investors must depend upon mathematical calculations to help them decide whether to buy, sell, or hold. What makes investing an art instead of a science is the fact that so many variables determine the quality, growth, and earning power of a company that no single set of mathematically calculated valuation models can accurately project the future course of stock-market prices.

Many of the following topics, which are important in evaluating a company, are nonquantifiable. Before investors can consider investing in a company's common stock, they should make a careful study of the company so that their decisions will be the most informed possible. Each aspect must be analyzed, and the importance of each must be weighted before the investor can make a final decision on investment. The remainder of this chapter will describe the various aspects of a company that must be considered.

The Company's Capital Structure

One of the first items a potential investor should be concerned with in the study of a company's balance sheet is the condition of the capital structure. When investors evaluate the capital structure of a company, they are investigating the right-hand side of the balance sheet. The financial risk of a firm can be a serious problem for any company that fails to construct its debt and equity financing prudently.

The proportion of debt financing in the firm's financial structure can have an impact on the investment decision. A large debt-to-equity ratio indicates that the firm has relied heavily on the debt markets to finance its growth relative to the owners or reinvestment of earnings. A large debt relative to equity indicates that there are substantial fixed charges that the firm must be able to meet annually, which could threaten to undermine the financial condition of the firm during a prolonged business decline. It may also indicate that the firm has relied heavily on debt financing for future growth, and that any future capital that may be needed might be obtainable only in equity markets and perhaps at great expense.

Chapter 4 indicated the type of analysis that an investor can undertake to determine the degree of financial risk inherent in a firm. Nevertheless, some investors seek firms with high financial leverage because the growth in sales (and earnings) can exert positive leverage on common-stock performance. For example, many firms that are heavily leveraged experience a considerably more rapid increase in earnings than in sales growth. Because this increases the level of financial risk that the investors are assuming, they should be aware of the possible effects this may have on their common-stock holdings.

The investor must also consider the makeup of the firm's current debt structure. Traditionally, firms finance a large portion of their fixed assets from long-term debt and equity. If a firm alters this approach, it may present a problem in attempting to follow the concept of matching appropriate assets with their corresponding liabilities. If the firm is financing current assets out of long-term debt, it may be paying too much on the borrowed funds relative to their income-producing ability.

A larger problem exists if the firm is financing a large portion of fixed assets through current liabilities. This practice runs a substantial risk of generating a shortage of cash, and technical bankruptcy can result. For example, the current liabilities will have to be paid in the very near future, but the corresponding funds have been placed in fixed assets, which are not liquid. Because of these risks, it is best to invest only in firms that are balancing their assets and liabilities in a proper and orderly manner.

The Company's Short-Term Financial Position

The short-term financial position of a company determines its ability to pay bills on time to avoid a loss of goodwill between the firm and its suppliers and lenders. It also reflects the ability of the firm to take advantage of possible fortuitous conditions by maintaining a strong cash or working capital position.

A firm's working capital is its investment in current assets, such as cash, marketable securities, accounts receivable, and inventory. The firm's working capital position is important because the current-asset accounts will have to generate sufficient cash for the firm to retire its current liabilities and finance its day-to-day operations. Net working capital is a common measurement of the excess liquid assets available to the firm and is represented by the difference between current assets and current liabilities.

Many of the financial relationships were discussed previously in this chapter in terms of several key ratios that the investor can use in determining the financial position of a firm. Correct interpretation of these ratios is crucial in arriving at an informed investment decision.

The Company's Competitive Position

A most important aspect of a company that should be analyzed for long-term investors is the competitive position compared with other firms in the same industry. This analysis should combine a sales and financial approach to the company's position. It is of importance to be aware of the competitive makeup of the industry and to determine the degree of competitiveness or oligopolistic characteristics.

The investor can examine the market share of the company under review and compare this with its competitor's share to determine if the firm is in a leadership position within the market served or if it is just one of many strong competitors or producers. This competitive aspect is important, because market leaders generally can resist adverse economic and financial conditions better than secondary firms in an industry. The firm's ability to retain a competitive business advantage over smaller marginal producers can be of significant importance to the investor. Additionally, the investor should determine how the capital structure of the potential firm compares with that of its competitors. In some industries, particularly high technology, changes can occur quickly in product demand and a competitive, popular product today can be obsolete almost overnight. In such an industry, a firm's ability to raise funds quickly to finance the development of a new product can be important in retaining or improving its competitive position.

The Company's Operating Efficiency

There are literally thousands of types of companies in which investors can place their funds, and these firms make many thousands of different products, all in a somewhat different way. By analyzing the income statements of the prospective investment, the investor can determine a number of important things about the company. Among them are the company's operating efficiency and its potential for risk in terms of an adverse impact of a declining demand for its product.

Several of the ratios outlined previously are important for the investor in determining the company's operating efficiency. For example, the asset turnover ratios of a firm and its chief competitors will give the analyst some idea of how fully management is utilizing assets. If the ratio is lower for the company than its competitors, it may indicate the firm is not utilizing its assets to the fullest and has unused excess capacity.

Most of the ratio analysis that may be computed for a firm has its value in comparison with data for other firms in the industry and with some reasonable norms for prudent financial management. For example, an important comparative statistic for firms within the same industry is the gross profit margin on sales. If it is assumed that the product sold by competitors is basically the same and sells for the same price, then any difference in the gross profit margin will be a result of the firm's production efficiency. Certainly, the firm with the higher gross profit margin will have done a better job controlling the variable costs associated with the manufacture of the product. Therefore, that firm will be in a stronger position to absorb drops in the selling price of the product should they occur in the future.

The investor can also derive information about the general administrative expenses of the different firms from their income statements. Expressing these expenses as a percent of sales allows the investor to determine whether one of the firms within an industry is operating in a more efficient manner (provided, of course, that none of the firms is the beneficiary or the victim of special circumstances).

It is also possible to determine from the income statement whether a company is involved in a capital- or labor-intensive industry. Capital-intensive industries are far less able to adjust their expenses quickly than are labor-intensive firms because the majority of expenses are fixed in nature. Therefore, capital-intensive industries tend to be more susceptible to losses that result from fluctuations in the demand for their product.

Analysis of Management

Certain characteristics of a firm's upper-level management should concern investors during analysis. Because top management is responsible for the operating policies of the firm, it is most important for investors to be able to estimate how long present management and its policies will remain in control. In addition, the financial policy followed by the current management is important to the overall analysis. If the policy is conservative, it may indicate that financial leverage has been underutilized.

It is difficult to determine whether management is exceptional, but over the long run, management's decision-making capabilities will be demonstrated by the company's overall performance relative to its industry and economic conditions. The impact of management on the long-run performance of the company's common stock is most difficult to quantify. Nevertheless, well-qualified management can be one of the firm's most important assets.

Analysis of Growth Potential

If an investor is concentrating investments in industries and companies known for their ability to enjoy a long-run growth trend, a portion of the investment return will be dependent upon the ability of those firms and industries to continue to grow. It is important that the investor have some experience in determining the growth components of an investment.

If the firm is involved in a relatively new industry, it is possible that its product market has not yet been fully developed. As the market size increases, the firms within the industry should grow simply by retaining their share of the market. As long as the total market size is increasing, the firms within the industry should easily be able to continue to grow.

On the other hand, a firm may be part of an industry that has become saturated with competing firms, and no longer is there an increase in the overall market size. In that case, a firm will only be able to grow in its present industry if it is able to increase its share of the existing market. Any of the firms in such an industry may decide to attempt to increase their market share, but such growth can only come at the expense of other firms. This situation would lead to increased price competition among those firms best situated to participate in such action, which generally reduces the overall profitability of the industry. Therefore, if the market size exhibits no sign of future growth, it may be advisable for the investor to avoid investing in the smaller firms in such an industry and perhaps avoid investing in the industry altogether. Many analysts have pointed to the automotive industry as one that has difficulty in increasing the overall size of its unit sales, because the analysts believe that the relative saturation point has been achieved. Therefore, the only form of revenue growth that can occur in such an industry would be through increased price or for participating firms to increase their shares of the market.

Growth through Diversification

A firm can also conduct its future growth by diversifying. Diversification can take three courses: (1) expanding into related products, (2) expanding into fields unrelated to present product lines, or (3) enlarging a company's vertical integration by expanding into areas that supply the firm's present needs or into marketing its products directly to consumers. By moving into related fields, the company would remove the danger of being restricted to one area that might be adversely affected by the economy but would still be involved in its main area of expertise. This process would reduce but not eliminate the investor's risk, because fluctuations in the business cycle in one product line may also be felt in related industries.

If the company attempts to integrate in a vertical manner, it will find that it is still subject to the risk of declining product demand. However, it may be better able to survive any sales decline because it will have reduced the threat of being caught in a profit pinch between high prices from suppliers and the inability to sell sufficient amounts of its product. One part of the operation might be able to subsidize other parts in the integrated structure. For example, a steel mill may decide to engage in vertical integration by purchasing an ore mine through which it will directly own control of the natural resources.

A difficult type of growth for management is conglomerate diversification. Conglomerates are combinations of many unrelated businesses under one corporate umbrella. The risk in such a policy is that a firm may very well move into a field in which it has no expertise and face the danger of poor profit margins and loss. Many conglomerates have become unwieldy because there are so many unrelated companies that top-level management has difficulty controlling the total operation. However, if such a pattern of growth can be successfully handled, the firm can enjoy a considerable lessening of business risk, because the difficulties of one company will not necessarily affect other business divisions.

Analysis of Earnings

The foundation of any fundamental security analysis must revolve around the earning power of the company under review. The importance of earnings for the investor cannot be overemphasized. The entire concept of calculating

Figure 6-1 Corporate Profits (Seasonally Adjusted Annual Rates, Quarterly)

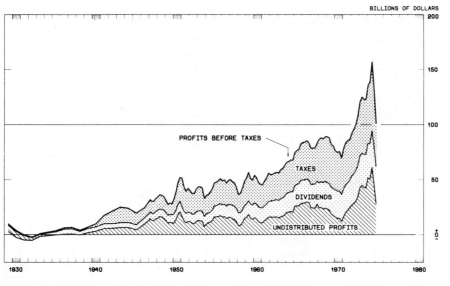

Source: Federal Reserve System, *Federal Reserve Chart Book, 1982.*

a security's investment value is built around an accurate projection of earnings and earnings per share. If there is no earnings growth, there can be no dividend growth. Figure 6-1 illustrates the correlation of dividends with earnings.

Earnings per share will normally be reported in two ways on a corporate income statement: primary and fully diluted. **Primary** earnings per share are computed by taking the net earnings available to common stockholders and dividing that sum by the average number of common shares outstanding during the year.

Fully diluted earnings per share are determined by adding to the amount available to common stockholders any dividends paid to holders of convertible preferred stock and the after-tax increase in earnings of any interest paid to holders of convertible bonds. This new sum is then divided by the average number of shares outstanding for the year, plus the number of shares the convertible securities could be exchanged for, plus the number of shares that could be issued on any unexercised warrants or options.

Table 6-2 is an example of the calculations for primary and fully diluted earnings per share. In this example, fully diluted earnings per share is important to the investor because it is less than the primary earnings per share and will generally be the resulting figure over the long run if the conversion aspect of the security issues is successful. If diluted earnings per share is greater than primary earnings per share, it can be effectively ignored

Table 6-2
Calculation of Earnings Per Share

ABC Company: Capital Structure
  $100 million of 7% debentures
  $100 million of 8% convertible debentures (1 bond = 8 shares)
  $50 million of 7% convertible preferred $100 par value
    (1 share = 8 common shares)
  $150 million of common stock, $50 par value
  $200 million of retained earnings

ABC Company: Income Statement (000 omitted)

Sales	$1,000,000
Cost of goods sold	650,000
General & administrative expenses	250,000
EBIT	$ 100,000
Interest expense	15,500
Taxes (48%)	40,560
Net income	$ 43,940

Primary EPS (000 omitted)

Net income	$ 43,940
less: Preferred dividends	3,500
Available to common	$ 40,400
No. of outstanding shares	3,000
EPS	$13.48

Diluted EPS (000 omitted)

Net income available to common	$ 40,000
plus: preferred dividends	3,500
plus: interest on convertible bonds	8,000
less: taxes on interest for convertible bonds	3,840
Revised earnings available to common	$ 48,100
Common shares outstanding	3,000
Common shares from conversion of bonds	800
Common shares from conversion of preferred stock	1,500
Total common shares outstanding assuming full conversion	5,300

Fully diluted EPS: $\dfrac{\$48,100}{5,300} = \$9.08$

because conversion can only improve the common-stockholder's position. However, it is not often that diluted earnings per share would be greater than primary earnings per share, and any analysis to determine the company's investment value should center on diluted earnings per share. This is important because the dividend-paying ability of a firm and management's decision to change the dividend payout may be affected by the difference between primary and diluted earnings per share.

Earnings per Share Growth

One item that should be examined by the investor is the growth trend in earnings per share and its determining factors. A constant rate of growth is a far more favorable sign of the firm's stability than a historically volatile earnings performance. Stable growth indicates a more controlled growth pattern for the products and will usually result in a higher price/earnings ratio for the common stock as a reward for the certainty of the earnings growth pattern and, therefore, the certainty of earnings forecasts and a dividend growth pattern.

If a firm's earnings growth rate has been increasing, it is generally indicative of the firm's successful participation in a growth industry. If this is the case for the common stock under review, investors should determine to the best of their ability how much longer they believe that the industry will continue its desirable growth before reaching the maturity stage. When and if the company and industry do mature, it is unlikely that the historical growth rate can be maintained. The sudden realization that the historical growth has decreased or ceased can cause a rapid reassessment of the stock's future value in the marketplace. The market price of the common stock can be expected to decline even though earnings may increase at the lowered rate in the future.

The investor should also be aware of the composition of the firm's earnings in the recent past. Extraordinary income and loss items on the income statement can completely change the appearance of the degree of success the firm has experienced. The investor must always filter out extraordinary items from the operating earnings in order to be able to determine the true earning capacity of the firm's normal operations. At times, some firms have attempted to offset a poor year by choosing to liquidate a successful past investment, thereby boosting reported earnings. Unfortunately, many individuals are concerned only with the total earnings for the company and do not recognize that a large portion may be the result of extraordinary gains.

Companies often decide to make a complete write-off of an unsuccessful project in one accounting period; that decision can result in extremely poor earnings and even a large loss. This often happens when a new management team takes over running a firm and does some housecleaning of its losing operations. Investors who do not recognize what management is attempting to do may quickly liquidate their common-stockholdings when they receive their earnings statements. The write-off of the asset may substantially improve the future earning performance of the company.

RCA Corporation's earnings dropped when they wrote off their losing computer operations in one accounting period. This was also true for the du Pont Corporation when they decided to discontinue the production of Corfam, which had lost money steadily for many years. Both companies' income statements for the periods in which the write-offs occurred were substantially below the previous period, but most investors were delighted with managements' decision. Future earnings had the potential for greater increases because the negative effects of those losing divisions had been eliminated.

The investor may also want to examine the effect of the firm's accounting methodology. Because so many firms follow so many different generally accepted methods of accounting, the investor should read the footnotes to the financial statements to determine which method the company is using. More sophisticated security analysts rewrite the financial statements to conform to their own opinions of what a prudent financial statement should contain. This is especially important if analysts are comparing several firms within an industry, because they must be sure that all statements are constructed on the same basis. Some of the most important differences are found in the methods used in the valuation of inventory and the depreciation of fixed assets.

The Company's Operating Leverage

The degree of operating leverage for a firm should be important to the potential investor in determining how vulnerable earnings are to price declines and reduced demand for the product. Firms in capital-intensive industries generally require a large level of sales to cover their fixed costs. Once this level of sales has been reached, large profits can be earned on each additional unit sold because there is very little variable expense. A firm in a capital-intensive industry is more subject to wider fluctuations in earnings than are labor-intensive firms when there is a change in the level of revenues.

A company in a labor-intensive industry can respond more quickly to changes in demand by decreasing its labor force. However, a firm in a capital-intensive industry cannot reduce the amount of fixed assets over the short run.

High fixed expenses in capital-intensive industries act as leverage and have a magnifying effect on that income owing to slight changes in sales. Figures 6-2 and 6-3 graphically illustrate the operating leverage effect for capital-intensive and labor-intensive firms. These illustrations show the positive effect on profit for each additional unit sold. Once the break-even point is reached, the capital-intensive firm has a larger percentage of profit increase than does the labor-intensive firm. However, the capital-intensive firm requires a higher level of revenues to reach its break-even point than does the labor-intensive firm.

Figure 6-2 Labor-Intensive Firm

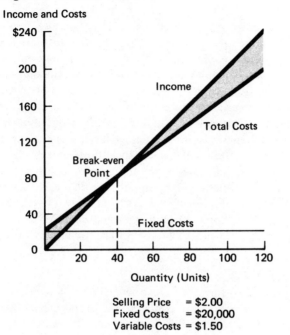

Income and Costs

Selling Price   = $2.00
Fixed Costs   = $20,000
Variable Costs = $1.50

Figure 6-3 Capital-Intensive Firm

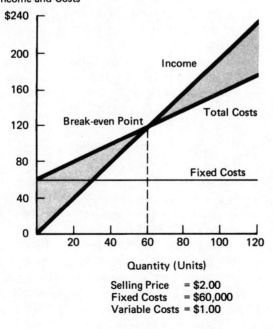

Income and Costs

Selling Price   = $2.00
Fixed Costs   = $60,000
Variable Costs = $1.00

The Company's Financial Leverage

Investors should be concerned with the extent to which financial leverage has accounted for the size of the firm's profit. If a substantial portion of the firm's income can be explained by leveraging on low-interest debt, the investors will want to know how long they can expect the benefit to continue. If a firm is earning 10 percent on total assets and has borrowed to purchase those assets at 6 percent, the future may not be favorable if the borrowed funds will soon be refinanced at a higher interest rate. Nevertheless, during the current period there is substantial positive leverage to the common stockholders, because they will also receive 10 percent on their investment funds, plus the excess earnings generated between the 6 percent cost of money and the corresponding 10 percent rate of return. As interest rates have increased over time, the advantages to a highly leveraged capital structure have diminished. Some firms experience negative financial leverage, where the rate of return on assets is less than the cost of borrowed funds.

Rate of Return on Investment

A firm's total rate of return on investment should be of central interest to any investor. Most investors are concerned with the rate of return on stockholder equity, which is generally higher than the rate of return on total assets if positive financial leverage exists. If a firm's rate of return on investment is low, it is entirely possible that the firm's problem is not a lack of efficiency but that it is operating in a mature, saturated industry. If the firm is unable to earn a reasonable rate of return, there is little reason for the investor to look to that firm's common stock as an investment. Nevertheless, many investors buy common stock of firms whose rate of return on assets and rate of return on equity are lower than 8 percent. It is easy to understand why these firms rarely show any desirable rate of long-term growth; under these circumstances, some investors would be better off in a savings institution.

Conclusion

Before investing, an investor who is concerned with analyzing a company must be aware of the importance of the interrelationship of many of the financial components of the decision-making process. Many of the topics discussed in this chapter can be studied in greater detail and are the subject of most security analysis textbooks. Investors who rely on surface financial information or who only look at the earnings-per-share growth rate may experience undesirable investment returns over the long run.

It is first of all important that investors have sufficient sources of accurate information for their analysis. As they approach the securities market, they should first analyze in detail the conditions of the economy and trend forecasts. Only if investors determine that the economic conditions are desirable should they proceed to select industries that they believe will be the strongest participants in an economic upswing. Then the investor should select from those industries the firms that are best able to take advantage of positive economic and industry trends. Finally, within those selected companies, investors should analyze securities that are most appropriate for their goals, and they should select from a firm's debt issues, preferred-stock issues, and common-stock issues.

KEY TERMS

annual report
assets
balance sheet
capital structure
common-stock security
  ratios
competitive position
cutoff price
debt structure
discount rate
diversification
earnings per share
extraordinary gains
financial leverage
financial position
financial ratios
financial services
financial statements
growth potential
growth rate

income statement
intrinsic value
investment counselor
investment value
leverage and capital
  structure ratios
liabilities
liquidity ratios
net worth
operating efficiency
operating leverage
profitability ratios
prospectus
rate of return on
  investment
return-on-investment
  ratios
10-K report
turnover ratio
write-offs

QUESTIONS

1. Why is financial data from financial institutions considered a better source than company reports?
2. Why is a company's prospectus important to an investor?
3. For what kind of information would banks be the best source?
4. What is a balance sheet?
5. What is the difference between current and fixed assets?
6. What is owners' net worth?
7. What is an income statement?
8. What is the importance of ratios?
9. What do liquidity ratios measure?
10. What do profitability ratios measure?
11. What is the importance of return-on-investment ratios?
12. What do leverage and capital structure ratios measure?
13. What do common stock security ratios measure?

14. Identify the two parts that make up the intrinsic value of a common stock.
15. What is the investment value formula for common stock? What is the objective of this formula, and what are its major problems?
16. Why are dividends used to compute a company's growth rate?
17. Explain two ways of determining the downside limit for a discount rate.
18. Why would an investor be concerned about a company's debt-to-equity ratio?
19. Why is a firm's competitive position important to an investor?
20. Identify ways to measure a firm's operating efficiency.
21. Explain the ways that a company can grow through diversification.
22. How are earnings per share reported on corporate income statements?
23. Explain the importance of stable earnings-per-share growth.
24. What should an investor look for when he is researching a company's earnings?
25. How does operating leverage influence a company's earnings?

SELECTED READINGS

BEAVER, WILLIAM, and DALE MORSE. "What Determines Price-Earnings Ratios?" *Financial Analysts Journal*, July–August 1978, 65–76.

BERNSTEIN, LEOPOLD A., and JOEL G. SIEGEL. "The Concept of Earnings Quality," *Financial Analysts Journal*, July–August 1979, 72–75.

COTTLE, MENNIS, and SCHUELKE. "Corporate Earnings—Long-Term," *Financial Analysts Journal*, July–August 1971, 22.

"The Death of Equities: How Inflation Is Destroying the Stock Market," *Business Week*, August 13, 1979, 54–59.

FISHER, L., and J. H. LORIE. "Rates of Return on Investments in Common Stocks," *Journal of Business*, January 1964, 1–24.

GRAHAM, BENJAMIN, D. L. DODD, and SYDNEY COTTLE. *Security Analysis*, 4th ed. New York: McGraw-Hill, 1960.

GRAHAM, BENJAMIN. *The Intelligent Investor*, 4th ed. New York: Harper & Row, 1972.

HAUGEN, ROBERT A. "Do Common Stock Quality Ratings Predict Risk?" *Financial Analysts Journal*, March–April 1979, 68–71.

MERRILL, LYNCH, PIERCE, FENNER & SMITH, INC. *How to Read a Financial Report*, 4th ed. New York: Merrill, Lynch, May 1979.

MURPHY, JOSEPH E., JR. "Some Effects of Leverage," *Financial Analysts Journal*, July–August 1968, 121.

TREYNOR, JACK L. "The Trouble with Earnings," *Financial Analysts Journal*, September–October 1972, 41–46.

7

Options and Futures

Up to this point we have covered investments in which the investor can participate directly. This chapter introduces options and futures, which are generally regarded as speculative investments and which have been of growing interest among the investing public.

Options are used in many different areas of business. Real estate options are probably the best known. In this case, a buyer is given an option to buy a particular property or building within a specified time at a predetermined price. The buyer pays a fee for the option privilege. The fee is usually considered part of the down payment if the option is exercised before its expiration date. Security options include option contracts, stock rights, stock warrants, and convertible securities. All security options have some similar qualifications: the options are purchased for a premium that entitles the buyer (or the holder of the option) to purchase or sell a certain amount of shares of stock (or in the case of futures, a certain amount of commodity) at a predetermined price within a specified time.

STOCK OPTIONS

Stock options are divided into two categories: (1) call options, which are options to buy stock, and (2) put options, which are options to sell stock. The investor should become familiar with the following terms used in the options market:

1. **Holder:** the buyer of an option
2. **Writer:** the seller of an option
3. **Premium:** the amount of money the holder pays the writer for the option
4. **Striking price:** the price at which the holder can exercise the option
5. **Expiration date:** the date at which the option expires
6. **Class:** options on the same stock
7. **Series:** options of the same class that have the same striking price and expiration date
8. **Straddles:** combinations of a call and a put on the same stock when striking prices are the same
9. **Spread:** combination of a call and a put on the same security when the striking price of the call is higher than that of the put (a spread can also refer to the situation in which an investor is the holder of a call on a certain stock and is also the writer of a call on the same stock but of a different series).
10. **One unit:** options are traded in units of 100 shares

An option buyer has the right or option to call (buy) or put (sell) a prescribed number of shares of given security at a specified price within a specified time. The life of an option varies, but the most common durations are 3, 6, and 9 months. The expiration date is usually the Saturday following the third Friday of that month. The standard option contract is written on 100 shares of stock.

If investors feel that the price of a stock will rise, they can buy a call, which will give them the right to buy the stock at the striking price before the expiration date of the option. When the price of the stock has risen, investors exercise their calls by buying 100 shares at the striking price. They can then resell the shares at a higher market price and realize a profit. If investors feel that the price of a stock will fall within the option period, they buy a put, which will give them the right to sell the stock at the striking price any time before the expiration date of the option. After the price has fallen, they buy 100 shares in the marketplace at the lower price and then sell them to the writer of the put at the specified higher striking price and realize a profit. If either of these two groups of investors had been wrong about the future price movement, they would not have exercised their option, but their losses would be limited to the price paid for the option.

Options are also attractive because they allow the investor to make a deferred purchase or sale of a security at a previously fixed price. Suppose that investors feel that a stock will rise quickly in a short time, but they do not have all the funds available at that time to purchase the security. By being able to buy a call on the stock, they are able to earn a profit if the stock does increase in price without having to pay the full price of the security at the earlier point in time.

Prior to the formation of the Chicago Board of Options Exchange (CBOE) in 1973, a purchaser or writer of an option had to deal with options brokerage firms that arranged option contracts generally tailor-made to each order. These option brokerage firms advertised heavily in the financial media in an attempt to attract potential purchasers and writers of options. Since the formation of the CBOE, the options business has expanded dramatically because the centralized marketplace has facilitated smoother operation and a considerably more liquid market. Throughout this discussion of the put and call option markets, we shall assume that there is no basic difference between purchasing an option and writing an option through an options brokerage firm or the brokerage firms that deal with central marketplaces such as the CBOE.

Options Brokers

To participate in an options market, the investor contacts a broker to buy or write an option on a certain stock. The investor specifies the series of the option, orders a call or put, and designates the premium he or she is willing to accept.

Price quotations are listed in the financial sections of newspapers. As an example, company XYZ has an option listed as follows:

	-JUL-		-OCT-		-JAN-		
	VOL	LAST	VOL	LAST	VOL	LAST	CLOSE
XYZ 80	13	$1\frac{1}{2}$	20	$2\frac{3}{4}$	a	a	$77\frac{5}{8}$

An investor who wishes to buy an option to purchase XYZ at a striking price of 80 and with an expiration date in October would have to pay a premium of $275 ($2\frac{3}{4} \times$ 100 shares).

The broker then arranges for a writer to write a contract either through the floor of the exchange or by contacting an options brokerage firm. If the brokers agree on the amount of the premium, a **matched trade** is made. The purchaser of the call options pays $275 for the option to buy 100 shares of XYZ at $80 per share. The writer of the call option receives $275 in cash as a fee for agreeing to write the call option. The $275 represents the price of the option; it is not a down payment on the stock if the holder decides to exercise the option.

To exercise the call option, the holder instructs the broker to contact the exchange's clearinghouse and to issue an exercise notice to a writer of the same class and series of options. The writer has a choice of either turning over the stock of the underlying issue or turning in a call option of the same class and series. The vast majority of options written are call options, although put options are growing in popularity as the option exchanges expand their operations to include these issues. Nevertheless, investors who wish to write or purchase put options can contact an options brokerage firm to handle the transaction.

The put option is the opposite of a call option. It allows the holder the privilege of selling 100 shares of a particular stock to the writer of the put option at a specified striking price. The holder of a put option hopes that the market price of the stock will go down so that he or she can buy 100 shares of the common stock and then put them (sell them) to the writer of the put option at the higher striking price. This allows the holder of the put option to participate in a declining market. The premium paid for the put option allows the writer to earn a return if the stock does not go down or to decrease the loss if the stock indeed moves down and the stock is eventually sold to the writer.

The Options Market

When an investor decides to purchase or write an option, they first study the listed option's quotation to see which options are available. The quotation gives the name of the stock, the striking price, number of options traded on the day reported, and the last asking price for the option for each closing date. The closing market price of the common stock is in the last column. Sometimes more than one separate option is available for one company's stock. In the XYZ option in the previous example, 20 options that expire at the end of October were traded at a price of $275 per option. Thirteen options that expire in July were traded at a closing price of $150 per option. There were no transactions for the January option. The last column shows that the common stock closed that day at $77 $\frac{5}{8}$ per share.

When an investor purchases a call option on the CBOE, one of three expiration months is chosen. When an investor buys or writes an option through an option brokerage house, the length of the option can be 30, 60, or 95 days, 6 months and 10 days, or 1 year.

The price of a premium is determined by the length of the option life, the price of the underlying common stock, the volatility of the common stock, and the size and nature of the market. The higher the price of the underlying common stock is and the longer the length of life for the option, the higher the price for the option. If an option has a high underlying common stock price relative to the striking price, the option costs more. The length of the option is important to the option price, because the longer the option, the more opportunity for gain because the underlying common stock may rise in value. The premium on an option for a highly volatile stock is higher than a premium for a more stable stock. If the stock market rises, premiums increase; if the stock market falls, premiums decrease.

The speculator's interest in purchasing options is the **leverage potential** that can be obtained and the limited dollar exposure to loss. For example, investors have a choice of either buying the stock of a company, as in the normal long position, or of buying options that they can either exercise at some future date before it expires or let expire if it is not to their advantage. To continue the XYZ example, for an October expiration, there were 20 options transacted at a price of $2\frac{3}{4}$ or $275 per option. If investors believe that the prospects for the common stock of XYZ are very good for a price rise between this transaction date and the third Friday in October, they have a choice of either going to their broker and purchasing 100 shares of XYZ at $77\frac{5}{8}$ per share, or $7,762.50, or purchasing an option for $275. The investors' cash outlay is considerably different in the two choices.

If the investor chooses to buy the option for $275, plus a normal commission of $25, the broker arranges the purchase and the investor owns an option that can be exercised any time before the third Friday in October. The striking price of $80 per share means that the investor who owns the option can purchase 100 shares of XYZ at $80 per share anytime he or she chooses up to the expiration date. If in the meantime XYZ common stock rises to a price of, say, $85 per share, the option holder can exercise the option to buy 100 shares at $80 per share. The option holder would want to exercise this privilege if the common stock were indeed at $85 per share. If the option holder exercised the option, 100 shares of XYZ would be bought for $8,000 from the option writer and instantly sold in the marketplace for $8,500 (100 shares times $85 per share). The profit on the transaction would be $500, less the price of the option and commissions, which would be approximately $300. Thus the investor would net $200 on the transaction for a gain of more than 66 percent. Meanwhile, the price of the common stock rose only approximately 10 percent.

The exposure for the option buyer is only the price of the option of $275 plus commission. If the price of XYZ, which was at $77\frac{5}{8}$, never moved higher than the exercise price of $80, the option buyer would not exercise the option and would lose the entire price of the option, or $275 plus the $25 commission.

Those who purchase options are interested in the leverage potential and the significantly lower risk exposure (illustrated in the preceding example). In the example of XYZ, the investor would need only $275 plus commission to buy an option, but would need $7,762.50 plus commission to buy 100 shares of XYZ outright.

The major drawback of options is that the option buyers are working against the clock because the underlying common stock must rise above $82\frac{3}{4}$ in order for them to break even. If the price of the stock does not go above $80 per share, option buyers do not exercise the options and they lose the price of the option. Therefore, many option purchasers wish to take a position in the longest available option, and in the case of the XYZ option with a striking price of $80, the longest available option is for the next January. Although the January option did not trade on this particular day, it would have carried a higher price than the October option owing to the longer time period.

Option Writer

Option prices are determined by supply and demand and by the acceptability of the premium to both the writer and buyer of the option. Every time an option is purchased there must be a writer to receive the premium. For example, in the case of the XYZ option with a striking price of $80, the purchaser of the option for $275, in essence, pays the writer a fee for the option. The writer of the option has earned $275, but he or she must stand ready and able to deliver 100 shares of XYZ if the purchaser calls the option away from the writer. Even if the 100 shares of XYZ are called away, the writer receives $8,000, has earned $275 less commissions, and has sold the stock at a higher market price than was available at the time the option was written ($77 $\frac{5}{8}$). The following illustrates the option writer's strategy in the XYZ example. If we assume that the option will not be called before the October expiration date, the writer will receive $405.00.

Option premium	$275.00
Commissions	− 25.00
Two quarterly dividends	+ 155.00
	$405.00

If the option is called before the expiration date, the writer will receive $642.50.

Cash received from option holder	$8,000.00
Cash received from premium and dividends less commissions	+ 405.00
	$8,405.00
Less cost of original shares of the option writer May 9 at 77 $\frac{5}{8}$ per share plus commissions	− 7,762.50
Net profit for option writer	$ 642.50

The option writer has earned $642.50 on the investment of $7,762.50, a 5-month profit of 8.3 percent or an annualized return of 20 percent. If the stock did not reach $80 per share, the writer would have received a total

of $405 and would have protected himself from a drop in the stock to
$73\frac{5}{8}$.

The strategy used by the option writer may be similar to that of the
buyer, but the writer's investment philosophy is very different. Option
writers are usually sophisticated investors, and they also have the capital
to cover the options they write.

When writers sell a call option on stock that they own, they are primarily interested in the premium income they will receive. They are not
especially concerned about a rise in the stock's price, even though their
stocks might be called and they would lose the profit potential that they
would have gained had they not sold an option. The writers are concerned
with the return on the stock. If the premium they receive on the option is
large enough to cover a drop in the price of the stock, they are satisfied.
By writing calls on their stock, they increase the return on the stock by the
amount of the premium. By writing puts on stock they wish to buy, they
can purchase the stock at a lower price because of the premium they receive
for the put. Thus, they are able to lower the effective purchase price.

Strategy for Option Investors

An option investor's basic objectives are to increase the return on investment
by using the leverage options provided or to protect a portion of the present
position of the underlying stock against a sudden market reversal by selling
a call option. There are many strategies and procedures that the investor
can use to obtain these objectives.

If investors believe that either the market or an individual stock will
rise, that is, if they are bullish on a stock, they may either buy the securities
outright or buy an option on the stock that they may exercise at some future
date. If they buy 100 shares of a particular stock and if, when the stock rises
they decide to sell, they receive a considerably less percentage gain on the
original investment than they would if they owned an option on the same
stock.

Hedging

Many investors use options as a form of hedging to protect their presently
owned stocks or options. If investors buy an option on XYZ at $80 and the
stock rises 15 points over a few months, they earn a paper profit of $1,500,
less the price of the option. Speculators may doubt that the stock can continue the rise as quickly, if at all, over the near term. If they were to sell
their option now, they would earn a rather large return but would forfeit
any future potential gain in the price of the option during its remaining life.
Instead of selling the call, they might buy a put on the stock of $95 for a
premium of say, $400, thus placing a floor on their profit level, which is the

difference between the striking price of the put and the striking price of the call, less the premiums of the put and call. In this case, if the call had a premium of $350 and if the premium of the put were $400, they would lock in a profit of $750, the difference between the price rise of $1,500 less the price of the put and call premiums. If the stock were to continue rising, the investor's profit would continue to grow and the put would never be exercised.

More conservative investors may use the hedge to protect a paper profit. For example, if they own 100 shares of stock that they purchased at $20 per share many months or years ago and the stock has risen to a price of $50 per share, they have a paper profit of $30 per share. Their total profit is $3,000. The investors believe that the stock has an opportunity for further appreciation, but they do not want to risk a market downturn should their prediction of a further price rise be incorrect. Therefore, they might purchase a put option for $300; in effect this amounts to an insurance policy. If the stock continues to rise from $50 per share to $60 or $70 per share, the investors continue to enjoy a further profit rise in the value of their stock. However, if the price of the common stock does indeed decline, the investors are protected by the option. As the market price falls from $50 down to $40 or $30 per share, they still make a profit on the put option and lose a similar amount on the value of their stock. Therefore, if the price declines, the investors have locked in their $3,000 profit, less the price of the put option of $300. If the price rises, they continue to fully participate in the additional profits, less the $300 put option premium, which, again, amounts to an insurance premium.

Some conservative investors buy a **straddle,** that is, they buy both a put and a call at the same striking price. The premium is higher than buying either a put or a call, but it is less expensive then buying a put and a call separately. Investors who buy a straddle are saying that they do not know which way the price of the stock (probably a volatile stock) will move, but they feel certain that the stock will experience a considerable move in the market. The disadvantage of their position is that they must experience a larger price move in the security before they reach their breakeven point. For example, the premium for a 6-month straddle at a market price of $50 might cost $600. This means that for the investor to profit the stock must rise above $56 per share or fall below $44 per share.

Covered and Naked Options

When writers write options on stocks they own, they are called **covered options;** such writers are primarily interested in increasing the rate of return on their own investments. When investors write options on stock they do not own, they are writing **naked options.** Their interest is in speculation. A naked-option writer writes calls in a declining market and writes puts in a rising market. The rate of return on a naked option will be potentially higher than that of a covered writer, because the naked-option writer can write options on margin and, hence, has considerably less capital tied up. The naked writer, however, faces substantially greater risk, as indicated by the following example.

If a naked writer writes a call on the October XYZ option price for $275 at a striking price of $80, the writer may be required to put up a margin of 50 percent, or $4,000 less the premium. If the stock rises above $80 per share and the option is called, the writer must go to the market and purchase 100 shares and deliver them to the holder of the call option for $8,000. If the stock never rises to $80, the writer has earned the $275 premium without tying up $8,000 in the ownership of stock. The high risk comes in when the stock moves up past $80 and the naked-option writer is forced to deliver called shares that he or she must buy at a price higher than the striking price. Many brokerage firms do not allow their customers to write naked options; they require that their customers be holders of the security before they are allowed to write either put or call options.

The Risk of Options

Very few of the options written are ever exercised. Because of market trends and the writers' skill in determining premiums, most options (approximately 70 percent) are not profitable enough to be exercised. Therefore, purchasing options can be very risky, and consistent profits are more likely to be made in writing options.

In addition, most options are not exercised because they are traded on a secondary market. When holders want to sell their options on the secondary market, they contact their brokers, who sell the options either through the clearinghouse of the exchange or through an options brokerage house. The option is purchased either by an investor who wishes to exercise the option or by a writer who is hedging his or her present position. An option holder may find it more profitable to sell the option outright than to exercise it and own the underlying common stock. It may be less expensive to sell the option, because the commission cost is higher for the execution of the common stock sale than it is for the sale of the option. A commission is generally charged for any option that is exercised.

In general, options are highly speculative investments, except perhaps when they are used as hedges. The CBOE has given great liquidity to the marketplace because the purchaser and seller of an option have the opportunity to close out their positions at any time by selling their position to other individuals entering the marketplace. It is not the intention here to cover all the intricate details of the options market. A potential investor is encouraged to write to the various options exchanges for information on current operating practices and to contact brokers who are options experts.

PREEMPTIVE STOCK RIGHTS

When a corporation determines that additional funds should be raised through the sale of common stock, it may offer its present stockholders the opportunity to purchase a proportional number of the new issue so that the stockholders can maintain their present percentage ownership of the company. This is called a **preemptive rights offering** and is required of companies whose charters dictate that they must issue rights.

As will be discussed extensively in Chapter 8, a company issuing securities in the primary market has a variety of ways in which to sell common stock if there is no preemptive rights requirement in the company's charter. The underwriting procedure is generally followed. Nevertheless, many companies issue rights that in essence represent an option to purchase common stock at a predetermined price. The company may offer stock rights because of an obligation to its present stockholders or because the company is closely held; that is, stockholders who own a substantial portion of the security want to be sure that they can maintain their present percent of ownership. Even if the new funds result in greater profits, which in turn increase the value of the market price of the stock over the long run, the individual stockholder's percentage of control would be reduced if he or she was unable or chose not to purchase a proportional share of the new issue.

For most firms the inflow of new funds from a common stock issue generally does not result in an immediate increase in profit. In the short run, some dilution in earnings per share may occur. Therefore, many companies that issue new shares of common stock compensate for this risk by establishing an exercise price for rights that is slightly lower than the current market price. This compensates shareholders for immediate dilution in earnings per share, but, more importantly, it represents a greater inducement to exercise these rights.

The recipient of rights has three choices: exercise the rights, sell the rights, or let the rights expire. Investors can exercise the rights by mailing the rights and the appropriate amount of cash per share to the company. The company then sends them shares of common stock. Or investors can sell the rights in the open market to another individual who will either exercise them or speculate on a price rise before expiration date. Because most rights are active for the few weeks they are on the market, it gives investors an opportunity to dispose of the rights if they do not want to exercise them. Or investors can let the rights expire, but this is generally an irrational choice because many of the rights that are allowed to expire have some value. The rational investor at least attempts to recover some funds by selling the rights in the open marketplace.

Stock rights are similar to options because they entitle the holder to buy stock at a certain price for a certain length of time. The life of most rights is very short (usually a few weeks) because the issuing company fears that a downward price movement of its common stock would not only make the rights worthless, but it would also jeopardize the sale of its new issue.

There are three important dates in the life of a stock right: the announcement date, the date of record, and the expiration date. On the **announcement date,** the board of directors declares the new offering, the amount of rights needed to purchase one share of new stock at the subscription price, and the value of the subscription price. On the **date of record,** the company closes its books and determines the owners of the old shares. Each owner of record is sent one right for each share of stock owned at the date of record. On the **expiration date,** all rights that have not been exercised expire and become worthless.

Between the announcement date and the date of record the common stock includes the value of the rights and trades **rights-on** (rights belong to the stock purchaser). After the date of record, the rights are mailed to the owners; therefore, the stock and the rights trade separately, the stock being traded **ex-rights** (stock purchased after the record date is not entitled to rights).

Value of Rights

Because a stock has a right attached to it when it trades rights-on, the price of the stock has two components: (1) the value that the market perceives the stock to be worth, and the (2) value of the attached right. The theoretical value of a right is given by the formula:

$$V = \frac{M - S}{N + 1}$$

where: V = value of one right
           M = price of the stock before the date of record
           S = subscription price
           N = number of rights needed to purchase one new share

For example, the XYZ corporation announced that it was issuing 500,000 new shares of common stock and that it was offering its present shareholders, who collectively owned 5 million shares, the opportunity to buy one new share at the subscription price of $40 for each 10 shares they owned before the date of record. If the stock is currently selling at $45 a share, the theoretical value of one right trading rights-on would be $V = (45 - 40) \div (10 + 1) = .45$. This means that the value of the stock itself would be lowered to $44.55 when the stock trades ex-rights, which is after the date of record.

When the date of record passes, the stock and rights trade separately and the value of the right is derived differently. The formula for the value of rights for stock trading ex-rights would be

$$V = \frac{M' - S}{N}$$

where M' is the price of the stock after the record date. The value of the XYZ rights would still be ($44.55 - $40) ÷ 10 = $.45.

Since the values of S and N are fixed, the theoretical value of the right depends upon the price of the stock. In reality, for a number of reasons rights often trade at values different from their theoretical value. The use of leverage in the investing of rights can increase the value of the rights substantially above its theoretical value. For instance, if the common stock of XYZ were to rise an additional 10 percent during the ex-rights period, from $44.55 to $49.00, the value of the right would increase by 100 percent to $.90 per right. In some circumstances rights can be bought on margin for as little as 25 percent; this increases the rate of return fourfold. The value of a right, being influenced by the price of the stock, will increase or decrease, depending upon the movements of the stock market.

A right is considered a short-term investment, and any gains or losses are short-term in nature. Investors who place funds in rights that appear worthless use them for short-term losses if the price of the common stock never rises above the exercise price of the rights.

As previously mentioned, rights generally trade substantially above their theoretical value because of the significant leverage potential. As the expiration date approaches, the premium of the right over its theoretical value diminishes, and the right trades continually closer to its theoretical value. Because of the leverage potential, speculators often deal exclusively with rights. It is a method of participating in the movement of common stock without tying up large sums of capital.

STOCK PURCHASE WARRANTS

Stock purchase warrants, known as warrants, are long-term call options on common stock that allow the holder to buy a certain number of shares of stock for a designated price. Warrants vary from one another in terms of length, detachability, and exercise price. Warrants are much like rights, but they have a considerably longer lifetime (years instead of weeks). Most warrants originate from the sale of corporate bonds and preferred stock. Warrants are most frequently attached to bonds, are sold as units at the original offering date, are used to attract buyers to the bond, and also have a lowering effect on the coupon rate of the bond. Several months after the bonds are issued, the warrants are detached and traded separately on their own merits.

Some warrants have no expiration date and, therefore, are perpetual because the terms exist until all warrants are exercised at the holder's option at some future date. Although almost all perpetual warrants are detachable and are traded separately, some warrants are not detachable and can only be exercised by trading the security to which they are attached.

A corporation issues warrants to induce investors to buy securities that they would not ordinarily accept because the returns are too low and because there is too much risk involved. In addition, corporations want the warrants to be exercised in the future because they enable them to raise equity capital. Warrants are not only speculative in nature, but they are also generally associated with speculative companies. Until 1970, warrants were not traded on the New York Stock Exchange, but they were traded on the over-the-counter market or the other regional or national exchanges, such as the American Stock Exchange. In 1970, however, when American Telephone and Telegraph issued warrants attached to a series of debentures, the New York Stock Exchange allowed the AT&T warrants to be listed for trading. This was a significant departure for the New York Stock Exchange and gave higher credibility to companies issuing warrants.

Value of Warrants

When a company issues warrants, it chooses an exercise price that is generally above the current market price because the company wants conversion to take place in the future at a higher market price than at the date of issue. If the new funds received from the sale of the units are invested wisely, the company should increase its future earnings. Since warrants will not be exercised when the stock is selling below the exercise price, the company is protected from premature earnings dilution.

The theoretical value of a warrant after the ex date can be expressed as

$$V_w = \frac{P_m - P_e}{N}; \text{ provided } P_e < P_m$$

where: V_w = warrant's value

P_m = current market price of common stock

P_e = price at which the warrant can be exercised

N = number of warrants needed to purchase one share

For example, if the stock of XYZ Company were currently selling in the marketplace for $20 a share, and if each warrant allowed the purchase of one share of common stock at $15 per share, the theoretical value of the

XYZ Company warrants would be $5 per warrant. If the common stock were selling below the exercise price of $15, the theoretical value of the warrant would be zero. In reality, warrants take on a value different from that predicted by the theoretical valuation model. The price of a warrant is determined by the price of the common stock in relation to the exercise price, the length of the life remaining for the warrant, and the leverage effect of buying warrants. Because the value of a warrant is so closely related to the price of the stocks, warrants affect the way the market judges the stock price. Investors know that the warrants' existence represents potential dilution. In essence, the price of the warrant is determined by the investor's expectation of how the price of the common stock will perform in the future. Therefore, if a warrant has a significant time remaining in its life, it will generally trade substantially above its theoretical value.

Leverage and Hedge Potential

The leverage potential of warrants is similar to the leverage potential of call options and stock rights because the value of a warrant will increase in almost the same dollar amounts as an increase in the underlying stock. Because of this leverage effect, the value of a warrant may be different from its theoretical value. For example, Greyhound Corporation issued warrants of 1.2 million shares, with each warrant entitling the holder to purchase one share of common stock for $30. The warrants expire on May 15, 1984. During 1982, the stock was selling at approximately $17 per share. According to the theoretical value, the warrant should be worth zero. However, the warrants traded for approximately $1.50 each. Investors are willing to pay $1.50 for a valueless warrant because it entitles them to buy the common stock at $30 at any time through May 15, 1984. Therefore, investors are expecting the price of Greyhound common stock to rise above the exercise price of $30 and, further, above $31.50 their break-even point. Speculators are willing to buy valueless warrants because, as the stock rises, the value of the warrants rises and the opportunity for substantial gains is inherent in the value of the warrant; they may also purchase the warrants for hedging purposes.

Most investors purchase warrants as a speculation, use the warrants as a hedge, or use them for insurance when they have sold a stock short and want some upside protection if the stock rises in price. If the investors are speculating, they probably have no intention of exercising the warrant; they would rather sell at a later date to another individual who may exercise the warrant.

Investors who purchase warrants for hedging purposes and have also sold the underlying common stock short expect the value of the stock to decline. They hedge their positions by purchasing the warrant if the stock increases. Not only do the warrants provide them with a ceiling on the amount they will have to pay to replace the borrowed stock, but they also provide them with a potential for profit should the value of the warrants appreciate faster than the price of the stock.

Generally, there is little difference between a warrant and a stock right except the length of life. Most speculators would rather deal with warrants because of their considerably longer life. Few purchasers of warrants would be considered investors.

CONVERTIBLE BONDS

Chapter 3 outlined the characteristics of convertible bonds and some of their advantages and disadvantages to investors. Convertible bonds are a form of option on common stock because the holders of the convertible bond can usually convert it into common stock at their option. The convertible bond entitles the holder to convert the bond into a specific number of shares of the issuing company's common stock. Much of the discussion on convertible bonds is also true of convertible preferred stock, which can also be converted at the option of the holder into a fixed number of shares of common stock. The discussion which follows is limited to convertible bonds.

A company usually issues convertible bonds for one of four reasons: (1) when the market for a common stock issue is poor, (2) when interest rates are high for corresponding straight bonds, (3) when one firm purchases another company and offers convertible bonds in trade for the acquired company's common stock, and (4) as delayed equity financing. Because of a bond's convertibility, a firm generally pays less interest on a convertible bond than it does on a regular straight bond of the same grade and maturity date. The company probably realizes more from floating a convertible bond issue than it does from issuing common stock directly, because investors consider the bond less risky than the stock and its convertible nature makes it easier to sell. Convertible bonds are used in mergers because they can be exchanged tax-free for common stock at the time of the merger.

Price Behavior of Convertible Bonds

A convertible bond has two separate bases of value: bond investment value and bond conversion value. The **bond investment value** results from the inherent value of the bond as a debt instrument and is entirely separate from its conversion characteristics. The **bond conversion value** results from the value of the common stock into which the bond may be converted at the holder's option. The actual price of a bond in the marketplace is higher than either of these basic values, because investors are normally willing to pay something extra for the chance, even if remote, that conversion will ultimately prove profitable. A convertible bond sells above its conversion value because, if there is a decline in the market price of the stock, the price of the bond will not decline lower than its straight bond investment value. Therefore, it offers the investor a downside protection that the owner of the common stock would not enjoy. This limits (but does not eliminate) the loss that would result from a drop in a stock's price. The size of the premium over investment value and over conversion value depends upon the investor's evaluation of the conversion privilege and the underlying common stock.

The relationship of market price to bond investment and bond conversion values is explained graphically in Figure 7-1. The horizontal axis indicates common stock prices and the vertical axis indicates the price of the bond. Suppose that a bond has a 10-year maturity remaining and is now callable at 105, that it has a coupon of 5 percent and a conversion price of $50 per share, which is equivalent to 20 shares for one bond (1000/50 = 20), and that equivalent straight-debt issues currently yield 6 percent. The investment value of the bond is approximated by the following formula (explained in Chapter 4):

$$.06 = \frac{50 + [(1000 - X)/10]}{(1000 + X)/2}$$

$$X = 923$$

The bond would not sell below its investment value of $923 unless the yield on equivalent straight-debt issues increased or the risk of the issuer in-

Figure 7-1 Theoretical Price Behavior of a Convertible Security

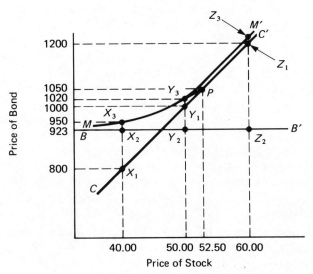

creased. The bond value floor is given as line BB' in Figure 7-1. If we assume that the price of the common stock is $40 per share, the conversion value of the bond would be $800 (20 × 40). This is given as point X_1 on line CC'. This does not mean that the market price of the bond is $800; it means that the conversion value is lower than the price of a straight bond, as indicated by point X_2. Furthermore, if the market wishes to pay a premium for the option value of the bond, it may sell at an even higher price than the $923 floor price, such as $950, which is indicated by the point X_3 on the actual price line of the convertible bond MM'.

If the common stock price were to rise to $50 per share, the investment value would not change unless the increase in the price of the stock was a result of reducing the riskiness of the firm or lowering all market rates of interest. In either case, the yield on equivalent straight-bond issues would fall, and the investment value of the bond would rise. If we assume, however, that these variables are held constant and that the difference in the stock price is caused by other reasons, such as favorable earnings in the future, the price of the bond would be worth $1,000, indicated by point Y_1 in Figure 7-1. The investment value of the bond would still be $923 (point Y_2); however, if the bond were to continue carrying a premium, the bond may sell for $1,020, indicated by point Y_3 on market value line MM'.

If the price of the common stock continued to rise to, say, $60 per share, the investment value would remain at $923 (point Z_2), all other things remaining the same. The conversion value would become $1,200 (20 × 60), indicated by point Z_1; this would be the theoretical market price of the issue. Note that the market price of the bond may still carry a premium and, therefore, trade at point Z_3. Many convertible issues, however, no longer carry a premium beyond point P because the issue is in the callable range beyond the price of $1,050. Hence, at point P the market price line MM' may join the conversion value line CPC'. When the market price of the common stock advances to $52.50, the conversion value of the bond should exactly equal the call price. Market bond prices could be justified above this price only if the market price of the common stock also advanced. Any premium over conversion value would be the expectation by the bondholder of higher prices and a more desirable yield than possible on the underlying common stock. Also, the bond would not be in the callable period.

Figure 7-1 shows the theoretical price behavior of a convertible security. It in no way represents the actual movement of a convertible bond. The investment value of a bond does not remain constant over its life. Changing interest rates in the marketplace cause the investment value of all classes of bonds to rise and fall in an inverse relationship. Nevertheless, Figure 7-1 does indicate the dynamics and relationship of a convertible bond to its underlying investment value and any changes in the price of the common stock.

Converting or Selling Convertible Securities

One reason for converting a security into common stock is that a convertible selling substantially above its call price may be called by the issuer at its predetermined call price. The holder may either convert to common stock or accept a cash payment at the call price or sell the bond to another investor who will exercise the option.

A second reason for converting a security into common stock is that a bond may rise in price because the market price of the underlying stock may advance to a point where its current yield is substantially below that of the common stock. At a certain level the bond's yield becomes undesirable and the ownership of the common becomes more desirable. This generally occurs when the price of the convertible bond sells substantially over par. Many who invest in convertible bonds instead of common stock choose to sell the bonds and reinvest the funds in other desirable convertible bond issues.

Conservative investors buy convertible bonds when interest rates are at a cyclical high, which dictates that bonds will have dropped in market price, and when common stock prices are at a cyclical low. This generally enables investors to establish a position at prices significantly below the par value of $1,000. The current yield on such bonds tends to be significantly higher than the yield for the corresponding common stock. Investors can then calculate the yield to maturity, which will be a combination of the annual interest received and the average price appreciation per year of the security to par.

Short of bankruptcy proceedings, the worst that could possibly happen would be that the bondholder would receive the current interest payments and a small appreciation per year to maturity. If the underlying common advances before the maturity date, the price behavior of the bond is much like that shown in Figure 7-1. However, if the common stock does poorly between the purchase date of the convertible bond and the maturity date, the investor is at least assured of a reasonable rate of return that would be far in excess of the return generally experienced by the underlying common stock.

Another desirable feature of convertible bonds is the limited risk on the downside if the common stock falls and interest rates rise. The investment value of the bond places a floor under the bond's price. At the bond's maturity the investor receives the face value of the bond, usually $1,000. In addition, the investor generally pays substantially lower brokerage commission on bond transactions than on an equivalent amount of common stock. However, the convertible bondholder does not usually experience the full impact of a rising market.

An investor must keep in mind that although a bond issue does have a lower limit, the downside risk can be substantial if the price of the underlying common stock plummets. The reason that a firm's common stock declines sharply in price is that the firm's financial situation has generally deteriorated and its earning capacity may be questionable. This increased riskiness would certainly raise the rate that a firm would have to pay on a straight-debt issue. Therefore, the investment value of all the firm's bonds will decrease, and the investment value floor will be lowered accordingly. As has been noted before, an increase in the general level of interest rates produces the same effect. In addition, a price deterioration in the common stock may dampen an investor's enthusiasm about the future. This will manifest itself in the form of a lower premium above conversion value. For example, as the price of a stock falls, the normal premium price of the convertible bond could be reduced. The price of the bond could decline faster than the price of the underlying common stock to a point where it will trade at its investment value. Nevertheless, unless investors are dealing with risky companies, convertible bonds offer conservative investors a stated rate of return on their investments. Convertible bonds can help meet stated goals and can increase the value of an investor's capital investment through price appreciation of the convertible bond purchased at a discount from par value.

THE FUTURES MARKET

The futures market is one of the fastest growing markets. For example, in the last decade, the dollar value traded in futures has increased tenfold. Probably in no other investment market can more money be made or lost more quickly than in the futures market. Futures are more speculative than stock options because they can be purchased on less margin, are considerably more volatile, and many are based on perishable commodities that are affected by uncontrollable events. The speculator promises to take or make delivery of a commodity at a predetermined price on a given future date.

Markets in which future crops are given a prearranged price are not new; they existed in China, Egypt, Arabia, and India thousands of years ago. The first commodity exchange in the United States was the Chicago Board of Trade, which opened in 1848. In the beginning, the exchange dealt only in cash exchanges and forward contracts (forward contracts only specify the quantity of the commodity and date of delivery). In the 1860s, the exchange began trading in futures contracts similar to those of today. Participants in the futures market are either hedgers or speculators. The commodity markets have none of the characteristics found in the investment markets.

Hedgers

Hedgers are growers, processors, warehousers, marketers of agricultural products, miners, smelters, dealers, large users of precious metals, numismatists, coin dealers, and individuals and firms engaged in international trade. They use the futures market principally to guarantee or protect the prices at which they buy or sell listed commodities for cash some weeks or months in the future.

The hedger frequently finds that the futures market also serves as a helpful financial management tool for stabilizing income, freeing working capital, reducing procurement costs, complementing other marketing plans, reducing inventory costs, insuring contract obligations, expanding bank borrowing ability, and providing for flexibility in the timing of purchase and sale. When a producer, processor, warehouser, and marketer can plan ahead successfully, products may be available at more stable and reasonable prices throughout the year.

Speculators

Speculators (the general public and professional traders) do not grow, process, or handle a product. Speculators use their risk capital to try to take advantage of price fluctuations in the futures market. They buy and sell futures contracts in an attempt to make profits, but the level of risk is exceptionally high. Speculators should only use money which, if lost, would not materially affect their ways of life or deny them the necessities or comforts of their normal lives. Most commodity firms will not open an account for a speculator unless his or her net worth is sufficient to absorb substantial losses.

Hedgers and speculators need each other. The speculator assumes the hedger's risk by (in most cases) taking the opposite side of the hedger's contract. If there were hedgers but no speculators, there would be little liquidity, entry and egress from the market would be difficult and costly, and there would probably be large price gaps between transactions.

Leverage of Futures

The reason futures markets offer the speculator great profit potential, with commensurate risk, is leverage: the ability to control large amounts of value with relatively little cash. When a trader establishes a position in futures, he or she is required to advance sufficient cash to guarantee fulfillment of the contract. This is not a part payment for the commodity, and it is not the amount related to the value of the commodity. Instead, it is margin, which represents security to cover any initial loss that may result from adverse price movements. The dollar amount of the margin is determined by market risk, which reflects price volatility.

Commodity exchanges establish the minimum initial deposit for each commodity and the maintenance deposit. When a loss on a particular market position has used up as much of the original security deposit as the maintenance schedule permits, the trader must bring his or her account back to the original level by depositing additional maintenance funds. (Some brokerage houses have higher initial and maintenance margin requirements than the commodity exchanges do.)

For example, if the original margin required is $1,500 and the maintenance margin is $1,000, a price move in excess of $500 against the trader will require a deposit of sufficient cash to bring the margin back to $1,500. If the trader does not respond sufficiently to the margin call, the broker would have the right to liquidate the contract. Conversely, any gain resulting from a favorable price move can be paid to the trader as it accrues. The trader does not have to wait until the position is liquidated.

Order Execution Process

A speculator who wants to buy or sell futures can go to a broker who specializes in the futures market and has a membership on one of the commodity exchanges. The commodity broker is engaged to transact business on the speculator's behalf. A commodities transaction is similar to buying and selling securities. The broker contacts the futures exchange's clearinghouse; the clearinghouse then matches buy offers with sell offers. When the transaction is completed, however, the clearinghouse then becomes the opposite of the buyer or the seller. That is, the buyer of the futures is buying from the clearinghouse, not from the seller, and the seller of the futures is selling to the clearinghouse, not to the buyer-speculator.

Commodity Quotations

Future contracts are sold on 50 different commodities on 11 different exchanges. Exhibit 7-1 is a partial listing of future prices in the more actively traded commodities as reported in the financial section of newspapers. In each section is the name of the commodity, the exchange the commodity is traded on, the unit the commodity is traded in, and the price per unit. For example, in the grains and feeds section are the commodities listed which trade on the Chicago Board of Trade (CBT); are sold in units of 5,000 bushels; and sell in cents per bushel. Below the commodity names are listed the months in which commodities are to be delivered and the prices. Wheat futures are delivered in March, May, July, September, and December. Also shown are the season's high and low prices per bushel and the price change

Exhibit 7-1

Futures Prices

Friday, June 25, 1982

Open Interest Reflects Previous Trading Day.

	Open	High	Low	Settle	Change	Lifetime High	Low	Open Interest

—GRAINS AND OILSEEDS—

CORN (CBT)—5,000 bu.; cents per bu.

OATS (CBT)—5,000 bu.; cents per bu.

SOYBEANS (CBT)—5,000 bu.; cents per bu.

SOYBEAN MEAL (CBT)—100 tons; $ per ton.

SOYBEAN OIL (CBT)—60,000 lbs.; cents per lb.

WHEAT (CBT)—5,000 bu.; cents per bu.

WHEAT (KC)—5,000 bu.; cents per bu.

WHEAT (MPLS)—5,000 bu.; cents per bu.

—WOOD—

LUMBER (CME)—130,000 bd. ft.; $ per 1,000 bd. ft.

PLYWOOD (CBT)—76,032 sq. ft.; $ per 1000 sq. ft.

—FINANCIAL—

BRITISH POUND (IMM)—25,000 pounds; $ per pound

CANADIAN DOLLAR (IMM)—100,000 dlrs.; $ per Cans

JAPANESE YEN (IMM)—12.5 million yen; $ per yen(.00)

SWISS FRANC (IMM)—125,000 francs-$ per franc

W. GERMAN MARK (IMM)—125,000 marks; $ per mark

EURODOLLAR (IMM)—$1 million; pts. of 100%

GNMA 8% (CBT)—$100,000 prncpal; pts., 32nds of 100%

—COFFEE (CSCE)**—37,500 lbs.; cents per lb.

COTTON (CTN)—50,000 lbs.; cents per lb.

ORANGE JUICE (CTN)—15,000 lbs.; cents per lb.

POTATOES (NYM)—50,000 lbs.; cents per lb.

SUGAR—WORLD (CSCE)—112,000 lbs.; cents per lb.

—METALS AND PETROLEUM—

Source: Reprinted with permission of The Wall Street Journal, © Dow Jones & Company, Inc. (1982). All right reserved.

from the previous day (recorded in cents). Fractional cents are important because of the quantity of the commodity being exchanged and the small margin required.

Regulation of Commodity Exchanges

The futures exchanges (and their clearinghouses) are regulated by the Commodity Exchange Authority, which is a division of the Department of Agriculture. The role of the Commodity Exchange Authority in regulating futures is similar to the role of the Securities Exchange Commission. The Commodity Exchange Authority determines the quality of the commodities and the trading procedures followed by the exchanges. It is also responsible for enforcing uniform standards for the commodities and the trading procedures. The Commodity Exchange Authority determines the hours of trading, the amount the price of the commodity can fluctuate within one trading day, the minimum margin requirements for a commodity, and the highest amount in which a commodity trader can establish a position. In short, the Commodity Exchange Authority is responsible for maintaining the integrity of the futures market.

Strategy in Trading Commodities

The hedger's basic goal is either to ensure the future price of a product or to predetermine the cost of goods needed to buy in the future. Suppose that a farmer grows wheat. He can either sell the wheat at the spot price (the cash market) when the wheat is harvested or he can sell it in the futures market at planting time or any other time before harvest. Perhaps he must make payment on his equipment and is concerned that the price of wheat will drop when he harvests his crop. If he decides that he must receive no less than $2.60 a bushel to meet expenses and if the futures price at the projected date of harvest for wheat is $2.64, he can sell the crop on the futures market, thereby locking in his revenue. If the farmer's assumptions are correct, he has assured himself of meeting expenses, plus a small profit per bushel. The farmer ensures himself a small profit, but he is giving up the opportunity of larger profits if the price of wheat in the cash market is higher at harvest time than the futures contract was at planting time. For this reason, a farmer usually hedges. Note also that the farmer runs the risk of not being able to produce a sufficient size crop to meet his promised future delivery. Therefore, many farmers sell only a portion of their estimated crop in the futures market.

A hedge consists of taking a long position in either the cash market or the future market and selling short an equal amount of the commodity in the other side of the market. The cash price is usually below the future price in a normal market, but sometimes a shortage arises and cash prices are higher. This is called an **inverted market.** Although cash prices and future prices can fluctuate a great deal, they usually move in the same direction. Any gain or loss from the long position is counterbalanced by the movement of the short position.

Example of a Speculator's Transaction

Speculation is very attractive to high-risk-oriented investors because futures can be purchased with as little as 5-percent margin and because there is a potential for large profits by using leverage. For example, a speculator can buy a contract on December wheat selling at $2.64 per bushel for a margin requirement of approximately $500, although the wheat he or she contracted for is valued at $13,200. If the price of wheat rises 10 cents per bushel in a relatively short time, the value of the total wheat contract increases by $500, which is a return of 100 percent on the speculator's initial margin.

Also, a small change in the daily futures price can lead to an extremely lucrative gain for the speculator. To continue the previous example, if the price of wheat for December contract rose $2\frac{1}{2}$ cents per bushel in one day, the speculator who owns the contract increases the value of the holdings by $125 on a $500 margin investment. That is an excellent gain for a one-day period. Speculators are drawn into the marketplace hoping to make a substantial return on their investment over an extremely short time.

It must be made very clear that an investor can lose more than his or her original investment. For example, if the price of wheat were to decline substantially over a few days, the investor could lose several times the original investment.

The investor should also know that a commission is charged for each transaction. Commissions for commodities are charged on a round-trip basis, not separately on the purchase and the sale. The round-trip commission for a wheat contract is approximately $35 to $40. Actually, the commission is small considering the potential for profit.

Speculators use a strategy similar to a hedging strategy when they want to protect the position of a future contract. However, speculators more often are interested in profit, not protection, and are more willing to risk large amounts to gain large profits. Speculators sometimes use a spread strategy; that is, they buy or sell futures on a commodity and take the opposite position (for an equal amount) on the same commodity but with a different delivery month. The object is to experience a price narrowing of the hedge.

Researchers who have studied speculators and their participation in the commodities futures market have often considered speculators to be gamblers. The erratic price behavior of most commodity contracts makes it extremely difficult for the speculator to predict the short-term price movement. It is generally accepted that approximately 70 percent of all futures contract trades are losing trades. However, the strategy is not to experience a majority of profitable trades but rather to limit the losses on the negative trades and to allow the profits to run up to high levels on the few profitable contracts.

Many speculators who approach the market systematically have made considerable profit, but only less than one-half of the transactions have been profitable. The difficulty arises not so much from determining the general price trend of commodities, but rather from being able to sustain a sharp loss when the market takes a small intermediate turn against the speculator's position. For example, if the price of wheat steadily rises to a seasonal high of $4.37 per bushel, many intermediate price swings usually occur. These swings cause the price to decline 10 or 20 cents a bushel, which is just enough to eliminate the speculator's total investment, even though in the long run the market price continues to advance. It is these short-term swings that cause most speculators to close out their positions and experience a large number of losing transactions.

The topics in this chapter, with the exception of convertible bonds, concern speculative investments. These topics have been included because most active investors will at one time or another have to decide whether or not to participate in the various markets. Therefore, prudent investment management dictates that individuals familiarize themselves in detail with each of these markets before venturing into them.

KEY TERMS

bond conversion value	leverage potential
bond investment value	matched trade
call option	naked options
commodity markets	option writer
convertible bond	preemptive rights
covered options	put option
futures	stock option
hedging	straddle
inverted market	warrants

QUESTIONS

1. What do all security options have in common?
2. What are the two kinds of stock options?
3. What are the advantages and disadvantages of options?
4. What determines the price of an option?
5. What is the major concern of the writer of call options?
6. What are the basic objectives of an option investor?
7. A call option is selling for $500 at a striking price of $50. Why might an investor buy an option instead of the underlying stock at $45?
8. What are preemptive stock rights?

9. What are the important dates in the life of a stock right?
10. How is the value of a right computed?
11. What is a warrant?
12. Why would a company issue warrants?
13. What is the theoretical value of a warrant?
14. What is a convertible bond?
15. What are the bases of value for a convertible bond?
16. What are the advantages of convertible bonds?
17. Why are futures so speculative?
18. What two groups participate in the futures markets? What are their objectives?

SELECTED READINGS

ALEXANDER, GORDON J., and ROGER D. STOVER. "Pricing in the New Issue Convertible Debt Market." *Financial Management*, Fall 1977, 35–39.

ANSBACHER, MAX G. *The New Options Market*. New York: Walker Publishing Co., 1975.

BOOKBINDER, ALBERT I. A. *Security Options Strategy*. Elmont, N.Y.: Programmed Press, 1976.

BRENNAN, M.J., and E. S. SCHWARTZ. "Convertible Bonds; Valuation and Optimal Strategies for Call and Conversion." *Journal of Finance*, December 1977, 1699–1715.

CLAUSING, HENRY. *The Dow Jones-Irwin Guide to Put and Call Options*. Homewood, Ill.: Dow Jones-Irwin, 1975.

CLEETON, CLAUD E. *Strategies for the Options Trader*. New York: Wiley, 1979.

Commodity Research Publications Corporation. *Understanding the Commodity Futures Markets*. New York: The Corporation, 1974.

CRETIEN, PAUL D., JR. "Convertible Premiums vs. Stock Prices." *Financial Analysts Journal*, November–December 1969, 90.

DAWSON, FREDERIC S. "Risk and Returns in Continuous Option Writing." *Journal of Portfolio Management*, Winter 1979, 58–63.

FINNERTY, JOSEPH E. "The Chicago Board Options Exchange and Market Efficiency." *Journal of Financial and Quantitative Analysis*, March 1978, 29–38.

GASTINEAU, GARY L. "An Index of Listed Option Premiums." *Financial Analysts Journal*, May–June 1977, 70–75.

MERTON, ROBERT C., MYRON S. SCHOLES, and MATHEW L. GLADSTEIN. "The Returns and Risks of Alternative Call Option Investment Strategies." *Journal of Business*, April 1978, 183–242.

OPTIONS CLEARING CORPORATION. *Prospectus—Exchange Traded Call Options*, Oct. 30, 1975 (obtainable from any exchange upon which options are traded).

POUNDS, HENRY M. "Covered Call Option Writing Strategies and Results." *Journal of Portfolio Management*, Winter 1978, 31–42.

REBACK, ROBERT. "Risk and Return in CBOE and AMEX Option Trading." *Financial Analysts Journal*, July–August 1975, 42–51.

SHELTON, JOHN P. "The Relation of the Price of a Warrant to the Price of Its Associated Stock." *Financial Analysts Journal*, July–August 1967, 88–99.

SOLDOFSKY, ROBERT M. "Performance of Convertibles." *Financial Analysts Journal*, March–April 1971, 61.

8

The Securities Markets

An investor can participate in either the primary or secondary security market. The securities markets provide a meeting ground for buyers and sellers. This chapter will examine the investment banking function and the places where securities are traded (national exchanges, over-the-counter market, the specialized markets).

PRIMARY MARKET

The **primary market** is a system of distributing new securities that originate in a company that needs funds to operate and expand. When a firm needs more funds than those provided by internally generated sources, such as net income and depreciation, it goes to the primary market to sell securities, usually bonds or stocks.

Since the new issue of the security involves a large amount of funds and the issuance of a large number of certificates, an investment banker is usually employed to organize the purchase and distribution of the company's securities.

There are two broad categories of issuers of new securities: (1) the noncorporate sector, which includes the U.S. government, U.S. government agencies, and state and local governments; and (2) the corporate sector, which includes manufacturing, commerce, transportation, public utilities, communication, and the real estate and financial industries. Exhibit 8-1 shows not only the magnitude of the securities issued, but also that various government issues constitute approximately two-thirds of the total security new issues in the last several years.

In the corporate sector, bonds have consistently netted a substantial part of total new issues. However, some bonds are issued simply to replace previously retired bonds; thus, sources of corporate investments are not as high as the total new issues shown in Exhibit 8-1.

The Investment Banker

The economic function that an investment banker performs is central to the smooth functioning of the American capital market system. The investment banker acts as a middleman between the user of the funds provided from the sale of securities and the investing public. Through the investment banker, new, long-term capital is obtained from a variety of sources (insurance companies, mutual funds, pension funds, and the investing public). Responsibilities extend to providing aid in financing, determining the most appropriate form of financing and the rate to be paid in the case of bonds, and establishing generally sound financial practices. The investment banker is responsible for thorough investigation of the issuer, the securities to be issued, and the formulation of investment judgement of the issuing company. In addition, the investment banker usually aids in maintaining a stable market by having someone ready to buy the securities immediately after the new issue is sold. The investment banker, therefore, plays an extremely important role in the capital formation process in our economy, both by making available to business and public bodies the funds required for the operation and growth of the economy and by obtaining these funds from the financial institutions that channel the savings of many millions of investors into these required uses.

Investment banking is separate from the brokerage business, but many of the large national brokerage houses have separate and subsidiary functions and act as investment bankers. The typical brokerage house operates on a commission basis. The broker assumes no responsibility for the outcome of the client's operations; his business is to execute orders on behalf of his client. The broker, of course, is interested in the customer's success or failure, for future business depends upon the outcome of prior transactions.

On the other hand, the investment banker's basic functions are advising, underwriting, and selling.

Exhibit 8-1

NEW SECURITY ISSUES of State and Local Governments

Millions of dollars

Type of issue or issuer, or use	1979	1980	1981	1981 July	Aug.	Sept.	Oct.	Nov.	Dec.	1982 Jan.ʳ	Feb.
1 **All issues, new and refunding**¹	**43,365**	**48,367**	**47,732**	**3,211**	**3,113**	**3,910**	**4,097**	**5,355**	**4,744**	**3,878**	**3,495**
Type of issue											
2 General obligation	12,109	14,100	12,394	1,075	1,000	560	748	1,315	749	1,056	1,028
3 U.S. government loans²	53	38	34	5	8	2	2	3		1	1
4 Revenue	31,256	34,267	35,338	2,136	2,113	3,350	3,349	4,040	3,995	2,822	2,467
5 U.S. government loans²	67	57	55	1	4	9	5	2	3	4	6
Type of issuer											
6 State	4,314	5,304	5,288	353	446	92	439	518	315	514	234
7 Special district and statutory authority	23,434	26,972	27,499	1,733	1,701	2,749	2,467	3,439	3,308	2,132	2,004
8 Municipalities, counties, townships, school districts	15,617	16,090	14,945	1,125	966	1,070	1,191	1,398	1,120	1,232	1,257
9 **Issues for new capital, total**	**41,505**	**46,736**	**46,530**	**3,200**	**2,460**	**3,904**	**4,009**	**5,318**	**4,683**	**3,722**	**3,455**
Use of proceeds											
10 Education	5,130	4,572	4,547	257	257	153	203	576	561	236	254
11 Transportation	2,441	2,621	3,447	537	.113	222	499	286	355	138	206
12 Utilities and conservation	8,594	8,149	10,037	844	524	1,626	700	757	955	1,178	1,257
13 Social welfare	15,968	19,958	12,729	712	770	515	953	1,873	1,813	889	731
14 Industrial aid	3,836	3,974	7,651	377	316	874	1,015	676	523	455	414
15 Other purposes	5,536ʳ	7,462ʳ	8,119	473	480	514	639	1,150	476	826	593

1. Par amounts of long-term issues based on date of sale.
2. Consists of tax-exempt issues guaranteed by the Farmers Home Administration.

NEW SECURITY ISSUES of Corporations

Millions of dollars

Type of issue or issuer, or use	1979	1980	1981 ʳ	1981 Aug.	Sept.	Oct.	Nov.	Dec. ʳ	1982 Jan.	Feb.
1 All issues¹	51,533	73,694	69,283	3,097	4,696	4,368	8,518	5,908	2,451 ʳ	2,906
2 Bonds	40,208	53,206	44,643	1,616	2,797	2,845	6,724	3,893	840 ʳ	1,537
Type of offering										
3 Public	25,814	41,587	37,653	905	2,198	2,582	6,560	3,576	614 ʳ	1,364 ʳ
4 Private placement	14,394	11,619	6,989	711	599	263	164	317	226	173
Industry group										
5 Manufacturing	9,678	15,409	12,325	308	452	21	2,054	954	185	138
6 Commercial and miscellaneous	3,948	6,693	5,229	390	201	617	949	850	168	59
7 Transportation	3,119	3,329	2,054	95	63	51	130	82	28	
8 Public utility	8,153	9,557	8,963	360	1,012	1,008	802	582	284	304
9 Communication	4,219	6,683	4,280	115	471	83	326	106		335
10 Real estate and financial	11,094	11,534	11,793	348	598	1,065	2,463	1,319	174 ʳ	701
11 Stocks	11,325	20,489	24,642	1,481	1,899	1,523	1,794	2,015	1,611 ʳ	1,369
Type										
12 Preferred	3,574	3,631	1,796	14	186	141	59	80	199 ʳ	145
13 Common	7,751	16,858	22,846	1,467	1,713	1,382	1,735	1,935	1,412 ʳ	1,224
Industry group										
14 Manufacturing	1,679	4,839	4,838	160	117	193	407	258 ʳ	129 ʳ	67
15 Commercial and miscellaneous	2,623	5,245	7,436	661	487	449	564	456	669 ʳ	420
16 Transportation	255	549	735	91	87	23	15	23	25	73
17 Public utility	5,171	6,230	5,486	248	514	438	405	604	449	703
18 Communication	303	567	1,778	12	369	7	85	95	58	2
19 Real estate and financial	12,931	3,059	4,371	310	325	412	318	580	281 ʳ	104

1. Figures, which represent gross proceeds of issues maturing in more than one year, sold for cash in the United States, are principal amount or number of units multiplied by offering price. Excludes offerings of less than $100,000, secondary offerings, undefined or exempted issues as defined in the Securities Act of 1933, employee stock plans, investment companies other than closed-end, intra-corporate transactions, and sales to foreigners.

Source: *Federal Reserve Bulletin*, May, 1982, p. A36.

Advisory Function

The investment banker provides advisory services for clients. For example, the statistics department answers inquiries from clients who may become potential underwriting clients. Generally, the investment banker works very closely with a potential client in trying to determine which type of security is the best to sell under the current market conditions and in trying to determine the best price. The investment banker also distributes research literature on various securities that may be of interest to clients. The literature may include economic, industry, and individual security analyses for the client to use as a basis for making an investment decision. In addition, the investment banker advises customers on income and estate tax problems in connection with security holdings.

Underwriting Function

The typical underwriting function of an investment banking house involves the direct purchase of a security issue from the issuer on terms agreeable to both the investment banking house and the issuer. A corporation that wants funds for long-term financing approaches an investment banker and begins negotiating with the banking house to underwrite the particular issue. Some issues, particularly utility, railroad, and municipal bonds, are usually purchased by an investment banker under competitive bidding. Other issues, generally industrial corporation stocks and bonds, are purchased on a negotiated basis between the issuer and the investment banker acting as the purchaser.

Many corporations have dealt with the same investment banking houses for years. Experience with successive issues tends to familiarize the banker with the affairs of the issuing company. As a result, more intelligent advice can be provided to the corporation on financial policy. The banker also feels a responsibility to the corporation, and the reputation of the banker often depends upon the success of the issues that are underwritten.

Generally, the investment banking house makes an exhaustive investigation before purchasing a new corporate issue. The investigation determines whether or not the company may be unsuccessful in future years. First, a preliminary survey of the financial statements and general history of the company is made. If this survey indicates that the security issue has merit, the investment banker then makes a more thorough investigation of the company's assets and internal affairs. Auditors may be employed to check the financial records and accounting practices. Specialists in marketing, engineering, and legal matters may also be brought in. If the results of the investment investigation are satisfactory, the officers of the issuing company and the officers of the investment banker determine the best security to sell to raise the desired capital and the appropriate interest rate, maturity date (if a bond issue), and price of the security. During the investigation a banker must always consider his ability to resell the issue to the investing public. There is a very narrow margin between the purchase price and the selling price of higher-grade securities.

Ordinarily, there is no competition among investment bankers once negotiations have begun, but corporate issuers may investigate other bankers at the preliminary stage of negotiations to determine whether or not they have the most interested investment banker for their proposed security offering. There is, of course, competition in performance. An investment banker who has a number of dissatisfied clients after an underwriting has been completed will suffer in future competition.

Selling Function

Once the underwriter and the issuing company have tentatively agreed to the terms of the security offering, the prospective issuing company registers its issue with the Securities and Exchange Commission, as required by the Securities Act of 1933. The investment banking firm then organizes a purchase group, which includes other investment banking houses that join with the major investment banker in purchasing the new issue. The originating investment banker is generally known as the **managing underwriter.** The investment banking firms that join to purchase the issue are known as the **purchasing underwriting group.**

Several days before the registration statement becomes effective, the managing underwriter of the purchase group organizes a larger selling group. This group consists of underwriters that agree to participate in the retail distribution of the proposed new issue. Membership in the selling group is generally determined by prior experience and is made up of firms that have good reputations for being able to retail a certain amount of a proposed issue. Often in large underwritings there may be several hundred firms in the selling group, depending upon the size of the new issue and the expected intensity of the sales effort required to distribute the issue. Several days before the registration statement becomes effective, the members of the purchase group sign a contract. The issuer agrees to buy a stipulated number of bonds or shares of stock at a price that has already been negotiated. Payment for the issue is generally made two or three weeks after the public offering date. Also, several days before the effective date of registration and issuance, the group agrees to sell the securities at a common offering price and to carry on the distribution of the issue in accordance with the provisions of the selling agreement.

An important and delicate task of the investment banker is to set the price at which the issue is to be sold to investors. Generally, the prices and yields are guided by those that prevail in the market for comparable issues of other companies. Underpricing an issue deprives the issuing company of funds that might otherwise have been raised. Overpricing may result in large losses for the underwriters. Only through experience does an underwriter obtain the ability to price a new issue correctly. The price must also reflect an underwriting spread or commission. This spread is determined by the difference between the offering price to the investing public and the proceeds to the issuing corporation. Spreads vary with the size of the issuing company, the type of issue to be distributed (stock or a bond), and the quality of the issue and issuer. Underwriting costs of floating a new issue may range from less than 1 percent for a high-grade corporate bond to as much as 25 percent for small unknown corporate stock issuers that would require intensive sales effort and considerably greater risk for the underwriter.

After the issue has been sold, a major duty of the underwriting group is that of stabilizing the market price. Investors who have purchased the new issue generally begin to trade the bonds or shares of stock through dealers and brokers. It is in the best interest of all concerned that the market price not sharply drop below the public offering price; therefore, there is a stabilization period for up to 30 days.

Best-Efforts Selling

There are times when an underwriter does not want to make a firm commitment to an issuing corporation. In this case, the investment banker 1does not take a risk but acts an agent for the issuing company. The banker agrees to sell the issue on a best-efforts basis. Such an arrangement is generally found in the distribution of corporate stocks issued by very speculative and risky firms. The flotation costs in such best-efforts selling are usually the payment for the sales services rendered, not for the underwriting risks.

Competitive Bidding

Another method for underwriting a new security issue is for the investment banker to enter competitive bidding instead of negotiating directly with the issuing company. Most state and local governments and many railroad and utility bond issues are sold by competitive bidding, as required by regulation. Approximately one-half of all corporate bonds and almost all state and municipal bonds are currently sold through competitive bidding. Competitive bidding stemmed from the desire to eliminate, or at least lessen, the possibility of monopoly in securities underwriting and the desire to obtain the best price and the smallest underwriting commission available.

Investment banking firms are organized to bid for new issues in much the same way that they form purchase groups to negotiate purchases. When it becomes known that an issue is to be offered for sale by bidding, several leading investment banking firms form groups to submit bids. Membership is tentative, and often there are changes in membership up to the date of bidding. The group members discuss the bidding price, but frequently the exact figure is not determined until the morning of the sale.

Bidding takes place at a time and place known to the investment bankers in advance, usually shortly before noon at the office of the issuer. Representatives from the various bidding groups meet with the appropriate corporate officials and submit sealed bids. After the fixed time for the sale, the bids are opened in the presence of the bidders, and the bid most favorable to the issuer is awarded. The favorable bid on a bond issue is the one that provides the lowest interest cost to the issuer, which is a combination of the issuing price and the coupon rate. When a common stock is sold, the highest price per share available to the issuing company is awarded. A sale is completed at that time with the highest bidder. The winning group then makes a public offering of the issue and accepts all the risks of distribution.

Standby Underwriting

A standby underwriting agreement usually originates from the issuance of common stock or convertible bonds to existing stockholders under preemptive rights. Preeemptive rights (discussed in Chapter 5) allow existing stockholders the privilege of purchasing a proportional amount of securities from a new offering. When the issuer of a new security does not wish to incur the risk that existing shareholders will not subscribe to the new issue, an underwriting group is formed to stand by to purchase the securities not subscribed to by existing stockholders. The additional stock is offered to existing stockholders on a subscription basis. The stockholders are permitted to subscribe to one new share of additional stock for a specified number of currently owned shares.

The subscription price of the new stock is generally somewhat lower than the market price of the outstanding security at the time of the offering. It is an inducement for stockholders to subscribe to the new issue. However, if some stockholders do not exercise their rights to subscribe, or if they do not sell their rights to someone who does, the new issue is not fully sold. There is the danger in a rights offering that the issue will not be fully subscribed, and the issuing company will not be able to raise the amount of capital that may already have been committed to certain capital budgeting projects. Therefore, a standby underwriting group is formed to provide that the investment bankers will purchase whatever amount of stock is not subscribed for by the exercise of rights. The issuer is assured that all the stock offered will be sold and that it will obtain the full amount of capital to be raised by the issue.

Investment bankers organize themselves for standby underwriting in much the same way they negotiate purchases and distribute the shares that are not subscribed. A commission is paid to the standby underwriting group on the entire issue. If stockholders subscribe to the entire issue, the underwriters are paid for the assurance that the funds will be available when required. If any shares are underwritten by the investment bankers, an additional commission is paid on that amount.

Regulation of New Security Issues

Whenever a company issues new securities, they are subject to federal and local regulation. After the stock market crashed in 1929, a large amount of government regulatory legislation was enacted to protect the investing public.

When new issues are registered, the Securities and Exchange Commission requires that the issuing company give investors copies of its prospectus. The **prospectus** is a printed document that provides investors with information on a new security issue and on the issuing company. Exhibit 8-2 shows the front cover of a Lockheed Corporation issue of 2 million common shares priced at $48.375 a share, dated March 23, 1982, with the help of many investment banking houses. At the bottom of the exhibit are the five managing underwriter investment banking firms. The prospectus is an abridged version of a required registration statement that is on file at the Securities and Exchange Commission. The prospectus is made available to investors because it is almost impossible for them to have access to the Security and Exchange Commission files. The penalties for not publishing a prospectus are severe. Security legislation requires that the issuing company provide full disclosure of all relevant information so that the purchaser will be able to make an informed decision. The responsibility remains with the buyer to determine the desirability of the issue. A company violates the law if it makes untrue statements of immaterial fact or fails to state a material fact that would have an impact on the analysis of the issuing company. See Chapter 11 for a discussion of security regulations.

Direct Placement of Securities

Direct sales of securities are made without investment banking or underwriting assistance. For example, the federal government sells their new issues directly to investors. Also, small firms, new firms, and firms that have speculative characteristics cannot often obtain or afford the services of an investment banker. These companies sell securities directly to interested investors, who may be employees and executives of the company.

The largest form of direct selling is that of **direct placement**, in which a corporation sells securities in large blocks directly to individual institutions. Many institutions, such as life insurance companies, negotiate directly with

Exhibit 8-2

2,000,000 Shares

≡☆Lockheed

Common Stock

The last reported sale price of the Common Stock of Lockheed Corporation ("Lockheed") on the New York Stock Exchange on March 22, 1982 was $48½ per share. See "Price Range of Common Stock."

THESE SECURITIES HAVE NOT BEEN APPROVED OR DISAPPROVED BY THE SECURITIES AND EXCHANGE COMMISSION NOR HAS THE COMMISSION PASSED UPON THE ACCURACY OR ADEQUACY OF THIS PROSPECTUS. ANY REPRESENTATION TO THE CONTRARY IS A CRIMINAL OFFENSE.

	Initial Public Offering Price	Underwriting Discount(1)	Proceeds to Lockheed(2)
Per Share	$48.375	$1.75	$46.625
Total Minimum	$ 96,750,000	$3,500,000	$ 93,250,000
Total Maximum(3)	$106,425,000	$3,850,000	$102,575,000

(1) Lockheed has agreed to indemnify the Underwriters against certain liabilities, including liabilities under the Securities Act of 1933.

(2) Before deducting expenses estimated at $325,000.

(3) Assumes full exercise of an option granted by Lockheed to the Underwriters to purchase on the same terms up to an additional 200,000 shares to cover over-allotments. See "Underwriting."

These shares are offered severally by the Underwriters as specified herein, subject to receipt and acceptance by them and subject to their right to reject any order in whole or in part. It is expected that certificates for the shares will be ready for delivery at the office of Goldman, Sachs & Co., New York, New York, on or about March 30, 1982.

Goldman, Sachs & Co.

The date of this Prospectus is March 23, 1982.

Source: *Lockheed Corporation Prospectus, March 23, 1982.*

the issuing company, thereby bypassing the underwriting services of the middleman. However, an investment banker often acts as an intermediary to bring the two parties together. The investment banker does not, however, underwrite the securities. Most private sales are made to one or a small number of buyers. Exhibit 8-1 indicates that of the total corporate bonds issued, approximately 20 percent are privately placed.

The method by which a company directly places its securities is very straightforward. The firm that wants to sell its new securities contacts a number of investing institutions, for example, life insurance companies, pension funds, and other kinds of financial institutions. When the firm finds an interested party, the firm's officers meet with the representatives of the investing institution to negotiate terms. Negotiations often become difficult and prolonged, because many details of the terms to be agreed upon must represent the interests of both the borrower and the lender.

There are several important advantages for corporate issuers that place their securities directly. Since direct placement is a private transaction, it does not have to be registered with the SEC. The time saved by placing securities directly may be important to an issuing corporation that needs funds quickly. In addition, the terms negotiated with a few sophisticated officers of financial institutions may be better suited to the issuer than the terms negotiated with an underwriter for a public offering. Another advantage to issuers is that they may deal directly with the purchasers of their securities after the transaction has been completed. From time to time there are business developments that prompt an issuer of a security to change the legal requirements of the security issue. If the change has no major adverse effect on the institutional investor's position, the change is usually easily arranged. Therefore, private placement offers flexibility in future negotiations of outstanding issues.

Direct placement of securities is often very desirable for companies that are not well known but are very sound financially. Some smaller firms need funds of a small dollar amount that would not attract an investment banker for a public offering because the underwriting commission would not cover the cost of the work involved.

Institutional investors frequently obtain a higher expected rate of return on a direct placement than they would by purchasing equivalent securities in the open market. In addition, corporate issuers will occasionally give institutional lenders an opportunity for equity participation through the option to convert debt securities to common stock. These options may be in the form of convertibles, warrants, or rights to buy additional stock at favorable prices that are generally fixed over a period of time. If the issuing company sustains a good earnings growth rate and if the price of the stock rises, the institutional lender may realize a profit on converting or exercising options, in addition to the interest income received on debt securities.

Direct placements have been criticized because the particular security to be issued does not undergo the test of the marketplace in order to obtain the best price. Another disadvantage of private placements is that distribution is limited, and future security offerings do not have an experienced investment community that knows how desirable or undesirable the company's securities are.

SECONDARY MARKETS

Secondary securities markets are found anywhere buyers and sellers come together to trade securities in an orderly manner at fair prices to both parties. To facilitate the transaction of securities between buyers and sellers, brokers or dealers act as middlemen to bring the two parties together.

Investors who approach the secondary markets to exchange securities may have originally obtained their stocks or bonds through the primary market. Investors who were neither able nor willing to buy securities through the primary market are now ready to bid on those securities.

Secondary markets are significantly larger than the primary markets in dollar volume. The ease with which an investor can sell a security and the reasonableness of the charges and costs in connection with these sales are important factors to consider before making an investment decision. Unless a security can be resold readily and at a reasonable price, the investment banker who is trying to sell a new issue may find that investors are reluctant to purchase, because they are not sure that there will be a ready market if they want to sell later. To overcome this problem, investment banking firms that underwrite and sell new issues usually help establish a resale market if other securities of the issuing firm are not already traded actively in the marketplace.

The establishment of the securities market for a particular company's securities is a benefit to investors in several ways. If a security is listed on an organized exchange or is actively traded in the over-the-counter market, it enjoys marketability and, therefore, is often acceptable as collateral for a loan if an investor has to borrow funds.

Functions of the Stock Exchanges

A stock exchange is an organization of individuals and firms established to trade among themselves in securities. Members of the securities exchanges generally act as brokers who execute orders sent to them by their clients. Brokers may, however, act as principals or dealers in purchasing and selling for their own accounts, but they are not permitted to take advantage of their positions. They must give precedent to orders held for others at the same price.

The primary purpose of a securities exchange is to provide a continuous and liquid market for the exchange of outstanding issues. The exchange also provides a means for determining fair prices, and it indirectly aids in financing industry by giving liquidity to publicly held security issues. National exchanges assure the investor of basic financial information and protection. They require that a company provide its shareholders with a statement of earnings and with balance sheet information that summarizes the company's financial position. National stock exchanges must register with the Securities and Exchange Commission, which affords added protection for stockholders.

Security exchanges are auction markets because brokers for sellers deal directly with brokers for buyers in competitive bidding and offering. The buyer's broker tries to obtain the lowest possible price; the seller's broker tries to obtain the highest possible price. Thus, prices change from one sale to the other according to the volume of securities offered and bid.

A securities exchange provides a continuous market for security issues. The market depends upon a large volume of sales and a narrow price range between the selling price and the buying price. A well functioning securities market insists upon the rapid execution of orders, and the rules of most stock exchanges encourage the implementation of these functions.

Since the price of a share of stock or bond is established by an auction market, there is no price setting by traders on the floor of the exchange or by negotiations off the floor. Since prices are established through bidding, the price at any one time tends to reflect a fair-market appraisal of the stock. Because the market for a security is continuous and the price is established by supply and demand, securities may be used as collateral for loans. Since the fair-market appraisal of any security is generally determined by supply and demand, regulatory agencies insist that all information on a security be available to the investing public before security transactions are made. Often when significant information is announced, there may be either a substantial increase or substantial decrease in the price of the security. This fluctuation is in response to the investment community's attempt to arrive at a new fair-market value for the company. Since the marketplace can be emotional, stock prices tend to swing in a wide range around a generally accepted value (the **intrinsic value**) of a security. Since it is difficult to determine an exact intrinsic value for a security and because different investors view the value of a company from different perspectives, price fluctuations can be various and acute.

There are approximately 12 security exchanges within the United States. The New York Stock Exchange and American Stock Exchange are the largest national marketplaces. There are a number of regional exchanges throughout the United States, but they are extremely small, with the exception of the Midwest Stock Exchange and the Pacific Coast Stock Exchange. Very few shares are traded on regional exchanges in relation to the total securities transacted.

The New York Stock Exchange

Certainly the best-known, largest, and most important stock exchange in the United States is the New York Stock Exchange (NYSE). It handles the greatest volume of business of all the organized exchanges, and its activities have a far-reaching impact on all the financial centers in the world. Table 8-1 indicates the importance of the New York Stock Exchange in relation to all the other exchanges. The NYSE captures 80 percent of the volume and 84 percent of the value of listed securities. Stock exchanges neither buy, sell, own, nor set the prices of securities. These activities are carried on by the members of the exchanges; the stock exchanges only provide the facilities and the rules by which members execute orders on behalf of their clients or for their own accounts.

The New York Stock Exchange was founded on May 17, 1792, when 24 brokers signed a partnership agreement (supposedly under the famous Buttonwood Tree). The agreement established a commission of one-quarter of 1 percent of the value of the securities traded, and it obligated the members to buy and sell securities only from one another. Until 1817, the exchange's business was conducted in an office of a New York coffee house. Then the exchange moved to new quarters at 40 Wall Street and took on the name of the New York Stock and Exchange Board. In 1863, the name was changed to the New York Stock Exchange. In 1903, the exchange moved to its present quarters at Broad and Wall streets.

The New York Stock Exchange is a voluntary incorporated association of members. A member of the exchange, with prior approval of the 21-man board of governors, may combine with other individuals to form a partnership or a corporation as a member organization and do business with the public. The member also may choose to do business for himself, but if he does, he cannot carry accounts for customers. The number of member organizations stood at 570 at the end of 1980.

Members own **seats of the exchange.** These seats may be transferred either by sale or assignment, subject to approval by the board of governors. The exchange membership has been 1,366 since 1953. Table 8-2 shows the prices for membership on the exchange. The record price paid for a seat on the New York Stock Exchange was $625,000 (February 1929). The price included the privilege to sell one-quarter interest in a new membership; thus the actual price for a single seat was $500,000. This price was surpassed several times in late 1968 and early 1969. The current record is $515,000. The lowest price in this century was $17,000 (1942). Table 8-2 shows that the price of a seat has been declining over the last decade. It has been suggested that increased competition from other security markets and the desire by many to eliminate all stock exchanges, except one central marketplace, have decreased the desirability of membership in the New York Stock Exchange.

Table 8-1
Shares Sold on Registered Exchanges

	Number of Shares (millions)			Percent of Total		
Year	NYSE	ASE	Other	NYSE	ASE	Other
1935	513.6	84.7	63.6	77.6%	12.8%	9.6%
1940	282.7	47.9	41.4	76.0	12.9	11.1
1945	496.0	152.4	96.1	66.6	20.5	12.9
1950	655.3	114.9	86.9	76.5	13.4	10.1
1955	820.5	243.9	148.0	67.7	20.1	12.2
1960	958.3	300.6	129.6	69.0	21.6	9.3
1965	1,809.4	582.2	195.3	69.9	22.5	7.5
1966	2,204.8	730.9	252.2	69.2	22.9	7.9
1967	2,885.8	1,290.2	327.8	64.1	28.6	7.3
1968	3,298.7	1,570.7	442.6	62.1	29.6	8.3
1969	3,173.6	1,341.0	448.8	63.9	27.0	9.0
1970	3,213.1	878.5	444.1	70.8	19.4	9.8
1971	4,265.3	1,049.3	601.1	72.1	17.7	10.2
1972	4,496.2	1,103.2	669.8	71.4	17.5	11.1
1973	4,336.6	740.4	653.2	75.7	12.9	11.4
1974	3,821.9	475.3	541.9	79.0	9.8	11.2
1975	5,056.5	540.9	637.6	81.1	8.7	10.2
1976	5,649.2	637.0	749.5	80.3	9.1	10.7
1977	5,613.3	651.9	758.2	799	9.3	10.8
1978	7,618.0	992.2	872.6	80.3	10.5	9.2
1979	8,675.3	1,161.3	1,026.2	79.9	10.7	9.4
1980	12,389.9	1,658.8	1,437.0	80.0	10.7	9.3
	Market Value of Shares (millions)			Percent of Total		
Year	NYSE	ASE	Other	NYSE	ASE	Other
1935	$13,335	$1,205	$ 736	87.3%	7.9%	4.8%
1940	7,166	643	595	85.3	7.7	7.0
1945	13,462	1,728	1,036	83.0	10.6	6.4
1950	18,725	1,481	1,571	86.0	6.8	6.7
1955	32,745	2,593	2,530	86.5	6.8	6.7
1960	37,960	4,176	3,083	83.9	9.2	6.8
1965	73,200	8,612	7,402	82.0	9.7	8.3
1966	98,565	14,130	10,339	80.1	11.5	8.4
1967	125,329	23,111	13,318	77.5	14.3	8.2
1968	144,978	34,775	16,605	73.8	17.7	8.5
1969	129,603	30,074	15,621	73.9	17.2	8.9
1970	103,063	14,266	13,579	78.7	10.9	10.4
1971	147,098	17,664	20,169	79.5	9.6	10.9
1972	159,700	20,453	23,873	78.3	10.0	11.7

Table 8-1 (continued)

Year	Market Value of Shares (millions)			Percent of Total		
	NYSE	ASE	Other	NYSE	ASE	Other
1973	146,451	10,430	21,156	82.3	5.9	11.9
1974	99,178	5,048	14,023	83.9	4.3	11.9
1975	133,819	5,678	17,595	85.2	3.6	11.2
1976	164,545	7,468	22,956	84.4	3.8	11.8
1977	157,250	8,532	21,421	84.0	4.6	11.4
1978	210,426	15,204	23,625	84.4	6.1	9.5
1979	251,098	20,596	28,279	83.7	6.9	9.4
1980	397,670	34,696	43,485	83.6	7.3	9.1

Source: Securities and Exchange Commission. Data as reprinted in *The New York Stock Exchange Fact Book,* 1981, p. 73.

A member organization doing business with the public must maintain a minimum net capital of $100,000 ($200,000 if the member is a corporate organization). The member firm must also maintain a net capital of $1 for every $15 of total debt and pay 1 percent of net commissions to the exchange, in addition to an initiation fee of $7,500 and annual dues of $1,500. Membership fees are the major source of revenue for the operation of the New York Stock Exchange.

Table 8-2
New York Stock Exchange Membership Prices

Year	High	Low	Year	High	Low
1875	$ 6.8	$ 4.3	1966	$270.0	$197.0
1885	34.0	20.2	1967	450.0	220.0
1895	20.0	17.0	1968	515.0	385.0
1905	85.0	72.0	1969	515.0	260.0
1915	74.0	38.0	1970	320.0	130.0
1925	150.0	99.0	1971	300.0	145.0
1935	140.0	65.0	1972	250.0	150.0
1945	95.0	49.0	1973	190.0	72.0
1955	90.0	80.0	1974	105.0	65.0
1960	162.0	135.0	1975	138.0	55.0
1961	225.0	147.0	1976	104.0	40.0
1962	210.0	115.0	1977	95.0	35.0
1963	217.0	160.0	1978	105.0	46.0
1964	230.0	190.0	1979	210.0	82.0
1965	250.0	190.0	1980	275.0	175.0

	Series Records				
Low	1876 and 1878	$4,000	High	1929	$625,000

Source: *The New York Stock Exchange Fact Book,* 1981, p. 74.

A member of the exchange may conduct business as an individual, a partnership, or a corporation. No one may become a partner or a stockholder of a member company without permission and approval of the governors, and each member firm must have one partner or stockholder who is an exchange member. At the end of 1980, there were 363 corporations and 207 partnerships operating as member organizations. Corporate memberships were not allowed until 1953. Since then the number of corporate memberships has grown substantially while the number of partnerships has diminished. The majority of corporate ownerships are made up of the large national brokerage houses and investment banking firms. At the end of 1975, there were 10 publicly held corporations whose stocks were being traded either on an exchange or over-the-counter.

Exchange Self-Governance

The New York Stock Exchange is governed by a 21-person board of governors, 10 of whom are from the securities industry and 10 of whom are from the public. The twenty-first member, the chairperson of the board, is elected by the 20 governors. As chief officer of the exchange, the chairperson devotes full time to its management. The chairperson must not be connected with any other business concern because there would be a conflict of interest.

The board of governors is vested with the power to suspend or expel any member for constitutional violations, fraud, unjust or inequitable conduct in connection with trading, or any act that may be detrimental to the exchange. Members may be disciplined by the board of governors for violating any of the high standards of business conduct or for offenses against the rules of the exchange, even if no civil statutes have been violated.

Exchange Members

The members of the exchange are divided into the following classes: commission brokers, floor brokers, floor traders, odd lot brokers, bond brokers, and specialists. Each class provides a function necessary to the smooth operation of the marketplace and is discussed next.

COMMISSION BROKER. From the typical investor's viewpoint, the commission broker is the most important member of the exchange because he trades primarily for the public. Most commission brokers are large, national retail brokerage firms that purchase memberships on the exchange for the main purpose of executing orders for their clients. The commission broker acts as an agent for a customer and earns a commission for the services performed. Most business conducted on the floor of the exchange by the commission broker is obtained through registered representatives of the member firms. The registered representative more commonly known as the **broker** or **account executive,** is an employee of a member firm engaged in retail soliciting of buy and sell orders in securities. Each firm that is a member of the New York Exchange or a member of any other exchange must have one partner or stockholder who is a member of that exchange.

FLOOR BROKERS. Floor brokers transact business on the floor of the exchange for exchange members who have more orders than they can handle at a particular time or who may need help in handling large orders. Floor brokers, better known as **two-dollar brokers,**[1] share the commission with the member firm. Although the floor broker does not ordinarily belong to a member firm, he or she must, of course, own a seat.

FLOOR TRADERS. Floor traders, more recently known as **registered traders,** buy and sell on the floor of the exchange for their own accounts. The floor trader does not represent outside customers and does not execute orders for other members of the exchange. He obtains his profit or loss from trading on relatively small price fluctuations. Many floor traders are there only part-time; most full-time floor traders are members of a firm. Floor traders help make a continuous market and stabilize prices, although for many years they have been criticized for not performing any important economic function.

Today, there are very few full-time traders, and their impact on the market is insignificant. In 1964, the activities of the floor trader were subject to very strict regulation enacted by the SEC. The new legislation restricted membership of floor traders to those having adequate capital and restricted their trading practices. For example, when the floor trader buys, the price paid must be above the last price executed on the exchange. When the floor trader sells, the selling price must be below the last price executed. In addition, floor traders must relinquish priority preference to other dealers so that their position on the trading floor will not give them any advantage over the investing public.

ODD-LOT BROKERS. Only lots of 100 shares are traded on the floor of the stock exchange. To facilitate small transactions of from 1 to 99 shares, an odd-lot broker acts as a principal. Odd-lot shares are not actually traded on the floor, but the price of the transaction is determined by the price of a round-lot sale at the time of transaction. Before 1976, one member firm handled almost all odd-lot business at the New York Stock Exchange. The odd-lot broker charged the investor an additional one-eighth of one point per share for dividing a round lot into the desired number of shares to be purchased.

Early in 1976, several retail brokerage houses began servicing the odd-lot business for their clients without the one-eighth point charge. This removed a significant portion of the odd-lot business from the odd-lot broker

---

[1]The term "two-dollar broker" originated from the fee brokers received for executing orders for member firms. More recently the commission averages more than twice the $2 per 100 share transactions, and there are approximately 200 floor brokers out of the total membership.

at the NYSE. In an attempt to counter the increased competition, the NYSE allowed the execution of odd-lot orders entered "at the opening" of the market at the same price as round lots. However, intraday trades continued to be assessed the one-eighth point differential. The New York Stock Exchange has assumed practically all the responsibility for odd-lot transactions, and the former odd-lot brokers have all but disappeared.

BOND BROKERS. There are approximately 2,000 bond issues currently listed on the New York Exchange. There are approximately 12 members that act as bond brokers. Bonds traded on the exchange are divided into two classes: free bonds and cabinet bonds. There are approximately 100 free bonds that are the most actively traded issues. All other bonds listed are classified as cabinet bonds because trading involves the use of metal cabinets where the records of bids and offers are kept for each issue. The bond-trading floor is in a separate room at the New York Exchange.

SPECIALISTS. The function of the specialist is one of the most interesting and important among the membership of the exchange. Specialists make the markets in the various securities issues and are charged with the responsibility of maintaining a fair and orderly market. Specialists are usually employees of privately owned firms that the exchange permits to specialize in certain stocks assigned to them. All trades must be transacted at the price set by specialists as they perceive the supply and demand for a particular security. At times, specialists may purchase for their own accounts, as opposed to merely matching buy and sell orders as they come before them from other exchange members. In their responsibility to maintain an orderly market, specialists usually buy securities in a declining market in order to support the price and sell securities when the market increases. Each specialist does business in one or more stocks that have been assigned to him or her. The number of stocks varies with the size of the specialist's firm. Sometimes specialists execute orders for other brokers and receive commissions for their services as agents. At other times, specialists buy and sell stocks for their own accounts; thus they act dealers. Often the specialist has to decide in a split second whether to act as a broker or act as a dealer for a particular transaction.

A specialist for a certain stock can always be found at a particular physical location on the floor of the New York Stock Exchange. This location is commonly known as the **post.** The specialist maintains a book in which he or she enters all price-limit orders brought by members of the exchange. A **price-limit order** is an order to buy or sell at not more than nor less than a stipulated price. This price is usually different from the current market quotation. For example, if an investor is willing to sell 100 shares of stock at $40 when the current bid price is $35, he or she places a price limit order to sell at $40. The broker cannot execute this order because the price stipulated is higher than the market price; the broker turns the order over to a specialist in the stock to execute at some future time when and if a transaction is first executed at $40 or higher. The specialist who receives a price-limit order enters it in the book along with other price-limit orders for the same stock. Some are orders to sell above the current price, and some are orders to buy below the current price.

When a member comes to the post with a market order to sell, the specialist must decide whether to buy the stock for his or her own account as a dealer or to buy it as a broker to fill a price-limit order. Here a conflict of interest could arise, but it could be eliminated if the specialist were prohibited from buying and selling for his or her own account. However, that solution is not satisfactory because transactions by specialists for their own accounts are often needed to provide reasonable **price continuity,** a condition in which the price at which the stock is bought and sold changes by no more than a small fraction of a point from one transaction to another.

The rules of the New York Stock Exchange have made specialists responsible for providing an orderly market and maintaining prices that have continuity from one transaction to another. To do this, specialists must buy for their own accounts to prevent a sharp downward change of price that might result from matching sell orders with buy orders in their lists of price-limit orders. In the same fashion, a sharp upward change of price on an execution might occur with a demand being met by a price-limit sell order substantially above the previous transaction. The Securities and Exchange Act provides that when the specialist acts as a dealer, transactions must be restricted "so far as practicable to those reasonably necessary to maintain a fair and orderly market."

Listing of Securities

The members of the New York Stock Exchange may use its facilities to trade only in security issues that have been listed. The Exchange has established requirements that companies must meet before their securities can be listed. These requirements have gradually become stricter, as indicated in Table 8-3. The Exchange also requires that adequate and reliable information on securities and on their issuers be disseminated to investors.

The New York Stock Exchange also requires that firms publish annual financial reports to their stockholders. These firms must also agree to keep the exchange authorities informed of any major developments in their corporate affairs. Each firm that applies for initial listing on the New York Stock Exchange is selected on its own merits. The criteria outlined in Table 8-3 indicate that the firm must be large enough, profitable enough, and have sufficient public ownership to make listing worthwhile. All listed companies must give their owners the privilege of voting; therefore, the Exchange requires that the company solicit proxies for all stockholders' meetings and provide all pertinent information that may affect security values or influence investment decisions. The requirements for continued exchange listing are

Table 8-3
NYSE Minimum Listing Requirements, Domestic Companies, 1958–1981
(Shares and dollars in thousands)

	Effective Date						
	April 23 1958	April 20 1961	March 19 1964	April 15 1965	May 23 1968	July 15 1971	May 20 1976
Net Income Latest Year	$1,000	$1,000	$1,200	$1,200	—	—	—
Net Income Preceding Year	—	—	1,200[•]	1,200[•]	—	—	—
Pre-Tax Income Latest Year	—	—	2,000[•]	2,000	$2,500	$2,500	$2,500
Pre-Tax Income Preceding 2 Years	—	—	2,000[•]	2,000[•]	2,000	2,000	2,000
Net Tangible Assets	8,000	10,000	10,000	10,000	14,000	16,000	16,000[♦]
Aggregate Market Value Shares Outstanding	8,000	10,000	—	—	—	—	—
Aggregate Market Value Publicly Held Shares	—	—	10,000	12,000	14,000	16,000	16,000[♦]
Shares Outstanding	—	—	—	1,000	1,000	—	—
Shares Not Concentrated (Publicly Held)	400	500	600	700	800	1,000	1,000
Number of Stockholders of Record	—	—	—	2,000	2,000	—	—
Number of Holders of Round Lots (100 Shares or more)	1,500[■]	1,500[■]	1,500	1,700	1,800	2,000	2,000

[•]Normally Earnings' yardsticks should have been exceeded for 3 years.
[■]Some credit given for odd-lot holdings. None in later years.
[♦]Value as of January 15, 1981
—no longer applicable.
Source: The New York Stock Exchange Fact Book, 1981, p. 31.

less stringent than the initial requirements; if, however, a company is no longer worthy of being listed because it is in financial difficulty, or if there are too few security transactions in the stock, the exchange may delist the stock.

Table 8-4 summarizes the types and numbers of companies listed on the New York Stock Exchange. At the end of 1980, there were 1,570 companies listed, and there was a total of 2,228 different security issues being traded, including preferred and common stock of U.S. and foreign companies. In addition to these common and preferred stock issues, there was a total of 3,057 bonds listed from among 1,045 U.S. and foreign companies. The vast majority of the bonds listed are U.S. government, New York State, and New York City bonds.

Importance of the New York Stock Exchange

Large American corporations in need of a ready market for their shares and sources of capital find that listing their securities on a national exchange is to their advantage. Smaller companies may find that trading in the over-the-counter market is sufficient. The New York Stock Exchange is the world's most important securities marketplace (see Table 8-5). For example, the New York Stock Exchange accounts for only one-tenth of 1 percent of the total corporations in the United States; as of 1977, however, the firms listed on the exchange account for approximately 41 percent of all assets, 43 percent of all sales or revenues, and approximately 69 percent of all net income of U.S. corporations. These figures dramatically illustrate the importance of the companies listed on the New York Stock Exchange and the importance of the exchange's function in aiding companies with the liquidity required for their securities.

Shareowner Profile

The New York Stock Exchange has made seven different studies that highlight the exchange's shareowner profile (see Table 8-6). As of the latest study (1980), approximately 30 million individuals owned stock and almost three-fourths of the total owned securities listed on the New York Stock Exchange. Shareholder ownership from the total population increased from 1 in 16 persons in 1952 to 1 in 5 persons in 1980.

Institutions continue to gain in dominance over the individual investor and have a significant impact on the volatility and price movements of many companies' securities. Table 8-7 indicates the major sources of New York Stock Exchange volume in terms of shares and in dollar value as divided among the exchange members, public individual investors, and the financial institutions and intermediaries.

Institutional investors hold approximately 55 percent of the total mar-

Table 8-4
Stocks Listed at the End of 1980 (Shares and value in millions)

	Common Stocks				All Stocks		
Industry	No. Cos.	No. Issues	No. Shares	Market Value	No. Issues	No. Shares	Market Value
Industrials	1,093	1,089	22,757	$953,495	1,344	23,168	$968,651
Aircraft	20	20	440	20,425	33	483	22,431
Amusement	18	18	295	11,941	21	298	11,976
Automotive	34	34	954	25,650	45	971	25,997
Building	52	52	606	18,095	72	635	19,010
Chemicals	77	77	2,113	86,469	97	2,128	87,105
Drugs, Cosmetics	35	35	1,312	58,604	40	1,327	59,080
Electronics, Electrical	132	132	2,693	140,087	161	2,743	141,952
Foods, Commodities	71	70	1,685	43,992	87	1,706	44,555
Furniture, Office Eq.	14	14	222	10,962	19	227	11,087
Leather, Shoes	11	11	99	2,838	12	100	2,943
Machinery, Metals	176	176	2,167	79,116	215	2,214	80,907
Mining	31	31	678	23,597	42	680	23,736
Paper, Publishing	60	60	1,056	36,411	74	1,081	37,388
Petroleum, Nat'l Gas	73	73	4,466	288,563	97	4,539	291,584
Retail Trade	106	105	1,723	35,408	119	1,744	36,085
Rubber	14	13	240	3,929	20	242	4,009
Steel	36	35	540	13,772	42	556	14,274
Textiles	46	46	308	5,903	49	310	5,925
Tobacco	8	8	285	13,250	13	301	13,838
Other	79	79	874	34,483	86	882	34,770
Transportation	65	61	1,065	37,565	86	1,121	38,822
Utilities	189	171	5,949	145,181	523	6,230	154,102
Finance, Real Estate	223	219	3,109	79,151	275	3,191	81,228
Grand Total	1,570	1,540	32,881	$1,215,393	2,228	33,709	$1,242,803

Warrants Listed at the End of 1980 (Warrants and value in millions)

	No. of Cos.	No. of Issues	No. of Warrants	Value
Warrants	11	12	36	$162

Source: *The New York Stock Exchange Fact Book,* 1981, p. 32.

ket value of all New York Stock Exchange listed securities. Table 8-8 shows a breakdown of selected institutional investors according to their dollar amount of ownership and their growing importance over the last quarter-century. A number of institutional categories are not included in Table 8-8 because there is no way to estimate their New York Stock Exchange security holdings. These categories include bank-administered personal trust funds, foreign institutions, mutual funds not registered with the SEC, investment counseling organizations, private hedge funds, and nonbank trusts. If it were possible to estimate the amount of stock held or managed by this group, total institutional holdings would probably be approximately one-half the total New York Stock Exchange volume.

Table 8-5
Comparison of NYSE Listed Corporations With All U.S. Corporations

Year	Number of Companies			Total Assets (billions)		
	All U.S.	NYSE	Percent	All U.S.	NYSE	Percent
1979	N/A	1,536	—	N/A	$3,057	—
1978	N/A	1,552	—	N/A	2,645	—
1977•	2,241,317	1,549	0.1%	$5,349	2,327	43.5%
1976	2,082,000	1,550	0.1	4,743	2,067	43.6
1975	2,024,000	1,531	0.1	4,268	1,793	42.0
1974	1,966,000	1,543	0.1	3,996	1,700	42.5
1973	1,905,000	1,536	0.1	3,649	1,491	40.9
1972	1,813,000	1,478	0.1	3,257	1,270	39.0
1971	1,733,000	1,399	0.1	2,889	1,125	38.9
1970	1,655,000	1,330	0.1	2,635	1,007	38.2
1969	1,659,000	1,290	0.1	2,446	887	36.3

Year	Sales or Revenues (billions)			Net income (billions)		
	All U.S.	NYSE	Percent	All U.S.	NYSE	Percent
1979	N/A	$2,363	—	N/A	132	—
1978	N/A	2,019	—	N/A	108	—
1977•	$4,103	1,779	43.4%	$134	93	69.4%
1976	3,636	1,583	43.9	111	82	73.9
1975	3,199	1,404	43.9	83	63	75.9
1974	3,090	1,332	43.1	84	69	82.1
1973	2,558	1,072	41.9	72	63	87.5
1972	2,171	905	41.7	57	49	86.0
1971	1,906	809	42.4	44	42	95.5
1970	1,751	734	41.9	33	37	♦
1969	1,680	687	40.9	43	39	90.7

•Preliminary
♦Percentage relationship not meaningful
Source: U.S. Treasury Dept. Statistics of Income as reprinted in *The New York Stock Exchange Fact Book*, 1981, p. 33.
N/A-Not Available

Table 8-6
Highlights of Eight NYSE Shareowner Surveys

	1952	1956	1959	1962	1965	1970	1975	1980
No. of individual shareowners (thousands)	6,490	8,630	12,490	17,010	20,120	30,850	25,270	29,840
No. owning shares listed on NYSE (thousands)	N/A	6,880	8,510	11,020	12,430	18,290	17,950	23,520
Adult shareowner incidence in population	1 in 16	1 in 12	1 in 8	1 in 6	1 in 6	1 in 4	1 in 6	1 in 5
Medium household income	$7,100	$6,200	$7,000	$8,600	$9,500	$13,500	$19,000	$27,750
No. of adult shareowners with household income:								
Under $10,000 (thousands)	N/A	N/A	9,340	10,340	10,080	8,170	3,420	1,720
$10,000 & over (thousands)	N/A	N/A	2,740	5,920	8,410	20,130	19,970	25,410
No. of adult female shar-owners (thousands)	3,140	4,260	6,350	8,290	9,430	14,290	11,750	13,530
No. of adult male shareowners (thousands)	3,210	4,020	5,740	7,970	9,060	14,340	11,630	14,030
Median age	51	48	49	48	49	48	53	46

N/A - Not available
Source: *The New York Stock Exchange Fact Book,* 1981, p. 47.

Table 8-7
Major Sources of NYSE Volume

	Shares		Value	
	1974	1976	1974	1976
NYSE members	24.3%	22.3%	25.5%	22.2%
Public individuals	31.1	33.2	23.1	23.1
Institutions/intermediaries	44.6	44.5	51.4	54.7

Note: Data cover the first quarter.
Source: *The New York Stock Exchange Fact Book,* 1981, p. 51.

Table 8-8
Estimated Holdings of NYSE Listed Stock by Selected Institutional Investors (billions)

Type of Institution	1949	1955	1960	1965	1970	1975
			Year End			
U.S. institutions:						
Insurance companies:						
Life	$ 1.1	$ 2.2	$ 3.2	$ 6.3	$ 11.7	$ 21.9
Non-life	1.7	4.2	6.0	10.1	12.2	11.3
Investment companies:						
Open end	1.4	6.3	12.4	29.1	39.0	35.2
Closed end	1.6	4.6	4.2	5.6	4.1	5.4
Noninsured pension funds:						
Corporate and other private						
State and local government	0.5	3.4	14.3	35.9	60.7	82.2
	●	0.1	0.3	1.4	9.6	22.8
Nonprofit institutions						
Foundations	2.5	6.9	8.0	16.4	17.0	22.1
Educational endowments	1.1	2.3	2.9	5.9	6.6	7.2
Other	1.0	2.5	4.4	7.7	9.0	8.7
Common trust funds	●	0.9	1.4	3.2	4.1	6.1
Mutual savings banks	0.2	0.2	0.2	0.5	1.4	2.3
Subtotal	$11.1	$33.6	$57.3	$122.1	$175.4	$225.4
Foreign institutions:◆						
Investment, Insurance, and Miscellaneous Cos.	—	—	—	—	—	$ 5.1
Market value of all NYSE-listed stock	$76.3	$207.7	$307.0	$537.5	$636.4	$685.1
Estimated % held by institutional investors	14.5%	16.2%	18.7%	22.7%	27.6%	33.6%

●Less than $50 million.
◆Not included are foreign banks, brokers and nominees. This institutional group held an estimated $18.5 billion of NYSE-listed stocks at the end of 1975. Miscellaneous institutions consist of pension funds and other employee funds or trusts.
Source: *The New York Stock Exchange Fact Book,* 1981, p. 50.

American and Regional Exchanges

The American Stock Exchange (AMEX) is the second largest exchange in the United States. Although the stocks of many large companies are listed on the AMEX, most companies listed on this exchange are either not large enough or would not qualify for the NYSE. Listing requirements for the AMEX are less stringent than for the NYSE, and they encourage applications from relatively young companies.

The AMEX had its beginning around the middle of the nineteenth century outdoors on Wall and Broad streets. It was known as the New York Curb Exchange because brokers met to trade shares on the curb of Wall Street.[2] As the number of companies listed expanded and as activity increased, a large amount of the sidewalk area on Wall and Broad streets was used for trading. When electronic communications became more commonplace, transactions from across the country were directed to a broker's office and then transmitted by hand signals from the offices above the street to the broker below. (Brokers for certain securities were identified by their very colorful clothing.) The exchange's activities became a source of attraction for visitors to the Wall Street area. All the exchanges, including the NYSE, carry on their business today much as the AMEX did outdoors in the nineteenth century. The rules, however, are much more stringent, and regulation has eliminated many of the past abuses.

There are approximately 500 members or seats on the AMEX. The cost of membership and the annual dues are lower than those of the NYSE. In addition, there are approximately 400 associate members who enjoy the privilege of conducting business through a regular member of the AMEX at a substantial commission savings.

Over 1,400 issues are traded on the AMEX, and the companies traded vary from very old, established firms to new, highly speculative issues. Frequently, companies first list their securities on the AMEX and then when they mature they move to the NYSE.

The AMEX is the nation's leading market for foreign securities. The exchange originated the use of American depository receipts (ADRs) for trading in foreign securities. ADRs are certificates issued by New York banks and trust companies against foreign shares that are deposited in the foreign branches of American banks. United States shareholders of foreign securities have all the rights and ownership privileges, even though they possess only ADRs as evidence of their stockholdings.

A number of regional and local stock exchanges provide a marketplace for a variety of securities with varying degrees of public participation and support. As indicated in Table 8-1, other exchanges conducted approximately 9 percent of the market value of the total securities traded on all exchanges

---

[2] The exchange moved indoors in 1924.

in the United States during 1980. The largest regional exchanges are the Midwest Exchange in Chicago, the Pacific Coast Stock Exchange in Los Angeles and in San Francisco, and the Philadelphia-Baltimore-Washington Stock Exchange. The remaining exchange business is conducted by a number of small local exchanges in Boston, Detroit, Cincinnati, Pittsburgh, Honolulu, Spokane, Salt Lake City, Richmond, Wheeling, and Colorado Springs. Most of the regional and local exchanges are organized much the same as the NYSE and AMEX. The number of securities traded on the small regional exchanges has been declining in recent years. Each regional exchange deals with approximately 500 companies; the smaller local exchanges list approximately 100. Many of the companies listed on regional and local exchanges also have their stock traded on the NYSE and AMEX. There is, however, no duplication of listing among the national exchanges. The price of shares traded on local exchanges is usually low, the volume of trading is small, seats and membership fees are inexpensive, and there are very few members of each exchange. Except for trading in securities listed on the NYSE or AMEX, trading is confined to local and regional issues.

Foreign Stock Exchanges

Around the world there are a number of exchanges that provide marketplaces for the publicly owned securities of capitalistic countries. Some of the more popular and active exchanges are the Toronto Stock Exchange, French Stock Exchange, London Stock Exchange, Tokyo Stock Exchange, and German Stock Exchange. The largest foreign exchange is the London Stock Exchange, which lists and trades more than six times the number of issues listed on the NYSE and has three times the number of members. Trading on foreign exchanges is similar to trading on exchanges in the United States. Purchasing stocks of foreign companies, however, adds new risks for the investor. In most cases, it is difficult to obtain information on securities traded on foreign exchanges, although there has been some improvement in recent years. In addition to the normal fluctuations in stock prices that occur on any exchange, the investor runs the risk of fluctuations in the various monetary values.

Over-the-Counter Market

A second major division of the secondary market is the **over-the-counter market** (OTC). The OTC market encompasses all securities not traded on national exchanges. Most of the trading is in corporate bonds, bank and insurance company common stocks, preferred stocks, and U.S. Treasury and municipal bonds. Business in the OTC market is not conducted in any one central marketplace. There are approximately 40,000 issues traded in the OTC market, and dealers and brokers trade directly with each other. Approximately 75 percent of the total transactions are in corporate stock issues, and 25 percent are in corporate and government bond issues. The OTC market does all the federal, state, and municipal bond business, over 80 percent of the corporate-bond business, and one-third of the corporate stock business.

An over-the-counter market exists wherever a securities firm makes a market in a security issue. A firm makes a market when it quotes a price at which it will buy or sell an issue to other members of the financial community or to investors. At the center of the OTC market are the whole-sale dealer firms that make markets by standing ready to buy and sell at quoted prices the securities in which they are registered by the National Association of Security Dealers. Some dealers specialize in bonds, some in stock, and others in only government issues. The wholesale market is largely an interdealer market, but the dealers also do business with retail firms that serve the public.

An individual investor who wishes to buy an OTC stock places an order with a firm that regularly handles a particular company's stock. The retail firm may purchase the stock for its own account from a dealer and then resell it to the customer at a marked-up price. If a firm does this, it must disclose to the purchaser that it is acting as principal and may not add on a commission. Most retail firms, however, act as brokers for their customers and buy at another dealer's offering price. They charge the customer the normal brokerage commission for their services.

Most of the stocks traded in the OTC market are stocks of small and relatively unknown companies or stocks that are closely held by a family. The majority of companies are inexperienced and may offer little or no investment or speculative interest. Several well-known and highly reputed firms, however, have not chosen to have their securities listed.

Many of the most actively traded OTC stocks that are of reasonably large national interest are quoted daily in the *Wall Street Journal* and large metropolitan daily papers. The market prices and volume are supplied by the firms that make a market in the securities and are reported through the NASDAQ (National Association of Security Dealers Automated Quotation) system. The NASDAQ system does not include all shares traded in the over-the-counter market, because it would be extremely difficult to include all 40,000 issues. Most of the unlisted stocks are quoted in local markets.

Recently, there has been significant progress in automating OTC markets quotations. Before NASDAQ existed, it was difficult to determine whether or not an investor was receiving the best price because a quote from one dealer in a particular OTC stock would be substantially different from a quote from another dealer in another part of the country. Not only was the price structure inadequate for investors, but no one knew for sure the extent of the market. The broker is always obligated to obtain the best possible price at the time of the transaction on behalf of the customer. Since many investors, brokers, and dealers did not actively compete in the marketplace in providing bids and offers, it was difficult to be sure that a completely competitive market existed for a particular security. NASDAQ has gone a long way in providing greater depth and liquidity to the marketplace and has contributed significantly to increasing competition.

The Third Market

Over-the-counter trading by nonmembers in common stocks listed on any of the national exchanges is known as the **third market.** Although most transactions involve large institution and security dealers, individuals are increasingly turning to this market. The main reason for the use of the third market is the possibility of saving on commissions on large orders. Listed securities may be traded off the exchanges without restrictions by broker-dealers who are members of the exchange.

The institutional market is very large and can have a tremendous impact on the stock market. The major participants in the institutional market are pension funds, bank trust departments, mutual funds, and insurance companies that have large blocks of securities to trade. The New York Stock Exchange, recognizing that a great deal of its potential business is being transacted in the third market, has attempted to develop techniques for handling large block transactions quickly in order to attract much of the third market business.

Future of the Secondary Markets

Recently, there has been a great deal of discussion about having one central marketplace. It has been said that a central market would be a more efficient marketplace, would be more liquid and marketable, and would eliminate fragmentation across the country. The assumption is that lower costs and fair prices, both in terms of security transactions and administrative costs, would result. NASDAQ would expand its operations by computerizing a nationwide market. It would consolidate ticker tapes for the NYSE, AMEX, national and regional exchanges, and the OTC market, including the third market. The substantial pressure to move in this direction comes from the belief that a central market would be in keeping with the free-enterprise, fully competitive position of our economic system. It could result in the elimination of the nation's stock exchanges.

KEY TERMS

account executive	price continuity
best-efforts selling	price-limit order
bond broker	primary market

broker   prospectus
commission broker   registered trader
competitive bidding   secondary market
direct placement   securities exchange
floor broker   specialists
floor trader   standby underwriting
investment banker   third market
listed securities   two-dollar broker
odd-lot broker   underwriter
over-the-counter-market

QUESTIONS

1. What is the primary market for securities?
2. What are the major functions of the investment banker?
3. Define best-efforts selling.
4. Define standby underwriting.
5. Define direct placement of securities.
6. What are the advantages of direct placement?
7. What are the disadvantages of direct placement?
8. Define secondary markets.
9. How does an investor benefit from a secondary market?
10. What are the functions of the stock exchanges?
11. What is a seat on the exchange? What has the price of seats declined lately?
12. Who are the members of the board of governors of the NYSE? How are they elected?
13. What are the different types of members of the exchange? What are their functions?
14. What requirements must be met in order to be listed on the NYSE?
15. What is the major importance of the NYSE to the national economy?
16. What is the AMEX? How do AMEX securities differ from NYSE securities?
17. What other exchanges are there?
18. What is the over-the-counter market?
19. What is the third market?

SELECTED READINGS

Annual Report of the Securities and Exchange Commission. Washington, D.C.: Government Printing Office. Annually.

BRANCH, BEN, and WALTER FREED. "Bid-Asked Spreads on the AMEX and the Big Board." *Journal of Finance*, March 1977, 159–163.

HERSHMAN, ARLENE. "Here Comes the New Stock Market." *Dun's Review,* April 1978, 65–70.

JESSUP, PAUL F., and UPSON, ROGER B. "Opportunities in Regional Markets." *Financial Analysts Journal,* July–August 1971, 28.

KEENAN, MICHAEL. *Profile of the New York Based Security Industry.* New York: New York University, Center for the Study of Financial Institutions, Monograph 1977-3.

MENDELSON, MORRIS. *From Automated Quotes to Automated Trading.* New York: New York University, Center for the Study of Financial Institutions, Bulletin nos. 80–82, March 1972.

New York Stock Exchange. *New York Stock Exchange Fact Book.* New York: The Exchange, annually.

PEAKE, JUNIUS W. "The National Market System." *Financial Analysts Journal,* July–August 1978, 25–33ff.

SCHWERT, G. WILLIAM. "Stock Exchange Seats as Capital Assets." *Journal of Financial Economics,* Januaury 1977, 51–78.

SKOUSEN, K. FRED. *An Introduction to the SEC,* 2nd ed. Cincinnati: South-Western, 1980.

SMIDT, SEYMOUR. "Inadequacies of NYSE Specialist System." *Commercial and Financial Chronicle,* June 10, 1971, 18–19.

STOLL, HANSR. "The Pricing of Security Dealer Services: An Empirical Study of NASDAQ Stocks." *Journal of Finance,* September 1978, 1153–1172.

9

The Brokerage Business

To transact business in the securities market, an investor must use the facilities of a brokerage firm unless he or she is a member of an organized exchange or is a registered dealer in securities. Almost all the larger national brokerage firms are members of the major stock exchanges. However, many brokers have not purchased membership on national exchanges and, therefore, must do business through exchange members in order to execute orders. For securities traded in the over-the-counter markets, membership is not necessary on any exchange. This chapter discusses the brokerage business, the functions a broker performs for a client, how orders are executed, and the mechanics of security trading.

TYPES OF BROKERAGE FIRMS

Brokerage firms and dealers in securities can be classified according to the three broad functions they perform. They function as (1) investment bankers, (2) as buyers and sellers of securities on behalf of customers, and (3) as principals making markets in securities.

As discussed in Chapter 8, brokerage firms may have an organization through which they act as underwriters of new security issues. The brokerage firm functions as an investment banker because it sells securities directly to the investing public without using the facilities of an exchange.

The broker functions as a principal and makes a market in the securities. This is generally done in over-the-counter issues, but it can also take place in listed securities.

A brokerage firm functions as a buyer and seller of securities for its customers. It is this function for which most brokerage firms are known by the investing public and the function with which the individual investor most frequently comes in contact.

A broker trading in securities listed on a stock exchange is acting as an agent on behalf of clients. Compensation for this service is in the form of commission, which varies among brokerage houses. It is important that the brokerage firm exercise care and demonstrate a reasonable amount of skill in filling the customer's order. The brokerage firm may be held liable for any losses that may result from its mistakes. The care with which the brokerage firm executes orders is determined by what is reasonable practice in the brokerage business. The exercise of the broker's skill requires that instructions be followed and the order placed in the market where the security is customarily traded in the fastest possible time. The brokerage firm is required to refrain from making secret profits on transactions or from crossing orders in its office by acting as both broker and dealer in the same transaction. All securities listed on an exchange must be traded on the floor of that exchange. They cannot be executed off the floor by the broker, except in certain circumstances. The brokerage firm cannot act as both broker and dealer in the same transaction because there could be a conflict of interest or a double commission might result.

If the securities to be traded are not listed on an exchange but are traded in the over-the-counter market, the broker might actually own the shares. He or she would be acting as a principal or dealer in the transaction. Many brokerage firms specialize in making a market in certain securities. In this case, the brokerage firm would sell the security to the customer at the asking price and would not charge a commission for handling the transaction. The brokerage firm makes its fee from the difference between the price it pays for the shares for its own account and the price at which it sells them to customers. The difference between the asked price and bid price is known as the spread and is the compensation for making a market in that security.

Over the years there has been a significant increase in regulation requiring brokerage firms to represent their customers honestly and legally. Chapter 11 reviews securities regulation, which covers the stock exchanges through the brokerage firms and the role of the National Association of Security Dealers.

BROKERAGE INFORMATION

A traditional function of a brokerage firm is providing customers with information to help them purchase suitable securities. Most brokerage firms inform their clients about individual companies and industries. The brokerage business is now changing its information policy. For example, on May 1, 1975, when the client and the brokerage firm were for the first time allowed to negotiate commission rates, many firms lowered their rates but reduced free research. Most brokerage firms retained a commission-fee structure that permitted the continuation of providing clients with research. Other firms charge on an individual basis for many of the services normally covered previously under the commissions charged. Many firms believe that they cannot serve clients adequately unless they provide them with information.

Most large brokerage houses continue to provide research reports on individual companies and industry analyses. These analyses are prepared by financial analysts in the brokerage firm's research department. The information is made available to retail customers through published reports that are generally available in the broker's office. Institutional investors are provided with a more complete research service, which is usually paid for by commission dollars. The cost for this service can sometimes be very high. Excerpts from institutional reports are often carried in the financial news. Individual retail customers can learn from these excerpts what the analysts' current feelings are toward industry or individual companies.

Most large brokerage firms also provide economic forecasts. Many experienced fundamental investors would quickly agree that it is difficult to invest without knowing the overall economic conditions within which companies operate.

Many large national brokerage firms analyze portfolios and recommend specific changes that would better meet an investor's objectives. (Usually, there is no fee for this service.) For example, if an investor wanted a financial analyst's recommendation on the securities he owned, he would ask his broker to appraise his investment portfolio.

A few brokerage firms also provide indirect investment management services. (There is a fee for this service.) For example, an investor who feels that he or she cannot manage a portfolio adequately may ask a brokerage firm to recommend an investment advisor. Most brokerage firms that provide this investment management service on a continuing basis usually employ the service of outside investment advisory firms. The brokerage house provides the standard brokerage services for that investment advisor. Only rarely does a broker actually perform a discretionary investment management service for a client and then only with written permission from the client. Most brokerage firms prohibit their account executives from performing discretionary investment management services.

SELECTING A BROKERAGE FIRM AND A BROKER

It is very difficult for the investor to differentiate between the brokerage firm and the broker. Both the broker and the firm must be suitable for the investor because they cannot work independently of each other. The conscientious investor should look for a reliable broker who works for a reliable brokerage firm. This may seem obvious, but for the individual investing for the first time, selecting a broker can be difficult. Many individuals are hesitant to interview a broker and the firm.

It is most important that a broker be engaged who will work closely with the investor at each step in the investment process. If the individual is new in the investment business, it is important that a broker be selected who is willing to spend time educating him or her in the fundamentals of investing.

A brokerage firm must have an unquestioned credit rating, and it must be of sufficient size and experience to be able to provide the necessary investment services. It is perhaps difficult for the novice investor to determine the credit rating and the reputation of a brokerage firm. It may be possible to determine these by asking discreet questions at various banks within the investment community.

Selecting a brokerage firm that provides adequate information and research facilities is paramount to a successful investment program. The information should contain data on general economic conditions, industry analysis, company analysis, and securities appropriate for the individual. The data should also include a historical analysis and economic and business forecasts for the industries selected.

Since order execution is of major importance to any investor, the brokerage firm should be able to deal in securities listed on the major exchanges and should be knowledgeable in the over-the-counter market. The brokerage firm should have membership in the national exchanges, and the broker should be a member of the National Association of Security Dealers. In addition, the brokerage firm should have a reputation that enables it to participate in underwriting syndicates, thus giving clients an opportunity to purchase new security issues. Because many small local brokerage firms do not have membership on exchanges and do not participate in very many national underwritings, the investor is limited in the ability to obtain good executions and new stock issues. Brokerage houses must have regular audits. These audits assure clients that their accounts are being handled properly. In addition, investigations are required if there is any suspicion of violations. Also, firms that are members of the major stock exchanges must have a minimum capitalization.

Once the individual has found a reliable brokerage firm, a qualified broker must be selected. This can be costly if an individual has to go from broker to broker until one is found who gives correct advice. Therefore, it is preferable to interview several brokers initially to find one who meets the client's needs.

It is important for a broker to give prompt and efficient service, that is, be able to confirm a purchase or sale within minutes and provide price quotations quickly. A broker who cannot give prompt service is not fulfilling a basic obligation.

A broker's integrity must be unquestioned, and it should be reflected in his or her reputation in the community. Lawyers, bankers, and independent investment counselors can provide the investor with a list of reputable brokers.

For most investors, it is important to select a broker who is experienced in the brokerage business and who is working for an established firm that has a record of good service. It is important to select a broker who is experienced in the securities markets and who has been through several business cycles. The new broker often lacks the necessary perspective to help the new investor. A seasoned broker will generally suggest long-term investments instead of suggesting that the client be an active trader moving in and out of securities. Active trading can be very expensive because commissions eat away at much of the profit. Therefore, it is important that the broker have the best interest of the investor uppermost in his mind.

OPENING A BROKERAGE ACCOUNT

Once the investor has selected a brokerage firm and a broker who understands his or her investment objectives, the next step is to open an account. Opening an account is relatively simple. The investor fills out a signature card that asks for occupation, employer, bank, and citizenship. Also, the broker has to know the type of account the investor wishes to open and the address where confirmations, monthly statements, annual reports, and proxy information are to be sent. The investor usually must be at least 21 years of age to open an account with a brokerage firm; in several states the age is 18 years. If the investor is under age, a guardian may buy securities until the child reaches legal age.

The applicant indicates whether he or she wants to open a cash or margin account. If the applicant opens a cash account, he or she is expected to pay cash for each purchase. If the applicant opens a margin account, the broker extends credit to meet part of the cost of purchases, subject to the rules that govern margin accounts. Margin accounts are discussed later in this chapter.

After each transaction in an investor's account, a confirmation of the transaction is sent to the investor immediately. Exhibit 9-1 shows a sample confirmation slip. Each investor receives a monthly statement showing all account activity during that month. The monthly statement itemizes each

Exhibit 9–1 Brokerage Confirmation Slip

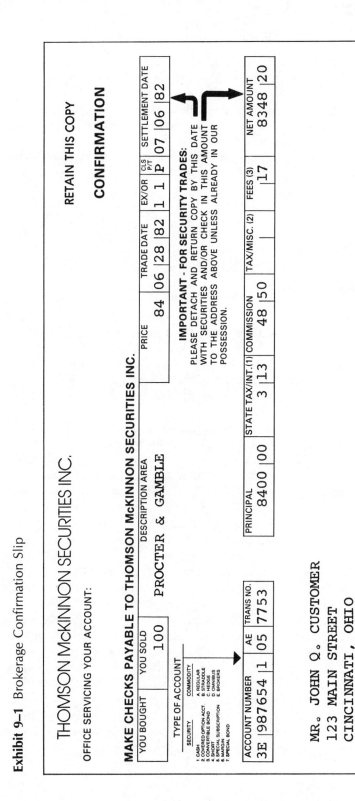

Courtesy of Thomson McKinnon Securities Inc.

transaction. It shows cash deposits and withdrawals and is the official record of the account. Many brokerage firms do not supply monthly statements when there has been no activity in a client's account.

A typical account is a cash account in which no credit is extended and all transactions are settled within five business days from the date of purchase. The confirmation slip, which is received a day or two after the transaction, includes the total amount due the brokerage firm and the payment date (see Exhibit 9-1).

Registering Securities

The broker has to know how the investor wants the securities registered. There are basically two forms of security registration: beneficial ownership and street name ownership. Securities may be registered in the investor's name as the beneficial owner. The investor's name as beneficial owner is printed on the stock or bond certificate. **Street-name ownership** is a term used by the securities industry to denote stock registered in the name of a brokerage firm or its nominee. Although the stock belongs to customers of the brokerage firm, the broker holds the stock in its name because it simplifies trading by the customer and completion of the transaction by the broker-dealer.

For example, when a customer wishes to sell stock that the broker is holding and that is registered in street name, the customer need only give the broker verbal instructions. The customer does not have to deliver the certificate to the broker, and the execution of a stock power to authorize transfer of the certificates is eliminated. Moreover, in many circumstances delivery by one broker to another broker of stock registered in street name and endorsed in blank constitutes good delivery. The transaction completion process is facilitated when securities are held in street name because the buying broker will accept from the selling broker securities registered in street name. The buying broker-dealer, in turn, may redeliver these securities to another broker-dealer without having to transfer ownership before delivery. Thus, numerous routine transfers are eliminated.

Because securities held in street name carry the brokerage house name, not the investors' name, the corporation whose stock or bonds are held sends dividends or interest checks to the brokerage house. When the brokerage house receives these payments on behalf of its clients, it credits the individual investors' accounts with those monies. Financial statements, proxy information, and other information are also channeled through the brokerage firm, which then remails them to the individual investors. Sometimes there are delays in the transfer process, but generally it works smoothly.

TYPES OF ORDERS

Once the investor has opened either a cash or a margin account and has determined how securities are to be held, he or she then places orders appropriate to the investment objectives. An investor's order can be executed either at the best prevailing price on the exchange or possibly at a price he or she determines.

Market Orders

Market orders are executed as fast as possible and at the best prevailing price on the exchange. An order is executed **at the market** but without limitation on price. For example, in a quotation of 20 bid, $20\frac{1}{2}$ asked, an order to buy at the market would be executed at $20\frac{1}{2}$ and an order to sell at the market would be executed at 20. Although the broker will try to get the best price possible on market orders, the broker cannot afford to delay because other orders may intervene.

The advantage of a market order is the speed at which it is executed. The disadvantage is that the investor does not know the exact execution price until after the broker receives confirmation of the order execution, usually several minutes after the execution. This disadvantage is most troublesome when dealing in very inactive or volatile securities.

Limit Orders

On limit orders, the investor places a price limit that the broker may not violate. For example, on a sell order, the broker must not sell for less than the price limit, but he may accept more. On a buy order, the broker must not pay more, but he may pay less than the price limit. Limit order overcome the disadvantage of the market order because the investor knows in advance the limits of the potential transaction. Thus, limit orders set the boundaries of the dollar risk the investor wishes to assume.

Assume, for example, that General Motors is currently trading at $45 per share and the investor wants to buy the stock soon, but he wants to be sure to obtain shares at not much higher than the current price. The investor has the opportunity to place a limit order to buy at any price and might select $45\frac{1}{4}$. This will allow the execution to rise one-quarter point higher than the last trading price of 45. (It is important to note here that common-stock price quotations are usually stated in eighths of a dollar, but they are not limited to one-eighth fluctuations at a time.) The limit order of $45\frac{1}{4}$ cannot be executed at any price higher than that, but it may be executed lower.

Generally, limit orders are placed **away from the market**; that is, the limit price is somewhat different from the prevailing price. There are a number of uses and many variations of the limit order. For example, if an individual owns GM and the price of the stock is at $45 per share, he may enter a limit order to sell at $46, hoping that the stock will reach that level. Obviously, the investor believes that the limit price will be reached and executed in a reasonable period of time. The chief disadvantage of the limit order is that the order may never be executed. If the limit sell price, in this case, is set close to the prevailing price, there is little advantage over using the market order. Furthermore, if the stock is moving either sharply upward or downward, to place a limit order very close to the market and risk not getting the trade executed is not good investing.

Investors often enter limit orders at the last known market price because most future transactions will be close to that price. Nevertheless, limit orders can at times result in no transaction being made, and the price may move away from the limit order, leaving the investor to reconsider placing another order. Limit orders are especially helpful in securities that have very few shares outstanding, for in these stocks the market price may fluctuate over a wide range. It is also advisable to use limit orders on small quantities of bonds, because many bond issues fluctuate substantially. When an investor trades in a well-known stock such as American Telephone and Telegraph, which has a very active daily volume, a market order is generally sufficient to obtain a reasonable order execution near or at the last known price. A good broker will advise a client on the correct use of limit and market orders, depending upon the security in question.

Stop Orders

A stop order, sometimes referred to as a **stop-loss order,** may be used either to protect a profit or limit a loss. In effect, a stop order is a special limit order, but it has very important differences in intent and application. A stop order to sell is treated as a market order when the stop price or a price below it is reached. A stop order to buy is treated as a market order when a stop price or a price above it is reached.

For example, if an investor purchased 100 shares of stock at 30 and the stock is currently selling at 50, the profit on paper, excluding taxes and commissions, would be $20 per share, or $2,000. The investor may wish to protect this profit without losing the long position in the security. The investor may believe that there is additional upside potential, but knows that paper profits can evaporate very fast in a down market and that a market moves in cycles. Therefore, he or she may wish to protect the position by entering a stop order to sell at a price below 50. The investor may choose a price of 47. If at some future time the market price falls to 47 or below, the investor's stop order becomes a market order, and he will be automatically sold out of the 100 shares at the next market price. Since the stop order becomes a market order, the investor may be sold out at 47, $47\frac{1}{2}$

or perhaps $46\frac{5}{8}$. In an orderly securities market, the price will be close to the stop of 47, which allows the investor to maintain a certain level of profit.

There are several possible dangers in using the stop. If the stop is placed too close to the market, the investor's position might be closed-out because of minor price fluctuation. If the stop order is placed too far away from the market, the stop order serves no reasonable purpose. In addition, because stop orders become market orders only after the proper price level has been reached, it is possible that the actual transaction will take place some distance away from the price the investor had in mind when he placed the order. In general, stop orders may be useful if they are used wisely by a knowledgeable investor, but they cannot rectify basically bad investment decisions. If stop orders are poorly placed, they can close out good investment positions.

Stop-Limit Orders

The stop-limit order is a device to overcome some of the uncertainty of the stop order. In the typical stop order, the investor does not know what the execution price will be after the order becomes a market order. A stop-limit order gives the investor the advantage of specifying the limit price. There are several variations of the stop-limit order. For example, the investor may wish to specify a maximum price he or she will pay in the case of a stop-limit buy or the minimum price acceptable in the case of a stop-limit order to sell. Therefore, a stop-limit order to buy is activated as soon as the stop price or higher price is reached. Then an attempt is made to buy at the limit price or lower. Conversely, the stop-limit to sell is activated as soon as the stop price or lower is reached. Then an attempt is made to sell at the limit price or higher. For example, if an investor has a long position in 100 shares of a stock at $30 and wishes to protect most of the profit, he might enter a stop limit to sell at 28. If and when the stock reaches 28 or below, his order is activated, and an attempt is made to sell at 28 or above; nothing below 28 would be accepted.

The danger in a stop-limit loss order is that the order may not be executed if the market moves downward. The end result may be a substantially greater loss. Very few investors find it wise to place stop-limit orders. They prefer only to enter the stop order.

TIME PERIOD FOR ORDERS

At the time the investor places an order, the period for which an order is to remain in force is specified. Most stock exchanges recognize two types of orders: the day order and open orders.

Day Orders

A day order remains active only for the trading day on which it is entered. Unless customers request otherwise, brokers enter all orders as day orders. Market orders are almost always day orders because they do not specify a particular price. In most cases, they are executed during that trading day. Many investors make frequent use of day orders because they know that conditions can change rapidly. They may want to reconsider their orders if they are not filled on the day they are placed.

Open Orders

Open orders, more commonly known as **good till canceled (GTC) orders,** remain in effect until either canceled by the customer or executed. Open orders are frequently used in conjunction with limit orders. An investor using an open or GTC order implies that he or she understands the supply and demand conditions of the stock in question and, therefore, feels sufficiently confident that, given enough time, the order may very well be executed on desired terms. As a matter of convenience to customers, a broker may accept an order good for a week, or for a month, or through a specified date. In such a case, the broker enters a GTC order with the specialist on the floor of the exchange and assumes responsibility for canceling the order at the specified time if the order is not executed. Many brokerage firms permit GTC orders to remain in effect for no longer than one month. The broker automatically confirms with the investor to ensure that the investor is aware of the open order's continued existence.

Open orders are risky because the circumstances surrounding the proposed transaction may change considerably and the contemplated action would no longer be advisable. For example, positive information may increase the stock's price so that a limit sell order is reached, but circumstances may have changed. A sell order may now be inappropriate and unwarranted, but the investor may not have time to cancel the open order. Conversely, negative information may depress the stock's price so that an open limit order to buy is activated. An open order is also risky, because the investor may forget about the order after a considerable amount of time has passed since the order was confirmed by the broker. The investor is responsible for any open order that has been placed and executed. Most brokerage firms give their investors confirmation slips of their open interests.

ODD-LOT ORDERS

Orders for the purchase or the sale of less than the established unit of trading on the various exchanges have been handled for many years through **odd-lot** dealers. For the great majority of stocks on the New York Stock Exchange, the unit of trading is 100 shares, called a **round lot.** In some limited cases, 10-share markets have been established for a group of stocks in which activity is limited for various reasons. Odd-lot transactions of listed stocks on the New York Stock Exchange are now handled mainly by the exchange. An odd-lot order usually covers from 1 to 99 shares. If an investor were purchasing 125 shares, 100 would be purchased as a round lot and 25 would be purchased as an odd lot. The price is set at $12\frac{1}{2}$ cents a share higher on purchase orders and $12\frac{1}{2}$ cents lower on selling orders than is quoted for the round-lot price. On odd-lot limit orders, execution does not take place until the round-lot price reaches the $12\frac{1}{2}$ cent differential. For example, an order to buy 25 shares at $27 is not filled until the regular price reaches $26\frac{7}{8}$. Similarly, an order to sell 25 shares at 27 is not filled until the regular price reaches $27\frac{1}{8}$. The odd-lot price differential of one-eighth of a point represents the compensation for dividing the shares into odd lots.

Odd-lot trading permits the investor who has limited financial resources to buy a modest number of shares in several corporations and thus obtain some diversification for his or her limited funds. The disadvantage is that the odd-lot price differential, plus the minimum commission charged, can comprise a significant percentage of the purchase and sale price on small orders, especially for low-priced securities.

To minimize the impact of commissions on odd-lot orders, some members of the New York Stock Exchange have sponsored a Monthly Investment Plan (MIP) through which investors may invest from $50 to $1,000 monthly or quarterly in common stocks. Commissions are at the normal rates charged by the brokerage firm. The montly investment plans vary from one firm to another. Also, some brokerage firms act as odd-lot dealers without charging the one-eighth differential. Also, market orders received by 9:45 A.M. to buy or sell will not be charged the odd-lot differential.

Trading in the over-the-counter market is usually done in 100-share lots, but the purchase of fewer than 100 shares is usually at the same price as a 100-share lot. In other words, no distinction is made between round lots and odd lots.

EXECUTION OF ORDERS

Once the individual investor has selected a brokerage firm and broker and the appropriate type of account, he or she gives the order to the broker. If, for example, the investor wants to buy 100 shares of General Motors (GM), he or she first asks the broker for the current price of the stock. The broker gives the client the high and low prices of the day, the price of the last transaction, and the current bid and asking prices. The bid represents the highest price to buy that the specialist on the floor of the exchange is willing to pay, and the asking price represents the lowest price to sell stock by the specialist.

The broker checks his stock-quote machine and reports back to the investor that GM is currently quoted at "45 to $\frac{1}{4}$." This means that the investor would pay $45\frac{1}{4}$ if he placed a market order to buy. If the asking price is appropriate, the investor places a market order. The written order is either wired by telegraphic transfer or phoned to the brokerage firm's New York Office. The order is then transferred by phone to a clerk on the floor of the exchange. The clerk, who is an employee of the brokerage firm, notifies by means of a signal board system, a partner of the brokerage firm who is a member of the exchange. (The communication system consists of huge boards mounted on the walls. Each member of the exchange has an assigned number that is posted on one of the boards. Any member of the exchange can be paged through an assigned number.) The member of the exchange then picks up the order from the clerk and takes it to the location on the floor where GM is being traded.

Each stock listed on the exchange is assigned to a particular U-shaped trading post where a specialist in that stock is located. Upon arrival at the **post**, the exchange member checks with the specialist to determine the current bid and asked prices of GM. Current bid and asked prices are usually posted at the specialist's location. The market order is then executed at the best obtainable price. Usually, the transaction is carried out through face-to-face contact with the specialist, that is, through a member partner representing the investor who wants to sell. They bargain with each other and finally reach a mutually satisfactory price. When a security market is active, there will generally be other members buying and selling the same security. Therefore, the transaction must take place at the post and at or between the posted bid and asked prices.

After the trade is made, the brokers note the transaction and with whom it was made by using the number from the broker's name badge. An employee of the exchange who reports all transactions notes the price and number of shares of the transaction and then fills out an optical scanning card that is immediately placed in the optical reader. The price of that transaction updates the ticker system and the quote machines located around the world. The member then advises the phone clerk and reverses the order-placing process so that the investor can be notified at what price the 100 shares of GM were purchased. This entire process occurs within minutes of the initial phone call made by the broker.

The Specialist's Role

In the preceding example, the purchase of GM was made from another broker. This is not always possible, and in such cases, the specialist must stand ready to act as a dealer. Specialists sell from their own accounts when there are more buyers than sellers, and they buy for their inventory when there are more sellers than buyers. Specialists play a key role in maintaining a stable market. They do not allow large price fluctuations in either direction and must have a great deal of experience, as well as a large capital requirement, to maintain an inventory in the stocks in which they specialize. In the GM example, had there not been another broker present, the specialist would have sold 100 shares of GM at the market asking price. This is not always true, however, when a large number of shares are either sold or bought. But when 100 shares are offered or wanted, the specialist must stand ready to handle that market order.

When limit orders or stop orders are placed away from the market, they are left with the specialist, who records them in a book and executes them in the order in which they were received. In these cases, the specialist acts as a broker by bringing buyers and sellers together instead of as a dealer trading for his own account.

SHORT SALES

An investor who anticipates a decline in the price of the stock attempts to make a profit by borrowing the stock from someone who owns it, selling the stock now, and buying it back later at a lower price. The broker to whom the order is given arranges to borrow the stock either from his own inventory or from inventory of customers who have agreed to allow their securities to be loaned for this purpose or from another broker who has stock available for lending. A **short sale** is the sale of stock that the seller does not own but which he or she expects to acquire in the future, it is hoped at a lower price.

When the broker borrows stock from a customer, the customer turns it over but continues to receive any dividends paid during the transaction. Instead of being paid by the company (the company now pays the purchaser of the shorted stock), the lender is paid the dividend by the short seller himself. Since the customer who lends the stock can demand return of the shares of stock at any time, he or she incurs no risk in lending. Most of the time the lending customer does not know that his stock has been borrowed for a short sale. Similarly, the buyer of the shorted stock not only may not know that the shares purchased were shorted, but also does not care, because he or she receives not only delivery of the shares but also any dividends paid on the stock.

For a short sale to take place, it must be designated a short sale when it is placed. It cannot be executed at a price lower than that established in the preceding regular sale. This requirement by federal regulation is important, because short sellers might otherwise be able to drive down the price of the stock through successive short sales. The Securities Exchange Act of 1934 requires that a short sale may only occur if the previous direction of the stock price change was higher. For example, if a seller decides to go short at 25 and the preceding trade was $24\frac{3}{4}$ there is no problem. If, however, the preceding trade took place at 25 and the last movement in the stock's price was down from $25\frac{1}{8}$, a short sale cannot be made. Therefore, short sales can only take place if the stock's price movement has been previously on an uptick.

There is no time limit on how long an individual may hold a short position, but the investor's account must maintain an adequate level of cash and collateral. As long as the price of the stock declines, the investor can buy the stock back (called **covering the short position**) at any time and realize a profit. If, however, the stock rises in price, the investor sustains an increasing loss as the price rises. The broker must have sufficient collateral in the investor's account to buy the stock back and cover the customer's short position at a higher price than the original short transaction.

Generally, because of the degree of risk involved, short sales have been recommended only for sophisticated investors. The risk lies in the fact that the maximum profit potential of a short sale is when the stock declines to zero. However, the maximum amount of loss that can be sustained in a short sale is infinite since, theoretically, the price of the stock can rise to infinity. As a practical matter, an investor can prevent this by using stop orders.

There has been considerable debate about the economic function that short selling performs in the marketplace. Some claim that it should be outlawed because it is detrimental to investment values; others believe that it provides not only a corrective check to abnormally high prices but also a protective cushion to declining prices. Short selling is much more prevalent when markets are weak or uncertain than when markets are strong. Generally, investors seek either shares of firms whose future prospects are dim, shares whose prices are volatile, or shares whose prices appear to be too high as candidates for short positions. Technical analysts believe that large short positions in a security can actually result in higher prices, because short sellers must eventually place buy orders to cover their positions. Therefore, when the short position of a firm's stock increases to a high level, it is generally thought that there will be an upward movement of the stock's market price.

The short position (the number of shares sold short and not covered as of a specific date) in individual listed stocks is computed regularly by the New York Stock Exchange (the middle of each month) and is published in the financial sections of leading newspapers.

MARGIN TRADING

The two main types of accounts with brokers are cash accounts and margin accounts. In a cash account, purchases are made outright for full ownership, and sales are made against immediate delivery of securities. In a margin account, securities purchased can be paid for by a mix of cash and borrowed funds or other securities. The principal reason for buying on margin is to leverage the amount of money invested. For the same amount of cash, the investor can control more shares on margin than if he or she had to put up the entire purchase price in cash.

To open a margin account, the buyer deposits with the broker cash or securities equal to a portion of the price of the security required (the margin). The broker advances the balance and charges the buyer interest on this balance. To finance this balance, the broker either uses his own capital or obtains funds by pledging the securities purchased with a bank as collateral for a loan. The charge for the borrowed funds is approximately one percentage point above the prevailing prime rate. As long as the value of the securities remains the same or higher, the investor never needs to repay the borrowed funds, but must pay interest monthly. Interest on margin loans is usually computed daily and is based on the cost of the broker's borrowed funds, which changes in accordance with fluctuations in the prime rate. New York Stock Exchange rules require that a minimum down payment of $2,000 or an equivalent amount of securities be made into the account before margin trading can take place. Some brokerage firms also have additional rules; for example, some firms require higher down payments.

The percent of margin in an individual investor's account can be expressed as follows:

$$\text{percent of margin} = \frac{\text{equity in account}}{\text{market value of securities}}$$

For example, if an investor buys $10,000 worth of securities and pays $6,000 cash, his margin is $6,000, or 60 percent of the total value of the shares purchased.

The Federal Reserve Board established margin requirements for the initial amount of equity a purchaser of listed securities is required to deposit. Table 9-1 shows the changes that have taken place in the initial margin requirements over the past several decades. The Federal Reserve requirements have varied between 40 and 100 percent since their inception in 1934. Margin requirements for stocks and convertible bonds are the same. Margin on straight bonds can be less than those on stocks and vary according to the bonds' overall quality. Prior to July 8, 1969, brokers were permitted to extend regulated credit on stocks and convertible bonds listed or traded only on registered exchanges. After that date, the Federal Reserve amended the regulations to permit brokers to extend regulated credits on a selected list of stocks traded over the counter.

The New York Stock Exchange has a minimum maintenance requirement of 25 percent, and most brokerage firms impose a 30 percent requirement. If the value of the securities begins to fall in the marketplace and if the customer is not maintaining the minimum maintenance requirement, he or she will receive a **margin call** requiring the customer either to put up additional cash or securities or to liquidate a sufficient amount of holdings to reestablish the maintenance requirement.

For example, let's assume that an individual investor having $10,000 in cash believes that a particular stock will rise 10 percent over the next few months. If the investor is correct and buys the stock for $10,000 in cash and sells it after three months for $11,000, he or she makes a profit of $1,000 (ignoring commission) or 10 percent on the original investment, all within 3 months. If, however, the investor wants to maximize financial leverage and purchases the same security on margin, he or she could invest the $10,000 and purchase $20,000 of the security, assuming a margin requirement of 50 percent. By borrowing the maximum permitted, the investor realizes a 10 percent gain in the value of the security over the 3-month period, but now the profit is $2,000 because the stock rises from $20,000 to $22,000. In this example the investor makes a larger profit than the $1,000 with the use of margin. Excluding the interest and commissions that would normally be charged, the profit before taxes would be $2,000 on the original cash investment of $10,000, which has doubled the profit both in terms of dollars and percent.

Interest is charged on the $10,000 loan over the 3-month period. For example, if the annual interest rate were 12 percent, the investor would be charged 3 percent on the $10,000 borrowed over the 3 months, or $300. This would reduce the $2,000 profit to $1,700, resulting in a 17 percent profit.

Trading on margin carries added risk. If the stock were to decline 10 percent, the investor would realize a 20 percent loss on the security, in addition to the 3 percent interest charge. The total loss would be 23 percent, plus the normal commissions.

The risk in trading on margin can be seen from the results of 1929

Table 9-1
Initial Margin Requirements: Percent of Total Value
Required to Purchase Stock

Effective	Rate	Effective	Rate	Effective	Rate
10/15/34	45%	1/17/51	75%	7/10/62	90%
2/1/36	55	2/20/53	50	11/6/63	70
11/1/37	40	1/4/55	60	6/8/68	80
2/5/45	50	4/23/55	70	5/6/70	65
7/5/45	75	1/16/58	50	12/6/71	55
1/21/46	100	8/5/58	70	11/24/72	65
2/1/47	75	10/16/58	90	1/3/74	50
3/30/49	50	7/28/60	70		

Source: *The New York Stock Exchange Fact Book*, 1981, p. 43.

when many brokerage firms required only a 10 percent margin. When the stock market had its sharp drop in the fall of 1929, investors who were operating on a 10 percent margin quickly found their entire equity positions eliminated. A 10 percent drop in the price of their securities completely eliminated their investment if they had borrowed the 90 percent balance. After the stock market crash and the Great Depression, the Federal Reserve imposed initial margin requirements, which were quickly raised. The fluctuating margin requirements, shown in Table 9-1, have been used by the Federal Reserve to regulate speculative influences on the stock market.

BOND TRADING

Bonds are traded on the New York Stock Exchange and on other exchanges, but the bulk of trading is in the over-the-counter market. The usual denomination of bonds is $1,000.

Bonds **payable to the bearer** are called **bearer bonds. Registered bonds** are recorded in the name of a particular person or persons. They may be registered as to principal only, or as to both principal and interest. Bonds registered as to both principal and interest are often called **fully registered bonds.** Bearer bonds and bonds registered as to principal have interest coupons attached, each of which has a due date. The bondholder clips or detaches the appropriate coupon and collects interest through a bank or broker. Since fully registered bonds have no interest coupons, interest checks are mailed directly to registered owners. Bondholders are beginning to appreciate the convenience of having registered bonds because they provide the following:

1. The collecting of all interest in a single check directly from the company.
2. The safety of registered over bearer form.
3. The simplicity of keeping track of fewer certificates.
4. The ability of the issuer to notify bondholders directly in case of redemption before maturity date.

Almost all bonds quoted and sold include interest to the date of delivery; that is, to arrive at the total cash outlay for the purchase of a bond, the interest accrued since the last interest payment date must be added to the quoted price, plus commissions. The seller of the bond is entitled to receive interest to, but not including, the date of payment; the buyer is entitled to receive interest from the date of purchase to the next payment date. Therefore, regardless of the current rate of interest or the yield base in which the bond is sold, the accrued interest is computed by prorating the current coupon. Bonds in default and income bonds are usually sold **flat,** that is, paying no current interest but carrying accumulated interest for the buyer from the last payment date, should any future payment be made.

DELIVERY AND SETTLEMENT

If a security is sold for regular delivery, the current practice on the exchanges and over-the-counter markets for all stock and corporate and municipal bonds is for delivery of securities sold and payment of securities purchased to be made on the fifth business day following the day of the transaction. The settlement date is indicated on the confirmation slip. Care should be taken that securities and funds are in the possession of the broker by or before the required date. The usual practice on U.S. Treasury and federal agency issues is for delivery and settlement on the next business day. A seller may arrange for other than the described delivery, but he or she may have to make a small sacrifice in price. The investor may have delivery made on a cash basis, meaning that delivery can take place on the same day. This can be important for the investor who wants to establish a gain or loss in the closing days of a taxable year.

Because delivery occurs on the fifth business day following the day of transaction, corporate records only show stockholders of record five business days prior to the actual settlement date. This is particularly important for the payment of corporate dividends, because the ex-dividend date precedes the payment date for dividends by five business days. The **ex-dividend date** is the date on which the stock's price is lowered automatically by the amount of the dividend to be paid to stockholders of record five business days later. For example, if a company pays a 25 cent quarterly dividend and the stock is trading at $30 per share and the stock goes ex-dividend, the specialist on the floor of the New York Stock Exchange or other exchanges will automatically reduce the price by one-quarter of a point to $29\frac{3}{4}$. This has the effect of giving no advantage to the individual who purchases the shares ahead of the ex-dividend date. In fact, many investors prefer to buy a security after it has gone ex-dividend so that they can purchase the stock at a lower market price and avoid paying tax on a dividend.

FEES AND COMMISSIONS

A portion of the price of buying and selling securities is the brokerage commission, which is charged all buyers and sellers. Prior to May 1, 1975, all commissions were set by the New York Stock Exchange, and all members had to charge at least those commissions. The commissions in effect on April 30, 1975, are shown in Table 9-2, which continues to be used as a basis for most institutional commission calculations. Since May 1, 1975, all commissions have been negotiated, and most firms have raised their rates for retail customers.

Because negotiated commissions are now permitted, a number of new brokerage firms have been created for the sole purpose of executing retail and institutional customer orders and giving discounts of up to 80 percent. These firms do not offer the investor any services, such as research, which many investors find necessary for the successful administration of their portfolios.

In the past there had been considerable pressure on the NYSE to allow commission rates to be negotiated, especially commissions on large orders. The fixed commission schedule in effect since 1959 caused a number of large institutional investors to transact business in the third and fourth markets, which resulted in a decrease in the amount of commissions earned by firms that were members of the NYSE. Since May 1, 1975, large discounts (from 30 to 80 percent off the regular fee schedules) have been given to institutional investors by the large brokerage houses.

In addition to commission charged on purchases and sales of securities, there are fees and taxes on the sale of common stock. Table 9-3 itemizes the fees charged nonresidents by the SEC and the state of New York when a stock is sold; Exhibit 9-1 shows the New York State tax and the SEC fee for the 100-share sale of Procter and Gamble.

Table 9-2
Commission Schedule, April 30, 1975

	Money Involved	Money Involved, %	Plus
(a) On orders for 100 shares	$2,000 and under	As mutually agreed	—
	Above $2,000 but under $2,500	1.3%	$ 12.00
	$2,500 and above	0.9%	$ 22.00
The minimum commission on any order for 100 shares could not exceed $65.			

	Money Involved	Money Involved, %	Plus
(b) On multiple round-lot orders	$2,000 and under	As mutually agreed	—
	above $2,000 but under $2,500	1.3%	$ 12.00
	$2,500 but under $20,000	0.9%	$ 22.00
	$20,000 but under $30,000	0.6%	$ 82.00
	$30,000 to and including $300,000	0.4%	$142.00
Plus, for each round lot	First to tenth round lot		$6.00 per round lot
	Eleventh round lot and above		$4.00 per round lot

Source: *The New York Stock Exchange Fact Book*, 1976, p. 59.

Table 9-3
Transfer Taxes: Nonresident New
York State Transfer Tax Effective
August 1, 1975

Selling Price per Share	Rate in Cents
Less than $5	0.78125
$ 5 to less than $10	1.56250
$10 to less than $20	2.34375
$20 or more	3.12500

Maximum tax on any single taxable sale
is $437.50.

SEC Fee: Transaction on any registered
exchange 1¢ for each $500 or fraction
thereof of the principal amount of
money involved in sales.

Source: The New York Stock Exchange Fact
Book, 1976.

FUTURE OF THE BROKERAGE BUSINESS

The securities business is changing rapidly, especially since the change to negotiated commissions beginning May 1, 1975. Also, potential changes in the makeup of the nation's stock exchanges relative to the over-the-counter markets are taking place in response to the driving forces within the investment community to have a central marketplace for all securities and a common, unified quotation system. These forces have caused the brokerage houses to think in terms of diversification in order to reduce their dependence on security commission business. Early stages of diversification have shown entry into areas such as life insurance sales, greater development of real estate syndication, and total personal financial planning. One of the more profitable areas of brokerage operation is investment banking, which has traditionally been a source of high profit margin. Today, many firms are expanding into commodity trading and the option and futures markets.

Currently most brokerage firms charge their clients a standard commission, whether or not the clients use the services. There is increasing pressure on the industry to **unbundle** the commission charges so that clients pay only for the services they use. For example, if a customer wanted to have his or her order executed, he or she would pay the lowest possible commission. If the customer wanted to have his or her order executed, maintain a margin account, have his or her securities held in safekeeping, have a street name account, and receive research information or any other service not directly related to the order execution, he or she would be billed on a per service item basis. Currently, there is a great deal of confusion within the brokerage industry, and it will take several years before the question of fees and services rendered is resolved.

KEY TERMS

bearer bond
beneficial ownership
brokerage firm
cash account
commission
day order
ex-dividend rate
fully registered bond
GTC order
limit order
margin account
market order

odd-lot order
open order
registered bond
round lot
short sale
specialist
spread
stop-limit order
stop order
street-name ownership
trading on margin

QUESTIONS

1. What is the spread in over-the-counter securities?
2. What are the two major brokerage functions?
3. What criteria should be used in selecting a brokerage firm and a broker?
4. What is the difference between a cash account and a margin account?
5. What are the two forms of security registration?
6. What are market orders?
7. What are limit orders?
8. What is the difference between a stop order and a limit order?
9. What are the risks involved in using a stop-limit order?
10. What are the two types of period orders?
11. What is the difference between odd-lot trading and round-lot trading?
12. What function does the specialist serve and how does he perform this function?
13. What is a short sale?
14. How is the margin percentage calculated?
15. How are bonds traded?
16. Explain negotiated commissions.

SELECTED READINGS

GROTH, JOHN C., WILBUR G. LEWELLEN, GARY G. SCHLARBAUM, and RONALD C. LEASE. "An Analysis of Brokerage House Securities Recommendations." *Financial Analysts Journal*, January–Februrary 1979, 32–40.

"Is It Time to Tighten Margin Rules?" *Business Week*, November 20, 1978, 138.

JACOB, NANCY, and RICH PETTIT. "Research Output and Capital Market Efficiency under Alternative Commission Rate Structures." *Journal of Financial Research*, Winter 1978, 45–60.

LOGUE, DENNIS E., and DONALD L. TUTTLE. "Brokerage House Investment Advice." *Financial Review*, 1973, 38–54.

MAHON, GIGI. "Sunny Side of the Street: Discount Brokers Increase Share of Trade." *Barron's*, June 11, 1979, 11ff.

MARCIAL, GENE G. "Margin Calls Rise as Share Prices Drop." *Wall Street Journal*, October 31, 1978, 13.

MCENALLY, RICHARD W., and EDWARD A. DYL. "The Risk of Selling Short." *Financial Analysts Journal*, November–December 1969, 73–76.

MOFFITT, DONALD. "Borrowing from Your Broker: How Margin Works to Inflate Investors Gains—And Losses." *Wall Street Journal*, October 15, 1979, 40.

SHEPARD, LAWRENCE. "How Good Is Investment Advice for Individuals?" *Journal of Portfolio Management*, Winter 1977, 32–36.

"Short Sales." *Financial World*, March 15, 1978, 62.

10

Investment Companies

The words **mutual funds** can be used in two ways: in a broad sense, they refer to investment companies in general; in a narrow sense, they refer to **open-end** investment companies only. In this text, we will be using "mutual funds" in the broad sense unless it is specified otherwise. Figure 10-1 shows the classification of investment companies in terms of different types of funds. A full explanation of those funds will follow.

HISTORICAL BACKGROUND

The idea of mutual funds originated and became very popular in Great Britain during the nineteenth century. Because mutual funds were highly speculative at the time, many of them failed and public interest subsided for some years. In the United States investors became interested in mutual funds around 1900, but there was little activity until 1924 when three investment companies were organized: Massachusetts Investors Trust, State Street Investment Corporation, and U.S. and Foreign Securities Corporation. All three companies are operating today.

The stock market crash of 1929 and the subsequent depression left almost all forms of investment in difficulty. Many mutual funds failed, es-

Figure 10-1 Classification of Investment Companies

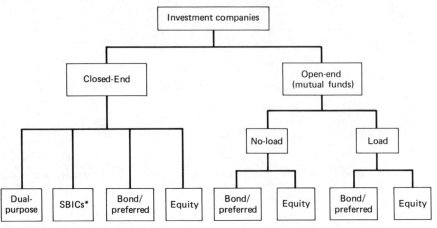

*SBICs — Small business investment companies

pecially those that used borrowed funds to gain leverage. Because the depression created a great deal of mistrust in the investment community, the government enacted the Federal Securities Act of 1933 and the Securities and Exchange Act of 1934. These acts, along with the formation of the Securities and Exchange Commission, began extensive investigation into the fraud and misrepresentation that had led to many of the difficulties during the late 1920s. These investigations led to the Investment Company Act of 1940, which is the foundation for the mutual fund industry today. The 1940 act places restrictions on the structure of investment companies and protects the investor by periodically reviewing the procedures followed by the various funds.

Investment companies are financial institutions organized under the Investment Company Act of 1940 for the sole purpose of managing capital. Many individuals or companies do not feel qualified to select stocks or bonds and establish portfolios of securities to meet their objectives. Investment companies help the investor participate in the securities market indirectly.

Investment companies, unlike such financial institutions as insurance companies or banks, accept savings from individuals and financial institutions and make investments according to their shareholders' objectives.

When investors own shares in a mutual fund, they own a proportional share of that securities portfolio. The shareholders have pooled their money to create the mutual fund. The fund, in turn, contracts with an investment management firm to manage the assets.

The two prime advantages in investing in mutual funds are security diversification and professional investment management. Professional investors and money managers generally agree that diversification is crucial in minimizing undue risk. But many investors do not have sufficient funds to invest in a widely diversified portfolio. Because mutual funds are able to purchase many securities, they are able to diversify.

Since most small investors do not feel qualified to administer their portfolios, they prefer to hire a professional, if the costs are not too great. Mutual funds spread the cost of professional investment management over a large number of shareholders in the fund. Because fund managers make security purchases in large quantities, they reduce the amount of brokerage commissions.

A mutual fund issues its own securities, which are usually common stock. These securities represent a proportionate amount of ownership in the portfolio. The individual securities purchased for the portfolio include both equity and debt issues of corporations and governments. The value of a share in the fund is based on the **net asset value,** which is determined by the market value of the portfolio held by the fund less any liabilities, and then divided by the total number of shares outstanding.

To meet its shareholders' objectives, the mutual fund hires a professional investment advisor to construct the securities portfolio. The investment advisor's primary responsibility is to analyze the markets, the economy, industries, and specific securities. Once he or she has made an analysis, the advisor undertakes the necessary purchase and sale of securities. Figure 10-2 shows the typical organization of a mutual fund.

Figure 10-2 Typical Organization of Mutual Funds

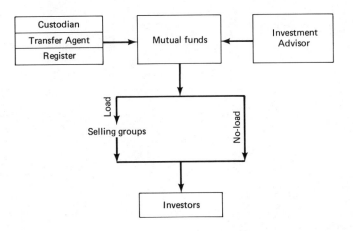

GROWTH OF THE MUTUAL FUND INDUSTRY

Since 1940, there has been rapid growth in the mutual fund industry, much of which can be attributed to the economy of the country after World War II. After the war the mutual fund industry began to expand rapidly, and

Table 10-1
Shareholder Accounts and Total Net Assets, 1965–1980

Calendar Year End	Number of Reporting Funds	Number of Accounts (In Thousands)	Assets (In Billions of Dollars)
1965	170	6,709.3	$35.2
1966	182	7,701.7	34.8
1967	204	7,904.1	44.7
1968	240	9,080.2	52.7
1969	269	10,391.5	48.3
1970	361	10.690.3	47.6
1071	392	10,901.0	55.0
1972	410	10,635.3	59.8
1973	421	10,330.9	46.5
1974			
Mutual Funds	416	9,970.4	34.1
Money Market Funds	15	103.8	1.7
1975			
Mutual Funds	390	9,712.5	42.2
Money Market Funds	36	208.8	3.7
1976			
Mutual Funds	427	8,515.1	45.0
Money Market Funds	50	177.5	3.9
1978			
Mutual Funds	444	8,190.6	45.0
Money Market Funds	61	467.8	10.9

Calendar Year End	Number of Reporting Funds	Number of Accounts (In Thousands)	Assets (In Billions of Dollars)
1979			
Mutual Funds	446R	7,482.2R	49.0R
Limited Maturity Funds*	2	3.5	3
Money Market Funds	76	2,307.9	45.2
1980			
Mutual Funds	458	7,212.0	58.4
Limited Maturity Funds*	10	16.5	1.9
Money Markets Funds	96	4,745.6	74.4

R — Revised
*Municipal Bond funds with less than two years maturity.

Note: Figures for shareholder accounts represent combined totals for member companies. Duplications have not been eliminated.

Source: Mutual Funds Fact Book, 1981, p. 11.

investor confidence grew. Post-World War II was one of the most powerful economic growth periods in our nation's history. Many people were successful with their investments, and people who did not have the knowledge to invest on their own flocked to mutual funds. Most investors who held their mutual fund investments over a relatively long time did not lose money, although a number of funds did record poor performance.

For the past few years, however, the industry has made a dramatic reversal in its growth. More people redeemed their shares than invested new funds. Because net redemptions exceeded net purchases, the growth of the mutual fund industry came to a halt. However, due to the high inflation rates people have experienced in the last few years, the public continued to gravitate toward financial assets that offered high yield, liquidity, and safety. Money market funds have grown rapidly. Table 10-1 shows how the industry has grown over the past 15 years. Table 10-2 shows the asset composition of money market funds for the years 1978 to 1980.

Table 10-2
Money Market Funds Asset Composition Year-End, 1978–80 (In Millions of Dollars)

	1978	1979	1980
Total Net Assets	$10.858.0	$45,214.2	$74,447.7
U.S. Treasury Bills	1.489.3A	1,621.3	2,920.4
Other Treasury Securities	.0	4,020.2A	554.2
Other U.S. Securities	.0	.0	4,753.6
Repurchase Agreements	.0	.0	5,642.8
Commercial Bank CD(1)	5,293.8B	18,128.4B	19,691.3
Other Domestic CD(2)	.0	.0	1,330.1
Eurodollar CD(3)	.0	.0	6,769.3
Commercial Paper	2,842.0	14,453.3	25,026.1
Bankers' Acceptances	764.7	4,844.9	6,534.6
Cash Reserves	68.2	67.0	165.9
Other	400.0C	2,079.1C	1.059.4
Average Maturity (4)	42	34	24
Number of Funds	61	76	96

(1) Commercial bank CDs are those issued by American banks located in the U.S.
(2) Other Domestic CDs include those issued by S&L's and American branches of foreign banks.
(3) Eurodollar CDs are those issued by foreign branches of domestic banks and some issued by Canadian banks; this category includes some one day paper.
(4) Maturity of each individual security in the portfolio at end of month weighted by its value.
A. Includes other US securities.
B. Includes other domestic CDs an Eurodollars deposits.
C. Includes repurchase agreements.

Source: Mutual Funds Fact Book, 1981, p. 36.

CLASSIFICATION OF INVESTMENT COMPANIES

Open-End Company

As indicated in Figure 10-1, there are two basic investment companies in existence today: the open-end fund and the closed-end fund. The open-end investment company represents more than 90 percent of the investment companies. Open-end investment funds stands ready to buy or sell their securities at any time. This means that the capitalization of the company is constantly changing as investors buy and sell their shares directly with the fund. Shares of an open-end investment company are valued at the fund's net asset value, as defined previously. Most open-end companies sell new shares at net asset value plus a **loading** or management fee; and they redeem shares approximately at net asset value.

Close-End Company

Closed-end investment companies have a fixed number of shares that can be owned by the investing public. The investor cannot buy or redeem shares directly with the investment company. The only way the investor can purchase additional shares or sell his or her shares is to buy from a shareholder or find an individual to buy his or her shares. Some closed-end funds are listed an organized exchanges and some are listed by brokerage houses in the over-the-counter market. The price for closed-end mutual fund shares is established by supply and demand.

Exhibit 10-1 shows, for each closed-end fund, its net asset value, traded price, and the percentage difference, which indicates whether the fund is traded at premium or at discount. Most often, the closed-end fund is traded at a price lower than its net asset value.

The most important distinction between an open-end investment company (mutual funds) and a closed-end investment company is the manner in which ownership shares are redeemed. By law, open-end companies must redeem their shares at the fund's current net asset value at the time the shareholder requests redemption. This is substantially different from closed-end companies, for which supply and demand for the fund determine the price per share. There are a few exceptions to the open-end redemption method. For example, a few funds charge a small redemption fee or redeem shares in exchange for stock certificates of a company held by the fund, and a few funds stipulate that redemption may be suspended under special circumstances.

Because an open-end company fund must stand ready to redeem shares when asked, it must have a constant in flow of cash to meet the demand for any shares sold back to the fund at net asset value. More recently, however, when redemptions exceeded purchases, many mutual funds were forced to sell portions of their securities portfolios to meet redemption cash demands.

Exhibit 10-1 PUBLICLY TRADED FUNDS

Publicly Traded Funds

Friday, April 2, 1982

Following is a weekly listing of unaudited net asset values of publicly traded investment fund shares, reported by the companies as of Friday's close. Also shown is the closing listed market price or a dealer-to-dealer asked price of each fund's shares, with the percentage of difference.

	N.A. Value	Stk Price	% Diff		N.A. Value	Stk Price	% Diff
Diversified Common Stock Funds				BancrftCv	23.73	21¾	− 8.3
				Castle	26.91	23⅛	−14.1
AdmExp	14.81	14	− 5.5	CentSec	9.90	7⅝	−23.0
BakerFen	84.11	64½	−23.3	Claremont	26.25	19⅝	−25.2
GenAInv	14.72	14¾	+ 0.2	CLAS	−4.50	..⅜	....
Lehman	12.74	12	− 5.8	CLAS Pfd	23.83	....	....
Madison	20.90	16⅞	−19.3	Cyprus	.23	7/16	+90.2
NiagaraSh	13.93	15⅝	+12.2	Engex	12.82	8½	−33.7
OseasSec	5.31	6¾	+27.1	Japan	9.77	8¼	−15.6
Source	24.83	21½	−13.4	Mexico(b)	4.99	4⅛	−17.3
Tri-Contl	21.95	19⅛	−12.9	Nautilus	21.42	19½	− 9.0
US&For	21.69	18¼	−15.9	NewAmFd	27.54	20¾	−24.7
				Pete&Res	27.03	28	+ 3.6
Specialized Equity and Convertible Funds				PrecMet	12.21	10⅞	−10.9
AmGnCv	28.77	27⅜	− 4.8	a-Ex-Dividend. b-As of Thursday's close. c-Merged. z-Not available.			
bASA	40.49	34½	−14.8				

Source: Reprinted with permission of The Wall Street Journal, © Dow Jones & Company, Inc. (1982). All rights reserved.

PORTFOLIO CLASSIFICATION OF FUNDS

Because investors purchase funds for a number of reasons, their portfolios can be classified according to their objectives. Investment companies that have different overall objectives have different performance records. The companies should not be judged on the same performance basis. For example, an investment company that attempts to maximize income with a modest degree of risk should not be evaluated on the same basis as a growth portfolio that attempts to maximize capital gains.

Common-Stock Funds

Common-stock funds invest most of their money in common stocks, but they occasionally invest in short-term government securities and commercial paper. There is a broad range of common-stock funds — from those that invest almost exclusively in high-quality blue-chip companies to those that invest solely in the new, unestablished companies.

Some of the more aggressive common-stock funds use various techniques to accelerate the growth of the fund. These funds may have a high turnover of securities, since many investment advisors rely on technical analysis in the purchase and sale of securities. To leverage the potential gains in the portfolio, these funds often use borrowed capital (in addition to the funds invested by the shareholders). Unfortunately, however, when the market declines, there is an accelerated decrease in the value of the portfolio. An investor who selects one of the performance common-stock funds should be able to assume a higher than normal degree of risk.

Balanced Funds

Balanced funds combine bonds and/or preferred stocks with the ownership of common stock, usually at some predetermined percentage relationship. Several balanced funds keep one-half of the portfolio in common stocks and one-half in bonds and preferred stocks. Balanced portfolios are more conservative than common-stock funds, and they generally do not have significant price movement either up or down.

The main purpose of balanced funds is to achieve an adequate return in the form of interest and dividends from the fixed portion of the portfolio, while at the same time gaining a modest growth in the common-stock portion. This approach to mutual funds has been successful over the years and appeals to the investor who wants both growth and income.

Income Funds

The purpose of income funds is to maximize current income. Growth in the value of the portfolio is of small importance. There are two basic groups within the income funds: (1) those that stress constant income at relatively low risk, and (2) those that attempt to achieve the maximum income possible, even with the use of leverage. Naturally, the higher the anticipated return of any investment, the higher the potential risk of the investment.

Investors in markets similar to that of 1981 to 1982 can expect to receive income of 12 to 14 percent from income funds. Some of these income funds are termed **bond funds** and have grown sharply in popularity during the mid to late-1970s. The popularity stems from the argument that if an investor can receive 12 percent return for modest risk with income securities, why should he assume a considerably higher risk in common stocks that have a historical return of approximately 9 percent? Few individual investors have achieved 12 percent per year over the past 15 years; therefore, income funds do have great appeal, especially when income yields are at high levels historically.

Specialized Funds

A number of funds invest predominantly in a specialized group of securities. Funds may specialize in securities of firms in certain industries, of producers of specific products, or of specific income-producing securities. Investors interested in a particular group of securities might want to invest in a specialized mutual fund.

Specialized mutual funds have not been very successful over the long run. Investors have been hesitant to choose a particular area for investing because one of the main objectives in selecting mutual funds is to obtain diversification.

Some specialized funds have purchased securities in the insurance industry, in the chemical industry, and in foreign securities. Most of the specialized funds prospered in the late 1950s and early 1960s, but they are not one of the main segments in the investment company industry today.

Leverage Funds

Leverage mutual funds are common-stock funds whose main objective is maximum capital appreciation. The special techniques these funds use make them speculative and risky. Leverage funds use borrowed funds to their utmost in order to increase the size of the value of the portfolio. They hope the gain received will exceed the cost of the borrowed funds, and the balance of the gain will benefit the shareholders.

Some leverage funds use the **short sale,** which permits the management of the fund to take advantage of declining markets to realize gains in the portfolio. The proper use of short sales decreases the loss of the portfolio in a declining market, but it also decreases the gain in a rising market if a proportionally large short position is maintained.

Some leverage funds use options, specifically, call options. Call options give the purchaser the right to buy a security at a predetermined price for a stipulated length of time, regardless of the fluctuation of the market price of the security on which the option is written. Because of the exceptionally high risk, call options are not used as often as borrowed funds and short sales are. Other quasi-options, such as stock warrants, are more often used because their life span tends to last several years; call options usually expire within one year.

Dual-Purpose Funds

Dual-purpose funds are a relatively new concept borrowed from Great Britain in the mid-1960s. These funds take advantage of leverage in a new and different way. The capital structure of a fund is divided exactly in half; thus, it is a closed-end investment company. Half the shares initially sold are purchased by investors who want income. The other half are purchased by investors who want growth. The funds initially received are pooled, and investments are made just as in any mutual fund. Any income derived from the portfolio goes to the investors who hold the income shares. They have twice the amount of their original investment working for them to produce income. The investors who own capital shares receive no income. Instead, they receive all the capital gain or loss that results from the investments of the total portfolio. Capital shares have twice the amount of funds working for them to achieve capital growth.

For example, if 1 million income shares of a dual-purpose fund are sold for $10 each and then an additional 1 million capital shares are sold for $10 each, the fund begins operations with a total of $20 million. Any income earned from the $20 million portfolio goes to the investors who are holding the 1 million income shares. Any capital gain or loss in the fund goes to the investors who are holding the 1 million capital shares. This provides a two-for-one leverage.

When the funds were first introduced in the mid-1960s, the investment community was hoping that the price of the shares traded in the market after the initial sale would not sell at a discount from their net asset value, as most other closed-end funds usually do. However, as time progressed, the dual-purpose fund shares, especially the capital shares, sold at a discount from net asset value, and many sold at a substantial discount. Many people criticize the funds' managers' investment philosophy. Critics argue that the managers are managing a conflicting situation, because they are trying to produce good income on the one hand and a high growth rate on the other. In the past, very few securities have produced a high yield while growing at a high rate. The lives of these funds expire during the 1980's.

Real Estate Investment Trusts

Real estate investment trusts (REITs) are a form of closed-end fund. All REITs are closed-end because the primary investment is in real estate ventures. As in all mutual funds, the investor's money is pooled, but the investment advisor makes real estate investments instead of security investments. There are several forms of real estate investment trusts, depending upon the type of real estate undertaken. For example, some REITs invest only in long-term mortgages, others in short-term mortgages, and still others in lending money for real estate construction. (REITs and their performance are discussed in Chapter 16.)

Money Market Funds

Money market funds were set up in 1972 and gained public recognition quickly. In 1982, the total assets were 200 billion dollars. These funds' portfolios consist solely of short-term money market instruments, such as bank certificates of deposit, U.S. Treasury bills, commercial paper, bankers' acceptance, and so on. The major advantages of this type of fund are its high yield, liquidity, and safety. A fund's yield is much better than that of a passbook savings account. However, the interest income produced by the funds depends heavily on interest-rate conditions in the economy. Also, because the funds offer check-writing privileges to the shareholders, they are considered as liquid as any savings account. Since market interest rates are relatively certain in the short-run, money funds are virtually immune to capital loss. Therefore, they are considered to have low risk and high safety.

MUTUAL FUND ACCOUNTS

The mutual fund industry has helped the small investor for the past 45 years. Once investors, determine the fund that best meets their objectives, they must decide the type of account to open. The three major types of accounts offered by most mutual funds are the regular, accumulation, and withdrawal accounts.

Regular Account

A regular account permits investors to purchase any number of shares of the mutual fund at any time they choose. The investors receive certificates stating that they are the owners of a proportion of the fund. The fund may place the shares in a bank vault for safekeeping. Investors do not need to take the responsibility of taking possession, but they may. In addition, investors can invest additional amounts of money. The fund issues full and fractional shares that can also be kept on deposit at a bank appointed as trustee. For most people, this procedure is preferred because it eliminates transferring certificates between the fund's transfer agent, the bank, and the investor.

Any income from the fund's investments is paid to the investor either quarterly or semiannually. In some cases, monthly checks are distributed. Many investors prefer taking dividends in additional stock instead of in cash, and instruct the fund to reinvest any distribution made by the fund.

Accumulation Account

As accumulation account has two plans: voluntary and contractual. The voluntary plan is flexible and allows the investor the convenient opportunity for periodic investing. Most accumulation accounts allow the investor to begin an account with a very small initial investment, but the investor is expected to add to the fund periodically.

In the contractual plan, the investor agrees to make a predetermined amount of investment in the fund at regular intervals for a predetermined period of time, for example, 10 or 15 years. However, the word contractual is misleading because the investor is not legally obligated to continue investing. In essence, both the contractual and the voluntary plans are similar to the regular account if the investor wishes to make sporadic payments or to make no additional payments. In principle, the idea behind the accumulation account is good because it tends to force investors to continue their investment programs.

A word of caution is necessary. Some contractual plans affect a sales charge of up to 50 percent of the payments made during the first year of the plan. The charge is reduced as the years progress. Therefore, once an accumulation plan is begun with a heavy load charge, it is extremely expensive to cancel or redeem the shares because, in essence, much of the sales charge has been prepaid. Recent Securities and Exchange Commission rulings have limited the scope and potential abuses of these plans.

Withdrawal Account

Mutual funds are generally considered vehicles by which funds can be accumulated over time in order to allow the investor to accomplish goals later in life, for example, for education of children or for retirement. The withdrawal plan allows the individual to withdraw funds on a regular basis. The investor automatically received monthly or quarterly income from the investment company. Many investors in their later years need withdrawal accounts to supplement Social Security and pension benefits. The income that would normally be produced by the mutual fund is estimated and paid to the investor on a regular basis. If the withdrawals are larger than normal dividends, the investor may be dipping into the capital portion of the investment. Over a period of time the investor can exhaust the assets of the account.

Therefore, the investor must take great care when the amount of the periodic withdrawal is established. Withdrawal is often stated in a percentage amount of the fund. Because the value of the fund fluctuates from time to time, the amount of the withdrawals would also fluctuate. This could be troublesome if the withdrawals were needed for retirement.

Regardless of the type of account chosen, the investor always has the privilege in an open-end mutual fund to make investments and withdrawals at any time. The accumulation and withdrawal plans aid the investor in a systematic program to help accomplish various goals.

MUTUAL FUND EXPENSES

Several expenses involved in the acquisition and ownership of an open-end company's shares are a sales charge (or load, paid by buyers of a load fund), redemption charges, administrative costs, management fees, and brokerage and custodial costs.

Open-end investment companies are classified according to the expenses involved when shares are purchased by the investor. There are load funds and no-load funds. The majority of funds are **load funds** which charge a fee when the shares of the fund are sold to the public.

The term **load** means that the fee is added to the net asset value of the shares in order to arrive at the purchase price. The sales fee is not deposited into the fund, but is paid entirely to another organization or individual, usually a brokerage firm, for the expenses they incur in selling the shares. In other words, the sales charge is a selling commission and is considered an expense to the investor. This fee usually ranges between 4 and 9 percent of the total purchase; the most common fee is 8.5 percent.

For example, if an investor paid $1,000 to a salesperson representing a mutual fund, $915 worth of shares would be purchased in the fund if the sales charge were 8.5 percent; the other $85 is the sales fee. The investor hopes that the fund's investment managers will invest the $915 along with the money of other investors to purchase securities that will increase in value over the long term. It is important to recognize that the load charge significantly detracts from the value of the fund in the beginning, as well as during the life of the investment. If the investor has a large amount to invest, he or she may be charged a smaller load fee, as shown in Table 10-3.

Table 10-3
Typical Sales Fees for Load Funds

Dollar Amount of Purchase	Sales Load,%
1– 12,499	8.50
12,500– 24,999	7.50
25,500– 49,999	5.75
50,000– 99,999	4.00
100,000–249,000	3.25
250,000–999,999	2.50
1,000,000–and over	1.00

No-load funds came into existence later than load funds, but they have grown more rapidly. These mutual funds do not have load fees because little sales effort is made to promote the funds's share sales except through direct advertising. No sales force has been contracted to sell the fund's shares.

Therefore, if an investor has $1,000 and selects a no-load fund, the entire $1,000 is placed in the fund. If the investor immediately turns around and redeems the shares, he or she receives the entire $1,000. As investors become more educated, they will not need salespeople to convince them of the benefits of mutual funds.

Between 1972 and 1976, a considerable number of load funds switched their status to no-load funds in hopes of attracting more investment funds. This was a clear sign of the impact no-load funds have made on the mutual fund industry. In addition, the heavy redemption that took place during the early 1970s was heaviest in load funds.

Exhibit 10-2 is a listing of open-end mutual funds. The first column shows the net asset value (NAV) per share. The second column, the offer price, indicates whether the fund is load or no-load. If a price is shown in the second column, the difference between the number and the NAV is the amount of the load charge. No-load funds are indicated in the second column by N.L. The third column shows the NAV change from the previous day's trading. Any change in the NAV reflects the changing value of the fund's security portfolio.

Redemption Charge

A number of funds, especially no-load funds, charge a small fee for redemption. The fee is usually charged if redemption occurs within 6 months of the purchase date. The fee is approximately one-half of 1 percent to 1 percent and is meant to discourage trading no-load fund shares. Some investors have tried to trade mutual fund shares in hopes of catching the swings in the market by riding an uptrend in the market for a few months and then selling out in time for a market downturn. The only difficulty with this approach is the problem of knowing when the market will make such up and down moves. Timing investment decisions has always been one of the most difficult aspects of investing, not only for the novice but also for the professional.

Administrative Costs

Administrative costs are the costs of running the fund. Sometimes they are borne by a management company, but they are usually paid from the income of the fund. Examples of these expenses are administrative and clerical salaries, office supplies, legal fees, custodial fees, periodic stockholders reports, office rental, and other such expenditures. When these expenses are charged against the fund as an expense, they reduce the value of the investors' holdings.

Exhibit 10-2

Mutual Funds

Wednesday, June 16, 1982

Price ranges for investment companies, as quoted by the National Association of Securities Dealers. NAV stands for net asset value per share; the offering includes net asset value plus maximum sales charge, if any.

	NAV	Offer Price	NAV Chg.
Able Assoc	13.05	N.L.	− .19
Acorn Fnd	21.93	N.L.	+ .05
ADV Fund	13.60	N.L.	− .03
Afuture Fd	12.92	N.L.	...
AIM Funds:			
Conv Yld	11.34	12.13	− .01
Edsn Gld	8.13	8.70	− .07
HiYld Sc	8.27	8.84	+ .01
Alpha Fnd	15.95	N.L.	− .02
Am Birthrt	10.66	11.65	− .04
American Funds Group:			
Am Bal	8.07	8.82	− .03
Amcap F	5.63	6.15	...
Am Mutl	10.54	11.52	− .03
Bnd FdA	10.85	11.86	− .01
Fund Inv	7.50	8.20	− .01
Gth FdA	9.74	10.64	...
Inc FdA	8.03	8.78	− .02
I C A	7.63	8.34	− .02
Nw Prsp	6.49	7.09	− .04
Wash Mt	6.68	7.30	− .01
American General Group:			
A GnCBd	5.77	6.31	...
AG Entp	10.74	11.74	...
Gn Exch	30.97	N.L.	− .05
Growtp	18.00	N.L.	+ .03
High Yld	8.42	9.03	+ .01
A G Mun	14.55	15.28	− .02
A GnVen	20.10	21.97	+ .03
Comstk	9.11	9.96	− .01
Fd Amer	8.62	9.42	− .02
Harbor	9.89	10.81	...
Pace Fd	25.66	28.04	− .05
Prov Inc	3.69	3.98	...
Am Grwth	6.76	7.39	...
Am Heritg	2.44	N.L.	+ .03
Am Ins Ind	4.66	5.09	+ .01
Am Invest	7.75	N.L.	− .09
AmInv Inc	8.68	N.L.	+ .02
Am MedAs	189.10	N.L.	− .54
AmNat Gw	3.39	3.70	+ .01
AmNtl Inc	14.79	16.16	− .03
Amway Mt	5.24	5.60	...
Archer Gvt	9.29	N.L.	− .02
Axe-Houghton:			
Fund B	7.76	8.43	− .01
Income	4.00	4.35	...
Stock Fd	7.49	8.19	− .01
BLC Gwth	12.43	13.59	− .13
BLCInc Fd	11.40	12.46	...
Babsn Inc	1.34	N.L.	...
Babsn Inv	10.56	N.L.	− .08
Beacon Gr	10.49	N.L.	− .05
Beacon Hll	11.97	N	L.	− .11
Berger Group Funds:			
100 Fund	11.57	N.L.	...
101 Fund	8.76	N.L.	+ .02
Boston Company:			
IPI Fund	9.55	10.32	− .03
Cap Apr	18.54	N.L.	− .11
Bos Found	9.28	10.42	− .04
Bull & Bear Group:			
Capam	9.12	N.L.	− .01
Capitl Sh	10.43	N.L.	− .03
Golcnd	9.54	N.L.	− .01
Calvin Bullock Funds:			
Bullock	13.61	14.87	− .06
Canadn	5.84	6.38	− .05
Div Shrs	2.45	2.68	− .01
Hi Incm	9.77	10.53	− .01
Income	8.99	9.83	− .02
Ntwide	8.43	9.21	− .04
Tax Free	8.20	8.61	− .02
Cap TNT	9.83	N.L.	− .04

	NAV	Offer Price	NAV Chg.
Income	4.06	4.38	− .01
Stock Fd	9.64	10.39	− .05
Eberstadt Group:			
Chem Fd	8.14	8.90	− .07
Enrgy R	8.32	9.09	− .15
Surveyr	11.50	12.57	− .11
Energy Utl	17.76	N.L.	+ .04
Evrgrn Fd	26.28	N.L.	− .02
Farm B Gr	12.46	13.62	− .05
FedrlSt Fd	36.78	N.L.	− .04
Federated Group:			
Am Lead	8.17	8.74	− .05
Exch Fd	23.77	N.L.	− .03
Hi Incm	10.15	10.86	− .02
Tax Free	7.59	N.L.	− .01
US Gvt S	x6.86	N.L.	− .06
Fidelity Group Funds:			
Asst Inv	13.14	N.L.	...
Bd Corp	6.08	N.L.	− .01
Congr St	37.64	N.L.	− .34
Contra	8.97	N.L.	− .10
Eq Incm	18.21	N.L.	− .06
Ex Fd f	29.35	N.L.	− .11
Fidel Fd	14.03	N.L.	− .04
Govt Sec	8.88	N.L.	− .02
Hi Incm	7.08	N.L.	− .01
High Yld	9.58	N.L.	− .03
Ltd Muni	7.21	N.L.	− .02
Mageln	18.89	19.28	+ .02
Muncpl	5.80	N.L.	− .02
Puritan	9.96	N.L.	− .03
Thrift Tr	9.05	N.L.	− .02
Trend	24.40	N.L.	− .22
Financial Programs:			
Dynam	6.88	N.L.	+ .01
Industl	3.75	N.L.	...
Income	6.77	N.L.	+ .02
Tax Free	12.69	N.L.	− .03
First Investors Fund:			
Bond Ap	13.00	14.02	− .02
Discovr	8.59	9.39	+ .04
Growth	6.26	6.84	− .01
Income	5.97	6.52	...
Nat Resr	4.76	5.20	− .06
Optn Fd	5.91	6.37	− .03
Tx Exmt	7.34	7.91	...
44 Wall St	11.97	N.L.	+ .03
44 WS Eqt	6.85	7.49	+ .03
F&M Grw	4.42	4.70	+ .01
Fnd Grwth	4.55	4.97	− .02
Founders Group Funds:			
rowth	6.71	N.L.	− .01
Income	11.75	N.L.	...
Mutual	7.11	7.41	− .32
Special	17.30	N.L.	...
Franklin Group:			
AGE Fd	3.16	3.41	...
D N T C	12.80	13.80	+ .06
Growth	7.14	7.70	− .03
Income	1.71	1.84	+ .01
Optn Fd	4.98	5.37	− .01
Tax Free	5.88	6.13	− .04
US GvSc	6.43	6.93	− .01
Utilities	4.68	5.05	+ .02
Res Capt	5.72	6.17	− .04
Res Eqty	4.88	5.26	− .03
Funds Incp Group:			
Cm IncS	7.91	8.60	...
Pilot Fd	7.55	8.21	+ .03
GT Pac Fd	13.42	N.L.	− .08
Gatewy Op	13.62	N.L.	− .07
Genl Elec Invest:			
Elf TxE	7.88	(z)	...
Elfn Tr	16.66	(z)	...

	Offer	NAV	NAV Chg.
Growth	9.18	10.03	− .02
High Yld	8.26	8.86	− .01
Int'l Fd	10.49	11.46	− .13
Muni Bd	6.49	6.81	− .01
Optn Inc	11.18	12.22	− .08
Summit	15.57	17.02	− .01
Technol	9.70	10.60	− .02
Total R	11.03	12.05	− .05
US GvSc	7.95	8.28	...
Keystone Mass Group:			
Cust B 1	13.42	14.02	− .02
Cust B 2	16.00	17.49	...
Disct B 4	6.78	7.41	...
Cust K 1	6.81	7.44	− .03
Cust K 2	5.45	5.96	− .02
Cust S 1	14.62	15.98	− .10
Cust S 3	6.11	6.68	− .01
Cust S 4	4.65	5.08	− .02
Intl Fnd	3.80	4.15	− .02
Tax Free	6.58	6.85	− .02
Mass Fd	10.11	11.05	− .01
Mn MkO	16.18	N.L.	+ .01
Lexington Group:			
Cp Ledrs	9.67	10.72	− .04
Gold Fd	2.25	N.L.	− .02
Gnma	7.06	N.L.	− .01
Growth	7.25	N.L.	...
Resrch	13.49	N.L.	+ .01
Lindner Fd	13.06	N.L.	− .01
Loomis Sayles Funds:			
Cap Dev	14.95	N.L.	+ .06
Mutual	13.86	N.L.	+ .02
Lord Abbett:			
Affilatd	7.02	7.57	− .02
Bnd Deb	8.65	9.45	− .01
Devl Gro	15.80	17.27	+ .03
Income	2.70	2.91	...
Lutheran Brotherhood:			
Broth Fd	10.49	11.46	− .06
Bro Inc	7.35	8.03	− .03
Bro MBd	x5.94	6.49	− .07
Broth US	7.79	8.51	− .01
Mass Financial Services:			
MIT	9.46	10.20	− .07
MIG	10.04	10.82	− .01
MID	13.70	14.77	− .02
MCD	7.39	7.97	+ .01
MFD	9.19	9.91	+ .01
MFB	10.88	11.73	...
MMB	7.40	7.77	− .03
MFH	5.71	6.16	...
MFI	10.25	11.05	− .02
Mathers	16.81	N.L.	− .18
Merrill Lynch:			
Basc Val	9.70	10.37	− .03
Captl Fd	14.63	15.65	− .08
EquiBd 1	8.71	9.07	− .03
Hi Incm	6.90	7.19	...
Hi QualP	9.45	9.84	− .02
Int TPrt	9.70	9.90	...
Muni Ins	5.95	6.20	− .02
Mun HY	7.68	8.00	− .02
Ltd Mat	9.74	9.84	...
Pacific	10.13	10.83	− .10
Sp'l Valu	8.28	8.86	+ .01
Mid Amer	5.49	6.00	...
Mdw Incm	9.94	N.L.	− .01
MSB Fund	15.37	N.L.	− .05
Mutl BnFd	9.26	10.12	− .02
Mutual Investing Funds:			
MIF Fd	7.63	8.25	− .03
MIF Gro	5.27	5.70	− .02
MIF Bd	8.26	8.93	+ .01
Mutual of Omaha Funds:			
Amer	10.16	N.L.	...
Growth	4.42	4.80	...
Income	8.00	8.70	...
Tax Free	8.99	9.66	...
MutlQl Fd	11.54	N.L.	− .05
Mutl Shars	37.86	N.L.	− .19
NaesTh Fd	32.56	N.L.	+ .01
NtlAvia Tc	7.52	N.L.	+ .01
Natl Indust	11.42	N.L.	− .05

	Offer	NAV	NAV Chg.
Intl Equi	12.40	13.55	− .10
Investr	7.61	8.32	− .02
Option	11.22	12.26	− .07
Tax Ex	16.61	17.44	− .05
Vista Fd	12.80	13.99	...
Voyage	10.68	11.67	− .02
Quaser As	31.07	N.L.	− .12
Rainbw Fd	2.91	N.L.	...
Revere Fd	6.70	N.L.	− .06
Safeco Group:			
Equity	8.30	N.L.	− .01
Growth	12.04	N.L.	+ .05
Income	9.51	N.L.	...
St Paul Funds:			
Captl Fd	9.36	9.96	...
Growth	10.21	10.86	+ .01
Specl Fd	15.62	N.L.	+ .01
Scudder Funds:			
Cptl Gro	10.29	N.L.	− .02
Commn	10.64	N.L.	− .03
Devl Fd	42.79	N.L.	− .10
Income	9.89	N.L.	...
Intl Fnd	15.25	N.L.	− .09
Muni Bd	6.46	N.L.	− .03
Specl Fd	40.13	N.L.	− .03
Security Funds:			
Bond Fd	7.11	7.31	...
Equity	5.27	5.76	− .02
Invest	7.79	8.51	...
Ultra Fd	6.50	7.10	+ .01
Selected Funds:			
Selct Am	6.90	N.L.	− .01
Selct Spl	13.26	N.L.	− .02
Seligman Group:			
Captl Fd	6.66	7.18	− .01
Com Stk	9.43	10.17	...
Growth	5.08	5.48	− .01
Income	10.20	11.00	− .02
Sentinel Group Funds:			
Bal Fund	7.12	7.78	− .01
Bond Fd	5.53	6.04	− .01
Com Stk	12.79	13.98	− .03
Growth	10.14	11.08	− .02
Sentry Fd	17.47	18.99	− .11
Sequoia	26.32	N.L.	+ .19
Shearson Funds:			
Apprec	11.89	12.52	+ .03
High Yld	16.06	16.91	− .01
Income	15.97	16.81	− .04
Mg Muni	11.17	11.76	...
N Direct	12.41	13.06	+ .05
Shrm Dean	5.86	N.L.	− .22
Sierra Gro	10.30	N.L.	...
Sigma Funds:			
Capitl Sh	7.66	8.37	− .05
Incm Shr	6.29	6.87	− .03
Invest Sh	11.26	12.31	− .04
Trust Sh	8.26	9.03	− .03
Venture	6.29	6.87	+ .01
Sm Barney	11.83	12.45	− .06
Sm BrIncG	7.62	8.02	− .01
So GenFnd	11.77	12.32	− .01
Sowest Inv	9.35	N.L.	− .03
SowInv Inc	4.11	N.L.	...
Sovern Inv	14.06	14.80	− .27
State Bond Group:			
CmSt Fd	4.39	4.80	− .02
Diversf	4.58	5.01	− .01
Progrss	6.51	7.11	− .03
StateF Bal	10.28	N.L.	− .08
State FrGr	7.45	N.L.	− .04
StateSt (a)	50.17	50.50	− .03
StStr Exch	55.44	N.L.	− .12
Steadman Funds:			
Am Ind	2.68	N.L.	...
Assoc Fd	.78	N.L.	− .01
Inves Fd	1.35	N.L.	...
Oceang	5.39	N.L.	− .01
Stein Roe Funds:			
Balanc	17.13	N.L.	+ .01
Bond Fd	8.02	N.L.	...
Capit Op	16.63	N.L.	...
Specl Fd	9.20	N.L.	− .05

Management Fees

An important expense incurred by all investment companies is the fee charged by the investment management company. The fund has contracted for the investment management company to perform the investment function, which includes analyzing the economy, the securities markets, and industries, and then selecting specific securities. The management fee usually ranges between two-tenths of 1 percent and six-tenths of 1 percent per year, depending upon the size of the fund. Most funds with assets over $1 billion charge less than one-half of 1 percent; smaller funds may charge higher rates. The fee is charged regardless of whether the fund is a load or no-load. It has no relation to any sales fee.

Almost all mutual funds hire outside investment advisors to manage their assets. The operations of the fund itself are clerical, marketing, and administrative in nature.

Brokerage and Custodial Costs

Brokerage fees are the same for mutual funds as they are for any investor transacting business in the securities markets. Investment managers must use brokers as must the individual investor. However, since the investment company usually makes transactions in large dollar amounts, the commission per dollar invested is considerably lower.

An investment company usually employs a custodial trustee to hold security certificates, collect dividends and interest, and make the necessary transfer of securities. Banks are usually appointed as custodial trustees.

DIVIDEND AND CAPITAL GAINS

Just as any individual periodically receives dividends from the companies in which he or she owns securities, investment companies receive dividends and interest. Investment companies also realize capital gains and losses over a long period of time as investment management advisors make changes in the portfolios. Unless otherwise directed, investment companies pay the majority of these receipts directly to the investor after the appropriate expenses have been deducted.

Most mutual funds offer the investor the alternative of either taking the distributions in cash or in additional shares of the fund. The option to reinvest distributions is only allowed in an open-end fund. Most funds make a distribution from dividends at least once a year. The yields from the dividends have ranged from 1.6 percent to as high as 12 percent for the more recent money market funds. Capital gains are derived from the purchase and subsequent sale of securities. Distribution of capital gains might not be made every year because in some years there may be no capital gains. Capital gain distributions represent a return of capital and do not originate from the earnings of the companies in the portfolio. The option to reinvest the distributions is usually urged in order to maximize future benefits. It is by reinvesting capital gains and dividends that mutual funds can grow significantly. Of course, if the investor needs income from the fund, as provided in the withdrawal plan, then reinvestment for future consumption through growth is unimportant.

SELECTION AND PERFORMANCE OF MUTUAL FUNDS

Not all mutual funds can be judged on the same basis because no one fund can meet the objectives of growth, income, and stability that various investors seek. The investors must articulate what they expect to achieve in their selection of a mutual fund. If the investor emphasizes growth, as most investors have done in the past, only funds whose primary goal is growth should be compared.

There are several ways to narrow the field from which to select the appropriate fund. One method is to seek the advice of a knowledgeable investment advisor. Another method is to research the investment services publications on mutual fund performance and selection. Most of the leading mutual fund advisor services are carried by libraries. The independent investment advisors usually charge a flat fee for advising clients on mutual fund selection.

Before making any investment decision, investors must obtain a copy of the fund's latest **prospectus,** which will fully acquaint them with the fund and its objectives. The prospectus includes the investment objectives and policies; names of the investment advisors; details of the investment advisory contract, including fee schedules and other expenses; names of the officers and directors and their backgrounds; federal taxes, capital gain and dividend distribution policies and options; investment restrictions of the portfolio; capital stock and voting rights of the mutual fund owners; valuation of the net assets; and financial statements of the fund.

Many financial services publish performance measurements of the mutual fund industry. Summaries of current performance are often found in most popular business magazines. Performance had been an overworked term during the 1960s, and almost every financial institution seemed to be striving for the best record of investment management. The game was hectic, especially since the securities markets ended the decade at just about the same level that they began in 1960. Money managers in the 1970s seem to be returning to the basic standards of measurement, looking for long-term results as their key to performance comparisons. This attitude was especially strengthened during the severe market drop of 1973 to 1974. Even for professionals, timing of the market during the 1960s and early 1970s was almost an impossible task. Fund managers who remain with a conservative long-run growth plan were much farther ahead then the newer, more performance-minded fund managers.

Many mutual fund reports carry presentations of the growth of investor portfolios. Figure 10-3 is an example of one of these presentations. In this example, an investment of $10,000 made in November 1954 would have grown to be worth $220,698 by April of 1981. However, had the investor reinvested all the dividends and capital gain distributions over the entire period through 1981, the original investment would have been worth $374,057. Had the investors taken all distributions in cash over the 26 year period, they would have received dividends of $63,066 and capital gains distributions of $90,293. Figure 10-3 is an important illustration because it shows the value of compounding.

In any long-term investment program, it is important to get started as early as possible, no matter how small the dollar amount. In the Templeton Growth Fund example, the first 5 or 6 years are slow growth in terms of absolute dollars, but as the years progress compounding gives the investment dramatic growth. Without question, patience is one of the important elements in investing. This is especially true when the securities markets are in a downturn.

The Templeton Growth Fund example helps explain how expensive a load fund can become over time. Had it been a no-load fund, $850 more would have been deposited in the fund in 1954 and it would have grown to be worth $408,805 instead of $374,057. The $34,748 difference is the true long-term cost of the load fee. However, it is important to note that there are many load funds whose performance is far superior to some no-load funds. In the case of Templeton Growth Fund, an investor would be better off owning the load fund, since its performance has been outstanding. Nevertheless, when a load fund and a no-load fund of comparable quality and management performance are being compared, it is difficult to understand why one would select a load fund. Because the majority of new funds entering the mutual fund industry are being directed toward no-load funds, the investment community seems to be convinced of the soundness of the argument.

To make an informed election of a mutual fund, the investor must not only review the past progress of the fund, but he must also keep in mind the fund's objectives. If the fund's past record has been poor, there may be little reason to expect significant progress in the years ahead, unless a new management team has been selected to manage the fund. When an investor evaluates investment performance, a sufficient number of years must be

Figure 10-3   Templeton Growth Fund, Ltd.

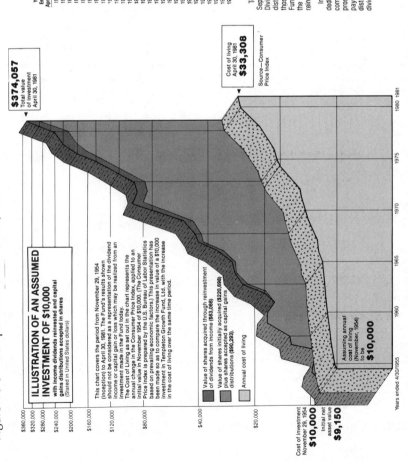

ILLUSTRATION OF AN ASSUMED INVESTMENT OF $10,000
with income dividends reinvested and capital gains distributions accepted in shares
(Stated in United States dollars)

This chart covers the period from November 29, 1954 (inception) to April 30, 1981. The Fund's results shown should not be considered as a representation of the dividend income or capital gain or loss which may be realized from an investment made in the Fund today.
The Cost of Living as set out in the chart represents the annual change in the Consumer Price Index, applied to an initial value in November 1954 of $10,000. (The Consumer Price Index is prepared by the U.S. Bureau of Labor Statistics based on prevailing economic factors.) This presentation has been made so as to compare the increase in value of a $10,000 investment in Templeton Growth Fund, Ltd. with the increase in the cost of living over the same time period.

$374,057 Total value of investment April 30, 1981

Cost of living April 30, 1981 **$33,308**
Source—Consumer Price Index

Cost of investment November 29, 1954 **$10,000**
Initial net asset value **$9,150**

Value of shares acquired through reinvestment of dividends from income **($63,066)**
Value of shares initially acquired **($220,698)** plus shares accepted as capital gains distributions **($90,293)**.
Annual cost of living

Assuming annual cost of living (November, 1954) to be **$10,000**

Years ended 4/30 1955 1960 1965 1970 1975 1980 1981

Value of Shares

Year Ended April 30,	Initially Acquired	Accepted as Capital Gains Distributions (cumulative)	Received Through Reinvestment of Dividends (cumulative)	Total Value
1955	$ 9,516	$ —	$ —	$ 9,516
1956	11,072	—	—	11,072
1957	10,889	—	—	10,889
1958	9,699	—	—	9,699
1959	14,457	—	—	14,457
1960	14,640	—	—	14,640
1961	19,398	—	—	19,398
1962	19,124	—	—	19,124
1963	17,477	—	—	17,477
1964	19,856	—	251	20,107
1965	25,712	—	325	26,037
1966	28,182	1	757	28,939
1967	28,365	—	1,123	29,488
1968	32,391	—	1,840	34,231
1969	42,548	—	3,019	45,567
1970	43,920	—	3,868	47,788
1971	48,312	—	5,116	53,428
1972	65,423	1,266	8,025	74,734
1973	85,095	3,667	11,376	100,138
1974	71,370	12,685	11,515	95,570
1975	73,383	13,043	12,492	98,918
1976	91,134	16,656	16,889	124,679
1977	112,271	22,238	22,681	157,190
1978	138,531	39,321	30,664	208,516
1979	160,034	46,371	37,476	243,881
1980	171,014	53,697	43,731	268,442
1981	220,698	90,293	63,066	374,057

Templeton Growth Fund, Ltd. was incorporated in Canada on September 1, 1954 and commenced operations November 29, 1954. Dividends from investment income were paid commencing in 1964 and distributions of capital gains were paid commencing in 1972. Prior to those years net income and realized capital gains were retained by the Fund. Income dividends and capital gains distributions are shown in the chart as reinvested at net asset value in accordance with the reinvestment policy described in the current prospectus.

Initial net asset value is the amount received by the Fund after deducting the maximum sales commission of 8½%. The actual sales commission on an investment of $10,000 is 7¾% as described in the prospectus. No adjustment has been made for any income taxes payable by shareholders. The total amount of capital gains distributions accepted in shares was $44,608; the total amount of dividends reinvested was $22,481.

Source: Templeton Growth Fund, Ltd., Prospectus, August 17, 1981.

Figure 10-4   Wiesenberger Mutual Fund Indexes

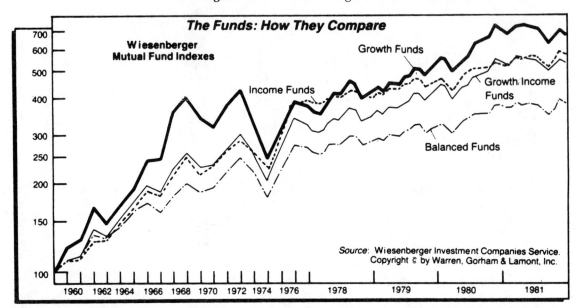

studied, because just one good or one bad year can distort the true per-formance of the fund's management. Figure 10-4 is a 23-year comparison of the price changes for various categories of mutual funds.

MEASURING PERFORMANCE

The most common and accepted method for measuring the investment re-sults of an investment company is based on the **per share values** from one period to the next. Every statistic is based on per share figures; therefore, all investors can apply the data to their holdings by multiplying the number of shares by the appropriate share data. The first step in measuring results is to record the final closing net asset value per share of the fund for the period. Add to this figure the dividend and capital gain distributions per share that were paid during the period being evaluated, usually a year. Deduct from the total of these figures the net asset value of the fund per share at the beginning of the year. The difference is either the appreciation or depreciation in the per share value of the fund. Divide this difference by the beginning of the year net asset value to arrive at a percentage expression of increase or decrease. For example,

Per share net asset value at year end	$11.82
Add: per share dividend distribution	.42
per share capital gain distribution	1.27
Total adjusted value	$13.51
Per share net asset value at beginning of year	12.21
Per share increase for period	$ 1.30

$$\text{Percentage increase for year } \frac{1.30}{12.21} = .106 \text{ or } 10.6\%$$

Without the adjustments for the distributions, the value of the fund would seem to decrease from the beginning of the year net asset value of $12.21 to the year-end net asset value of $11.82.

A number of studies have attempted to measure the performance of various types of funds categorized by objectives, asset size, load versus no-load, and risk levels. Table 10-4 is an example of the research on the performance of various mutual funds categorized by risk class. The risk classes were broken down into three different beta groupings. **Beta** is a measurement of the volatility of a security or group of securities in relation to the movement of the overall market.

The results of the study summarized in Table 10-4 are as might be expected. The investment objective is highly correlated with the risk class, as measured by the beta coefficient. The growth funds have a higher degree of risk, and the income-growth-stability funds have a lower degree of risk. One important conclusion is that although the riskier investment objectives are associated with higher rates of return over the period covered by the study (January 1960 through June 1968), there was no clear relation between rates of return and investment objective once risk is held constant. These conclusions are only one small aspect of the total research completed on the performance of mutual funds. Several research studies are included in the list of slected readings at the end of this chapter.

SECURING INFORMATION

The prospectus and the annual report, furnished by all mutual funds, are invaluable to the potential investor because they provide all the data necessary to make an assessment of a particular fund and to compare similar funds. If the investor does not want to personally conduct the research, the data compiled by such companies as Barron's or Wiesenberger Services,

Table 10-4

A Comparison of the Investment Performance of Selected Mutual Funds with Different Investment Objectives (January 1960 to June 1968)

Risk-Class (beta coefficient)	Number in Sample				Mean Return			
	Growth Funds[a]	Growth-Income Funds	Income-Growth Funds	Income-Growth-Stability Funds	Growth Funds[a]	Growth-Income Funds	Income-Growth Funds	Income-Growth-Stability Funds
Low risk (β = .5–.7)	3	5	4	16	.069	.101	.097	.091
Medium risk (β = .7–.9)	15	24	7	7	.112	.100	.100	.122
High risk (β = .9–1.1)	20	1	0	1	.138	.095	—	.135

[a]Investment objectives for 1967 as classified by Arthur Wiesenberger Services.

Source: Irwin Friend, Marshall Blume, and Jean Crockett, *Mutual Funds and Other Institutional Investors*, McGraw-Hill Book Company, 1970, p. 160.

Inc. may be used. Exhibit 10-3 is an example of data furnished quarterly by Barron's. Table 10-5 is an example of a fund comparison. The comparison enables the potential investor to scan hundreds of funds and then concentrate on the few that are most appealing.

Most potential investors should be able to select several funds that meet their objectives. If a no-load fund is selected, the large sales commission is saved. In the case of no-load funds, the investor must write directly to the mutual fund to obtain information and to make the investment. These funds do not use a middleman and depend upon direct communication with the investor.

Taxation of Investment Companies

Another important factor that should not be overlooked is the tax-exempt features possessed by most of the investment companies (but not the investors). This exemption is based upon the "conduit theory, in which the investment companies are thought of as a mere organized conduit between the shareholders (investors) and the diversified portfolio that they own. Therefore, for most of the investment companies that qualify under Subchapter M of the Internal Revenue Code, the investment companies are not considered as paying entities.

A regulated investment company for tax purposes is defined in terms of the following requirements:

1. Ninety percent or more of its gross income comes from dividends, interest, and net capital gains, with less than 30 percent from short-term profits.
2. It pays out at least 90 percent in dividends of its net investment income.
3. It is not a holding company and maintains a substantial degree of diversification as defined by law.

A qualified investment company, therefore, pays regular corporation rates on the undistributed portion and pays no income tax on either income or capital gains on the portion that is distributed to its shareholders as dividends. Investors are informed by the company as to the sources of the dividends that they receive. They are required to pay income tax on the portion that comes from interest, income, and/or short-term capital gains; and they pay capital-gain tax on the portion that comes from long-term capital gains.

KEY TERMS

accumulation account   money market fund
balanced fund   mutual funds
beta   net asset value

Exhibit 10–3

QUARTERLY MUTUAL FUND RECORD

QUARTER ENDED DECEMBER 31

Columns for each year (1981, 1980, 1979, 1978, 1977, 1976, 1975, 1974, 1973, 1972, 1971) show:
Net Asset Value per share / 12 mos. Divs from Income per share / 12 mos. Disb. fr. Cap. Gns(a)

Fund	1981 NAV	Divs	Cap	1980 NAV	Divs	Cap	1979 NAV	Divs	Cap	1978 NAV	Divs	Cap	1977 NAV	Divs	Cap	1976 NAV	Divs	Cap	1975 NAV	Divs	Cap	1974 NAV	Divs	Cap	1973 NAV	Divs	Cap	1972 NAV	Divs	Cap	1971 NAV
Acorn Fund	24.41	.88	2.44	29.72	.80	2.34	25.70	.44	1.33	18.73	.38		16.38	.24		14.10	.20		8.70	.20		6.82	.14		9.63	.06	1.12	13.85	.19	.26	13.18
Affiliated Fund	7.75	.56	.49	8.78	.51	.49	8.05	.45		7.41	.37		7.41	.37		8.49	.34		6.76	.26		5.12	.32		6.45	.31		7.32	.29	.20	6.97
Afuture Fund	14.10	.407	3.094	17.94	.45	3.279	16.40	.145		11.95	.059		10.00	.033		9.69	.018		8.14	.01		4.98			8.59			15.14			12.71
American Birthright Trust (e)	11.61	.51		13.48	.43		13.48	.30		9.66	.01		9.61			9.79			8.10			2.80	.08		7.82	.04		4.22	.10		7.46
American Gen. Comstock	11.33		2.44	13.08			10.29			7.22			6.36	.37		5.93	.10		4.50						3.46						4.11
American Gen. Enterprise	13.11	.14		15.20	.055		8.83	.15		5.97	.175		5.08	.10		5.56	.11		4.94	.19		3.84			5.70	.05		7.26	.10		6.92
American Gen. Venture Fd	19.25	.85	2.04	19.65	.66	2.49	17.75	.15	3.00	14.91	.41	2.53	14.25	.055		11.35			9.06			4.85	.225	.53	8.20	.17	.12	13.40	.156	.87	10.99
American Gen. Grth Fund (c)	7.08	.34	.25	7.36	.45	2.52	8.81	.35	.14	6.13	.24		5.89	.145		5.42	.16		4.32	.20		7.05	.30		5.46	.33		6.35	.085		6.72
American Industry Shs	9.34	.38		10.41	.36		9.09	.40		5.63	.11		9.24	.38		11.33	.31		9.65	.29		7.05	.07		9.27	.05		6.07	.02		
American Investors Fund	11.54			12.63	.05	.77	9.11	.09					5.65	.08		5.45	.05		4.08	.06		3.51			5.09	.05					5.50
American Inv. Inco. Fd.	9.51	1.43	.31	11.74	1.29	.55	11.61	1.13		11.22	1.03		11.99	1.06		12.13	.94		10.03	.42					12.71	.44		16.54	.36		9.35
American Mutual Fund	12.37	.61	.41	12.48	.58	.48	10.89	.52		9.82	.50		9.51	.47		10.16	.46		8.09	.45		5.85	.48		8.08	.34		11.52	.30		7.94
Axe-Houghton Fund B	8.07	.48	.10	8.28	.58	.18	7.72	.49	.12	6.00	.16		7.73	.40		8.06	.41		6.67	.42		3.88	.26		4.91	.23		5.55	.33	.27	5.64
Axe-Houghton Income Fd.	4.01	.45		4.23	.39		4.30	.37		4.58	.36		4.91	.36		5.02	.255		4.32	.24					5.36	.23		5.47	.13		6.01
Axe-Houghton Stock Fund	9.06	.06		9.67	.18		7.21	.20		5.60	.10		5.60	.10		6.38	.10		5.43	.16		4.61	.16		5.36	.14					
D. L. Babson Inco Tr	1.34	.166		1.43	.153		1.54	.14		1.64	.122		1.75	.12		1.82	.128		1.75	.13		1.73	.14		1.84	.14		2.04	.135		2.00
D. L. Babson Invest. Fd.	12.20	.41		13.41	.42		10.85	.35		9.57	.30		9.08	.25		10.07	.24		9.01	.22		6.38	.15		7.67	.17		12.05	.17		9.93
Beacon Hill Mutual Fd.	12.85	.07		12.68	.13		10.14	.07		9.48	.07		8.81	.06		8.80	.05		7.95	.16		7.84	.12		22.69	.80		30.01	.02	.70	11.57
Boston Co Capital Apprec	25.37	.77	1.07	28.57	.29	.27	23.74	.97		20.67	.69	.04	19.78	.46	.44	21.80	.32		19.23	.42				.25				11.51	.46	.193	24.75
Boston Foundation Fund	9.55	.89		10.83	.785		9.50	.65		8.92	.36		9.34	.505		9.69	.425		8.28	.40		8.87	.42		9.09	.40		16.31	.275		11.18
Broad Street Investing	12.07	.44	.95	13.99	.61	.88	12.05	.58	.59	10.65	.55	.60	11.18	.53		13.04	.50	.77	11.21	.49		8.71	.47		12.71	.44	.20	16.54	.36	.36	15.30
Bullock Fund	14.85	.76	.61	16.24	.64	.61	14.94	.62	.45	12.21	.51	.35	12.85	.48		13.53	.49		11.17	.47		8.72	.45		11.90	.37		11.52	.19	.40	15.07
Canadian Fund	7.75	.37		9.05	.29		8.45	.27		7.37	.26		7.73	.30		7.85	.32		8.31	.33		3.32			5.36	.087		7.13	.133		9.77
Capital Shares	12.70	.15		14.61	.17		9.81	.12		6.46	.105		6.31	.094		6.06	.084		7.88	.12					10.75						6.79
Century Shares Trust	12.17	.60		11.32	.56	.96	12.15	.50		11.20	.40		11.17	.33		12.05	.135		9.07	.305		8.48	.30		13.39	.18		16.31	.275	.35	14.14
Charter Fund	16.91	.98	1.577	19.25	.61		17.23	.505	1.53	13.60	.281	3.834	13.61	.187	1.026	14.12	.128	.99	10.06	.12		7.67	.138		10.71	.03	1.201	12.41	.50		10.00
Chemical Fund	9.52	.32	.30	10.60	.29		8.60	.23	.25	7.35	.22	.21	6.99	.19	.21	8.04	.18	.198	7.76	.20	.15	6.70	.10	.455	9.68	.14	.52	12.05	.43	.50	9.78
Colonial Fund	10.71	.61		11.49	.57		9.93	.54		8.94	.45		8.95	.46		9.99	.45		8.99	.45		7.70	.51		5.62	.185	.20	7.45	.07	.29	11.13
Colonial Growth Shares	7.68	.18		8.58	.18		6.21	.16		4.62	.15		4.51	.11		5.15	.07		4.56	.122		3.85	.09		7.77	.41		11.05	.123	.583	10.20
Commerce Income Shares	8.43	.55		9.97	.55	.625	8.73	.625		8.08	.55		8.39	.30	.092	9.32	.165		7.86	.09		6.61	.32					9.20	.29		9.20
Composite Bond & Stock	8.77	.70	.15	9.22	.62	.40	8.76	.56	.19	7.96	.53		8.48	.50	.10	9.16	.48		7.86	.48		6.52	.48		7.77	.41	.41	9.40	.29	.300	9.61
Composite Fund (d)	9.06	.49	.40	9.49	.35		8.40	.28		7.24	.24		7.51	.39		8.07	.37		7.10	.20		5.93	.14		6.67	.17		11.30	.29		10.93
Concord Fund	20.08	.75		20.33	.57		16.66	.56		13.04	.48		13.51	.39		12.07	.32		8.70	.16		5.93	.45		9.28	.21	.50	11.49	.40		11.87
Decatur Income Fund	12.93	1.14	1.13	14.46	.95		13.28	.56	.17	11.84	.75		11.84	.46		11.72	.435		9.52	.62		6.99	.40		9.28	.62		12.38	.33	.78	12.52
Delaware Fund	15.22	.41	.67	14.91	.69		12.44	.58		10.55	.55		10.84	.535					9.10	.41		8.79	.36		8.79	.36		8.79			
De Vegh Mutual Fund	44.91	1.365	1.32	53.93	1.15		38.78	1.17		30.77	1.004		30.28	.88		32.61	.79		29.29	1.043		22.25	.655		28.86	.735	1.226	35.94	.66		37.04
Directors Capital Fund	2.43			2.01			2.71						4.18	.025		4.18	.054		3.71	.17		3.05	.187		4.66	.187	.564	7.32			7.08
Dividend Shares	2.62	.15		2.97	.16		2.69	.135		2.65	.12		2.77	1.12		3.28	1.00		2.89	.125		3.32	.125		3.28	.115		4.10	.11		3.78
Dodge & Cox Bal. Fund	22.05	1.59	.17	25.23	1.41	.31	22.35	1.27	.24	21.19	1.16	.24	21.19	1.12		23.06	1.00		19.25	.99		15.63	.94		20.64	.94	.62	24.49	.79		22.88
Dreyfus Fund	14.94	.61	1.97	16.78	.57	.745	14.11	.445	.725	12.35	.47	.51	12.94	.44	.18	12.93	.36		10.48	.33		8.24	.25		10.57	.265		13.94	.31		12.54
Eaton & Howard Bal. Fd.	7.80	.54	.18	9.13	.50	.13	7.80	.468	.29	7.71	.465		7.94	.453		9.01	.428		7.98	.42		6.96	.42		6.06	.42	.65	10.99	.416	.45	10.40
Eaton & Howard Income Fd.	4.10	.545		4.60	.53		5.09	.523		5.62	.476		6.07	.471		6.20	.454		5.46	.44		4.90	.434		6.06	.425	.327	6.77	.434	.052	6.61
Eaton & Howard Stock Fd.	10.83	.58		11.98	.49		10.01	.405		8.89	.382		8.70	.377		9.73	.305		8.66	.307		7.38	.307		6.89	.28		8.94	.09		14.26
Eaton Vance Growth Fd.	6.08	.23	2.61	9.02	.22		7.75	.18		6.79	.15		6.12	.12	.46	6.55	.11		5.54	.17		4.88	.17		6.89	.28		8.64	1.50		8.64
Energy Fund	17.63	1.12	2.11	23.45	.86	1.96	18.78	.44	.70	13.59	.577	.623	10.84	.47		14.59	.46		11.69	.46		9.11	.40		7.99	.36		12.99	.25		12.22
Evergreen Fund	34.78	.30	2.76	38.36	.07		28.32	.042	4.13	23.50	.128		16.88	.251	1.19	14.63	.076		9.83			6.14		.052	7.81	.04		10.58	.045	1.267	10.77
Fairfield Fund	7.41	.84	.104	7.94			5.03			4.02	.092		3.73	.092		4.18	.054		3.18		.096	2.34	.092		3.22			4.54			4.31
Fidelity Fund	18.01	.85	1.39	20.97	.86		17.00	.79		15.75	.71		15.46	.67		16.68	.81		15.01			10.01	.555	.05	14.52	.53		18.44	.51		16.63
Fidelity Puritan Fd	10.37	.91	1.07	11.20	.77		10.41	.70		9.93	.665		10.40	.645		11.26	.665		9.32	.575		7.60	.555		9.30	.54		10.71	.32		10.44
Fidelity Trend Fund	29.43	.77		31.87	.76		26.03	.84	1.61	22.55	.515		21.02	.49		22.24	.40		18.70	.375		14.18	.36		21.20	.32		28.19	.28		24.94

Source: *Barron's*, February 15, 1982.

Table 10–5

Mutual Funds: Approximate Percent of Change in Net Assets per Share with Capital Gains Reinvested (Total Return) and Income Dividends

	Total Net Assets 12/31/81 ($ Million)	12 Months 1981	Year 1980	5 Years 1977 to 12/31/81	10 Years 1972 to 12/31/81	Classification of Assets (Percent) 12/31/81			Percent Yield Last 12 Months
						Cash + Govt	Bonds + Prfd	Common Stock	
II. Growth Current Income Funds									
Affiliated Fund	1,580.6	0.1	24.2	54.4	156.7	4	0	96	5.3
Amer Mutual Fund	496.5	7.8	25.3	88.1	184.8	22	2	76	4.4
Analytic Optioned Equity Fund	8.2	7.0	20.3			8	0	92	4.4
Broad Street Investing Corp.	346.6	–2.6	30.2	60.2	113.4	16	2	82	4.6
Bullock Fund	125.4	–0.5	25.4	60.3	99.1	7	3	90	4.2
Colonial Fund	58.0	–3.1	24.3	41.0	63.9	23	5	72	5.2
**Commerce Income Shares (1977)	46.8	3.2	24.5			68	7	25	10.3
Composite Fund	24.1	4.4	26.4	73.6	80.5	15	0	85	4.2
Delaware Fund	226.8	9.5	25.9	69.3	108.7	37	18	45	6.5
Dividend Shares	236.6	–0.5	23.2	31.6	69.1	3	0	97	5.3
Dodge Cox Stock Fund	19.0	–2.0	33.2	62.2	104.5	5	0	95	4.6
**Eaton Howard Stock Fund (1979)	67.2	–5.5	24.8	36.8	20.3	7	0	93	5.0
Elfun Trusts	265.0	0.8	30.8	87.1	83.6	12	9	79	4.8
Evergreen Total Return Fund	16.7	9.0	26.8			5	23	72	5.5
Fidelity Fund	490.2	–3.3	33.9	62.5	108.5	6	7	87	4.4
Financial Industrial Fund	272.6	–14.2	27.8	69.0	139.4	9	24	67	5.5
Founders Mutual Fund	115.9	–7.6	27.5	22.5	60.4	2	0	98	5.0
**Fundamental Investors (1978)	316.5	–1.2	21.3	38.4	47.5	11	0	89	5.0
Gen Elec S S Program	506.5	–6.3	22.6	33.6	26.4	16	0	84	4.9
General Securities	10.4	1.7	23.9	61.3	99.5	6	17	77	7.3

	Total Net Assets 12/31/81 ($ Million)	12 Months 1981	Year 1980	5 Years 1977 to 12/31/81	10 Years 1972 to 12/31/81	Classification of Assets (Percent) 12/31/81			Percent Yield Last 12 Months
						Cash + Govt	Bonds + Prfd	Common Stock	
Gould (Edson) Fund	3.7	−10.2	40.5	60.0	186.8	3	0	97	0.0
Guardian Mutual Fund	169.0	−4.7	28.1	80.2	52.3	11	0	89	5.6
Hamilton Funds Series H-DA	224.8	−7.9	25.3	30.9	126.0	8	12	80	4.0
Investment Co of America	1,592.4	0.9	21.2	62.9		22	0	78	4.3
Investment Trust of Boston	56.0	−18.7	43.9	41.5	85.6	12	0	88	2.6

II. Growth Current Income Funds (Continued)

	Total Net Assets 12/31/81 ($ Million)	12 Months 1981	Year 1980	5 Years 1977 to 12/31/81	10 Years 1972 to 12/31/81	Cash + Govt	Bonds + Prfd	Common Stock	Percent Yield Last 12 Months
Investors Stock Fund	1,294.6	−6.6	26.4	38.4	59.5	34	0	66	6.1
ISI Trust Fund	102.5	−0.9	7.7	49.3	109.7	81	3	16	11.4
ISTEL Fund	121.1	−9.6	41.4	90.6	118.6	42	0	58	4.5
Keystone S-1 (High Grade)	59.3	−13.9	23.8	20.6	33.5	3	0	97	4.1
Lutheran Brotherhood Fund	27.1	4.2	21.1	41.0	67.2	17	17	66	6.5
Mann (Horace) Fund	60.2	−7.4	36.3	51.5	65.5	9	1	90	1.9
Mass Financial Dev FD	146.3	−13.5	40.7	91.4	84.3	11	12	77	3.2
Mass Investors Trust	1,015.4	−5.2	30.2	44.0	68.8	5	2	93	4.7
Merrill Lynch Capital Fd	119.5	11.8	24.8	83.0		19	3	78	5.8
National Industries Fund	29.4	−11.1	35.8	66.5	82.6	19	3	78	2.6
National Stock Fund	224.1	−4.1	32.5	60.7	131.4	7	3	90	4.7
Nel Equity Fund	10.9	5.7	20.5	69.0	112.4	30	4	66	3.4
North Star Stock Fund	16.9	−1.0	34.5	69.3	74.2	22	0	78	4.4
One William Street Fund	282.5	−0.2	28.4	78.1	105.9	12	0	88	4.0
Philadelphia Fund	180.4	−8.9	37.0	106.4	164.0	16	8	76	4.3
Pine Street Fund	39.1	−7.8	33.9	50.2	103.6	18	4	78	4.7
Pioneer Fund	1,025.7	−3.0	30.7	88.7	225.4	4	1	95	4.0
Pioneer II	458.4	8.6	28.5	161.3	444.5	8	2	90	3.4
Safeco Equity Fund	31.5	−4.9	27.6	80.2	147.4	17	8	75	6.2
St. Paul Capital Fund	46.1	−0.3	57.0	115.4	133.5	34	2	64	4.3

Selected American Shares	72.2	−0.9	21.6	35.5	23.2	17	24	59	6.5
Sentinel Common Stock FD	265.0	6.1	22.6	57.8	132.6	8	0	92	6.5
Sigma Investment Shares	48.3	5.7	27.7	61.4	108.2	8	5	87	4.6
Southwestern Investors	17.1	5.9	35.6	75.6	111.7	7	0	93	3.6
Sovereign Investors	8.5	7.9	20.2	57.5	109.3	12	0	88	5.8
State Street Investment	386.4	−1.7	24.9	77.8	113.0	(1)	1	100	3.5
Steadman Investment Fund	14.9	−11.5	28.9	20.1	27.8	19	0	81	3.6
Stratton Growth FD	6.8	−6.6	32.3	59.0		5	2	93	2.5
Technology Fund	478.8	−14.3	49.8	105.2	149.7	12	3	85	2.6
Twentieth Century Select Inv.	37.8	1.3	47.8	280.0	474.5	1	2	97	0.6
Unified Mutual Shares	7.1	−7.0	23.3	44.1	41.9	14	7	79	6.8
Vance Sanders Investors FD	132.8	4.7	20.1	62.1	110.1	12	22	66	6.1
Vanguard Index Trust	91.2	−8.5	31.9	39.1		0	0	100	5.3
Wall Street Fund	6.5	−7.4	21.0	39.1	41.0	4	0	96	3.1
Washington Mutual Investors	359.3	7.6	24.0	58.2	145.7	4	3	93	5.1
Total	$14,499.2								
Averages		−2.2	28.9	65.9	112.0				4.7

Source: Wiesenberger Services, Inc. Warren, Gorham, and Lamont, Inc., 1633 Broadway, N.Y., N.Y. 10019, All Rights Reserved

closed-end company   no-load fund
common-stock fund   open-end company
dual-purpose fund   per share value
income fund   prospectus
investment company   regular account
leverage fund   REITs
load fund   specialized fund

QUESTIONS

1. What are the major advantages of mutual funds?
2. What is an open-end company?
3. What is a closed-end company?
4. Describe the following mutual funds classifications: common stock funds, balanced funds, income funds, specialized funds, and leverage funds.
5. What are dual-purpose funds? What seems to be the inherent problem of these funds?
6. What are REITs?
7. What are the three major mutual fund accounts? How does each differ from the other two?
8. What are load funds?
9. What are no-load funds?
10. What are the costs in running a mutual fund?
11. How do open-end funds deal with dividends and capital gains?
12. How should an investor choose a mutual fund?
13. How do you calculate the percentage of increase or decrease for the year?
14. What sources of information are important concerning mutual funds?
15. What is the major tax advantage of a mutual fund?

SELECTED READINGS

ANDREDER, STEVEN S. "Money Market Funds — Yield-Sensitive Investors Flock to Them." *Barron's*, October 15, 1979, 4–5, 16.

BOLAND, JOHN C. "Switch in Time: Holders of Mutual Funds Try to Profit by Swapping." *Barron's*, December 18, 1978, 11–12 ff.

FRIEND, IRWIN, MARSHALL BLUME, and JEAN CROCKET. *Mutual Funds and Other Institutional Investors.* New York: McGraw-Hill, 1971.

GLENN, ARMON. "Switch to No-Load." *Barron's*, June 6, 1977, 5 ff.

Investment Company Institute. *Mutual Fund Fact Book.* New York: The Institute, annually.

KIM, TYE. "An Assessment of the Performance of Mutual Fund Management: 1969–1975." *Journal of Financial and Quantitative Analysis*, September 1978, 385–406.

KON, STANLEY J., and FRANK C. JEN. "The Investment Performance of Mutual Funds: An Empirical Investigation of Timing, Selectivity, and Market Efficiency." *Journal of Business*, April 1979, 263–289.

ROENFELDT, RODNEY L., and DONALD L. TUTTLE. "An Examination of the Discounts and Premiums of Closed-End Investment Companies." *Journal of Business Research*, Fall 1973, 129–140.

THOMPSON, REX. "The Information Content of Discounts and Premiums on Closed-end Fund Shares." *Journal of Financial Economics*, June–September 1978, 151–180.

WIESENBERGER, ARTHUR G. *Investment Companies*. New York: annually.

11

Securities Regulation

Before 1933, regulation of the securities industry was limited to state security laws because there were no federal security laws. However, the state security laws had many drawbacks. Listed companies were not required to furnish financial and accounting information to their shareholders or to the general public. When fraud did take place, it was often too late for the state to prosecute those people responsible for they had already left the state and, hence, were not subject to its jurisdiction. Consequently, widespread misrepresentation in financial statements was commonplace, and manipulation and fraud in security trading were widespread. All these abuses in the securities markets contributed to the overvaluation of securities and the market crash of 1929 and, consequently, the federal government regulations of 1933.

Some of the most commonly seen abuses were wash sales, corners on the market, pools, and excessive usage of debt. A **wash sale** is a fictitious transaction in which no change of ownership takes place. Manipulators of a wash sale know that investors will view a certain security favorably if they observe a price rise coupled with increased activity in that issue. Therefore, they agree to create a fictitious transaction (buy and sell) at a stipulated price (usually higher than the normal market price) in order to create market activity in that security. However, the buyer, by agreement, incurs no financial obligation to the seller. Therefore, the sale is purely fictitious. The purpose is to make the security appear in a strong position and to deceive interested investors. To **corner the market** in a security means that a person buys all that security that is for sale. Since this person then has the total control of the security, he or she may liquidate it at a higher price for appreciation (or capital gains). **Pools** refer to an association of people who agree to manipulate some security's price and, hence, benefit from the activities. The objective of the pool is to accumulate holdings in a particular issue at a low price and then to sell them to the public later at a higher price. Once the objective is achieved, the pool is dissolved. All these fraudulent activities are prohibited by the Security Exchange Act of 1934.

Under Franklin Roosevelt's administration beginning is 1933, the Senate conducted an investigation into banking practices and security market operations. The resulting Securities Act of 1933 was enacted to control such abuses and excesses. Enforcement of the act was the responsibility of the Federal Trade Commission until 1934, when the Securities and Exchange Commission was created by the Securities Exchange Act.

Four more securities laws were passed between 1935 and 1940, and the 1934 Exchange Act was amended by the Securities Act Amendment of 1964. The pendulum swung from the excesses of the 1920s to what is now considered one of the nation's most heavily regulated periods.

These complex security laws involve a profusion of legal definitions, rules, exemptions, and other provisions. This chapter highlights important aspects of the regulatory environment for the securities industry.

SECURITIES AND EXCHANGE COMMISSION

The SEC was created to serve as the enforcement agent for security laws. It is authorized under Chapter 10 of the Federal Bankruptcy Act to appear as a party to reorganization proceedings either on its own motion, if approved by a federal judge, or at the request of a judge.

The commission consists of five members, not more than three of whom may belong to the same political party. The members are appointed by the president of the United States with the advice and consent of the Senate for 5-year staggered terms. The president also designates the chairman of the commission. The commission reports annually to Congress.

The SEC staff consists of lawyers, accountants, engineers, security analysts, and examiners. It is divided into divisions and offices, including nine regional offices, each under the direction of officials appointed by the commission. The SEC regional offices investigate complaints or other indications of possible violations of law in securities transactions. Complaints from investors or the general public to the regional offices are the principal means of detecting violations of security laws. The regional offices also have the authority to inspect the books of brokers and dealers at any time to check for compliance with security rules.

Generally, SEC investigations are fact-finding inquiries. If it is determined that the law has been violated, the commission can pursue several courses of action. It can seek a civil injunction by applying to a U.S. district court for an order restraining the acts in violation of the law. In the case of fraud or other willful law violations, the commission contacts the Department of Justice, which may present the evidence to a federal grand jury and institute criminal proceedings. The SEC can also impose administrative remedies by denying, suspending, or revoking registration of brokers and dealers, or by suspending or expelling members from exchanges or from the National Association of Security Dealers.

The many security regulations would be meaningless were it not for the broad powers bestowed on the SEC to administer them. However, the commission does not function alone. It cooperates closely with other federal, state, and local law enforcement agencies.

The board of governors of the Federal Reserve System works with the SEC by setting margin requirements. Margin trading is the buying of securities on credit. When the securities market and the economy need stimulation, the margin requirement is reduced; conversely, when they need to be slowed down, margin requirements are tightened. Thus, the power to change margin requirements is an effective government tool for regulating the economy.

SECURITIES ACT OF 1933

The policy of the 1933 act is basically one of disclosure, enabling investors to make financial decisions based on the facts at hand. The act, often referred to as the **Truth in Securities Act,** has two objectives: (1) to provide investors with financial and other information concerning securities offered for public sale, and (2) to prohibit misrepresentation, deceit, and other fraudulent acts and practices in the sale of securities. The basic provisions of the 1933 act are as follows:

1. To protect investors by requiring that key information be disclosed to investors.
2. To require corporations wishing to sell securities in interstate commerce to file a registration statement containing extensive information concerning both the issue and the corporation.
3. To subject all corporate officers and directors, attorneys, appraisers, and accountants associated with the undertaking (i.e., as signers of the registration statement) to the provision of the act.
4. To hold all these responsible individuals liable for any material misstatements or omissions of material facts.

The responsibility for appraisal of investments is left to the individual investor, with the aid of such private advice as he or she wishes to or can obtain. But under the act, the SEC determines the kinds of information that must be given to the public by an enterprise that seeks to obtain public investment. Although the SEC does not make judgments on the merits of the securities, it does see to it that the firm floating a new issue of stock does not mislead the investor. Therefore, the SEC has the responsibility of taking appropriate action to stop and to punish those who attempt to avoid furnishing information or who attempt to sell securities on the basis of misrepresentation or misinformation.

Registration Statement

Before a new security offering can be made to the general public, a registration statement must be filed with the SEC. A prospectus is the principal part of the registration statement, thus eliminating much duplication between the registration statement required by the SEC and the prospectus to be offered to the public.

The issuing firm's registration statement discloses information such as a description of its properties and business, a description of the security offered and its relationship to other securities offered by the registrant, certain information about the company's management, and certified financial statements for several preceding years. It also includes details about the issuer's arrangements for bonuses, stock options, and profit sharing; copies of the firm's articles of incorporation, bylaws, and trust indentures; and agreements with the investor banker. Furthermore, the SEC may require any other statements and information that may materially affect the value of the securities.

The 1933 act requires that the first written offer of a security be a prospectus. The purpose of the prospectus is to supply the investor with up-to-date data concerning the security offered.

The registration statement and the prospectus become public information when they are filed with the commission, but it is unlawful to sell securities until the effective date of the registration, which is generally 20 days after filing. If the SEC discovers any deficiency in the disclosure requirements, a stop order is issued extending the waiting period until the deficiency is corrected.

Within the 20-day waiting period, or until the registration statement becomes effective, written communication with potential investors is restricted to the **preliminary prospectus**[1] or to a **tombstone advertisement.** The tombstone announcement derives its name from the starkness of its

---

[1]The preliminary prospects is often called a **red herring** because of the legend written vertically on the cover of the document in red ink stating that the document does not constitute an offer to sell. The red herring is the same as the final prospectus except that the security prices and other information not yet available are omitted.

contents, which are specified by the commission. It permits potential customers to be reached so that a prospectus can be delivered when available and requested.

The **statutory** or **final prospectus** is made available for use as a selling document once the registration becomes effective. It contains all pertinent information about the company and the issue, including the offering price.

Exemptions

Certain issues are exempt from registration.

A Private Offering.

As a rule of thumb, if there are fewer than 25 offerees (i.e., individuals contacted regarded a potential purchase) and if the securities are held by the investor for investment purposes rather than for immediate public resale, the offering would probably qualify as a private offering.

Another qualifying factor is the degree of sophistication possessed by the offerees. In other words, it is important to determine whether the offerees can judge the merit of a security offering without the added protection of the prospectus.

Other factors considered are the size and manner of the offering. Most private placements are with large institutional investors such as banks or insurance companies.

An Intrastate Offering.

To qualify as an intrastate offering, each purchaser must be a resident of the state, and the company must be incorporated and doing business within the state in which the placement is made. Any exception to these conditions (e.g., if a share is sold to an out-of-state purchaser) is a violation of this exemption, and the entire offering is placed under the provisions of the 1933 act. In addition, these shares must not be resold to out-of-state purchasers for as long as 1 or 2 years after the original sale, as determined by each state.

Small Public Offerings.

An offering not in excess of $300,000 in any one year is exempt, but certain formalities similar to a regular registration must be taken. This is sometimes called the **short form** of registration.

Other.

Securities of municipal, state, federal, and other government agencies, banks, charitable institutions, and carriers subject to the Interstate Commerce Act are exempt from the complete registration requirements of the 1933 act.

SECURITIES ACT AMENDMENTS OF 1964

The SEC conducted an investigation of the securities market that culminated in the publication in 1964 of the *Report of Special Study of the Securities Markets*. This, in turn, led to the passage of the Securities Act Amendments of 1964, which make extensive changes in the Security Exchange Act of 1934. The 1964 amendments extended the exchange act to cover those OTC companies dealing in interstate commerce that have more than 500 shareholders and assets in excess of $1 million. The SEC is also given greater disciplinary control over OTC violators of securities laws.

In addition, the 1964 amendments strengthen the rules of the New York Stock Exchange, the National Association of Securities Dealers, and other self-regulatory security organizations.

Exemptions from the 1964 amendments are granted to securities listed and registered with a national exchange, registered investment companies, insurance companies, banks, savings and loan institutions, and foreign issuers.

The proxy rules of the exchange act were extended to a large number of publicly owned unlisted companies that had never made public disclosure of some of the information that must be set forth in a proxy statement subject to SEC rules. Management of these corporations quite often did not send out proxies in order to avoid having to comply with SEC proxy regulations. Therefore, the 1964 amendments require these companies to send their shareholders information comparable to that sent to shareholders of listed companies.

SECURITIES EXCHANGE ACT OF 1934

The basic function of the securities market is to bring buyers and sellers together. To maintain a free and orderly market, both the purchasers and the sellers of securities must be assured that the market is free from manipulative schemes or fraudulent practices. Therefore, the philosophy of the 1933 act was extended to the secondary market by the Securities Exchange Act of 1934 (the Exchange Act).

The basic purpose of this act is to protect investors by curbing excessive speculation and eliminating unfair practices in security exchanges. Although the 1933 act regulates new nonexempt issues, the Exchange Act regulates the secondary markets; that is, it regulates the buying and selling of existing securities on the exchanges and in the over-the-counter markets.

It requires that all exchanges be licensed by the SEC and that all securities sold on the exchanges be registered both with the SEC and with the listing exchange. Registration is effected by submitting an application similar to, but less extensive than, the registration statement required by the 1933 act. In addition, reports must be filed annually and quarterly with the SEC to keep the exchanges, the SEC, and investors informed. The annual report, called the **10-K report,** covers extensive details, such as transactions in the company's securities by insiders or principal shareholders (individuals owning over 10 percent of the voting securities), and includes certified financial statements. The quarterly report, called the **10-Q report,** contains unaudited financial statements.

The exchanges require that all listed companies submit a listing application. As part of that application, the company enters into a listing agreement with the exchange setting forth certain requirements such as the mailing of certified annual reports to stockholders and the publication of interim unaudited earnings statements. Copies of these reports, together with copies of the quarterly and annual reports filed with the SEC, are filed with the stock exchange. The exchange act requires that the exchanges have adequate provisions for disciplining its members for violations of the listing agreement.

Credit Requirements

As mentioned before, a major factor contributing to the great crash of the securities markets in 1929 was the excessive use of debt. Many speculators purchased securities by borrowing up to 90 percent of the cost of the security. When the market went down from 1929 to 1932, many securities prices declined to one tenth of the original purchased price. Many speculators who had overextended their credit went bankrupt. The banks who lent money to these speculators could not sufficiently cover the debt by selling the securities (collateral) whose value had declined so much. To avoid further losses, banks tried to liquidate those shares by dumping them on the market; this, in turn, worsened the situation. To prevent history from repeating itself, the SEA of 1934 authorized the Federal Reserve Board to regulate credit in security markets. The Federal Reserve then wrote Federal Reserve Regulations T and U to cover the initial margin requirements.

Regulation T stipulates the minimum percentage of collateral that would be acceptable to cover the purchase or short sale of a security. It is 50 percent at the present time. Thus, a person cannot borrow more than

50 percent (100 percent minus the margin of 50 percent) of the market value of the security that is purchased. Maintenance margin, which is established by the major exchanges, is 25 percent now. Some brokers even require a higher margin, about 30 percent, for maintenance. The combination of a high initial margin and a low maintenance is supposed to reduce the probability of widespread liquidation of securities. Regulation U extends the same initial margin requirements to commercial banks that Regulation T imposes upon broker accounts. In 1968, the Federal Reserve Board introduced Regulation G to lenders other than brokers, dealers, or banks.

Proxy Solicitations

Every shareholder entitled to vote at a shareholders' meeting or to express consent or dissent without a meeting may authorize another person or persons to act for him by proxy. The exchange act provides for SEC control of the solicitation of proxies.

Proxies are solicited by management or by minority groups (those that do not hold enough shares to control policy) to win approval of certain corporate actions or to elect a slate of directors. In such solicitations, all material facts concerning the matters on which holders are asked to vote must be disclosed, and holders must be afforded the opportunity to vote yes or no on each matter. Before the proxy material is sent to the shareholders, it must be filed with the SEC for examination.

Tender Offer Solicitations

Tender offers and take-over bids are subject to SEC regulations. A **tender offer** is made to stockholders to purchase their stock. That is, an individual or corporation desiring to acquire a substantial number of another corporation's outstanding shares may make a tender offer to that corporation's shareholders. Therefore, any person or corporation acquiring stock that results in ownership in excess of 5 percent of the outstanding securities of that class (common or preferred) must file with the SEC and disclose to the company such pertinent information as the purpose of the acquisition and the method by which it was financed.

Insider Trading

Certain corporate information that is not available to the general investing public could be used to the advantage of insiders (directors, officers, and owners of more than 10 percent of the corporation's stock) if it were not for SEC rules governing insider trading. Insiders are required to file reports with the SEC and with the listing exchange disclosing their security holdings. They must also file additional reports in any month during which there is any change in their holdings. Any profit resulting from the purchase or sale of such securities within a 6 month period from the date of an important corporate event may be recovered by the company or a shareholder on behalf of the company if transactions resulted from insider information.

PUBLIC UTILITY HOLDING COMPANY ACT OF 1935

The Public Utility Holding Company Act of 1935 provides for the registration of holding companies engaged in the electric utility business or in the retail gas business. Natural gas pipeline companies and other nonutility companies that are subsidiaries of registered holding companies also fall within the jurisdiction of this act. Registration accomplishes the same results as the exchange act in that an initial registration statement is submitted with the commission and is kept up to date by annual reports. But unlike the other security laws, this act is designed primarily to protect consumers in general, rather than the investor in particular.

Under this act, a public utility group must meet the following requirements:

1. It must be an integrated system. That is, its properties must be integrated geographically.
2. It must have a simplified capital and corporate structure. For example, it may not have a subsidiary whose subsidiary is, in turn, a holding company. [2]
3. It must abide by the provisions of the act relating to intercompany transactions.
4. It must report all holdings of, and transactions in, the company's stock by corporate insiders. [3]
5. It must follow SEC requirements relating to the sale and issuance of securities, dividend payments, and other factors that affect the public interest.

TRUST INDENTURE ACT OF 1939

The Trust Indenture Act requires that evidences of indebtedness (bonds, debentures, and so forth) may not be offered to the public unless they are issued under a trust indenture that has been filed with the commission. The purpose of the act is to provide protection for debt-security holders and to give adequate power to the appointed trustees.

All corporations making a public offering of $1 million or more in debt securities issued under an indenture during any 36 month period or making a public offering in excess of $250,000 in debt securities not issued under

---

[2] This arrangement is known as a **second-degree holding company.**

[3] This provision is the same as the provision of the Securities Exchange Act relating to insider trading.

an indenture during any 12 month period must abide by the provisions of this act.

The trustee must submit annual reports to the debt-security holders and must report to them within 90 days if an interest payment, principal repayment, or sinking-fund payment is to be omitted or if the corporation has committed an act of bankruptcy.

Under the Trust Indenture Act, the qualifications and duties of the trustees and the duties of the corporation are clearly defined, as are the form and content of the trust indenture.

INVESTMENT COMPANY ACT OF 1940

Between 1934 and 1940, the number of investment companies increased rapidly, and their methods of operation varied considerably. (For a full description of investment companies, see Chapter 10.) The Investment Company Act was devised to remedy the many abusive practices of investment trusts.

This act requires registration and full disclosure of investment companies not registered under the 1933 act or the exchange act and prevents speculative abuses. It requires honest and unbiased management and adequate capital structures and limits on the amount and number of issues of bonds and preferred stock.

Directors must be elected by the shareholders. However, vacancies may be filled by the board if at least two-thirds of the directors holding office at the time of the appointment were elected by holders of the outstanding voting securities of the company.

Investment management contracts are approved by the shareholders and are renewed annually or may be canceled by directors or shareholders with 65 day notice.

At least 75 percent of the investment company's assets must be invested in securities, but only 5 percent of the total assets can be invested in any one issuer. The remaining 25 percent of the company's assets need not be diversified; that is, they may be invested in the securities of a single issuer.

Other provisions of this act relate to such matters as load charges (selling commissions), proxies, the prospectus, annual reports, and redemption of investment company shares.

INVESTMENT COMPANY AMENDMENTS ACT OF 1970

After extensive investigation, the SEC released a comprehensive report on mutual funds in December 1966. The report suggested a number of important revisions in the Investment Company Act of 1940 and in the regulatory power granted the SEC under that statute relative to mutual funds. Its chief recommendations were abolition of front-end load contractual plans, limitation of sales charges to a maximum of 5 percent (4.75 percent of the offering price), requirement of reasonable management fees, and control or elimination of **give-ups,** whereby part of the sales commission earned by selling dealers is given up to other dealers who have provided services to the funds' managers or to smaller dealers unable to develop a large volume of sales.

After long and controversial hearings, Congress passed the Investment Company Amendments Act of 1970. However, it fell considerably short of meeting the SEC recommendations. Important differences from the recommendations included the following:

Neither the front-end load plans nor the 50 percent sales charge in the first year were eliminated. However, investors can rescind the entire transaction within 45 days, and during the first 18 months, shareholders can receive a refund of their payments, less a 15 percent service charge.

Sales charges were not limited to a specific maximum, but the offering price of mutual-fund shares may not include an "excessive" sales load. Rules relating to sales commissions are to be formulated by the National Association of Security Dealers.

Management fees are not specified but generally must be computed on the net asset value of the fund being managed. Fees based on performance are prohibited unless they increase and decrease in proportion to an index of security prices.

Fiduciary duty (the obligation to guard the interests of shareholders with honesty and prudence) is imposed on the officers and directors of investment companies and their advisers.

NATIONAL ASSOCIATION OF SECURITIES DEALERS

The Maloney Act of 1938 amended the exchange act to allow brokers and dealers to regulate themselves through the National Association of Securities Dealers (NASD) in lieu of direct regulation by both the SEC and the exchange with which they are registered. However, registration with the SEC is still required.

The NASD is the only trade organization in the country that has regulatory powers. Its main purpose is to promote high standards of commerce and honor in the securities business. Its major function is the continuous inspection of the books and records of members to ascertain whether the rules have been or are being violated. The SEC, although allowing the dealers and brokers self-regulatory power, still has the final decision over NASD rules and disciplinary actions.

The NASD is not merely another rule-making arm of the government; rather, it strives to place its members on a high professional level by establishing ethical as well as legal standards. Penalties for violations of NASD rules may take the form of a fine, suspension, or expulsion. Because membership in the NASD requires registration with the SEC and with state authorities where applicable, membership can be revoked not only for violation of NASD ethical or legal standards but also for violations of state or federal security laws.

Loss of NASD membership causes economic hardships because it prevents joint underwritings with NASD members and forbids compensation by a member to an individual whose membership has been revoked or suspended. NASD membership is essential if a broker or dealer is to operate profitably in the OTC market. For example, NASD members are given a wholesale price, whereas nonmember brokers or dealers are charged the same prices charged to the general public.

The delinquent member may appeal NASD action through the SEC. The commission reviews the NASD decision and may uphold the action, waive the penalty, or impose a more severe sentence.

SECURITIES INVESTOR PROTECTION ACT OF 1970

This act, amended in 1978, provides protection for investors against loss due to failure of a brokerage firm through a nonprofit, government agency, the Securities Investor Protection Corporation (SIPC). SIPC now can insure accounts at brokerage firms up to $500,000. SIPC is financed by assessing members (almost all the brokers-dealers have joined) up to 1 percent of their commission revenues, and it can borrow up to $1 billion from the U.S. Treasury if additional funds are needed. The SIPC, under the SEC's supervision, is also required to consult closely with the stock exchanges and NASD in order to detect approaching difficulties in securities firms. If the SIPC finds a brokerage firm that is financially troubled or failing to meet its obligations to its customers, the SIPC will apply to a federal court to appoint a trustee to take over, and perhaps liquidate, the troubled firm. The trustee then promptly notifies customers to file claims for the amounts owed them and settles all claims accordingly.

INVESTMENT ADVISERS ACT OF 1940

Any person or organization acting as a security adviser, either directly or by written advice, for compensation must be registered with the SEC. However, certain advisers are exempt from registration, including bankers, attorneys, teachers, and accountants; those who advise only insurance companies or investment companies; and those who had fewer than 15 clients during the last 12 months and who do not generally represent themselves to the public as investment advisers.

Investment advisers may not receive compensation based on a sharing of the clients' capital gains or capital appreciation. Generally, fees for investment advice are either a flat rate, as is the case with subscriptions to investment publications, or a percentage of the assets involved.

If the investment adviser violates any of the requirements of this act, the SEC may deny, suspend, or revoke the adviser's registration. The commission may also obtain injunctions restraining violators of the act and may recommend that the Department of Justice prosecute the investment adviser for fraudulent misconduct or willful violation of the provisions of the act.

BANKRUPTCY ACT, CHAPTER 10

Chapter 10 of the Bankruptcy Act provides a procedure for corporate reorganization. It is the function of the SEC to study the reorganization plan and to submit a report on whether the plan is feasible and equitable. The SEC will serve as a disinterested adviser to the court if requested to do so by the judge in the reorganization proceedings.

The SEC will conduct a thorough investigation of the debtor's operations, financial condition, future prospects, and so forth, and then submit to the court its recommendation on whether the plan is feasible and equitable. Because the SEC serves in an advisory capacity only, the judge will either accept or reject the report. If the report is accepted by the judge, it is given to the creditors and security holders of the debtor company, and they decide whether the plan is acceptable.

REGULATION BY THE BROKERS

National Association of Securities Dealers

The Maloney Act of 1938 amended the exchange act to allow brokers and dealers to regulate themselves through the National Association of Securities Dealers (NASD) in lieu of direct regulation by both the SEC and the exchange with which they are registered. However, registration with the SEC is stilled required.

The NASD is the only trade organization in the country that has regulatory powers. Its main purpose is to promote high standards of commerce and honor in the securities business. Its major function is the continuous inspection of the books and records of members to ascertain whether the rules have been or are being violated. The SEC, although allowing the dealers over NASD rules and disciplinary actions.

The NASD is not merely another rule-making arm of the government; rather, it strives to place its members on a high professional level by establishing ethical as well as legal standards. Penalties for violations of NASD rules may take form of a fine, suspension, or expulsion. Because membership in the NASD requires registration with the SEC and with state authorities where applicable, membership can be revoked not only for violation of NASD ethical or legal standards but also for violations of state or federal security laws.

Loss of NASD membership causes economic hardships because it prevents joint underwritings with NASD members and forbids compensation by a member to an individual whose membership has been revoked or suspended. NASD membership is essential if a broker or dealer is to operate profitably in the OTC market. For example, NASD members are given a wholesale price; whereas nonmember brokers or dealers are charged the same prices charged to the general public.

The delinquent member may appeal NASD action through the SEC. The commission reviews the NASD decision and may uphold the action, waive the penalty, or impose a more severe sentence.

STATE BLUE-SKY LAWS

The 1933 act provides for state regulation of security issues, even though the issuing company may be registered under the federal security laws. In some cases, state security laws may govern where an exemption exists under federal security laws.

State **blue-sky laws** regulate the offer and sale of securities within the state's boundaries.[4] Such regulation takes a variety of forms, further complicating the registration process because each security issue must be registered in any state in which the securities are to be sold. Furthermore, most states require that brokers and dealers in securities be registered or licensed in the individual states.

Several states stipulate the securities in which savings banks, insurance companies, and fiduciaries operating within that state may invest. This compilation of eligible securities, called a **legal list,** is published annually by the state banking department or commission.

A more lenient investment guideline adopted by some states is called the **prudent man rule,** which means that a trustee should exercise the same

---

[4] The phrase **blue sky** originated in 1917 in a case in which the judge described "speculative schemes which have no more basis than so many feet of blue sky."

degree of care while investing other people's money that a prudent person would exercise in the management of his or her own affairs in similar conditions.

In most states, registration takes one of three forms:

1. By qualification. Affirmative action by the blue-sky official is required in issuing a license or certificate.
2. By notification. The issuer notifies the state official of the pending security offer, and if no action is taken by the state official after a lapse of time, the registration becomes effective automatically.
3. By coordination. Copies of the information filed with the SEC are sent to the state official, and registration becomes effective in that state when it becomes effective with the SEC. This is the simplest form of state registration and is available for issues registered under the 1933 act and in states that have adopted the Uniform Securities Act.

The Uniform Securities Act was approved by the SEC in 1956 and has been adopted in many states. It is intended to simplify and unify the various state security laws. If the securities division within a particular state does not approve a security offering that has been registered through the SEC, the offering cannot be sold in that state. Usually, the SEC and most states simply require registration to ensure full disclosure of all material facts concerning the security being offered and the issuing company. However, some states make judgments concerning the appropriateness of the issue for their residents. If the securities division does not think the offering appropriate, even though full disclosure has been made, it may disapprove the issue for sale.

State security laws are criticized for failure of the state officials to formulate procedures for the guidance of the security industry and to make adequate disclosure of administrative practices with regard to these security laws.

REGULATION BY THE EXCHANGES

In addition to the New York Stock Exchange and the American Stock Exchange in New York, there are 12 regional exchanges registered with the SEC. Each exchange has certain standards for listing, but the NYSE's listing standards are the most stringent. These standards are designed to ensure that there will be an adequate auction market for the listed security.

The NYSE represents about 84 percent of the total dollar volume on registered exchanges. There are certain advantages to listing with the NYSE (the **Big Board**) that encourage many companies to strive to meet its listing requirements. A company whose stock is listed on the NYSE receives considerable exposure through daily market quotations; stocks listed with the

NYSE generally sell at higher multiples than stocks listed on other exchanges; and it is considered prestigious to be listed with the NYSE.

The exchanges have minimum qualitative and quantitative standards that must be met before the company can be eligible for listing. Once eligibility is established, the company enters into a listing agreement that covers such points as options, proxies, warrants, disclosure, security redemptions, dividends, and interest. Furthermore, the listed company must abide by the extensive exchange bylaws and regulations in order to maintain its eligibility. If at any time the board of governors of the exchange believes that it is not in the public interest to list a company's stock, that company is suspended or delisted.

FINANCIAL REPORTING REQUIREMENTS

An investor's primary source of information about a company is its external financial statements. The company is evaluated by the use of various financial ratios or, perhaps, certain trend data. Thus, financial statements are vitally important in making investment decisions.

To illustrate how the market responds to changes in financial data, consider how the market price of a share of stock is generally based on some multiple of earnings per share (*P/E ratio*). The more optimistic investors are concerning a company's long-run potential earnings, the higher the P/E ratio will be. Therefore, if increased earnings per share meet or exceed expectations, there is generally an increase in the market price of the common stock over the long run.

What is to prevent management from inflating P/E ratio figures in order to force up the price of the company stock? Such manipulation of financial data is largely prevented by the SEC's power to prescribe the form and content of financial statements filed by reporting companies and to specify the methods to be followed in their preparation.

One of the SEC's major objectives is to improve accounting and auditing standards for registered companies. The SEC is the only government agency primarily concerned with financial reporting to investors. It requires companies subject to its jurisdiction to follow accounting practices certified as generally accepted by independent public accountants (CPAs).

Regulation S-X, the SEC's principal accounting regulation, sets forth the required form and content of financial statements to be filed as a part of the registration statement and annual reports. There is also a requirement that the financial statements be certified in order to assure compliance with SEC reporting requirements. To certify financial statements, a CPA issues an opinion the fairness of the presentation. The CPA (or auditor) will consider such factors as whether generally accepted accounting principles are consistently applied and whether all relevant information concerning the company's financial position and performance is sufficiently disclosed.

The auditor is subject to liability if the examination has not been performed in accordance with generally accepted auditing standards. If any material errors are contained in the registration statement, the auditor (along with those signing the registration statement) becomes liable to anyone who relies on such information.

The SEC works closely with the accounting profession and, as a matter of policy, allows the profession to orginate accounting standards. However, the SEC occasionally submits notices of new and amended rules, regulations, and opinions relating to questions of accounting, auditing, or administrative policy with respect to financial statements and other matters of importance to the accounting profession.

KEY TERMS

blue-sky laws	proxy solicitation
Chapter 10	prudent man rule
corner the market	registration statement
Exchange Act	Securities and Exchange Commission
fiduciary duty	SIPC
insider trading	statutory (or final) prospectus
intrastate offering	tender offer
legal list	10-K report
margin requirements	10-Q report
pool	tombstone prospectus
preliminary prospectus	Truth in Securities Act
private offering	wash sale

QUESTIONS

1. What is the SEC?
2. What are margin requirements? Who sets them, and what is their importance?
3. Why is the Securities Act of 1933 called the *Truth in Securities Act?*
4. What is the registration statement?
5. What is the prospectus?
6. What is the function of the Securities Exchange Act of 1934?
7. What are the 10-K and the 10-Q reports?
8. What is a tender offer?
9. What is the Public Utility Holding Company Act of 1935?
10. What is the purpose of the Investment Company Act of 1940?
11. What are the major provisions of the Investment Advisers Act of 1940?
12. What is Chapter 10?

13. What are the most important aspects of the Investment Company Amendments Act of 1970?
14. What are blue-sky laws?
15. What are the advantages of listing on the New York Stock Exchange?
16. What is the NASD?

SELECTED READINGS

BLOOMENTHAL, HAROLD S. *Securities and Federal Corporate Law.* New York: Clark Boardman Co., 1972.

Blue Sky Law Reporter and *Federal Securities Law Reporter.* Commerce Clearing House, Chicago: (both loose-leaf).

GRUBE, R. CORWIN, O. MAURICE JOY, and DON B. PANTONE. "Market Response to Federal Reserve Changes in the Initial Margin Requirement." *Journal of Finance*, June 1979, 659–674.

KROGH, HAROLD C. "The Securities Investor Protection Corporation: Financial Stringency in Securities Firms." *CPCU Annals*, March 1977, 78–85.

LOSS, LOUISE. *Securities Regulation*, 2d ed. Boston: Little,Brown, 1969.

ROBINSON, GERALD J., and KLAUS, ELLPLER. *Going Public.* New York: Clark Boardman Co., 1974.

Securities and Exchange Commission. Annual reports.

Securities and Exchange Commission. *Special Study of Securities Markets.* Washington, D.C.: The Commission, 1963 (especially Part 4 or Part 5, Chap. XI).

Securities and Exchange Commission. *Study of Unsafe and Unsound Practices of Brokers and Dealers.* Washington, D.C.: The Commission, 1971.

SKOUSEN, K. FRED. *An Introduction to the SEC*, Cincinnati: South-Western, 1976.

"Which Way Regulation?" *Barron's*, May 28, 1979, 4–5ff.

12

Economic and Industry Analysis

To be successful over the long run, an investor must have access to pertinent, timely information on which to base investment decisions. All financial decisions that an individual makes should be based on fundamental data from reliable sources which, if properly understood and applied, can greatly increase the chances for success. Many individual investors have done poorly in the stock market, and one factor contributing to this has been a lack of proper investigation of the available information. While no amount of experience or analysis can enable a person to be absolutely certain about the price movement of any specific security, the accumulation of available information and proper analysis are central to success in the investment process. Chapters 3 to 7 provided an investment process for security analysis. This chapter will center on the framework for economic and industry analysis based on the pertinent information that is available to the public.

The determination of the desirability of the economic climate is the beginning of the analytical portion of the investment process. It is important to know that the value of a particular company's stock is closely related to the present and future success of the larger industry of which the company is a part. The success of the industry, in turn, will be closely tied to the level of national economic activity. For example, the number of new cars that the auto industry can sell in any given year will be limited by a portion of the aggregate disposable consumer income. Each firm's profits, in turn, will reflect the industry's total earnings according to its market share. For this reason, investors should not only examine the present condition of a particular firm, but they must also forecast the firm's future performance in the perspective of how its industry will be affected by foreseeable trends in the national economy.

CLASSIFICATION OF INFORMATION

Financial information may be classified by type, which is a very general category, and by source, which will provide more specific data. It is important for a student of the market to become familiar with these materials. In much the same way that good craftsmen are skilled in the use of the tools of their trade, intelligent investors are skilled in the evaluation of those sources of information that will provide the necessary background and data for wise decision making.

Classification of information by type encompasses the following:

1. General business and economic data
2. General investment data
3. Specific industry data
4. Specific company data
5. Specific security data

None of these areas should be ignored in the investment process. Each plays an important role in establishing the basis for an investment decision.

Classification of information by source includes the following:

1. Published books
2. General and business periodicals
3. Government publications and documents
4. Investment and financial periodicals and newspapers
5. Financial information services
6. Financial institutions, including brokerages and investment banks
7. Investment advisory firms
8. The company whose security is being analyzed

In using investment information, it is important to be alert to any biases that a particular source might have. For example, the company itself, in annual and quarterly reports, prospectuses, and news releases, is unlikely to present a dark picture of its own future. In contrast, most of the data given in more general publications and in the publications of established financial institutions are sufficiently reliable, because the continued existence of these organizations depends on their independent presentation of the facts. Federal and state legislation has helped ensure the reliability of such material, but no amount of legislation can ensure that the individual investor will make the best use of the available information. However, investors who make good use of such information have a much greater chance of success in the purchase of specific securities and, therefore, of a better overall performance of their investment programs.

General Business and Economic Data

The most readily available source of information on general economic and business conditions is the daily newspaper. Its business section supplies a wide variety of information about both the domestic and international economies. Prominent weekly magazines such as *Time, Newsweek,* and *U.S. News & World Report* also devote special sections to the state of the economy. More comprehensive interpretations may be gleaned from the *Wall Street Journal,* the *New York Times,* and the *Washington Post.* Other publications devoted to these matters include *Barron's, Business Week,* the *Commercial and Financial Chronicle, Forbes,* the *Magazine of Finance,* and *Financial World.* All report on key government and economic indicators that should form the basis of an investor's analysis of the general economic climate.

The U.S. government, through its many agencies, publishes a great deal of material concerning economic conditions. The Federal Reserve System's *National Summary of Business Conditions* is available at no charge from the Publication Services, Board of Governors, Federal Reserve System, Washington, D.C. 20551. (Just include your name and address with your request.) *Economic Indicators,* published by the U.S. Government's Council of Economic Advisors, is available from the Superintendent of Documents, U.S. Government Printing Office, Washington, D.C. Most libraries carry extensive amounts of government economic data and reports.

Exhibits 12-1 through 12-4 offer samples of representative sources of data concerning the state of the economy.

Certain private organizations, including large insurance companies, also publish data on general economic conditions under the general heading of **forecasts.** The Ford Foundation, of necessity, keeps tabs on economic projections and obligingly publishes information. Once again, however, it is important to be wary of any bias that might exist in letters published by privately sponsored organizations or foundations, which may reflect political pursuits more than they reflect economic realities.

General Investment Data

Closely related to economic and business data are the market data reflected in the major stock market averages. These averages register the current climate or sentiment of investors. Economists generally agree that inter-

Exhibit 12-1

Economic Indicators (Seasonally Adjusted Annual Rates; Dollar Figures in Billions)

ECONOMIC INDICATORS

Seasonally Adjusted Annual Rates—Dollar Figures in Billions

	Annual Data 1981	Annual Data 1982	% Increase E1981	% Increase E1982	1981 IV	1982 I	1982 II	1982 III	1982 IV	E1983 I	% Ann. Rate of Increase 4th Q 1981	% Ann. Rate of Increase E 1st Q 1982
Gross National Product												
GNP (billions of dollars)	$2,925.5	$3,099.6	11.4	5.9	2,998.4	3,007.3	3,044.0	3,124.0	3,223.0	3,306.0	4.6	1.2
Ann. Rate of Increase (%)	11.4	5.9	...	...	4.6	1.2	5.0	10.9	13.3	10.7	...	...
Ann. Rate of Increase—Real GNP (%)	2.0	-1.4	...	...	-4.5	-4.4	-1.2	3.7	5.4	3.1	...	...
Ann. Rate of Increase—GNP Deflator (%)	9.2	7.4	...	...	9.5	5.9	6.3	7.0	7.5	7.4	...	...
Components of GNP												
Personal Consumption Expenditures	1,875.8	2,009.5	11.1	8.2	1,908.3	1,951.0	1,997.0	2,026.0	2,084.0	2,131.0	5.3	9.3
Durable Goods	232.0	250.8	9.5	8.1	226.4	238.0	247.0	258.0	260.0	262.0	-15.5	22.1
Nondurable Goods	743.2	775.7	10.0	4.4	760.3	762.7	767.6	778.4	794.0	807.8	4.9	1.3
Services	882.6	986.5	12.4	11.8	921.5	951.7	973.0	996.1	1,025.3	1,051.5	11.7	13.7
Gross Private Domestic Investment	450.5	438.3	14.0	-2.7	443.3	411.0	422.0	448.0	472.0	498.0	-16.0	-26.1
Residential Structures	105.5	108.5	0.3	2.8	94.2	94.0	100.0	115.0	125.0	136.0	-22.8	-0.8
Nonresidential Fixed Investment	328.8	333.5	11.1	1.4	339.8	332.0	330.0	332.0	340.0	352.0	5.7	-8.9
Change in Business Inventories	16.2	-3.8	...	...	9.4	-15.0	-8.0	1.0	7.0	10.0	...	...
Govt. Purchases of Goods & Services	591.2	632.8	10.6	7.0	622.0	628.3	627.0	630.0	646.0	655.0	24.5	4.1
National Defense	154.3	180.9	17.2	17.2	169.7	173.1	178.7	180.9	190.7	198.9	47.1	8.3
Other Federal	75.9	75.2	12.9	-0.3	83.5	82.2	73.3	71.1	74.3	69.1	78.9	-6.1
State & Local	261.0	376.8	7.5	4.4	368.7	373.0	375.0	378.0	381.0	387.0	7.0	4.7
Net Exports	26.0	19.0	...	...	24.7	17.0	18.0	20.0	21.0	22.0	...	...
Income & Profits												
Personal Income	2,404.1	2,589.3	11.3	7.7	2,486.5	2,508.9	2,553.5	2,611.7	2,683.5	2,746.9	7.5	3.7
Personal Taxes	388.2	394.0	14.7	1.5	398.0	392.6	401.8	382.9	398.6	406.9	-1.8	-5.3
Disposable Income	2,016.0	2,195.3	10.7	8.9	2,088.5	2,116.3	2,151.2	2,228.9	2,284.8	2,340.1	9.4	5.3
Savings Rate (%)	5.3	5.9	...	...	6.1	5.3	5.5	6.5	6.2	6.4	...	...
Corporate Profits Before Taxes*	233.8	186.0	-4.8	-20.4	214.6	178.6	172.9	189.5	202.9	217.0	-29.7	-52.0
Corporate Profits After Taxes*	155.8	127.2	-4.5	-18.4	145.2	122.9	119.3	129.1	137.5	148.9	-25.5	-48.6
Prices & Interest Rates												
Ann. Rate of Incr.—Consumer Prices (%)	10.3	6.0	...	...	7.8	3.2	4.5	5.0	6.0	7.0	...	...
Ann. Rate of Incr.—GNP Deflator (%)	9.2	7.4	...	...	9.5	5.9	6.3	7.0	7.5	7.4	...	...
Rate on 3-Month Treasury Bills (%)†	14.0	11.8	...	...	11.8	12.7	11.8	11.0	11.8	12.8	...	...
Corporate Bond Yields AA (%)†	14.3	14.1	...	...	14.8	15.1	14.0	13.5	14.0	14.4	...	...
Prime Rate (%)†	18.9	15.7	...	...	17.0	16.2	16.2	15.1	15.2	16.5	...	...
Production & Other Key Indicators												
Index of Indus. Production (1967=100)	150.9	143.9	-2.6	-4.6	146.2	141.1	141.8	144.7	148.0	150.5	-16.7	-13.2
Housing Starts (million units)	1.1	1.2	-15.3	-5.6	0.9	0.9	0.9	1.3	1.4	1.4	-34.4	42.2
Retail Car Sales (million units)	8.6	8.4	-4.2	-2.4	7.4	8.2	7.6	8.6	9.2	9.3	-57.5	56.0
Unemployment Rate (%)	7.6	9.2	...	...	8.4	8.7	9.5	9.6	9.0	8.8	...	...

E-Estimated. †Average for period. NA-Not available. *Subject to revision due to Economic Recovery Act of 1981. Note: Figures may not add because of rounding.

Source: Standard & Poor's Corporation, *Outlook*., April 14, 1982, p. 820.

Exhibit 12-2

Business Indicators: Charts and Forecasts

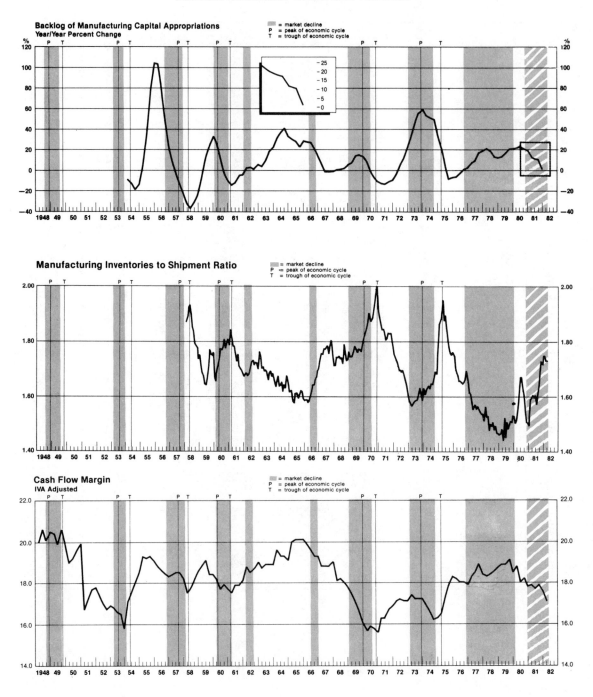

Exhibit 12-2 (cont.)

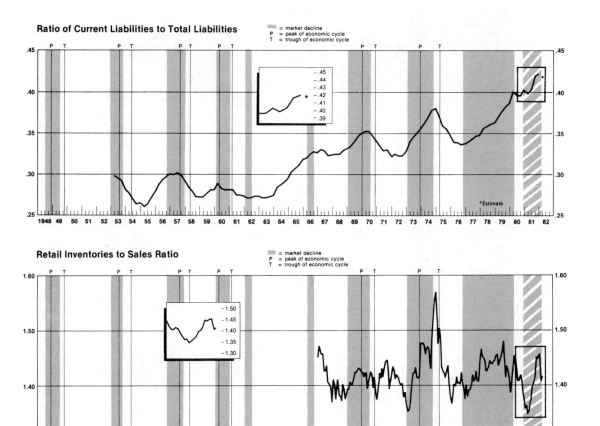

Exhibit 12-3

Fixed Income Research Department

MAURY N. HARRIS
Vice President &
Money Market Economist
(212) 730 – 5163

In this issue: – Maury Harris interprets the significance of the House budget resolution.
– Elaine Solloway reviews recent trends in weekly unemployment insurance claims.
– Gerald Zukowski analyzes the recent trend of M2 growth.

Budgets and Bonds

The House of Representatives' surprise approval of a budget resolution on June 10 is a constructive factor for bond prices. To be sure, the budget outlook is still unsettled. After the House and Senate resolve their differences on broad spending and revenue totals, the controversial specifics still must be enacted. However, by way of contrast, in recent weeks it had appeared that a majority of the House of Representatives might not be able to soon agree on any one fiscal policy course. Now the deliberative process is back on track. This hastens the day when investors can regain confidence that Federal deficits will be contained over coming years. And as confidence in fiscal policy starts to be restored, investors will part with their money at lower interest rates.

The Significance of The House Vote

Before investors' confidence in fiscal policy can be renewed, though, Congress must be more decisive. Over the late-May to early-June period a sagging bond market was importantly tied to the breakdown in the House budget negotiations. The passage of the House Republican version of the budget, though, demonstrated a reunification of the conservative, bipartisan coalition that supported the fiscal 1982 spending cuts.

Some Lingering Doubts

Of course, the budget picture is still unsettled. The hard task of filling in many tax and spending details remains. Moreover, even after a budget is passed, there still will be doubts over specific magnitudes of Federal borrowing. For example, the Congressional Budget Office (CBO) estimates that the $99.3 billion House Republican budget deficit would be $109.8 billion with what the CBO sees as more realistic technical assumptions.

Still, at the least, investors can reasonably expect an arresting of the budget trends dictated by the "current services" budget. It points to rising -- rather than falling -- deficits in 1983 and beyond without new initiatives on the tax and spending fronts. The ultimate budget deficit that is passed for fiscal 1983 will seem unusually high from an historical perspective. But adoption of a budget deficit package in the low $100 billion range will require some visible departures from past tax and spending policies. And these significant changes in political behavior will not go unnoticed, or unrewarded, by the investment community.

Volume 7, Issue 24   June 14, 1982

Source: Paine Webber Mitchell Hutchins, The Liberty Street Review, Fixed Income Research Department, Volume 7, Issue 24.

Exhibit 12-4

ECONOMIC AND FINANCIAL INDICATORS

	Latest period	Preceding period	Year ago
Federal Reserve Condition Report, Mil $, June 9, 1982			
Loans and securities, total	620,565	623,221	574,440
U.S. Treasury securities, total	38,056	36,945	43,687
Other loans, gross	482,366	r483,115	431,730
Commercial & Industrial	209,577	209,058	176,507
Real estate	129,196	r129,098	117,977
Financial institutions, total	41,443	42,140	39,482
Nonbank brokers & dealers	6,682	6,455	6,108
Total Assets	827,782	r851,062	783,482
Demand deposits, total	158,263	r179,476	193,215
Domestic commercial banks	16,671	r23,721	35,362
Savings deposits, total	80,709	80,795	78,929
Time deposits, total	301,904	r300,532	255,003
Total Liabilities	771,430	r794,659	731,108
Federal Reserve Bank Changes, Mil $, June 23, 1982:			
Gov't. securities bought outright	130,497	131,418	120,971
Federal agency issues bought outright	9,002	9,002	8,707
Borrowings from Fed	1,015	931	2,302
Seasonal Borrowings	254	r222	307
Extended credit	96	104	
Float	2,079	r2,047	2,614
Total reserve bank credit	152,809	r152,056	145,983
Treasury gold stock-z	11,149	11,149	11,154
Currency in circulation	146,314	r146,915	136,652
Treasury deposits with Fed banks	3,730	2,950	3,021
Reserves with Fed banks	24,649	r24,122	27,464
Total reserves including cash	39,835	r39,564	40,684
Required reserves	39,554	39,344	40,270
Net borrowings from Fed	665	605	1,995
Excess reserves	281	r220	414
Free reserves	− 384	r− 385	− 1,581
Money Supply (M1) bil $, June 16, 1982:	452.5	r454.8	r428.8
Monetary Base, bil $, June 23, 1982:	172.0	r172.3	164.4
Federal Reserve Interest Rates, % June 23, 1982:			
Federal Funds	14.17	14.24	19.20
Treasury bill (90 day)	12.70	12.20	14.69
Commercial paper (dealer, 90 day)	14.40	13.67	16.24
Certfs of Deposit (resale, 90 day)	15.00	14.10	17.03
Eurodollar (90 days)	16.09	15.03	18.00
Money Market Funds, bil $, June 23, 1982:			
Total Assets	202.9	202.4	124.7
Mutual Funds, % March, 1982:			
Liquidity Asset Ratio	10.9	10.4	8.3
Treasury Statement, bil $, June 21, 1982:			
Gross Federal Debt	1,069.3	1,075.2	966.8
Statutory Debt Limit	1,079.8	1,079.8	985.0

p-Preliminary. r-Revised. sa-Seasonally adjusted. z-Actual.

Source: *Barron's.*, June 28, 1982.

Exhibit 12-5

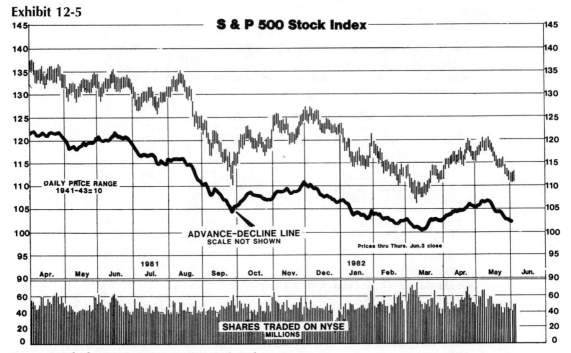

Source: Standard & Poor's Corporation, Outlook, Volume 54, No. 23.

mediate-term movements in the stock market are leading indicators of the future movement of the economy. The validity of this position is demonstrated in Exhibit 12-5, which indicates a movement in the stock market that preceded an actual shift in overall corporate profits. Exhibit 12-6 is an example of the type of weekly market data available to the investor.

Specific Industry Data

All companies operating in the economy are classified according to their appropriate industry category, which is usually based on the firm's major business or sales activity. In recent years, however, many companies have diversified to such an extent that it is not possible to determine their main operation. Such companies are known as **conglomerates,** and a major portion of their growth has been attributed to acquisition of and mergers with other companies, rather than through internal growth.

Not all industries move in the same direction as the economy, nor do all industries have the same expected future growth rate as that of the economy in general. Thus, in making any specific investment decisions, it is important to study the current condition and future prospects of the particular industry in which investment is contemplated. Certain industries are expected to have a much greater future growth rate than the economy as a whole; others are considered mature and should level off or decline in the future.

Some industries are **cyclical;** that is, they tend to expand and contract as the economy expands and contracts. The building and automobile industries, airlines, steel, textiles, and consumer goods are all cyclical. Those industries that are resistant to the general economic swings are considered **defensive** industries. Foodstuffs, soaps, utilities, and natural resources are all defensive industries. Exhibits 12-7 through 12-9 are examples of industry summaries. More comprehensive analyses can be obtained from the research departments of brokerage houses, from business publications such as those mentioned earlier in this chapter, and from the specialty reports issued by investment research companies.

Process of Investment Analysis

After investors have examined the relevant information regarding the economy and the industry, they need to distinguish whether the present economy is growing or regressing, which factors are most affected by present conditions, and what impact they will have on the economy as a whole.

The next step will be to determine how long the trends will continue and what future trends can be anticipated. The investor will want to develop at least a 1-year perspective on these questions, although estimates for the next several years are also important in guiding investment strategy. If recession is forecast, the investor may decide that common stocks are undesirable and may concentrate on limited-income securities as an alternative or may decide not to invest at all and instead keep the funds in some sort of short- or intermediate-term investment. Conversely, if a period of growth and prosperity is forecast, common stocks might provide the best method of participating in such growth. Moreover, the investor will want to pay particular attention to any segments of the economy that will grow faster than the economy as a whole.

Then the investor must determine which industries are most likely to participate in the economic growth (or be most negatively affected by adverse economic trends). Usually, a firm within an expanding industry will grow with an expanding economy and provide a relatively favorable investment opportunity. In recent years, expansion has occurred in the computer and household products industries. Many firms in these industries, such as IBM and Procter and Gamble, have prospered even though the economy has moved forward and backward in the economic cycle.

Finally, the investor will narrow the search to finding particular firms within strong industries that seem best able to participate in that industry's growth at an acceptable level of risk. The investor has at this point answered several crucial questions: What stage is the economy presently in? How will

Exhibit 12-6.

BARRON'S MARKET LABORATORY

Dow-Jones Hourly Averages

30 Industrials

June	21	22	23	24	25
Opening	786.72	789.95	801.75	814.69	807.93
11:00	789.19	793.47	800.23	813.55	806.70
12:00	792.24	792.43	798.90	816.59	807.65
1:00	795.66	797.56	797.56	817.73	806.13
2:00	794.14	792.81	802.13	814.12	806.03
3:00	792.90	795.76	803.08	810.12	806.13
Close	789.95	799.66	813.17	810.41	803.08
High (h)	797.85	801.46	815.35	821.63	812.12
Low (h)	784.25	787.67	795.76	805.56	800.61
Change	+1.33	+9.71	+13.51	-2.76	-7.33

Wk's net change +14.46 (h) H 821.63 L 784.25

20 Transportation Cos.

	21	22	23	24	25
Opening	304.33	302.91	308.98	317.97	316.62
11:00	305.38	304.18	310.03	317.60	316.02
12:00	306.21	304.56	308.98	319.02	315.50
1:00	306.73	304.41	308.75	319.92	316.10
2:00	305.83	304.63	310.55	317.60	315.72
3:00	305.31	305.98	311.23	316.47	316.47
Close	303.73	307.78	316.70	317.00	315.35
High (h)	308.45	308.98	317.37	321.57	318.65
Low (h)	301.41-	301.78	306.65	313.85	313.62
Change	-1.28	+4.05	+8.92	+0.30	-1.65

Wk's net change +10.34 (h) H 321.57 L 301.41

15 Utilities

	21	22	23	24	25
Opening	106.65	106.04	106.13	106.39	106.70
11:00	106.61	106.04	106.39	106.22	106.57
12:00	106.65	105.96	106.30	106.30	106.83
1:00	106.30	105.83	106.09	106.74	106.87
2:00	106.35	105.87	106.04	106.78	106.83
3:00	106.13	105.87	106.09	106.70	106.48
Close	106.13	106.30	106.13	106.83	106.57
High (h)	107.22	106.78	106.83	107.39	107.39
Low (h)	105.43	105.26	105.61	105.78	106.13
Change	-0.57	+0.17	-0.17	+0.70	-0.26

Wk's net change -0.13 (h) H 107.39 L 105.26

65 Stocks

	21	22	23	24	25
Opening	306.16	306.18	310.47	315.90	314.20
11:00	306.97	307.30	310.55	315.46	313.70
12:00	307.88	307.14	309.93	316.70	313.89
1:00	308.61	307.01	309.48	317.26	313.74
2:00	308.05	307.20	310.95	315.85	313.60
3:00	307.53	308.21	311.36	314.63	313.66
Close	306.45	309.77	315.09	314.90	312.73

Dow-Jones Weekly Averages

Stock Averages

	First	High	Low	Last	Chg.
Indus	789.95	813.17	789.95	803.08	+14.46
Trans	303.73	317.00	303.73	315.35	+10.34
Utils	106.13	106.83	106.13	106.57	-0.13
Comp	306.45	315.09	306.45	312.73	+5.95

Bond Averages

	First	High	Low	Last	Chg.
20 Bonds	58.48	58.68	58.42	58.45	-0.59
10 Util	56.06	56.24	55.62	55.62	-1.34
10 Ind	60.88	61.28	60.70	61.28	+0.17

Dow-Jones Averages for 1982

Stock Averages

	First	High	Low	Last	Chg	%
Ind	882.52	882.52	788.62	803.08	-71.92	-8.22
Trp	379.68	379.68	303.73	315.35	-64.95	-17.08
Util	109.83	116.95	103.61	106.57	-2.45	-2.25
Cmp	349.60	349.60	306.45	312.73	-35.07	-10.08

Stock averages are compiled daily by using the following divisors: Industrials, 1.314; Transports, 1.668; Utilities, 2.875; 65 Stks Comp., 6.036.

Bond Averages

	First	High	Low	Last	Chg	%
20 Bds	56.93	60.27	55.67	58.45	+1.37	+2.40
10 Util	55.40	59.18	53.80	55.62	-0.24	-0.43
10 Ind	58.47	61.57	57.36	61.28	+2.97	+5.09

Dow-Jones Price-Earnings Ratio

	June 25 1982	May 25 1982	June 25 1981	June 25 1980
Industrials	8.3	8.8	8.1	7.3
Tmsprt Cos	9.0	8.6	9.3	9.6
Utilities	5.9	6.3	6.9	7.4

Per share earnings for 12 months ended Mar. 31.

Week's Market Statistics

	Last week	Prev. week	Last year
Sales NYSE, th sh	262,964	244,406	223,459
Sales ASE, th sh	18,750	20,950	28,400
Sales OTC, th sh-a	128,808	122,473	162,875
Dow-Jones groups:			
30 Ind, th sh	21,625	31,030	15,517
20 Transp, th sh	7,607	5,923	5,297
15 Util, th sh	4,907	4,336	4,513
65 Stks, th sh	34,139	41,289	25,327
20 Most Active Stocks:			
Average price	33.40	32.61	40.37
% vol to total vol	16.83	18.09	12.41
20 Low Priced Stocks-v:			
Index	771.71	768.2	854.2
Volume, th sh	3,284.7	2,744.2	2,976.4
%vol to DJI vol	14.46	8.22	18.02
NYSE volume report, June 11, 1982:			
Buy/sell, th sh-w	267,349	183,899	260,559
Total shorts, th sh	21,763.9	14,839.0	20,276.6
Public shorts, th sh	3,944.5	c2,559.7	3,360.5
Member trading, June 11, 1982:			
Member shrt, th sh-x	17,819.4	12,279.3	16,916.1
Speclst shrt, th sh	7,600.7	4,183.0	7,936.2
Purchases, th sh	71,359.6	51,425.5	66,418.2
Sales, th sh-z	74,628.9	53,330.7	69,988.2
Net buy/sell, th sh	3,269.3	-1,905.2	-3,570.0
% vol to NYSE vol	27.30	28.48	26.18
Odd-lot trading, June 11, 1982:			
Purchases, th sh	1,067	785	1,375
Purchases, th $	29,571	21,037	50,919
Sales, th sh-z	2,126	1,630	2,998
Sales, th $	58,834	47,218	105,249
Short sales, actual	5,474	4,075	7,319
Bond vol, NYSE, th$	111,529	117,639	90,498
Stock offerings th$	479,375	2,559,469	2,887,035
Barron's Best Gr	84,250	116,487	564,040
bond yields-v	13.37	13.31	12.50
Barron's Intrm Gr bond yields-v	14.95	14.71	13.89
Barron's Confidence Index (Ratio Best Gr to Intrm Gr Bonds)	89.4	90.5	90.0
Spread between yields for Barron's Best Grade Bonds & Dow Jones Industrial Stock Avg.	-6.42	-6.23	-7.00

Weekly Composite Diary

Week ended June 25, 1982

	NYSE	AMEX	NASDAQ
Issues Traded	2,101	920	3,360
Advances	1,148	432	1,144
Declines	683	325	804
Unchanged	270	163	1,412
New Highs	49	25	....
New Lows	252	101	....

NYSE Common Stock Diary

June	21	22	23	24	25
Issues Traded	1,487	1,483	1,487	1,480	1,468
Advances	636	700	895	624	381
Declines	514	438	290	551	755
Unchanged	337	345	302	305	332

NYSE Composite Diary

	21	22	23	24	25
Issues Traded	1,855	1,852	1,875	1,849	1,811
Advances	757	821	1,036	772	468
Declines	639	583	426	660	902
Unchanged	459	448	413	417	441
New Highs	3	13	23	29	13
New Lows	118	100	55	35	60
Sales, th shs	58,721	65,627	72,821	65,223	45,251

Amex Composite Diary

	21	22	23	24	25
Issues Traded	754	761	785	741	698
Advances	253	268	368	267	201
Declines	272	250	194	261	246
Unchanged	229	243	223	213	251
New Highs	2	5	11	12	8
New Lows	42	32	23	19	22
Sales th shs	4,293	4,117	4,944	4,316	3,559

NASDAQ OTC Market Diary

	21	22	23	24	25
Issues Traded	3,363	3,363	3,363	3,363	3,360
Advances	363	629	611	243	333
Declines	638	343	243	386	518
Unchanged	2,362	2,391	2,289	2,366	2,569

Source: *Barron's*, February 15, 1982.

Exhibit 12-6 (cont.)

High (h)	309.99	310.72	316.08	318.88	316.00
Low (h)	304.24	305.00	308.28	312.48	311.51
Change	− 0.33	+ 3.32	+ 5.32	− 0.19	− 2.17

Wk's net change +5.95 (h) H 318.88 L 304.24

(h)-Averages of the highs and lows reached at any time during the day by the individual stocks.

Shares Traded on N.Y. Exchange

Thous. shares

10-11	11,950	13,260	14,390	14,820	11,580
11-12	9,760	9,520	10,940	10,490	5,740
12- 1	8,660	6,800	7,210	7,710	5,660
1- 2	5,080	4,800	6,870	7,400	4,370
2- 3	6,280	8,290	7,840	7,640	4,920
3- 4	8,640	12,620	15,460	7,800	6,470
Total	50,370	55,290	62,710	55,860	38,740

By Groups-Thous. shares

30 Ind	4,522.1	4,343.6	4,880.1	4,535.4	3,343.8
20 Tran	1,053.3	1,237.4	3,020.4	1,692.6	603.0
15 Util	1,088.0	1,193.2	722.8	1,031.2	871.8
65 Stock	6,663.4	6,774.2	8,623.3	7,259.2	4,818.6

Ratio of 10 Most Active Stocks (Composite) to total trading, % of total:

15.19	12.84	11.42	12.02	17.68

Average closings (Composite) of 10 Most Active Stocks:

31.06	39.26	32.15	38.46	37.16

Weekly Trading by Markets in NYSE Listed Stocks

	Shares	Warrants
NYSE	262,963,612	760,000
Midwest	17,143,900	....
Pacific	10,699,400	....
NASDAQ	9,959,260	....
Phila.	4,004,300	....
Boston	1,809,800	....
Cincinnati	997,400	....
Instinet	59,300	....

NYSE Odd-Lot Trading

June	18	21	22	23	24
Purch th shs	114.8	128.2	125.8	132.6	125.1
Sales, th shs	262.0	277.6	259.5	281.0	264.6
Short sales, shs	1,494	647	610	988	1,405

NASDAQ OTC Indexes

Index	6/25/82	% Chg.
Industrial	195.25	+ 1.64
Composite	170.48	+ 1.18
Bank	130.75	− 1.15
Insurance	171.66	+ 0.20
Other Finance	157.75	+ 0.06
Transportation	149.68	+ 2.63
Utilities	196.22	+ 5.56

(February 5, 1971, equals 100.00)

NYSE Most Active Stocks

High	Low		Sales	High	Low	Last	Chg.
69⅛	23¾	CitiSvc	9,389,100	55⅞	52⅞	55	+ 1⅞
36⅞	20	NLT	4,419,300	36⅞	26	36⅞	+ 8⅞
34	12¼	MesaPt	3,927,900	14¾	13½	13½	− 3
66⅛	48⅜	IBM	3,260,800	61½	58¼	60¼	+ 1⅞
56	33⅞	GMot	2,653,200	47⅛	45⅜	46	+ ⅜
61½	50	ATT	2,624,000	51	50	50¼	− ⅜
29⅝	21¾	Citicrp	2,450,900	25¾	24¼	25	+ ¼
36	26⅞	Exxon s	2,141,400	27⅞	27	27⅜	+ ⅛
39⅛	26	Tandy	2,055,300	29¼	27	27½	+ ⅜
77⅞	60⅝	EsKod	2,004,000	74	68⅜	72⅝	+ 4
23⅝	15¾	RCA	1,996,200	18½	15¾	17¾	+ 2
48½	23⅛	SuprOil	1,849,200	30⅛	25⅛	29¾	+ 4⅛
102½	67⅛	Digital	1,741,500	71¾	67⅛	69	+ 1½
23	17⅞	CarPw	1,733,400	20¼	19¾	19⅞	− ⅛
7⅝	3⅛	Chryslr	1,660,500	7¼	6⅜	6⅞	+ ⅜
22¾	12	SonyCp	1,614,000	13⅝	12¾	13¼	+ ⅛
13⅜	7⅜	UnBrnd	1,586,200	8⅛	7½	7¾	− ¼
47⅛	27	PhilPet	1,584,300	31½	28⅛	31	+ 1¾
71	37⅝	Schlmb	1,572,800	41⅜	38⅛	38⅞	+ ½
34⅜	19⅞	DowCh	1,520,000	20⅝	19⅞	20	+ ¼

STOCK EXCHANGE VOLUME TRENDS

	NYSE Up	NYSE Down	QCHA (%)	Amex Up	Amex Down	QCHA (%)	NASDAQ Up	NASDAQ Down
June21	23,593,200	19,812,200	+ .12	1,062,500	1,718,500	+ .01	4,594,000	7,838,300
22	35,425,000	12,571,800	+ .41	1,645,300	1,069,300	+ .38	9,456,900	3,754,000
23	46,693,100	10,671,900	+ 1.12	3,008,100	646,100	+ .96	14,949,500	2,924,700
24	21,143,500	28,389,700	+ .25	1,193,700	1,746,700	+ .18	9,630,300	5,122,100
25	9,310,000	24,867,600	− .50	1,337,600	1,056,600	+ 0.	5,667,100	6,981,300

Supplied by QUOTRON.

Prices and Yields on Dow-Jones Averages:

30 Ind	803.08	788.62	992.87
30 Ind. %	6.95	7.08	5.50
20 Transp	315.35	305.01	419.37
20 Transp, %	4.42	4.57	3.28
15 Util	106.57	106.70	108.76
15 Util, %	11.42	11.41	9.75
20 Bonds, %-v	14.55	14.36	13.71
10 Util, %-v	15.38	15.05	14.26
10 Ind, %-v	13.72	13.68	13.17
Municipal Bond yield,%	13.41	13.46	11.69

a-NASDAQ. c-Correction. v-Week ended Thursday. w-Shares and warrants. x-Includes specialists short sales. z-Includes short sales.

Dow-Jones Bond Averages

June	21	22	23	24	25
20 Bonds	58.48	58.42	58.60	58.68	58.45
10 Util	56.06	56.13	56.24	56.15	55.62
10 Ind	60.88	60.70	60.95	61.20	61.28
U.S. Govts.	83.91	84.02	83.84	83.69	83.65

New York Exchange Bond Diary

Issues Traded	912	862	955	847	787
Advances	235	269	274	289	270
Declines	497	399	482	359	354
Unchanged	180	194	199	199	163
New Highs	8	10	13	8	11
New Lows	40	29	24	19	22
Sales, ths $	25,020	21,120	27,170	21,910	16,320

New Highs	18	26	47	36	29
New Lows	188	130	46	54	69
Sales, ths shs	23,177	25,294	30,960	26,903	22,471

Other Market Indicators

NYSE Comp.	61.73	62.29	63.26	63.12	62.72
Ind.	69.98	70.77	72.07	71.84	71.36
Util.	36.76	36.72	36.81	36.82	36.60
Tran.	51.60	52.23	53.52	53.37	53.10
Fin.	61.66	62.07	62.69	62.87	62.64
Amex Index	245.68	249.12	255.13	253.82	252.43
OTC-a Comp.	168.00	169.05	170.86	171.12	170.48
Ind.	191.67	193.29	196.03	196.35	195.25
Insur.	169.64	169.71	171.06	171.94	171.66
Banks	131.63	131.48	131.59	131.20	130.75
S&P 500 Comp.	107.20	108.30	110.14	109.83	109.14
400 Ind.	119.88	121.18	123.38	122.92	122.09
Value Line	118.04	118.74	120.35	120.45	119.76

a-NASDAQ.

Amex Most Active Stocks

High	Low		Sales	High	Low	Last	Chg.
21¼	3 13-16	DomeP	2,142,500	4⅞	3 13-16	4¾	+ ½
38	24	Wang B	772,000	27¾	25⅞	27¾	+ ⅞
25	12⅜	ChftD g	453,500	16⅞	16½	16¾	+ ¼
7⅞	4⅛	IntBknt	432,100	5¼	4⅛	5¼	+ ⅞
25⅝	8⅞	GlfCd g	375,300	11⅝	10⅛	11	+ ⅝
30⅜	9⅝	CrystO	288,500	13⅝	10¾	11	− ⅞
10	3¼	TchSym	276,300	10	8⅞	9½	+ ⅝
3½	1⅛	ChmpH	272,800	3	2¾	3	+ ¼
4⅞	1½	IntgEn n	248,700	1¾	1½	1⅝	.....
31⅛	16	Vrbtm s	247,900	31⅛	27⅛	30	+ 2¼

NASDAQ OTC Most Active Stocks

	$ Volume	Last	Chg.
MCI Communications	142,534,000	45⅛	+ 5
Tandem Computers	30,722,000	23¾	+ 1
Amer Internat'l Grp	30,579,000	57¾	− ½
Intel Corp	29,761,000	30½	+ 1½
Olympia Brewing Co	16,934,000	21⅞	+ 2
St Paul Cos	16,128,000	35⅞	− ⅜
Tandon Corp	13,323,000	32	+ 2¼
Pabst Brewing	12,312,000	20½	− ⅛
Apple Computer	10,215,000	13¼	+ ⅜
Inter Medics Inc	7,981,000	31⅞	+ 1⅞

Source: *Barron's*, June 28, 1982.

Exhibit 12-7

A strong line-up of potential blockbusters suggests a profitable summer for the filmmakers.

Having learned to live with television, the movie companies now are joining, not fighting, a new rival in video games.

For the year ahead, *General Cinema, Outboard Marine* and *Warner Communications* look like timely choices.

COMPOSITE STATISTICS: RECREATION INDUSTRY

1977	1978	1979	1980	1981	1982	© Arnold Bernhard & Co., Inc.	84-86E
7946.9	9291.5	10318	11143	11873	*12230*	Revenues ($mill)	*14000*
14.3%	14.9%	14.0%	12.2%	13.7%	*13.5%*	Operating Margin	*14.5%*
222.7	254.8	277.0	318.8	324.8	*380*	Depreciation ($mill)	*475*
454.5	612.7	724.7	572.0	733.0	*745*	Net Profit ($mill)	*1000*
41.9%	41.1%	38.2%	37.6%	37.5%	*37.0%*	Income Tax Rate	*37.0%*
5.7%	6.6%	7.0%	5.1%	6.2%	*6.1%*	Net Profit Margin	*7.1%*
1651.2	1929.8	2374.2	2467.3	2500.3	*2575*	Working Cap'l ($mill)	*3000*
1183.3	1250.5	1427.4	1309.4	2031.7	*2350*	Long-Term Debt ($mill)	*4500*
3233.7	3780.8	4552.0	5029.4	5623.5	*6200*	Net Worth ($mill)	*8375*
11.4%	13.2%	13.3%	10.0%	10.8%	*9.5%*	% Earned Total Cap'l	*10.0%*
14.1%	16.2%	15.9%	11.4%	13.0%	*12.0%*	% Earned Net Worth	*12.0%*
11.0%	13.1%	12.7%	8.0%	9.4%	*8.5%*	% Retained to Comm Eq	*9.5%*
23%	22%	30%	30%	29%	*30%*	% All Div'ds to Net Prof	*25%*
8.4	7.3	6.7	10.8	11.7		Avg Ann'l P/E Ratio	*11.0*
11.9%	13.7%	14.9%	9.3%	8.6%		Avg Ann'l Earn's Yield	*9.1%*
2.7%	2.7%	3.1%	2.8%	2.4%		Avg Ann'l Div'd Yield	*2.5%*

A Summer Revival For Films

The motion picture industry is again demonstrating that attractive product, more than general prosperity, is what builds revenue and profit. Unemployment and general gloom must have played a part in the poor theatrical box office figures for the recent Christmas holiday season. That, however, is not where theater operators lay all the blame. What's needed is pictures with qualities able to restore audiences.

Recently, the producers have been coming through with more commercially acceptable output. The success of the new offerings is reflected in an upsurge in theater admissions. Though comparisons were negative early this year, the overall box office take for the first five months of 1982 was up 18%. May figures alone were 34% ahead. We think this year's prospects for movie makers are bright.

Computerized Competition

Besides "free" television, alternative home amusement forms that have rapidly gained in popularity include pay-cable movies, video cassettes, video discs, and video games. Filmmakers have all taken steps to participate in these entertainment forms, which eventually must become powerful forces in the recreation industry. *Warner Communications*, for example, had disappointing results in its film division last year. Yet the company left all of its motion picture competitors far behind in overall profit growth. That's because *Warner* owns Atari, which dominates the burgeoning video game industry.

Already video game revenues exceed those of the film industry, and they're on a path that might double in three to five years. Most filmmakers learned the hard way, from television, that it's better to join the competition than fight it. So they're joining the video game movement in one way or another.

Columbia (soon to be acquired by Coca-Cola) owns pinball-machine-maker D. Gottlieb, which will be reorienting output in line with the developing new market. *MCA* is forming a video games division that surely will come up with something based on its famous *Jaws* property. *Disney's* coming movie, *Tron*, follows a video game theme and provides a ready name for a new game cassette. Whether any of these companies will be able to follow in Atari's footsteps, however, is hardly a certainty.

E.B.S./N.R.W.

INDUSTRY TIMELINESS: 50 (of 93)

RECREATION EQUIPMENT INDUSTRY

The recession is hurting companies in the recreation equipment industry. But diversification, high interest rates, falling fuel prices, and a relatively short time span between downturns make this slump different from previous recessions. On balance, most companies in this group won't suffer quite as much this time around.

There is no question that companies in this industry are feeling the current recession's pinch. But there are some differences from previous downturns. For one thing, companies in this group are now more diversified. In 1981, *AMF*, for the first time, did more nonleisure than leisure business. *Brunswick*, on the other hand, took a major step backward on the road to diversification when it sold its medical products business to American Home Products. Nevertheless, the trend certainly has been, and will continue to be, toward becoming less dependent on cyclical recreation products.

Business is generally weak across the board but there are some pockets of strength. Outboard motors aren't doing too badly, especially in the high-horsepower range. In this business, consumer perception of the improved availability of fuel has gone a long way toward making up for a down economy. (Compare 1982's relatively strong outboard sales with business in the first half of 1980, when the economy was doing OK but long lines at gas stations panicked boating enthusiasts.)

Another oddity of the current recession is the high cost of capital. This is hitting big-ticket items especially hard—yacht or even lawn mower purchasers usually need financing. *AMF* is the most vulnerable to this phenomenon. But *Brunswick* is suffering as well, since interest rates are also hurting bowling capital equipment sales.

Finally, since the previous recession ended only a year before the current one began, many companies had cost-cutting measures already in place when the economy turned down. So margins haven't deteriorated as badly as in past economic slumps. Inventory levels have stayed low for the same reason. This is true for all of the big guns in the industry—*AMF*, *Brunswick*, and *Outboard Marine*.

Just as many companies in this group aren't having as poor a year as they might, their stocks haven't done too badly either. *Outboard Marine* and *Wometco Enterprises* have been hot equities over the past six months, a difficult period for many stocks. (Strong performances haven't been common to all stocks in this group though: *AMF* has been making new lows almost daily.) We don't expect these stocks to do as well over the next 12 months. But patient investors can choose from a number of equities with above-average 3- to 5-year potential. *AMF* and *Technicolor* stand out in this class. *D.K./K.C.B.*

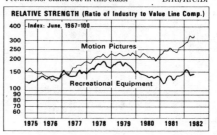

RELATIVE STRENGTH (Ratio of Industry to Value Line Comp.)
Index: June, 1967=100
Motion Pictures
Recreational Equipment

Exhibit 12-8

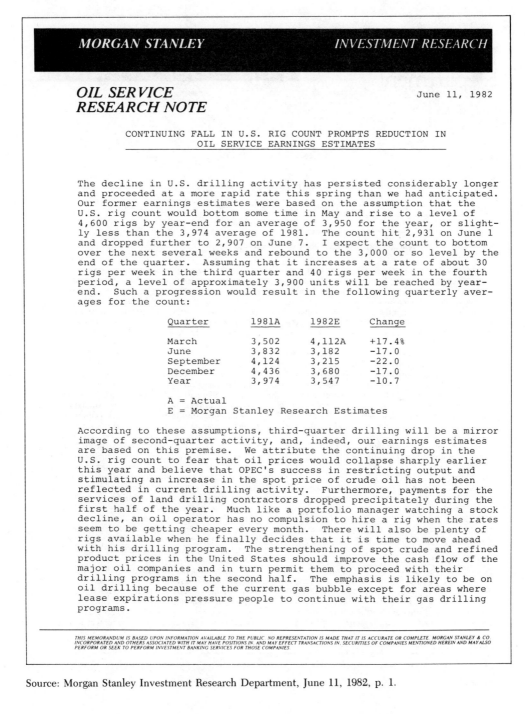

MORGAN STANLEY   INVESTMENT RESEARCH

OIL SERVICE   June 11, 1982
RESEARCH NOTE

CONTINUING FALL IN U.S. RIG COUNT PROMPTS REDUCTION IN
OIL SERVICE EARNINGS ESTIMATES

The decline in U.S. drilling activity has persisted considerably longer
and proceeded at a more rapid rate this spring than we had anticipated.
Our former earnings estimates were based on the assumption that the
U.S. rig count would bottom some time in May and rise to a level of
4,600 rigs by year-end for an average of 3,950 for the year, or slightly less than the 3,974 average of 1981. The count hit 2,931 on June 1
and dropped further to 2,907 on June 7. I expect the count to bottom
over the next several weeks and rebound to the 3,000 or so level by the
end of the quarter. Assuming that it increases at a rate of about 30
rigs per week in the third quarter and 40 rigs per week in the fourth
period, a level of approximately 3,900 units will be reached by year-
end. Such a progression would result in the following quarterly averages for the count:

Quarter	1981A	1982E	Change
March	3,502	4,112A	+17.4%
June	3,832	3,182	-17.0
September	4,124	3,215	-22.0
December	4,436	3,680	-17.0
Year	3,974	3,547	-10.7

A = Actual
E = Morgan Stanley Research Estimates

According to these assumptions, third-quarter drilling will be a mirror
image of second-quarter activity, and, indeed, our earnings estimates
are based on this premise. We attribute the continuing drop in the
U.S. rig count to fear that oil prices would collapse sharply earlier
this year and believe that OPEC's success in restricting output and
stimulating an increase in the spot price of crude oil has not been
reflected in current drilling activity. Furthermore, payments for the
services of land drilling contractors dropped precipitely during the
first half of the year. Much like a portfolio manager watching a stock
decline, an oil operator has no compulsion to hire a rig when the rates
seem to be getting cheaper every month. There will also be plenty of
rigs available when he finally decides that it is time to move ahead
with his drilling program. The strengthening of spot crude and refined
product prices in the United States should improve the cash flow of the
major oil companies and in turn permit them to proceed with their
drilling programs in the second half. The emphasis is likely to be on
oil drilling because of the current gas bubble except for areas where
lease expirations pressure people to continue with their gas drilling
programs.

Source: Morgan Stanley Investment Research Department, June 11, 1982, p. 1.

Exhibit 12-9

The
Research
Department

June 22, 1982

CHEMICAL INDUSTRY

Second-Quarter Estimates

- **Second-period results projected to show an average decline of 39%; first-half results projected to decline 36%.**
- **No business improvement seen yet.**
- **We remain neutral on chemicals as a group, short term.**

Table 1 shows projected second-quarter and first-half comparisons for our universe of 12 major chemical companies. The estimates provided are in line with recent indications from their respective managements and, we imagine, are thus similar to the results which will be anticipated by many on the Street. Therefore, we would say that as earnings are reported, stocks may react positively or negatively in the short term to the extent that actual results exceed or fall short of our projections. For now, it appears that the average performer in our group will show a year-to-year decline in earnings of 39% in the quarter and 36% in the half. In other words, second-period comparisons, on average, will be slightly worse than even those of the depressed first period.

Expected results for the quarter and half have forced us once again to revise downward our earnings estimates for the 1982-83 period. Updated projections are shown in Table 2. Using these new numbers, we have also attempted to regroup the companies with respect to our estimated present values, following the recent downward movement in the market. Our methodology is described in the table. The judgments offered represent only our views about one-year trading opportunities, and are not intended to serve as a sophisticated analysis of long-term investment merit. For example, as discussed in our May 24 Industry Review, we believe that between the 1982-83 period and the 1985-86 period, the chemical industry's ROA will be rising from a cyclical trough to a cyclical peak, resulting in above-average earnings growth during that time. Therefore, we would be positive on the group long term, since a 12% discount from the market multiple seems a low valuation to apply to trough earnings.

For the near term, however, we remain neutral. It is tempting when things seem blackest to pull the trigger and recommend purchase, since historically this has proven to be a useful time to buy. For example, any investors who bought chemicals early in 1970, at the depths of that recession, made out very well, beating the market averages handily for six consecutive years. But, loath as we are to miss a classic buying opportunity, we still feel certain restraining influences.

It is our impression that the Street generally is still, after going on three years, in a mode of cutting earnings estimates. Projections which seemed reasonable as recently as a month or two ago now appear unrealistically high, and this cannot be a bullish circumstance. Also, our own newly revised estimates assume some business recovery in the second half; without such a rebound, they may have to be cut further. And so far, not one division of one company we follow reports that it sees any such upturn beginning. Finally, in our May 24 review we stated our belief that the dollar was overvalued and subject to a decline, which would be a benefit both to domestic operating rates and the translation of results from foreign operations. However, following a significant decline in April, the dollar has recently strengthened again and is now 3% higher than it was on March 31, relative to an unweighted basket of five European currencies.

In fact, some producers report a deterioration in second-quarter business from first-period levels. Such instances would include the troubled chemicals business at Celanese, which saw some loss of export volumes recently, the fibers business at Du Pont, and both chemicals and agricultural products at Stauffer.

Industry Comment _____

Source: Kidder Peabody & Co., Inc. Research Department, June 22, 1982, p. 1.

the economy change? When will particular industries be affected by these changes? What firms can participate positively in these future forecasts?

Two critical decisions are implicit to this analysis: (1) when to invest in order to participate in growth trends and to avoid large losses resulting from declines in economic or industry activity, and (2) where to invest in order to benefit most fully from that growth. This involves the selection of industries and firms most likely to prosper and to share in that growth, keeping in mind that not all segments of the economy will grow at a uniform rate and that not all industries will share equally in overall economic expansion. Analysis of these issues will indicate whether common stocks or bonds are preferable to alternative investments.

Analysis involves projections based on past data, planned courses of action, expert judgment, and, to varying degrees, luck. At the very best, the projections are estimates and, therefore, contain elements of risk. The best information available will be dated because of the inevitable time lag incurred in collecting and processing the data. Furthermore, the technical process involved is often exceedingly complex. Nevertheless, information on the anticipated performance of the national economy and the industries within it is essential if the investor is to make an intelligent investment decision that will minimize overall risk.

In the process of investment analysis, general economic analysis describes the environment within which the firm must operate, while industry analysis identifies and describes those components of the economy that are critical to the industry's performance. Together they provide the investor with a basis for further examination of companies operating within that industry under various economic conditions.

ECONOMIC ENVIRONMENT

Gross National Product

No tool is more basic to analyzing the current condition of the national economy and to providing a basis for predictions than the **gross national product** (*GNP*). The GNP represents the current market value of all goods and services produced by the nation over a given period of time. It breaks this production down into categories of **national income** and **product accounts**. These accounts indicate where total income for every segment of the economy comes from and goes to in terms of aggregate receipts and expenditures and how production is distributed among product groups and markets.

Exhibit 12-10 illustrates the elements that make up the GNP and national income. The Federal Reserve System publishes the most current GNP data in the monthly *Federal Reserve Bulletin*.

Exhibit 12-10
Gross National Product and Income: Billions of Current Dollars; Quarterly Data Are at Seasonally Adjusted Annual Rates

GROSS NATIONAL PRODUCT AND INCOME
Billions of current dollars except as noted; quarterly data are at seasonally adjusted annual rates.

Account	1979	1980	1981	1981 Q1	Q2	Q3	Q4	1982 Q1p
GROSS NATIONAL PRODUCT								
1 Total	**2,413.9**	**2,626.1**	**2,925.5**	**2,853.0**	**2,885.8**	**2,965.0**	**2,998.3**	**2,995.1**
By source								
2 Personal consumption expenditures	1,510.9	1,672.8	1,857.8	1,810.1	1,829.1	1,883.9	1,908.3	1,950.7
3 Durable goods	212.3	211.9	232.0	238.3	227.3	236.2	226.4	236.8
4 Nondurable goods	602.2	675.7	743.2	726.0	735.3	751.3	760.3	766.1
5 Services	696.3	785.2	882.6	845.8	866.5	896.4	921.5	947.8
6 Gross private domestic investment	415.8	395.3	450.5	437.1	458.6	463.0	443.3	392.6
7 Fixed investment	398.3	401.2	434.4	432.7	435.3	435.6	434.0	432.6
8 Nonresidential	279.7	296.0	328.9	315.9	324.6	335.1	339.8	339.8
9 Structures	96.3	108.8	125.7	117.2	123.1	128.3	134.3	134.1
10 Producers' durable equipment	183.4	187.1	203.1	198.7	201.5	206.8	205.5	205.7
11 Residential structures	118.6	105.3	105.5	116.7	110.7	100.5	94.2	92.7
12 Nonfarm	113.9	100.3	100.0	111.4	105.4	94.9	88.4	87.1
13 Change in business inventories	17.5	−5.9	16.2	4.5	23.3	27.5	9.4	−40.0
14 Nonfarm	13.4	−4.7	13.8	6.8	21.5	23.1	3.7	−38.8
15 Net exports of goods and services	13.4	23.3	26.0	29.2	20.8	29.3	24.7	23.8
16 Exports	281.3	339.8	367.3	367.4	368.2	368.0	365.6	359.0
17 Imports	267.9	316.5	341.3	338.2	347.5	338.7	341.0	335.1
18 Government purchases of goods and services	473.8	534.7	591.2	576.5	577.4	588.9	622.0	628.0
19 Federal	167.9	198.9	230.2	221.6	219.5	226.4	253.3	255.7
20 State and local	305.9	335.8	361.0	354.9	357.9	362.5	368.7	372.3
By major type of product								
21 Final sales, total	2,396.4	2,632.0	2,909.4	2,848.5	2,862.5	2,937.6	2,989.0	3,035.1
22 Goods	1,055.9	1,130.4	1,272.3	1,247.5	1,257.0	1,298.3	1,286.4	1,261.7
23 Durable	451.2	458.6	506.9	501.4	516.9	525.2	484.2	461.8
24 Nondurable	604.7	671.9	765.4	746.1	740.1	773.0	802.2	799.9
25 Services	1,097.2	1,229.6	1,371.7	1,317.1	1,344.7	1,390.5	1,434.4	1,459.3
26 Structures	260.8	266.0	281.6	288.4	284.1	276.3	277.5	274.1
27 Change in business inventories	17.5	−5.9	16.2	4.5	23.3	27.5	9.4	−40.0
28 Durable goods	11.5	−4.0	7.4	−4.2	18.5	18.6	−3.3	−37.5
29 Nondurable goods	6.0	−1.8	8.8	8.6	4.8	8.9	12.7	−2.5
30 MEMO: **Total GNP in 1972 dollars**	**1,483.0**	**1,480.7**	**1,510.3**	**1,516.4**	**1,510.4**	**1,515.8**	**1,498.4**	**1,483.6**
NATIONAL INCOME								
31 Total	**1,963.3**	**2,121.4**	**2,347.2**	**2,291.1**	**2,320.9**	**2,377.6**	**2,399.1**	**n.a.**
32 Compensation of employees	1,460.9	1,596.5	1,771.6	1,722.4	1,752.0	1,790.7	1,821.3	1,844.9
33 Wages and salaries	1,235.9	1,343.6	1,482.8	1,442.9	1,467.0	1,498.7	1,522.5	1,538.8
34 Government and government enterprises	235.9	253.6	273.9	267.1	270.5	274.7	283.2	287.1
35 Other	1,000.0	1,090.0	1,208.8	1,175.7	1,196.4	1,224.0	1,239.2	1,251.7
36 Supplement to wages and salaries	225.0	252.9	288.8	279.5	285.1	292.0	298.8	306.1
37 Employer contributions for social insurance	106.4	115.8	134.7	131.5	133.2	135.6	138.4	142.3
38 Other labor income	118.6	137.1	154.1	148.0	151.8	156.3	160.4	163.8
39 Proprietors' income[1]	131.6	130.6	134.8	132.1	134.1	137.1	135.9	129.0
40 Business and professional[1]	100.7	107.2	112.4	113.2	112.5	112.4	111.5	110.8
41 Farm[1]	30.8	23.4	22.4	18.9	21.7	24.7	24.4	18.2
42 Rental income of persons[2]	30.5	31.8	33.6	32.7	33.3	33.9	34.5	34.8
43 Corporate profits[1]	196.8	182.7	191.7	203.0	190.3	195.7	177.6	n.a.
44 Profits before tax[3]	255.4	245.5	233.3	257.0	229.0	234.4	212.8	n.a.
45 Inventory valuation adjustment	−42.6	−45.7	−27.7	−39.2	−24.0	−25.3	−22.3	−10.6
46 Capital consumption adjustment	−15.9	−17.2	−13.9	−14.7	−14.7	−13.4	−12.8	−9.7
47 Net interest	143.4	179.8	215.4	200.8	211.0	220.2	229.7	237.9

1. With inventory valuation and capital consumption adjustments.
2. With capital consumption adjustments.

Source: Department of Commerce, Survey of Current Business; as Reprinted in Federal Reserve Bulletin, May, 1982, p. A52.

Exhibit 12-11

Personal Income and Savings: Billions of Current Dollars; Quarterly Data Are at Seasonally Adjusted Annual Rates

PERSONAL INCOME AND SAVING

Billions of current dollars; quarterly data are at seasonally adjusted annual rates. Exceptions noted.

Account	1979	1980	1981	1981 Q1	1981 Q2	1981 Q3	1981 Q4	1982 Q1[p]
PERSONAL INCOME AND SAVING								
1 **Total personal income**	**1,943.8**	**2,160.2**	**2,404.1**	**2,319.8**	**2,368.5**	**2,441.7**	**2,486.5**	**2,512.7**
2 Wage and salary disbursements	1,236.1	1,343.7	1,482.7	1,442.9	1,467.0	1,498.5	1,522.5	1,539.0
3 Commodity-producing industries	437.9	465.4	512.7	501.3	508.1	520.2	521.0	521.2
4 Manufacturing	333.4	350.7	387.3	377.4	386.7	393.9	391.0	390.3
5 Distributive industries	303.0	328.9	361.1	351.9	357.8	365.3	369.5	373.5
6 Service industries	259.2	295.7	335.0	322.5	330.5	338.5	348.7	357.0
7 Government and government enterprises	236.1	253.6	273.9	267.1	270.5	274.5	283.3	287.3
8 Other labor income	118.6	137.1	154.1	148.0	151.8	156.3	160.4	163.8
9 Proprietors' income[1]	131.6	130.6	134.8	132.1	134.1	137.1	135.9	129.0
10 Business and professional[1]	100.8	107.2	112.4	113.2	112.5	112.4	111.5	110.8
11 Farm[1]	30.8	23.4	22.4	18.9	21.7	24.7	24.4	18.2
12 Rental income of persons[2]	30.5	31.8	33.6	32.7	33.3	33.9	34.5	34.8
13 Dividends	48.6	54.4	61.3	58.0	60.2	63.0	64.1	64.7
14 Personal interest income	209.6	256.3	308.5	288.7	300.9	315.7	328.7	338.5
15 Transfer payments	249.4	294.2	333.2	319.6	324.2	342.2	347.0	354.1
16 Old-age survivors, disability, and health insurance benefits	131.8	153.8	180.4	169.8	172.0	188.5	191.2	194.5
17 LESS: Personal contributions for social insurance	80.6	87.9	104.2	102.3	103.1	105.0	106.5	111.2
18 EQUALS: Personal income	1,943.8	2,160.2	2,404.1	2,319.8	2,368.5	2,441.7	2,486.5	2,512.7
19 LESS: Personal tax and nontax payments	302.0	338.5	388.2	372.0	382.9	399.8	398.0	397.4
20 EQUALS: Disposable personal income	1,641.7	1,821.7	2,016.0	1,947.8	1,985.6	2,042.0	2,088.5	2,115.3
21 LESS: Personal outlays	1,555.5	1,720.4	1,908.4	1,858.9	1,879.0	1,935.1	1,960.5	2,003.3
22 EQUALS: Personal saving	86.2	101.3	107.6	88.9	106.6	106.9	128.0	112.1
MEMO: Per capita (1972 dollars)								
23 Gross national product	6,588	6,503	6,570	6,619	6,581	6,585	6,494	6,417
24 Personal consumption expenditures	4,135	4,108	4,171	4,191	4,162	4,184	4,150	4,182
25 Disposable personal income	4,493	4,473	4,526	4,511	4,517	4,535	4,541	4,534
26 Saving rate (percent)	5.2	5.6	5.3	4.6	5.4	5.2	6.1	5.3
GROSS SAVING								
27 **Gross saving**	**412.0**	**401.9**	**455.5**	**442.6**	**465.3**	**469.4**	**444.7**	**n.a.**
28 Gross private saving	398.9	432.9	480.1	451.1	475.3	486.2	507.7	n.a.
29 Personal saving	86.2	101.3	107.6	88.9	106.6	106.9	128.0	112.1
30 Undistributed corporate profits[1]	59.1	44.3	50.8	55.7	52.0	52.8	42.9	n.a.
31 Corporate inventory valuation adjustment	− 42.6	− 45.7	− 27.7	− 39.2	− 24.0	− 25.3	− 22.3	− 10.6
Capital consumption allowances								
32 Corporate	155.4	175.4	197.7	187.5	194.6	201.1	207.7	211.7
33 Noncorporate	98.2	111.8	123.9	119.0	122.0	125.4	129.1	132.1
34 Wage accruals less disbursements	.0	.0	.0	.0	.0	.0	.0	.0
35 Government surplus, or deficit (−), national income and product accounts	11.9	− 32.1	− 25.7	− 9.7	− 11.2	− 17.9	− 64.1	n.a.
36 Federal	− 14.8	− 61.2	− 62.4	− 46.6	− 47.2	− 55.7	− 100.0	n.a.
37 State and local	26.7	29.1	36.7	36.9	36.1	37.8	35.9	n.a.
38 Capital grants received by the United States, net	1.1	1.1	1.1	1.1	1.1	1.1	1.1	.0
39 **Gross investment**	**414.1**	**401.2**	**454.7**	**446.0**	**458.3**	**469.6**	**444.8**	**392.4**
40 Gross private domestic	415.8	395.3	450.5	437.1	458.6	463.0	443.3	392.6
41 Net foreign	− 1.7	5.9	4.2	8.8	− .2	6.5	1.5	− .2
42 **Statistical discrepancy**	**2.2**	**− .7**	**− .8**	**3.4**	**− 6.9**	**.2**	**.2**	**.2**

1. With inventory valuation and capital consumption adjustments.
2. With capital consumption adjustment.

Source: Department of Commerce, Survey of Current Business; as Reprinted in Federal Reserve Bulletin, May, 1982, p. A53.

The *Survey of Current Business* published by the Bureau of Economic Analysis of the Department of Commerce uses the GNP data as the basis for its own detailed analysis. Exhibit 12-11 illustrates the breakdown of the various income accounts and their historical trends.

Figure 12-1 graphically illustrates recent trends in the major components of GNP. Even though the investor is most concerned with forecasts based on GNP data projected for one year, GNP can also be used for longer-term estimates. Because of large fluctuations in the rate of inflation, it is useful to express GNP in terms of constant dollars when comparing one year with another.

Because GNP breaks down total economic activity into its income and expenditure elements, it can provide inportant clues to how the various areas of industrial activity are likely to be affected by variations in the GNP accounts. For example, the expenditure accounts indicate areas in which personal consumption expenditures were made, the level and distribution of investment, the extent to which the government bought goods and services, and the net total of goods and services imported and exported. A company that deals primarily with personal services would be interested in examining the trend in the total amount of personal consumption expenditures for consumer services. An industry that is heavily involved in government defense projects must be evaluated in light of the level and trends in government expenditures. Much of the forecasting data published to aid business decision making are expressed in terms of the national income accounts.

It is important to recognize that GNP forecasts are subject to error. There has been little error in forecasts of overall GNP because it tends to change in a predictable manner. However, attempting to forecast components of GNP can be very difficult because some fluctuate widely from year to year. In addition, errors in forecasting GNP or its components are often increased with the length of time covered by the prediction.

Economic Indicators

Even though GNP is a basic predictive tool, it has a limited ability to predict aberrations in the business cycle. **Economic indicators** serve as a basic device for predicting cyclical movements.

The National Bureau of Economic Research (NBER) has developed a comprehensive list of 77 cyclical indicators broken down into three broad categories: leading, lagging, and coincident indicators. Figure 12-2 concisely identifies these indicators by the economic process to which they are most closely related and by their cyclical timing.

The **leading** indicators have historically peaked or fallen to their low points (troughs) approximately 6 months before the total economy has made a similar change. The **lagging** indicators, however, tend to peak and fall approximately 6 months after the general economy has reached its turning

Figure 12-1
Gross National Product or Expenditure: Real Product, Change from Preceding Quarter; Seasonally Adjusted at Annual Rates

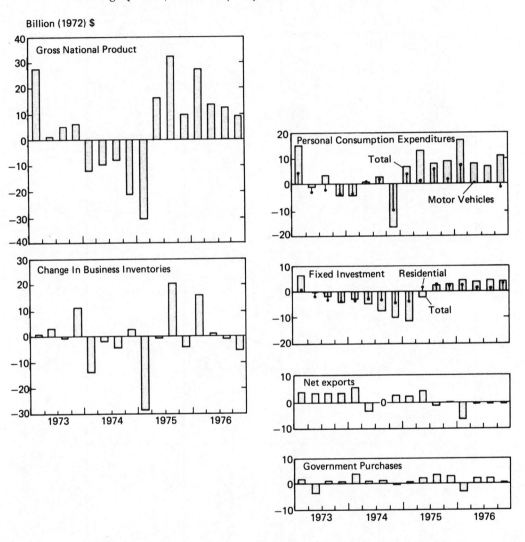

point. The **roughly coincident** indicators reach their high and low points at about the same time as the general economy. To make the economic indicators a more manageable and useful tool, the NBER has produced an abbreviated list of 26 indicators: 12 leading, 8 roughly coincident, and 6 lagging. Table 12-1 summarizes the composition of this shorter list.

The movements of the components making up this short list are graphically illustrated in each month's issue of *Business Conditions Digest* (published by the Bureau of the Census, Department of Commerce). Rather

Figure 12-2

Cross-Classification of Cyclical Indicators, by Economic Process and
Cyclical Timing

Economic Process / Cyclical Timing	I. EMPLOYMENT AND UNEMPLOYMENT	II. PRODUCTION, INCOME, CONSUMPTION, AND TRADE	III. FIXED CAPITAL INVESTMENT	IV. INVENTORIES AND INVENTORY INVESTMENT	V. PRICES, COSTS, AND PROFITS	VI. MONEY AND CREDIT
LEADING INDICATORS	Marginal employment adjustments		Formation of business enterprises New investment commitments	Inventory investment and purchasing	Sensitive commodity prices Stock prices Profits and profit margins Cash flows	Flows of money and credit Credit difficulties
ROUGHLY COINCIDENT INDICATORS	Job vacancies Comprehensive employment Comprehensive unemployment	Comprehensive production Comprehensive income Comprehensive consumption and trade	Backlog of investment commitments		Comprehensive wholesale prices	Bank reserves Interest rates
LAGGING INDICATORS	Long-duration unemployment		Investment expenditures	Inventories	Unit labor costs	Outstanding debt Interest rates

Source: Bureau of Economic Analysis, Department of Commerce, *Business Conditions Digest*, March, 1982.

Table 12-1
Short List of NBER Cyclical Indicators, by Timing

	Timing	
Leading(12)	Lagging(6)	Roughly Coincidental(8)
1. Average work sheet for production workers in manufacturing (hours)	1. Unemployment rate, persons unemployed 15 weeks or more	1. Personal income
2. Average weekly initial claims for state unemployment insurance	2. Business expenditures for new plant and equipment	2. GNP in current dollars
3. Net business formation	3. Book value of manufacturing and trade inventories	3. GNP in constant dollars
4. New orders in durable goods industries	4. Labor cost per unit of output in manufacturing	4. Industrial production
5. Contracts and orders for plant and equipment	5. Commercial and industrial loans outstanding as reported weekly by large commercial banks	5. Manufacturing and trade sales
6. New building permits for private housing units	6. Bank rates on short-term business loans	6. Sales of retail stores
7. Change in book value of manufacturing and trade inventories		7. Employees on nonagricultural payrolls
8. Industrial materials prices		8. Unemployment rate, total
9. Stock prices of 500 leading common stocks		
10. Corporate profits after taxes		
11. Ratio of price to unit labor cost in manufacturing		
12. Change in consumer installment debt		

Source: Adapted from NBER data.

Figure 12-3   Composite Index of Indicators and Their Components

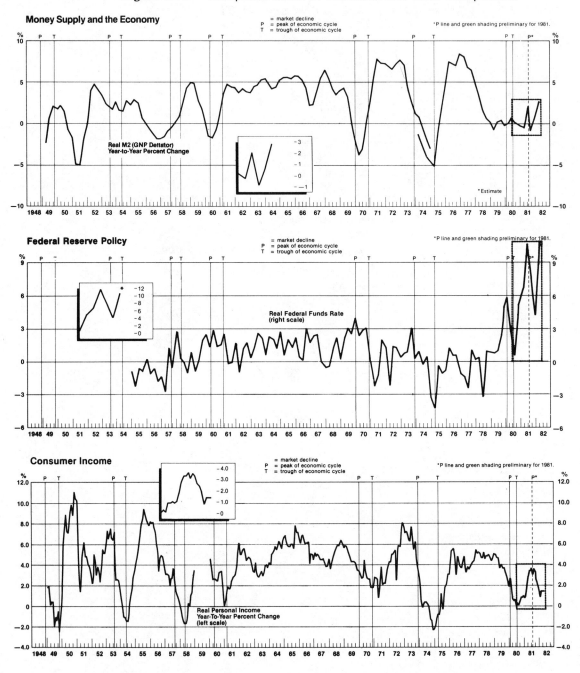

Source: Bureau of Economic Analysis, Department of Commerce, Business Conditions Digest, March, 1982.

than examine the individual movement of each of the 26 indicators, it is possible to combine the movement of several indicators into a composite or consensus index called a **diffusion index,** as shown in Figure 12-3. Figure 12-4 provides detailed information on how to interpret the various indicator charts.

It is also possible to develop diffusion indexes that portray the movements of the elements that go into the formation of an indicator.

How can leading indicators display changes in direction before the general economy? Some leading indicators reflect both investment decisions that anticipate an upswing in business and investment decisions that help to promote that upswing. For example, new business formations anticipate the existence of an expanded market that it is hoped will absorb the increased production, provide new jobs, and consume additional materials in its expansion. Conversely, the effects of the decisions that determine lagging indicators will linger beyond changes in the economy. For example, it will take a fixed period of time to repay outstanding bank loans that contributed to capital expansion, even though business conditions may worsen before the debt is repaid.

Even though economic indicators can reasonably predict cyclical movements, they are neither foolproof nor comprehensive. The indicators predict the direction of change, but they do not indicate how great that change will be or how long it may last. During a short period of time, a single indicator may display many small peaks and troughs, although its general movement may be consistent. Furthermore, there is a time lapse between the collection of data and their usage, thereby shortening the predictive horizon of the indicators. In short, the economic indicators are not always accurate; they are simply one of several tools useful for economic analysis.

Econometric Models

One of the more recent predictive devices is the **econometric model,** which combines economic theory, statistics, and mathematics to produce a sophisticated prediction of the economy. These predictions indicate not only the direction of change but also the precise quantities of change. A computerized model of the economy is constructed on the basis of variables included in the economic model itself (called **endogenous variables**) and the effects of changes in variables determined outside the system of equations that describe the model (**exogenous variables**).

Because the econometric model is in a stable condition, an exogenous variable can be altered, and the effects of its variation on the economy can be observed. For example, during the initial stage of the oil embargo by the Organization of Petroleum Exporting Countries in late 1973, several econometric models were used to try to predict the effect of greatly increased oil prices on the economy. The effects of changes in other key economic variables can be similarly analyzed. The better-known econometric models include those constructed by the Massachusetts Institute of Technology,

Figure 12-4 How to Read Charts

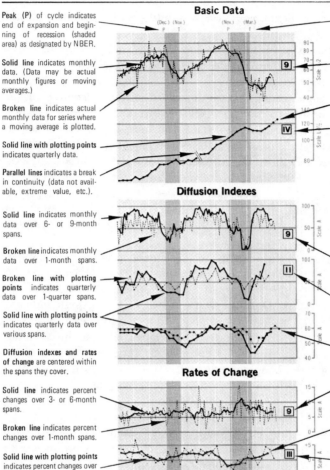

Peak (P) of cycle indicates end of expansion and beginning of recession (shaded area) as designated by NBER.

Solid line indicates monthly data. (Data may be actual monthly figures or moving averages.)

Broken line indicates actual monthly data for series where a moving average is plotted.

Solid line with plotting points indicates quarterly data.

Parallel lines indicates a break in continuity (data not available, extreme value, etc.).

Solid line indicates monthly data over 6- or 9-month spans.

Broken line indicates monthly data over 1-month spans.

Broken line with plotting points indicates quarterly data over 1-quarter spans.

Solid line with plotting points indicates quarterly data over various spans.

Diffusion indexes and rates of change are centered within the spans they cover.

Solid line indicates percent changes over 3- or 6-month spans.

Broken line indicates percent changes over 1-month spans.

Solid line with plotting points indicates percent changes over 3- or 4-quarter spans.

Trough (T) of cycle indicates end of recession and beginning of expansion as designated by NBER.

Arabic number indicates latest month for which data are plotted. ("9" = September)

Dotted line indicates anticipated data.

Roman number indicates latest quarter for which data are plotted. ("IV" = fourth quarter)

Various scales are used to highlight the patterns of the individual series. "Scale A" is an arithmetic scale, "scale L-1" is a logarithmic scale with 1 cycle in a given distance, "scale L-2" is a logarithmic scale with two cycles in that distance, etc.

Arabic number indicates latest month for which data are used in computing the indexes.

Roman number indicates latest quarter for which data are used in computing the indexes.

Dotted line indicates anticipated quarterly data over various spans.

Arabic number indicates latest month used in computing the changes.

Broken line with plotting points indicates percent changes over 1-quarter spans.

Roman number indicates latest quarter used in computing the changes.

Source: Bureau of Economic Analysis, Department of Commerce, Business Conditions Digest, March, 1982

Michigan State University, the University of Chicago, the Wharton School of Business of the University of Pennsylvania, and, more recently, Data Resources Incorporated. These organizations' predictions are regularly published in various financial news sources and are followed closely by economists in the investment community.

As promising as econometric models may be, they are still a relatively recent development and display definite limitations. Predictions generally are accurate only over short-term forecasting periods. Tremendous investments in computer and data-collection facilities are necessary for their proper implementation, and high degrees of technical and theoretical sophistication are necessary to compose and maintain a meaningful model. Finally, econometric models have experienced the same sort of data lag characteristic of economic indicators. Obviously, the conclusions of any single predictive device should not be accepted without question. Rather, the various tools of economic analysis must be employed in concert and must be examined critically by the potential investor.

INDUSTRY-WIDE PROJECTIONS AND EVALUATIONS

Dimensions of an Industry

The growth of some industries has kept pace with the growth of GNP. Other industries have exceeded that rate; still others have grown at a slower rate than the rate of GNP. In general, a firm's growth will parallel that of the industry of which it is a part. For these reasons, investors need to select industries that keep pace with the growth of GNP if their investment objectives are more growth oriented than income oriented.

Because the selection of an industry is an important step in the investment process, the investor must identify what is meant by an industry. Most basically, an industry is defined by two dimensions: (1) the similarity of the products produced, and (2) the homogeneity of the technological process employed in that production. On that basis, coal mining might be considered both part of the mining industry (based on the process employed) and part of the fossil fuel industry (based on the product).

Industrial groups based on broad processes can be broken down into more precisely defined product classes. GNP is partially expressed in terms of product categories, which makes it easier to relate shifts in GNP accounts to changes in industrial performance. For example, manufacturing can be broken down into durable and nondurable goods and can then be even more finely segmented. However, this process can and does lead to several alternate schemes of industrial classification.

Dow-Jones Classifications

One of the more frequently quoted classification schemes is that used to describe compactly changes in the average market value of a limited group of publicly held stocks traded on the New York Stock Exchange. The

Dow-Jones averages divide the majority of stocks into three broad investment groups: industrials, transportation, and utilities. Even though each
group does not include all firms within each category, the stocks selected
are said to be of sufficient importance to indicate the general direction of
changes within each category. Exhibit 12-12 shows the movement in the
three Dow-Jones categories over a selected period.

The **industrials** category includes 30 companies in a variety of industries in the areas of mining, manufacturing, and merchandising. These industries display distinctive growth patterns, some expanding, some declining.
Some have growth rates exceeding the rate of growth of GNP; others fall
behind GNP.

The **transportation** category includes airlines, railroads, and trucking
and shipping companies. Because these particular fields are carefully regulated by the federal government, their success is affected to a material
degree by political decisions. For example, it is likely that many railroads
will continue to experience severe financial strains, and quasi-government
ownership is likely in some geographic areas. However, some long-haul
railroads have managed to maintain competitive success over the past decade
without government intervention.

Public utilities experienced stable rates of growth until the mid-1970s.
Even though projections of energy demand have been revised to a slower
growth rate from earlier estimates, great expansion in plant and equipment
will continue through the 1980s to suppy the necessary level of energy
required by the economy. The **utilities** category is mainly composed of
investor-owned telephone, gas, and electric companies. However, despite
necessary expansion, the investment performance of these companies' securities has been greatly modified by the ill effects of inflation, the magnitude
of the capital investments involved, ecological considerations, and lags in
regulated rate adjustments.

Standard Industrial Classifications (SIC)

The federal government has developed an extremely comprehensive
industrial classification system in order to convey the vast amount of information it collects in a systematic manner. A large part of this information
is published in the comprehensive economic census of the United States,
Bureau of the Census, *Census of Manufacturers*. Basically, the SIC system
classifies an industry according to the primary activity in which it is engaged,
using the format presented in Table 12-2.

These major groups are further broken down into three-digit industries
and four-digit groups, each level more precisely describing the industry's
major activity. The SIC not only identifies the various industrial categories
but also provides information such as the number of firms in the field, the
number of employees and production workers in the field, and the value

Exhibit 12-12

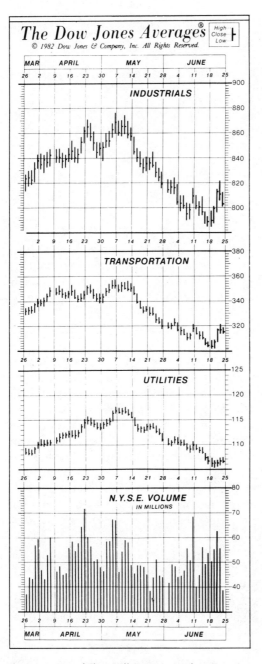

Table 12-2
Subdivisions of the Standard Industrial Classification

Industrial Division		Major Groups
A	Agriculture, forestry, and fisheries	01–09
B	Mining	10–14
C	Contract construction	15–17
D	Manufacturing	19–39
E	Transportation, communication, electric, gas, and sanitary services	40–49
F	Wholesale and retail trade	50–59
G	Finance, insurance, and real estate	60–67
H	Services	70–89
I	Government	91–94
J	Nonclassifiable establishments	99

Source: Department of Commerce data.

of their products. Table 12-3 illustrates the information contained in the *Annual Survey of Manufactures*. Given such information, an investor can estimate the scope and magnitude of various industries over time.

Selected Business Indexes of the Federal Reserve Board

One of the most instructive and widely known means of utilizing an industrial classification scheme to discern shifts in industrial performance is through analyzing the information contained in the index of industrial production published by the Federal Reserve Board. The index compares the total market value of current production categories with the total for a base year. For example Table 12-4 shows that total industrial production through August 1981 equaled 152.8, which represents an increase of 52.8 percent over the base year of 1967. Table 12-4 further breaks down the components of industrial production, allowing the investor to examine various shifts in the components. The data presented in Table 12-4 are a summary of much more detailed information contained in other publications. For example, there is a row labeled Consumer Goods; other publications break down these data into durables and nondurables. These categories are further broken down to give data for actual product classifications such as appliances, furniture, and clothing.

This type of information can be valuable in helping the investor to understand the trend of the economy. The indexes can quickly identify those areas of industrial production that have expanded most (relative to the base year). For example, in 1980 consumer goods increased 45.4 percent over the base year, whereas equipment increased by only 45.2 percent since 1967. Total industrial production had increased 47 percent during the same period. If these trends were to continue, the investor would want to select

Table 12-3 Statistics for Industry Groups and Industries: 1980 and 1979.

Statistics for Industry Groups and Industries: 1980 and 1979

(For explanation of column captions, see appendix)

SIC code	Industry group and industry	All employees — Number (1,000) [A]	All employees — Payroll (million dollars) [B]	Production workers — Number (1,000) [C]	Production workers — Hours (millions) [D]	Production workers — Wages (million dollars) [E]	Value added by manufacture (million dollars) [F]	Cost of materials (million dollars) [G]	Value of industry shipments (million dollars) [H]	New capital expenditures (million dollars) [I]	End-of-year inventories (million dollars) [J]	Standard error of estimate (percent) for column[1] — A	F	I
	ALL INDUSTRIES, TOTAL r . . .	21,040.2	328,887.9	14,537.8	28,324.3	192,881.5	747,480.5	999,157.5	1,727,214.6	61,533.0	239,050.6	1	1	1
20	FOOD AND KINDRED PRODUCTS. .	r1,552.2	r21,678.0	r1,101.4	2,178.0	13,837.6	68,732.7	167,980.9	235,974.7	5,034.2	20,572.9	1	1	2
21	TOBACCO PRODUCTS	58.6	906.0	47.7	90.1	667.9	5,342.7	5,240.1	10,601.3	237.2	3,642.3	1	1	3
22	TEXTILE MILL PRODUCTS r . .	842.1	8,823.5	732.3	1,461.7	6,941.3	18,154.4	27,106.9	45,135.5	1,329.3	5,984.4	1	1	7
23	APPAREL, OTH, TEXTILE PRODS.	1,306.2	10,624.2	1,129.5	1,997.4	7,937.9	21,709.7	21,440.4	45,029.9	523.8	6,047.0	1	2	3
24	LUMBER AND WOOD PRODUCTS . .	742.5	9,042.2	632.2	1,221.0	6,989.9	20,107.0	30,063.2	49,826.3	2,067.8	5,847.4	1	2	4
25	FURNITURE AND FIXTURES . . .	r482.9	r5,361.9	397.5	769.8	r3,814.2	10,998.8	10,299.5	r21,067.0	525.6	3,388.9	2	2	3
26	PAPER AND ALLIED PRODUCTS. .	657.8	10,810.0	509.1	r1,030.3	7,635.6	27,136.3	37,807.9	65,199.4	r4,447.0	6,826.4	1	1	3
27	PRINTING AND PUBLISHING. . .	1,223.0	16,952.6	698.4	1,294.0	8,760.6	40,004.4	22,637.3	62,667.4	r2,449.0	5,230.2	1	1	2
28	CHEMICALS, ALLIED PRODUCTS .	895.0	16,515.9	552.0	1,106.0	8,849.9	70,356.0	78,291.9	147,673.7	7,976.0	17,322.5	1	1	1
29	PETROLEUM AND COAL PRODUCTS.	157.5	3,418.0	106.2	222.0	2,188.7	r28,847.0	121,452.6	r148,366.6	3,272.9	7,653.1	2	2	1
30	RUBBER, MISC. PLASTICS PROD.	753.7	10,146.4	592.9	1,150.2	6,938.7	23,112.4	24,238.5	46,847.9	2,208.2	5,949.4	1	1	4
31	LEATHER, LEATHER PRODUCTS. .	238.6	2,085.4	206.6	362.4	1,542.4	4,246.5	4,809.4	9,002.6	130.3	1,391.7	2	3	3
32	STONE, CLAY, GLASS PRODUCTS.	654.2	9,896.5	521.7	1,035.8	7,232.8	24,467.6	22,013.2	45,962.8	2,606.1	5,348.6	3	3	10
33	PRIMARY METAL INDUSTRIES r .	1,190.3	23,995.9	952.9	1,887.9	18,184.0	50,882.1	87,973.6	137,379.4	r5,129.3	22,600.0	1	1	5
34	FABRICATED METAL INDUSTRIES r	1,671.0	25,609.6	1,286.4	2,538.9	17,552.7	56,892.6	57,971.7	113,597.2	r3,345.2	18,816.0	1	1	2
35	MACHINERY, EXCEPT ELECTRIC .	2,409.8	40,681.6	1,640.5	3,266.9	24,305.4	92,527.6	77,969.6	166,470.2	6,817.0	36,780.9	1	1	2
36	ELECTRIC, ELECTRONIC EQUIP .	1,953.3	29,144.4	1,387.6	2,588.3	16,592.8	66,476.3	52,230.6	116,031.9	4,565.7	22,551.7	1	1	1
37	TRANSPORTATION EQUIPMENT . .	1,923.7	38,493.9	1,381.5	2,758.8	25,199.5	80,387.8	124,489.4	201,625.0	r6,853.8	31,096.6	1	1	1
38	INSTRUMENTS, RELATED PRODS r	601.1	9,329.1	370.8	722.9	4,561.7	24,598.1	13,852.7	37,740.2	r1,419.2	7,694.2	2	2	2
39	MISC. MANUFACTURING INDUS. .	443.0	5,014.0	338.8	641.9	3,147.9	11,934.7	11,268.1	23,015.6	595.4	4,306.4	2	2	4
--	ADMINISTRATIVE AND AUXILIARY .	1,283.7	30,358.8	-	-	-	-	-	-	-	-	1	(x)	(x)
20	FOOD AND KINDRED PRODUCTS. .	r1,552.2	r21,678.0	1,101.4	2,178.0	13,837.6	68,732.9	167,980.9	235,974.7	5,034.2	20,572.9	1	1	2
201	MEAT PRODUCTS.	317.3	4,289.0	261.6	517.9	3,307.3	9,442.0	52,260.4	61,638.7	549.5	1,847.4	1	2	14
2011	MEATPACKING PLANTS . . .	146.5	2,419.6	117.5	241.3	1,887.4	5,156.1	38,073.1	43,191.3	234.8	964.6	2	3	4
2013	SAUSAGES,OTHER PREPARED MEATS	62.0	957.0	46.6	92.9	672.1	2,364.8	7,454.9	9,830.1	136.5	502.5	4	4	5
2016	POULTRY DRESSING PLANTS. .	94.9	789.0	85.5	160.4	646.6	1,661.5	5,790.3	7,408.6	151.9	318.6	2	2	49
2017	POULTRY AND EGG PROCESSING .	13.8	123.4	12.1	25.2	101.1	259.5	942.1	1,208.7	26.2	61.6	5	4	8

319

Table 12-3 (cont.)

Code	Industry														
202	DAIRY PRODUCTS	152.6	2,161.1	85.5	180.7	1,134.8	6,908.7	23,413.7	30,209.0	423.3	1,447.6	3	3	3	5
2021	CREAMERY BUTTER	2.0	29.7	1.5	3.3	20.3	81.9	967.5	1,046.4	8.2	27.7	1	33	12	17
2022	CHEESE, NATURAL AND PROCESSED	28.3	354.0	22.6	45.2	278.4	1,221.6	6,492.8	7,654.4	99.8	664.4	3	6	6	13
2023	CONDENSED AND EVAPORATED MILK	13.2	205.9	9.6	22.9	139.5	1,018.5	2,616.6	3,591.4	57.6	244.6	4	9	4	13
2024	ICE CREAM AND FROZEN DESSERTS	19.9	277.4	12.3	24.3	151.9	1,712.6	1,678.8	2,393.7	46.3	164.4	6	8	13	13
2026	FLUID MILK	89.2	1,294.2	39.6	85.1	544.8	3,874.2	11,658.0	15,523.5	211.5	346.5	3	4	13	8
203	PRESERVED FRUITS AND VEGETABLES	243.8	2,811.4	206.0	391.1	2,164.3	9,100.5	15,665.2	24,688.3	662.9	5,319.6	2	1	3	6
2032	CANNED SPECIALTIES	26.3	345.1	21.5	42.8	265.5	1,308.9	2,051.5	3,361.0	73.1	579.2	2	3	3	7
2033	CANNED FRUITS AND VEGETABLES	82.4	939.6	71.4	135.9	761.8	2,813.6	5,338.1	8,128.3	200.4	2,536.6	3	6	5	11
2034	DEHYD. FRUITS, VEGETABLES, SOUP.	14.0	177.6	11.6	21.1	124.4	598.2	758.0	1,311.5	44.8	315.7	5	1	4	7
2035	PICKLES, SAUCES, SALAD DRESSING.	25.1	318.5	20.8	39.3	231.9	1,302.9	2,326.5	3,630.9	73.6	541.8	6	3	8	3
2037	FROZEN FRUITS AND VEGETABLES	51.9	525.2	45.7	83.5	423.6	1,531.6	2,441.3	3,959.1	119.2	938.4	8	2	8	3
2038	FROZEN SPECIALTIES	44.2	505.4	35.1	68.5	357.2	1,545.3	2,749.8	4,297.5	151.7	407.7	3	3	2	22
204	GRAIN MILL PRODUCTS	r 114.3	r 1,838.9	r 80.8	170.2	1,215.9	7,831.4	18,040.2	25,782.3	599.0	2,095.1	4	2	1	4
2041	FLOUR, OTHER GRAIN MILL PRODS.	15.3	255.5	11.2	25.2	181.3	942.5	3,281.2	4,218.3	68.4	402.0	1	3	1	7
2043	CEREAL BREAKFAST FOODS	16.3	347.2	14.1	28.6	280.0	1,859.6	1,261.3	3,095.7	92.0	214.9	3	5	3	16
2044	RICE MILLING	5.5	76.4	4.1	8.5	46.2	356.1	1,057.0	1,397.4	47.7	376.0	1	1	2	9
2045	BLENDED AND PREPARED FLOUR	r 8.6	129.0	r 6.1	13.7	83.4	435.9	743.2	1,172.4	22.7	91.0	2	1	3	19
2046	WET CORN MILLING	10.8	216.1	7.5	14.9	152.7	847.5	1,615.5	2,442.4	140.0	208.8	3	3	4	1
2047	DOG, CAT, AND OTHER PET FOOD	18.6	290.0	13.7	28.2	191.9	1,397.0	1,830.2	3,230.0	76.9	229.2	3	4	3	5
2048	PREPARED FEEDS, NEC.	39.3	524.7	24.0	51.0	280.5	1,992.6	8,251.8	10,226.1	151.3	573.1	1	5	4	10
205	BAKERY PRODUCTS	231.4	3,375.4	138.0	272.3	1,775.8	8,328.7	6,126.8	14,445.5	381.4	488.3	2	2	2	5
2051	BREAD, CAKE, RELATED PRODUCTS	184.4	2,730.2	101.9	203.5	1,318.3	6,224.6	4,515.3	10,737.6	290.4	281.5	2	2	2	6
2052	COOKIES AND CRACKERS	47.0	645.1	36.1	68.8	457.4	2,104.1	1,611.5	3,707.8	91.0	206.7	3	3	3	6
206	SUGAR, CONFECTIONERY PRODUCTS	99.1	1,329.9	80.6	156.9	978.1	4,689.6	7,898.8	12,640.3	290.5	1,719.7	1	1	2	2
2061	RAW CANE SUGAR	7.0	102.1	5.7	9.4	83.0	601.0	491.3	842.8	39.4	95.8	8	7	1	8
2062	CANE SUGAR REFINING	9.8	189.7	7.1	14.8	132.9	601.0	2,102.0	2,715.0	36.4	242.8	1	1	1	1
2063	BEET SUGAR	9.7	141.0	8.1	16.5	112.5	375.5	967.5	1,347.8	56.9	426.1	1	1	2	4
2065	CONFECTIONERY PRODUCTS	54.9	646.6	45.6	85.2	469.3	2,284.5	2,801.1	5,069.1	98.7	579.8	2	2	3	5
2066	CHOCOLATE AND COCOA PRODUCTS	10.7	156.1	8.5	16.9	111.2	686.5	1,240.0	1,902.9	31.5	236.4	3	1	1	1
2067	CHEWING GUM	7.0	94.4	5.6	10.5	69.0	468.3	296.9	762.7	27.6	138.9	1	1	1	1
207	FATS AND OILS	43.5	677.8	31.7	67.8	453.9	2,992.1	14,917.8	17,695.8	253.9	2,037.5	2	2	3	3
2074	COTTONSEED OIL MILLS	5.4	60.0	4.3	9.4	43.0	231.6	733.6	938.2	17.7	276.7	5	5	1	10
2075	SOYBEAN OIL MILLS	10.2	161.6	7.3	15.3	105.1	907.9	8,296.5	9,085.3	93.5	1,150.7	3	3	3	2
2076	VEGETABLE OIL MILLS, NEC	1.4	19.4	1.0	2.1	13.4	103.7	306.4	397.6	9.2	89.7	1	1	8	4
2077	ANIMAL AND MARINE FATS AND OILS	13.8	205.5	10.2	22.0	137.0	671.4	1,309.7	1,984.1	50.6	83.6	6	8	8	13
2079	SHORTENING AND COOKING OILS	12.8	231.2	8.9	19.0	155.0	1,077.5	4,271.6	5,290.6	82.9	435.7	1	2	2	5
208	BEVERAGES	201.9	3,436.6	103.6	207.2	1,696.1	12,328.2	17,189.1	29,342.5	1,433.1	3,605.2	2	1	3	3
2082	MALT BEVERAGES	43.9	1,051.8	31.3	61.4	752.7	3,190.5	5,177.1	8,352.5	644.7	537.5	1	1	23	29
2083	MALT	1.5	37.7	1.1	2.2	14.9	429.2	...	538.3	56.8	162.8	23	19	9	8
2084	WINES, BRANDY, BRANDY SPIRITS	12.0	177.5	7.7	14.9	99.0	764.6	1,281.7	1,954.4	77.7	769.0	9	7	9	7
2085	DISTILLED LIQUOR, EXCEPT BRANDY	15.4	260.4	12.0	23.6	190.7	1,435.6	2,995.5	1,172.1	47.3	1,172.1	2	3	2	6
2086	BOTTLED AND CANNED SOFT DRINKS	119.0	1,751.0	45.2	91.6	544.5	5,016.1	7,563.5	12,544.0	565.2	676.4	4	2	6	3
2087	FLAVORING EXTRACTS, SIRUPS, NEC.	10.1	158.1	6.3	13.5	86.0	1,661.2	1,302.0	2,957.9	41.4	287.4	5	3	3	23
209	MISC. FOODS, KINDRED PRODUCTS	148.3	1,758.0	113.7	214.0	1,111.4	7,217.0	12,468.9	19,532.2	440.8	2,012.5	2	3	2	5
2091	CANNED AND CURED SEAFOODS	16.1	178.9	14.3	25.1	144.9	471.0	1,320.9	1,800.3	35.8	393.4	3	6	6	19
2092	FRESH OR FROZEN PACKAGED FISH	36.1	318.6	31.1	54.4	232.3	954.8	2,408.2	3,355.9	58.3	541.4	4	4	3	9
2095	ROASTED COFFEE	11.4	198.9	7.2	14.8	117.6	1,748.3	4,222.5	5,944.8	60.4	379.5	3	3	2	11
2097	MANUFACTURED ICE	5.6	53.4	3.7	8.4	30.0	118.4	39.5	157.2	10.6	7.4	11	12	56	56

Source: *Annual Survey of Manufactures*, Department of Commerce, 1980, p. 9.

320

Table 12-4 Nonfinancial Business Activity   Selected Measures

NONFINANCIAL BUSINESS ACTIVITY   Selected Measures

1967 = 100; monthly and quarterly data are seasonally adjusted. Exceptions noted.

Measure	1979	1980	1981	1981 July	Aug.	Sept.	Oct.	Nov.	Dec.	1982 Jan.r	Feb.	Mar.p	Apr.e
1 **Industrial production**[1]	**152.5**	**147.0**	**151.0**	**153.9**	**153.6**	**151.6**	**149.1**	**146.3**	**143.4**	**140.7**	**142.7**	**141.5**	**140.7**
Market groupings													
2 Products, total	150.0	146.7	150.6	153.0	152.6	151.0	149.4	147.5	146.2	142.9	144.5	143.7	143.3
3 Final, total	147.2	145.3	149.5	152.1	151.5	150.0	148.9	147.2	146.3	142.8	144.2	143.5	143.3
4 Consumer goods	150.8	145.4	147.9r	150.7	149.6	147.8	146.5	144.0	142.0	139.6	141.7	141.7	142.5
5 Equipment	142.2	145.2	151.8	154.1	154.0	152.9	151.4	151.5	152.1	147.2	147.7	146.0	144.5
6 Intermediate	160.5	151.9	154.4	156.2	156.8	154.6	151.4	148.7	145.9	143.4	145.8	144.2	143.1
7 Materials	156.4	147.6	151.6	155.3	155.2	152.5	148.5	144.6	139.0	137.2	139.9	138.2	136.8
Industry groupings													
8 Manufacturing	153.6	146.7	150.4	153.2	153.2	151.1	148.2	145.0	142.0	138.5	140.8	139.9	139.4
9 Capacity utilization (percent)[1,2] Manufacturing	85.7	79.1	78.5	79.8	79.6	78.3	76.6	74.8	73.1	71.1	72.1	71.5	71.1
10 Industrial materials industries	87.4	80.0	79.9	81.9	81.7	80.0	77.7	75.5	72.4	71.4	72.6	71.6	70.8
11 Construction contracts (1977 = 100)[3]	121.0	106.0	107.0	99.0	99.0	100.0	101.0	92.0	112.0	115.0	97.0	105.0	n.a.
12 Nonagricultural employment, total[4]	136.5	137.6	139.1	139.6	139.7	139.9	139.6	139.1	138.5	138.1	138.3r	137.9r	137.6
13 Goods-producing, total	113.5	110.3	110.2	111.3	111.3	111.2	110.1	109.1	107.7	106.4	106.6	105.6r	104.8
14 Manufacturing, total	108.2	110.4	104.2	105.6	105.4	105.4	104.1	102.9	101.5	100.5	100.3	99.0	99.0
15 Manufacturing, production-worker	105.3	99.4	98.5	100.1	99.9	99.8	98.1	96.4	94.5	93.2	93.1	92.2r	91.6
16 Service-producing	149.1	152.6	155.0	155.2	155.2	155.6	155.7	155.6	155.3	155.5	155.7r	155.7r	155.6
17 Personal income, total[5]	308.5	342.9	381.5	384.0	387.8	390.9	392.8	395.6	395.6	396.5	399.1r	400.8	n.a.
18 Wages and salary disbursements	289.5	314.7	347.3	347.8	351.4	353.7	355.4	357.8	356.5	358.6	361.2r	361.4	n.a.
19 Manufacturing	248.6	261.5	288.9	292.1	294.3	294.9	293.7	292.0	288.8	289.3	292.4r	291.5	n.a.
20 Disposable personal income[5]	299.6	332.5	379.6	369.7	372.9	375.5	379.6	382.0	381.8	384.0	385.9	388.3	n.a.
21 Retail sales[6]	281.6	303.8	330.6r	333.8	338.8	338.9	331.1	333.3	334.1	326.0	334.9	332.9	337.4
Prices[7]													
22 Consumer	217.4	246.8	272.4	274.4	276.5	279.3	279.9	280.7	281.5	282.5	283.4	283.1	n.a.
23 Producer finished goods	217.7	247.0	269.8	271.8	271.5	271.5r	274.3r	274.7r	275.3	277.4	277.4r	276.9	n.a.

1. The industrial production and capacity utilization series have been revised back to January 1979.
2. Ratios of indexes of production to indexes of capacity. Based on data from Federal Reserve, McGraw-Hill Economics Department, and Department of Commerce.
3. Index of dollar value of total construction contracts, including residential, nonresidential, and heavy engineering, from McGraw-Hill Information Systems Company, F. W. Dodge Division.
4. Based on data in *Employment and Earnings* (U.S. Department of Labor). Series covers employees only, excluding personnel in the Armed Forces.
5. Based on data in *Survey of Current Business* (U.S. Department of Commerce).

6. Based on Bureau of Census data published in *Survey of Current Business.*
7. Data without seasonal adjustment, as published in *Monthly Labor Review.* Seasonally adjusted data for changes in the price indexes may be obtained from the Bureau of Labor Statistics, U.S. Department of Labor.

NOTE. Basic data (not index numbers) for series mentioned in notes 4, 5, and 6, and indexes for series mentioned in notes 3 and 7 may also be found in the *Survey of Current Business.*
Figures for industrial production for the last two months are preliminary and estimated, respectively.

Source: *Federal Reserve Bulletin,* May, 1982, p. A46

investments that will participate in the greatest growth. However, growth does not always mean profitability, and the investor must be careful to choose profitable industries and firms.

Other indexes contained in Table 12-4, such as nonagricultural employment, indicate how many people are employed producing goods and services and are therefore receiving wages that will eventually be expended. National growth depends upon an employed population both producing and buying goods and services. The index of total retail sales provides some indication of how freely the consumer is spending and reflects consumer confidence in the immediate future. When retail sales decline, it can serve as a warning, indicating an economic slowdown because consumers either have less to spend or are less willing to spend what they have. Similarly, construction contracts reflect the level of building in the economy from period to period. When the building level falters, the effects are often reflected throughout the economy.

Other indexes, such as the consumer price index, have been of particular concern in the mid-1970s because they reflect the degree of inflation the economy has experienced. For example, the consumer price index of 281.5 at the end of 1981 indicates a 181.5 percent increase in prices over 1967. The economy is improved only when the increase in production or any GNP account is greater than the rate of inflation. In other words, real economic growth must always be measured in terms of noninflated figures. Therefore, most economic analyses should contain adjustments for all increases in prices as reflected in the appropriate price indexes. Increases in the consumer price index mean a loss of purchasing power for the consumer and a false indication of economic growth. Also, inflation rates will vary within product categories. For example, fuel costs might rise at a greater rate than rents. Expressing the GNP in terms of deflated constant 1967 dollars (or some other base year) reduces the distortion that inflation creates.

Major Considerations in Predicting Industry Performance

Several factors are essential in analyzing any industry because they provide important indications of how well the industry is likely to perform in the future.

The first of these factors is the examination of the historical performance of the industry under consideration. In particular, sales and earnings performance are of special importance because they play a key role in determining the market value and dividend performance of any given stock. An additional factor is just how long the industry has existed in its present organizational state. An industry that has not proved its ability to withstand adverse economic situations might falter or fail under difficult economic conditions or increased competition. The seasoned company is generally best able to meet the impact of changes in the economic climate.

Historical Performance

Historical data can also be important in providing the bases for calculating the magnitude and stability of an industry's sales and earnings. Such data can answer a question such as, How much variance in sales and earnings has the industry experienced in the past? Even though average performance may be adequate, the industry might be subject to great variations in earnings. Finally, the cost structure of an industry must be considered. The investor needs to know how much of an industry's total debt is fixed. The higher the proportion of fixed debt, the larger the sales volume necessary for the industry to reach the break-even point. Even though it is not always correct to assume that historical trends will continue into the future, an analysis of this sort provides an important basis for making performance predictions.

Product Stability

The degree of product stability within an industry is another factor that must be considered. Whereas historical data indicate the past demand for the industry's product, the nature of the product and its technological sophistication must be examined to determine whether future demand will remain stable or change rapidly. For example, industries based on fad products, such as the Hula-Hoop, will vanish quickly. However, more stable industries such as the steel industry or the chemical industry have long-established product demands. However, even these more stable industries have fluctuating profitability from year to year primarily because of changes in the price structure and to a lesser extent in the demand for their products.

An industry must always strive for technological advances because superior substitutes are continuously entering the marketplace and can drive out firms or substantial segments of an industry that have not kept up. For example, the demand for gaslights was greatly reduced by the introduction of electric lights. The steam locomotive industry has disappeared altogether. Certainly, investment in an industry likely to experience this type of decline would be a poor choice. The investor must continuously examine the likelihood that an industry's product line will be subject to replacement by superior products or shifts in consumer demand.

Competitive Influences

The analyst will also be concerned with the degree to which the industry's market is protected against competition. Several important factors will reduce the entry of new firms into the existing industrial market.

If the consumer has developed a definite preference for the products of an existing firm or group of firms, this can result in a competitive advantage for the firms' more popular products. When this is the case, new firms entering the identical market will most likely be unable to charge a price comparable to that charged by existing firms or will be forced to spend a great deal on sales promotion and advertising in order to establish an acceptable market share and price level. Even in those industries where entry is not difficult, brand name distinction can create an advantage that discourages competition.

Existing firms may be able to produce a product at a lower cost than a competitor because of absolute cost advantages arising from patent ownership, control of key resources, greater ability to obtain funds and equipment, or superior management skills. Some cost advantages may arise because of economics of scale. This implies that total costs decrease with larger levels of production. Therefore, existing firms likely to be producing at high levels of output may be able to control a large share of the market. A competitor attempting to enter the marketplace will be at a cost disadvantage unless it can gain a large market share in a relatively short period of time. Generally, the less susceptible an industry is to competitive inroads, the safer the industry and its individual companies are as investment vehicles.

Labor Considerations

An investor must also examine factors affecting the labor force. Labor conditions can greatly influence an analyst's forecast of business conditions for a particular industry. When labor performs a large or critical part of the production process, the investor must be concerned with the effect of a strike. The history of labor negotiations within an industry can be of some help in determining the degree of difficulty that companies may face in negotiating contracts. Industries with large fixed costs, resulting from high levels of capital required for plant and equipment, will experience severe losses in the event of an extended strike because fixed costs continue regardless of the level of production or revenue. In industries with low fixed costs, some fixed costs will still be incurred during a strike, and the loss of customers can greatly harm the industry.

Government Intervention

An investor must evaluate the government's policy toward the particular industry under examination, because government involvement can greatly influence the industry in a number of ways. It can promote the industry through research grants, favorable tax legislation, tariffs designed to restrict foreign competition, and a number of additional legislative and executive actions that protect the industry, reduce its costs, and stimulate investment in it. The American textile industry, for example, is greatly influenced by the degree of legislative protection it receives in the form of import tariffs.

On the other hand, the government may burden an industry with restrictive regulations concerning the ecology, safety, size of firms, and pricing. The railroad and natural gas industries provide two more recent examples of how government intervention in an industry can critically affect private profit performance. It has been alleged that the government's inability to pass appropriate legislation has negatively affected the short-run performance of certain industries.

Nevertheless, government intervention has aided greatly in the stabilization of certain industries that could otherwise become quite chaotic. For example, the airline industry has its routes regulated so that all air carriers are not flying between the most profitable city pairs only. Regulation of utilities is important to ensure that only one electric utility operates in a particular geographic area. This eliminates the potential problem of having four or five different companies running their own sets of electrical wires down each street, each providing service within the same community.

Investment Decision

All the factors just discussed must be considered in light of the current market price of the stock and its earning potential. Future earnings are difficult to predict, but the current price-earnings ratio (the P/E ratio) will give some indication of how well the current market price of the securities within an industry reflects investor confidence and expectation in terms of total future returns. For example, an industry or firm might indicate substantial potential for future growth, but there is a point at which the prices of the securities within that industry are relatively too high to justify their purchase. Conversely, the securities of an industry likely to experience only modest gains might be reasonable purchases if their price is low enough and the estimated future returns are subject to little probable variation.

The investor must examine the industry to determine whether market psychology has overvalued or undervalued the group relative to the market and the industry's ability for growth. The interaction of investors and speculators in the marketplace can, many times, drive prices exorbitantly high or low relative to their true value. Much of the market movement is a result of changes in investors' perception of what a firm or industry is really worth, rather than a result of changes in the fundamental factors likely to affect an industry's future earnings.

Many times stock prices will run up in response to particular industry developments. For example, the introduction of the Wankel engine caused a number of related securities within certain industries to jump in price. Groups of investors and speculators concluded that these industries were on the brink of substantial growth because of the new engine. However, after certain information was obtained about the engine's reliability and the ease with which it could be introduced into the production system of existing manufacturing operations, the market prices of these industries' stocks returned to more modest levels in recognition of the long-run impact of such a product introduction.

The investor attempting to ascertain the desirability of a purchase in any industry must discern how much of the existing price truly reflects the opportunity for future earnings and how much reflects speculative demand. Investors should also consider such diverse factors as how consumer preferences and income distributions might change and how much of an influence future foreign competition is likely to have on the introduction of certain products. It is only through systematic appraisal of these factors that an investor can expect to make an accurate industrial analysis leading to an intelligent investment decision.

Patterns of Industrial Performance

Business Cycle

An investor should be aware that industries often exhibit identifiable and somewhat predictable patterns of growth and decline over varying periods. Even though it may prove impossible to predict the exact magnitude and timing of major changes, knowledge of their existence will at least help the investor to identify the current stages of industrial development and to understand the dynamics involved.

One pattern of growth is not related to the periodic and somewhat predictable swings in the general level of business activity. The pattern is that for **growth industries.** Their earnings increase at high levels, usually without much variation in response to changes in the business cycle. Major technological improvements or the marketing of important new products or services often sparks this type of growth. Computers and dry-process photocopiers have exhibited this type of growth over the past several decades. Investors have found the high-growth industries to be of particular interest partly because they provide a hedge against cyclical fluctuations. These industries have decreased the necessity of accurate timing of purchases for the investor because their stock prices do not tend to follow any business cycle.

Cyclical industries, however, display growth patterns directly related to the general business cycle. When the economy is in general expansion, these industries follow such expansion closely; in times of economic contraction, these industries suffer a comparable decline. This is largely because the purchase of certain goods related to these industries can be delayed until the economy improves. This is the case with consumer and manufactured durables and applies to a significant degree to income elasticity of demand.

On the other hand, some industries are called **defensive industries** because demand for their products remains rather stable regardless of cyclical declines in the business cycle. Because of this, they may be desirable as income investments rather than as investments for capital gains. At times, earnings of defensive industries may actually increase in a period of general decline. Food and utility items are the two common examples of defensive industries because income elasticity for their products is generally low and earnings of representative companies are relatively stable.

It is possible for some industries to display both a growth and a cyclical pattern, growing steadily for a time and then displaying patterns of earnings performance that will vary with the economy. Often, major technological improvements stimulate new periods of growth. Obviously, the analyst must recognize that such diverse growth patterns exist and are closely related to the business cycle. Establishing which historical pattern best fits the industry presently under consideration can help the investor to avoid placing funds in that industry if a material decline in earnings is likely to occur or to avoid missing a good opportunity if expansion is likely.

The introduction of the television receiver had wide market acceptance in the 1950s as the price of the product was reduced, thus stimulating demand. Several firms within that market experienced rapid expansion in sales and earnings during the period. However, by the late 1960s, demand for both black and white and color television sets had reached a point where further demand corresponded closely to the business cycle.

Industrial Life Cycle

Often an industry will display a distinct growth pattern over its history called the **industrial life cycle.** This cycle is graphically portrayed in Figure 12-5 and is divided into three primary stages: infancy, growth, and maturity.

INFANCY PERIOD. During the infancy stage, demand for the industry's product increases rapidly. New firms enter the market to seek their share of the profit. The competition is heavy, and prices tend to be unstable. As the number of firms increases, prices and profits tend to fall with higher levels of production. Many inefficient firms fail because of heavy start-up costs and price competition. Large losses are not uncommon for many firms during their initial years of operation. These firms are often absorbed by more successful survivors if they are having financial difficulties but retain some technological advantages. Consequently, only a few firms of the best quality remain, and some may begin to dominate the industry as the infancy period comes to an end. Because of the high risk of failure, speculators rather than investors tend to supply the needed capital during this period.

GROWTH PERIOD. During the growth period, growth continues, but at a slower, more orderly rate than during the infancy period. The market tends to be dominated by the firms that emerged from the infancy period

Figure 12-5 Industrial Life Cycle

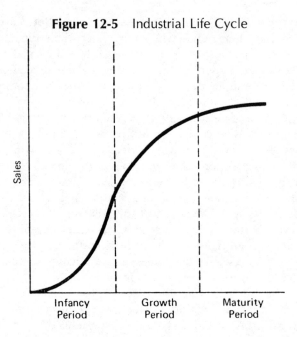

with a reasonable amount of marketing and financial strength. These firms are often larger and usually display stronger and more stable capital structures that allow them to begin to pay regular dividends and to expand their operations. Competition continues, but the established firms have generally demonstrated their ability to compete, survive, and grow. The length of this period can range from several years to many decades. For these reasons, this stage is sometimes called the **period of investment opportunity.** The industry continues to grow, but the growth is much more predictable and less subject to uncertainty and wide fluctuations. The investors are less likely to lose their entire investment because of business failure, and they can still enjoy the benefits of the industry's growth.

MATURITY PERIOD. During the maturity stage, the industry's rate of growth declines to a more moderate level. In some cases, growth may cease entirely, and total industrial output may even decline. The industry loses its capacity to grow. In this period, an industry's growth may well fail to keep pace with increases in the GNP and may suffer most when GNP declines. However, some industries may actually experience a new growth because of important technological innovations.

The final transition to the maturity stage may be difficult to discern over a short period of time, but, in general, an investor will want to withdraw funds when this stage begins.

Although these three stages are generalizations and do not apply in every circumstance, they describe a sufficient number of industrial growth patterns to justify careful, cautious consideration in selecting industries for investment. For example, many analysts conclude that the auto industry has gone through all three stages of the industrial life cycle and that the maturity stage turned into a more stagnant stage in the early 1970s. It is difficult for the industry to maintain its historic growth rate since World War II because there are only so many automobiles that a family unit is willing and able to purchase. Furthermore, the energy crisis of the early 1970s is changing the type of automobile required. Therefore, the automobile manufacturing companies have had to make rapid and expensive changes to respond to market demand.

Factors Influencing Industry Growth and Decline

A number of factors contribute to the end of a firm's growth cycle and the beginning of its decline. The factors that can influence a company negatively include increasingly higher labor costs, improved technology or automation, changes in the social habits of the buying public, government regulations and changes initiated by legislation, and market saturation. These factors often begin to develop early in an industry's life cycle, but they may or may not materially affect industrial profits and render the industry obsolete during its growth stage.

If demand for the industry's product declines, a price reduction may help to maintain the product's competitive position. However, high labor costs may prevent a company from taking such action. Broad changes in social habits may cause the industry's product to become unpopular, and substitute products will fill demand. Legislative action by the government, such as tax credits and rate regulations, can significantly affect certain industries. These few factors serve to emphasize that an industry's growth is likely to be limited unless it successfully adapts to alterations in its own structural makeup and key environmental changes.

The significant technological improvements that are often the very basis for an industry's rapid expansion tend to be concentrated in the early stages of the industry's growth. Technological improvements may drastically change the original product, and, therefore, primary demand for the original product can be greatly altered and increased. However, an industry generally reaches a point when further enhancement of demand is unlikely to occur and future growth becomes limited. For example, the once costly pocket calculator, which sold to a narrow market, increased its market position because of reductions brought about by improvements in microelectronics.

Industries that expand more rapidly than the national economy, partly because of cost advantages, sometimes find their ability to reduce total costs limited. Many times, the cost of factor inputs beyond their control will not experience similar reductions. To this degree, a slower rate of economic growth retards industrial expansion. New industries that produce directly competitive substitutes or that compete for materials may develop. Finally, there are practical limits to how much of the product each customer can consume. For these and other reasons, it is unlikely that increased growth will continue for long periods of time for products attempting to serve a well-defined market.

Tools for Assessing Industrial Growth and Predicting Future Trends

An investor has a critical interest in the answers to two questions: How has an industry grown in the past? How well can it be expected to grow in the future? The investor is interested in how an industry has grown in comparison with its own past sales and earnings history and how its performance compares with the growth of GNP or other relevant aggregate statistics, such as national income or disposable personal income. Throughout this process, the investor will be especially interested in determining which industries have either grown as fast as or faster than GNP, because they may offer the best investment potential.

To begin this process, a **sales index** can be constructed that compares a representative base year with all others, thus expressing sales as a percentage. For instance, if base-year sales equal $200 million and 1976 sales equal $250 million, the 1976 index would equal 250/200, or 125 percent. This index can be quickly compared with GNP index figures to reveal how the particular industry's growth compares with the growth of GNP. The same comparison can be made with other measures of the national economy, such as the indexes of national and disposable personal income. Furthermore, sales can be expressed as a percent of GNP.

These relationships can be portrayed graphically through the process of regression and correlation analysis. Regression analysis examines two variables (such as GNP and sales), plots the relationship of these variables at definite points in time on a graph, and mathematically constructs a regression line that best fits or describes the general pattern implied by these points. This creates a clear and simple picture of how sales have been related to GNP and implies how they might be related in the future if the pattern remains constant. Such an analysis can be accurate for short predictions but is less reliable for longer periods.

Multiple regression analysis relates the effect of several variables interacting on some item such as sales. Computers are often utilized to construct regression lines. Standard & Poor's utilizes this process in the course of its industrial survey. Table 12-5 illustrates the types of indexes that are constructed by regression analysis. The construction of these indexes and regression lines provides important information. They indicate how quickly an industry is growing, both in absolute terms and in comparison with closely selected business indexes. How stable this growth pattern is can be esti-

Table 12-5

Home Furnishings Industry Statistics

	[1]Production Indexes (adjusted)				[2]Retail (season. adj.)				[3]Value of Ship. Mattresses, Bedsprings and Dual-purpose Sleep Furniture		[3]Wholesale Price Indexes			
	Total Home Goods		Carpeting and Furniture		Sales Furniture & Appliances		Inventories Furniture and Appliances				Household Furniture		Floor Coverings	
	(1967 = 100)				(million dollars)				(million dollars)		(1967 = 100)			
	1975	1976	1975	1976	1975	1976	1975	1976	1974	1975	1975	1976	1975	1976
Jan.	117.5	126.8	135.1	139.2	2,040	2,273	5,026	4,789	81.11	67.18	145.4	150.8	123.8	130.3
Feb.	114.0	127.0	132.3		2,051		4,861		78.40	69.74	145.5	150.5	123.6	130.8
Mar.	112.3		127.9		2,046		4,659		85.24	77.11	145.3	150.8	123.6	130.8
Apr.	115.9		127.8		2,132		4,545		88.13	85.05	145.4		123.4	
May	117.8		128.6		2,139		4,520		96.68	85.35	145.3		123.1	
June	118.8		131.1		2,168		4,565		91.02	84.77	145.3		123.1	
July	121.0		135.5		2,171		4,677		836.0	82.47	145.4		123.9	
Aug.	121.9		136.0		2,202		4,686		100.79	98.39	145.5		126.6	
Sept.	125.0		137.6		2,214		4,701		91.56	101.66	146.1		126.8	
Oct.	123.6		137.9		2,241		4,749		99.72	108.81	147.8		126.9	
Nov.	124.2		139.3		2,349		4,718		73.16	82.28	148.5		126.9	
Dec.	124.5		137.2		2,337		4,798		64.51	77.43	149.6		127.2	
Year	120.1		133.7		20,090				1,033.92	1,020.24	146.3		124.9	

[a]Includes carpets, furniture, major household appliances, radio and television.

Source: Standard & Poor's Corporation, Outlook, Volume 54, No. 23.

mated. They also show how cyclical the industry is and allow for some prediction of future levels of growth. However, it is important to make certain that the firms and periods selected are representative of the industry under consideration. If this is the case, the performance of individual firms can be assessed against industrial data.

Predicting Sales

An analysis of appropriate indexes can lead directly to a reasonable estimate of future sales for an industry. For example, sales can be estimated as a fixed percent of GNP, plus or minus the range of deviation from historical data. If GNP increased by 6 percent and sales constitute 2 percent of GNP, then sales for the industry would increase proportionately. Another method of predicting future sales is to extrapolate the regression line into the future. A simpler method is to construct a trend line of past sales in relation to the expectation of GNP or even more precisely with the appropriate component of GNP. Finally, some estimate of per capita sales could be made. If future per capita sales could be forecast and combined with a forecast of future population, total sales also could be estimated. For example, if each American expected to spend an average of $1.45 on toothbrushes by 1990 and the population in 1990 is estimated at 260 million, the industry's sales should equal approximately $377 million.

It is important to be very careful in extrapolating historical data and in using historical data as a rigid measurement, because industries from time to time have experienced patterns that fluctuate from historical data. Nevertheless, for most estimates of an industry's profitability, which is the main determinant of security prices, it is necessary to have a reliable method of predicting sales. Sales are the focal point for all forecasting for an industry or company.

Input-Output Analysis: A Tool for Predicting Demand

Input-output analysis is a massive statistical resource that can be used to estimate the inputs necessary to produce a given output and the composition of that total output in terms of product categories and demand markets. The federal government has compiled detailed data on these items for all major American industries. In Table 12-6 the Coal column indicates that for every dollar used to produce coal, inputs of $.60 in labor, $.20 in electricity, and $.20 in chemicals are required. The Coal row indicates that $.70 of coal must be produced to satisfy the needs of the electric power industry and that $.20 worth of coal will be required by the chemical industry. The government tables are much more detailed but similarly constructed.

Table 12-6
Input-Output Table

Type of Input	Distribution of Industrial Output		
	Electricity	Coal	Chemicals
Electricity	$ .05	$ .20	$ .30
Coal	.70	—	.20
Chemicals	.10	.20	.35
Labor	.15	.60	.15
Total	$1.00	$1.00	$1.00

This information is important to industry analysis because it allows the investor to estimate the effects of a change in output on all those industries that supply the necessary input. Furthermore, if an industry's output increases, the distribution of that additional output can be estimated for the various product categories that require it. The importance of input-output analysis increases as industries become more interdependent in an expanding industrial climate that is becoming more technologically oriented.

Use of Investment Service Materials

Much of the discussion in this chapter has dealt with general theories, principles, and patterns. Commercial investment services regularly publish professionally produced industry-wide analyses or surveys and supplement them with investment opinions and suggestions. This information is extremely helpful to the individual investor in making prudent investment decisions. These surveys vary in their degrees of comprehensiveness and sophistication and are thus tailored to meet the needs of many kinds of investors. Most of these sources assess an industry's future outlook and describe its magnitude and economic importance. They outline an industry's mode of operations, its current difficulties, and the probable developments that may significantly affect its performance over the next several years. These surveys, then, describe what the industry does, how it is classified, the breadth of its activity, the extent of its profitability, and its most probable future growth potential. Because this information is important to the investment process, the individual investor should become familiar with the various sources of industry analysis provided by investment services.

Sources of industry evaluation and opinion are especially valuable to the individual investor because she or he is generally unable to construct the vast amounts of data necessary for an accurate appraisal. The services available to the individual investor employ large staffs of financial analysts who specialize in a limited number of industries, and the reports are based on sophisticated industrial and economic analyses.

As was mentioned in the beginning of this chapter, a great deal of public investment information is available. In addition to government publications, private companies such as Moody's, Standard & Poor's, and Value Line generally provide reasonably sophisticated industrial and economic analyses for the average investor. Nevertheless, the investor should supplement these data with analyses obtained from brokerage house studies or independent research organizations.

Table 12-7
Mutual Funds' Portfolio Diversification
(Percent of Total Common Stock by Industries, 1970, 1975, 1980)

	1970	1975	1980
Agricultural Equipment	0.14%	0.41%	0.88%
Aircraft Mfg. & Aerospace	0.90	1.71	2.26
Air Transport	1.47	1.91	1.32
Auto & Accessories (excl. Tires)	3.15	2.42	1.01
Building Materials & Equip.	4.31	2.41	1.85
Chemicals	5.46	8.15	5.51
Communications (TV, Radio, Motion Pictures)	0.90	1.90	1.57
Containers	0.44	0.46	0.28
Drugs & Cosmetics	5.96	8.04	6.96
Elec. Equip. & Electronics (excl. TV & Radio)	6.45	4.46	8.52
Foods & Beverages	4.59	3.89	2.52
Financial (incl. Banks & Insurance)	9.12	7.21	7.56
Machinery	1.42	1.72	1.56
Metals & Mining	3.60	3.12	3.00
Office Equipment	7.53	7.87	7.47
Oil	10.41	14.20	22.39
Paper	1.69	3.03	1.87
Public Utilities (incl. Telephone & Natural Gas)	10.52	5.48	4.83
Railroad	1.43	1.55	1.21
Railroad Equipment	0.30	0.30	0.58
Retail Trade	5.27	3.46	3.60
Rubber (incl. Tires)	1.75	1.13	0.32
Steel	0.24	2.07	1.22
Textiles	0.48	0.46	0.13
Tobacco	2.05	2.41	1.62
Miscellaneous*	10.42	10.23	9.96
TOTALS	100.00%	100.00%	100.00%

Note: Composite industry investments drawn from the portfolios of 40 of the largest investment companies as of the end of calendar year 1980 whose total net assets represented 41.0% of total net assets of all Institute member companies excluding all short term funds.
*Includes diversified industrial companies not readily assignable to specific industry categories.

Source: 1981 Mutual Fund Fact Book, p. 29.

Many investors are interested in what the professional money managers are doing at a particular time. For example, the billions of dollars invested by mutual funds, pension funds, bank trust departments, and insurance companies can indicate where the professional money managers believe the best opportunities for overall returns can be obtained. These data are published frequently in the financial literature; the most popular data are compiled by the Investment Company Institute. Each quarter mutual funds report their holdings, major purchases, and sales. From these reports, investors can ascertain indications of any shifts in investment emphasis by these professional managers. Table 12-7 lists the major industry holdings of institutional investors.

It must be noted that, although many of the large financial institutions employ large and well-paid staffs of financial analysts, many of their performance records have been quite disappointing. In other words, the mere presence of a professional staff does not guarantee successful performance in the securities market. Nevertheless, knowledge of the important economic and industry data can significantly help individual investors to reduce various investment risks substantially and achieve their investment goals.

KEY TERMS

coincident indicators	forecasts
conglomerate	gross national product (GNP)
consumer price index	growth industry
cyclical industry	industrial life cycle
defensive industry	industry analysis
diffusion index	input-output analysis
Dow-Jones averages	lagging indicators
econometric model	leading indicators
economic analysis	period of investment opportunity
economic indicators	sales index
financial information	Standard Industrial Classifications

QUESTIONS

1. What are the fundamental questions of economic and industrial analysis?
2. What is the GNP?
3. What are barometric indicators?
4. How do economic indicators work?
5. How can an indicator display changes in direction before the general economy changes?
6. What are econometric models?
7. How is an industry defined?
8. What are the Dow-Jones classifications?

9. What are the standard industrial classifications?
10. What is the importance of the consumer price index?
11. What are the most important factors to an investor when analyzing an industry?
12. What other factors are important in influencing an investor's decision concerning an industry?
13. Describe the three major growth patterns.
14. What is the industrial life cycle? Describe the three primary stages of the cycle.
15. What is input-output analysis?

SELECTED READINGS

AMBACHTSHEER, KEITH P. "U.S. Stock Prices and Interest Rates: The Three to Five Year View." *Financial Analysts Journal*, November–December 1977, 38–46.

BUTLER, HARTMAN L., JR., and J. DEVON ALLEN. "The Dow Jones Industrial Average Reexamined." *Financial Analysts Journal*, November–December 1979, 23–30.

FERRETTI, ANDREW P. "The Economist's Role." *Financial Analysts Journal*, January–February 1969, 35.

GRAY, WILLIAM S., III. "Developing a Long-Term Outlook for the U.S. Economy and Stock Market." *Financial Analysts Journal*, July–August 1979, 29–39.

LIVINGSTON, MILES. "Industry Movements of Common Stocks." *Journal of Finance*, June 1977, 861–874.

MOAR, ROY E. "Economics and Investment Analysis." *Financial Analysts Journal*, November–December 1971, 63.

PALMER, MICHAEL. "Money Supply and Stock Prices." *Financial Analysts Journal*, July–August 1970, 19.

REILLY, FRANK K., and EUGENE DRZYCIMSKI. "Alternative Industry Performance and Risk." *Journal of Financial and Quantitative Analysis*, June 1974, 423–446.

REILLY, FRANK K., and EUGENE F. DRZYCIMSKI. "Aggregate Market Earnings Multipler over Stock Market Cycles and Business Cycles." *Mississippi Valley Journal of Business and Economics*, Winter 1974–1975. 14–36.

WENGLOWSKI, GARY M. "Industry Profit Analysis—A Progress Report and Some Predictions." *The Economic Framework for Investors*. Charlottesville, Va. Financial Analysts Research Foundation, 1975, 19–30.

Regular reading of the following publications is also recommended: *Barron's, Federal Reserve Bulletin, Forbes, Moody's Industrial Manual, The New York Times, Value Line Investment Survey*, and *The Wall Street Journal*.

13

Market Analysis and Timing

Throughout this text the emphasis has been on the fundamentalist's approach to the market, the approach that relies upon economic and financial statistics and information as the bases for investment decisions. The fundamentalist investigates a company's financial statements, dividend records, growth, management ability and policies, competitive forces, and the many related factors discussed in Chapter 6. This chapter centers on an alternative approach to predicting stock price behavior: **technical analysis.** Technical analysis is often used as a supplement to a fundamental analysis, rather than as a substitute for it. However, those who are pure technicians concentrate on price and volume movements to determine investment decisions. Nevertheless, technical analysis can, and often does, confirm the conclusions of fundamental analysis.

The technician bases decisions on the forces of supply and demand as reflected in the price patterns and volume of trading in the market. Technicians do not consider the qualitative aspects that are central to the fundamentalist's approach. Technicians are concerned neither with the financial condition of a firm nor with its earning power. They simply study the patterns of price and volume and use these trends to predict whether prices are moving higher or lower and by what degree. In essence, technicians believe that all factors known by the participants in the marketplace will be reflected in the price movement of the security and that a trend may exist that will persist for some period of time.

Most fundamental analysts generally look to the broad-based technical indicators to supplement their analysis and to confirm their beliefs. This chapter will examine some of the better-known technical market theories and tools used by the technician. Although not directly related to technical analysis, timing approaches to investment decisions are significant. Therefore, a discussion of different approaches to timing of the investment decision is included in this chapter.

MARKET ANALYSIS

Market analysis is important to the technician who wants to determine the overall direction of the market before proceeding to the technical analysis of individual stocks. Generally, technical analysts have a higher degree of accuracy in forecasting the trends of the overall market than individual securities within that market. Therefore, the analysts are concerned with the overall direction of the market because they know that a well-diversified portfolio of individual security issues generally reflects the overall movement of the market.

The Dow Theory

Market analysis originated around the turn of the twentieth century when Charles Dow formulated the Dow theory. Dow, who was editor of the *Wall Street Journal*, felt that the stock market followed definite trends and that these trends could be identified by following the movements of a certain group of stocks that were representative of the market. The Dow theory has become more sophisticated through the years, but Dow's idea that a group of major representative stocks could be used to follow the movement of the entire market is still its basic premise. Dow stated that the market is always to be considered as having three types of movements, all operating at the same time: (1) the general day-to-day movement; (2) the short-swing movement, running from 2 weeks to 9 months or more; and (3) the main movement, lasting for at least 4 years.

Although the Dow theory has often been applied to predicting the movements of individual stocks, it was originally intended for use in forecasting future movements of the entire market. At its simplest, the theory states that future movement of the market can be predicted by examining past movements of the Dow-Jones Industrial Average of 30 stocks and the Dow-Jones Transportation Average of 20 stocks. By examining past momentum and amplitude of the movements of these averages, the Dow theorists believe that they can predict what the market for all stocks will do.

The difficulty in the theory lies in being able to discriminate among the three types of movements that occur in these averages. The term **primary trend** refers to the movement lasting at least 4 years. When prices are rising, this is termed a **bull market;** during periods of declining prices, it is termed a **bear market.** However, the exact length of the primary trend cannot be forecast in advance with any high degree of accuracy. Nevertheless, Dow theorists, without exception, believe that investors should always strive to follow the course of primary trends.

The **secondary reaction** (movements lasting 2 weeks to 9 months) is found within bull and bear markets and will correct from one-third to two-thirds of a previous market advance or decline. Investors should generally not seek to profit from secondary reactions. The risks are inherently high because these reactions generally take a position against the major market move.

Dow theorists believe that the day-to-day variations in price contain no information whatsoever and should be completely ignored because they reflect trading patterns caused by a wide variety of factors.

Different Market Phases

Dow-theory bull markets are broken down into three phases. The first stage is the **recovery stage** during which prices begin to rise from very depressed levels. The second stage can last a long time and it usually contains the largest advance in stock prices, which are responding to favorable economic conditions. The third stage of a bull market occurs when prices overreact and stocks become overvalued in relation to their intrinsic value or other market measurements. During this third stage, Dow theory signals announce the end of the bull market and the beginning of a bear market. However, many investors get caught up in the rapidly rising prices and fail to recognize the potential for adverse price movements.

According to the Dow theory, a bear market also has three stages. In the first stage, market prices fall. This is a reaction to the overinflated prices of the third stage of a bull market. In the second phase, business conditions begin to match the performance of the stock market and fears of economic uncertainty begin to spread. Stock prices begin to reach low levels that were thought impossible only a short time earlier. As the economic decline continues, an ever increasing concern spreads throughout the investment community, and individuals begin to sell heavily, creating the third stage of a bear market, during which prices reach extremely low levels in relation to the stock's intrinsic value. At these levels, the Dow theory signals the end of the bear market and the possible conditions for a bull market to begin.

Dow Theory Signals

There are a number of signals that the Dow theory gives to show the beginning and the end of a primary trend. A bull market is said to begin when the Dow-Jones averages rise from a bottom to a secondary high, fall to a low that is higher than the previous low, and then rise until the previous high is exceeded. Bear market signals occur when the Dow-Jones averages fall from a high, reach a reactionary low, rise to a point that is lower than the previous high, and then fall farther than the previous low point. These indicate that the market's strength is either increasing or subsiding.

Dow theorists believe that the Dow-Jones Industrial and Transportation Averages must have similar patterns in order to produce a valid Dow signal. Dow signals need not appear in both averages at the same time, but both averages should move in the same general direction. When the two averages do signify a trend reversal, a Dow confirmation has been given and is many times referred to in the financial press.

If one average does not confirm the other, Dow theorists are alerted to the **possible** reversal in a primary trend. In such cases, they may wait until the other average confirms the change. Without this confirmation, they interpret the primary trend as remaining intact.

Criticism of the Dow Theory

Although there are many advocates of the Dow theory, there are also many critics. If the Dow theory worked perfectly, all investors would base their decisions on it. Some of the problem areas are as follows:

1. Price averages do not always make clear-cut formations on the chart. Thus, distinguishing between primary and secondary movements is not as easy as the theory suggests. There are many differences among Dow theorists about what is happening.
2. Studies indicate that buying all securities used to plot the Dow-Jones Industrial Average and holding them will achieve better results than trading the same securities based on the primary turns in the market. The difference in results is basically in the brokerage costs of buying and selling.
3. Others detract from the Dow theory by saying that it lacks precision in forecasting price movements, especially in forecasting the peaks and troughs in the cycle of stock market prices. The theory also lacks precision because it fails to indicate which securities to buy and sell.
4. Also questionable is the relevance of the transportation average. When the Dow theory was originated, the rail industry played a much greater part in the national economy than it does today. Even with the substitution of six airlines and three trucking stocks for nine previous railroad companies in the transportation average, it is not certain that the use of the average performance of twenty companies with very special revenue and cost aspects is likely to help an investor to predict accurately what stocks generally will do.

Regardless of the criticisms that have been leveled against the Dow theory, the investor might want to know what it forecasts for the future, if for no other reasons than that so many people continue to base investment decisions on it and that, historically, it has had a reasonable record of forecasting.

MARKET INDEXES

Dow-Jones Averages

The Dow-Jones averages are the best-known stock indexes, and as such, are the most influential among investors. When people refer to the Dow-Jones averages, they are usually referring to the Dow-Jones Industrial Average (DJIA). However, there are three other averages: the Dow-Jones Transportation Average (DJTA), the Dow-Jones Utility Average (DJUA), and the Composite Average of the stocks of the three averages. The DJIA is made up of 30 stocks, the DJTA includes 20 stocks, and the DJUA is based on 15 stocks; thus, the Composite Average reflects the movement of 65 stocks.

Firms selected for inclusion in the averages are leaders in their respective industries and are representative of the larger firms in those industries. The companies used in the averages are changed when it is felt that a company on the list no longer reflects the conditions in its industry as well as another company might, or when an industry loses its position of influence in the economy, in which case some of the firms in the average will be replaced. For example, until 1970, the transportation average was called the **railroad average.** Because of the decline of the railroads' influence on the economy, nine railroads were deleted from the average and six airlines and three trucking companies were added. Table 13-1 lists the 65 stocks that make up the three averages.

COMPUTATION OF DOW-JONES AVERAGES. The calculation of Dow-Jones averages uses a price-weighted approach. For each average, the index is simply the arithmetic mean of the stock prices of the constituent companies. Originally, the computation of the Dow-Jones Industrial Average was determined by adding the individual stock prices and dividing the total by 30. However, when a stock split, 30 could no longer be used as the divisor. The owner of one share of stock selling at 60 that split two-for-one still held $60 worth of stock, but the price was $30 per share. If 30 were still used as the divisor, the Dow-Jones Average would drop without a corresponding decrease in the value of any of its stocks. To rectify this situation, the divisor was determined by adjusting for stock splits. Once this figure was determined, it was used to divide the new total to get the appropriate average.

Below is a simplified illustration of the determination of the divisor. Suppose that there are three firms making up a stock average: companies

Table 13-1
Stocks Included in Dow-Jones Averages

Thirty stocks used in Dow-Jones Industrial Average

Allied Corp.	General Electric	Owens-Illinois
Aluminum Co.	General Foods	Procter & Gamble
Amer Brands	General Motors	Sears Roebuck
Amer Can	Goodyear	Std Oil of Calif
Amer Express	Inco	Texaco
Amer Tel & Tel	IBM	Union Carbide
Bethlehem Steel	Inter Harvester	United Technologies
Du Pont	Inter Paper	US Steel
Eastman Kodak	Merck	Westinghouse Elect
Exxon	Minnesota M&M	Woolworth

Twenty Transportation Stocks

American Airlines	McLean Trucking	Santa Fe Indust
Burlington North	MoPac Corp	Southern Pacific
Canadian Pacific	Norfolk & Southern	Transway Int'l
Carolina Freight	Northwest Airlines	Trans World
Consolid Freight	Overnite Transp	UAL Inc
CSX Corp.	Pan Am World Air	Union Pac Corp
Delta Air Lines	Rio Grande Ind	
Eastern Air Lines		

Fifteen Utility Stocks

Am Elec Power	Consol Nat Gas	Panhandle Eastern
Cleveland E Illum	Detroit Edison	Peoples Energy
Colum-Gas Sys	Houston Indust	Phila Electric
Comwlth Edison	Niag Mohawk Pow	Pub Serv E&G
Consol Edison	Pacific Gas & El	Sou Cal Edison

X, Y, and Z. If their market prices per share are added together and divided by 3, the average is 20.

Company X	$30
Company Y	$20
Company Z	$10
Total	$60
Divisor	3
Average	20

Now suppose everything remains the same except that company X has a two-for-one stock split. Since in this case, the market does not move up or down, the average index should remain the same. Therefore, it is necessary to adjust the divisor for the stock split.

Company X	$15
Company Y	$20
Company Z	$10
Total	$45
Divisor	d
Average	20

$$d(\text{divisor}) = \frac{\text{total after the split}}{\text{average before the split}} = \frac{45}{20} = 2.25$$

The new divisor should be 2.25 instead of 3.

Over the years, each new split within the averages has caused a decrease in the divisor. In 1982, the divisor for the Dow-Jones Industrial Average was 1.314, which has decreased considerably from the original value of 30 because of the various stock splits over the last 80 years. Therefore, if the current market prices of all 30 stocks are added together and divided by 1.314, one would obtain the current Dow-Jones Industrial Average.

Since the series is price weighted, the impact from a change of a higher-priced stock on the average index will be greater than that of a lower-priced stock. Take the previous example of three companies, and now suppose that the company X's stock goes up by 10 percent. If there were not a split, the average index would be 21:

Company X	$33	($= 30 \times 1.10$)
Company Y	$20	
Company Z	$10	
Total	63	
Divisor	3	
Average	21	

But if there is the split, the average index is 20.67:

Company X	$16.5	($= 15 \times 1.10$)
Company Y	$20	
Company Z	$10	
Total	46.5	
Divisor	2.25	
Average	20.67	

From this example, it is clear that the same event (company X's stock goes up by 10 percent) could have a different impact on the average if there is a stock split. However, the total market value of company X is not changed by its stock split. Therefore, the "importance" of company X being in the group should not change either. But the price-weighted approach makes company X less important after the stock split. This tendency of downward bias is a major drawback of Dow-Jones averages for using the price-weighted method.

As individual figures, the Dow-Jones averages do not mean much to an analyst because their purpose is to show movement over time. Figure 13-1 is a bar chart of two of the leading market indicators, the Dow-Jones average of 30 industrials and the Standard & Poor's Composite Index of 500 stocks, covering the period from August 1973 to the beginning of 1976.

Standard & Poor's Index

Contrary to Dow-Jones's price-weighted method, Standard & Poor's stock price index takes on a value-weighted approach. Value is determined by the market price per share of a stock, times the number of stocks outstanding. Standard & Poor's stock price index is made up of 500 stocks. Its movement is compared with the base years of 1941 to 43. The 500 stocks are divided into four sections: 400 industrial stocks, 40 utility stocks, 20 transportation stocks, and 40 financial stocks. The current index figure is obtained by dividing the total market value of those stocks in the series at the present time by that of the initial value of the base, then times 10. Mathematically,

$$\text{S\&P index} = \frac{\sum P_t Q_t}{\sum P_0 Q_0} \times 10$$

where

P_t = closing prices for stocks in the series on day t

Q_t = number of outstanding shares on day t

P_0 = closing prices for stocks in the series on base day

Q_0 = number of outstanding shares on base day

The advantage of Standard & Poor's index is that it is more comprehensive than the Dow-Jones average. The Standard & Poor's average is often used to confirm a movement of the Dow-Jones average. Because the Standard & Poor's index contains many lower-priced stocks, it can be more volatile. Analysts who follow the Standard & Poor's index believe that when it rises faster than the Dow-Jones average it serves as a strong indicator of a bullish trend, and that if the opposite is true, it is likely that a bear market is at hand. Figure 13-1 includes the Standard & Poor's Composite Index of 500 stocks, which has moved in relatively the same direction as the Dow-Jones but not at the same magnitude.

New York Stock Exchange Index

A newer market index, originated in 1966, is the New York Stock Exchange common-stock index, which includes all stocks listed on that exchange. This index is calculated similarly to the Standard & Poor's index.

Figure 13–1 Daily Basis Stock Charts

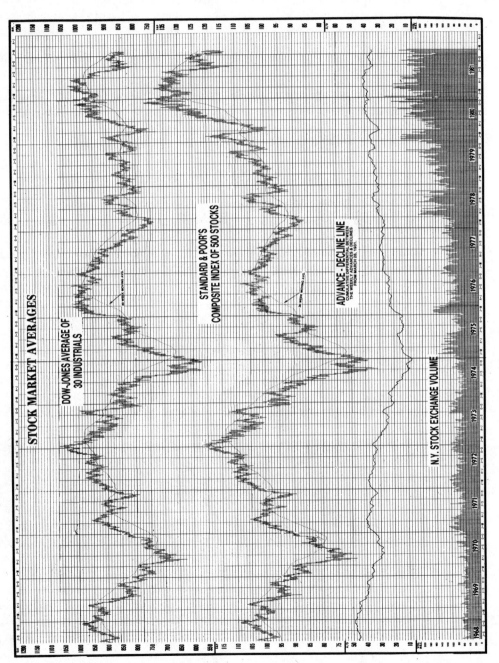

Chart courtesy of *Trendline*, a division of Standard & Poor's Corporation, February 2, 1982, p 5.

The price of the stock is multiplied by the number of shares outstanding, and the aggregate total of all the shares of stock is expressed as a percentage of the base year. The base date for this index is December 31, 1965, and the base is 50. In addition to the index of all the stocks, separate indexes are calculated for different segments of the market, such as finance, transportation, and utilities.

Trading Rules

Many rules concerning the problem of timing (i.e., when to buy and when to sell) are used by technicians. Also, there are many interpretations of each of these trading rules. Usually, a technician will use a combination of rules in making timing decisions.

The General Motors Index

The General Motors index is a one-stock index and is based on the simplest of theories. It states that any time GM makes either an intermediate high (and subsequently dropped off slightly) or an intermediate low (and subsequently rallied slightly) a market signal may have taken place. If, after an intermediate high, 4 months pass without that high being penetrated, stocks of all companies should be sold because the market is due to turn down. If, after an intermediate low, 4 months pass without the low being penetrated, stocks should be purchased because the market is in or is approaching a bullish phase.

The rationale of this theory is that GM is an important bellwether for the entire economy because many industries are dependent upon the success of the automobile industry. If GM's stock is falling, it is unlikely that the market as a whole can continue to rise, and vice versa. One questionable aspect of this theory is the use of the 4 month interval instead of a shorter one. The selection of a 4 month interval seems fairly arbitrary, but to the true followers of the theory it is a reasonable length of time for forecasting future trends and has had a reasonable degree of success in the past.

Barron's Confidence Index

This index, published weekly in *Barron's,* is the ratio of the average yield to maturity of 10 high-grade corporate bonds selected by *Barron's* to the average yield to maturity of 40 bonds of various grades selected by Dow-Jones. The basic idea of this index runs parallel to the concept of the yield spread between higher- and lower-grade bonds. When investors are pessimistic (confidence is low), they view the low-grade bonds as being riskier and so require a higher return. Therefore, the yields of both high- and low-grade bonds move up, but the spread (the differential) between the two is increased. Therefore, the confidence index, which is a ratio of the yield of high-grade bonds to the yield of low-grade bonds, is decreased. When investors' confidence rises, the spread is narrowed; hence, the ratio is increased and the confidence index is higher. Proponents of the confidence index argue that it is a reasonably accurate indicator of either a move away from or a move toward risky investments and that such moves show up in the bond markets before they are reflected in the stock market. Thus, conditions in the bond markets supposedly precede those in the stock market.

For example, suppose that the average yield on *Barron's* list of high-grade bonds is 6 percent and that the average yield on the Dow-Jones 40 bonds is 8 percent. The confidence index would then be 6 percent divided by 8 percent, or 75 percent. If in the next several months the respective yields on *Barron's* list and the Dow-Jones 40 changed to 5.8 percent and 7 percent, respectively, the confidence index would then be 5.8 divided by 7, or approximately 83 percent. The increase of 8 percentage points would then mean confidence had increased and should soon be reflected in stock prices.

Although this theory sounds straightforward, correct interpretation is, as usual, very important. An investor must decide how high is high and how low is low in interpreting the level of the indicator. An indicator may be higher than it ever has been in the past yet lower than it will ever be again. Finally, and again typically, deciding when and where the index will reach its top or bottom has proved to be extremely difficult, as is the case with most such theories.

Mutual-Fund Liquidity Theory

This theory suggests that mutual-fund liquidity can often be used to predict turning points in the stock market. High liquidity presumably means that the mutual funds will soon be putting their cash to work by buying stock. Low liquidity means that the funds are fully invested and that a top may be near. Mutual-fund liquidity is measured by the percent of total mutual-fund assets held in cash or equivalents as reported by the investment company institute. These figures must be adjusted to exclude the holdings of the relatively new money market funds, which consist entirely of short-term money market instruments.

Data on the aggregate cash position of mutual funds go back to 1955. For most of this period, mutual-fund liquidity theory has proved to be a useful indicator of future market conditions. The general risk is that when the cash position of the funds exceeds 9 percent of total assets, the market is providing an unusually good buying opportunity and a bearish signal is given when the cash ratio falls below 5 percent. Historically, mutual funds have appeared to act in a fashion generally attributed to the small investor or the odd lotter, that is, reaching a fully invested position at the top of the market cycle and having the most reserve buying power at the bottom.

During the first half of the 1970s, the experience of the mutual funds tended to confirm this liquidity theory. At the end of 1974, the cash position of mutual funds (excluding money market funds) was 15.8 percent of total net assets, which was the highest level recorded since 1955. It was at the end of 1974 that the stock market ended the second-sharpest bear market in its history. These figures correspond closely to the liquidity theory, which would have indicated 1974 to be an excellent time to purchase common stock. Also, the cash position was 5.1 percent of total net assets in 1972 when the market was at its all-time high after the 3-year bull market from the lows experienced in 1970.

NYSE and AMEX Volume Ratios

Most of the stocks listed on the American Stock Exchange are smaller or represent younger companies than those listed on the New York Stock Exchange. The traders on the two exchanges are different, with more individuals trading shares on the American Stock Exchange (AMEX) and more institutions trading on the New York Stock Exchange (NYSE) as a percent of total volume. The American Exchange has a reputation of listing more speculative securities, and some market analysts believe that the ratio of the volume on the AMEX to the volume on the NYSE can be used to predict trends in market prices.

The ratio is determined by dividing the volume of the AMEX by the volume of the NYSE. Because the volume on the AMEX is less than that on the NYSE, the ratio is usually between 0 and 1. The higher the ratio is, the higher the volume of the AMEX compared with that of the NYSE. When the ratio reaches 0.6 or better, the technician considers it to be a strong indicator that the market will decline in the near future. The reason given for this phenomenon is that a higher ratio is the result of a speculative market. When the ratio reaches 0.6, the market will begin to decline because the increase of speculation will finally cause the bull market to collapse.

Short-Interest Ratio

The **short-interest ratio** is a monthly calculation of the total number of shares sold short at a particular time divided by the average daily volume of shares traded during the previous month. The ratio is almost always between 0.3 and 2.0. Taking a short position in an individual security is generally considered a bearish step. Those who are engaged in selling short a particular stock are expecting a price decline and hope to realize a profit when they eventually cover the short position.

However, for the market as a whole, a low or falling short-interest ratio is generally a bearish sign. A low short-interest ratio is less than 1.0. Analysts feel that this indicates that the market is in an overbought condition. A rising short-interest ratio is considered a bullish sign because the greater the level of short positions, the greater the future demand for those shares will be because shares sold short must eventually be covered by stock purchases. When the short-interest ratio is 1.5 or above, it is considered by technicians to be a bullish signal; when the ratio approaches 2.0, it is considered an extremely strong indicator of a market reversal.

When short sales are large relative to the average daily volume, technicians conclude that the market is oversold and that an upward correction should be forthcoming. Short interest must be related to volume, because short interest in an active market must be larger than in a slow market in order to give the same technical strength. The short-interest ratio theory is also relevant for individual issues. The analyst would proceed by obtaining the monthly short-interest figures for individual stocks, which are published monthly in major financial newspapers, and would relate them to average daily volume figures for the stocks. The short-interest ratio has been relatively accurate in times when it has reached less than 0.5 and a level of greater than 2.0. Historically, the market has made major market turns at these points.

Odd-Lot Trading Theory

This technical theory, sometimes called the **theory of contrary opinion,** was originated by Garfield A. Drew in 1940. He believed that the general public was not sufficiently sophisticated to compete with professional investors because they lacked the knowledge and ability to make investment decisions with emotional detachment.

The theory states that the collective investment decisions of small investors (those who buy in odd lots, which consist of less than 100 shares) are more likely to be wrong relative to the direction of the market. The informed investor should therefore determine what the small investor is doing and then use this information as an indicator that the market may be moving in the opposite direction.

Most analysts of odd-lot data place primary emphasis on the ratio of odd-lot selling volume to odd-lot buying volume. Volume is usually expressed in the number of shares traded, rather than in dollar amounts, and is published daily in most financial newspapers. This ratio is based on a 10-day moving average to make underlying trends more discernible. In addition, this ratio should be compared with some market index or average to make its trend meaningful.

When the odd-lot public tends toward selling or when odd-lot selling increases relative to buying, the ratio will rise. Proponents of this theory state that the ratio will rise sharply at or near an important stock market bottom because fear prompts odd-lot traders to liquidate their positions at the very time shares should be bought. The ratio will decline when odd-lot traders tend toward buying shares in greater numbers than they sell them. The ratio displays this pattern at important market tops because overenthusiam prompts people to purchase shares at the very time they should be selling. When the Dow-Jones Industrial Average moves opposite to the odd-lot ratio, a classic buy or sell signal is usually given. When they move parallel to each other, odd-lotters are acting correctly.

200-Day Moving Average

The 200-day moving average is a Dow theory tool that can be used with charts as a means of smoothing the short-term movements and that gives a long-term trend to the average. The average for the market, industry, or stock is derived by taking the previous 200 trading days of price information. After each trading day, the first price in the 200-day average is dropped, the most recent price is added, and the sum is averaged for the new 200-day period. The analyst examines the movement of this average in order to help determine a forecast for future prices for the market, industry's, or particular company's stock.

The 200-day moving average is most often used to detect turning points in the market. A turning point at the top of the market is forecast when one of three events occurs:

1. If, following a rise, the 200-day moving average flattens out or declines, and if the price of the stock or market penetrates the 200-day average line from the top, a sell signal is flashed.
2. If a stock price rises above the 200-day moving average line while that average line is still falling, the forecast is also bearish.
3. If actual price movement is below the 200-day line and, after advancing toward it, it then fails to go through the line and starts to turn down again, the forecast is bearish.

These three situations could be turned around, and buy signals would then be flashed.

Figure 13-1 indicates a 200-day moving average for the Dow-Jones Industrial Average and the Standard & Poor's Composite Index of 500 stocks. Note that both averages break through their 200-day moving average in January 1975, thus indicating the end of the bear market and confirming a new bull market. Many investors follow the 200-day moving average to help them determine the major market trends of a particular company or the market as a whole. Their belief causes them to have a common-stock portfolio only when a 200-day average is increasing. When the average begins to decline, they unload all common stock in their portfolios.

Breadth of Market Movements

Technicians are interested in the proportions of stocks that advance compared with those that decline. The convenient way of charting this information is by using an advance-decline line. The number of advances and declines of stocks traded on the New York Stock Exchange is published daily in the financial sections of most newspapers. From these figures, the analysts note whether stocks advanced or declined on balance, then add or subtract that amount to or from the current level of the chart, and draw the connecting line. The advance-decline line reflects cumulative net advances and declines on the market.

One main use of the advance-decline line is a double check on the popular market indicators, which are often overly influenced by a small proportion of all stocks. As long as both the advance-decline line and the market indexes are moving together, they confirm one another. When they begin to diverge, a significant market development may be indicated.

According to users of the advance-decline line, a peak will occur before the market index changes. The technician believes this to be true because it is felt that the blue-chip stocks, so important in popular market averages, are the last to turn down when a bull market has ended. The technicians indicate that the upward movement of the entire market generally reaches a peak before the popular averages reach that conclusion and, therefore, **leads** the popular averages. A general market rise is usually indicated at the bottom of a bear market, if the popular averages continue to fall but the advance decline line begins to rise.

A variation of the advance-decline line is the advance-decline ratio, which is determined by subtracting the number of declines from the number of advances and then dividing that figure by the number of declining issues. Some technicians consider this index a guide to the internal strength of the market. An increase in this ratio is taken to be bullish and a decrease is taken to be bearish.

There is much debate over the usefulness of the advance-decline series as a price-forecasting tool. There are times when the advance-decline line appears to have worked when it has given the wrong prediction. A classic example of its being correct is its forecast in 1929 when the number of stocks advancing from February 1929 to August 1929 were declining in comparison with the number of declining issues, yet the Dow-Jones Industrial Average continued to surge to new highs. And in 1973, it was accurate in predicting the historic peak of the market.

Figure 13-1 also includes the advance-decline line for the New York Stock Exchange, indicating a relatively close correlation to the major indicators.

ANALYSIS OF MARKET PRICE

Almost all technical analysts believe that there are definite patterns in the movement of stock prices, but few agree on what the patterns are, and more important, how they can be used to advantage. Almost all technicians caution investors that the patterns are not completely reliable. The stock market seems to exhibit trends that last weeks and even months, not just a day. When the stock market is in one of these trends, either up or down, it is relatively easy to predict daily movements.

Technical analysts chart price movements because charting visually assists them in detecting evolving patterns in price behavior. Two of the most widely used charting procedures are point and figure charting and bar charting. They are the technician's tools for analyzing individual stocks.

Point and Figure Charting

From the technical standpoint, point and figure charting is one of the simplest methods of charting, but it is also the least understood method. The major features of this method of charting a security are that it has no time dimension, it disregards fractional changes in the stock price, and it requires a stock to reverse direction by a predetermined number of points before it changes direction as recorded on the chart.

Figure 13-2 illustrates the results of point and figure charting for nine different companies listed on the American Stock Exchange. The vertical axis represents a change in the price of the stock, and the horizontal axis represents a change in the direction of the price of the stock. For example, the Carnation Company's chart covers the period from the end of 1974 through the beginning of 1975. Note that the price moves sharply higher from a level of $50 per share to over $75 per share. The Carolina Pipeline Company's chart covers a period from 1969 through the beginning of 1975. Note that the horizontal axis does not cover the same time period for each security. It represents the change of direction of the price of the common stock over time.

Although there are a number of variations on the basic approach to point and figure charting, Figure 13-2 represents one of the more typical methods. Generally, when prices are rising, the chartist uses an ×; as long as the price continues to rise, the chartist continues to place an × in the next price interval above the previous one. Only when the stock price moves in an opposite direction is a new mark recorded to the right. If the new

Figure 13-2 Point and Figure Charts

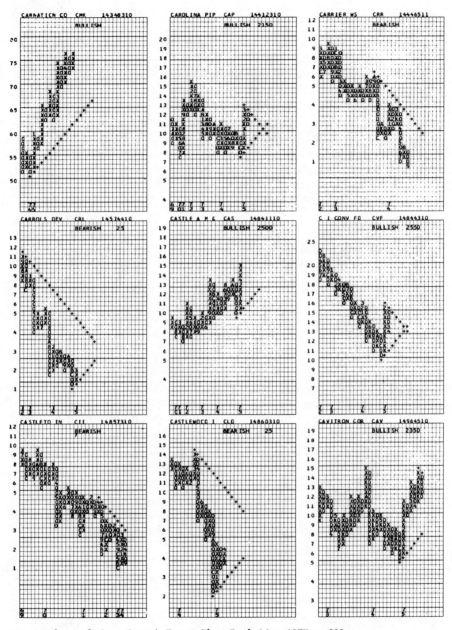

Source: Chartcraft, Inc., *Point & Figure Chart Book*, May, 1975, p. 203.

direction is down, the chartist records an O. If the price continues to decline, he continues to place an O under the previous one as the price moves lower into each new price interval.

It is important to note that the chartist does not take time or volume into account and that a price that has very little volatility may remain in a very tight price range. Thus, the technician has very little marking to do on the chart. The intervals on the vertical axes for the nine companies in Figure 13-2 are very different, depending upon the price range of the stocks involved. For example, Carnation Company uses one space for each dollar change in the price of the common stock; Carolina Pipeline Company uses one space for every 50-cent change in the price of the security.

Technicians use point and figure charting to look for trends and points where there may be a change in the primary direction of the stock. If they ignore the time element, the analyst can determine the forces of supply and demand and can often determine where support for the stock is and where overhanging supply may be. Analysts generally call these two interpretations **resistance and support levels.**

Bar Charting

The second most widely used method of charting is bar charting. The vertical axis of a bar chart represents the measure of price movement and the horizontal axis represents time. The horizontal axis can be marked off in any dimension the analyst wishes, for example, in days, weeks, or months. Instead of just plotting the points on the bar chart at a point in time, the analyst plots a vertical line to represent the range of prices of the stock during the period. If the analyst were plotting daily data, the top of the vertical line would represent the high price of the stock during the day and the bottom of the line would represent the low price of the stock during the same day. Very often a small horizontal line is drawn across the bar to denote the closing price at the end of the time period. The analyst will usually include at the bottom of the bar chart the volume information for the same period that the price information is recorded. Figure 13-3 shows four bar charts. These charts were plotted daily and give the daily price movement and the corresponding volume.

Interpreting Charts

Both point and figure chartists and bar chartists have found key patterns to look for in determining a stock's most probable price action. Analysts have identified an unlimited number of chart patterns. The six shown in Figure 13-4 represent some of the more common patterns that analysts look for.

Figure 13-3 Bar Charts

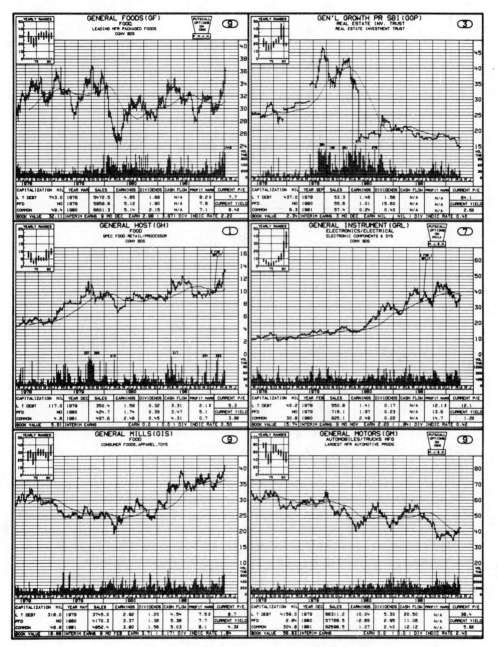

Source: Standard & Poor's Corporation, *Trendline, Daily Basis Stock Charts*, April, 1982, p. 102.

Figure 13-4   Technical Chart Patterns

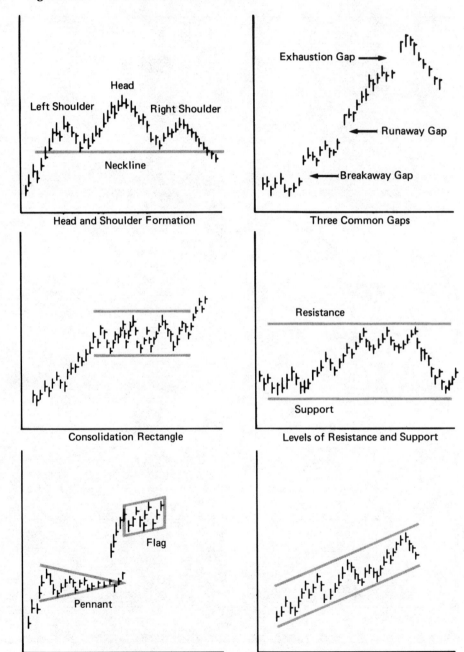

Head and Shoulder Formation

Three Common Gaps

Consolidation Rectangle

Levels of Resistance and Support

Two Identifiable Formations

Uptrend Channel

A head and shoulders formation is common at market tops. An inverse head and shoulders formation is common toward the end of a bear market. For example, in Figure 13-1 there is an inverse head and shoulders formation for the Dow-Jones Industrial Average: the left shoulder formation occurring in September, the head in October, and the right shoulder in early November 1974. At the time, this inverse head and shoulder formation received wide attention from the technical analysts because many believed that it possibly signaled the end of the long bear market begun in February 1973. We now know that it did indeed signal the end of the bear market, even though in December the market tested its previous low and then increased sharply over the next 7 months.

Also in Figure 13-1 there is a consolidation rectangle formed between July 1975 and December 1975. At that time the market was digesting its gains during the first six months of 1975. Technical analysts believe that a consolidation rectangle like this gives support to a further market advance, as indicated in early 1976.

The other chart patterns in Figure 13-4 can be found in a number of the charts and can be used for both bar charts and point and figure charts, although they are usually used with bar charts. Investors who are interested in a full discussion of the technical approach and the interpretation of chart patterns can find a great number of publications available for an in-depth study of the field. Some of these are listed in the Selected Readings at the end of the chapter.

APPROACHES TO INVESTMENT TIMING

Many experienced investors know that it is easier to select the individual companies in which to invest than it is to determine the right time to invest. If investors want to maximize their profits, they must not only purchase the right security, but they must also know the right time to purchase and sell.

Although all investors know the importance of timing, it is difficult for them to determine when it is the right time to buy or sell. Experienced investors know that most stock prices fluctuate widely during a particular business cycle, but, nevertheless, they often react in a way opposite to one that would enable them to benefit from these fluctuations.

Ideally, investors should buy when prices are low and sell when prices rise to levels higher than their normal fluctuations. However, investors hesitate to buy when prices are low because they fear that prices may fall disastrously lower or they fear that prices will not move higher. When prices are exceptionally high, investors hesitate to sell because they want to maximize their profits and they feel that the price may rise higher. Some investors are motivated by greed.

It requires exceptional discipline to purchase securities when prices are low and pessimism about the fate of the economy or company prevails and to sell when stock prices are high and optimism prevails. Investors not only find it difficult to overcome their emotions, but they also find it difficult to determine the course of future fluctuations of security prices.

Many widely used mechanical techniques have been employed to ease the problem of timing and to minimize the emotions involved in investing. To apply one of these methods, investors must recognize their limitations in the accuracy of timing and be willing to leave a large portion of the timing decision to a technical formula plan.

Dollar Cost Averaging

A relatively simple, yet generally effective strategy to minimize the risk of incorrect timing is dollar cost averaging. **Dollar cost averaging** uses timing diversification, which is the practice of periodically spacing purchases and sales of a security over time. By spreading the securities purchases over a period of time in generally equal dollar amounts, investors are suggesting that they do not know when the market will rise and fall and therefore buy at equal intervals and settle for the average market price.

In dollar cost averaging, the investor places an equal amount of funds in a common stock or in groups of stocks at some regular time interval, regardless of the market price. The provision that equal amounts be applied to purchases is central to the dollar cost averaging plan. The effect of equal amounts and regular intervals for purchase results in the investor's buying more shares when prices are low than when prices are high. When prices fluctuate, the investor who follows this plan acquires stock at an average cost per share that is less than the average market price of the stock.

Table 13-2 illustrates the theory behind the dollar cost averaging plan and assumes a cyclical trend in the stock market. The price movement of the stock begins at $10 per share in time period 1, rises 20 percent, declines to $10 per share, then drops 20 percent to $8 per share, and then returns to $10 per share. At each interval $1,000 is invested. The total number of shares purchased is 508 and at the end of the fifth period they have a total market value of $5,080. It can be seen from this example that the average market price of the stock is $10 per share [(10 + 12 + 10 + 8 + 10)/5 = 10], which is greater than the $9.84 average cost per share ($5000/508 = $9.84).

The dollar cost averaging theory states that as long as prices are moving in a sideways or increasing manner, the investor will always experience a market value higher than the total amount invested. A major requirement of the dollar cost averaging program is that it be long enough to allow investors time to acquire sufficient shares in both up and down markets. Dollar cost averaging is best suited for investors who have regular funds available for purchasing securities, who have little desire to forecast stock prices, and who recognize their limited ability in timing their decisions. The

Table 13-2
Dollar Cost Averaging

Time Period	Amount Invested	Market Price	No. of Shares Purchased
1	$1,000	$10	100
2	1,000	12	83
3	1,000	10	100
4	1,000	8	125
5	1,000	10	100
	$5,000		508

Total market value after fifth period = (508 × $10) = $5,080

major disadvantage of the dollar cost averaging plan is that because it requires regular and equal investments, many investors are unable to participate. In addition, the plan does not really deal with the difficulties of timing. It only attempts to minimize the risk of timing. Many experienced investors put little weight in the dollar cost averaging plan because the annual rate of return may be inferior to that of a savings institution.

Formula Timing Plans

Formula timing plans try to make the timing decision on investment automatic for the investor. The plans consist of rules for when purchases and sales will be made and how large those purchases and sales should be. Formula plans eliminate the emotions involved in making the timing decision, because formula plans dictate what actions are to be taken. Formula plans call for investors to divide their investment portfolio funds into two portions: an aggressive portion and a defensive portion. The aggressive portion usually consists of common stock that must be more volatile than the defensive portion. The defensive portion usually consists of bonds because they are stable. The aggressive portion of the portfolio will generally rise more rapidly and to a greater extent than the defensive portion of the portfolio when the general securities markets are rising. The volatile section of the portfolio will generally fall more quickly when the securities markets are declining. Generally, the larger the difference is between the movements of the two portfolio sections, the larger the profit a formula plan may yield.

The rules of a formula plan often make an investor do what the majority of the investors might not otherwise do in the market. The selection of a formula plan and the determination of the appropriate ground rules make investors consider and outline their investment objectives and policies. The central purpose of the implementation of a formula is to relieve the pressure on investors to forecast changes in security prices.

Formula plans are not universally successful, and there are no guarantees to their successful implementation and outcome. Although formula plans may solve part of the timing problem, they do not aid investors in selecting a specific security for their portfolios. A formula plan must be inflexible, but this inflexibility makes it difficult for investors to know whether or not they should adjust the plan to new conditions that may be present in the investment environment. As with dollar cost averaging, formula plans must be implemented over a long period of time during which the securities markets have an opportunity to rise and fall in response to the economic cycle.

The central tenet of formula plans evolves around the relationship of the aggressive portion to the defensive portion of the portfolio. The market value of each portion of the portfolio will change relative to one another as certain market conditions are experienced. There are three basic formula plans. Each plan is different in its provisions for transferring funds from the aggressive portion of a portfolio to the defensive portion, or vice versa. The formula provisions automatically force the investor to sell volatile securities when their value rises and to buy those securities when their value falls.

Constant Dollar Plan

The constant dollar formula plan specifies that the dollar value of the stock portion of the portfolio will remain constant. Therefore, when the values of common stocks rise, to keep the value of the aggressive portfolio portion constant, the investor must sell some shares from the aggressive portion and transfer the proceeds to the defensive portion. When the prices of stocks fall, the opposite is done. Because the major advantage of the constant dollar value plan is its simplicity, the investor is easily able to determine the amount to invest from time to time. However, the percentage of the total funds that this constant amount will represent in the aggressive portion of the portfolio will vary at different levels of common stock values.

The constant dollar formula plan does not require forecasting the extent to which upward market increases may reach, but it does require forecasting the extent of downward fluctuation, because the conservative portfolio must be large enough so that funds are always available for transfer to the stock portion as its value decreases. This requires determining how low common stock prices might go. The required size of the conservative portfolio can then be determined.

Constant Ratio Plan

The constant ratio formula plan specifies that the ratio of the value of the aggressive portion of the portfolio to the value of the conservative portion of the portfolio will be held constant. This automatically forces the investor to sell stocks when their values rise in order to keep the ratio of their values to the conservative portion constant. Similarly, when the values of stocks fall, the investor is forced to transfer some funds from the conservative portion of the portfolio to purchase more common stocks.

In the constant ratio plan, the aggressive portfolio portion is kept as a constant proportion of the total value of the funds; therefore, there will always be funds in the conservative portfolio that can be transferred to the aggressive portfolio to purchase stocks if the common stocks continue to decline in value. Thus, unlike the constant dollar formula plan, the constant ratio formula plan requires no forecast of the low level to which stock prices might fluctuate. The constant dollar value plan does, however, call for a consistent level of aggressiveness in transfer to and from the stock portion of the portfolio. The very nature of the constant ratio relationship causes the purchase of stocks to become less aggressive as prices decline, because the constant ratio is applied to the total funds that are decreasing in value. The constant ratio plan also calls for less aggressive sales when the prices of stocks increase, because the total value of the fund grows and the constant ratio allows a larger dollar value for the stock portfolio.

During a substantial rise or sustained fall, the constant ratio plan will generally result in higher profits for the investor than either the constant dollar formula plan or the variable ratio plan (to be discussed next), because the ratio automatically places the investor in a more optimal position. However, over the entire cycle of stock prices, the constant ratio plan is not as satisfactory as the other two formula plans because it calls for transferring funds into and out of the stock portfolio most aggressively near the median of the fluctuation instead of near its turning points.

Variable Ratio Plan

The basic strategy of the variable ratio plan is to change the ratio of stocks to the total portfolio based on current market values as prices fluctuate. The purpose of the plan is to sell stocks in a rising market and to increase the proportion (buy stocks) in a declining market. For example, suppose that toward the end of a bull market, an investor holds 10 percent of the portfolio in stocks and 90 percent in bonds. If the market were to reverse itself, the investor would sell bonds and would continue to buy stocks, so that at the bottom of a bear market the investor would hold 90 percent of the portfolio in stocks and 10 percent in bonds.

In implementing a variable ratio plan, investors must make decisions. They must first decide what the median value is to be, that is, when should the percentage of stocks equal the percentage of bonds. They must decide when to buy and when to sell and how often and by what magnitude to recalculate the ratio. In determining a median value (in effect, determining the ratio) a trend line should be established. A **trend line** is the point at which an investor believes that the stock market and the bond market are in equilibrium. An investor's strategy might be to place 50 percent in stocks at or near the trend line, 45 percent in common stock when the price index moves 5 percent above the trend line, and 60 percent in common stock when the price index drops 10 percent below the trend line.

Although formula timing plans require that investors make some forecast of market movement, they reduce their forecastings to a minimum. Once a trend line has been determined, investors can easily determine when they should buy or sell stock.

There are many modifications of basic formula plans, but the general thrust is to move the investor in the overall approach to the timing of security purchases and sales. Many investors need some type of program to help them decrease their exposure to common stock at high points in the market and begin to increase their exposure to common stock after a market has declined substantially. Almost all investors who have had a reasonable amount of experience in stock market recognize this as one of the most difficult parts of the investment process. Whether or not investors wish to use a timing plan, they must recognize the fact that determining appropriate times to decrease their exposures in the common stock market and at other times to increase their exposures is central to a successful investment program. The study of the timing issue can greatly aid the investor in recognizing its importance.

DISAGREEMENT WITH TECHNICAL ANALYSIS

Efficient Market Hypothesis

A "good" or "efficient" market, in the eyes of investors or theorists, should meet the following criteria:

1. It should make available information regarding price and volume for past transactions and current market conditions. It also assumes that new information comes to the market in a random and independent fashion.
2. It should provide **liquidity.** That is, investors should be able to buy and/or sell an asset quickly (**marketability**) at a certain price (**certainty**). This implies price continuity, which means no large price changes between trades.
3. In terms of the **internal efficiency** of the market, the investor will minimize the cost of transaction.
4. It should provide **external efficiency**, which means that prices adjust quickly to new information regarding securities, as well as the supply and demand in the market.

In general, in an efficient market security prices adjust rapidly to the infusion of new information, and current stock prices fully reflect all available information, including the risk involved. Therefore, it is implied that the expected return is consistent with risk. Consequently, contrary to the technicians' belief that the current stock price movement is completely determined by its past movement, in an efficient market, the current stock price movement is an unbiased reflection of all the pertinent information concerning this stock and the whole market.

Eugene Famma, in his 1970 article in the *Journal of Finance*, proposed a "fair game" model in which he distinguished among three different forms of the **efficient market hypothesis** (EMH), according to the degrees in which market prices "fully reflect" all information:

1. The weak form of the efficient market hypothesis assumes that current stock prices fully reflect all stock market information, including the historical sequences of prices, price changes, and any volume information. Therefore, it is implied that any trading rule that depends on past price changes or past market data to predict future price changes should be of little value. Hence, if our market is indeed consistent with the weak form of EMH, technical analysis would be useless.

2. The semistrong form of the EMH assumes that security prices adjust rapidly to the release of all new public information; that is, stock prices "fully reflect" all public information. Therefore, investors acting on important new information after it is public cannot derive above-average profits from the transaction, taking into consideration the cost of trading, because the security price already reflects the effect of the new public information.

3. The strong form of the EMH assumes that stock prices fully reflect both public and private information. It requires not only "efficient" markets but, also, "perfect" markets in which all information is available to everyone at the same time. Therefore, no group of investors (such as corporate insiders, stock exchange specialists, or professional money managers) can consistently derive above-average profits.

Numerous empirical studies using statistical tests have been done on these forms of EMH. The results generally support the statement that our equity market is efficient for the great majority of investors.

Random-Walk Hypothesis

The basic assumption of market and technical analysis is that the history of the stock market repeats itself. According to the technicians, the future value of a stock is dependent not only upon its past price action but also upon the price action of the whole market. The random-walk hypothesis contradicts this assumption because it is based on the fact that stock price action has no repetition; that is, the movement of the stock is independent of any previous movement. Supporters of this theory believe that, because future prices of stocks are not dependent upon current prices, future trends are unpredictable.

The random-walk hypothesis is an outgrowth of efficient market theories. These theories hold that the stock market is an efficient market because buyers of stocks are rational and because all buyers have the same objective: to maximize profit. There is free flow of information and the market reacts instantaneously to any new information; therefore, the market price of a stock truly reflects its intrinsic value. Prices of stocks are at, or very near, their intrinsic value or fair market value at any time. When speculators receive new information on a stock, they may overreact, but this overreaction will be quickly corrected. In the short run, however, the overreaction will cause the market to move in an unpredictable or random manner. The basic random-walk hypothesis states that market prices will move randomly around the intrinsic value for the stock. If this is true, it then becomes extremely difficult to predict short-run moves in the market and seems to discredit the theory that stock prices will at times move excessively above or excessively below their true value.

Proponents of the random-walk hypothesis believe that empirical tests that compare randomly selected stocks were as effective (or noneffective) at predicting future trends as were the results of technical analysis. Technicians argue that the test results are not valid because the experimenter did not apply technical analysis as it is really used in the marketplace. Nevertheless, since none of the theories used by the technicians and none of the procedures used by the fundamentalists are without error, it is difficult for the informed investor to take a wholly positive or wholly negative attitude toward any of the positions. Instead, investors should attempt to understand the positive tenets of each of the theories, because they will help them understand current market conditions so that they will be able to more accurately form a basis for their portfolio approaches.

Technical versus Fundamental Approach

Theoretically, the technical approach and the fundamental approach use opposing bases to analyze trends in the stock market, but, in reality, most analysts use both fundamental and technical market analysis to arrive at their investment decisions. Fundamental analysis is used to determine the future earnings potential that can be the basis of the determination of a stock's intrinsic value. Much of the technical analyst's procedure is centered in its attempt to help the investor with the timing of stock purchases or sales. It is difficult for most informed investors to ignore competely the technical approach to the stock market because all the tools used have been reasonably reliable over recent market cycles.

An experienced investor knows that it is difficult to make money in the stock market if his position is contrary to the overall market trend. After having studied a particular security carefully, many analysts determine that, even though the stock price continues to fall, the security has an excellent opportunity for price appreciation because of the underlying fundamental condition. This can be a frustrating experience for analysts, because they believe that the fundamentals are appropriate for investment. Those analysts have failed to recognize that the overall trend of the market may be down and that practically all the stocks are following the overall trend. However, if their analyses are correct and if the company continues to maintain its good fundamental characteristics, the investors will generally be rewarded over the long term but must suffer the intermediate-term market decline.

KEY TERMS

advance-decline line
advance-decline ratio
bar charts
Barron's Confidence Index
bear market
bull market
constant dollar plan
constant ratio plan
dollar cost averaging
Dow Jones averages
Dow theory
efficient market hypothesis
formula plans
General Motors Index
market analysis
market index
mutual fund liquidity

New York Stock Exchange
  Index
NYSE and AMEX volume
  ratios
odd-lot trading theory
point and figure charts
primary trend
random-walk hypothesis
secondary reaction
short-interest ratio
Standard & Poor's
  Composite Index
technical analysis
trading rules
200-day moving
  average
variable ratio plan

QUESTIONS

1. Explain the difference between the fundamentalist's approach and the technician's approach to evaluating stocks.
2. How did market analysis originate? What is the basic idea of this theory?
3. What are the Dow-Jones averages?
4. How does the Standard and Poor's Index differ from the Dow-Jones average? How is the Standard and Poor's Index used?
5. Why is the General Motor's Index considered the simplest index to interpret?
6. Explain how Barron's Confidence Index is computed. What does this index indicate?
7. What is the mutual fund liquidity theory?
8. Explain the basic ideas of the volume theories.

9. What is the short-interest ratio and why would a low ratio be considered a bearish sign?

10. Why is the odd-lot trading theory called the "theory of contrary opinion"?

11. Explain how an investor might use an advance-decline line.

12. What is the random-walk hypothesis?

13. What are the two most widely used charting procedures and what are the differences between the two procedures?

14. Why would an investor use a dollar cost averaging plan?

15. Explain the philosophy behind a formula timing plan.

16. What is a constant dollar plan?

17. What is a constant ratio plan?

18. What is a variable ratio plan?

SELECTED READINGS

AKEMANN, CHARLES A., and WERNER E. KELLEY. "Relative Strength Does Persist!" *Journal of Portfolio Management*, Fall 1977, 38–45.

BARRON's. "Market Laboratory," weekly feature in *Barron's,* a publication of Dow-Jones, Inc.

CHENG, PAO L., and M. DEETS KING. "Portfolio Returns and the Random Walk Theory." *Journal of Finance*, March 1971, 11.

COOTNER, PAUL H., ed. *The Random Character of Stock Market Prices*. Cambridge, Mass.: M.I.T. Press, 1967.

EDWARDS, ROBERT D., and JOHN MAGEE. *Technical Analysis of Stock Trends*, 5th ed. Springfield, Mass.: John Magee, 1957.

GRANT, DWIGHT. "Market Timing: Strategies to Consider." *Journal of Portfolio Management*, Summer 1979, 41–46.

HARDY, C. COLBURN. *Investor's Guide to Technical Analysis*. New York: McGraw-Hill, 1978.

LERRO, ANTHONY J., and CHARLES B. SWAYNE, JR. *Selection of Securities: Technical Analysis of Stock Market Prices*, 2nd ed. Morristown, N.J.: General Learning Press, 1974.

LEUTHOLD, STEPHEN C., and KEITH F. BLAICH. "Warped Yardstick: The Amex Index Distorts Moves Both Up and Down." *Barron's*, September 18, 1972, 9ff.

LORIE, JAMES H., and MARY T. HAMILTON. *The Stock Market: Theories and Evidence*. Homewood, Ill.: Irwin, 1973.

MALKIEL, BURTON G. *A Random Walk Down Wall Street*, college ed. rev. New York: Norton, 1975.

NEILL, HUMPHREY B. *The Art of Contrary Thinking.* Caldwell, Idaho: Caxton Printers, 1967.

PINCHES, GEORGE E. "The Random Walk Hypothesis and Technical Analysis." *Financial Analysts Journal*, March–April 1970, 104–110.

WALLICH, HENRY C. "Random Walk and Security Analysts." *Financial Analysts Journal* March–April, 1968, 159–162.

14

Traditional Security Portfolio Management

The field of portfolio management for the securities markets is drawn from two basic approaches. These two approaches are traditional portfolio management and modern portfolio theory. While there is a considerable amount of common ground shared by the two approaches, substantial division between proponents of each position exists.

The purpose of Chapter 14 (and Chapter 15, which follows) is to familiarize the reader with the significant differences between the two approaches and to appreciate and understand their basic roots and points of similarities and differences. Modern portfolio theory came into being in the 1950s and has gradually worked its way into the decision-making process among the investment management firms who administer the vast majority of the investment funds in the United States.

The purpose of the text is not to be a proponent of either approach in an absolute sense, but rather to allow a basic appreciation of the two approaches. The person entering the investment management field today who lacks an understanding of these two approaches to portfolio management will indeed be lacking. It is important to recognize that the majority of the investment community continues to embrace traditional approaches to portfolio management. This is perhaps because of the lack of understanding by the majority of investment managers of the relatively recently introduced modern portfolio theory. As new investment managers, who have much more exposure to the new developments in portfolio theory, move up the ranks in investment management firms and financial institutions, certainly additional emphasis will be given to the newer approaches. However, extreme caution needs to be undertaken in the study of the new theory. Much of the thrust of modern portfolio theory comes from theorists at a number of universities and research institutions. Much of the theory has not been tried to any extensive degree and, therefore, has not been seen in the full light or been thoroughly tested in the marketplace.

A major criticism of modern portfolio theory is that it requires the ability to understand the mathematical models in order to successfully manage a portfolio. This constitutes a severe constraint on the application of the theory to the "real world." A great deal of the theory works well on paper, but when the realities of the marketplace are brought to bear on the portfolio decision, modern portfolio theory has been of limited use.

Nevertheless, a substantial amount of the results from modern portfolio theory have been of help to the portfolio manager, since large quantities of data can be processed by the computer and can greatly reduce the uncertainty of traditional portfolio management. The criticism that currently is leveled against the traditional portfolio manager is that they have very little reason, if any, in many cases for selecting the combination of securities that they place in a portfolio. To a large degree it is a cafeteria approach — a little of this and a little of that. This approach does not try to balance an investor's needs against the riskiness of the overall portfolio, but instead lumps a variety of industry groups into "safe" and "risky" categories. Some old-timers in the traditional field still believe in the "good old days" and have failed to recognize, as have most traditional nonprofessionals, that the investment environment is ever changing. An examination of the "forest" is more important, in the long run, than an examination of the "trees." Portfolio managers who still believe that blue-chip companies can provide the investor with superior market performance have failed to do the necessary homework. Those who have intently studied the underlying strengths and weaknesses of blue-chip companies can see quite clearly that they will experience subpar performance over the long run. The key to the success of the portfolio manager who follows the traditional approach is to be sure that the detailed steps of security analysis are followed carefully. Many fail to take the time to fully understand the dynamics involved in the prospects for each security issue and for each industry.

Investing is primarily an art and not a science. Lack of proper understanding of this truth is the beginning of an investor's downfall, since the investor will tend to follow a variety of schemes and perhaps even quantitative methodology, hoping that somewhere he or she will find the perfect approach to above-average investment returns. Serious and rational investors should learn early that their investment life span is only 40 years or so in length and they need to be concerned with the business of managing the portfolio for the long-run financial goals of themselves and their families. If an investor wastes the first 10 or 15 years of his or her investment career, working on a scheme to "strike it rich," the investor will have lost out on a substantial portion of the financial benefits that could have been derived during the years that are so important in establishing a financial base for the remainder of their lives.

TRADITIONAL STEPS IN PORTFOLIO MANAGEMENT

The traditional approach to securities portfolio management usually contains three major steps: (1) to identify the suitable portfolio objective, (2) to select the appropriate securities to be included in that portfolio, and (3) to monitor the performance of the portfolio constantly and make adjustments if necessary. This chapter is designed to demonstrate this process in a more detailed fashion.

To identify the suitable objective of the portfolio, the investor needs to determine his or her goals: constant and stable income, preservation of capital, high potential for capital appreciation in the future, or some combination with emphasis either in the direction of income or growth. Chapter 2 provided a background discussion on the financial objectives for investment management. The basic goal for every investor is to achieve the highest expected total return (in the form of either income and/or capital appreciation) subject to the level of risk the investor is able and willing to assume. Due to different characteristics among investors, different investors will have different goals in terms of income and/or growth. The list that follows captures the idea of a variety of goals by categorizing different types of investors according to their needs, from the most income concerned to the most growth oriented. This list is not conclusive but attempts to illustrate the most basic types of investors. Readers may find themselves between any two basic types or a combination of two or three types.

TYPES OF INVESTORS

Spectrum of Types of Investors According to Their Objectives

The following presents a possible spectrum of types of investors:

1. Widow with limited net worth and dependent children.
2. Retired person with modest net worth and little income from traditional resources (such as pensions and Social Security).

3. Unemployed individual who needs income to replace salary and/or unemployment compensation.
4. Children with assets received from gifts, saving for future educational costs.
5. Retired individual with substantial net worth, who needs preservation of the investment capital.
6. Salaried individual with supplemental income needs.
7. Employed individual with sufficient salary to cover yearly needs, who is more interested in growth but does not desire a high level of risk.
8. Employed individual with sufficient salary and substantial net worth, whose emphasis is placed exclusively on high growth.

The expected total return of a portfolio is derived from either the income and/or future appreciation, but the magnitude of the rate of return is dependent upon the risk level of the portfolio. The concept of risk-return trade-off still holds here. For the various types of risks, reference to Chapter 1 will be helpful. In general, investors whose primary concern is income will have less capacity to assume risk than those whose concern is more on future growth. Investors placed in the middle range of the spectrum will be concerned primarily with the safety of the capital invested, but can assume a moderate level of risk. Therefore, a spectrum of risk level, ranging from low risk to moderate risk and then to high risk, can be constructed corresponding to the spectrum of types of investors and consequently to the spectrum of objectives ranging from income to growth. However, the final determination of the level of risk that investors should place themselves in depends not only on the capacity of the investor to assume the risk, but also on the psychological factors that determine the willingness of the investor to assume a certain level of risk.

Refer to Chapter 2 for discussions on individual investor's psychological constraints. For example, an employed individual with sufficient salary to cover his or her yearly needs, who also has a substantial amount of net worth, can, theoretically, assume a high level of risk, yet due to the particular psychological factors he or she may have, the investor might be concerned most about the safety of capital. Therefore, the investor will not be willing to assume a high level of risk. The final determination may very well be a moderate level of risk for this investor. In this case, the investor should realize that the expected total return will be lower than for a higher level of risk, which he or she may be able to assume. On the contrary, a retired person with modest net worth and little income from traditional retirement resources may desire to take on a higher level of risk than he or she is able to assume. In this case, the investor should carefully examine the situation and his or her own limitations, and realize that the higher level of risk may result in jeopardy to his or her financial future.

After the final decision is made on the risk level, the next step is to determine the types of securities that are appropriate for the assumed level of risk. The following list provides a variety of types of securities ranging from low risk to high risk.

TYPES OF SECURITIES

A generalized spectrum of types of securities includes the following:

1. Federal Treasury securities
2. Federal Agency securities
3. Investment-grade corporate bonds
4. Common stocks with high dividend (such as public utilities' common stock)
5. Lower-grade (speculative) corporate bonds
6. Preferred stocks
7. Municipal bonds
8. Convertible bonds
9. Common stocks of cyclical companies
10. Common stocks with low dividend and high growth
11. Common stocks with no dividend and hyper growth

Again, the investor should realize that a bond portfolio containing federal government securities and investment-grade corporate bonds has very little risk; therefore, the expected yield is lower than the expected return from a well-diversified common stock portfolio. On the other hand, companies in the growth stage retain a large portion of their earnings for expansion purposes and, therefore, distribute little or no dividend to the common stockholders and have great potential for reward; but the risk of failing to attain the anticipated return is also great.

The next step is to perform a fundamental analysis of the securities of each type selected to meet the risk level. The fundamental approach contains an economic analysis, industry analysis, and company analysis. This approach is explained in detail throughout Chapters 4, 6, 7, and 12. A sufficiently diversified portfolio contains about 15 to 25 securities, and should not be overly weighted in one industry, one company, or, in the case of a bond portfolio, should not be disproportionately weighted in certain maturity dates so as to minimize the exposure to future interest-rate risk. Generally, different industry representation should occur in any of the three general risk categories. For example, for a low-risk bond portfolio, the diversified industries might be government bonds (treasury as well as agency) and corporate bonds that include utility, telephone, industrial, and banking and finance.

A moderate-risk portfolio may contain public utility companies' common stocks, securities of blue-chip companies from mature industries, such as auto, paper, chemical, and steel, and convertible bonds. A high-growth (high-risk) stock portfolio would most likely contain stocks from companies whose growth in sales and in expected earnings is significantly greater than that of the average market return. The industries might be electronics, drugs, computers, office equipment, semiconductors, and precision instruments. However, no one industry or company can stay in the growth stage indefinitely. As time progresses, some industries and companies will move to the mature stage, while some new industries and new companies will emerge as examples of future growth. When this situation occurs, investors should eliminate those maturing industries or companies from their portfolio and replace them with newer industries and companies in order to maintain a growth-oriented portfolio.

MONITORING THE PORTFOLIO

This leads to the significance of monitoring the performance of the portfolio. Apart from the reason previously stated, other exogeneous changes will lead to changes in the expected return and the risk characteristics of an industry, company, or type of security. Examples might be changes in technology, in company management, in federal government monetary policy, in prices of resources (input factors), or even in the political situation of a foreign country. There are hundreds of factors that may have impact on the price and the risk characteristics of the securities in the marketplace. Effective management of the portfolio therefore requires a constant monitoring of the performance of each of the securities included in the portfolio, and adjustments should be made to maintain the objective of the portfolio.

Figure 14-1 summarizes the process of traditional securities portfolio management just described. Some investors may start out with relatively low funds; this process then becomes substantially inhibited. However, this investor should either select an appropriate mutual fund (see Chapter 10 for a detailed discussion) or select a small portfolio with a handful of securities to begin with. Obviously, the risk level is higher than that of a sufficiently diversified portfolio with 15 to 25 securities. However, should additional funds become available, the person should increase the size of the portfolio to achieve sufficient diversification and optimal performance of the portfolio. In some instances, investors may change the objectives of the portfolio, owing to changes in their needs or in their assumed risk level. If changes do occur, the entire process should be repeated, and the appropriate securities should be selected to adjust for the new parameters.

Thus far, the description is concentrated on the individual investors' side. However, a large amount of capital is invested in the marketplace by institutional investors such as mutual funds, closed-end investment companies, retirement funds, which include pension, profit sharing, defined benefit, IRA, Keogh, endowments, and foundations, and certain insurance company assets. The most significant difference between the institutional investors and the individual investors is that the latter is taxable whereas many of the former are nontaxable.

This difference in taxability makes a strong contrast between individuals and institutions in terms of portfolio strategies, although the basic

Figure 14-1 Process of Traditional Security Portfolio Management

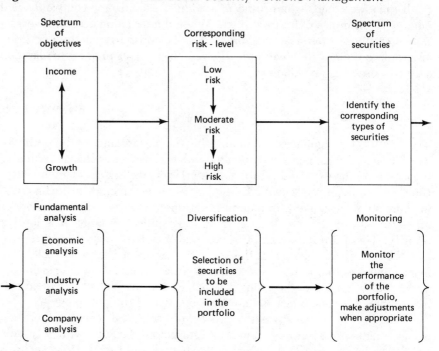

process still applies to both. Because individual investors are subject to taxation, income and capital appreciation are treated differently owing to different taxes applied on ordinary income and on capital gains and losses. Since most funds managed by institutions are not subject to taxation, income and capital appreciations are treated in the same fashion; therefore, it is irrelevant as to which comprises more of the total return for the institutional portfolio. Consequently, it is only the total return and the risk level that determines the selection of the types of securities. For example, if the total return on bonds exceeds the total expected return on common stock, the institutional portfolio, in theory, should not contain any stocks at all. This was indeed the case in the early 1980s when the rates of investment-grade corporate bonds reached 17 percent. Very little incentive remained for the inclusion of blue-chip common stocks whose expected return ranged from 12 to 15 percent in the eyes of the managers of institutional portfolios.

However, it is not implied that institutional investors are indifferent to the objectives of income versus growth. For example, for university endowment funds or other charitable organizations, the objective is definitely placed toward the orientation of income. For retirement funds, where the participants are of a wide range of ages and salary levels, there will be little preference for income or growth over the other.

An additional contrast between individuals and institutions is that, given the same portfolio, institutions will have a wider range of expected return on the portfolio than will individuals. Because if the portfolio has a loss, the individual can take a tax benefit from the capital loss, thereby reducing the magnitude of the negative return; if the portfolio has a gain, the individual will pay tax on the capital gain, and thereby the return is also reduced. Following the same logic, it can be concluded that individuals tend to take on a higher level of risk owing to the reduction of dispersion of possible returns brought about by taxation. On the other hand, because of its nontaxable nature, an institution may achieve the same level of return with a lesser degree of risk than an individual would.

Tax-free institutional portfolios do not need to assume as high a level of risk as an individual to achieve the same desired level of return. Also, most institutional investors manage retirement funds or public money; therefore, they select a moderate-risk posture and tend not to deviate much from the market rate of return owing to the sensitive nature of the assets.

The average annual total return on Standard & Poor's 500 Composite Stock Index represents the market rate of return or the performance of an unmanaged market portfolio. Exhibit 14-1 shows a listing of the S&P 500 companies with their associated weights in the portfolio. The weight of each company is determined by the proportion of the market value of the company to the market value of the entire market (i.e., the total market value of these 500 companies). From time to time, there are changes, such as companies being deleted from or added to the market portfolio. Also, due to fluctuations in the market values, weights associated with these companies will change accordingly. A superior money manager should be able to consistently "beat the market," that is, to perform better than the market. Investors (or money managers) who are not confident of their ability should purchase an **index fund,** which is a mutual fund with the portfolio that represents the market rate of return.

Exhibits 14-2 and 14-3 illustrate typical institutional portfolios for two different investment objectives. Exhibit 14-2 is a portfolio of securities designed with the emphasis on income; Exhibit 14-3 is constructed with the main objective being growth. These two exhibits are mutual fund portfolios of 1982. The purpose of these illustrations is not to judge here whether or not these portfolios are superior, since time has passed and portfolio changes should be made continually, but rather to see how a professional portfolio manager would group securities of various industries together in an attempt to achieve the stated goal(s).

From looking at a portfolio, there is no way, on the surface, to know the approach that the manager took to achieve the resulting portfolio. In the previous two exhibits, either the traditional or modern theory approach could have been taken. The most important factor over time is whether or not the original goal has been achieved. This is the only criterion that has

Exhibit 14-1

Listing of S&P 500 Companies According to the Investment Strategy Format

	S&P Mkt. Wt. %
Credit Cyclicals	**1.78**
Bldg. Mat. — Diversified	0.21
American Std.	0.08
Crane Co.	0.03
Masco Corp.	0.10
Bldg. Mat. — Air Conditioning	0.05
Fedders Corp.	0.01
Trane Co.	0.04
Bldg. Mat. — Cement	0.07
Alpha Portland Inds.	0.00
Ideal Basic Inds. Inc.	0.02
Kaiser Cement	0.02
Lone Star Inds. Inc.	0.03
Bldg. Mat. — Roofing/Wallboard	0.20
Johns Manville Corp.	0.03
Masonite Corp.	0.03
National Gypsum Co.	0.04
United States Gypsum	0.06
Walter Jim Corp.	0.04
Mobile Homes	0.06
Fleetwood Enterprises	0.02
Redman Inds. Inc.	0.02
Skyline Corp.	0.02
Home Building	0.07
Centex	0.04
Kaufman & Broad Inc.	0.01
U. S. Home Corp.	0.02
Savings & Loan	0.10
Ahmanson H.F. & Co.	0.03
First Charter Finl. Cp.	0.04
Great Western Finl. Corp.	0.03
Forest Products	0.88
Boise Cascade	0.08
Champion Intl. Corp.	0.09
Evans Prods. Co.	0.02
Georgia Pac. Corp.	0.18
Louisiana Pac. Corp.	0.07
Potlatch	0.04
Weyerhaeuser Co.	0.41
Misc. Building	0.15
Armstrong World Ind.	0.05
Owens Corning Fibergl.	0.08
Sherwin Williams Co.	0.03
Consumer Growth	**14.42**
Cosmetics	0.60
Alberto Culver Co.	0.01
Avon Products Inc.	0.22
Chesebrough-Pond's Inc.	0.14
Faberge Inc.	0.01
International Flav&Fra	0.10
Revlon Inc.	0.13
Soft Drinks	1.04
Coca Cola Co.	0.50
Dr Pepper Co.	0.03
General Cinema	0.05
Pepsico Inc.	0.44
Royal Crown Cola Co.	0.02
Drugs	4.80
American Home Prods. Cp.	0.69
Bristol Myers Co.	0.45
Lilly Eli & Co.	0.58
Merck & Co.	0.68
Pfizer & Inc.	0.50
Schering Plough Corp.	0.20
Searle G.D. & Co.	0.22
SmithKline Beckman	0.70
Squibb Corp.	0.23
Sterling Drug Inc.	0.18
Upjohn	0.16
Warner Lambert Co.	0.22
Entertainment	0.90
Columbia Pictures Inds.	0.08
Disney Walt Prodtns.	0.24
MCA Inc.	0.16
Metro Goldwyn Mayer Film	0.05
Warner Communications	0.36
Leisure Time	0.12
AMF Inc.	0.05
Brunswick Corp.	0.03
Handleman Co. Del.	0.01
Outboard Marine Corp.	0.03
Questor Corp.	0.02
Restaurants	0.59
Church's Fried Chicken	0.05
Dennys Inc.	0.04
Marriott Corp.	0.12
McDonald's Corp.	0.33
Wendy's Intl.	0.05
Auto Parts—After Mkt.	0.23
Champion Spark Plug Co.	0.04
Echlin Mfg. Co.	0.03
Genuine Parts Co.	0.16
Radio-TV Brdcstg.	0.64
American Broadcasting	0.13
Capital Cities Commun.	0.12
CBS Inc.	0.14
Cox Broadcasting	0.10
Metromedia Inc.	0.10
Taft Broadcasting Co.	0.04
Publishing, Newspapers	0.69
Dow Jones	0.18
Gannett Inc.	0.22
Knight Ridder Newspprs	0.12
Times Mirror Co.	0.17
Hospital Supplies	2.07
Abbott Labs	0.45
American Hosp. Supply	0.26
Bard C. R. Inc.	0.04
Baxter Travenol Labs	0.30
Becton Dickinson & Co.	0.11
Johnson & Johnson	0.92
Retail Stores—Drugs	0.31
American Stores Co.	0.05
Eckerd Jack Corp.	0.08
Revco D. S. Inc.	0.07
Rite Aid Corp.	0.05
Walgreen	0.05
Photography	1.54
Eastman Kodak Co.	1.46
Polaroid Corp.	0.08
Hospital Management	0.55
Amer. Medical Intl.	0.09
Hospital Corp. of America	0.20
Humana Inc.	0.17
Natl. Medical Entrp.	0.09
Misc. Consumer Growth	0.35
Tandy Corp.	0.35
Consumer Cyclicals	**8.23**
Textiles—Apparel Mfg.	0.25
Blue Bell Inc.	0.04
Cluett Peabody & Co.	0.02
Hart Schaffner, Marx	0.02
Jonathan Logan Inc.	0.01
Levi Strauss Co.	0.12
V.F. Corp.	0.04
Textile Products	0.22
Burlington Inds. Inc.	0.08
Cone Mills Corp.	0.02
Lowenstein M. & Sons	0.01
Reeves Bros Inc.	0.02
Springs Mills Inc.	0.03
Stevens J. P. & Co. Inc.	0.03
West Point-Pepperell	0.03
Shoes	0.28
Brown Group Inc.	0.04
Genesco Inc.	0.01
Interco Inc.	0.08
Melville Corp.	0.15
Toys	0.06
Ideal Toy Corp.	0.01
Mattel	0.03
Milton Bradley	0.02
Tonka Corp.	0.00
Household Furnish./Appl	0.28
Bassett Furniture	0.02
Maytag Co.	0.05
Mohasco Corp.	0.01
Roper Corp.	0.0
Whirlpool Corp.	0.13
White Consolidated	0.04
Zenith Radio Corp.	0.03
Retail Stores—Dept.	0.92
Allied Stores Corp.	0.07
Associated Dry Goods Cp.	0.05
Carter Hawley Hale Str.	0.05
Dayton Hudson Corp.	0.21
Federated Dept. Stores	0.26
Macy R. H. & Co. Inc.	0.14
Marshall Field & Co.	0.04
May Dept. Stores Co.	0.11
Retail Stores— Gen. Mercdsg.	1.49
K Mart Corp.	0.27
Penney J. C. Inc.	0.32
Sears Roebuck & Co.	0.83
Woolworth F W Co.	0.07
Finance—Personal Loans	0.16
Beneficial Corp.	0.05
Household Intl.	0.11
Hotel—Motel	0.25
Hilton Hotels Corp.	0.12
Holiday Inns Inc.	0.12
Ramada Inns Inc.	0.02
Publishing	0.67
Dun & Bradstreet	0.23
Harcourt Brace Jovanov.	0.01
Macmillan Inc.	0.02
McGraw Hill Inc.	0.16
Meredith Corp.	0.02
SFN Cos.	0.02
Time Inc.	0.19
Air Transport	0.38
American Airls. Inc.	0.06
Delta Air Lines	0.15
Northwest Airls. Inc.	0.07
Pan Amern. World Awys.	0.03
UAL Inc.	0.06
Misc. Consumer Cyclicals	0.53
ARA Services Inc.	0.04
Borg Warner Corp.	0.14
Gulf and Western Inds.	0.13
RCA Corp.	0.18
Singer Co.	0.03
Auto	2.08
American Mtrs. Corp.	0.03
Chrysler Corp.	0.06
Ford Mtr. Co. Del.	0.35
General Mtrs. Corp.	1.65
Auto Pts. — Orig. Equip. Ex. Aerospace	0.33
Dana Corp.	0.13
Eaton Corp.	0.10
Libbey Owens Ford Co.	0.03
Timken Co.	0.07
Tires	0.35
Firestone Tire & Rubber	0.07
Goodrich B.F. Co.	0.05
Goodyear Tire & Rubr.	0.21
Uniroyal Inc.	0.03
Defensive Consumer Staples	**7.91**
Soaps	1.37
Clorox Co.	0.04
Colgate Palmolive Co.	0.18
Procter & Gamble Co.	0.88
Purex Corp.	0.04
Unilever N.V.	0.23
Distillers	0.50
Heublein Inc.	0.10
National Distillers & Chem.	0.08
Seagram Ltd.	0.19
Walker (Hiram) Consumers Home Ltd.	0.12
Tobacco	1.65
American Brands Inc.	0.27
Philip Morris Inc.	0.78
Reynolds R.J. Inds. Inc.	0.61
Foods	3.73
Archer-Daniels-Midland	0.13
Beatrice Foods Co.	0.23
Borden Inc.	0.12
Campbell Soup Co.	0.14
Carnation	0.15
Consolidated Foods	0.11
CPC Intl. Inc.	0.21
Dart & Kraft	0.36
General Foods Corp.	0.23
General Mills Inc.	0.25
Gerber Prods. Co.	0.03
Great Atl. & Pac. Tea	0.03
Heinz H.J. Co.	0.19
Hershey Fd.	0.08
Jewel Cos. Inc.	0.05
Kellogg Co.	0.24
Kroger Co.	0.10
Lucky Stores Inc.	0.09
Nabisco	0.26
Norton Simon Inc.	0.07
Pillsbury	0.12
Quaker Oats Co.	0.10
Ralston Purina Co.	0.19
Safeway Stores Inc.	0.10
Stokely Van Camp Inc.	0.01
Winn Dixie Stores Inc.	0.11
Wrigley Wm. Jr. Co.	0.03
Sugar Refiners	0.05
Amalgamated Sugar Co.	0.01
Amstar	0.03
Holly Sugar Corp.	0.01
Beverages — Brewers	0.43
Anheuser Busch Inc.	0.30
Coors Adolph Co.	0.05
Pabst Brewing Co.	0.02
Schlitz Jos. Brewing Co.	0.06
Misc. Staples	0.19
Esmark Inc.	0.07
Gillette Company	0.12
Capital Goods	**6.49**
Pollution Control	0.32
Browning Ferris Inds.	0.07
Peabody Intl.	0.01
Waste Management	0.16
Wheelabrator-Frye Inc.	0.06
Zurn Industries	0.02
Machinery — Construction Mat. Handling	0.52
Bucyrus Erie Co.	0.03
Caterpillar Tractor Co.	0.41
Clark Equipment Co.	0.03
Hyster	0.02
Rexnord Inc.	0.02
Non-Consumer Electronics — Major Cos.	2.04
General Elec. Co.	1.77
Westinghouse Elec. Corp.	0.27
Agricultural Machinery	0.26
Allis-Chalmers	0.02
Deere & Co.	0.22
International Harvester	0.01
Massey Ferguson Ltd.	0.01
Machine Tools	0.11
Acme Cleveland Corp.	0.01
Brown & Sharpe Mfg. Co.	0.01
Cincinnati Milacron	0.06
Giddings & Lewis Inc.	0.02
Monarch Mach. Tool Co.	0.01
Machinery — Industrial/Specialty	0.60
Briggs & Stratton Corp.	0.04
Chicago Pneumatic Tool	0.01
Combustion Engr. Inc.	0.11
Cooper Inds. Inc.	0.17
Ex-Cell-O Corp.	0.04
Foster Wheeler Corp.	0.05
Ingersoll Rand Co.	0.11
Joy Mfg. Co.	0.06
Railroad Equipment	0.19
ACF Inds. Inc.	0.04
Amsted Inds. Inc.	0.03
General Signal Corp.	0.12
Auto Trucks & Parts	0.29
Cummins Engine Inc.	0.03
Fruehauf Corp.	0.03
PACCAR	0.07
Signal Co.	0.15
Misc. Capital Goods	2.15
Black & Decker	0.07
Corning Glass Works	0.13
Fluor Corp.	0.17
IC Inds. Inc.	0.05
International Tel. & Tel.	0.40
Litton Industries	0.19
Minnesota Mng. & Mfg. Co.	0.76
Teledyne	0.27
Textron Inc.	0.09
Capital Goods — Technology	**11.93**
IBM	4.58
International Bus Mach.	4.58
Electronics — Semiconductors	0.98
AMP Inc.	0.24
Intel Corp.	0.17
Motorola Inc.	0.27
National Semiconductor	0.06
Texas Instrs. Inc.	0.25
Electronics — Instrumentation	0.91
Hewlett Packard Co.	0.68
Perkin Elmer Corp.	0.10
Tektronix Inc.	0.12
Bus. Equip./Service (Ex. IBM)	2.06
Burroughs Corp.	0.18
Control Data Corp. Del.	0.12
Data General	0.04
Datapoint	0.03
Digital Equip. Corp.	0.52
Honeywell Inc.	0.19
NCR Corp.	0.15
Pitney Bowes Inc.	0.06
Sperry Rand Corp.	0.13
Storage Technology	0.10
Wang Labs.	0.21
Xerox Corp.	0.33
Electrical Equipment	0.76
Emerson Elec. Co.	0.36
Gould Inc.	0.13
Grainger (W.W.)	0.07
McGraw Edison Co.	0.06
Square D Co.	0.09
Thomas & Betts Corp.	0.05
Auto Parts Orig. Equip-Aerospace Related	0.33
Bendix Corp.	0.13
TRW Inc.	0.20
Aerospace	1.57
Boeing Co.	0.21
General Dynamics Corp.	0.17
Grumman Corp.	0.04
Martin Marietta Corp.	0.13
McDonnell Douglas Corp.	0.17
Raytheon Co.	0.35
Rockwell Intl. Corp.	0.27
United Technologies Cp.	0.25
Communication — Equip./Manuf.	0.49
Harris Corp.	0.10
MA Communication	0.11
Northern Telecom.	0.18
Rolm Corp.	0.06
Scientific Atlanta	0.04
Computer Services	0.25
Automatic Data Processing	0.10
Computer Sciences	0.02
Electronic Data Systems	0.10
Tymshare	0.03
Energy	**21.76**
Oil Well Services	2.95
Baker Intl. Corp.	0.25
Dresser Inds. Inc.	0.19
Halliburton Co.	0.46
Hughes Tool Co.	0.17
McDermott J. Ray	0.11
NL Inds. Inc.	0.19
Schlumberger Ltd.	1.59
Offshore Drilling	0.25
Global Marine Inc.	0.05
Reading & Bates Offsh. Dr.	0.05
Sedco Inc.	0.09
Western Co. of North Amer.	0.06
Coal	0.15
Eastrn Gas & Fuel Assoc.	0.06
North Amer. Coal Corp.	0.01
Pittston Co.	0.07
Westmoreland Coal Co.	0.01
Crude Oil	1.18
General Amern. Oil Tex.	0.10
Louisiana Ld. & Expl. Co.	0.13
Mesa Petroleum	0.14
Superior Oil Co.	0.47
Texas Oil & Gas	0.34
Oil International	8.63
Exxon Corp.	3.06
Gulf Oil Corp.	0.75
Mobil Corp.	1.24
Royal Dutch Pete Co.	1.18
Standard Oil of Calif.	1.43
Texaco Inc.	0.97
Oil—Domestic	8.17
Atlantic Richfield Co.	1.25
Cities Svc. Co.	0.36
Getty Oil Co.	0.53
Phillips Pete Co.	0.58
Shell Oil Co.	1.41
Standard Oil Co. Ind.	1.62
Standard Oil Co. Ohio	1.15
Sun Inc.	0.52
Union Oil Co. Calif.	0.76
Misc. Energy	0.42
Tenneco Inc.	0.42
Basic Industries	**6.97**
Aluminum	0.53
Alcan Alum. Ltd.	0.19
Aluminum Co. Amer.	0.23
Kaiser Alum. & Chem. Cp.	0.07
Reynolds Metals Co.	0.05
Paper	0.89
Crown Zellerbach Corp.	0.06
International Paper Co.	0.22
Kimberly Clark Corp.	0.17
Mead Corp.	0.05
Scott Paper Co.	0.09
St. Regis Paper Co.	0.10
Union Camp Corp.	0.13
Westvaco Corp.	0.07
Containers—Metal/Glass	0.33
American Can Co.	0.06
Continental Group Inc.	0.11
Crown Cork & Seal Inc.	0.04
National Can Corp.	0.02
Owens Illinois Inc.	0.09
Containers—Paper	0.13
Bemis Company	0.01
Diamond Intl. Corp.	0.07
Federal Paper Brd. Inc.	0.02
Maryland Cup Corp.	0.03
Misc. Metals	0.49
Amax Inc.	0.18
Hudson Bay	0.02
Inco Ltd.	0.10
Phibro Corp.	0.20
Copper	0.25
Asarco Inc.	0.07
Newmont MNG Corp.	0.11
Phelps Dodge Corp.	0.06
Steel	0.64
Armco Inc.	0.13
Bethlehem Stl. Corp.	0.10
Inland Stl. Co.	0.05
Interlake Inc.	0.02
National Stl. Corp.	0.04
Republic Stl. Corp.	0.04
United States Stl. Corp.	0.25
Wheeling Pitts Steel	0.01
Chemicals	2.46
Dow Chem. Co.	0.52
Du Pont E I DeNemours	1.00
Hercules Inc.	0.10
Monsanto Co.	0.32
Stauffer Chem. Co.	0.12
Union Carbide Corp.	0.39
Misc. Basic Industries	0.16
Northwest Inds.	0.16
Chemical (Misc.)	0.90
Akzona Inc.	0.01
Allied Corp.	0.15
American Cyanamid Co.	0.18
Celanese Corp.	0.10
F M C Corp.	0.10
Grace W. R. & Co.	0.22
PPG Inds. Inc.	0.14
Fertilizers	0.19
Beker Inds. Corp.	0.01
First Miss. Corp.	0.03
International Min. & Chem.	0.10
Williams Cos.	0.06
Financial	**5.77**
Life Insurance	0.38
Capital Hldg. Corp. Del.	0.08
Jefferson Pilot Corp.	0.07
Lincoln Natl. Corp. Ind.	0.11
NLT Corp.	0.12
Property-Liability Ins.	0.56
Chubb Corp.	0.06
Continental Corp.	0.16
SAFECO Corp.	0.08
St. Paul Cos. Inc.	0.11
United States Fid & Gty.	0.15
Multi-Line Insurance	1.60
Aetna Life & Cas. Co.	0.36
American Gen. Ins. Co.	0.12
American Intl. Group	0.45
CIGNA Corp.	0.36
CNA Finl. Corp.	0.08
Travelers Corp.	0.22
Banks—NYC	1.15
Bankers Trust N. Y. Corp.	0.09
Chase Manhattan Corp.	0.18
Chemical New York Corp.	0.10
Citicorp	0.40
Manufacturers Hanover	0.12
Morgan J. P. & Co. Inc.	0.25
Banks—Ex NYC	1.03
BankAmerica Corp.	0.31
Continental Ill. Corp.	0.13
First Chicago Corp.	0.09
First Interstate	0.14
First Intl. Bancshares	0.14
First Natl. Boston Corp.	0.05
First Pa. Corp.	0.01
Mellon Natl. Corp.	0.07
N. C. N. B. Corp.	0.04
Northwest Bancorporation	0.06
Financial Misc.	0.81
American Express Co.	0.50
Heller Walter E. Intl.	0.03
Merrill Lynch	0.13
Transamerica Corp.	0.16
Gold Mining	0.23
ASA Ltd.	0.04
Campbell Red Lake Mns.	0.06
Dome Mines Ltd.	0.08
Homestake Mng. Co.	0.05
Transportation	**1.90**
Railroads	1.59
Burlington Northern Inc.	0.21
CSX Corp.	0.21
Missouri Pacific Corp.	0.12
Norfolk & Westn. Ry. Co.	0.18
Santa Fe Inds. Inc.	0.16
Southern Pac. Co.	0.10
Southern Ry. Co.	0.16
Union Pacific Corp.	0.43
Air Freight	0.14
Emery Air Freight Corp.	0.02
Federal Express	0.11
Tiger International	0.02
Truckers	0.18
Consolidated Freightway	0.06
McLean Trucking Co.	0.01
Roadway Express Inc.	0.09
Yellow Fght. Sys. Inc.	0.02
Utilities	**12.83**
Telephone	6.63
American Tel. & Tel. Co.	5.64
Centel Corp.	0.10
Continental Tel. Corp.	0.12
General Tel. & Electro	0.59
United Telecommunication	0.18
Electric Utilities	4.77
American Elec. Pwr. Inc.	0.35
Baltimore Gas & Elec.	0.12
Central & So. West Corp.	0.16
Commonwealth Edison Co.	0.37
Consolidated Edison N.Y.	0.29
Detroit Edison Co.	0.16
Duke Power Co.	0.26
Florida Pwr. & Lt. Co.	0.19
Middle South Utils. Inc.	0.23
New England Elec. Sys.	0.08
Niagara Mohawk Pwr. Cp.	0.15
Northn. Sts. Pwr. Minn.	0.10
Ohio Edison Co.	0.14
Pacific Gas & Elec. Co.	0.40
Phil. Elec. Co.	0.20
Public Svc Co. Ind. Inc.	0.12
Public Svc Elec. & Gas	0.22
Southern Calif. Edison	0.36
Southern Co.	0.30
Texas Utils. Co.	0.31
Virginia Elec. & Pwr. Co.	0.18
Wisconsin Elec. Pwr. Co.	0.08
Gas Distributors	0.65
American Nat. Res. Co.	0.09
Brooklyn Un. Gas Co.	0.02
Columbia Gas Sys. Inc.	0.14
Consolidated Nat. Gas	0.11
Enserch Corp.	0.13
ONEOK	0.04
Pacific Ltg. Corp.	0.08
Peoples Gas Co.	0.03
Gas Pipelines	0.78
El Paso Co.	0.13
Northern Nat. Gas Co.	0.15
Panhandle Estn. Pipe L.	0.15
Southern Nat. Res. Inc.	0.14
Texas Estn. Corp.	0.15
Texas Gas Transmission	0.06

5/31/82

The information set forth herein was obtained from sources which we believe reliable, but we do not guarantee its accuracy. Neither the information, nor any opinion expressed, constitutes a solicitation by us of the purchase or sale of any securities or commodities.

Source: Merrill Lynch, Performance Monitor, June, 1981.

Exhibit 14-2 Portfolio of Vance, Sanders Income Fund, Inc.

PORTFOLIO OF INVESTMENTS — December 31, 1980

Face Amount		Cost	Value (Note 1A)
	U.S. GOVERNMENT AND AGENCIES — 3.3%		
$500,000	U.S. Treasury Bonds, 8⅜s, 2000	$ 483,750	$ 368,750
	FOREIGN GOVERNMENT — 10.0%		
$500,000	Government of Canada, 9¼s, 1982	$ 470,713	$ 401,150
500,000	Government of Canada, 9½s, 2001	443,124	327,502
500,000	Province of Ontario, 9¾s, 2009	495,625	397,500
	Total Foreign Government	$ 1,409,462	$ 1,126,152
	NON-CONVERTIBLE BONDS — 62.9%		
	Broadcasting — 4.0%		
$500,000	RCA Corp., 10.20s, 1992	$ 515,000	$ 445,625
	Finance — 3.1%		
$450,000	General Motors Acceptance Corp., 8⅞s, 1999	$ 471,938	$ 344,813
	Petroleum — 3.6%		
$500,000	Imperial Oil Limited, 9¾s, 2009	$ 499,030	$ 398,750
	Telephone — 8.3%		
$250,000	Chesapeake & Potomac Telephone Co. (Md.), 8⅞s, 2009	$ 266,825	$ 188,750
500,000	Chesapeake & Potomac Telephone Co. (W.Va.), 9¼s, 2019	493,750	386,875
200,000	New York Telephone Co., 11⅝s, 2019	190,000	180,000
250,000	Southern Bell Telephone & Telegraph Co., 8⅝s, 2018	241,875	178,750
		$ 1,192,450	$ 934,375
	Utilities — 23.7%		
$200,000	Baltimore Gas & Electric Co., 12⅞s, 1990	$ 200,000	$ 195,000
450,000	Carolina Power & Light Co., 12¼s, 2009	450,000	411,750
500,000	Commonwealth Edison Co., 9⅛s, 2008	491,236	366,250
450,000	Illinois Power Co., 9s, 2000	469,915	360,000
100,000	Northern Indiana Public Service Co., 11¾s, 2009	100,000	91,000
450,000	Potomac Electric Power Co., 9½s, 2005	478,983	343,125

Face Amount		Cost	Value (Note 1A)
	NON-CONVERTIBLE BONDS — Continued		
$500,000	Public Service Company of Colorado, 9⅜s, 2005	$ 359,650	$ 378,125
450,000	Union Electric Co., 8⅞s, 2006	458,208	326,250
250,000	Virginia Electric & Power Co., 10s, 2005	274,063	197,500
	Total	$ 3,282,055	$ 2,669,000
	Miscellaneous — 20.2%		
$500,000	Burlington Northern Inc., 8.60s, 1999	$ 402,500	$ 370,000
500,000	Crown Zellerbach Corp., 9¼s, 2005	499,880	390,625
500,000	Diamond Shamrock Corp., 9⅛s, 2000	496,440	393,750
450,000	Great Northern-Nekoosa Corp., 8.70s, 2008	448,875	333,000
500,000	Philip Morris, Inc., 9⅛s, 2003	491,250	385,625
500,000	Rockwell-International Corp., 9⅜s, 1996	499,375	400,000
	Total	$ 2,838,320	$ 2,273,000
	Total Non-Convertible Bonds	$ 8,798,793	$ 7,065,563
	CONVERTIBLE BONDS — 7.0%		
	Consumer Products and Services — 2.1%		
$250,000	Anheuser-Busch Companies, Inc., 9s, 2005	$ 242,500	$ 232,500
	Office and Business Equipment — 2.9%		
$250,000	Digital Equipment Corp., 8⅞s, 2005	$ 302,500	$ 329,375
	Transportation — 2.0%		
$250,000	Pan American World Airways, Inc., 9⅞s, 1996	$ 263,875	$ 228,750
	Total Convertible Bonds	$ 808,875	$ 790,625

Shares		Cost	Value (Note 1A)
	COMMON STOCKS — 14.3%		
	Drugs and Medical — 2.7%		
15,000	Warner-Lambert Co.	$ 276,512	$ 301,875
	Insurance — 2.1%		
10,000	Continental Corp.	$ 242,563	$ 241,250
	Transportation — 1.3%		
12,000	U.S. Truck Lines, Inc. of Delaware	$ 182,563	$ 147,750

Shares		Cost	Value (Note 1A)
	COMMON STOCKS — Continued		
	Utilities — 8.2%		
8,000	Baltimore Gas & Electric Co.	$ 205,301	$ 158,000
6,500	Central Telephone and Utilities Corp.	166,530	159,250
10,000	New England Electric System	219,648	206,250
8,700	Ohio Edison Co.	173,293	103,313
12,000	Philadelphia Electric Co.	196,500	151,500
10,000	Public Service Company of Colorado	181,471	142,500
	Total	$ 1,142,743	$ 920,813
	Total Common Stocks	$ 1,844,381	$ 1,611,688

Face Amount		Cost	Value (Note 1A)
	SHORT-TERM OBLIGATION — 2.5%		
$283,000	General Motors Acceptance Corp., due 1/2/81	$ 282,721	$ 282,721
	Total Investments	$13,627,982	$11,245,499
	Cost for Federal Income Tax Purposes	$13,580,491	

Source: Vance, Sanders Income Fund, Inc., Prospectus, April 30, 1981, pp. 18-19.

Exhibit 14-3   Portfolio of Eaton Vance Growth Fund, Inc.

PORTFOLIO OF INVESTMENTS — August 31, 1981

COMMON STOCKS — 100.0%

Shares		Value (Note 1A)	Shares		Value (Note 1A)
TECHNOLOGICALLY-BASED INDUSTRIES — 34.5%					
Medical — 13.0%			**Metals and Mining — 3.8%**		
25,000	Baxter Travenol Laboratories, Inc.	$ 1,243,750	231,700	Poseidon Limited	$ 1,156,183
300,000	Sankyo Co., Ltd.	1,080,600	210,000	Tubos deAcero deMexico, S.A. ADR*	787,500
75,000	Squibb Corporation	2,090,625			$ 1,943,683
115,000	Warner-Lambert Company	2,170,625	**BUSINESS/CONSUMER**		
		$ 6,585,600	**PRODUCTS AND SERVICES — 20.5%**		
Office and Business Equipment — 11.0%			**Retailing — 6.6%**		
19,000	Data General Corporation*	$ 855,000	115,000	Color Tile Inc.	$ 1,193,125
35,000	Dataproducts Corp.	857,500	45,000	Payless Cashways, Inc.	953,438
12,500	Digital Equipment Corporation*	1,137,500	40,000	Rite Aid Corporation	1,180,000
20,000	International Business Machines	1,100,000			$ 3,326,563
125,000	Mohawk Data Sciences Corp.*	1,640,625			
		$ 5,590,625	**Publishing and Printing — 5.1%**		
Electronics — 9.6%			58,324	Bowne & Company, Inc.	$ 860,279
60,000	Burndy Corporation	$ 1,117,500	40,500	Multimedia, Inc.	1,270,687
40,000	Intel Corporation*	1,125,000	22,500	Reynolds and Reynolds Company	427,500
80,000	Kyoto Ceramic Co., Ltd.	1,241,520			$ 2,558,466
13,000	Tektronix, Inc.	602,875	**Building — 4.3%**		
9,000	Texas Instruments Incorporated	769,500	35,600	Fischbach Corp.	$ 1,286,050
		$ 4,856,395	52,800	Scovill Inc.	917,400
Aerospace — 0.9%					$ 2,203,450
15,100	McDonnell Douglas Corp.	$ 462,437	**Consumer Products — 2.5%**		
NATURAL RESOURCES — 32.7%			28,000	Philip Morris, Inc.	$ 1,281,000
Energy — 17.3%			**Food — 2.0%**		
24,000	Atlantic Richfield Co.	$ 1,134,000	48,825	Archer-Daniels-Midland Co.	$ 817,819
55,000	Equitable Gas Co.	1,663,750	8,500	Wetterau Incorporated	177,969
40,000	InterNorth Inc.	1,220,000			$ 995,788
30,000	Mountain Fuel Supply Co.	1,061,250			
50,000	Phillips Petroleum Co.	1,912,500	**FINANCIAL SERVICES — 12.3%**		
40,000	Transco Companies, Inc.	1,780,000	**Insurance — 12.3%**		
		$ 8,771,500	22,500	American International Group, Inc.	$ 1,276,875
Chemicals — 6.8%			54,000	Corroon & Black Corp.	1,120,500
50,000	Ethyl Corp	$ 1,250,000	48,000	Farmers Group, Inc.	1,311,000
85,500	Lawter International, Inc.	897,750	19,000	General Re Corp.	1,330,000
10,800	MacDermid Incorporated	280,800	50,000	USLIFE Corp.	1,168,750
23,600	Nalco Chemical Co.	1,008,900			$ 6,207,125
		$ 3,437,450		**TOTAL INVESTMENTS**	$50,642,582
Petroleum Equipment and Services — 4.8%					
40,000	Big Three Industries Inc.	$ 1,230,000	*Non-income-producing security.		
20,000	Halliburton Co.	1,192,500			
		$ 2,422,500			

Source: Eaton Vance Growth Fund, Inc., Prospectus, December 22, 1981, p. 15.

any value as to the appropriateness of any approach to portfolio management. Only sufficient time will judge whether or not the investor's objective(s) have been achieved within the risk parameters drawn by the investor, or by the mutual fund managers, as in the case of these two sample portfolios.

The following chapter outlines the modern portfolio theory approach to investment management. The important point to keep in mind when examining either approach is that acceptable positive results over the long run can only be achieved from continually analyzing and monitoring the portfolio and the economic and industry environment in which the investor operates. For only in the long-run can the true investment results be counted. Performance results obtained from one year or from a portion of a business cycle are never sufficient in a test of superiority of either approach and/or the ability of a certain investment management.

KEY TERMS

index fund   risk-return trade-off
investor type   security type
modern portfolio theory   traditional portfolio management

QUESTIONS

1. Describe the basic tenets of traditional security portfolio management.
2. What are the important considerations for investors in determining their investment objectives?
3. What is the relationship of income objective and growth objective to the riskiness of a portfolio?
4. How does the investor determine the riskiness of a common stock?
5. Describe the important differences in portfolio rates of return between the institutions and the individuals.
6. What would be the approach for monitoring the portfolio after it is initially constructed?
7. Why might an investor prefer an unmanaged market portfolio such as an index fund?

SELECTED READINGS

BAKER, H. KENT, MICHAEL B. HARGROVE, and JOHN A. HASLEM. "An Empirical Analysis of the Risk-Return Preferences of Individual Investors." *Journal of Financial and Quantitative Analysis*, September 1977, 377–389.

BLOCK, FRANK E. "Elements of Portfolio Construction." *Financial Analysts Journal*, 25, no. 3, 1969, 123–139.

CROWELL, RICHARD A. "Risk Measurement: Five Applications." *Financial Analysts Journal*, 29, no. 4, 1973, 81–87.

JENNINGS, EDWARD H. "An Empirical Analysis of Some Aspects of Common Stock Diversification." *Journal of Financial and Quantitative Analysis*, March 1971, 797–813.

McCLAY, MARVIN, "A Rational Approach to Debt/Equity Allocation." *Journal of Portfolio Management*, Fall 1976, 50–56.

MILLER, EDWARD M. "Portfolio Selection in a Fluctuating Economy." *Financial Analysts Journal*, May–June 1978, 77–83.

15

Modern Portfolio Theory

Throughout this text we have been concerned with the investor's rate of expected return in relation to the risk level the investor is able to assume. The purpose of this chapter is to expose the reader to the more popular modern quantitative approaches to portfolio management. A more complete and in-depth exposure to the theoretical tenets and potential applications is available in a number of advanced texts and journals.

A major task for the investor is to estimate the highest level of risk he or she is able to assume. Estimates of one's ability to take risks are essentially subjective, although quantitative data are used in making estimates. A corresponding part of the problem of investment management is to select an individual security issue with risk such that the risk level of the portfolio will be the highest that the investor can afford to assume. For almost all investors, this is a difficult task because they must first select from among all security issues at a given level of risk and then choose those that they believe will provide the optimum risk-return relationship.

The investor should attempt to select security issues whose returns are least likely to be adversely affected by the same hazards in the economy and in an industry. By not selecting securities that can be adversely affected by the same hazards, the investor can assemble a securities portfolio that represents a lower level of risk than an arithmetic average of the risks of the issues that comprise the portfolio.

MARKOWITZ'S CONTRIBUTION

The basic elements of modern portfolio theory emanate from a series of propositions concerning rational investor behavior set forth by Harry M. Markowitz in 1952. Markowitz's great contribution was to analyze the implications of the fact that, although investors seeks high expected returns, they generally wish to avoid risk. Since there is overwhelming evidence that risk aversion characterizes most investors, especially most large investors, rationality in portfolio management necessitates that account be taken not only of expected returns for a portfolio, but also of the risk involved.

Once the level of risk the investor is willing to assume is established, the Markowitz portfolio model provides a theoretical framework for the systematic selection of optimum portfolios. Markowitz applied the complex mathematics of quadratic programming to the question of how most effectively to diversify portfolio holdings. He based his portfolio diversification theory on the fact that the riskiness of portfolios depends not only upon the attributes of securities considered individually, but also upon their interrelationships.

The theme of Markowitz's work is that investors conduct themselves in a rational manner that reflects their aversion to assuming more risk without being adequately compensated by an increase in the expected return. The investor, at any expected return, will prefer a portfolio that has the least risk, and at any given risk level, will prefer the portfolio that has the highest expected return. Risk, as defined by Markowitz, is the variability of expected return around the mean.

The Efficient Frontier

The notion of efficient portfolios is illustrated in Figure 15-1. The vertical axis measures the expected return of a portfolio, and the horizontal axis measures its associated risk. The shaded area represents all possible portfolios that can be obtained from a given set of securities. The portfolios lying on the curve ACE are efficient because they offer the maximum return for a given level of risk and a minimum risk for a given level of return. Portfolio B is inferior to portfolio A because the investor can receive the same expected return at less risk. Portfolio C is superior to Portfolio D because it can receive a higher expected return for the same amount of risk. The Markowitz analysis assumes that any rational investor prefers efficient portfolios to all

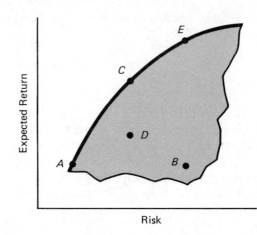

other portfolios. The particular portfolio the investor chooses depends upon the investor's constraints and the risk he or she is willing and able to assume.

Markowitz observed that investors try to minimize deviations from the expected portfolio rate of return by diversifying their portfolios, that is, by holding either different types of securities and/or securities of different companies. He noted, however, that holding different issues does not significantly reduce the variability of the portfolio's expected rate of return if the income and market prices of these different issues contain a high degree of positive covariance, that is, if the timing, duration, and magnitude of their fluctuations are similar. Effective diversification is only achieved if the portfolio is comprised of securities that do not fluctuate in a similar fashion as they react to external stimuli, for example, economic changes.

This principle can be more readily understood by considering a simple two-stock portfolio having equal amounts invested in each of two issues. If the two stocks were positively correlated, the price movement would resemble Figure 15-2. If they were negatively correlated, the price movement would resemble Figure 15-3. In this case, when one security price rises, the other declines in exactly the same proportion, and vice versa. By combining these two issues into one portfolio, variance in the portfolio's return is completely eliminated.

A general rule can now be formulated for a two-security portfolio: When the correlation of price movement between the two securities is not perfectly positive, the variance in the portfolio's return is less than if the portfolio contained only one of the two securities.

Obviously, practical problems go far beyond the consideration of a two-security portfolio. Therefore, the basic principle must be expanded to include all possible portfolio combinations available for selection. For each

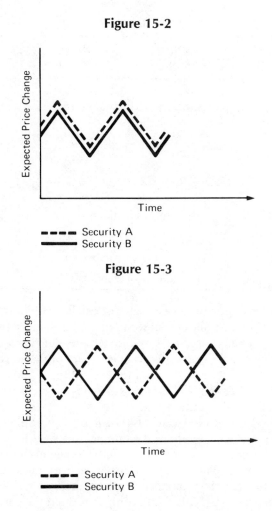

Figure 15-2

Figure 15-3

portfolio considered, it is necessary to calculate not only the expected return, but also the expected variance in the return over the time period under review.

RISK AND RETURN ON THE PORTFOLIO

The return on the portfolio is the weighted average of the returns on its component securities. The weight of each security is the fraction of the total value of the portfolio of which it is a part. Table 15-1 illustrates this relationship (the expected rate of return equals R_i).

Table 15-1

Security	Proportion Invested	Rate of Return	$X_i R_i$
(i)	(X_i)	(R_i)	.03
1	.25	.12	.04
2	.25	.16	.04
3	.50	.08	
Total	1.00		.11

$$R_p = X_1 R_1 + X_2 R_2 + X_3 R_3 + \ldots + X_n R_n = \sum_{i=1}^{n} X_i R_i$$

where: R_p = return of portfolio

X_i = proportion invested

R_i = rate of return expected

n = number of securities

The relationship between estimates of risk for individual securities and estimates of risk for portfolios is not so simple. One commonly used measure of risk is the variability measured by the variance (or the square root of it, the standard deviation). This is the weighted sum of the squared deviations of a variable around its expected value where the weights are the probabilities that the deviations will occur. It provides a measure of the spread or dispersion of the distribution.

Although the expected rate of return on a portfolio is a weighted average of the expected rates on the component securities of a portfolio, the variance of a portfolio is not a weighted average of the variances of the component securities. The variance of each security does matter, but it is also necessary to know the relationship among changes in the rates of return on the component assets. This relationship is termed the **covariance**. It has already been indicated that as long as two securities are not perfectly and positively correlated with each other, the effect of risk will be reduced.

The application of modern portfolio theory begins with judgments on individual securities and how their price changes in relation to each other vary over time. These judgments must be predicated on reasonable expectations of future uncertain developments. The security analyst and portfolio manager must translate their investment research analysis into estimates of future rates of return and assign probability weightings to the likelihood of the returns actually occurring. The modern practice of assigning probabilities and specifying covariances substantially extends traditional analytical procedures. However, the tenets of modern portfolio theory continue to be based on the fundamental analysis of companies, industries, and overall economic forces that affect the outlook for stock prices.

General Principles of Diversification

As mentioned before, although the expected return for the portfolio is simply the weighted average of the expected returns on its securities, the risk of a portfolio is not equal to the weighted average of the risks of its component securities. Instead, it depends not only on the risks of its component securities, but also on the extent to which they are affected similarly by underlying events. Usually, as the previous example has shown, the risk of a portfolio is less than the weighted average of the risks of its component securities owing to the effect of diversification.

General principles of diversification can be stated as follows:

1. When the portfolio contains securities whose returns are perfectly positively correlated, $r_{ij} = 1$, diversification does not help.
2. When the portfolio contains securities whose returns are perfectly negatively correlated, $r_{ij} = -1$, diversification eliminates the risk completely.
3. When the portfolio contains uncorrelated securities, $r_{ij} = 0$, the insurance principle, that is, risk pooling applies.

The correlation between the returns on security i and on security j is defined mathematically as

$$r_{ij} = \frac{\text{cov}(R_i, R_j)^1}{(S_i)(S_j)}$$

where: R_i = return on security i

R_j = return on security j

S_i = standard deviation of returns of security i

S_j = standard deviation of returns of security j

---

[1] Cov (R_i, R_j) the covariance of rates of return between security i and security j, is

$$E\{[R_i - E(R_i)][R_j - E(R_j)]\}$$

where $E(R_i)$, the expected value of return on security i, is

$$\sum_{t=1}^{n} (P_t)(R_{it})$$

P_t, the probability of the tth event, is

$$\sum_{t=1}^{n} P_t = 1$$

and R_{it} is the rate of return on security i when the tth event takes place. Equivalently,

$$\text{cov}(R_i, R_j) = \sum_{t=1}^{n} P_t\{[R_{it} - E(R_i)][R_{jt} - E(R_j)]\}$$

For example, assume that there are only two events: 1 and 2. Event 1 has 40 percent chance of occurrence, whereas event 2 has 60 percent chance of occurrence. Also, assume that there are only two securities evenly contained in the portfolio, A and B. Further assume that, when event 1 takes place, security A will have a return of 10 percent, whereas security B will yield 12 percent.

When event 2 takes place, security A yields 20 percent, and security B, 10 percent. Table 15-2 summarizes the situation and shows the return of the portfolio as well as its reduced risk (in terms of standard deviation) due to diversification.

Table 15-2

(1) Event	(2) Probability	Return (%) (3) A	(4) B	(5) = .5 × (3) + .5 × (4) Portfolio
1	.4	10	12	11
2	.6	20	10	15
Expected return (%):		16	10.8	13.4
Standard deviation (%):		4.9	0.98	1.96

Covariance $(R_A, R_B) = -.00048$

Correlation: $r_{AB} = \dfrac{-.00048}{(4.9\%)(.98\%)} = -.983$

As the result of diversification, the portfolio contains 50 percent of security A and 50 percent of security B and has a risk level of 1.96 percent as measured by its standard deviation. Due to a high negative correlation, the risk level is reduced from 2.94 percent [= (.5)(4.9%) + (.5)(.98%)], the standard deviation of this portfolio if no diversification is effective, to 1.96% when diversification is effective.

When a portfolio is expanded to include more than two securities, Markowitz offers a mathematical computer technique that permits the determination of the most probable rates of return on numerous possible portfolio combinations of the individual securities and the associated possible range of deviations from these most likely returns. However, once an efficient portfolio is constructed, it will not retain its optimum status for a long period of time because stock prices fluctuate. Thus, the computer program must be continually rerun, and a new, efficient portfolio composition must be determined each time. High-speed computer capability has also enabled the investor to utilize different assumptions about expected return, variance, and covariance for various combinations of individual securities.

The Markowitz approach has been criticized from both theoretical and practical points of view. One criticism concerns the assumption that rational investors are actually risk averters. The argument holds that it is irrational for investors to accept an opportunity whereby they might receive a 5 percent or 23 percent return over one that might result in either a 7 percent or 21 percent return, when both offer an expected return of 14 percent.

A closely related consideration is whether or not the variance is the most appropriate measure of risk. Most of the empirical work stimulated by Markowitz uses short-term price volatility to determine whether the expected rate of return from a security should be assigned a high or low expected variance. If investors have limited liquidity constraints, and if they are truly long-term holders of securities, then short-term price volatility per se does not pose a risk to the investors. Instead, in this case, the question of concern is one of ultimate price realization and not short-term volatility.

There are some practical limitations to using Markowitz's techniques. First, because many practicing investment managers could not understand the conceptual mathematics involved, they became suspicious of the academic approach to portfolio management and thought that the approach was essentially unsound. Second, although security analysts and portfolio managers are accustomed to thinking about expected rates of return, they are much less comfortable about assessing the possible ranges of error in their expectations and are generally unaccustomed to distinguishing covariances among securities.

There is, however, a growing awareness among portfolio managers of the relevance and use of many of the mathematical portfolio techniques that have evolved over the last 20 years. Nevertheless, even those practicing analysts and portfolio managers who have attempted to apply the mathematical portfolio techniques to the everyday management of security portfolios have found the techniques less than optimal in reducing or identifying all risks associated with portfolios. Much of the criticism centers around the issue of whether or not any reasonable degree of accuracy can be achieved in portfolio management by using these mathematical techniques, because investing continues to be considered an art, not a science. Many extreme mathematically oriented portfolio theorists have a tendency to believe that the best possible portfolio decisions are those that are made with the aid of various mathematical techniques, but the majority of practicing portfolio managers recognize the limitations of these mathematical techniques. Success in portfolio management still hinges on the successful merging of both traditional and modern portfolio management.

An additional limitation in the use of the Markowitz model is that each time a change in the existing portfolio comes under consideration the entire population of securities must be reevaluated to preserve the desired risk-return relationship. This, in turn, requires a large number of subsequent mathematical calculations.

Even more significant than the voluminous mathematical computations required for the Markowitz model are the portfolio alterations required to achieve constant portfolio efficiency. There may be so many alterations that the costs would be uneconomic.

Despite its shortcomings, Markowitz's contribution to modern portfolio theory cannot be minimized. Markowitz forced others in the investment field to consider that some measure of risk, and not just the expected rate of return, should be considered when dealing with investment decisions.

CAPITAL MARKET LINE

A natural extension of the Markowitz analysis was to consider the problem of building portfolios that include riskless assets, portfolios purchased in part with borrowed funds, and portfolios containing risky assets paid for in full with the investor's equity.

Introducing a riskless asset into a portfolio presents some interesting consequences. Generally, a riskless asset yield is defined as the current yield on treasury bills. In Figure 15-4 the return on a risk-free asset is designated by R_f on the vertical axis. Sharpe[2] and Tobin[3] pointed out that if this alternative exists, it is possible to select portfolios at a given point on the line R_fB defined by the return of the riskless asset and the point of tangency with the efficiency frontier of portfolios of risky assets.

The tangency point, X, is said to be the optimum combination of the risky securities. Because if we combine the riskless point, R_f, with any other portfolio, the result is a risk-return combination lying on a lower, hence less desirable, level than the point X. The line R_fXB is called the **capital market line**. Portfolios represented by points between R_f and X on this line indicate that the investors are lending (lending money to the federal government). Points beyond point X on the capital market line indicate that the investors are using leverage (i.e., borrowing).

However, this model assumes that investors can borrow and lend at the same rate (i.e., the risk-free rate) without limit. In fact, such assumption is not practical. Usually, investors will have to borrow at a higher rate, or they are restricted in the amount of borrowing. When borrowing rate, b,

[2]William F. Sharpe, "A Simplified Model for Portfolio Analysis," *Management Science*, January 1963, 277–293.

[3]James Tobin, "Liquidity Preference as Behavior Towards Risk," *Review of Economic Studies*, February 1958, 65–86.

Figure 15-4   Efficient Frontier with Leverage

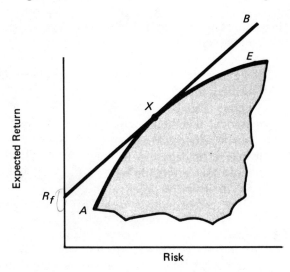

is higher than the lending rate, R_f, the efficient investment strategies are as shown in Figure 15-5.

The efficient frontier is the curve $AXBE$. The risk-free rate of return, R_f, makes risky portfolios between A and X on the frontier curve less desirable, because the combinations of the riskless asset and the market portfolio, X, provide higher levels of return for the same level of risk. The curve between X and B is still efficient. The ability to borrow money at rate b makes those formerly efficient portfolios between B and E uninteresting. Therefore, the capital market line is now two lines: R_fX, and BC plus a curve between X and B. Investors who choose to lend can select portfolios on line R_fX. Those who want to borrow can select portfolios on line BC.

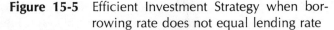

Figure 15-5   Efficient Investment Strategy when borrowing rate does not equal lending rate

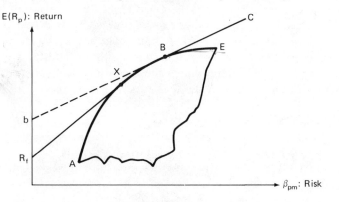

Finally, those investors who choose not to borrow nor to lend stay on the curve between X and B. The unique point that represents the specific portfolio the investor chooses is then determined by the level of risk the investor is willing and able to assume.

Capital-Asset Pricing Model (CAPM)

To define Markowitz's efficient set of portfolios, it is necessary to know each security's expected return, its variance, and its covariance with every other security. If the efficient set were to be selected from a list of 1,000 securities, it would be necessary to have 1,000 statistics for the expected return, 1,000 variances, and 499,500 covariances.

Because of this practical difficulty, Markowitz's model was of very little interest until Sharpe suggested a simplification. Instead of measuring the covariance of every pair of securities under consideration for possible investment, he built upon Markowitz's suggestions that each security's price movements could be related to a broad common stock market index such as the Standard & Poor's 500 Stock Index. This immediately reduced the number of calculations involved in determining efficient portfolios, and it vastly simplified the practical complications of the basic theory.

Sharpe further indicated that this approach could separate risk into two distinct elements: systematic (nondiversifiable) risk and nonsystematic (diversifiable) risk. Market risk, or **systematic, nondiversifiable risk,** is that portion of the stock's price or portfolio investment that can be attributed to movement of the market as a whole. **Nonsystematic, diversifible risk** is that portion of price movement unique to the specific asset. These two risk elements were discussed in Chapter 1.

Not all companies are positioned to respond to broad market movements with the same degree of sensitivity. Important market events change the value of some companies more than others. This may reflect the relative degree of financial leverage, operating leverage, comparative P/E ratios, and so forth. Whatever the case, the market sensitivity relationship can be measured and can be illustrated by partitioning the return on common stock into its two basic elements: a market component and a specific stock component. Therefore, another way to measure the risk of a portfolio is by using its component securities' **beta,** which measures the relative sensitivities of the securities to the change in the market.

Assumptions of the Capital-Asset Pricing Model

The approach, which is termed the capital-asset pricing model, developed by Sharpe in 1963 to 1964, is designed to price individual securities (capital assets) within a portfolio context. Some of the important assumptions made in the original version of the CAPM are as follows:

1. Every investor has the same informaton and analyzes it in the same way. Therefore, everyone agrees with each other about the future prospects for securities.
2. The investors' only concern is risk of and return on the securities.
3. Transaction costs are ignored.
4. Every investor is able to borrow and/or lend money at the "risk-free" rate.
5. Taxes are assumed to have no noticeable effect on investment policy.

According to the CAPM, the relevant aspects of a security are its contribution to the return of an efficient portfolio, and its contribution to the risk of an efficient portfolio. As a basic belief, in major market moves, most securities move in the same direction, although at different rates. Therefore, the sensitivity of a security's price to change in the overall market is of crucial importance. It constitutes the major component of the security's contribution to the portfolio risk. This element is captured by the idea of beta.

Security Characteristic Line

To be more explicit, the CAPM asserts that there is a statistically linear relationship between the expected excess return over the risk-free rate on the market portfolio and the expected excess return on any portfolio or individual security over the risk-free rate. The market portfolio is a combination of all securities, each in proportion to the market value outstanding. Under the assumptions of the original CAPM, efficient investment strategies include only 1. the market portfolio, 2. borrowing and/or 3. lending. Mathematically,

$$E(R_i) - R_f = \alpha_i + \beta_{im}[E(R_m) - R_f]$$

where

R_i = return on security i

R_f = risk-free rate of return

R_m = return on the market portfolio

β_{im} = sensitivity of the security's price to the overall market; the security's beta value

α_i = expected risk-adjusted excess return

Notice that the value of α_i can be negative, as shown in the graph (a) of Figure 15-6 or zero, as shown in graph (b); or it can be positive as shown in graph (c). The straight line illustrated in this figure is called the security's characteristic line, which has a slope equal to the security's beta value, β_{im}. In the case of (a), the security underperforms the market. Case (b) indicates that the security's return is the same as its normally expected rate of return. This is the case of market equilibrium. In case (c), the security outperforms the market ("beats the market"). The same relationship holds

Figure 15-6 Characteristic Line

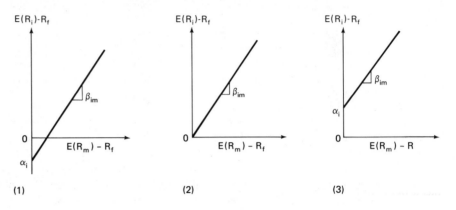

(1)   (2)   (3)

for any portfolio relative to the market portfolio. The characteristic line for a portfolio can be constructed in the same fashion:

$$E(R_p) - R_f = \alpha_p + \beta_{pm}[E(R_m) - R_f]$$

where R_p = the return on the portfolio.

Furthermore, $$\alpha_p = \sum_{i=1}^{n} w_i \alpha_i$$

$$\beta_{pm} = \sum_{i=1}^{n} w_i \beta_{im}$$

where w_i = proportion of the market value of the portfolio p invested in security i, assuming that p contains n different securities

If α_p is greater than zero, the portfolio will beat the market. Similarly, if α_p is negative, the portfolio underperforms the market. When the market is in equilibrium, α_p equals zero[4], and so does α_i for any security i in the

---

[4] Assume a portfolio contains both risk-free securities, such as-treasury bills, and risky assets, such as a market portfolio; then, in equilibrium condition,
$$E(R_p) = (1 - k)R_f + k[E(R_m)]$$
$$\beta_{pm} = (1 - k)0 + k(\beta_m)$$
Since $\beta_m = 1$, by definition, $\beta_{pm} = k$, which is the proportion of the portfolio invested in risky assets. Substituting β_{pm} for k, we obtain
$$E(R_p) = (1 - \beta_{pm}) R_f + \beta_{pm} E(R_m) \qquad (1)$$
$$= R_f + \beta_{pm}[E(R_m) - R_f]$$
Since $E(R_p) - R_f = \alpha_p + \beta_{pm}[E(R_m) - R_f]$ according to the characteristic line equation. After rearrangement of the equation,
$$E(R_p) = \alpha_p + R_f + \beta_{pm}[E(R_m) - R_f] \qquad (2)$$
From (1) and (2), $\alpha_p = 0$ results, if the market is in equilibrium.

market. Hence, the characteristic line equations are reduced to

$$E(R_i) = R_f + \beta_{im}[E(R_m) - R_f] \quad \text{for any individual security}$$
$$E(R_p) = R_f + \beta_{pm}[E(R_m) - R_f] \quad \text{for any portfolio}$$

Plotting these two equations results in the security market line (SML) and the capital market line (CML), as shown in Figure 15-7.

According to the SML graph, security A has a beta value of 0.5, and will have an expected return, $E(R_p)$, equal to $R_f + .5[E(R_m) - R_f]$. For example, if the T-bill rate is 15 percent and the expected return on the market portfolio is 18 percent, the expected return on security A is 16.5 percent [15% + .5(18% − 15%)]. The expected return on security B, which has a beta value of 1.5, is 19.5 percent [15% + 1.5(18% − 15%)].

The same relationship can be expanded to cover the case of a portfolio. Therefore, if the expected return on the market portfolio can be estimated and the value of the risk-free rate is known, by determining the portfolio's beta (the weighted average of its component securities' betas), the expected return of the portfolio can be obtained.

FATE OF MODERN PORTFOLIO THEORY

Before Markowitz infused portfolio management with a high degree of sophistication, portfolio practioners used rules of thumb and intuition to arrive at their portfolio decisions. Using a risk-reward framework in his pioneering efforts, Markowitz adapted mathematical programming and statistical analysis to portfolio management. The literature of portfolio construction theory following Markowitz's original research has grown at a very rapid rate, and a great many variations of portfolio models have been developed.

Figure 15-7

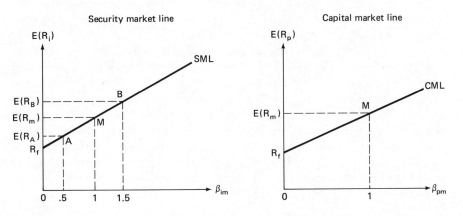

There are some limitations on the effort being made by modern port-folio theorists in their quest to construct efficient portfolios, that is, portfolios with the highest expected rate of return at a given level of risk. The portfolios require statistical inputs. Once the inputs are obtained, the remainder of the solution is a problem in logic and mathematics. If the inputs are correct, the logic is generally valid and the mathematical methods properly applied produce the desirable output. However, the critical element is the **accuracy** of the inputs.

Random-walk theorists believe that the future rate of return is com-pletely unpredictable because stock prices over the short-term move un-predictably. Therefore, they feel that valid inputs are impossible and that portfolio construction is no more than an exercise in mathematics. However, financial analysts believe that they can predict future rates of return within some acceptable range of accuracy. For many financial analysts, the range of frequency distribution of expected rates for stock has been very accept-able. However, a range of expected rates of return is not generally accepted as input for modern portfolio construction. The difficulty is that most esti-mates are subjective and can have large margins of error. Both the traditional financial analyst and the quantitative portfolio manager have often been criticized because the inputs they use for portfolio construction may contain large margins of error.

The difficulty centers in the vast number of unpredictable events that can cause sizable changes in realized rates of return from securities during a particular period of time. Management's mistakes sometimes do come to light. For example, a company that has been highly profitable and is gen-erally regarded as having a very bright future must absorb huge write-offs of unprofitable ventures. The company's earnings per share figures that for a number of years have been steadily increasing annually may suddenly decline or go below zero, with a sharp corresponding decline in market price, which gives little validity to previous market forecasts. History is littered with such cases. Certainly, basic changes in an industry that may have long been regarded as a growth industry may result in an end to growth due to demand slackening, product prices sagging, and overall expenses rising at a faster rate than changes in revenues.

The period from the late 1960s through the early 1980s gave analysts many a nightmare because their ability to predict the effects of events on portfolio performance was less than desirable. This was true for both the traditional as well as the quantitative portfolio managers, because the un-quantifiable forces against the market left the investors with little comfort. Although advances in modern portfolio theory have been of great help in analyzing historic risk inherent in the market and groups of securities, its inability to predict the future currently gives its methods little advantage over the more traditional portfolio approaches.

beta
capital-asset pricing model
capital market line
covariance
diversification
efficient frontier
expected return
market component
nonsystematic risk

risk aversion
riskless asset
risk pooling
security characteristic line
security market line
standard deviation
stock component
systematic risk
variance

QUESTIONS

1. Why should an investor look at a security in the context of his or her total portfolio rather than individually?
2. Explain the basic premise of Markowitz's theory and portfolio model.
3. What is Markowitz's definition of risk? Why might diversification not be effective in dealing with risk?
4. Describe modern portfolio theory.
5. What criticisms have been made of Markowitz's theory?
6. Explain the efficient frontier theory. How does this theory relate to Markowitz's basic premise?
7. How can an investor receive the desired level of yield of a portfolio on the efficient frontier but at less risk?
8. Markowitz's portfolio model was criticized for practical reasons. How did Sharpe simplify this model?
9. Theoretically, the investor invests at the point on the market characteristic line that gives him the combination of yield and risk that allows him to maximize his net worth and make a satisfactory return. Why might an investor not operate at this point?
10. Sharpe divided risk into different components. What are these components?
11. Why are ranges of expected rates of return generally unacceptable as inputs for modern portfolio construction?

SELECTED READINGS

BLACK, FISHER. "Random Walk and Portfolio Management." *Financial Analysts Journal*, 27, no. 2, 1971, 16–22.

BLUME, MARSHALL E. "Betas and Their Regression Tendencies." *Journal of Finance*, June 1975, 787–795.

————. "Betas and Their Regression Tendencies: Some Further Evidence." *Journal of Finance*, March 1979, 265–267.

HAGIN, ROBERT L. *The Dow-Jones-Irwin Guide to Modern Portfolio Theory*. Homewood, Ill.: Dow Jones-Irwin, 1979.

MARKOWITZ, HARRY M. *Portfolio Selection*, New York: Wiley, 1959. Also "Portfolio Selection," *Journal of Finance*, March 1952.

MARTIN, JOHN D., and ARTHUR KEOWN. "A Misleading Feature of Beta for Risk Measurement." *Journal of Portfolio Management*, Summer 1977, 31–34.

McCLAY, MARVIN. "The Penalties of Incurring Unsystematic Risk." *Journal of Portfolio Management*, Spring 1978, 31–35.

MODIGLIANI, FRANCO, and GERALD A. POGUE. "An Introduction to Risk and Return." *Financial Analysts Journal*, 30, no. 2, 1974, 68–80.

ROLL, RICHARD, "Ambiguity When Performance Is Measured by the Securities Market Line." *Journal of Finance*, September 1978, 1051–1070.

ROSS, STEPHEN A. "The Current Status of the Capital Asset Pricing Model." *Journal of Finance*, June 1978, 885–901.

SHARPE, WILLIAM F. "A Simplified Model for Portfolio Analysis." *Management Science*, January 1963, 277–293.

————. "Bonds versus Stocks: Some Lessons from Capital Market Theory." *Financial Analysis Journal*, November–December 1973, 74–80.

16

Real Estate Investments

Real estate is one of the most familiar forms of investment. The places in which we live and work are someone's investments in real estate. Housing construction is the largest single item of national wealth, representing over one-tenth of the nation's total output. Between 1980 and 2000, the United States will spend approximately $1,500 billion on new and renewal nonfarm housing. In addition, $1,000 billion will be spent on commercial, industrial, and utility expansion and renovation.

The demand for real estate is closely related to the size of the population and the level of disposable personal income. By 1985, the population should approach 250 million, and by 2000, 285 million, despite a declining birthrate. This trend tremendously increases the demand for all types of real property, especially housing. In addition, 85 percent of this growth will be concentrated in 12 major metropolitan areas. These areas constitute only 10 percent of the total land acreage yet contain 65 percent of the population. In urban areas, increased housing and increased government housing subsidies will be required. The trend has been toward larger and more complex units. Disposable personal income generally rises and falls with GNP.

Generally, the more money a consumer has, the more that is spent on real estate. This is particularly true in periods of prosperity and growth.

Conversely, the real estate industry suffers during periods of tight money and recession. This has been true for the last 50 years, although proportionately less of the dollar has been spent on home ownership. Future levels of disposable personal income are more difficult to predict, but they are generally expected to rise, and the field of real estate should benefit as a result.

MAJOR AREAS OF REAL ESTATE INVESTMENT

Real estate is composed of several distinct areas of investment opportunity. Land is the most common. It is purchased for motives such as development, capital gains from general appreciation in value, or for its productive income use, as in the case of farmland. Undeveloped land is land for which no use has been set and consists of three main types: vacant land, unused farmland, and reclaimed land. Each demonstrates special investment characteristics and risks.

Once an investor constructs an improvement of any type on the land, it becomes real property. Homes represent the most widespread investment in real property. The 1980 census established that approximately 95 percent of all occupied housing units were nonfarm. Of these, 62 percent were owner occupied; 38 percent were rented properties.

Real property may be held for the production of income in the form of rents on apartments, office complexes, farms, or any other rentable property. The investor may hold property, not because it produces significant income, but in the anticipation of selling the property at a later date to realize a capital gain. Vacant lots are usually held for this purpose. Investments in property held for business or trade can offer desirable returns. Finally, real estate brokers and subdividers often hold property for sale to customers.

ADVANTAGES OF REAL ESTATE INVESTMENT

Real estate offers some important advantages. Financing is usually flexible and easily obtainable if the borrower's credit is adequate and if the property is of sufficient value. Furthermore, the buyer can effectively utilize mortgage debt and invest only a small portion of his own funds. Intelligently selected real estate should appreciate in value and provide direct rental or business income, as well as significant tax advantages. Real estate values tend to increase with the general price level and therefore provide some protection against loss resulting from inflation. Even if the property is poorly chosen or if general economic conditions worsen, it is unlikely that rental income will cease entirely, and the owner will still be able to write off depreciation and maintenance charges against his or her income.

This is more than can be said of many other poorly selected investments, such as stocks, which might lose all value and earning power. During times of prosperity, the owner of real property benefits from the fact that consumers have more money to spend on a relatively fixed short-run supply of land and buildings. Increased demand and buying power tend to increase the value of general property holdings. Also, during extended periods of inflation, the use of long-term debt will reduce the effective cost by repaying with depreciated dollars.

DISADVANTAGES OF REAL ESTATE INVESTMENT

Real estate investment does, however, create some special problems and disadvantages. The general principles of appreciation, income, and tax advantages may be simple to understand, but their profitable application demands a knowledge of the complexities involved. The management of real property holdings often demands greater commitment of time and energy than do most other forms of investment. Also, the investment of most real estate purchases requires large amounts of capital commitments for long periods of time that preclude wide diversification of investments. This investment normally is not subject to quick liquidation. Instead, the seller must find a buyer willing to accept the sales price, which may be difficult in times of depressed values and tight money. Furthermore, the renegotiation of loan arrangements can be time consuming and depends upon a great number of conditions. Because of the great sums of capital involved, a major mistake made in real estate investment can financially ruin an investor.

RESIDENTIAL PROPERTY: THE BUY OR RENT DECISION

The purchase of a home is a common investment and deserves special examination by a potential buyer. The basis of the examination generally is a comparison of the benefits and expenses arising from renting an apartment or buying a home. The apartment dweller has one major living expense: rent. In addition, the renter usually pays modest fees for utilities and insurance on the furnishings. Major appliances, carpeting, and air conditioning equipment are usually supplied with the apartment and are covered by the rent payment. Additional direct operating expenses are negligible.

The homeowner, however, incurs a wide variety of additional expenses. Home ownership is economically justified only if the additional benefits exceed the expenses. The benefits arise mostly through tax savings on interest expenses and property taxes and the general appreciation of the property value.

Table 16-1 compares renting an apartment at $350 per month with purchasing a home at $60,000. The comparison covers a 5-year period and assumes the sale of the real estate at that time. The 5-year period is used because most families change residence at least once during the first 5-year period after marriage. The figures are based on data supplied by realtors during 1981 and are conservatively stated (e.g., a 12 percent loan rate, modest utility bills, and a 20 percent cash down payment on the real estate). For simplicity's sake, a few assumptions are made in the example: the mortgage is for 30 years, the individual's opportunity cost is also at 12

Table 16–1
Comparison of Cost of Home Ownership versus Renting an Apartment

5-Year Totals	Apartment		Home	
	Cash Outflow After Tax	Cash Outflow	After Tax[a]	
Rent $350 per month	$21,000	$ 0	$ 0	
Interest on loan	0	28,502	21,376	
Principal payments	0	1,121	1,121	
Taxes	0	6,000	4,500	
Insurance	450	600	600	
Utilities (excluding phone)	3,600	6,000	6,000	
Repairs on building and equipment	0	2,000	2,000	
Income lost on down payment	0	7,200	5,400	
Closing costs when buying (3% of mortgage)	0	1,440	1,320[b]	
7% sales commission when sold	0	4,200	4,200	
Closing costs when selling	0	200	200	
Total cash outflow	$25,050		$46,717	
less principal returned at time of sale			-1,121	
Net cash outflow	$25,050		$45,596	
Plus cost of lost income from higher cash outflows on home versus apartment			2,466[c]	
Total Net Cost	$25,050		$48,062	
Differential between home and apartment = $23,012				

[a] Assumes a 25% tax rate.

[b] About one-third of the closing costs when buying are tax deductible $(1,440/3) \times .25 = 120$. $1,440 - 120 = 1,320$.

[c] $(45,596 - 25,050) \times 12\% = 2,466$.

percent, and there is no time value of money associated with the cash flows. The purpose of the exhibit is to present the general logic used in what has become a typical decision for many people. Each individual decision will demand financial comparisons unique to the situation.

For the selected example, the only way the purchase of the home is more economically desirable over renting the apartment, for the 5-year period based on conservative data, would be for the real estate to appreciate by more than $23,012 when sold, which is equivalent to an annual compounded growth rate of approximately 7 percent. To give the illustration more validity, one should also consider the great number of additional expenditures that are associated with owning a home, for example, purchasing appliances, additional furniture, decorating, garden equipment, and lawn-care equipment. These additional expenditures only increase the cash outflow and, therefore, necessitate a much larger percent of increase in the value of the house to overcome the advantages of the apartment.

The decision to buy a home is often made on the basis of life-style rather than on economics. Specific cases vary substantially from the data presented in Table 16-1. The length of time the house will be owned and the rate of price appreciation dramatically affect the buy versus rent decision.

INDIRECT OWNERSHIP OF REAL ESTATE

An investor might choose not to invest in real estate directly. Some projects require too much capital, too great a risk, or too much supervision and managerial talent for one person or family. Large projects such as housing developments are often so complex that they demand the pooling of money and talents. For these and other reasons, an investor might seek equity ownership in a real estate firm that will make the investment on the investor's behalf. An investor may invest indirectly by purchasing equity interest in one of several types of companies that specialize in real estate investment, for example, in real estate syndicates, in real estate investment trusts, and in real estate corporations. These companies offer a wide variety of opportunities, professional management, diversification, and levels of risk.

Real Estate Syndicate

During the early 1950s, real estate development greatly increased and a new source of investment funds evolved: the public syndicate. A **syndicate** is a group of investors who pool their funds for real estate investment. The number of partners may vary from several friends to an unlimited number of individual investors. Most syndicates are limited partnerships, which offer the important legal advantage of limiting an investor's liability to his direct dollar investment. Syndicates may also be in the form of corporations or trusts, although these legal forms are less common. The limited partnership offers an additional important advantage in that it escapes corporate taxation. All income and loss in the limited partnership are passed through to the individual owners and are therefore taxed as individual income or loss. The corporation, however, is taxed first for its own profits; then the individual stockholder is taxed on his or her share of the corporate profits paid in dividends.

Real estate syndicates flourished during the 1950s and continue to be popular. Yields on investments can be increased through using accelerated depreciation, which gives the investor tax advantages.

The desirability of real estate is centered in the expenses that create a tax shelter because they lower the investor's taxable income bracket. As income is generated from the investment, it is applied to the mortgage and various operating expenses and depreciation. When the investment no longer generates sufficient depreciation by accelerated methods and when the interest expense declines to a point where the investment fails to provide a significant tax shelter, the property is usually sold, at a profit if possible.

The capital gain on a property is taxed at a long-term capital rate that is one-half of the taxpayer's ordinary rate. Proceeds from the sale are reinvested in other property, and the cycle begins again with accelerated depreciation and high interest payments. In this manner, syndicates avoid repaying the tax saved through accelerated depreciation. Not all syndicates have been successful at this process, and by the late 1960s, they were less important than trusts.

Real Estate Investment Trusts

Real estate investment trusts (REIT) are similar to closed-end investment companies (discussed in Chapter 10). They issue public shares, many of which are traded over the counter, although some are listed on various stock exchanges. The funds raised from the sale of stock are invested in real estate property or mortgages. These trusts enable indirect investment in a wide variety of diversified holdings and offer the investor professional management. Even though trusts are similar to investment companies, there are important differences. According to the Real Estate Investment Trust Act of 1960, to qualify as a real estate investment trust for special tax considerations, a trust must distribute at least 90 percent of its ordinary taxable income to shareholders to avoid taxation as a separate corporate entity. These funds, as well as any capital gains distributed to stockholders, are exempt from federal taxation for the trust. The two general types of REITs are those that specialize in investing in real property and land (**equity trusts**) and those that make loans of various durations to builders, property buyers, and developers (**mortgage trusts**).

Under certain economic conditions and with proper management, real estate trusts can be good investments and offer significant benefits, such as favorable tax treatment. In 1968, REITs had total assets of over $1 billion and were paying annual cash returns of 6 to 9 percent. They also provided owners with an established market for their shares. However, sizable management fees can be encountered. More importantly, a financially sound trust can be greatly affected by alterations in the general market for borrowed funds. If the money supply is tight, trusts might have to borrow short-term funds at high rates to meet contractual long-term loan agreements at lower rates. The profitability of the trust can be seriously affected if these conditions exist for a long time. Steady inflation reduces the buying power of the trust's mortgage reserve funds. For these and other reasons, investment in REITs can be risky; therefore, the individual investor should seek expert advice on REIT investments.

Several years ago there was a decline and collapse of many sizable real estate investment trusts because they had become greatly overextended. The building boom of the late 1960s and early 1970s was accelerated by the REITs, which had substantial sums of money. Contractors were eager to build as long as funds were available. However, many projects constructed by REITs went unsold or could not be rented because the amount of new units available for occupancy far exceeded demand. During the early 1970s, almost all REITs found themselves in grave financial conditions; and in 1974, 19 of the 20 largest percentage stock market losers on the New York Stock Exchange were REITs. Despite the past poor record, recent years have seen a resurgence in interest in REITs. The desire of investors to seek avenues to combat inflation has made them more attractive.

Real Estate Corporations

A number of corporations deal exclusively in real estate holdings. Unlike the case of trusts, real estate corporations must pay tax whether or not they pay substantial dividends to shareholders. The corporation is taxed on the income, but instead of disbursing substantial portions of the income, the firm may reinvest profits for further expansion.

The overall yield on real estate companies would generally be less than the yields on trusts because of a lower level of distributed earnings and less tax advantages.

Like trusts, real estate companies are vulnerable to the same effects of a tight or an easy money market, a depressed construction industry, and high inflation levels. For similar reasons, many real estate companies have gone into bankruptcy in recent years. Investment in real estate companies should receive the same degree of careful investigation as investment in REITs, with an emphasis upon the expected conditions of future money markets, the forecasted level of building activity, and inflation levels.

The corporate form combines economic power and diversification superior to that of the limited partnership and is less encumbered by regulatory restrictions than the REITs. In fact, early real estate syndicates often have converted to the corporate form of organization because several advantages outweigh the possible single tax advantage of the partnership form.

FINANCIAL ANALYSIS AND FUNDING OF REAL ESTATE INVESTMENT PROJECTS

Real Estate Valuation and Appraisal

Distinction between Price and Value

From the buyer's point of view, a good investment in a parcel of real estate will largely be determined by the price that must be paid, the potential value of the property, and any cash flows generated during the period in which the property is held. Value, the key issue, is different from price. The buyer or seller's objective is to determine whether or not the price truly reflects the value of the property. If it does not, financing may be difficult to obtain and either the seller or buyer will be at a disadvantage. Market value is concerned with determining the present value of future benefits to be derived from property ownership in the form of rents or other cash flows. Both present and possible future uses should be considered when valuing a real estate investment. For example, a residential property might become a business site; a private home might become a rental home. Market price and market value may differ. Market price is the dollar value attributed to the property at the time of a transaction and it represents an individual's opinion of the property's true value.

Appraisal Principles

An appraisal, which is an estimation and opinion of value, can be little more than an informal opinion or it can be a highly sophisticated analysis. An appraisal is used to determine the fairness of the market price. In its definition of market value, the American Institute of Real Estate Appraisers includes the highest price estimated in terms of money that a property will bring in the open market, a reasonable time to find a purchaser, and a purchaser who buys with the knowledge of all the uses with which the real estate can be adapted.

A professional written appraisal provides information on neighborhood characteristics, trends in population, employment, and income in the geographic area where the property is located. In addition, the size, shape, topography, and specific location of the site and structure are considered in determining how suitable the property is for its intended use and the value for which the property should be given. A total valuation is made to determine the stability of the property's value and its income-producing potential. The appraiser also considers the maximum potential return based on the land being put into its highest and best use and compares this with present usage rates of return for comparable real estate.

Appraising Users and Methods

Most real estate appraisals are conducted either by real estate brokers or by professional real estate appraisers. The two groups often use methods that differ significantly in sophistication. Real estate brokers usually use simple rules of thumb that quickly determine whether or not a market price is reasonable.

The **gross rent multiplier** (GRM) is a simple formula used to price income-producing property. It suggests that the market price should be within a dollar range dictated by a multiple of gross rentals. The multiple is derived by comparing the recent selling prices of similar properties in the same market area with gross rents. For example, the multiple for a small unfurnished apartment building might be seven times the gross rental income. Therefore, if annual rentals are $12,000, the selling price might be approximately $84,000. If the building is new, in excellent repair, and has some deluxe features (modern appliances and/or a swimming pool), the multiple may be as high as ten times the gross rents. In some areas of the country where property values increase at an above-average rate, the GRM may be considerably higher than the average for comparable buildings in other parts of the country. The GRM is a rough estimate of the value of an income-producing real estate property, and it assumes consistent operating and debt expenses within the limits of a typical comparable income-producing piece of real estate. Although the GRM is useful and generally reliable, it is only one of the devices used in professional appraising.

An improvement on the GRM is the **net income multiplier** (NIM), which takes into account variations in operating expenses. This calculation is similar to the price-earnings ratio for common stocks, which divides price by net income. In this case, net income is arrived at after operating expenses are deducted. Mortgage interest expenses, taxes, or depreciation are not deducted. In the case of gross rental income of $12,000, if we assume operating expenses of $5,000, the net operating income would be $7,000. Dividing $7,000 into the price of $84,000 yields a NIM of 12 ($84,000 ÷

$7,000 = 12$). The NIM is often expressed as a capitalization rate, which is the NIM inverted, which yields $\frac{1}{12}$, or a capitalization rate of .083. Like the GRM, the NIM is a useful general guide to market prices. A more detailed appraisal should also be conducted.

Another rule of thumb in appraising real estate is that the average net earning power is calculated as a percentage of the purchase price. For example, assume that an estimate of normal annual rental value can be obtained based on $400 a month on a two-unit apartment building. The total annual rent would be $4,800. From this $4,800 must be subtracted expenses such as operating costs, which include utilities, tenant services, maintenance expenses, insurance, taxes, and depreciation. If these expenses totaled $2,500, the net income would equal $2,300 per year. If the purchase price of the property was $36,000, the net earning power would be expressed as $2,300/$36,000 or 6.39 percent. The annual net earning power generally should not be less than 5 percent; however, this is determined by the investor's opportunity cost and the method and amount of depreciation.

Multipliers are also established for particular geographic areas and are based on some physical unit of measure, for example price per front foot or per cubic foot. Raw land in a suburban neighborhood might sell for $55 per front foot; whereas land in a business district of a downtown metropolitan city might sell for $1,000 per front foot. These multipliers are called **sales price multipliers** and evolve directly from local market conditions. Although useful and easy to determine, none of these multipliers estimates the investor's total yield on an investment, and the evaluation is not accurate enough to base a final purchase decision on.

The American Institute of Real Estate Appraisers is the major professional society for specialists in the appraisal field. The appraiser uses one or more of three major methods of valuation: the market approach, the income approach, or the replacement cost approach. A thorough appraisal estimates value by using all three methods and using each method as a cross-check on the accuracy of the other two methods, thereby indicating areas for further analysis and explanation. The results of the three methods should indicate values that fall within a narrow range of each other.

MARKET APPROACH TO VALUE. The market approach systematically compares the prices of similar land and similar properties recently sold or currently available and is used extensively for residential and nonincome property. It is important to define the relevant market carefully by the type of structure and location, making sure that the properties are actually comparable. For example, large office buildings may be so similar that a statewide market could be used as a basis of comparison, using properties from several cities of similar size. Homes may vary so greatly that the market may be confined to an immediate neighborhood.

The greater the number of sales used and the greater their comparability, the more accurate the appraisal will be. Because there will always be some degree of noncomparability, appraisal must be adjusted to reflect unique characteristics of the property, differences in age, location, and physical condition, the terms of past sales (including financing), and the time lapse between present and past sales data.

INCOME APPROACH TO VALUE. The income approach is the most sophisticated technique usually used in evaluating income property. Basically, the appraiser attempts to determine the present worth of the estimated future stream of income. In short, the appraiser attempts to determine the present value of all future cash flows derived over the remaining life of the property.

The appraiser attempts to capitalize the stream of income as a process whereby he converts the estimated cash flow into a value for the property. The income approach consists of two steps: (1) determine a stablized projected net annual cash flow, based on comparable market rents, historical expense data, and the tax shield from depreciation, and (2) determine an appropriate capitalization rate based on the expected yield and risk of the income-producing property. The projected income is divided by the capitalization rate to determine the market value. Assume that the capitalization rate is 11 percent and that the estimated cash flow is $11,000 per year. The property's value would be estimated at $100,000 ($11,000 ÷ .11 = $100,000). The various multipliers are often compared with the capitalized income value approach estimate as a cross-check on the accuracy of the appraisal process.

REPLACEMENT COST APPROACH TO VALUE. The replacement cost method, the most common method used to appraise residential property, is often used when income is not considered and market data are unavailable. This approach is used to estimate the value of churches and public buildings.

The appraiser first determines the cost of replacing the property. He or she usually uses a cost per foot construction standard for a particular type of construction and property. The standard is adjusted for local differences. Next, estimates of the total accumulated depreciation are deducted from the replacement cost. Finally, the present market value of the land is determined by comparing markets and adding that value to the depreciated replacement cost of buildings to determine the total value of the property. The substitution principle of real estate holds that the value of a piece of real property cannot exceed its cost of replacement.

Sources of Real Estate Finance

Principles of Debt Utilization in Real Estate Investing

If the valuation and appraisal process determines that a particular piece of real estate shows adequate yield potential to warrant investment, the next concern is the acquisition of necessary funds. Because large sums are usually involved in real estate investments, very few individuals can supply all the funds needed to complete a real estate purchase. Even if the funds were available from personal sources, an investor might still improve an investment return by borrowing the funds.

Financing allows an investor to contribute only a portion of the total purchase price. Very seldom must more than 35 percent of the total property purchase value be paid in cash. Sometimes government-backed loans allow borrowing up to 100 percent of the purchase price. Using secondary loan sources, an investor may only be contributing 10 or 20 percent of the purchase price. However, depreciation rates for tax purposes (for the investor) on income-producing property are calculated on the full property value, not just the owner's cash investment. Similarly, the benefits of property appreciation go entirely to the owner, not to the lender. This is debt leverage: benefiting from the use of another's money. More specifically, the full benefit of income-producing property accrues to an investor who contributes only part of the purchase funds.

Before deciding how much debt to use, a number of factors should be considered. If property values rise, the borrower generally benefits from using leverage. If values fall, the debtor is still obligated for fixed-interest expenses and principal repayments based on the original amount. In this situation, leverage compounds the investor's loss. Furthermore, interest expenses on residential property are deductible for tax purposes. Finally, the investor might be able to invest the cash not applied to the property purchase at a rate of return exceeding the interest expense of the balance of the funds needed, thus yielding a positive net return for the investor.

Mortgages

Mortgages are the most common form of real estate financing. A mortgage is a formal, legally binding lien against a piece of real estate to secure the payment of a debt. In most instances, a mortgage establishes a given piece of property as collateral for a loan, evidenced by the execution of a mortgage note. The lender is known as the **mortgagee;** the borrower is known as the **mortgagor.** A mortgage may be short-term (generally from 1 to 5 years) or long-term (over 5 years). The repayment period on residential loans usually ranges from 15 to 30 years. Short-term mortgages are most commonly used when the borrower anticipates selling the property within the term of the loan or when the borrower seeks funds for a small, unproved new high-risk business.

Mortgage loans also vary by the rate at which they are amortized. The **amortization rate** refers to the speed with which the principal of the loan is paid. Most residential loans are fully amortized. The borrower makes periodic payments against both the principal and the interest due. At the end of the loan period, the principal is fully paid. These mortgages are called

self-liquidating or **fully amortized** and are required with loans insured by the Federal Housing Authority and Veteran's Administration.

The mortgage lien establishes the legal interest of the mortgage holder in the collateral for the loan. If the borrower defaults on any portion of the loan, the mortgage holder cannot expect to be entitled to any additional property of the borrower other than the property that was mortgaged at the time of the loan. For this reason, preexisting mortgages, unpaid real property taxes, special assessments, and certain other claims must be settled before the senior mortgage holder can seek judgment against the borrower. The property can be sold for the payment of overdue property taxes, which are given the status of a first mortgage ahead of all other mortgages in terms of priority of claim. Subordinated mortgage holders must wait in line for whatever may remain after taxes and mortgage liens are paid. In most states, an unrecorded mortgage does not establish its priority of lien over subsequent junior mortgages. For this and other reasons, it is essential that mortgage agreements be executed in proper legal form, signed, and properly recorded.

When a mortgage is fully repaid, it becomes invalid. At that time, the lender should sign a mortgage release to make formal recognition of the cancellation of debt.

A mortgage holder may sell his or her interest against the property to another person at any time, in which case the proceeds and conditions of the mortgage apply to the new holder. The lender may sell a mortgage to secure a short-term loan by refinancing. The debtor may also sell his or her rights in the property. The sale is contingent upon the mortgage holder's approval of the purchaser. The mortgage holder may demand renegotiation of the mortgage terms to reflect the credit worthiness of the new mortgage holder. If the sale is approved, the new owner becomes obligated to the original mortgage holder.

Default is most commonly the result of the property holder's failure to make payments, usually interest payments, against the mortgage. Default also results from the property holder's failure to pay property taxes. In such cases, the mortgage holder must bring suit against the debtor, gain a favorable judgment by the court, and request the court to sell the property at public auction. The proceeds from the auction are applied against the mortgage debt. This is the process of **foreclosure** on mortgaged property.

Mortgage creditors are paid in order of the seniority of liens; property taxes and special assessments have top priority. The debtor is entitled to all proceeds over and above the total debt on the property. In many states, a debtor can reacquire his or her property after foreclosure by paying the amount of debt, plus interest. This period varies from between 6 months to 2 years; a few states allow no such period. This is legally described as the debtor's **statutory right of redemption.** Furthermore, most states allow the debtor to remain on the property until this period has elapsed. For this must make up the difference from another source. If the loan is approved, reason and because the mortgage holder hopes to resell the property at a higher price, he himself usually buys the property at public auction. Obviously, foreclosure proceedings are complex, time consuming, and a poor way to recover funds or to escape debt.

It is unusual, but a mortgage holder can even go further in pursuing recourse against a defaulting borrower. The central issue of the contractual agreement between the buyer and seller is the note that itemizes obligations and conditions. The mortgage merely secures the note. In theory, all individuals who sign a note obligate themselves and all their property as security for the note. A lender could, therefore, seek a deficiency judgment against the signators for any debt remaining after the property has been sold. Although this is uncommon, an investor should be aware of such possibilities.

At times, an investor may be unable to raise adequate funds, even by combining financial reserves with borrowed funds. The lender may view the applicant as an excessive personal risk, the value of the property as inadequate or uncertain, or the money market as tight and funds unavailable for this particular type of real estate loan. In this case, a borrower might obtain funds through a secondary credit source, that is, through a **second** or **junior mortgage.** For example, an investor might be able to contribute 20 percent of the purchase price and a lending institution might be willing to provide 70 percent. A second mortgage lender would contribute the remaining 10 percent. Because he would be repaid upon default only after the first mortgage holder's obligation has been satisfied 100 cents on the dollar, the second mortgage holder would run a greater risk. Therefore, interest charged on this loan would be substantially higher than on the first mortgage.

Because of the substantial risk involved, major lending institutions do not deal in second mortgage loans. The Federal Housing Authority will not insure the mortgage of any property subject to a secondary lien. Speculative mortgage companies, mortgage dealers, and private lenders, however, do provide funds for second mortgages. Some lending institutions provide second mortgage funds at rates comparable to those on first mortgages, given the condition that the first mortgage is already held by the same institution. In this situation, the junior lien position does not diminish the creditor's overall position.

In the first half of 1982, first mortgage institution loans nationally ranged between 15.6 and 18.5 percent. The term of a second mortgage is shorter (usually not exceeding 5 years) than that of a first mortgage. Sometimes, the seller of the property himself grants the buyer a second mortgage.

Second mortgage funds are used much more often in connection with income-producing properties, such as housing projects and apartment buildings, than with residential purchases. Local dealers in second mortgage money make their services known through advertising in community newspapers and through personal contact with local real estate brokers, agents, and officers of lending institutions.

Land Contracts

The most common alternative to mortgage financing is land-contract financing. **Land contracts** (also called **installment sales contracts**) are agreements in which the purchaser of property takes immediate possession and the seller retains title until the full purchase price has been paid and all contract conditions are met. The purchaser usually pays a much smaller down payment than required with mortgage financing. The balance of the purchase price is paid in installments. The term of the loan is usually shorter than that of the mortgage loan and is specified at the outset.

Often the seller finances the purchase through a land contract and then helps the buyer refinance it with mortgage debt at a later date. In this sense, the land contract is supplemental to, not a replacement for, long-term mortgage debt.

Both the purchaser and seller retain their privileges to sell their rights in the property without affecting the obligations of a properly written and recorded land contract. The new titleholder of the land is entitled to receive the payments and is obligated to transfer the deed at the proper time. To receive the deed, the new purchaser must accept the terms of the original contract and make all payments. However, the original seller's rights are senior in priority of claim over any other mortgages or debt obligations the borrower may enter into after the contract is signed. Furthermore, if the purchaser defaults in payments, the seller takes possession of the property without cumbersome foreclosure proceedings. In many states, the funds the seller has applied to the sale up to that point are considered rent; therefore, the seller has acquired no accumulated equity. For this reason, land-contract sales are most prevalent in more highly risky situations such as vacant land sales, when the buyer cannot secure an adequate conventional mortgage, when the down payment is insufficient for a financial institution, or when the property does not provide adequate collateral for a loan. Land contracts are frequently used for farmland for which it is difficult to obtain mortgage funds at reasonable rates. Land contracts for residential property became popular in the early 1980s when tight money and high interest rates made conventional financing difficult.

Alternative Credit Devices

Businesses and investors who own income-producing properties use a number of alternative means of financing projects: leases, sales and leasebacks, leasehold mortgages, and real estate bonds.

Leasing a property may be more advantageous than the outright purchase of a piece of property. A lease is a formal agreement between two parties in which one party provides an asset that is to be used by another party at an agreed-upon periodic payment. Leasing reduces the amount of capital needed by a user, who might not be able to secure adequate funds. Leasing allows use of the property even though it is impossible to purchase the real estate.

Some firms use sale and leaseback arrangements in which a company in need of funds sells the property to an investor and then leases the property back on agreed terms. Such leases can run as long as 40 years, and the lease payments are set so that the investor will be fully repaid the purchase price and will gain a financial return comparable to an alternative investment with the same degree of risk. The advantages to the company that sells the property and then leases it back are that its funds are not tied up in the equity of the property and it is able to receive a tax deduction on the full lease payment; the owner can deduct only the interest payment and an appropriate amount of depreciation each year. The desirability of the sale and leaseback arrangement is determined by an analysis of the appropriate cash flows.

At times, a company borrows against a mortgage using both the building and an imputed value of the lease as collateral. This is called **leasehold mortgage financing.** The funds are used to improve or expand the property. Because the rights of the lender are generally subordinated to those of the lessor (the party that grants the lease), many conditions are imposed upon such a mortgage arrangement. The financial reliability of the tenant and the value of the property and lease must be well established.

Many times, a lending institution will examine a lease to determine its imputed value, which is derived by analyzing the length of the lease and the value of the future cash flows that will be generated from the lease payments. If these are sufficient and if the building is of substantial worth and condition, the lending institution may provide funds to the borrower.

An additional source of credit is in the form of real estate bonds, which are means by which corporations can secure large sums of money from various sources. These are corporate bonds sold to investors with a particular piece of property mortgaged to secure the note or bonds. For example, if a firm needed $20 million to construct a new plant, the firm would contact an underwriter to float the $20 million issue. The new plant would provide the necessary collateral. The mortgage would provide the trustee of the bond a deed of trust that would be the security for the bondholders should the company default in any interest or mortgage payments required under the bond indenture. If default were to occur, the trustee would act on behalf of the bondholders in bringing legal action against the issuer of the bonds.

Government-Insured Mortgages

In many cases, the federal government actually insures a lender so that the mortgage debt will be paid if the borrower defaults. In general, the interest rate and necessary down payment are lower and the terms are longer on a federally insured loan than on a noninsured or **conventional** loan. Obtaining the loan usually depends upon the appraised value of the property, which is determined by an appraiser employed or appointed by the federal agency involved.

These insurance programs have greatly broadened the real estate market, made purchase terms easier for the borrower and less risky for the lender, and in many cases have reduced the likelihood of default. The enormous proportion of the real estate losses during the 1930s pointed to the need for such programs and convinced the federal government that a broadened and stable real estate market is of value to the overall health of the national economy.

The federal government is involved in 20 major programs of real estate finance and development through the Department of Housing and Urban Development (HUD). The two that exert the greatest influence on commercial mortgage loans are the Federal Housing Administration (FHA) and the Veteran's Administration (VA).

Anyone who has an adequate credit rating, the necessary down payment, and income sufficient to maintain the mortgage payments qualifies for an FHA-insured loan. First the loan must be approved by a regular lending institution, and then the property must be appraised for a value acceptable to justify the amount of the loan. In the early 1980s, maximum mortgages the FHA would insure for a one- to four-family dwelling was $85,000.

Most conventional mortgages must be paid within 25 to 30 years. Most FHA and VA loans have terms of 30 years on single-family dwellings. Most banks and insurance companies will lend only between 67 and 75 percent of the appraised value because of legal and policy restrictions. Savings and loans can lend up to 90 percent of appraised value; the remaining percentage is the down payment. The amount of the down payments on FHA-insured loans are graduated. The necessary down payments vary, but average from 3 percent of the first $25,000 of appraised value, 10 percent on the next $10,000 of appraised value, and 20 percent on payments over $35,000 up to the maximum. Down payments for conventional mortgages nationally average close to 25 percent of the value of the property.

A Veteran's Administration mortgage is similar in benefits to FHA, but the applicant must be a veteran. As with an FHA loan, the VA applicant applies to a regular loan agency first. The property is appraised, and, if the price exceeds the appraised value, the loan is not approved or the buyer the VA guarantees the lender a specified percentage of the loan up to a maximum amount. The VA guarantees 60 percent of a mortgage loan up to their current maximum, which is adjusted annually. These amounts can be changed by congressional action, and in some geographically limited areas the VA has loaned money to individuals directly rather than only providing a guarantee.

A VA loan generally runs for 30 years on home loans and may be repaid early without penalty to the borrower. Down payments are negotiated between the veteran and the lender, and in many cases, no down payments are required because of the 60-percent guarantee by the VA to the lending institution.

The major disadvantage of both VA and FHA-insured loans is the red tape involved. Furthermore, during times of tight money and high interest rates, lending institutions are less likely to approve such loans, preferring to place their money in higher-yielding investments. Interest rates for both FHA and VA loans are set by a government agency and vary from time to time. In addition to the interest charged, FHA-insured loans and VA loans add one-half of 1 percent insurance fee. Institutions often add various charges, commonly called **points,** to increase the effective yield on the loans. (One point equals 1 percent of the mortgage loan amount.) Because of the complexities and often lower rates of interest involved, many institutions avoid making FHA and VA loans. Often, only large savings and loans associations will deal in these loans.

Conventional Loans

Conventional or noninsured mortgage loans comprise the bulk of borrowed funds in America. Their rates are generally higher, the terms are shorter, and the down payment is higher than on insured loans. Interest rates vary with changes in the money supply. The major institutional sources of consumer mortgage funds are the savings and loan associations and commercial banks. For 1981, commercial banks held approximately 18.3 percent of the total mortgage debt; mortgage loans accounted for approximately 15 percent of their total assets. Because in many states usury laws limit the maximum amount of interest a bank may charge individuals, many banks practically exclude themselves from home mortgage lending and confine their lending efforts to corporations.

Savings and loan associations (which can lend up to 90 percent of appraised value) specialize in residential lending, investing the majority of their assets in private mortgage money. During 1981, savings and loan institutions held approximately 34.2 percent of the total outstanding mortgage debt. Savings and loan associations are not bound by the same state usury limitations as commercial banks are; therefore, they have much more flexibility in the residential mortgage market.

Secondary Mortgage Money Market

It is important to note that a great deal of investment in real estate mortgage money takes place on a secondary level after the mortgage transaction between the original buyer and seller has taken place. This market is called the **secondary mortgage money market.** Huge sums of mortgage moneys are bought and sold like any other investment; their value at any particular time is determined by the size of the initial loan, its rate of interest, and the comparative rates of interest for similar-sized investments in the marketplace. For example, a savings and loan association might lend $30,000 for 25 years at 6 percent interest. Riskless government bonds might be selling at similar rates of return. Six months later, the savings and loan might find itself low on liquid funds and may choose to sell its rights in the mortgage. If interest rates have risen, a purchaser (such as an insurance company) might purchase the mortgage at a discount from the balance due.

After the sale of the mortgage, the savings and loan institution has cash to invest in other loans. The sale of mortgages is a means of increasing the amount of mortgage money in the market. Large institutions that have substantial amounts of cash or semiliquid securities (such as life insurance companies and trust funds) are the major forces in this market. Because these financial institutions are not able to make direct loans to individuals, the savings and loan institutions make the initial loan; the financial institutions may then purchase them in the secondary mortgage money market.

At the beginning of 1982, of the total assets of all U.S. life insurance companies, 27 percent (about $135 billion) was invested in mortgage loans. An additional 3.4 percent of total assets (about $17 billion) was invested in direct real estate holdings.

The secondary mortgage money market serves either to greatly accelerate or to retard the amount of mortgage money available to final borrowers. This function of the secondary market is so significant that the federal government has directly involved itself, primarily through its two agencies: the Federal National Mortgage Association (FNMA, generally called Fanny Mae) and the Government National Mortgage Association (GNMA, generally called Ginny Mae). Fanny Mae's primary purpose is to buy up outstanding FHA, VA, and conventional loans in the secondary market, thereby increasing the amount of total funds available for mortgage lending. This function is especially important during times of tight money or higher rates of return on alternative investments. At a later time, when the market conditions improve, Fanny Mae may resell the mortgages, thus removing funds from the mortgage marketplace.

Fanny Mae has been a private profit-seeking corporation whose stock trades on the New York Stock Exchange. Fanny Mae obtains its primary source of capital from owners' and borrowed funds in order to buy existing mortgages. However, the federal government appoints one-third of the 15-

member board of directors and can partially regulate the management of Fanny Mae through legislative directives established by the National Housing Act of 1968. Sellers of mortgages to Fanny Mae and to institutions that service Fanny Mae must buy fixed amounts of stock in the corporation. Potential mortgage sellers to Fanny Mae periodically bid against each other for funds on the basis of their yield to Fanny Mae and are assessed fees for the services rendered by Fanny Mae. Only large institutions qualify to sell mortgages to Fanny Mae. Therefore, although it is a private corporation, its government control and influence are very apparent.

Ginny Mae enters the secondary mortgage in another manner. It guarantees timely payment of principal and interest on certificates issued against privately assembled pools of government-insured mortgages. These certificates are called **certificates of participation.** The guarantees that secure these certificates are backed by the full faith and credit of the federal government, making them superior in grade to AAA corporate bonds.

The pool of mortgages itself must be worth a minimum of $2 million and have similar interest rates and maturities. An investor may purchase certificates in minimum amounts of $25,000 face value and in increments of $10,000 thereafter. These securities can be traded like common stock. The securities themselves are sold like bonds. The greater the discount for which the security can be purchased, the greater the effective yield. For example, a 14 percent certificate purchased at 90 percent of par value would have a current yield of 15.6 percent on a 30-year maturity.

Ginny Mae charges the insurer a fee of one-half of 1 percent per year of the mortgage loan for insuring the mortgage. Therefore, if a pool were based on 14 percent mortgages, the securities would be issued for $13\frac{1}{2}$ percent. As interest and principal are paid on the pooled mortgages, the insurer passes through to each certificate holder his pro rata share of the receipts. Prepayments and foreclosure proceeds are also passed through to the owners. Because any defaults are immediately made up by Ginny Mae, practically speaking, these are riskless securities. By making payments monthly instead of semiannually, as with bonds, the effective rate of return can be higher through reinvestment and more frequent compounding.

Individual as Lender

An individual investor might choose to become a direct lender or to deal in purchasing and reselling mortgage funds. Individual lenders are especially important in investments involving higher relative risk, such as unproved businesses and income-producing property, vacant lots, and individuals who have limited means. The terms of these first mortgage loans are generally shorter than those of institutions, usually not over 10 years.

Sellers and developers who accept a mortgage as partial payment on the property they sell are, in effect, providing individual sources of mortgage funds, as in the case of land contracts. Individuals are most important as sources of funds for second mortgages. Major lending institutions do not generally make second mortgage loans because of the high risk involved. This leaves mortgage dealers, mortgage companies, and individual investors to provide these funds.

Even though individual mortgage lending and secondary mortgage purchasing can yield worthwhile returns, there are disadvantages peculiar to the field. Large amounts of investment capital are required and usually will be returned rather slowly. The property itself must be supervised to assure that it is properly maintained, thereby protecting the investor's collateral. The value at which an existing mortgage can be sold will depend upon circumstances that are beyond the investor's control. An investor who needs cash is usually forced to sell the mortgage at a discount. An investor must have a good technical understanding of the mortgage mechanism and the workings of the mortgage market.

If the mortgagor defaults, the long and complicated process of foreclosure usually leaves the investor with only marginal returns, if any at all. In short, individual mortgage investment may be profitable, but it entails large sums, long pay-back periods, extended supervision, limited liquidity, and considerable technical knowledge and familiarity with the marketplace.

Usually, an investor finds it easier to buy government-backed mortgage participation certificates, which yield a reasonable return and carry almost no risk. This leaves the risk and supervision to another party more experienced and better able to assume the risk. Because the certificates can be readily resold, they offer superior liquidity. Such an investment would require much less knowledge and care in selection than direct mortgage holdings. The size of the necessary investment can be considerably less because certificates are sold in amounts of $25,000. However, as in all cases of reduced risk, the yield on certificates will not be so high as with individually negotiated loans, although they will be comparable to other investments of similar risk. At the end of 1981, Ginny Mae certificates were yielding approximately 16 percent, depending upon the stated interest rate of the pooled funds involved.

TAXATION OF REAL ESTATE INVESTMENTS

Depreciation, Taxes, and Interest

Real estate investments offer significant tax advantages. The primary advantage is that income can be sheltered through tax reductions that are allowed when depreciation methods are used. **Depreciation** is the write-off of the cost of property against income. Depreciation reduces the cash tax payments during the early years of an investment. The cash savings can be applied against the mortgage debt and then reinvested elsewhere. In general, property held for trade or business on the production of income is eligible for accelerated depreciation. However, the property need not actually be producing income. Land is not depreciable, although certain capital assets other than buildings (such as equipment) may be depreciated. The amount depreciable usually equals the price paid less any estimated salvage value.

Various accelerated depreciation methods are used, depending upon the type of property involved, and vary between 125 and 200 percent declining balance depreciation rates. Depreciation depends upon the amount of the depreciation base, the useful life of the property, and the method of depreciation used.

The Economic Recovery Tax Act (ERTA) of 1981 authorized the Treasury secretary to provide recovery rates for "15-years on real property," which reflect the 175% declining balance method of depreciation (200% for low-income housing). For example, if an individual bought a factory for $200,000 on December 1, 1981, and the land is worth $20,000, then this person's write-off for 1981 with respect to this real property is $1,750 ($[(200,000 - 20,000)/15] \times 1.75 \times \frac{1}{12}$).

If an individual uses the accelerated method to recover the cost of depreciable real property, the nature of any gain he or she may realize when the property is disposed of will depend on whether the property is residential or nonresidential. If the property is residential, the gain will be recaptured as ordinary income only to the extent that the deductions under the accelerated method exceed those that would have been allowable if a straight-line method was used over the 15-year period. On the other hand, if a straight-line method was applied originally, any gain realized on the disposition of the property will be capital gain. Due to the differential treatments on potential gains from disposition, the decision to use either the accelerated depreciation method or the straight-line method requires more considerations. However, as a rule of thumb, an individual should probably always use the 15-year straight-line method of capital cost recovery for commercial property, and the accelerated method for residential property in order to maximize the tax shelter. Personal residential property is not subject to depreciation tax reduction, but real estate taxes and mortgage interest expenses are tax deductible. Furthermore, taxes on capital gains on residential sales can be delayed or avoided if a new residence of equal or greater value is purchased or if construction is begun on a new dwelling within 18 months from the date of the sale of the previous residence.

Delay of the Capital Gains Tax

Income can be further sheltered by taking advantage of an installment or deferred payment sale on real estate. An installment sale taxes any gain only as payments are received from the purchaser. This keeps the seller from being put in a higher taxable income bracket. For example, if 35 percent of the sales price of a piece of real estate represents a gain, then only 35 percent of each dollar payment received, excluding interest, is subject to taxation. No more than 30 percent of the total sales price (including the down payment) can be received in the first year of sale. The installment sale delays taxable gain until the cash is received and it spreads the gain over several years.

When business or investment properties of like kind are exchanged, any taxable gains can usually be deferred until the property is sold. For example, if a business purchased for $30,000 were exchanged for a $40,000 business of similar nature, the $10,000 gain would be deferred.

As important as tax advantages are, there are restrictions and limitations. As already pointed out, the tax advantages of residential property ownership are more limited than those of commercial property holdings. The 1969 tax reform law significantly reduced the amount of money that could be saved from accelerated depreciation. The law states that if a property is sold within 100 months of purchase, the accumulated excess depreciation must be recaptured at ordinary income tax rates. In effect, taxes formerly deferred must be paid. Increasingly less must be repaid each month thereafter, up to 200 months. Therefore, the tax savings of writing off depreciation at a higher rate and then selling at a gain midway through the depreciation cycle is greatly reduced. In addition the Internal Revenue Service insists that a property owner incur a certain proportion of ownership expenses (generally 15 percent of revenues) before interest can be deducted.

KEY TERMS

accelerated depreciation	mortgage
amortization rate	mortgagee
appraisal	mortgage trusts
default	mortgagor
depreciation	net income multiplier (NIM)
equity trust	points
Fanny Mae	real estate bonds
Federal Housing Administration (FHA)	real estate corporation
foreclosure	real estate investment trust (REIT)
Ginny Mae	real estate syndicate
gross rent multiplier (GRM)	real property
income approach	replacement cost approach
installment sales contract	sale and leaseback
land contracts	sales price multiplier
lease	secondary mortgage money market
leasehold mortgage financing	second (or junior) mortgage
market approach	statutory right of redemption
market price	Veteran's Administration (VA)
market value	

QUESTIONS

1. To what two variables is the demand for real estate closely related?
2. What is real property, and what is the largest investment in real property?
3. What are some of the advantages of holding real estate?
4. What are some of the disadvantages of owning real estate?
5. When does it pay for an investor to buy instead of rent?
6. What are the three major categories of real estate investment companies, and what is the nature of each?
7. What is the difference between price and value? What is appraisal?
8. What are the GRM and the NIM?
9. What are the three major methods of valuation?
10. What are mortgages? What are self-liquidating or fully amortized mortgages?
11. What are land contracts?
12. What is a lease? What are the advantages of a sale and leaseback arrangement?
13. What are conventional loans, and what financial institutions make the most conventional loans?
14. What are FHA and VA loans?
15. What is the secondary mortgage market? Explain the roles of Fanny Mae and Ginny Mae in the secondary mortgage market.
16. List some of the tax advantages in owning real estate.

SELECTED READINGS

ALLEN, ROGER H. *Real Estate Investment and Taxation*. Cincinnati: South-Western, 1980.

BEATON, WILLIAM R., and TERRY ROBERTSON. *Real Estate Investment*, 2d ed. Englewood Cliffs, N.J.: Prentice-Hall, 1977.

BLECK, ERICH K. "Real Estate Investments and Rates of Return." *Appraisal Journal*, October 1973, 535–547.

CASE, FRED E. "The Attraction of Home Ownership." *Journal of the American Real Estate and Urban Economics Association*, Spring 1979, 39–44.

COOPER, JAMES R., and STEPHEN A. PYHRR. "Forecasting the Rates of Return on an Apartment Investment: A Case Study." *Appraisal Journal*, July 1973, 312–337.

GANIS, DAVID R. "All about the GNMA Mortgage-Backed Securities Market." *Real Estate Reveiw*, Summer 1974, 55–65.

"How to Get the Equity out of Your Home." *Business Week*. October 29, 1979, 200–202.

LEEBERT, PHIL. "Real Estate: The Opportunities Are off the Beaten Track." *Financial World*, January 15, 1979, 49–51.

MARK, MORRIS, et al. "Pitfalls in Real Estate Accounting." *Financial Analysts Journal*, January–February 1972, 29–36.

MOFFITT, DONALD. "How Figuring 'Residual' Value of Land Helps Real-Estate Investors Make Better Purchases." *Wall Street Journal*, December 11, 1978, 40.

NORGAARD, RICHARD L. "Are GNMAs a Good Investment?" *Journal of Portfolio Management*, Fall 1978, 49–52.

ROULAC, STEPHEN E. "Can Real Estate Returns Outperform Common Stocks?" *Journal of Portfolio Management*, Winter 1976, 26–43.

17

Taxation and Estate Planning

Among the many factors that an investor must consider when investing funds is the rate at which the returns will be taxed. At one time taxes had little effect on investment decisions, but today's rates make tax treatment of investment returns a most important factor. The American tax structure is far too complex to be covered adequately in one chapter of any book. Therefore, this chapter will cover only the general tax factors that are of central importance to the investor.

INCOME TAXES

All income that a person receives is subject to federal income tax unless it is from a source specifically exempt by law. To the investor this means that all returns, whether in the form of dividends, interest, or realized appreciation in market value, as taxable. The federal income tax is a progressive tax that begins at 11 percent and ends at 50 percent. The increasing tax rate is applied to each marginal dollar received.

Marginal and Average Tax Rates

There is a significant difference between the marginal tax rate and the average tax rate for the individual. The marginal tax rate is the percentage of each additional dollar of income received that is owed to the Internal Revenue Service. As shown in the tax schedules of Exhibit 17-1, a married taxpayer filing a joint return and having taxable income of $24,600 pays the government 25 cents of every additional dollar of income. This 25 percent is the taxpayer's marginal tax rate.

Many people confuse the marginal and average tax rates. The marginal rate rises in steps, but the average rate is always rising. For the preceding taxpayer with $24,600 in taxable income, the average tax rate is 3,465/24,600 or 14.09 percent. The average tax rate is not very relevant to the investor, since all investment returns will be taxed at the marginal rate.

Ordinary Income

Most of the income a taxpayer receives in the form of wages, dividends, or interest is classified as ordinary income and taxed at the marginal rates shown in Exhibit 17-1. Ordinary income is all the taxable income an individual receives that is not classified as capital gain.

Capital Gains

Capital gains are returns derived from appreciation in the value of a capital asset and are realized when the asset is liquidated. Stocks and bonds, which are typical investment vehicles, are considered capital assets. If a security is held for more than 1 year, it is considered a long-term holding. In calculating income taxes for a given year, gains and losses on long-term and short-term securities are treated differently.

All long-term gains and losses are netted to arrive at a single long-term realized figure. The same is done for all short-term gains and losses. If the two netted values differ (one a gain, the other a loss), they are netted to arrive at a single figure. For example, during a taxable year,

Total of all long-term gains	$10,000
Total of all long-term losses	(6,000)
Total of all short-term gains	8,500
Total of all short-term losses	(4,000)

Exhibit 17-1
Tax Rate Schedules

Married Individuals Filing Joint Returns and Surviving Spouses

			1984
Taxable Income	Amount of tax	+	Rate on excess
0— $3,400	–0–		–0–
$ 3,400— 5,500	–0–		11%
5,500— 7,600	$231		12
7,600— 11,900	483		14
11,900— 16,000	1,085		16
16,000— 20,200	1,741		18
20,200— 24,600	2,497		22
24,600— 29,900	3,465		25
29,900— 35,200	4,790		28
35,200— 45,800	6,274		33
45,800— 60,000	9,772		38
60,000— 85,600	15,168		42
85,600—109,400	25,920		45
109,400—162,400	36,630		49
162,400—215,400	62,600		50
215,400—.	89,100		50

The netted long-term and short-term results are

Net long-term gain	$4,000
Net Short-term gain	4,500

The two are the same; both are gains and no further netting is necessary. Net capital gains are treated as follows:

1. A net long-term gain and a net short-term gain: The long-term gain is taxed at preferential rates and the short-term gain is taxed in full as ordinary income. Only 40 percent of a long-term capital gain is included as ordinary income. Sixty percent of the gain is not taxed.
2. A net long-term gain and a net short-term loss: The two are netted; if the gain is larger than the loss, the gain receives the preferential rate treatment.
3. A net long-term loss and a net short-term gain: The two are netted; if the gain is larger than the loss, the gain is taxed in full as ordinary income.

Exhibit 17-1

Tax Rate Schedules continued

Unmarried Individuals (Other than Surviving Spouses and Heads of Households)

Taxable Income	Amount of tax	+	Rate on excess*
0— $2,300	–0–		–0–
$ 2,300— 3,400	–0–		11%
3,400— 4,400	$121		12
4,400— 6,500	241		14
6,500— 8,500	535		15
8,500— 10,800	835		16
10,800— 12,900	1,203		18
12,900— 15,000	1,581		20
15,000— 18,200	2,001		23
18,200— 23,500	2,737		26
23,500— 28,800	4,115		30
28,800— 34,100	5,705		34
34,100— 41,500	7,507		38
41,500— 55,300	10,319		42
55,300— 81,800	16,115		48
81,800—108,300	28,835		50
108,300—.	42,085		50

*The amount by which the taxpayer's taxable income exceeds the base of the bracket.

Source: Internal Revenue Service

Capital Losses

Net capital losses are treated differently from net gains. All of a net gain is taxable in the year it is realized, but a maximum of $3,000 per year of losses in excess of gains may be declared as deduction against taxable income. If the loss is greater than $3,000 in a given year, it can be carried forward for use in offsetting future gains and to provide further deductions in succeeding years. Furthermore, just as long-term gains receive preferred treatment, long-term losses receive reduced benefits. The annual capital loss deduction may be from long-term or short-term losses, but short-term losses are deducted dollar for dollar and long-term losses are deducted at a one-for-two rate against taxable income. It takes $2 of long-term loss to realize a $1 itemized deduction from taxable income. Any long-term loss carryover is, however, treated dollar for dollar in offsetting future gains.

Individual's Capital Gain and Loss Calculations

As indicated, capital losses (of an individual) can be offset against capital gains and may generally be used to reduce taxable income up to a maximum of $3,000. If the loss is not used up, it can be carried over to successive years. The following examples will help to illustrate the calculations.

Example 1: Assume that an individual has $8,000 of adjusted gross income before treatment of capital gains and losses. He realizes $2,000 of long-term capital gain and $1,500 of short-term capital loss during the taxable year. The $2,000 gain is offset by the $1,500 loss and the net result is a $500 long-term capital gain. Only 40 percent is taxable: therefore, adjusted gross income becomes $8,200.

Example 2: An individual has a realized gain of $2,800 on a sale of a capital asset held for two months. She sells no other capital asset during that year. She has a short-term capital gain of $2,800 on that transaction and a net short-term capital gain of $2,800 for the year. Because it is a short-term capital gain, adjusted gross income increases by $2,800.

Example 3: An individual has a realized long-term capital gain of $2,000 and a long-term capital loss of $3,000 for the entire year. These two are netted and the result is a $1,000 long-term capital loss of which only 50 percent can be used to reduce adjusted gross income. The remaining $500 is lost forever.

Example 4. An individual has a realized long-term gain of $2,000, a long-term capital loss of $8,000, and a short-term capital loss of $1,800 for the year. The investor first of all offsets the long-term gain against the long-term loss, resulting in a $6,000 long-term loss. The reduction in adjusted gross income is in the amount of $3,000 and comes from $1,800 of short-term loss and $2,400 of the long-term loss. The unused long-term loss of $3,600 is carried over to the next taxable year either to offset a gain, or half the amount is used to lower adjusted gross income.

Income Averaging

Income averaging is an elective device that allows a taxpayer who receives an unusually large amount of income in one year to be taxed in a lower bracket. This is achieved by taxing only a portion of the increased income at that particular rate.

Because of the progressive income tax rate structure under which individual tax rates vary from a low of 11 percent to a high of 50 percent, taxpayers whose incomes fluctuate widely from year to year are at a disadvantage in comparison with those whose incomes remain relatively stable. Under this graduated taxing system, a person who has high and low incomes in different taxable years usually pays more taxes than a person who has the same amount of total income spread evenly over the same period.

This disparity in tax treatment also carries over into the area of deductions. For example, a loss deducted in a low-income year does not provide the same benefit under the progressive rates as the same loss deducted in a high-income year. The same principles apply to any exemption or personal deduction. Furthermore, if losses or deductions are great enough, and the income low enough, part or all of the benefits of the loss or deduction may be lost forever.

Years ago, Congress recognized the tax inequities inherent in the uneven flow of income and took steps to alleviate the problem by enacting several relief provisions. These provisions, however, offered only limited relief and were restricted to special types of long-term income and to particular classes of taxpayers. For instance, the averaging rules covered only special situations, such as income from inventions or artistic works, back pay, and damages from patent infringement, breach of contract, or injury under the antitrust laws. (There are also other income-leveling provisions, such as the carryback and carryover of a net operating loss or a capital loss.)

In 1964, Congress extended the benefits of income averaging to a broader class of individuals and made it available for virtually all types of income. The revised laws set up a new, comprehensive averaging formula as follows:

1. Find the **averagable income,** that is, the excess of the current year's taxable income over a base. The base is 120 percent of the average taxable income for the 4 years preceding the current year (base period years). (A shorter method of arriving at the base figure is to take 30 percent of the total taxable income for the base period years.) In determining the average, the correct taxable income for a base period year is to be used (whether or not assessments or refunds are barred by the statute of limitations). The taxable income may not be less than zero.
2. Compute a tax on the base determined in (1).
3. Compute a tax on the sum of the base and one-fifth of the averagable income in (1).
4. Multiply the difference between the taxes in (2) and (3) (this difference is the tax on one-fifth of the averagable income) by 5 to get the tax on the averagable income.
5. The total tax is equal to the sum of the tax in (2) on the base and the tax in (4) on the averagable income.

Aspects of a Taxable Income to Be Considered

An investor may gain from dividends because the first $100 of common stock dividend income is not taxable (or the first $200 from jointly owned securities, when filing a joint return). In contrast, all interest income is fully taxable at the taxpayer's highest marginal rate. However, interest from municipal bonds is not taxable for federal income tax purposes, which makes them attractive to investors in high marginal tax brackets.

ESTATE PLANNING

The purpose of estate planning is to conserve as much income and principal as possible for the family and its heirs. Primary obstacles to reaching this goal may be the federal estate and gift taxes. (State taxes are discussed in a later section.) Whenever interests in property or the benefits to be derived from that property are conveyed from one party to another, those interests or benefits may be subject to federal taxes. The methods by which these taxes can be reduced will be discussed in this section.

Estate Taxes

Before an individual's estate is distributed after death, it is subject to federal estate taxes. The federal estate tax is a progressive tax running from a low rate of 18 percent on the first $10,000 to a top marginal rate of 50 percent on that portion of the taxable estate in excess of $5 million. Everything of value that a person owns, both tangible and intangible, is considered part of the estate and may therefore be subject to taxation. Since estate taxes may cause undue hardship on some decedent's heirs, there are a series of deductions and exemptions that reduce the gross taxable estate. Table 17-1 provides data for computing the federal estate tax.

Deductions and Exemptions

One of the largest deductions from which an estate may benefit is the marital deduction. This deduction is available only to an estate left by a married decedent. The law allows for an unlimited deduction from the adjusted gross estate of anything left to the spouse. Therefore, if everything is left to the spouse, no federal estate tax will occur. However, when the surviving spouse dies no marital deduction will be available, unless remarriage has occurred.

All expenses incurred in settling an estate, as well as all debts left by the decedent, are deductible from the gross estate. Charitable bequests also reduce the estate tax liability. Any testamentary gift that an individual leaves to a charitable institution is deductible in full.

Before the Economic Recovery Act of 1981 was enacted, each estate was entitled to a $175,000 exemption from the adjusted gross estate. The 1981 act replaced these provisions with equal rates for estate and gift taxes and a unified tax credit that will gradually rise until it reaches its permanent

Table 17-1
Table for Computation of Estate Tax

Rate Schedule

If the amount with respect to which the tentative tax to be computed is:	The tentative tax is:
Not over $10,000	18 percent of such amount.
Over $10,000 but not over $20,000 ...	$1,800, plus 20 percent of the excess of such amount over $10,000.
Over $20,000 but not over $40,000 ...	$3,800, plus 22 percent of the excess of such amount over $20,000.
Over $40,000 but not over $60,000 ...	$8,200, plus 24 percent of the excess of such amount over $40,000.
Over $60,000 but not over $80,000 ...	$13,000, plus 26 percent of the excess of such amount over $60,000.
Over $80,000 but not over $100,000 ..	$18,200, plus 28 percent of the excess of such amount over $80,000.
Over $100,000 but not over $150,000	$23,800, plus 30 percent of the excess of such amount over $100,000.
Over $150,000 but not over $250,000	$38,800, plus 32 percent of the excess of such amount over $150,000.
Over $250,000 but not over $500,000	$70,800, plus 34 percent of the excess of such amount over $250,000.
Over $500,000 but not over $750,000	$155,800, plus 37 percent of the excess of such amount over $500,000.
Over $750,000 but not over $1,000,000	$248,300, plus 39 percent of the excess of such amount over $750,000.
Over $1,000,000 but not over $1,250,000	$345,800, plus 41 percent of the excess of such amount over $1,000,000.
Over $1,250,000 but not over $1,500,000	$448,300, plus 43 percent of the excess of such amount over $1,250,000.
Over $1,500,000 but not over $2,000,000	$555,800, plus 45 percent of the excess of such amount over $1,500,000.
Over $2,000,000 but not over $2,500,000	$780,800, plus 49 percent of the excess of such amount over $2,000,000.
Over $2,500,000	$1,025,800 plus 50% of the excess over $2,500,000.

Source: Internal Revenue Service.

level in 1987. Any portion of this tax credit used to offset gift taxes cannot be used to offset estate taxes. As shown in Table 17-2, the tax credit will provide an "equivalent" exemption of $600,000 in 1987 and thereafter. In other words, unless a gross estate exceeds $600,000, no federal estate tax is due.

Table 17-2
Credit against Estate Taxes

Year	Tax Credit	Equivalent Exemption
1981	$ 47,000	$175,625
1982	62,800	225,000
1983	79,300	275,000
1984	96,300	325,000
1985	121,800	400,000
1986	155,800	500,000
1987	192,800	600,000

Source: Internal Revenue Service.

State Taxes and the Credit

In addition to the federal estate tax, in most states the estate of a decedent must pay an estate tax to the state of residency. In some states the tax is nominal, but in others the tax can be a relatively large sum. Generally, taxes paid to states and their subdivisions can be deducted from the federal estate taxes. The estate tax allows a maximum credit for state taxes. The credit varies with the size of the estate. The credit may only be taken for the smaller of either the state tax paid or the allowable credit. Because the size of the tax may differ widely from state to state, choosing a place of residency is an important aspect in estate planning. For example, Florida has adopted an estate tax exactly equal to the allowable federal credit. Table 17-3 shows how the credit for state death taxes is calculated.

Wills

One of the most important legal documents that an individual will ever sign in his or her will. Instead of going into the technical aspects of a will, this section will deal only with the general need for a will. Each state has its own laws concerning the validity of a will. An individual's personal property comes under the jurisdiction of the state of residency. Real property may come under the jurisdiction of the state in which it is located.

A will provides an individual with a means of detailing exactly how he or she wishes to have the estate's assets distributed. If a decedent does not have a valid will, he or she is considered to have died **intestate.** In this case, the state's statutes of descent and distribution are invoked, and the state divides the estate among eligible beneficiaries in accordance with a predetermined order of succession. The following is an example of the statute in Ohio for the order of distribution of the estate of an individual dying intestate:

Table 17-3
Credit for State Death Taxes

(A) Taxable Estate Equaling	(B) Taxable Estate not Exceeding	For Total Maximum Credit	
		Credit on Amount in Column (A)	Rate of Credit on Excess over Amount in Column (A)
			%
—	$ 40,000	—	—
$ 40,000	90,000	—	.8
90,000	140,000	$ 400	1.6
140,000	240,000	1,200	2.4
240,000	440,000	3,600	3.2
440,000	640,000	10,000	4.0
640,000	840,000	18,000	4.8
840,000	1,040,000	27,600	5.6
1,040,000	1,540,000	38,800	6.4
1,540,000	2,040,000	70,800	7.2
2,040,000	2,540,000	106,800	8.0
2,540,000	3,040,000	146,800	8.8
3,040,000	3,540,000	190,800	9.6
3,540,000	4,040,000	238,800	10.4
4,040,000	5,040,000	290,800	11.2
5,040,000	6,040,000	402,800	12.0
6,040,000	7,040,000	522,800	12.8
7,040,000	8,040,000	650,800	13.6
8,040,000	9,040,000	786,800	14.4
9,040,000	10,040,000	930,800	15.2
10,040,000	—	1,082,800	16.0

Source: Internal Revenue Service

(A) If there is no surviving spouse, to the children of such intestate or their lineal descendants, per stirpes;

(B) If there is a spouse and one child or its lineal descendants surviving, one-half to the spouse and one-half to such child or its lineal descendants, per stirpes;

(C) If there is a spouse and more than one child or their lineal descendants surviving, one-third to the spouse and the remainder to the children equally, or to the lineal descendants of any deceased child, per stirpes;

(D) If there are no children or their lineal descendants, three-fourths to the surviving spouse, one-fourth to the parents of the intestate equally, or to the surviving parent; if there are no parents, then the whole to the surviving spouse;

(E) If there is no spouse and no children or their lineal descendants, to the parents of such intestate equally, or to the surviving parent;

(F) If there is no spouse, no children or their lineal descendants, and no parent surviving, to the brothers and sisters, whether of the whole or of the half blood of the intestate, or their lineal descendants, per stirpes;

(G) If there are no brothers or sisters or their lineal descendants, one-half to the paternal grandparents of the intestate equally, or to the survivor of them, and one-half to the maternal grandparents of the intestate equally, or to the survivor of them;

(H) If there is no paternal grandparent or no maternal grandparent, one-half to the lineal descendants of such deceased grandparents, per stirpes; if there are no such lineal descendants, then to the surviving grandparents or their lineal descendants, per stirpes; if there are no surviving grandparents or their lineal descendants, then to the next of kin of the intestate, provided there shall be no representation among such next of kin;

(I) If there are no next of kin, to stepchildren or their lineal descendants, per stirpes;

(J) If there are no stepchildren or their lineal descendants, escheat (reverts) to the state.

In some instances a person may feel that the state can do as good a job as he or she can in dividing his estate and thus does not write a will. Rarely is this a wise decision. The state does not have complete knowledge about an individual's family life; therefore, the individual should not surrender to the state power to allocate assets. The individual has the best knowledge of his or her own affairs and, therefore, is in a position to make the best decision as to the disposition of assets.

There is a need for a will especially when minor children are involved. If there is no will, the state appoints a guardian for the children and a custodian of the funds, even though one spouse survives. Court authorization is usually required before funds can be expended. A will only passes assets that are solely in the name of the decedent. Assets held in joint survivor form or in a trust at the time of death are not distributed according to the will, but by the way the asset is titled.

Trusts

The use of trusts has become a widespread practice for the management and transfer of an estate at death. All trusts are of one of two basic classifications, either *inter vivos* (living) or *testamentary*. An **inter vivos trust** is established during the lifetime of the grantor. When a grantor establishes an *inter vivos* trust, he or she is able to include in the trust agreement any terms he or she chooses. If the grantor is the recipient of the trust income or if he or she retains any rights to the income or the trust principal, the trust is considered as part of the taxable estate at death (revocable trust). If the grantor retains no interet of any kind in the trust, the trust is considered a gift to its beneficiaries (irrevocable trust).

A person may have any number of reasons for establishing an *inter vivos* trust, either for his or her own benefit or for the benefit of others. Examples are to obtain the use of professional management for one's assets, to avoid the delays of probate at the time of death, to avoid the majority of attorney and executor fees at the time of death, to gain insight into how a trustee or beneficiary may act, prior to death, or to avoid the publicity of probate.

A trust may be established to avoid paying taxes on a portion of one's income. A short-term trust, or Clifford trust, is a revocable trust that enjoys a life of no less than 10 years and 1 day. The grantor transfers property to the trustees and has no control over it, or rights to it, for the life of the trust. The trustee distributes the trust income to the beneficiaries of the trust, who pay the income taxes on it. This trust vehicle is often used by taxpayers who pay high marginal rates on income. They usually name their children or other relatives as beneficiaries and thus shift income to a lower marginal tax rate. Since the principal can revert to the grantor after 10 years, it is part of the grantor's estate.

A **testamentary trust** is established by a decedent's will. The advantages are the same as those of an **inter vivos** trust, but people usually have different reasons for establishing a testamentary trust. For example, they want to prevent the beneficiary from disposing of specific property during their lifetimes, and still allow that beneficiary the use of any income from the property, they have no confidence in the beneficiary's ability to manage and protect the property, or they want to retain control over the assets after they die.

Because a testamentary trust is created upon death under terms stated in the decedent's will, all assets go through the probate court and are subject to both attorney and executor fees. For this reason, many attorneys suggest living trusts containing all the provisions of the will that would have created the testamentary trust. Then, upon death, the living trust changes from revocable to irrevocable and accomplishes the same provisions as would a testamentary trust.

Power of a Trustee

The trustee of a trust agreement has only those powers given by the grantor in the trust document. It is imperative that the trustee be given enough authority to be able to act in the best interests of the beneficiaries. When a grantor is creating a trust agreement, he or she should state very specifically how much power the trustee may have over income distribution and invasion of the principal.

It is possible to give the trustee the power to decide how much of the trust's income should be distributed each year. This stipulation may, of course, give the trustee too much power, and in some states it may not be possible because some states prohibit trusts from accumulating income. A most important decision is whether or not to give the trustee power to invade the principal (corpus) and utilize the trust for the beneficiaries' best interest. If the trustee were not given this power, he or she would not be able to provide financial help when it may be desperately needed. Because a grantor cannot anticipate all future conditions, the trust agreement should provide flexibility.

Powers of Appointment

It is possible to give to someone other than oneself or the trustee the power to determine the beneficiaries of a trust and to decide how much each beneficiary should receive. There are two powers of appointment: general power and special power. The holder of a general power of appointment has the power to determine everything about a trust's beneficiaries and can even dispose of the trust's assets by giving them to himself.

A special power of appointment can be exercised only in the interest of a limited group or class of individuals. The person holding this power may distribute the assets of a trust only to a specified group of beneficiaries, but he may decide how much each beneficiary is to receive.

The reason for granting the power of appointment is to provide the trust with an extra measure of flexibility. The power provides a means whereby a decision made today can be changed if time proves that the decision is impractical. The problem with the power of appointment is that once the grantor has died there is no way of guaranteeing that the power will be exercised in the manner the decedent would have wanted. Furthermore, there is the additional problem that if the trust instrument is not drawn properly the holder of a general power may have the assets of the trust included in his or her own estate.

Estate Liquidity

Since estate taxes could amount to a rather large sum, having sufficient cash to pay the tax could present a major problem. This is particularly true when a large portion of the estate is tied up in nonliquid assets, such as land, real property, or a business. A part of good estate planning involves arranging to pay any anticipated tax and prevents the forced liquidation of good investments.

It is possible, though highly unlikely, for an individual to adopt a plan of carrying cash balances large enough to pay estate taxes, but this may be poor investment management. Therefore, another type of asset should be considered. Investing funds in corporate securities is one means of providing the liquidity needed to cover estate taxes. Securities are marketable and earn income until cash is needed. Unfortunately, if the market is depressed the day the securities are needed, it may not be the best time to have to sell them.

Investing in government securities may be a good way to accumulate funds. For example, one may invest in **flower bonds** (obligations of the federal government that are valued at face for estate tax purposes and may be used at face value in lieu of cash to pay the tax). The major drawback of flower bonds is that very few are available today, and those that are available sell at a high premium over investment value because of their tax payment usage.

Perhaps the most widely used means of guaranteeing cash to pay a decedent's estate taxes is adequate life insurance. However, the choice of a beneficiary must be carefully considered. If an individual is named as beneficiary, he or she receives the proceeds of the life insurance policy, but those funds would only be immediately available for the tax if the policy beneficiary were also a major beneficiary of the estate. However, if the estate is the beneficiary of the policy, the liquidity is there, but the funds might be tied up in probate proceedings and will increase the attorney and executor fees. If the beneficiary of an insurance policy is also a major beneficiary of the estate, it may be desirable to have the beneficiary become the owner of the policy. This reduces the size of the taxable estate because the proceeds are not considered part of the decedent's estate because the decedent did not own the policy at the time of death. This reduction in the taxable estate provides more funds to pay the estate taxes.

Gift Giving

An individual may give $10,000 each, tax free, to as many individuals as he or she desires every year. In addition, it is possible to double one's tax-free, gift-giving capacity by using gift splitting. This allows a husband and wife to double their exemption to $20,000 per recipient per year by electing to give a gift together. If the amount exceeds $10,000, a gift tax is imposed on the donor, not the recipient. Over and above this amount, college tuition and medical costs for another person may be gifted if paid directly to the institution providing the service.

Interest-Free Loans

Of growing interest to many individuals is the interest-free loan. In many instances an individual may not want to give assets to another but may want to help them financially. This can be desirable in the case of a parent supplying funds to a child. Most parents when transferring money to a child simply write a check for the amount agreed upon.

However, for most individuals a transfer of money can be very expensive. For example, if the transfer of money is in the amount of $1,000, the donor needed to earn much more than this amount to have $1,000 available after tax (assuming the donor has taxable income). At an interest rate of 10 percent, and assuming a 50 percent tax bracket, the individual would need to devote $20,000 of assets to be able to write the $1,000 check ($20,000 × 10% interest rate = $2,000 × 50% tax = $1,000). If instead, however, the parent loaned $10,000 to the child at no interest, and assuming the child earned 10% interest on the assets and did not have any other taxable income, then $1,000 could be available for the planned expenditure. This utilized half the assets than previously required, and the lender can acquire the loaned assets at any time since the borrower has signed a demand note.

RETIREMENT PLANNING

As a result of the sweeping pension reform bill signed by Congress in September 1974, many workers have the opportunity to do some tax-sheltered retirement planning on their own in a broader manner than before. The two basic retirement plans available to the individual are the Keogh Plan and the Individual Retirement Account, which were modified by the Economic Recovery Act of 1981.

Individual Retirement Account (IRA)

To qualify for an IRA, an individual must be receiving earned income and be either self-employed or employed by someone else. An individual who qualifies can set aside 100 percent earned income up to a maximum of $2,000 for each year. The amount set aside in a retirement fund is deducted from the taxpayer's taxable income and, therefore, is deferred from taxation.

The 1976 Tax Reform Act provided for the establishment of an IRA for the nonworking homemaker in recognition of the family contributions made by the nonworking spouse. The law places a ceiling on the size of the tax-deductible contribution to an IRA for a nonworking spouse, which is $250. Therefore, a total of $2250 could be set aside for a married couple where only one spouse is employed. If both spouses are employed, they each may set up their own IRA with the $2,000 maximum.

An employed individual may establish an IRA regardless of whether or not he or she is in any other plans. For example, if the individual has a company-paid retirement plan, a tax-sheltered annuity, and a Keogh Plan he or she can still establish an IRA.

Keogh Plan (HR10)

To qualify for the Keogh Plan an individual can be self-employed or can shelter side income if he or she is a member of an employer tax-deferred retirement plan. However, if a self-employed person wants to establish a Keogh retirement plan, all employees who have been working for the self-employed person for at least 3 years must also be covered. The contributions to the plan must be made by the owner. The maximum tax-deductible contribution per individual is $15,000. An individual may make a deductible contribution of either 7.5 percent of the first $200,000 or 15 percent of the first $100,000 to reach the $15,000 maximum. The employer may choose any percentage from zero to 15 percent each year and must use the same percentage for each employee.

Provisions of the Pension Reform Act

In both the IRA and Keogh plans the funds placed in the retirement fund have the advantage of tax-sheltered accumulation. Only when the individual retires and begins to withdraw funds are the funds taxed. At the time they are withdrawn, the funds are subject to ordinary income tax, whether their sources are contributions, interest, dividends, or capital gains. The benefits of these plans before retirement are greatest for those individuals in the highest tax bracket. Nevertheless, all participants benefit from the tax-deferred nature of the plans.

Participants in either plan normally cannot begin withdrawing funds before age 59½, and they must begin withdrawing no later than the calendar year in which they reach age 70½. The amount to be withdrawn is calculated by the life expectancy of the youngest of the participants or spouse at the time withdrawals begin. A faster rate is permitted, but a rate slower than the calculated life expectancy is not. If the participant dies before any or all of the funds have been withdrawn for retirement, all proceeds from the fund pass to the beneficiaries, but income tax will need to be paid by the recipient.

If the participant begins to withdraw funds before he or she reaches the age of 59½, a penalty of 10 percent is imposed, and the funds become subject to income taxation. The only exception to this rule against early withdrawal is because of disability; then the penalty is waived.

A participant in either the IRA plan or the Keogh plan may take advantage of one of the following basic methods for investing his or her funds:

1. A formal trust can be created if it is administered by another party. (The participant is not allowed to have access to the funds before retirement.) A bank or savings institution usually acts as custodian and administrator, but the participant may direct the bank or savings institution to invest in

whatever he or she chooses. Several brokerage houses have begun providing custodial services so that the individual can direct the investment of funds into securities. Most brokerage firms charge a nominal 1/5th of one percent per year on the value of the fund to cover administrative expenses over and above those normally associated with a brokerage account.

2. An annuity contract can be purchased from an insurance company. The contract, however, is not transferable and it cannot be used as collateral for a loan.

3. U.S. government retirement bonds can be purchased. They are usually purchased through any Federal Reserve Bank or branch and are in small denominations.

4. Mutual funds can invest the retirement funds. Mutual fund companies generally use a savings institution that acts as the custodian of the funds.

Estate and retirement planning is a very complex subject. The concerned investor must begin planning early in life in order to minimize the tax impact during his or her years of earning power as well as after death. Expert advice on tax and legal matters is of the utmost importance if an estate plan is to be successful.

KEY TERMS

average tax rate	Keogh Plan
capital gains	marginal tax rate
capital losses	ordinary income
estate planning	powers of appointment
flower bonds	revocable trust
income averaging	short-term trust
Individual Retirement Account	testamentary trust
inter vivos trust	trust
interstate	trustee
irrevocable trust	

QUESTIONS

1. What is the marginal tax rate?
2. What is the difference between ordinary income and capital gains?
3. What is the difference between a long-term holding and a short-term holding?
4. Explain the treatment of net capital gains for tax purposes.
5. Explain the treatment of net capital losses for tax purposes. Why are short-term losses more advantageous than long-term losses?
6. What preferential treatment do long-term capital gains receive for tax purposes? Give an example.

7. Assume that an individual had taxable ordinary income of $27,000 and that he or she filed a joint return. Using Exhibit 17-1, determine how much income tax he or she would pay if he or she (a) had a long-term gain of $2,000, (b) had a long-term loss of $2,000, (c) had a short-term loss of $2,000.

8. Why would a taxpayer who has a fluctuating income pay more taxes over a number of years than a taxpayer who has a relatively stable annual income?

9. Would a taxpayer pay the same amount of income tax on dividends and interest received as he or she would on his salary? Why might municipal bonds be an attractive investment?

10. What is a person's estate? Define marital deduction from estate taxes.

11. What deductions are legal for estate taxes?

12. How is the real property of a decedent treated differently from personal property? What does it mean to die intestate?

13. Explain the difference between the two classifications of trusts.

14. Define revocable trusts, irrevocable trusts, and short-term trusts.

15. The grantor of a trust can cite another person to administer the trust. How do the powers of a trustee differ from those of a holder of a general power of appointment and those of a holder of a special power of appointment?

16. An individual can avoid estate taxes by reducing the size of the estate. Explain what a gift tax is. What alternatives are there to not paying a gift tax?

17. In estate planning, liquidity of assets is important because there should be cash available to pay the estate taxes. Enumerate the different methods used to provide estate liquidity.

18. What is an Individual Retirement Account? What is a Keogh Plan?

SELECTED READINGS

Chartered Financial Analysts Research Foundation. *Pension Fund Investment Management.* Homewood, Ill.: Dow Jones-Irwin, 1969.

DREYFUS, PATRICIA A. "Tax Shelters with Inflation Hedges." *Money,* February 1980, 59–65.

DYL, EDWARD A. "Capital Gains Taxation and Year-End Stock Market Behavior." *Journal of Finance,* March 1977, 165–175.

Explanation of Economic Recovery Act of 1981. Chicago: Commerce Clearing House, 1981.

Explanation of Pension Reform Act of 1974. Chicago: Commerce Clearing House, 1974.

1982 Federal Tax Course. Chicago: Commerce Clearing House, 1981.

"How the New Tax Law Changes Your Investment Planning." *Business Week*, November 11, 1978, 172–174.

MOFFITT, DONALD. "How Tax-Loss Sales Can Cost You Gains." *Wall Street Journal*, December 18, 1978, 34.

NICHOLAS, DONALD R., and BRUCE D. FIELITZ. "Awareness of Marginal Income Tax Rates among Taxpayers." *Mississippi Valley Journal of Business and Economics*, Spring 1973, 39–46.

SCHOEPLIN, ROBERT N. "The Effect of Pension Plans on Other Retirement Saving." *Journal of Finance*, 25, no. 3, 1970, 633–637.

U.S. Master Tax Guide. Latest annual edition. Chicago: Commerce Clearing House.

Wills, Estate, and Trust Service. Englewood Cliffs, N.J.: Prentice-Hall, 1982.

Appendices

Appendix A–1
The Sum of One Dollar

Year	1%	2%	3%	4%	5%	6%	7%	8%	9%	10%
1	1.010	1.020	1.030	1.040	1.050	1.060	1.070	1.080	1.090	1.100
2	1.020	1.040	1.061	1.082	1.102	1.124	1.145	1.166	1.188	1.210
3	1.030	1.061	1.093	1.125	1.158	1.191	1.225	1.260	1.295	1.331
4	1.041	1.082	1.126	1.170	1.216	1.262	1.311	1.360	1.412	1.464
5	1.051	1.104	1.159	1.217	1.276	1.338	1.403	1.469	1.539	1.611
6	1.062	1.126	1.194	1.265	1.340	1.419	1.501	1.587	1.677	1.772
7	1.072	1.149	1.230	1.316	1.407	1.504	1.606	1.714	1.828	1.949
8	1.083	1.172	1.267	1.369	1.477	1.594	1.718	1.851	1.993	2.144
9	1.094	1.195	1.305	1.423	1.551	1.689	1.838	1.999	2.172	2.358
10	1.105	1.219	1.344	1.480	1.629	1.791	1.967	2.159	2.367	2.594
11	1.116	1.243	1.384	1.539	1.710	1.898	2.105	2.332	2.580	2.853
12	1.127	1.268	1.426	1.601	1.796	2.012	2.252	2.518	2.813	3.138
13	1.138	1.294	1.469	1.665	1.886	2.133	2.410	2.720	3.066	3.452
14	1.149	1.319	1.513	1.732	1.980	2.261	2.579	2.937	3.342	3.797
15	1.161	1.346	1.558	1.801	2.079	2.397	2.759	3.172	3.642	4.177
16	1.173	1.373	1.605	1.873	2.183	2.540	2.952	3.426	3.970	4.595
17	1.184	1.400	1.653	1.948	2.292	2.693	3.159	3.700	4.328	5.054
18	1.196	1.428	1.702	2.026	2.407	2.854	3.380	3.996	4.717	5.560
19	1.208	1.457	1.753	2.107	2.527	3.026	3.616	4.316	5.142	6.116
20	1.220	1.486	1.806	2.191	2.653	3.207	3.870	4.661	5.604	6.727
21	1.232	1.516	1.860	2.279	2.786	3.399	4.140	5.034	6.109	7.400
22	1.245	1.546	1.916	2.370	2.925	3.603	4.430	5.436	6.658	8.140
23	1.257	1.577	1.974	2.465	3.071	3.820	4.740	5.871	7.258	8.954
24	1.270	1.608	2.033	2.563	3.225	4.049	5.072	6.341	7.911	9.850
25	1.282	1.641	2.094	2.666	3.386	4.292	5.427	6.848	8.623	10.834
30	1.348	1.811	2.427	3.243	4.322	5.743	7.612	10.062	13.267	17.449
35	1.417	2.000	2.814	3.946	5.516	7.686	10.676	14.785	20.413	28.102
40	1.489	2.208	3.262	4.801	7.040	10.285	14.974	21.724	31.408	45.258
45	1.565	2.438	3.781	5.841	8.985	13.764	21.002	31.920	48.325	72.888
50	1.645	2.691	4.384	7.106	11.467	18.419	29.456	46.900	74.354	117.386

Year	11%	12%	13%	14%	15%	16%	17%	18%	19%	20%
1	1.110	1.120	1.130	1.140	1.150	1.160	1.170	1.180	1.190	1.200
2	1.232	1.254	1.277	1.300	1.322	1.346	1.369	1.392	1.416	1.440
3	1.368	1.405	1.443	1.482	1.521	1.561	1.602	1.643	1.685	1.728
4	1.518	1.574	1.630	1.689	1.749	1.811	1.874	1.939	2.005	2.074
5	1.685	1.762	1.842	1.925	2.011	2.100	2.192	2.288	2.386	2.488
6	1.870	1.974	2.082	2.195	2.313	2.436	2.565	2.700	2.840	2.986
7	2.076	2.211	2.353	2.502	2.660	2.826	3.001	3.185	3.379	3.583
8	2.305	2.476	2.658	2.853	3.059	3.278	3.511	3.759	4.021	4.300
9	2.558	2.773	3.004	3.252	3.518	3.803	4.108	4.435	4.785	5.160
10	2.839	3.106	3.395	3.707	4.046	4.411	4.807	5.234	5.695	6.192
11	3.152	3.479	3.836	4.226	4.652	5.117	5.624	6.176	6.777	7.430
12	3.498	3.896	4.334	4.818	5.350	5.936	6.580	7.288	8.064	8.916
13	3.883	4.363	4.898	5.492	6.153	6.886	7.699	8.599	9.596	10.699
14	4.310	4.887	5.535	6.261	7.076	7.987	9.007	10.147	11.420	12.839
15	4.785	5.474	6.254	7.138	8.137	9.265	10.539	11.974	13.589	15.407
16	5.311	6.130	7.067	8.137	9.358	10.748	12.330	14.129	16.171	18.488
17	5.895	6.866	7.986	9.276	10.761	12.468	14.426	16.672	19.244	22.186
18	6.543	7.690	9.024	10.575	12.375	14.462	16.879	19.673	22.900	26.623
19	7.263	8.613	10.197	12.055	14.232	16.776	19.748	23.214	27.251	31.948
20	8.062	9.646	11.523	13.743	16.366	19.461	23.105	27.393	32.429	38.337
21	8.949	10.804	13.021	15.667	18.821	22.574	27.033	32.323	38.591	46.005
22	9.933	12.100	14.713	17.861	21.644	26.186	31.629	38.141	45.923	55.205
23	11.026	13.552	16.626	20.361	24.891	30.376	37.005	45.007	54.648	66.247
24	12.239	15.178	18.788	23.212	28.625	35.236	43.296	53.108	65.031	79.496
25	13.585	17.000	21.230	26.461	32.918	40.874	50.656	62.667	77.387	95.395
30	22.892	29.960	39.115	50.949	66.210	85.849	111.061	143.367	184.672	237.373
35	38.574	52.799	72.066	98.097	133.172	180.311	243.495	327.988	440.691	590.657
40	64.999	93.049	132.776	188.876	267.856	378.715	533.846	750.353	1051.642	1469.740
45	109.527	163.985	244.629	363.662	538.752	795.429	1170.425	1716.619	2509.583	3657.176
50	184.559	288.996	450.711	700.197	1083.619	1670.669	2566.080	3927.189	5988.730	9100.191

Appendix A–2
The Sum of an Annuity

Year	1%	2%	3%	4%	5%	6%	7%	8%	9%	10%
1	1.000	1.000	1.000	1.000	1.000	1.000	1.000	1.000	1.000	1.000
2	2.010	2.020	2.030	2.040	2.050	2.060	2.070	2.080	2.090	2.100
3	3.030	3.060	3.091	3.122	3.152	3.184	3.215	3.246	3.278	3.310
4	4.060	4.122	4.184	4.246	4.310	4.375	4.440	4.506	4.573	4.641
5	5.101	5.204	5.309	5.416	5.526	5.637	5.751	5.867	5.985	6.105
6	6.152	6.308	6.468	6.633	6.802	6.975	7.153	7.336	7.523	7.716
7	7.214	7.434	7.662	7.898	8.142	8.394	8.654	8.923	9.200	9.487
8	8.286	8.583	8.892	9.214	9.549	9.897	10.260	10.637	11.028	11.436
9	9.368	9.755	10.159	10.583	11.027	11.491	11.978	12.488	13.021	13.579
10	10.462	10.950	11.464	12.006	12.578	13.181	13.816	14.487	15.193	15.937
11	11.567	12.169	12.808	13.486	14.207	14.972	15.784	16.645	17.560	18.531
12	12.682	13.412	14.192	15.026	15.917	16.870	17.888	18.977	20.141	21.384
13	13.809	14.680	15.618	16.627	17.713	18.882	20.141	21.495	22.953	24.523
14	14.947	15.974	17.086	18.292	19.598	21.015	22.550	24.215	26.019	27.975
15	16.097	17.293	18.599	20.023	21.578	23.276	25.129	27.152	29.361	31.772
16	17.258	18.639	20.157	21.824	23.657	25.672	27.888	30.324	33.003	35.949
17	18.430	20.012	21.761	23.697	25.840	28.213	30.840	33.750	36.973	40.544
18	19.614	21.412	23.414	25.645	28.132	30.905	33.999	37.450	41.301	45.599
19	20.811	22.840	25.117	27.671	30.539	33.760	37.379	41.446	46.018	51.158
20	22.019	24.297	26.870	29.778	33.066	36.785	40.995	45.762	51.159	57.274
21	23.239	25.783	28.676	31.969	35.719	39.992	44.865	50.422	56.764	64.002
22	24.471	27.299	30.536	34.248	38.505	43.392	49.005	55.456	62.872	71.402
23	25.716	28.845	32.452	36.618	41.430	46.995	53.435	60.893	69.531	79.542
24	26.973	30.421	34.426	39.082	44.501	50.815	58.176	66.764	76.789	88.496
25	28.243	32.030	36.459	41.645	47.726	54.864	64.248	73.105	84.699	98.346
30	34.784	40.567	47.575	56.084	66.438	79.057	94.459	113.282	136.305	164.491
35	41.659	49.994	60.461	73.651	90.318	111.432	138.234	172.314	215.705	271.018
40	48.885	60.401	75.400	95.024	120.797	154.758	199.630	259.052	337.872	442.580
45	56.479	71.891	92.718	121.027	159.695	212.737	285.741	386.497	525.840	718.881
50	64.461	84.577	112.794	152.664	209.341	290.325	406.516	573.756	815.051	1163.865

Year	11%	12%	13%	14%	15%	16%	17%	18%	19%	20%
1	1.000	1.000	1.000	1.000	1.000	1.000	1.000	1.000	1.000	1.000
2	2.110	2.120	2.130	2.140	2.150	2.160	2.170	2.180	2.190	2.200
3	3.342	3.374	3.407	3.440	3.472	3.506	3.539	3.572	3.606	3.640
4	4.710	4.779	4.850	4.921	4.993	5.066	5.141	5.215	5.291	5.368
5	6.228	6.353	6.480	6.610	6.742	6.877	7.014	7.154	7.297	7.442
6	7.913	8.115	8.323	8.535	8.754	8.977	9.207	9.442	9.683	9.930
7	9.783	10.089	10.405	10.730	11.067	11.414	11.772	12.141	12.523	12.916
8	11.859	12.300	12.757	13.233	13.727	14.240	14.773	15.327	15.902	16.499
9	14.164	14.776	15.416	16.085	16.786	17.518	18.285	19.086	19.923	20.799
10	16.722	17.549	18.420	19.337	20.304	21.321	22.393	23.521	24.709	25.959
11	19.561	20.655	21.814	23.044	24.349	25.733	27.200	28.755	30.403	32.150
12	22.713	24.133	25.650	27.271	29.001	30.850	32.824	34.931	37.180	39.580
13	26.211	28.029	29.984	32.088	34.352	36.786	39.404	42.218	45.244	48.496
14	30.095	32.392	34.882	37.581	40.504	43.672	47.102	50.818	54.841	59.196
15	34.405	37.280	40.417	43.842	47.580	51.659	56.109	60.965	66.260	72.035
16	39.190	42.753	46.671	50.980	55.717	60.925	66.648	72.938	79.850	87.442
17	44.500	48.883	53.738	59.117	65.075	71.673	78.978	87.067	96.021	105.930
18	50.396	55.749	61.724	68.393	75.836	84.140	93.404	103.739	115.265	128.116
19	56.939	63.439	70.748	78.968	88.211	98.603	110.283	123.412	138.165	154.739
20	64.202	72.052	80.946	91.024	102.443	115.379	130.031	146.626	165.417	186.687
21	72.264	81.698	92.468	104.767	118.809	134.840	153.136	174.019	197.846	225.024
22	81.213	92.502	105.489	120.434	137.630	157.414	180.169	206.342	236.436	271.028
23	91.147	104.602	120.203	138.295	159.274	183.600	211.798	244.483	282.359	326.234
24	102.173	118.154	136.829	158.565	184.166	213.976	248.803	289.490	337.007	392.480
25	114.412	133.333	155.616	181.867	212.790	249.212	292.099	342.598	402.038	471.976
30	199.018	241.330	293.192	356.778	434.738	530.306	647.423	790.932	966.698	1181.865
35	341.583	431.658	546.663	693.552	881.152	1120.699	1426.448	1816.607	2314.173	2948.294
40	581.812	767.080	1013.667	1341.979	1779.048	2360.724	3134.412	4163.094	5529.711	7343.715
45	986.613	1358.208	1874.086	2590.464	3585.031	4965.191	6879.008	9531.258	13203.105	18280.914
50	1668.723	2399.975	3459.344	4994.301	7217.488	10435.449	15088.805	21812.273	31514.492	45496.094

Appendix A–3
The Present Value of One Dollar

Year	1%	2%	3%	4%	5%	6%	7%	8%	9%	10%
1	.990	.980	.971	.962	.952	.943	.935	.926	.917	.909
2	.980	.961	.943	.925	.907	.890	.873	.857	.842	.826
3	.971	.942	.915	.889	.864	.840	.816	.794	.772	.751
4	.961	.924	.888	.855	.823	.792	.763	.735	.708	.683
5	.951	.906	.863	.822	.784	.747	.713	.681	.650	.621
6	.942	.888	.837	.790	.746	.705	.666	.630	.596	.564
7	.933	.871	.813	.760	.711	.665	.623	.583	.547	.513
8	.923	.853	.789	.731	.677	.627	.582	.540	.502	.467
9	.914	.837	.766	.703	.645	.592	.544	.500	.460	.424
10	.905	.820	.744	.676	.614	.558	.508	.463	.422	.386
11	.896	.804	.722	.650	.585	.527	.475	.429	.388	.350
12	.887	.789	.701	.625	.557	.497	.444	.397	.356	.319
13	.879	.773	.681	.601	.530	.469	.415	.368	.326	.290
14	.870	.758	.661	.577	.505	.442	.388	.340	.299	.263
15	.861	.743	.642	.555	.481	.417	.362	.315	.275	.239
16	.853	.728	.623	.534	.458	.394	.339	.292	.252	.218
17	.844	.714	.605	.513	.436	.371	.317	.270	.231	.198
18	.836	.700	.587	.494	.416	.350	.296	.250	.212	.180
19	.828	.686	.570	.475	.396	.331	.277	.232	.194	.164
20	.820	.673	.554	.456	.377	.312	.258	.215	.178	.149
21	.811	.660	.538	.439	.359	.294	.242	.199	.164	.135
22	.803	.647	.522	.422	.342	.278	.226	.184	.150	.123
23	.795	.634	.507	.406	.326	.262	.211	.170	.138	.112
24	.788	.622	.492	.390	.310	.247	.197	.158	.126	.102
25	.780	.610	.478	.375	.295	.233	.184	.146	.116	.092
30	.742	.552	.412	.308	.231	.174	.131	.099	.075	.057
35	.706	.500	.355	.253	.181	.130	.094	.068	.049	.036
40	.672	.453	.307	.208	.142	.097	.067	.046	.032	.022
45	.639	.410	.264	.171	.111	.073	.048	.031	.021	.014
50	.608	.372	.228	.141	.087	.054	.034	.021	.013	.009

Year	11%	12%	13%	14%	15%	16%	17%	18%	19%	20%
1	.901	.893	.885	.877	.870	.862	.855	.847	.840	.833
2	.812	.797	.783	.769	.756	.743	.731	.718	.706	.694
3	.731	.712	.693	.675	.658	.641	.624	.609	.593	.579
4	.659	.636	.613	.592	.572	.552	.534	.516	.499	.482
5	.593	.567	.543	.519	.497	.476	.456	.437	.419	.402
6	.535	.507	.480	.456	.432	.410	.390	.370	.352	.335
7	.482	.452	.425	.400	.376	.354	.333	.314	.296	.279
8	.434	.404	.376	.351	.327	.305	.285	.266	.249	.233
9	.391	.361	.333	.308	.284	.263	.243	.225	.209	.194
10	.352	.322	.295	.270	.247	.227	.208	.191	.176	.162
11	.317	.287	.261	.237	.215	.195	.178	.162	.148	.135
12	.286	.257	.231	.208	.187	.168	.152	.137	.124	.112
13	.258	.229	.204	.182	.163	.145	.130	.116	.104	.093
14	.232	.205	.181	.160	.141	.125	.111	.099	.088	.078
15	.209	.183	.160	.140	.123	.108	.095	.084	.074	.065
16	.188	.163	.141	.123	.107	.093	.081	.071	.062	.054
17	.170	.146	.125	.108	.093	.080	.069	.060	.052	.045
18	.153	.130	.111	.095	.081	.069	.059	.051	.044	.038
19	.138	.116	.098	.083	.070	.060	.051	.043	.037	.031
20	.124	.104	.087	.073	.061	.051	.043	.037	.031	.026
21	.112	.093	.077	.064	.053	.044	.037	.031	.026	.022
22	.101	.083	.068	.056	.046	.038	.032	.026	.022	.018
23	.091	.074	.060	.049	.040	.033	.027	.022	.018	.015
24	.082	.066	.053	.043	.035	.028	.023	.019	.015	.013
25	.074	.059	.047	.038	.030	.024	.020	.016	.013	.010
30	.044	.033	.026	.020	.015	.012	.009	.007	.005	.004
35	.026	.019	.014	.010	.008	.006	.004	.003	.002	.002
40	.015	.011	.008	.005	.004	.003	.002	.001	.001	.001
45	.009	.006	.004	.003	.002	.001	.001	.001	.000	.000
50	.005	.003	.002	.001	.001	.001	.000	.000	.000	.000

Appendix A–4
The Present Value of an Annuity

Year	1%	2%	3%	4%	5%	6%	7%	8%	9%	10%
1	.990	.980	.971	.962	.952	.943	.935	.926	.917	.909
2	1.970	1.942	1.913	1.886	1.859	1.833	1.808	1.783	1.759	1.736
3	2.941	2.884	2.829	2.775	2.723	2.673	2.624	2.577	2.531	2.487
4	3.902	3.808	3.717	3.630	3.546	3.465	3.387	3.312	3.240	3.170
5	4.853	4.713	4.580	4.452	4.329	4.212	4.100	3.993	3.890	3.791
6	5.795	5.601	5.417	5.242	5.076	4.917	4.767	4.623	4.486	4.355
7	6.728	6.472	6.230	6.002	5.786	5.582	5.389	5.206	5.033	4.868
8	7.652	7.326	7.020	6.733	6.463	6.210	5.971	5.747	5.535	5.335
9	8.566	8.162	7.786	7.435	7.108	6.802	6.515	6.247	5.995	5.759
10	9.471	8.983	8.530	8.111	7.722	7.360	7.024	6.710	6.418	6.145
11	10.368	9.787	9.253	8.760	8.306	7.887	7.499	7.139	6.805	6.495
12	11.255	10.575	9.954	9.385	8.863	8.384	7.943	7.536	7.161	6.814
13	12.134	11.348	10.635	9.986	9.394	8.853	8.358	7.904	7.487	7.103
14	13.004	12.106	11.296	10.563	9.899	9.295	8.746	8.244	7.786	7.367
15	13.865	12.849	11.938	11.118	10.380	9.712	9.108	8.560	8.061	7.606
16	14.718	13.578	12.561	11.652	10.838	10.106	9.447	8.851	8.313	7.824
17	15.562	14.292	13.166	12.166	11.274	10.477	9.763	9.122	8.544	8.022
18	16.398	14.992	13.754	12.659	11.690	10.828	10.059	9.372	8.756	8.201
19	17.226	15.679	14.324	13.134	12.085	11.158	10.336	9.604	8.950	8.365
20	18.046	16.352	14.878	13.590	12.462	11.470	10.594	9.818	9.129	8.514
21	18.857	17.011	15.415	14.029	12.821	11.764	10.836	10.017	9.292	8.649
22	19.661	17.658	15.937	14.451	13.163	12.042	11.061	10.201	9.442	8.772
23	20.456	18.292	16.444	14.857	13.489	12.303	11.272	10.371	9.580	8.883
24	21.244	18.914	16.936	15.247	13.799	12.550	11.469	10.529	9.707	8.985
25	22.023	19.524	17.413	15.622	14.094	12.783	11.654	10.675	9.823	9.077
30	25.808	22.397	19.601	17.292	15.373	13.765	12.409	11.258	10.274	9.427
35	29.409	24.999	21.487	18.665	16.374	14.498	12.948	11.655	10.567	9.644
40	32.835	27.356	23.115	19.793	17.159	15.046	13.332	11.925	10.757	9.779
45	36.095	29.490	24.519	20.720	17.774	15.456	13.606	12.108	10.881	9.863
50	39.197	31.424	25.730	21.482	18.256	15.762	13.801	12.234	10.962	9.915

Year	11%	12%	13%	14%	15%	16%	17%	18%	19%	20%
1	.901	.893	.885	.877	.870	.862	.855	.847	.840	.833
2	1.713	1.690	1.668	1.647	1.626	1.605	1.585	1.566	1.547	1.528
3	2.444	2.402	2.361	2.322	2.283	2.246	2.210	2.174	2.140	2.106
4	3.102	3.037	2.974	2.914	2.855	2.798	2.743	2.690	2.639	2.589
5	3.696	3.605	3.517	3.433	3.352	3.274	3.199	3.127	3.058	2.991
6	4.231	4.111	3.998	3.889	3.784	3.685	3.589	3.498	3.410	3.326
7	4.712	4.564	4.423	4.288	4.160	4.039	3.922	3.812	3.706	3.605
8	5.146	4.968	4.799	4.639	4.487	4.344	4.207	4.078	3.954	3.837
9	5.537	5.328	5.132	4.946	4.772	4.607	4.451	4.303	4.163	4.031
10	5.889	5.650	5.426	5.216	5.019	4.833	4.659	4.494	4.339	4.192
11	6.207	5.938	5.687	5.453	5.234	5.029	4.836	4.656	4.487	4.327
12	6.492	6.194	5.918	5.660	5.421	5.197	4.988	4.793	4.611	4.439
13	6.750	6.424	6.122	5.842	5.583	5.342	5.118	4.910	4.715	4.533
14	6.982	6.628	6.303	6.002	5.724	5.468	5.229	5.008	4.802	4.611
15	7.191	6.811	6.462	6.142	5.847	5.575	5.324	5.092	4.876	4.675
16	7.379	6.974	6.604	6.265	5.954	5.669	5.405	5.162	4.938	4.730
17	7.549	7.120	6.729	6.373	6.047	5.749	5.475	5.222	4.990	4.775
18	7.702	7.250	6.840	6.467	6.128	5.818	5.534	5.273	5.033	4.812
19	7.839	7.366	6.938	6.550	6.198	5.877	5.585	5.316	5.070	4.843
20	7.963	7.469	7.025	6.623	6.259	5.929	5.628	5.353	5.101	4.870
21	8.075	7.562	7.102	6.687	6.312	5.973	5.665	5.384	5.127	4.891
22	8.176	7.645	7.170	6.743	6.359	6.011	5.696	5.410	5.149	4.909
23	8.266	7.718	7.230	6.792	6.399	6.044	5.723	5.432	5.167	4.925
24	8.348	7.784	7.283	6.835	6.434	6.073	5.747	5.451	5.182	4.937
25	8.422	7.843	7.330	6.873	6.464	6.097	5.766	5.467	5.195	4.948
30	8.694	8.055	7.496	7.003	6.566	6.177	5.829	5.517	5.235	4.979
35	8.855	8.176	7.586	7.070	6.617	6.215	5.858	5.539	5.251	4.992
40	8.951	8.244	7.634	7.105	6.642	6.233	5.871	5.548	5.258	4.997
45	9.008	8.283	7.661	7.123	6.654	6.242	5.877	5.552	5.261	4.999
50	9.042	8.305	7.675	7.133	6.661	6.246	5.880	5.554	5.262	4.999

Glossary

Accrued interest.   Interest that has accumulated on a bond since the last interest payment was made. The buyer of the bond usually pays the market price plus accrued interest.

Annuity.   A series of payments of a fixed amount for a specified number of years.

Assets.   Everything that a corporation owns or that is owed to it.

Balance sheet.   An itemized statement of a firm's financial position at a given point in time, which itemizes assets, liabilities, and equity.

Barron's Confidence Index.   The ratio of the average yield to maturity (YTM) of ten high-grade corporate bonds to the average YTM of forty bonds selected by Dow Jones; considered by some technical analysts to be an indicator of future trends in the stock market.

Bear market.   A term referring to declining prices on the stock market.

Bearer bond.   A bond that does not have the owner's name registered on the books of the issuing company and that is payable to the holder.

Beta value.   A numerical value that measures the historical volatility of a stock relative to the market norm.

Blue-chip stocks.   Stocks issued by companies known nationally for the quality and wide acceptance of their products or services, and for their ability to make money and pay dividends.

Blue-sky laws.   A popular name for laws various states have enacted to protect the public against securities fraud.

Bond.   Basically, an IOU or promissory note of a corporation. A bond is evidence of a debt on which the issuing company usually promises to pay the bond-holders a specified amount of interest for a specified length of time, and to repay the loan on the expiration date.

Book value per share.   An accounting term. Book value of a stock is determined from a company's records, by adding all assets (generally excluding such intangibles as goodwill), then deducting all debts and other liabilities plus the liquidation price of any preferred issues. The sum arrived at is divided by the number of common shares outstanding, and the result is book value per common share.

Broker.   An agent who handles the public's orders to buy and sell securities, commodities, or other property. For this service, a commission is charged.

Bull market.   A term referring to rising prices on the stock market.

Business risk.   Variability in performance dependent upon such factors as the efficiency of management in the general operations of the firm, the firm's competitive position, its growth rate, and its stability.

C

Call feature.   A mechanism that allows the issuer to repurchase bonds (or preferred stock) at a stated price. The *call price* will always be set above the face value of the security.

Capital gain.   Returns derived from appreciation in the value of a capital asset; the gain is realized when the asset is sold.

Capital market.   The mechanism through which long-term funds are made available by suppliers to those who wish to borrow funds. Individuals, businesses, and governments participate in the market, primarily through the organized securities exchanges.

Capital structure.   The proportions of debt and equity by means of which a firm is financed. This information is listed on the right-hand side of the balance sheet.

Closed-end investment company.   An investment company with a fixed number of shares that can be owned by the public. The company does not redeem shares; as a result, the securities are traded in the market, with price determined by supply and demand.

Collateral.   Securities or other property pledged by a borrower to secure repayment of a loan.

Collateral trust bond.   A bond secured by collateral deposited with a trustee. The collateral is often the stocks or bonds of companies controlled by the issuing company, but may be other securities.

Commercial paper.   Short-term, unsecured promissory notes issued by a corporation, with a maturity of up to 270 days, and usually in denominations of $100,000 or more. The purchaser can expect a yield that is higher than the yield available on most other marketable securities, and the issuer usually pays a lower interest rate than would be available through most commercial banks.

Commission.   The broker's basic fee for purchasing or selling securities or property as an agent.

Commission broker.   An agent who executes the public's orders for the purchase or sale of securities or commodities.

Common stock.   Securities that represent an ownership interest in a corporation. If the company has also issued preferred stock, both common and preferred have ownership rights.

Compound interest.   The process of applying interest in succeeding periods not only on the initial principle but also on the interest accumulated from preceding periods.

Conglomerate.   A heavily diversified company that cannot be placed in any one industry or operational category.

Consumer price index.   An index number that measures the extent to which prices paid by city wage earners for a typical bundle of commodities have changed in comparison to a specified base year. Although it is actually a very specialized measure, it is most often referred to in consideration of price stability.

Convertible security.   A bond, debenture, or preferred share that may be exchanged by the owner for common stock or another security, usually of the same company, in accordance with the terms of the issue.

Corporation.   A form of business organization, operating under a charter granted by a state, in which the owners, or shareholders, have limited liability. Corporate earnings are taxed at a special rate.

Coupon bond.   Bond with interest coupons attached. The coupons are clipped as they come due and are presented by the holder for payment of interest.

Coupon rate.   The stated rate of interest on a bond.

Current yield.   See *Yield.*

Cyclical.   Refers to the tendency of operations of a firm to expand or contract as the economy expands or contracts.

D

Debenture.   A promissory note issued by a company and usually not secured by a mortgage or lien on any specific property.

Declaration date.   The date on which a corporate board of directors declares its intention to pay a dividend.

Defensive stock.   A stock included in a portfolio because of its resistance to cyclical trends.

Depreciation.   Normally, charges against earnings for the purpose of writing off the cost, less salvage value, of an asset over its estimated useful life. It represents no cash outlay and results in a tax savings.

Diversification.   Spreading investments among different companies in different industries.

Dividend.   The payment designated by the board of directors to be distributed among the shares of stock outstanding. The payment may be made in cash or in shares of the firm's stock.

Dividend-coverage ratio.   The ratio of a firm's annual net income to preferred dividends payable annually. This ratio provides an indication of the firm's ability to meet its obligations to preferred stockholders.

Dow Theory.   A theory of market analysis based upon the performance of the Dow Jones industrial and transportation stock price averages. The theory says that the market is in a basic upward trend if one of these averages advances above a previous important high, accompanied or followed by a similar advance in the other. When the averages both dip below previous important lows, this is regarded as confirmation of a basic downward trend. The theory does not attempt to predict how long either trend will continue.

Down tick.   A term used to designate a transaction made at a price lower than that of the preceding trade.

E

Effective rate of interest.   A recalculation of the stated interest rate to reflect the time value of money.

EPS.   Earnings per share.

Equity.   The ownership interest of common and preferred stockholders in a company.

Ex-dividend.   A synonym for "without dividend." The buyer of a stock selling ex-dividend does not receive the recently declared dividend.

F

Face value.   The value of a bond that appears on the face of the bond, unless the value is otherwise specified by the issuing company. Face value is ordinarily the amount the issuing company promises to pay at maturity. Sometimes referred to as par value.

Financial intermediary.   The individual or institution fulfilling the function of intermediary between suppliers and demanders of capital.

Financial risk.   Risk arising from the inclusion of debt in a firm's capital structure.

Fundamental analysis.   Anaylsis of industries and companies based on such factors as sales, assets, earnings, products or services, markets, and management. As applied to the economy, fundamental research includes consideration of gross national product, interest rates, unemployment, inventories, savings, etc.

Futures.   A form of speculative investment in the commodities market in which the investor promises to pay a specified price for a predetermined amount of the commodity at a future date.

G

General-obligation bonds.   Bonds issued by a (nonfederal) goverment entity that are backed by the issuer's full faith and credit and are unconditionally guaranteed through the issuer's ability to levy taxes.

GNP.   Gross national product—a measure reflecting all the productive activity in a particular country during a specified period of time, usually one year.

Good-till-cancelled order (GTC).   An order to buy or sell that remains in effect until it is either executed or canceled.

Gross-rent multiplier (GRM).   A formula used to price income-producing property, which calculates a price as a multiple of annual gross rental income on the property.

H

Holding-period yield.   The returns an investor receives during the period he holds an investment. This rate reflects all income received as well as any changes in the price of the security during that period.

I

Income bond.   Generally, income bonds promise to repay principal but to pay interest only when earned. In some cases, unpaid interest on an income bond may accumulate as a claim against the corporation when the bond becomes due.

Income statement.   A statement of a firm's revenues and expenses for a specified period of time, which includes profit or loss for the period.

Indenture.   A written agreement under which bonds and debentures are issued, setting forth maturity date, interest rate, and other terms.

Interest.   Payments a borrower pays a lender for the use of his money. A corporation pays interest on its bonds to its bondholders.

Interest-coverage ratio.   The ratio of a firm's annual earnings available for interest payments (EBIT) to its annual interest payable on debt. This ratio is often considered before the purchase of securities issued by a firm.

Interest rate.   The ratio, for a specified period of time, of the interest earned to the principle invested.

Interest-rate risk.   The risk of loss of principal as a result of fluctuations in the interest rate paid on newly issued securities.

Intrinsic value.   An estimation of the true value of a security, made by an analyst after a thorough investigation. If the intrinsic value is higher than the current market price, the security is a worthwhile investment.

Investment.   The use of money for the purpose of making more money, to gain income or increase capital, or both.

Investment banker.   Also know as an underwriter. He is the middleman between the corporation issuing new securities and the public.

Investment company.   A company or trust that uses its capital to invest in other companies. There are two principal types: the closed-end and the open-end or mutual fund.

L

Leading indicator.   Various ratios and indexes that are believed by technical analysts to provide an indication of future movement in stock market prices.

Legal list.   A list of investments, selected by various states, in which certain institutions and fiduciaries, such as insurance companies and banks, may invest. Legal lists are often restricted to high-quality securities meeting certain specifications.

Leverage. A term commonly used in investments to describe the use of borrowed funds to magnify a gain or loss on the principal amount invested.

Liabilities. All claims against a firm's assets, such as short- or long-term debt, wages payable, etc.

Limit order. An order to buy or sell a stated amount of a security at a specified price, or at a better one, if possible.

Liquidation. The process of converting securities or other property into cash. Also, the dissolution of a company, with cash remaining after sale of its assets and payment of all indebtedness being distributed to the shareholders.

Liquidity. The ability to readily convert a security to cash without losing any of the principal invested in it.

Liquidity-preference theory. A theory explaining higher interest rates on long-term securities by stating that the principal determinant of interest rates is investor aversion to risk.

Load fund. A mutual fund whose shares sell at a price higher than the net asset value. The added charge represents a sales fee, which is paid to an outside organization to cover selling expenses.

Long position. A term referring to the ownership of securities.

M

Margin. The amount the customer must pay when he uses his broker's credit to buy a security. The minimum requirement is established by Federal Reserve regulations.

Margin call. A demand upon a customer to put up money or securities with the broker when a purchase is made or when a customer's equity in a margin account declines below a minimum standard.

Margin trading. Buying stocks or bonds partially on credit.

Market order. An order to buy or sell a stated amount of a security at the most advantageous price obtainable after the order is placed.

Market risk. The risk of loss of capital resulting from changes in security prices.

Marketability. The degree to which there exists an active market for a security, in which it can be readily traded with minimal price changes.

Matched trade. A term referring to agreement between the writer and the purchaser of a call option on the amount of the premium (purchase price).

Merger. A combination of two or more firms into one company.

Mortgage. A lien against a piece of property, which usually establishes the property as collateral for a loan.

Mortgage bond. A bond secured by a mortgage on a property. The value of the property may or may not equal the value of the so-called mortgage bonds issued against it.

Municipal bond. A bond issued by a state or political subdivision, such as a county, city, town, or village, or by a state agency or authority. In general, interest paid on municipal bonds is exempt from federal income taxes and state and local income taxes within the state of issue.

Mutual fund.   An investment company in which individual investors have pooled their money in order to provide diversification and professional management for their funds. Each contributor receives shares issued by the fund in proportion to the amount of the investment.

N

NASD.   The National Association of Securities Dealers, Inc. An association of brokers and dealers in the over-the-counter securities business.

Net asset value (NAV).   A term, usually used in connection wih investment companies, meaning net asset value per share. It is common practice for an investment company to compute its assets daily, or even twice daily, by totaling the market value of all securities owned. All liabilities are deducted, and the balance is divided by the number of shares outstanding. The resulting figure is the net asset value per share.

Net income multiplier (NIM).   A formula similar to GRM except that it incorporates net rental income, thereby including variations in operating expenses in the calculation of the selling price.

Net working capital.   A measure of a firm's excess liquid assets, a figure that is the difference between current assets and current liabilities.

Net worth.   The difference between the assets and liabilities of a firm; the portion of a firm's value to which stockholders have claim.

No-load fund.   A mutual fund that has no sales charges added to the price of its shares; the shares, therefore, sell at their net asset value.

Nominal yield.   A contracted or stated interest rate, undeflated for price level changes; also known as coupon yield for bonds, or dividend yield on common-stock investments.

NYSE Index.   A composite index covering price movements of all common stocks listed on the New York Stock Exchange. The composite index is supplemented by four industry-group indexes: industrials, transportation, utilities, and finance.

O

Odd lot.   A unit of stock trading involving fewer than 100 shares; transactions of this type usually carry an additional charge as well as the regular commission.

Odd-lot trading theory.   See *Theory of contrary opinion*.

Open-end investment company.   An investment company that will buy or sell its securities at any time, a policy that results in frequent changes in the capitalization of the fund. Mutual funds are open-end investment companies.

Options.   The right to buy (call) or sell (put) a fixed amount of a given stock at a specified price with a limited period of time. The purchaser hopes that the stock's prices will go up (if he bought a call) or go down (if he bought a put) by an amount sufficient to provide a profit greater than the cost of the contract and the commission and other fees required to exercise the contract.

Over-the-counter market (OTC).   A market for securities that are not listed on the organized exchanges; transactions are primarily made over the telephone. The OTC is the principal market for U.S. government and municipal bonds.

P

Par.   In the case of preferred shares and bonds, par often signifies the dollar value upon which dividends on preferred stocks, and interest on bonds, are calculated.

Partnership.   A business organization owned by two or more individuals; the partners generally have unlimited liability, and the firm's earnings are taxed at their personal income tax rates.

Portfolio.   The combination of securities or assets in which an individual or an institution invests.

Preferred stock.   A class of stock with a claim on the company's earnings before payment may be made on the common stock. Preferred stock is entitled to dividends at a specified rate and usually takes priority over common stock if a company liquidates.

Present value.   The value, today, of a future payment (or stream of payments) discounted at a specified discount rate. The procedure is the inverse of compounding.

Price-earnings ratio (P/E).   The price of a share of stock divided by earnings per share for a twelve-month period. For example, a stock selling for $50 a share and earning $5 a share is said to be selling at a price-earnings ratio of 10 to 1.

Primary trend.   An important factor in the Dow Theory, this trend represents stock-market movement lasting at least four years.

Principal.   The amount of money on which interest is earned by a depositor or investor, or on which interest is paid by a borrower.

Proprietorship.   A business organization owned by one person.

Prospectus.   That portion of the document submitted to the SEC for registration of new security issues that may be distributed to potential buyers.

Proxy.   Written authorization given by a shareholder to someone else to represent him and vote his shares at a shareholder's meeting.

Purchasing-power risk.   Loss on income and principal of an investment as a result of decreased purchasing power of the dollar (inflation).

R

Random-walk hypothesis.   A theory that stock prices do not move in repeating patterns and therefore price movements cannot be predicted.

Real estate investment trust (REIT).   A fund that issues public shares of stock, then invests the proceeds in real estate and distributes any income or capital gains to shareholders.

Record date. The date on which one must be registered as a shareholder on the stock book of a company in order to receive a declared dividend or, among other things, to vote on company affairs.

Recovery stage. The period during which stock prices begin to rise after "bottoming out"; the first stage of a bull market.

Registered bond. A bond that is registered on the books of the issuing company in the name of the owner. It can be transferred only when endorsed by the registered owner.

Registered trader. A member of an exchange who trades in stocks on the floor for an account in which he has an interest.

Return. See *Yield.*

Revenue bonds. Bonds issued by a state or municipality that are not backed by the issuer's full faith and credit but, instead, will be repaid from funds generated by the project they were issued to finance.

Rights. The privilege given by a company to its shareholders to buy, ahead of others, the new securities it issues in proportion to the number of shares each stockholder owns. The piece of paper evidencing this privilege is called a right. Stockholders who exercise these rights can maintain the same percentage ownership in the company that they held before the new securities were issued.

Risk. The possibility that the returns expected from a certain project or investment will vary from current expectations. The term is used interchangeably with *uncertainty.* Risk is most often measured by standard deviation or coefficient of variation of expected returns.

Round lot. A unit of trading or a multiple thereof. On the NYSE, the unit of trading is generally 100 shares in stocks.

S

SEC. The Securities and Exchange Commission, established by Congress to help protect investors. The SEC administers the Securities Act of 1933, the Securities Exchange Act of 1934, The Securities Act Amendments of 1975, the Trust Indenture Act, the Investment Company Act, the Investment Advisers Act, and the Public Utility Holding Company Act.

Secured bonds. Debt issues that are backed by claims against specific assets owned by the issuer.

Short position. The opposite of a long position; the position of an investor who has sold short, but has not yet replaced (or covered) the borrowed securities.

Short sale. A stock transaction reflecting the seller's expectation that the stock's price will drop. The seller sells stock belonging to another firm or investor and promises to replace it in the future. The short seller expects to be able to purchase the replacement stock at a market price lower than that of his initial sale.

Sinking fund. Money regularly set aside by a company to redeem its bonds, debentures, or preferred stock from time to time as specified in the indenture or charter.

Small-investor syndrome. The tendency for small investors, who are generally considered to be less knowledgeable than professional traders, to sell securities just before market prices begin to rise, or to buy securities at market peaks, just before prices begin to fall.

Specialist. A member of the New York Stock Exchange who has two functions: to maintain an orderly market, insofar as reasonable practicable, in the stocks in which he is registered as a specialist; and to act as a broker's broker.

Spread. The difference between the price paid for a security by an investment banker and the price for which he sells it. The term also refers to the case in which the striking price on a call option is higher than that of a put option on the same security.

Standard & Poor's Index. A stock-market index reflecting the market value of stocks listed on the NYSE.

Stock dividend. A dividend paid in securities rather than cash. The dividend may be additional shares of the issuing company, or shares of another company.

Stock split. The division of the outstanding shares of a corporation into a larger number of shares. Although each shareholder will own more shares after the split, his proportionate equity in the company will remain the same.

Stop order. An order to buy at a price above or sell at a price below the current market. Stop sell orders are generally used to limit loss or protect unrealized profits on a holding. A stop order becomes a market order when the stock sells at or beyond the specified price and, thus, may not necessarily be executed at the stop price.

Street-name account. Securities held in the name of a broker instead of in his customer's name are said to be carried in a street-name account.

Striking price. The price at which the holder of an option can exercise it.

Subordinated debentures. Debt issues representing claims against an issuer's unsecured assets, which may be settled only after all secured creditors' and debenture holders' obligations have been fulfilled.

Systematic risk. The proportion of variability in returns on a security caused by factors affecting all securities of the same kind.

T

Technical analysis. Analysis of the market and stocks based on supply and demand. The technician studies price movements, volume, and trends, and patterns that are revealed by charting these factors, and attempts to assess the possible effect of current market action on future supply and demand for securities and individual issues.

Tender offer. A formal offer made by a firm to purchase its own shares or shares of another company at a specified price. A tender offer is often used when one firm is attempting to take over another, to circumvent the opposition of the management of the firm whose stock is being sought.

Terminal value. The value of an investment at the end of the period during which it is held. An investor's objective is to maximize the terminal value of his investment.

Theory of contrary opinion (Odd-lot trading theory). A theory based on the belief that small investors (those who trade in odd lots) are most likely to make the wrong investment decision and that therefore, the market should move in a direction opposite to that indicated by small-investor decisions.

Treasury bills.   Short-term obligations of the U.S. Treasury. They are issued weekly and carry a low yield because they are virtually risk-free.

Treasury notes.   Obligations of the U.S. Treasury with a maturity of one to seven years, providing a low yield because of the low level of risk.

Treasury stock.   Stock issued by a company but later reacquired. It may be held in the company's treasury indefinitely, reissued to the public, or retired.

Trustee (bond).   The third party to a bond indenture, who is responsible for overseeing the issuer's fulfillment of the conditions of the indenture. The role is often filled by the trust department of a commercial bank.

Two-dollar broker.   Members on the floor of the NYSE who execute orders for other brokers having more business at that time than they can handle themselves, or for firms that do not have an exchange member on the floor.

U

Unbiased expectation theory.   A theory that explains higher interest rates on long-term securities by stating that the yield on any security today is the geometric mean of all one-year yields expected to exist between today and the security's maturity date.

Underwriter.   The investment banker who fulfills the function of (1) guaranteeing the issuer of a security that it will receive at least a specified amount; (2) accepting the risk that the security will not sell or that the price will fluctuate adversely during the initial distribution period.

Unsystematic risk.   The portion of total risk that is unique to each firm; the two primary components are business and financial risk.

Up tick.   A term used to designate a transaction made at a price higher than the preceding transaction.

V

Volume theories.   Theories used to predict stock-market conditions, which are based on changes in the volume of trading.

W

Warrant.   A certificate giving the holder the right to purchase securities at a stipulated price, either within a specified time limit or perpetually. Sometimes a warrant is offered with a security as an inducement to buy, and may, after a specified period, be detached from the security and traded separately.

Working capital.   A firm's investment in current assets, such as cash, marketable securities, inventory, and accounts receivable.

Y

Yield.   Also know as *return*. The dividends or interest paid by a company expressed as a percentage of the current price. A stock with a current market value of

$40 a share and paying dividends at the rate of $2 is said to return 5 percent ($2/$40). The current return of a bond is figured the same way: A 3 percent $1,000 bond selling at $600 offers a current-yield return of 5 percent ($30/$600).

Yield to call. The rate of return that may be expected (on an annual basis) on a callable security.

Yield to maturity. The rate of return that an investor will realize on an annual basis if he buys a security and holds it to maturity.

Index